Human Resource Management

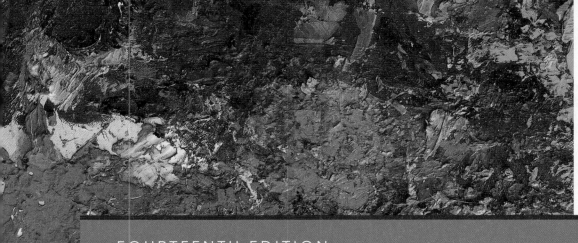

FOURTEENTH EDITION

Human Resource Management

ROBERT L. MATHIS
University of Nebraska at Omaha

JOHN H. JACKSON
University of Wyoming

SEAN R. VALENTINE
University of North Dakota

CENGAGE
Learning®

Australia • Brazil • Mexico • Singapore • United Kingdom • United States

**Human Resource Management,
Fourteenth Edition**
Robert L. Mathis, John H. Jackson and
Sean R. Valentine

Senior Vice President, LRS/Acquisitions &
Solutions Planning: Jack W. Calhoun

VP, General Manager: Social Science and
Qualitative Business: Erin Joyner

Product Director: Mike Schenk

Senior Product Manager: Michele Rhoades

Senior Content Developer: Michael
Guendelsberger

Product Assistant: Tamara Grega

Senior Brand Manager: Robin LeFevre

Marketing Coordinator: Michael Saver

Manufacturing Planner: Ron Montgomery

Art and Cover Direction, Production
Management, and Composition:
PreMediaGlobal

Senior Media Developer: John Rich

Rights Acquisition Director: Audrey
Pettengill

Senior Rights Acquisition Specialist, Text
and Image: Deanna Ettinger

Cover Image: © Hemera/Thinkstock

Internal Design Image (Global Icon):
SCPhotographie/The Image Bank/Getty
Images

Library of Congress Control Number: 2013932025

ISBN-13: 978-1-133-95310-4

ISBN-10: 1-133-95310-7

Cengage Learning
200 First Stamford Place, 4th Floor
Stamford, CT 06902
USA

Cengage Learning is a leading provider of customized learning
solutions with office locations around the globe, including Singapore,
the United Kingdom, Australia, Mexico, Brazil, and Japan. Locate your
local office at: **www.cengage.com/global**.

Cengage Learning products are represented in Canada by
Nelson Education, Ltd.

To learn more about Cengage Learning Solutions, visit **www.cengage.com**.

Purchase any of our products at your local college store or at our
preferred online store **www.cengagebrain.com**.

Printed in Canada
1 2 3 4 5 6 7 17 16 15 14 13

DEDICATIONS

TO

Jo Ann Mathis
for managing efforts on this book, and
Julie Foster and Lee Skoda as key supporters.

R. D. and M. M. Jackson,
who were successful managers of people for many years.

Page and Will, for their love and support, and family
and friends who have helped through the years.

BRIEF CONTENTS

TABLE OF CONTENTS

SECTION 2
Jobs and Labor 109

SECTION 3

Training, Development, and Performance 257

SECTION 4

Compensation 365

SECTION 5

Employee Relations 479

PREFACE

In comparing the 14th edition of *Human Resource Management* with the first edition the evolution that has occurred in the HR field is very apparent. By carefully researching and recording the changes in this book it has become the leader in both the academic and professional segments of the market, we are told, and the authors are very gratified that their efforts are appreciated by so many.

The book is a longtime standard in HR classes. We have paid close attention to an appropriate reading level, chapter lengths, use of examples, and other devices to make the book "student friendly." It is also worth noting that the authors have all won teaching awards, which certify a knowledge of what it takes to communicate this material whether orally or in a written fashion.

Casual comments from colleagues reveal a lack of clarity about how one successfully revises a textbook in a field that changes as rapidly as Human Resources. There are many hundreds of articles in the academic and professional literatures that have appeared in the three years since the last book was researched. When the business examples from *The Wall Street Journal*, *Business Week*, and other trade publications are added, the number is staggering. Some of these articles, and certainly the themes that appear in them, represent the changing nature of the subject matter and must be added to our knowledge of the field. Certainly, they must be added to a university text that purports to summarize the field. This book has tried to do that for many editions and has again. You can be confident it contains the most current HR content possible.

The field of HR management is different from some other business topic areas. There is a definite academic/theoretical/research

component that represents new knowledge evidence, and viewpoints in the field, and that is explored, but HR is a very applied professional area too. Just ask the HR leaders that deal with the issues covered here on a daily basis. That professional focus results in this book being widely used in preparation for certification in the HR profession. Our approach has always been that both perspectives are very important in understanding the field, and this strategy is continued in the 14th edition.

With this edition, we welcome a new author. Sean Valentine is an accomplished scholar who has a special interest and expertise in HR and ethics. You will note more consideration of the ethical implications of some HR decisions and areas. He is a strong addition to the author team.

THE FOURTEENTH EDITION

HR takes place in an environment that changes rapidly and impacts the field resulting in needed changes to the book between editions. The 14th edition identifies these changes and how they are being dealt with in the field. A few of the big-picture changes in the 14th edition follow. There are just too many to list all of the changes here that have been necessary, but you will find them in the text.

The Changing Workforce

The workforce that is available for employers to hire greatly affects the day-to-day operation of many HR functions. At this writing unemployment is high, and businesses tell us the needed training and skills for many jobs are simply not available in the workforce. The ethnic and gender mix of potential employees continues to change, the long anticipated retirement of the baby boomers seems to be on hold, and workforce participation rates are dropping. Since understanding these larger trends helps to understand the workforce available to hire, the 14th edition has added a section in Chapter 4—Workforce, Jobs, and Job Analysis—on the workforce that includes profiles, participation rates, skills gaps, and more.

Measuring HR Effectiveness

The trend toward holding HR accountable not only continues but has expanded, and may be the main distinction between HR having the much discussed "seat at the table" and not. The days when someone could be viewed as a successful HR manager because "they just love working with people" are long gone. Benchmarking, metrics, and now analytics are a part of the analysis of how well HR is doing its job. The 14th edition uses a metrics icon to indicate where material on measuring HR is covered throughout the book. Measurement of what HR does is to be welcomed as it can document how HR contributes to organizational goals in a tangible way.

Global Economies

It is probably trite to point out that business is global now and that has changed HR. Offshoring, global M+A, and, of course, all the cultural challenges are not new. But China's continuing success, some manufacturing operations coming back to the United States, and Europe's financial tribulations are new and affect HR. The 14th edition covers global issues throughout the chapters. Feedback from users indicates that many prefer that approach since a separate chapter on global HR often went uncovered in their classes. The material is too important to be ignored, so it is integrated. Globally related material is indicated with a global icon.

HR Ethics

The study of ethics has achieved a toe hold in the academic business world, and HR is a fertile area for the practical application of ethics material. The potential for unethical dealings in compensation, staffing, EEO, and other areas is large, and problematic. At a minimum, beginning to think about these issues can provide a basis for discussion and a realization that some issues do have this dimension associated with them. There is an HR ethics icon where HR ethics issues are covered.

ORGANIZATION OF THE BOOK

- Each chapter opens with an "HR Headline" designed to introduce chapter material with a real company dilemma or problem. Learning objectives are provided at the beginning of each chapter.
- There is a new case to close each chapter and three additional supplemental cases available for each chapter on the book's Web site.
- Chapters contain a mix of three boxed features designed to do different things: *HR Perspectives* provides real examples of how a company dealt with the issue covered. *HR Skills and Applications* provide a "how to do it" view of the material. Finally, *HR Ethics* highlights ethical issues.
- Each chapter ends with a point by point "Summary."
- "Critical Thinking Challenges" provides questions and exercises to apply what has been learned in each chapter. This is available at the end of each chapter.

Material is organized around five sections:

- The Environment of Human Resource Management
- Workforce, Jobs, and Staffing
- Training, Development, and Performance
- Compensation
- Employee Relations

The 14th edition presents both the continuity and changes occurring within Human Resource Management. The chapters in each section will be highlighted next along with some of the topics of note in each.

Section One: The Environment of Human Resource Management

Section one contains chapters emphasizing the changing environment in which HR operates, and how HR can adapt. *Chapter 1* explains why HR is needed and where employees can actually be a core competency for an organization. Basic HR functions and current HR challenges are covered. Ethics and HR as a career field are discussed. Differences in HR in small and large organizations and the important role of productivity are among the topics expanded in this edition. *Chapter 2* deals with two primary ways of dealing with the changing environment—strategy and HR planning. The strategic planning process and HR's role in it are covered. A process for doing HR planning including environmental analysis, assessing internal and external labor markets, and managing imbalances are identified. The chapter closes on HR metrics and analytics and presents benchmarking and balanced scorecard ideas. Good and bad strategy distinctions, HR analytics, and the HR audit are among topics added or expanded. *Chapter 3* deals with the EEO environment, including the legal requirements, concepts, and vocabulary. This comprehensive chapter also contains material on dealing with the challenges presented by EEO issues. Gender equity in compensation, discrimination based on sexual orientation, and religious discrimination/accommodation were expanded.

Section Two: Workforce, Jobs, and Staffing

Section two looks at people, the jobs they do and bringing the two together for the purpose of accomplishing work. *Chapter 4* profiles the United States' workforce participation rates and skills gaps, before turning to the nature of jobs including job design and redesign, flexibility, telework, and work–life balance. The chapter then presents the most comprehensive coverage of job analysis available in a basic HR text. Treatment of the workforce is all new, as is the presentation of jobs, and flexible jobs. *Chapter 5* looks at the individual/organizational relationship and retention. Individual performance factors including a very brief summary of the leading work motivation ideas and the psychological contract are identified. Absenteeism and turnover including measurement issues are covered. The discussion then turns to retention and management options for improving retention. The focus on individual performance factors is virtually all new as is employee engagement and loyalty, and drivers of retention for top employees. *Chapter 6* considers labor markets and recruiting. A pro/con look at online recruiting and the other recruiting methods commonly used is followed by a comprehensive look at measuring the success of recruiting. Recruiting and employer ethics and the use of technology and social media in recruiting are expanded. *Chapter 7* looks at placement, selection testing, interviewing, and background investigations among other topics. New to this edition is person-organization fit as part of the attraction-selection-attrition framework.

Section Three: Training, Development, and Performance

Section three considers bringing people along in their careers in organizations through training, talent management, and career and performance management. *Chapter 8* explores different potential strategies for training in the organization. A comprehensive model of the training process leads ultimately to training delivery and evaluation. New to this edition are issues associated with sales training, expansion of e-learning (online training) based on new research, and the increased use of simulation and games in training. *Chapter 9* looks at talent management, succession planning, and career issues. The topics have been very much in the literature since the last edition. This is reflected through the entire chapter with special emphasis on integrating talent management into the organization's strategy and ideas for keeping high performers invested in their jobs. *Chapter 10* considers identifying and measuring employee performance. Performance appraisal with all its pros and cons are covered as well as hints for the appraisal interview. In this edition, ethical issues surrounding performance appraisal are viewed, and the voluminous new literature in performance has been reviewed and integrated.

Section Four: Compensation

Section four summarizes compensation, incentives, and benefits. *Chapter 11* teaches basic compensation, total rewards, and development of a pay system. New to the 14th edition are strategic compensation decisions, linkage of pay to motivation theories, and current compensation challenges including the use of two-tier wage systems. *Chapter 12* considers variable pay (incentives) and executive pay. Individual, group, and organizational incentive systems are reviewed and the controversial topic of executive compensation is presented. New to this edition are clawbacks, commissions, "say-on-pay", and exit packages changes. *Chapter 13* explains benefits including types, what can be expected by an employer from benefits administering? New or expanded content includes international benefits, the Patient Protection and Affordable Care Act, outsourcing benefit administration, and self service.

Section Five: Employee Relations

Section five covers risk and safety, employee rights and responsibilities, and unions. *Chapter 14* looks at threats to the well-being of both organizations and employees. OSHA, legal requirements for well-being, safety management, and security concerns are specified. New to this edition are medical marijuana, counterproductive employee behaviors, and expansion of the drug testing material. *Chapter 15* looks at rights existing in the employment agreement including privacy rights, workplace monitoring, investigations, and discipline.

Expanded in the 14th edition are alternative dispute-resolution techniques and material on employee rights and ethical issues. *Chapter 16* evaluates the union/management relationship through labor laws, history, collective bargaining, and grievance management. New since the last edition is material on politics and unionization, changes in union membership, and union tactics.

APPENDICES

To keep the chapters sized appropriately, but yet provide additional specific information, the book contains 7 appendices. These provide details on the PHR/SPHR body of knowledge, HR literature, EEO laws, uniform guidelines, illegal pre-employment inquires, EEO enforcement, and HR job descriptions.

SUPPLEMENTS
Instructor's Resource CD

The Instructor's Resource CD puts all of the core resources in one place. The IRCD contains the Instructor's Manual, Test Bank, Examview, and PowerPoint presentation slides.

- *Instructor's Manual*: The instructor's manual represents one of the most exciting and useful aids available. Comprehensive teaching materials are provided for each chapter—including overviews, outlines, instructor's notes, suggested answers to end-of-chapter Review and Applications Questions, suggested questions for the "HR Headline," "HR Outline," "HR Best Practices," and "HR On-the-Job" features, suggested answers to the end-of-chapter case questions, and suggested questions and comments on the supplemental cases for each chapter.
- *Test Bank*: The test bank contains more than 1,800 questions, including multiple choice, true/false, and essay questions. Questions are additionally identified

by type—definition, application, and analytical—and also include AACSB tags for general (NATIONAL) and topic-specific (LOCAL) designations.

- *ExamView*: The easy-to-use ExamView testing software contains all of the questions in the test bank. Instructors can add or edit questions, instructions, and answers. Questions may be selected by previewing them on screen, selecting them randomly, or selecting them by number. Instructor can also create quizzes online whether over the Internet, local area network, or a wide area network.
- *PowerPoint Slide Presentation*: The PowerPoint presentation contains approximately 400 slides to aid in class lectures. They can also be downloaded from the Instructor's Web site.

Study Guide

Designed from a student's perspective, this useful guide provides aids that students can use to maximize results in the classroom and on exams, and, ultimately, in the practice of human resources. Chapter objectives and chapter outlines aid students in reviewing for exams. Study questions include matching, true/false, idea completion, multiple-choice, and essay questions. Answer keys are provided for immediate feedback to reinforce learning.

CengageNOW

This powerful and fully integrated online teaching and learning system provides instructors with flexibility and control, saves valuable time, and improves outcomes. Students benefit by having choices in the way they learn through a unique personalized learning path made possible by CengageNOW.

- *Homework, assignable and automatically graded*
- *Integrated e-book*
- *Personalized learning paths*

- *Interactive course assignments*
- *Assessment options, including AACSB learning standards achievement reporting*
- *Test delivery*
- *Course management tools, including Grade Book*

Speak with your Cengage Learning sales representative about integrating CengageNOW into your courses. Visit www.cengage.com/now today to learn more.

ACKNOWLEDGMENTS

The success of each edition of *Human Resource Management* can largely be attributed to our reviewers, who have generously offered both suggestions for improvements and new ideas for the text. We sincerely thank the following reviewers:

Dr. Casimir Barcyk	*Purdue University—Calumet*
Robyn A. Berkley, Ph.D.	*Southern Illinois University—Edwardsville*
Sherri Bias	*Christopher Newport University*
Barry A. Friedman	*SUNY Oswego*
Inez Giles	*University of Maryland University College*
Joel C. Levy	*Purdue University—Calumet*
Mike Roberson	*Eastern Kentucky University*
Romila Singh	*University of Wisconsin—Milwaukee*

The authors also wish to thank the publishing team at Cengage Learning: Mike Schenk, Product Direct or; Michele Rhoades, Senior Product Manager; Mike Guendelsberger, Senior Content Developer; John Rich, Senior

Media Developer; and Robin LeFevre, Senior Brand Manager.

As the authors, we are confident the 14th edition of *Human Resource Management* will continue to set the standard for the Human Resource field. As the users of the text, we certainly hope you agree.

Robert L. Mathis, SPHR
John H. Jackson
Sean R. Valentine

© Hemera/Thinkstock

The Environment of Human Resource Management

1 Human Resource Management in Organizations

CHAPTER

Learning Objectives

After you have read this chapter, you should be able to:

1 Define human capital.
2 Identify where employees can be used as a core competency.
3 Show the seven categories of HR functions.
4 Provide an overview of four challenges facing HR today.
5 Explain how organizational ethical issues affect HR management.
6 Explain the key competencies needed by HR professionals and why certification is important.

© Hemera/Thinkstock

HR/HEADLINE

Human Resource Management Done Well

© Peter Yates/REA/Redux

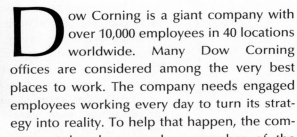

Dow Corning is a giant company with over 10,000 employees in 40 locations worldwide. Many Dow Corning offices are considered among the very best places to work. The company needs engaged employees working every day to turn its strategy into reality. To help that happen, the company's Human Resources department has been made a member of the company's Executive Council. The company believes it cannot reach its potential unless investment is made in its people. After all, employees are the source of all ideas, actions, and performance. Hiring the right people and getting them in the correct jobs, communicating with them, and developing them for greater opportunities are keys to the company's success. However, if company-wide efforts are to be successful in a competitive world, all the human resources decisions must strike a balance among the needs of employees, the economics of the business, and organizational performance.

To measure the extent to which the Human Resources department at Dow Corning is doing its job, elements of human resource (HR) performance are measured and benchmarked against how well competitors are doing in these areas. One common metric regarding human capital is turnover (the rate at which people leave the company). Historically in Dow Corning's U.S. operations, turnover has been about 2% annually, well below average. The average tenure at Dow Corning is 11 years. Employees who start with the company out of high school and are still there 20 or 30 years later are not uncommon.

The HR challenges facing Dow Corning, however, are not unlike those facing most businesses today.

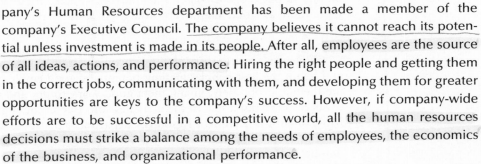

- Finding the right people, especially in developing countries
- Communicating complex information like salary, benefits, and program design around the worldwide operation

3

- Designing opportunities for career advancement within countries and across the entire organization
- Finding meaningful rewards that also encourage the behaviors needed

Some companies hold that their most important assets walk out the door each evening. How does Dow Corning make sure they come back the next morning? The company asked employees why they stay and the employees answered: The people they work with, the opportunities to move up, workplace flexibility, and interesting work keep them there.[1]

Human beings are a necessary, varied, and sometimes problematic resource that different organizations use to a greater or lesser degree. For some organizations, talented employees are the cornerstone of a competitive advantage. If the organization is to compete on the basis of new ideas, outstanding customer service, or quick, accurate decisions, having excellent employees is critical. Of course, not every organization must compete on the basis of having the best employees, but even for those that do not, employees are a major source of organizational performance, problems, growth, resistance and lawsuits.

Productive, creative, and reliable people working in a flexible organization at rewarding work should be the goal for a company in getting the most out of the money spent on its employees. Such organizations often earn the reputation as good employers and as a result have more and better potential employees available than competitors. But how does an employer accomplish such a goal?

When an organization employs people certain things must be done to recruit and retain the best people. Finding potentially good employees, training them, paying them appropriately, giving them good work to do, and providing opportunities to succeed are but a few of the activities someone in the organization must address. Most often it is a Human Resources department that does so.

But even doing such traditional HR activities well is not enough to earn a reputation as a desirable place to work. A company that can do these things well and also look ahead to address the challenges coming, operate ethically, and maintain high productivity can see its human resource practices earn an advantage over competitors.

LO1 Define human capital.

1-1 ■ WHAT IS HUMAN RESOURCE MANAGEMENT?

What is now called human resource management has evolved a great deal since its beginnings circa 1900. What began as a primarily clerical operation in larger companies concerned with payroll and employee records faced changes with the social legislation of the 1960s and 1970s. "Personnel departments," as they came to be called, became concerned with the legal ramifications of policies and procedures affecting employees. In the 1990s, globalization and competition began forcing

Human Resource departments to become more concerned with costs, planning, and the implications of various HR strategies for both organizations and their employees. More recently human resource operations in some companies have been involved with mergers and acquisitions, outsourcing, and managing vendors of certain traditional HR activities such as payroll and executive search. HR may also advise the CEO or chairman of the board in filling vacancies among executives and directors.[2]

Human Resource (HR) management
The design of formal systems in an organization to manage human talent for accomplishing organizational goals.

Human Resource management is designing formal systems in an organization to manage human talent for accomplishing organizational goals. Whether a big company with 10,000 employees or a small nonprofit organization with 10 employees, those employees must be paid, which means an appropriate and legal compensation system is needed. Employees also must be recruited, selected, trained, and managed. Each of these activities requires thought and understanding about what may work well and what may not. Research on these issues and the knowledge gained from successful approaches form the basis for effective HR management.

1-1a Why Organizations Need HR Management

Not every organization has an HR department. In a company with an owner and 10 employees, for example, the owner usually takes care of HR issues. However, despite the obvious differences between large and small organizations, the same HR issues must be dealt with in every organization.

In a sense *every* manager in an organization is an HR manager. Sales managers, head nurses, drafting supervisors, college deans, and accounting department supervisors all engage in HR management, and their effectiveness depends in part on the success of organizational HR systems. It is unrealistic: however: to expect a nursing supervisor to know about the nuances of equal employment regulations or how to design a compensation system. For that reason, larger organizations frequently have people who specialize in these activities which form the HR function or department.

Cooperation between operating managers and the HR department is necessary for HR efforts to succeed. In many cases, the HR department designs processes and systems that the operating managers must help implement. The exact division of labor between the two varies from organization to organization. Throughout this book there will be examples of how HR responsibilities in various areas typically are divided in organizations having HR departments. The suggestions will appear as figures (e.g., see Figure 1-1). That figure shows how the responsibilities for selection interviewing might be divided between an HR department and the other managers in the organization.

1-1b Human Capital

Organizations must manage four types of assets to be successful:

- *Physical assets*: buildings, land, furniture, computers, vehicles, equipment, and so on.
- *Financial assets*: cash, financial resources, stocks, bonds or debt, and so on.
- *Intellectual property assets*: specialized research capabilities, patents, information systems, designs, operating processes, copyrights, and so on.

FIGURE 1-1 Typical Division of HR Responsibilities: Selection Interviewing

HR Department	Managers
• Develops legal, effective interviewing techniques • Trains managers in conducting selection interviews • Conducts interviews and tests • Sends top applicants to managers for final interview • Checks references • Does final interviewing and hiring for certain job classifications	• Advise HR of job openings • Decide whether to do own final interviewing • Receive interview training from HR unit • Do final interviewing and hiring where appropriate • Review reference information • Provide feedback to HR department on hiring/rejection decisions

© Cengage Learning 2014

- *Human assets*: individuals with their talents, capabilities, experience, professional expertise, relationships, and so on.

All these assets are important to varying degrees in different organizations. But the human assets are the "glue" that holds all the other assets together and guides their use to achieve results. Certainly, the cashiers, supervisors, and other employees at Wendy's or Lowe's or the doctors, nurses, receptionists, technical professionals, and other employees at a hospital allow all the other assets of their organization to be used to provide customer or patient services. Effective use of the firm's human capital may explain a significant part of the difference in higher market value between companies.

Human capital is not just the people in organizations—it is also what those people contribute to organizational success. Broadly defined **human capital** is the collective value of the capabilities, knowledge, skills, life experiences, and motivation of an organizational workforce.

Sometimes human capital is called *intellectual capital* to reflect the thinking, knowledge, creativity, and decision making that people in organizations contribute. For example, firms with high intellectual capital may have technical and research employees who create new intellectual property such as biomedical devices, formulate pharmaceuticals that can be patented, or develop new software for specialized uses. All these organizational contributions illustrate the potential value of human capital. However, it should also be noted that unlike intellectual property that the organization *does* own (e.g., patents) it does *not own* its human capital.

A fundamental question is whether better human resource management strategies create higher market value for companies, or whether financially successful companies have more resources to allocate to human capital initiatives. It can be argued that hiring the right people, supporting their creative thinking and productivity, and combining it all with the right technology should build superior business performance and shareholder value.[3] However, the relationship between these two perspectives is more complex than that. In fact, it appears that the way the HR practices *are implemented* affects results.[4] Generally, better HR practices should improve firm performance if implemented properly, and having superior human capital can indeed influence company performance.[5]

Human capital
The collective value of the capabilities, knowledge, skills, life experiences, and motivation of an organizational workforce.

1-1c Managing Human Resources in Organizations

Human resources/human capital (or more simply people) who work in organizations may have valuable contributions they can make to the organization's mission. But these contributions will occur only if people have a reasonable opportunity to contribute. Employees must be placed into the right job, be trained, and given feedback if they are to do well. As noted earlier, it is not just the HR department that does these things, but a team effort between operating managers and the HR department, if one exists.[6] Managing people ultimately has to do with the choices the HR department and managers make from among the wide range of possible choices on the formal policies, practices, and methods for managing employees.[7] Examples of such systems and policies are pay system design, performance measurement, vacation policy, and hiring processes.

Human Resources in Smaller Organizations In the United States and worldwide, small businesses employ more than half of all private-sector employees and generate many new jobs each year. In surveys over several years by the U.S. Small Business Association (SBA), the issues identified as significant concerns in small organizations were consistent: not having enough qualified workers, the rapidly increasing costs of employee benefits, payroll taxes, and compliance with government regulations. Notice that all these concerns have an HR focus, especially when governmental compliance with wage/hour, safety, equal employment, and other regulations are considered.

When new employees are to be hired in a small organization, line managers usually do the recruiting, selecting, and orientation. These HR activities, however, reduce the amount of time managers have available to focus on their regular jobs. As a result, when such activities become more frequent, hiring someone to do them allows managers to spend more time on things only they can do. At about 80–100 employees, small organizations typically find that they need to designate someone to specialize in HR issues. Other HR positions are added as specialists (e.g., in compensation, training, or recruiting) as the company grows larger. The need for HR grows as an organization grows until it evolves into a specialty with specialists assigned to specific duties. However, for HR to be most useful it must remain firmly attached to the operating management of the organization. Without that attachment HR functions cannot reach their potential.

How Human Resource Management Is Sometimes Seen in Organizations HR departments have been viewed in different ways, both positive and negative. HR management is necessary, especially to deal with the huge number of government regulations enacted over the past decades. However, the need to protect corporate assets against the many legal issues often makes the HR function an enforcement role, which may be seen as negative, restrictive, and not focused on getting the business of the organization done.

The legal compliance role can create negative views of HR staff in others. The negative perception that some employees, managers, and executives have is that HR departments are too bureaucratic, detail-oriented, and costly and are comprised of naysayers. These critics do not see HR as making significant organizational contributions. Unfortunately, these views are accurate in some workplaces. Frequently, HR is seen as being more concerned about *activities* than *results*, and HR efforts are seldom seen as linking employee, managerial, and business performance.[8]

Despite such concerns, the HR function *can be* a very important contributor to strategic success if done well.[9] HR must be part of any organization, so it makes sense to see that it is done well.

1-1d Human Resource as a Core Competency

The development and implementation of specific strategies must be based on the areas of strength in an organization. Referred to as *core competencies*, those strengths are the foundation for creating a competitive advantage for an organization. A **core competency** is a unique capability that creates high value at which an organization excels.

Core competency
A unique capability that creates high value at which an organization excels.

Certainly, many organizations have identified that their HR practices differentiate them from their competitors and that HR is a key determinant of competitive advantage. Recognizing this, organizations as diverse as FedEx, Nordstrom, and Dow Corning have focused on human resources as having special strategic value for the organization.

The same can be true with small companies as well. For example, small community banks have added numerous small- and medium-sized commercial loan customers because those banks emphasize that their customers can deal with the same employees directly every time they need help, rather than having to call an automated service center in another state, which is the case with some larger nationwide banks. The focus here is on using people (loan officers) as a core competency.

LO2 Identify where employees can be used as a core competency.

1-2 ■ WHERE EMPLOYEES CAN BE A CORE COMPETENCY

If employees are really to be a core competency for an organization, how might that occur? The possible areas for using employees as a core competency are many, but the focus here will be on three common areas, as shown in Figure 1-2—productivity, customer service/quality, and organizational culture.

1-2a Productivity

MEASURE

Productivity can be a competitive advantage because when the costs to produce goods and services are lowered through high productivity, lower prices can be charged. The result is better sales. Better productivity does not necessarily mean more output. Perhaps fewer people (or less money or time) are used to produce

FIGURE 1-2 Where Employees Can Be a Core Competency

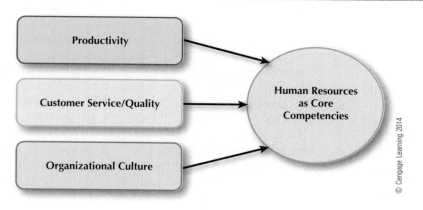

© Cengage Learning 2014

Productivity
Measure of the quantity and quality of work done, considering the cost of the resources used.

the same amount. In its most basic sense, **productivity** is a measure of the quantity and quality of work done, considering the cost of the resources used. A useful way to measure the productivity of a workforce is to determine the total cost of people required for each unit of output.[10] For example, a retailer may measure productivity as a ratio of employee payroll and benefits to sales, or a bank may compare the number and dollar amount of loans made to the number of loan officers employed. This example provides a metric of productivity per loan officer.

Unit labor cost
Computed by dividing the average cost of workers by their average levels of output.

A useful way of measuring the productivity of human resources is to consider **unit labor cost**, which is computed by dividing the average cost of workers by their average levels of output. Using unit labor costs, one can see that relatively high wages will not affect competitiveness if high productivity levels are achieved. Low unit labor costs can be a basis for a strategy focusing on Human Resource competency. Productivity and unit labor costs can be evaluated at the global, country, organizational, departmental, or individual level.

Improving Productivity Productivity at the organizational level ultimately affects profitability and competitiveness in a for-profit organization and total costs in a not-for-profit organization. Perhaps of all the resources used in organizations, the ones most closely scrutinized are human resources. Many HR management efforts are designed to enhance productivity, as Figure 1-3 indicates. Among the major ways to increase employee productivity are as follows:

- *Organizational restructuring* involves eliminating layers of management and changing reporting relationships as well as cutting staff through downsizing, layoffs, and early retirement buyout programs.
- *Redesigning work* often involves having fewer employees who perform multiple job tasks. It may also involve replacing workers with capital equipment or making them more efficient by use of technology or new processes.[11]
- *Aligning HR activities* means making HR efforts consistent with organizational efforts to improve productivity. This alignment includes ensuring that staffing, training and development, performance management, compensation, and other HR activities are not working to offset productivity.[12]
- *Outsourcing analyses* require HR to conduct cost-benefit analysis to examine the impact of outsourcing. Additional factors may include negotiating with outsourcing vendors, ensuring that contractors domestically and internationally are operating legally and appropriately, and linking organizational employees to the outsourcing firm's employees.[13]

1-2b Customer Service and Quality

In addition to productivity, both customer service and quality significantly affect organizational effectiveness and can be an HR focus for a core competency. Having managers and employees focus on the customers' needs contributes significantly to achieving organizational goals and maintaining a competitive advantage. In most organizations, service quality is greatly influenced by the individual employees who interact with customers.[14] For instance, organizations with high employee turnover rates may see slow sales growth. It seems customers consider continuity of customer service representatives important in their buying decisions.[15]

FIGURE 1-3 HR Approaches to Improving Productivity

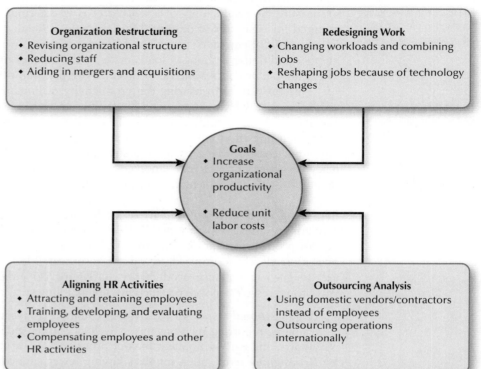

Organization Restructuring
* Revising organizational structure
* Reducing staff
* Aiding in mergers and acquisitions

Redesigning Work
* Changing workloads and combining jobs
* Reshaping jobs because of technology changes

Goals
* Increase organizational productivity
* Reduce unit labor costs

Aligning HR Activities
* Attracting and retaining employees
* Training, developing, and evaluating employees
* Compensating employees and other HR activities

Outsourcing Analysis
* Using domestic vendors/contractors instead of employees
* Outsourcing operations internationally

Customer Service Unfortunately, overall customer satisfaction has declined in the United States and other countries. One example illustrates the importance of service excellence. Within the first six months after being hired, a new CEO at Home Depot directed that labor costs and staffing in the company stores be reduced. As a result, a significant number of long-standing customers complained about not being able to find employees to help them, having to wait a long time to check out, and encountering shortages of merchandise on shelves. At the same time, Lowe's, a major competitor, expanded its staff and advertised its *customer service.* The result was that Lowe's sales and profitability grew significantly, while Home Depot's "cost-cutting" approach created customer problems and significantly affected the performance of the firm. After several years, the Home Depot CEO resigned, and Home Depot took steps to repair its customer service image.

Quality Delivering high-quality services and/or products can significantly influence organizational effectiveness. Whether producing automobiles, as General Motors and Toyota do, or providing cellular phone service, as Verizon and AT & T do, a firm must consider how well its products and services meet customer needs. Therefore, many organizations have emphasized efforts to enhance quality. These programs seek to get tasks done correctly and efficiently so that high quality is delivered by employees. The problems with quality that some U.S. auto manufacturers have had, compared with other firms such as Toyota and Honda, illustrate the important effect of quality on sales, revenue, costs, and ultimately organizational effectiveness. Attempts to improve quality have worked better for some organizations than for others, but usually can be impacted by HR efforts.

1-2c Organizational Culture

Organizational culture
Consists of the shared values and beliefs that give members of an organization meaning and provide them with rules for behavior.

The ability of an organization to use its human capital as a core competency depends at least in part on the organizational culture that is operating.[16] **Organizational culture** consists of the shared values and beliefs that give members of an organization meaning and provide them with rules for behavior. These values are inherent in the ways organizations and their members view themselves, define opportunities, and plan strategies. Much as personality shapes an individual, organizational culture shapes its members' responses and defines what an organization can or is willing to do.

The culture of an organization is seen in the norms of expected behaviors, values, philosophies, rituals, and symbols used by its employees. Culture evolves over a period of time. Only if an organization has a history in which people have shared experiences for years does a culture stabilize.[17] A relatively new firm, such as a business existing for less than two years, probably has not yet developed a stable culture.

Culture is important because it tells people how to behave (or not to behave). It is relatively constant and enduring over time. Newcomers learn the culture from senior employees; hence, the rules of behavior are perpetuated. These rules may or may not be beneficial, so culture can either facilitate or limit performance.

Managers must consider the culture of the organization before implementing HR practices. Otherwise, excellent ideas can be negated by a culture that is incompatible. In one culture, external events might be seen as threatening, whereas in another culture the same changes are challenges requiring immediate responses. The latter type of culture can be a source of competitive advantage.

Organizational culture can be seen as the "climate" of the organization that employees, managers, customers, and others experience. This culture affects service and quality, organizational productivity, and financial results. From a critical perspective, it is the culture of organization, as viewed by its employees, that affects the attraction and retention of competent workers. Alignment of the organizational culture with what management is trying to accomplish determines whether human capital can indeed be a core competency.

L03 Show the seven categories of HR functions.

1-3 ■ HR MANAGEMENT FUNCTIONS

HR management is designing the *formal systems* that are used to manage people in a work organization. Usually, both HR managers and line managers provide input into the policies, regulations, and rules that give guidance on HR matters. For example: How many days of vacation does an employee receive after three years? There is no "right answer" except for a given organization that is trying to devise a vacation policy. But the vacation policy that is finally designed is one of the "formal systems" used to manage people in work organizations. Such systems need to be formal, that is agreed upon and written down for all to see. Try to picture the chaos that would result if every supervisor in a very large company could set his or her own vacation policy!

FIGURE 1-4 HR Management Functions

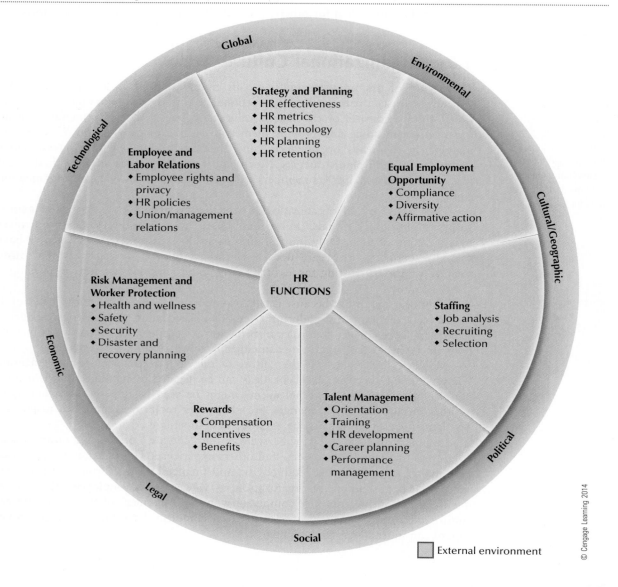

Grouping the areas where HR typically has to have formal systems yields seven interlocking functions, as shown in Figure 1-4. These functions take place in a unique organizational format that is influenced by external forces: global, environmental, cultural/geographic, political, social, legal, economic, and technological in nature. The seven HR functions that must be done can be visualized as follows:

- Strategy and Planning
- Equal Employment Opportunity
- Staffing
- Talent Management
- Rewards

- Risk Management and Worker Protection
- Employee and Labor Relations

Each of these functions consists of several areas covered in the forthcoming chapters of this book as follows:

- *HR Strategy and Planning*: As part of achieving organizational competitiveness, *strategic planning* for the organization and HR's role in those strategic plans are a good starting place. Dealing with workforce surpluses and shortages and predicting human capital needs and availabilities are challenges here. How well HR does what it plans to do is measured by HR metrics and analytics and is covered in Chapter 2.
- *Equal Employment Opportunity*: *Compliance* with federal, state, and even local equal employment opportunity (EEO) laws and regulations affects all other HR activities. The nature of these laws is discussed in Chapter 3.
- *Staffing*: The aim of staffing is to provide a sufficient supply of qualified individuals to fill jobs in an organization. The nature of the workforce, job design and job analysis lays the foundation for staffing by identifying what people do in their jobs and how they are affected by them. Relationships between individuals and the employing organization affect performance and retention of employees. Turnover helps determine how many new employees will be needed, an important bit of information when recruiting applicants for job openings. The selection process is concerned with choosing qualified individuals to fill those jobs. These staffing activities are discussed in Chapters 4, 5, 6, and 7.
- *Talent Management and Development*: Beginning with the *orientation* of new employees, talent management and development includes different types of *training*. *HR development* and *succession* planning for employees and managers are necessary to prepare for future challenges. *Career planning* identifies paths and activities for individual employees as they move within the organization. Assessing how well employees are performing their jobs is the focus of *performance management*. Activities associated with talent management are examined in Chapters 8, 9, and 10.
- *Rewards*: *Compensation* in the form of *pay*, *incentives*, and *benefits* rewards people for performing organizational work. To be competitive, employers develop and refine their basic *compensation* systems and may use *variable pay programs* as incentive rewards. The rapid increase in the cost of *benefits*, especially health care benefits, will continue to be a major issue for most employers. Compensation, variable pay, and benefits activities are discussed in Chapters 11, 12, and 13.
- *Risk Management and Worker Protection*: Employers must address various workplace risks to ensure protection of workers, meet legal requirements, and respond to concerns for workplace *health* and *safety*. Also, workplace *security* has grown in importance along with *disaster and recovery planning* HR implications of these activities are examined in Chapter 14.
- *Employee and Labor Relations*: The relationship between managers and their employees must be handled legally and effectively. *Employer and employee rights* must be addressed. It is important to develop, communicate, and update *HR policies and procedures* so that managers and employees alike know what is expected. In some organizations, *union/management relations* must be addressed as well. Activities associated with employee rights and labor/management relations are discussed in Chapters 15 and 16.

What Do Human Resource Managers Do?

The reality of what HR managers do on a weekly basis can be seen by looking at the diary of one manager. The activities help define HR management in a very "real world" way. Here are *some* activities an HR manager in a 700-employee firm dealt with during one week:

• Resolved an employee complaint about "offensive" pictures being shown by a co-worker.
• Met with the CEO to plan compensation budgets for the following year.
• Met with an outside lawyer regarding a racial discrimination complaint by a former employee who had been terminated because of performance problems.
• Negotiated with the provider of health care insurance benefits to bring a projected 22% increase in premiums down to a 14% increase.
• Reviewed an employee performance appraisal with a supervisor and discussed how to communicate both positive feedback and problem areas.

• Advised an executive on the process for terminating a sales manager whose sales performance and management efforts were significantly below the sales goals set.
• Addressed a manager's report of an employee's accessing pornographic websites on his company computer.
• Hosted an employee recognition luncheon.
• Discussed an employee succession plan for the Customer Operations Division, consisting of 400 employees.
• Discussed with the other members of the executive leadership team (the CEO, the CFO, and division heads) an employee staffing plan for the following year and ways to reduce employee turnover.

Many other topics were part of this HR manager's job that week. However, that list illustrates one fact: "there are a wide range of issues that are part of the regular work in HR management."

These functions are translated into daily activities for the HR department if one exists and for operating managers if an HR department does not yet exist. The HR Perspective: What Do Human Resource Managers Do? shows typical activities during a week in the life of an HR manager in a medium-sized company to illustrate what HR managers do relative to some of the functions just introduced.

1-4 ■ ROLES FOR HUMAN RESOURCE DEPARTMENTS

If an organization has a formal HR group (perhaps a department) there are typically three different roles that group might play in the organization. Which of the roles predominates or whether all three roles are performed depends on what management wants HR to do and what competencies the HR staff has demonstrated. The potential mix of roles is shown in Figure 1-5.

• *Administrative*: Focusing on clerical administration and recordkeeping, including essential legal paperwork and policy implementation

FIGURE 1-5 Mix of Roles for HR Departments

- *Operational and employee advocate*: Managing most HR activities in keeping with the strategies and operations that have been identified by management and serving as employee "champion" for employee issues and concerns
- *Strategic*: Helping to define the business strategy relative to human capital and its contribution to organizational results

While the administrative role traditionally has been the dominant role for HR, the emphasis on the operational and employee advocate role is growing in most organizations. The strategic role requires the ability and orientation to contribute to strategic decisions and a recognition by upper management of those skills. This practice is less common but reportedly growing.

1-4a Administrative Role for Human Resource

The administrative role of HR management has been heavily oriented to processing information and recordkeeping. This role has given HR management in some organizations the reputation of being staffed by people who primarily tell managers and employees what *cannot* be done usually because of some policy or problem from the past. If limited to the administrative role, HR staff are primarily clerical and lower-level administrative aides to the organization. Two major shifts driving the transformation of the administrative role are greater use of technology and outsourcing.

Technology and Administrative Human Resource More HR functions are becoming performed electronically or are being done using Web-based technology. Technology has changed most HR activities, from employment applications and employee benefits enrollments to e-learning. There will always be a record-keeping responsibility. It can, however, be done electronically or outsourced.

Outsourcing Administrative Human Resource Some HR administrative functions can be outsourced to vendors. This outsourcing of HR administrative activities has grown dramatically in HR areas such as employee assistance (counseling), retirement planning, benefits administration, payroll services, and outplacement services. The primary reasons why HR functions are outsourced are to save money on HR staffing, and to take advantage of specialized vendor expertise and technology. These activities are being outsourced to firms both in the United States and worldwide.

1-4b Operational and Employee Advocate Role for Human Resource

HR has been viewed as the "employee advocate" in some organizations. As the voice for employee concerns, HR professionals traditionally may serve as "company morale officers," but they spend considerable time on HR "crisis management," dealing with employee problems that are work-related. Employee advocacy helps ensure fair and equitable treatment for employees regardless of personal background or circumstances. Sometimes the HR advocate role may create conflict with operating managers. However, without the HR advocate role, employers could face even more lawsuits and regulatory complaints than they do now.[18]

The operational role requires HR professionals to cooperate with various departmental and operating managers and supervisors to identify and implement needed programs and policies in the organization. Operational activities are tactical in nature. Compliance with equal employment opportunity and other laws is ensured, employment applications are processed, current openings are filled through interviews, supervisors are trained, safety problems are resolved, and wage and benefit questions are answered. These efforts require making certain that HR operations carry out the strategies of the organization.

1-4c Strategic Role for Human Resources

The strategic role means that HR is proactive in addressing business realities, focusing on future business needs, and understanding how the need for human capital fits into those plans and needs. HR may not help formulate strategies for the organization as a whole; rather it may merely carry them out.

HR management can become a strategic contributor to the "business" success of organizations, because even not-for-profit organizations, such as governmental and social service entities, must manage their Human Resources in a business-like manner. In fact, it has been suggested that the HR function could be managed as its own business within the organization with senior HR executives selected from outside HR experience. Doing this means that these individuals have a business focus, not just HR experience.

Part of the strategy for HR should be knowing what the true cost of human capital is for the employer. For example, in some situations it costs twice a key employees' annual salary to replace her if she leaves. Turnover is something HR can help control, and if it is successful in saving the company money with good retention and talent management strategies, those may be important contributions to the bottom line of organizational performance.

The role of HR as a *strategic business partner* is often described as "having a seat at the table," and contributing to the strategic direction and success of the organization. That means HR is involved in *devising* strategy in addition to *implementing* strategy. That contribution requires financial expertise and financial results, not just employee morale concerns or administrative efficiencies.[19]

A significant concern is whether HR executives are equipped to help plan and meet financial requirements.

Some examples of areas where strategic contributions can be made by HR are:

- evaluating mergers and acquisitions for organizational "compatibility," structural changes, and staffing needs
- conducting workforce planning to anticipate the retirement of employees at all levels and identify workforce expansion in organizational strategic plans
- leading site selection efforts for new facilities or transferring operations to international outsourcing locations on the basis of workforce needs
- instituting HR management systems to reduce administrative time, equipment, and staff costs with technology
- working with executives to develop a revised sales compensation and incentives plan as new products or services are rolled out to customers
- identifying organizational training opportunities that will more than pay back the costs

LO4 Provide an overview of four challenges facing HR today.

1-5 ■ HUMAN RESOURCES MANAGEMENT CHALLENGES

As the field of HR management evolves, a challenging environment provides pressure for even more and faster change. Challenges are to be found in economic forces leading to cost pressures/job changes, globalization, changes in the workforce, and technology advancement.

Competition keeps pressure on business organizations to keep costs down so that prices will not become excessive and customers lost. Global competitors, technology changes, and cost concerns are also reflected in changing jobs. As work must be done differently jobs must change as well and are sometimes lost. Jobs are seldom static but rather changing and evolving along with the organization.

1-5a Competition, Cost Pressures, and Restructuring

An overriding theme facing managers and organizations is to operate in a "cost-less" mode, which means continually looking for ways to reduce costs of all types—financial, operations, equipment, and labor. Pressures from global competitors have forced many U.S. firms to close facilities, use international outsourcing, adapt their management practices, increase productivity, and decrease labor costs to become more competitive.

These shifts have caused some organizations to reduce the number of employees, while at the same time scrambling to attract and retain employees with different capabilities than were previously needed. For examples, see HR Perspective: Competition, Bankruptcy, and Restructuring.

The human cost associated with downsizing has resulted in increased workloads, some loss of employee loyalty, and turnover among the remaining employees. The shifts in the U.S. and global economy in the past years have changed the number and types of jobs present in the United States. The last recession affected many industries including automotive and financial firms. In general, the United States has continued to have private and public sector jobs that fall within the service economy, and many of the additional jobs to be filled in the next several years will be in the service industry rather than in manufacturing firms.

Competition, Bankruptcy, and Restructuring

When American Airlines finally declared bankruptcy it was the last of the traditional airlines to do so. Bankruptcy allowed American to cut costs. The entire airline industry is under powerful competitive financial pressure to keep fares low and costs down as well. At the time of filing bankruptcy, American's annual labor costs were at least $800 million higher than its rivals. Those rivals had used their previous bankruptcies to get their labor (and other) costs down well below American's. However, bankruptcy did not allow American to eliminate all of the advantages held by its biggest rivals—it may have waited too long to seek protection. By holding off bankruptcy for so long, American may have missed its best opportunity to merge, although a merger did finally come about.

The steel industry is another example of economic changes affecting employees. The U.S.

steel industry became viable only after several painful bankruptcies that allowed companies to reduce pension obligations, cut jobs, and restructure debt. A smaller more nimble industry has been very competitive. However, globally weak steel demand and a glut caused by Chinese steel mills more than doubling production forced the world's largest steel company ArcelorMittal to cut its operations. Output had to be cut 20% and the company's market share dropped by almost 40%. It is idling plants in Spain, Poland, Luxembourg, Germany, France, and Belgium to make adjustments.

The Belgium plant alone laid off 581 employees. Competition, costs, and the need to restructure keeps pressures on business organizations for change and that affects employees; HR deals with that impact on employees.[20]

Job Shifts The growth in some jobs and decline in others illustrate that shifts that are indeed occurring. Figure 1-6 lists occupations that are expected to experience the greatest growth in percentage and numbers for the period ending in 2020. Most of the fastest-growing occupations percentage-wise are related to health care. However, when the growth in the number of jobs is compared to the percentage growth, an interesting factor is evident. The highest growth of jobs by percentage is in occupations that generally require more education and training. But much of the largest growth in absolute numbers of jobs is in areas requiring less education and jobs that are lower-skilled.

Another example of the shifting economy is the types of jobs that have the greatest decline in numbers. They include postal employees, farmers/ranchers, fast-food cooks, and sewing machine operators. These declines reflect shifts in economic factors and how those jobs are being combined with others or eliminated because of technology or business changes.[21]

Skills Shortages Various regions of the United States face significant workforce shortages because of an inadequate supply of workers with the skills needed to perform emerging new jobs. It may not be that there are too few people—only that there are too few with many of the skills being demanded. For instance, the hardest jobs to fill today are engineers, nurses, technicians, certain teachers, and sales representatives.

FIGURE 1-6   Selected Fast-Growth Jobs for the Period Ending 2020

Percentage Increase in Jobs		Increase in Job Numbers	
Personal/home care aides	70%	Registered nurses	712,000
Biomedical engineers	62%	Retail salespersons	707,000
Veterinary technologists	56%	Food preparations workers	398,000
Physical therapy assistants	46%	Customer service reps	338,000
Market research analysts	41%	Childcare workers	262,000
Brick masons	41%	Elementary school teachers	249,000
Cost estimators	36%	Janitors	246,000
		Construction laborers	212,000
		Accountants	191,000

Source: U.S. Bureau of Labor Statistics, www.bls.gov.

Even though many Americans are graduating from high school and college, employers are concerned about the preparation and specific skills of new graduates. Test results show that students in the United States perform slightly above average in math and science, but *well below* students in some other directly competitive nations. Also, graduates with degrees in computer science, engineering, and the health sciences remain in short supply relative to the demand for them. Unless major improvements are made to U.S. educational systems, U.S. employers will be unable to find enough qualified workers for the growing number of skilled jobs. However, some groups in the population feel that it is the job of business to offer jobs to people without much regard for their skills.[22]

GLOBAL

1-5b Globalization

Many U.S. firms, both large and small, generate a substantial portion of their sales and profits and sales from other countries. Firms such as Coca-Cola, Exxon/Mobil, Microsoft, and General Electric derive half or more of total sales and profits from outside the United States. However, the reverse is also true. For example, Toyota, based in Japan, has grown its market share and increased its number of jobs in the United States and North America. Also, Toyota, Honda, Nissan, and other Japanese automobile manufacturers, electronics firms, and suppliers have maintained operations in the United States, whereas Chrysler and General Motors have had to reduce major operations.

Research suggests that about 400 mid-sized cities in emerging markets will generate 40% of global growth in the next 15 years. Many of these cities are relatively unknown in the West.[23] The globalization of business has shifted from trade and investment to the integration of global operations, management, and strategic alliances, which has significantly affected the management of human resources. Individuals from other countries are now being recruited as employees. There are three types of global workers: expatriate, host-country national, and third-country national.

An **expatriate** is a citizen of one country who is working in a second country and employed by an organization headquartered in the first country. Experienced expatriates can provide a pool of talent that can be tapped as the organization expands its operations more broadly into even more countries.

A **host-country national** is a citizen of one country who is working in that country and employed by an organization headquartered in a second country. Host-country nationals often know the culture, politics, laws, and business customs better than an outsider would.

A **third-country national** is a citizen of one country who is working in a second country and employed by an organization headquartered in a third country. For example, a U.S. citizen working for a British oil company as a manager in Norway is a third-county national. Staffing with third-country nationals shows a truly global approach.

Attracting global talent, however, has a downside; it has created political issues. For instance, U.S. employers are having a difficult time hiring enough engineers and educated technology workers, because U.S. federal legislation has restricted the number of high-skilled workers to be admitted from other countries.

Wage Comparisons Across Countries Many economic factors are linked to different political, legal, cultural, and economic systems. For example, in many developed countries, especially in Europe, employment restrictions and wage levels are high. When labor costs in the United States are compared with those in Germany and/or the Philippines, the differences are significant, as Figure 1-7 shows. As a result of these differences, many U.S. and European firms are moving jobs to lower-wage countries.

Expatriate
A citizen of one country who is working in a second country and employed by an organization headquartered in the first country.

Host-country national
A citizen of one country who is working in that country and employed by an organization headquartered in a second country.

Third-country national
A citizen of one country who is working in a second country and employed by an organization headquartered in a third country.

FIGURE 1-7 Hourly Wage Compensation for Production Workers

Source: U.S. Bureau of Labor Statistics, www.bls.gov.

Critics of globalization cite the extremely low wage rates paid by some international firms and the substandard working conditions that exist in some underdeveloped countries such as those found in Apple computer factories in China.[24] Various advocacy groups have accused global firms of being "sweatshop employers." As a result, some global employers have made efforts to ensure that foreign factories adhere to higher HR standards, but others have not. Global employers counter that even though the wage rates in some countries are low, their employees often receive the highest wages, and experience the best working conditions that exist in those countries. Also, they argue that more people have jobs in the host countries, which allows them to improve their living standards.

Legal and Political Factors Firms in the United States, Europe, and elsewhere are accustomed to relatively stable political and legal systems. However, many nations function under turbulent and varied legal and political systems. International firms in many industries have dramatically increased security measures for both operations and employees. Terrorist threats and incidents have significantly affected airlines, travel companies, construction firms, and even retailers such as McDonald's. HR management gets involved in such concerns as part of its transnational operations and risk-management efforts.

Compliance with laws and company actions on wages, benefits, union relations, worker privacy, workplace safety, and other issues illustrates the importance of HR management when operating transnationally. As a result, HR professionals conduct comprehensive reviews of the political environment and employment laws before beginning operations in a country. The role and nature of labor unions should be a part of that review. HR practices are different in different countries. But there are changes occurring especially in Europe, converging on a common set of HR practices because of legal and political influences.[25]

Common Challenges for Global Human Resources While HR practices differ in countries there is commonality in how successful companies handle global HR. Those successful approaches include increasing productivity, cutting costs, and investing in local talent while increasing retention rates.[26] Although individual companies do not all necessarily respond to all HR challenges exactly the same way, research suggests that all must face and overcome a common set of difficulties when an organization has a global presence.[27] The areas of difficulties are as follows:

Strategy: Companies feel they do not communicate their strategy clearly to all markets and so find it difficult to be locally flexible as they expand.

People: Executives feel their companies are not good at transferring lessons from one country to another and are not sufficiently effective at recruiting, retaining, training, and developing people in all geographic locations.

Complexity: Complexity arises as standardization of processes clashes with local needs, and sharing the cost of distant centers increases the expense of local operations.

Risk: Emerging market opportunities expose companies to unfamiliar risks that may be difficult to analyze, which results in sometimes rejecting approaches they perhaps should have done.

Global operations require a somewhat different business model.[28] Certainly, global HR presents challenges that are different from those encountered by local HR operations.[29]

1-5c A Changing Workforce

Chapter 4 will present a more comprehensive profile of the workforce, but the following will introduce some of the changes in the workforce that present challenges for human resources. The U.S. workforce is more diverse racially and ethnically, more women are in it than ever before, and the average age of its members is increasing. As a result of these demographic shifts, HR management in organizations has had to adapt to a more varied labor force both externally and internally. The changing workforce has raised employer concerns and requires more attention to resolve these concerns.[30]

Racial/Ethnic Diversity Racial and ethnic minorities account for a growing percentage of the overall labor force, with the percentage of Hispanics roughly equal to or greater than the percentage of African Americans. Immigrants will continue to expand that growth. An increasing number of individuals characterize themselves as *multiracial*, suggesting that the American "melting pot" is blurring racial and ethnic identities.

Racial/ethnic differences have also created greater cultural diversity because of the accompanying differences in traditions, languages, religious practices, and so on. For example, global events have increased employers' attention to individuals who are Muslim, and more awareness and accommodation for Islamic religious beliefs and practices have become a common concern.

Gender in the Workforce Women constitute about 50% of the U.S. workforce, but they may be a majority in certain occupations. For instance, the membership of HR professionals in the Society for Human Resource Management (SHRM) is more than 75% female. Additionally, numerous women workers are single, separated, divorced, or widowed, and are "primary" income earners. A growing number of U.S. households include "domestic partners," who are committed to each other though not married, and who may be of the same or the opposite sex.

For many workers in the United States, balancing the demands of family and work is a significant challenge. Although that balancing has always been a concern, the increased number of working women and dual-career couples has resulted in greater tension for many workers, both male and female. Employers have had to respond to work/family concerns to retain employees. Responses have included greater use of job sharing, the establishment of child-care services, increased flexibility in hours, and work–life programs.

Aging Workforce In many of the more economically developed countries, the population is aging, resulting in a significantly older workforce.[31] In the United States, during the second decade of the twenty-first century, a significant number of experienced employees will be retiring, changing to part-time work, or otherwise shifting their employment. Replacing the experience and talents of longer-service workers is a challenge facing employers in all industries. This loss of longer-service workers is frequently referred to as a "brain drain," because of the capabilities and experience of these workers. Employers are having to develop programs to retain them, have them mentor and transfer knowledge to younger employees, and find ways for them to continue contributing by limited means.[32]

Growth in Contingent Workforce *Contingent workers* (temporary workers, independent contractors, leased employees, and part-timers) represent about one-fourth of the U.S. workforce.[33] Many employers operate with a core group of regular employees who have critical skills, and then expand and shrink the workforce by using contingent workers.

The number of contingent workers has grown for many reasons. One reason is the economic factor. Temporary workers are used to replace full-time employees, and many contingent workers are paid less and/or receive fewer benefits than regular employees. For instance, omitting contingent workers from health care benefits saves some firms 20% to 40% in labor costs.[34]

Another reason for the increased use of contingent workers is that it may reduce legal liability for some employers. As more employment-related lawsuits are filed, employers have become more wary about adding regular full-time employees. By using contract workers, including those in other countries, employers may reduce many legal issues regarding selection, discrimination, benefits, discipline, and termination.

1-5d Human Resource and Technology

In the 1980s most large companies used a mainframe computer to run a Human Resource Information System (HRIS). These systems processed payroll, tracked employees and their benefits, and produced reports for HR managers. All of this was run by Information Technology (IT) people. In 1989 a software package called PeopleSoft became wildly popular—it allowed HR to run its own reports and make changes without help from IT. Today SaaS (Software-as-a-Service) runs in a vendor's data center or in the cloud and the self-service it allows has probably done more to change the work of HR than anything else.[35]

Technology's Advantages The rapid expansion of HR technology serves two major purposes in organizations. One relates to administrative and operational efficiency and the other to effectiveness.[36] The first purpose is to improve the efficiency with which data on employees and HR activities are compiled. The most basic example is the automation of payroll and benefits activities. Another common use of technology is tracking EEO/affirmative action activities. Beyond those basic applications, the use of web-based information systems has allowed the HR unit in organizations to become more administratively efficient and to communicate more quickly with employees.

Another purpose of HR technology is related to strategic HR planning. Having accessible data enables HR planning and managerial decision making to be based to a greater degree on information rather than relying on managerial perceptions and intuition, thus making organizational management more effective.

Technology with its varied uses is greatly impacting the way HR activities are performed. To illustrate, numerous firms provide a web-based employee self-service program to their worldwide staffs. Employees can go online to access and change their personal data, enroll in or change benefits programs, and prepare for performance reviews.

Using technology to support HR activities increases the efficiency of the administrative HR functions and reduces costs. Managers benefit from the availability of relevant information about employees. Properly designed systems provide historical information on performance, pay, training, career progress, and disciplinary actions. On the basis of this information, managers can make better HR-related decisions. To maximize the value of technology, systems should be integrated into the overall IT plan and enterprise software of the organization.[37]

Technology can be used to support every function within human resource management.[38] Recruiting and selection processes have changed perhaps the most dramatically with web-based job boards, online applications, and even online interviewing. Training is now conducted with the aid of videos, podcasts, web-enabled training programs, and virtual classrooms. Employee self-service has simplified benefit enrollment and administration by allowing employees to find health care providers and file claims online. Succession planning and career development are enhanced with real-time information on all employees and their potential career progression. One of the most important ways in which technology can contribute to organizational performance is through the collection and analysis of HR-related data. Identifying trends and modeling future conditions help managers to plan and optimize human resources.

Social Media The explosive growth of the Internet has resulted in many employees and managers using wikis, blogs, tweets, text messaging, and other techniques. In a wiki, which is a widely available website for individuals to make comments, employees can communicate both positive and negative messages on many topics. Employers have used wikis to increase the exchange of ideas and information among a wide range of individuals.

Blogs are web logs kept by individuals or groups to post and exchange information on a range of topics. People create and use more than one million blogs daily. The subjects of blogs vary. An example of company use would be CEOs or HR executives exchanging information with employees immediately on operational or other important occurrences.

Another technology tool is Twitter, which is a microblog that allows people to send and receive tweets, a quick message of less than 140 characters; through these messages individuals quickly send information to others. Some firms use tweets to send out policy changes, competitive services details, and many other organizational messages. However, individuals in an organization can also use tweets inappropriately and send critical, obscene, or even harassing details to other employees.

Firms must establish policies and regulations on how all of this technology can and should be used.[39] For example, IBM has established guidelines directing that the use of tweets must be responsible and protect privacy. Individuals are responsible for correcting mistakes made by individual tweets.

The Risks of Social Media The risk of social media is becoming apparent to employers and some fear that its use will lead to disclosure of trade secrets such as customer lists and many other problems. Users of Facebook approach communication in a casual way with little regard for privacy.[40] Items posted on a blog or Facebook can easily become public. Many other potential problems exist with social media at work.[41] Yet there are signs that it will become mainstream within most companies.[42] Indeed, companies are using social media for everything from enhancing employee interaction[43] to pinpointing leadership qualities in management candidates.[44] By creating appropriate standards of use companies can see responsible utilization of technology.

ETHICS

L05 Explain how organizational ethical issues affect HR management.

1-6 ■ ORGANIZATIONAL ETHICS AND HUMAN RESOURCE MANAGEMENT

Closely linked with the strategic role of HR is the way managers and HR professionals influence the ethics of people in organizations. How those ethics affect work and lives for individuals may aid in producing more positive work outcomes.

FIGURE 1-8 HR and Organizational Ethics

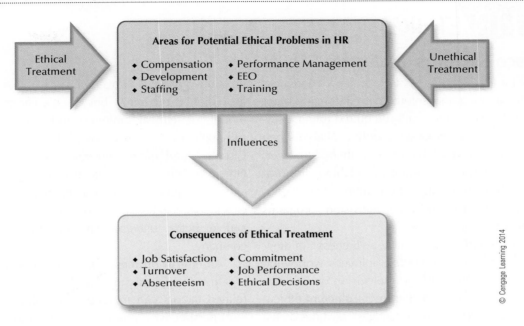

As Figure 1-8 indicates, violating HR protocols can lead to organizational and individual consequences.[45]

Attention to ethics has grown in the past few years, as evidenced by the corporate scandals at numerous financial and investment firms in the United States and globally. These scandals illustrate that ethical lapses are not just symbolic; they affect employers and employees. The expansion of the Internet electronic job boards and postings has led to more publicity about ethical issues. An increase in ethics issues has been identified by the Ethics Resource Center. One survey of 3,000 U.S. workers found that within a year, 52% had seen one incident of misconduct and 36% had observed two or more ethical violations. The survey also reported that almost 70% of employers had done ethics training.[46]

1-6a Ethical Behavior and Culture

Writers on business ethics consistently stress that the primary determinant of ethical behavior is organizational culture, which, as mentioned earlier, is the shared values and beliefs in an organization. Every mature organization has a culture, and that culture influences how executives, managers, and employees make organizational decisions. For example, if meeting objectives and financial targets is stressed, then it should not be a surprise when executives and managers fudge numbers or falsify cost records. However, a positive ethical culture exists in many organizations. When the following four elements of ethics programs exist, ethical behavior is more likely to occur:

• A written code of ethics and standards of conduct
• Training on ethical behavior for all executives, managers, and employees

HR ETHICS

Cisco Systems Trains on Ethics

Until a few years ago, Cisco Systems conducted ethics training and enforcement like many other firms by using organization-required training sessions. Those sessions were only available when someone was available to teach them. However, Cisco now uses a constantly available ethics program through its internal communications (intranet), Internet, and even television programs similar to *American Idol*.

To conduct its ethics awareness training, Cisco enables its 60,000 employees worldwide to view the *Ethics Idol* via television on its intranet. Cartoon individuals present different ethical situations and then have "judges" give decisions. Employees vote on the best answer to each ethical situation. After the employees vote, Cisco's ethics office professionals then give the best answer based on Cisco company standards and compliance requirements.

Merging ethics issues, technology, and regular interactive training has led to better understanding

of ethics among Cisco employees. Other firms have similar programs, but Cisco's efforts are a model of ethical training and engagement. Although many firms have ethics programs, Cisco's broad efforts illustrate how expanding ethical training can be effective. Using creative and entertaining self-paced training to teach ethics concepts has led to more ethical behavior, and a better understanding of ethics in the company.[47]

An ethical business culture is based first on organizational mission and values. Other related factors can include shareholders, long-term perspectives, process integrity, and leadership effectiveness.[48] The roles of boards, CEOs, other executives, and HR leaders are vital in setting the culture for ethics globally as well as locally. Training of employees is crucial, and with the use of innovative training, Cisco Systems has emphasized the importance of ethics to the company.

- Advice to employees on ethical situations they face, often made by HR
- Systems for confidential reporting of ethical misconduct or questionable behavior

1-6b Ethics and Global Differences

ETHICS

GLOBAL

Differences in legal, political, and cultural values and practices in different countries often raise ethical issues for global employers that must comply with both their home-country laws and the laws of other countries. With the changes in the global economy in the past few years, the Organization for Economic Cooperation and Development (OECD), has emphasized the effects of ethics. The OECD has recommended that global multinational firms establish and implement stricter ethical standards to aid business development.[49]

The different legal, political, and cultural factors in other countries can lead to ethical and legal conflicts for global managers. Some global firms have established guidelines and policies, for example, to reduce the payments of bribes, but even those efforts do not provide detailed guidance on handling all the situations that can arise.

1-6c Role of Human Resources in Organizational Ethics

Organizations that are viewed as ethical in the way they operate have better long-term success. People in organizations face ethical decisions on a daily basis, and HR management plays a key role as the "keeper and voice" of organizational ethics. Instead of relying just on HR policies or laws, people must be guided by their own values and personal behavior "codes," including these two questions:

- Does the behavior or result meet all applicable *laws*, *regulations*, and *government codes*?
- Does the behavior or result meet both *organizational standards* and *professional standards* of ethical behavior?

There are many different views about the importance of HR in ensuring that ethical practices, justice, and fairness are embedded in HR practices. Figure 1-9 identifies some of the most frequent areas of ethical misconduct involving HR activities.

Ethical issues pose fundamental questions about fairness, justice, truthfulness, and social responsibility. Just complying with a wider range of requirements, laws, and regulations cannot cover every ethical situation that executives, managers, HR professionals, and employees will face. Yet, having all the elements of an ethics program may not prevent individual managers or executives from engaging in or failing to report unethical behavior. Even HR staff members may be reluctant to report ethics concerns, primarily because of fears that doing so may affect their current and future employment.[50]

Critical for guiding ethical decisions and behavior is training. Firms such as Best Buy, Caterpillar, and others have training for all employees via the Internet or in person. The HR ethics box shows an example. How to address difficult and conflicting situations is part of effective HR management training efforts. To help HR professionals deal with ethical issues, the Society for Human Resource Management has developed a code of ethics for its members and provides information on handling ethical issues and policies.[51]

FIGURE 1-9 Examples of HR-Related Ethical Misconduct

Compensation	Employee Relations	Staffing and Equal Employment
◆ Misrepresenting hours and time worked ◆ Falsifying work expense reports ◆ Showing personal bias in performance appraisals and pay increases ◆ Allowing deliberate inappropriate overtime classifications ◆ Accepting personal gains/gifts from vendors	◆ Employees lying to supervisors and coworkers ◆ Executives/managers e-mailing false public information to customers and vendors ◆ Misusing/stealing organizational assets and supplies ◆ Intentionally violating safety/health regulations	◆ Discriminatory favoritism in hiring and promotion ◆ Sexual harassment of other employees ◆ EEO discrimination in recruiting and interviewing ◆ Conducting inappropriate background investigations

HR Ethics and Sarbanes-Oxley The Sarbanes-Oxley (SOX) Act was passed in 2002 by Congress to make certain that publicly traded companies follow accounting controls that could reduce the likelihood of illegal and unethical behaviors. Many HR issues must be managed in line with SOX. The biggest concerns are linked to executive compensation and benefits, but SOX sections 404, 406, 802, and 806 require companies to establish ethics codes, develop employee complaint systems, and have antiretaliation policies for employees who act as whistle blowers to identify wrongful actions. HR has been involved in routing people through the massive compliance verification effort that has occurred.

L06 Explain the key competencies needed by HR professionals and why certification is important.

1-7 ■ HUMAN RESOURCES MANAGEMENT COMPETENCIES AND CAREERS

The intent of this book is not to train all who read it to be an HR manager. Most will take this knowledge and work at another job in the organization but understand the duties HR must accomplish and which they must often share. Given that, it is useful to understand the necessary competencies and certifications for HR managers.

1-7a Human Resource Competencies

The transformation of HR toward being more strategic and professional has implications for the competencies needed.[52] HR professionals at all levels need the following:

- Strategic knowledge and impact
- Legal, administrative, and operational capabilities
- Technology knowledge and usage abilities

Senior HR leaders may need additional capabilities and competencies. According to an overview from an SHRM study, senior HR leaders also need (a) more business, strategic, HR, and organizational knowledge; (b) ability to lead changes because of credibility; and (c) ethical behavior and results orientation/performance.[53]

For individuals with HR as their career, these competencies help establish their value as professionals.[54]

1-7b Human Resource Management as a Career Field

HR generalist
A person who has responsibility for performing a variety of HR activities.

HR specialist
A person who has in-depth knowledge and expertise in a limited area of HR.

A variety of jobs exists within the HR career field, ranging from executive to clerical. As an organization grows large enough to need someone to focus primarily on HR activities, the role of the **HR generalist** emerges—that is, a person who has responsibility for performing a variety of HR activities. Further growth leads to the addition of **HR specialists**, or individuals who have in-depth knowledge and expertise in limited areas of HR.[55] The most common areas of HR specialty, in order of frequency, are benefits, employment and recruitment, and compensation. Appendix G contains examples of HR-related job descriptions of both a generalist and a specialist.

HR jobs can be found in corporate headquarters as well as in field and subsidiary operations.[56] A compensation analyst or HR director might be found at a corporate headquarters. An employment manager for a manufacturing plant and a European HR manager for a global food company are examples of field and subsidiary HR professionals. These two types of jobs have different career appeals and challenges.

1-7c Human Resource Professionalism and Certification

Depending on the job, HR professionals may need considerable knowledge about employment regulations, finance, tax law, statistics, and information systems.[57] In most cases, they also need extensive knowledge about specific HR activities. The broad range of issues faced by HR professionals has made involvement in professional associations and organizations important. For HR generalists, the largest organization is the Society for Human Resource Management (SHRM). Public-sector HR professionals tend to be concentrated in the International Personnel Management Association (IPMA). Two other prominent specialized HR organizations are the WorldatWork Association and the American Society for Training and Development (ASTD).

One characteristic of a professional field is having a means to certify that members have the knowledge and competence needed in the profession. The CPA for accountants and the CLU for life insurance underwriters are examples. Certification can be valuable to individuals and useful to employers as they select and promote certified individuals. The most well-known certification programs for HR generalists are administered by the Human Resource Certification Institute (HRCI), which is affiliated with SHRM. More than 100,000 professionals have an HRCI certification.

HRCI Certification The most widely known HR certifications are the Professional in Human Resources (PHR) and the Senior Professional in Human Resources (SPHR), both sponsored by HRCI. Annually, thousands of individuals take the certification exams. HRCI also sponsors a Global Professional in Human Resources (GPHR) certification. Eligibility requirements for PHR, SPHR, and GPHR are shown in Figure 1-10.

Additionally, eligible individuals must pass the appropriate exam. Appendix A identifies test specifications and knowledge areas covered by the PHR and SPHR exams. Readers of this book can identify specific competencies for the HRCI outline to aid them in earning a PHR or SPHR. Certification from HRCI also exists for global HR professionals in the GPHR. Global certification recognizes the growth in HR responsibilities in organizations throughout the world and covers appropriate global HR subject areas noted through SHRM.

WorldatWork Certifications The WorldatWork Association has certifications emphasizing compensation and benefits. The four certifications are as follows:

- Certified Compensation Professional (CCP)
- Certified Benefits Professional (CBP)
- Certified Work–Life Professional (CWLP)
- Certified Global Remuneration (CGR)

Other Human Resource Certifications Increasingly, employers hiring or promoting HR professionals are requesting certifications as a "plus." HR certifications give HR professionals more credibility with corporate peers and senior managers. Additional

FIGURE 1-10 HR Certifications at a Glance

The certification exams test on experience-based knowledge; therefore, you must possess a **minimum of two years of professional (exempt-level) HR experience.***

	Professional in Human Resources (PHR®)	Senior Professional in Human Resources (SPHR®)	Global Professional in Human Resources (GPHR®)
Exam Eligibility Requirements	Minimum of two years of professional (exempt-level) HR experience.	Minimum of two years of professional (exempt-level) HR experience.	Must hold a current PHR or SPHR certification.
	At least 51% of your daily work activities are within the HR function.	At least 51% of your daily work activities are within the HR function.	At least 51% of your daily work activities are within the HR function.
Profile of a Successful Candidate*	Has two to four years of professional (exempt-level) generalist experience.	Has six to eight years of progressive professional (exempt-level) experience.	Has at least two years of professional (exempt-level) experience in international HR practices.
	Focuses on program implementation rather than creation.	Designs and plans rather than implement.	Has core knowledge of the organization's international HR activities.
	Focuses within the HR function rather than organization-wide.	Makes decisions that have an impact within and outside the organization.	Develops and implements international HR strategies that affect international HR assignments and operations.

© Cengage Learning 2014

*In addition to meeting the exam eligibility requirements, successful exam candidates usually have the above work experience.

certification programs for HR specialists and generalists are sponsored by various organizations, and the number of certifications is being expanded. For specialists, some well-known programs include the following:

- Certified Recognition Professional (CRP) sponsored by the Recognition Professionals International
- Certified Employee Benefits Specialists sponsored by the International Foundation of Employee Benefits Plans
- Certified Professional in Learning and Performance sponsored by the American Society for Training and Development
- Certified Safety Professional (CSP) and Occupational Health and Safety Technologist (OHST) sponsored by the American Society of Safety Engineers
- Certified Graphics Communications Manager (CGCM) and Certified Mail Manager (CMM) sponsored by the International Personnel Management Association

Most individuals who want to succeed in the field update their knowledge continually. One way of staying current in HR is to tap information in current HR literature and relevant associations, as listed in Appendix B of this book. Overall, certifying knowledge is a trend in many professions, and HR illustrates the importance of certification by making many types available. Given that many people may enter HR jobs with limited formal HR training, certifications help both individuals and their employers to make HR management a better performing part of their organizations.

SUMMARY

- HR management should ensure that human talent is used effectively and efficiently to accomplish organizational goals.
- All organizations need HR management, but larger ones are more likely to have a specialized HR function.
- Organizations need HR because the HR functions must be done by *someone* in all organizations.
- Human capital is the collective value of the capabilities, knowledge, skills, life experiences, and motivation of an organizational workforce.
- HR management activities can be grouped as follows: strategic HR management; equal employment opportunity; staffing; talent management; compensation and benefits; health, safety, and security; and employee and labor relations.
- HR departments can take administrative, operations, and/or strategic roles in the organization.

- As an organization core competency, Human Resources has a unique capability that can create high value and differentiates an organization from competitors in areas such as productivity, quality/service, and organizational climate.
- Numerous HR challenges exist currently, including organizational cost pressures, globalization, a changing workforce, and technology.
- Ethical behavior is crucial in HR management, and HR professionals regularly face many ethical issues and consequences both domestically and globally.
- All levels of HR professionals need competencies in strategic knowledge and impacts; capabilities in legal, administrative, and operational areas; and technology abilities. Senior HR leaders need these areas plus others to be effective.
- Current knowledge about HR management is required for professionals in the HR career field, and professional certification has grown in importance for HR generalists and specialists.

CRITICAL THINKING CHALLENGES

1. Discuss several areas in which HR can affect organizational culture positively or negatively.

2. Give some examples of ethical issues that you have experienced in jobs, and explain how HR did or did not help resolve them.

3. Why is it important for HR management to transform from being primarily administrative and operational to becoming a more strategic contributor?

4. Assume you are an HR director with a staff of seven people. A departmental objective is for all staff members to become professionally certified within a year. Using Internet resources of HR associations, such as www.shrm.org and www. WorldatWork.org, develop a table that identifies four to six certifications that could be obtained by your staff members, and show the important details for each certification.

5. Your company, a growing firm in the financial services industry, is extremely sensitive to the issues surrounding business ethics. The company wants to be proactive in developing a business ethics training program for all employees both to ensure the company's reputation as an ethical company in the community and to help maintain the industry's high standards. As the HR Director and someone who values the importance of having all employees trained in the area of business ethics, you are in charge of developing the ethics training program. It needs to be a basic program that can be presented to all employees in the company. Resources for business ethics information can be found at www. business-ethics.org/primer1.html.

A. What legislative act prompted many U.S. companies to develop internal ethical policies and procedures?

B. What are key concepts related to business ethics that should be considered in the development of the ethics training program?

CASE

Rio Tinto: Redesigning HR

Rio Tinto is a mining and minerals company headquartered in London. The multibillion-dollar company employs over 98,000 people worldwide and operates in more than 60 different sites in over 50 countries.

When the 2008 global recession hit it was clear that a reduction in workforce would be necessary for the company to survive, and 14,000 employees and contractors were let go. HR had been involved in the initial business discussions and understood that the reduction in force (RIF) was necessary.

For the first time, Rio Tinto's HR used a co-ordinated approach globally. Previously, executives and HR directors in the individual business units would have all approached the downsizing differently. But this time with a common approach, the downsizing took place in an efficient, ethical, and sensitive manner, using regional severance policies and a comprehensive database and measurement tools to track the impact of the redirections. High-potential leaders and people with critical skills were identified and were moved around internally to retain them. Managers were trained to help the "survivors" stay focused. Previously the process would have taken two or three times as long it was estimated, and employee engagement and morale would have taken a much harder hit.

Rio Tinto had undertaken a strategic analysis and reformation of the HR functions before the RIF that made the favorable results possible. The analysis looked at HR functions for both effectiveness and efficiency. All HR functions needed to be delivered at a lower cost while maintaining quality. Previously most HR professionals would have spent their whole career in one plant. Today they move across product groups, locations, and assignments fostering a more consistent culture. A senior HR council to provide leadership and guidance was started. This helped with a consistent HR philosophy that supported policies and standards for the whole company.

Efficiencies were achieved by using more digital processes and adding self-service tools for employees. Bringing together disparate HR departments across multiple business units increased speed and lowered costs. Further, the company moved from a defined benefit pension plan to a defined contribution plan to conserve cash through reduction in long-term pension liabilities.

Rio Tinto feels that using their human capital better, organizing teams, developing talent, and supporting innovation and creativity can help make the company's people a source of potential competitive advantage. The company's HR professionals gained new skills relative to helping productivity in the workforce. The value of a 1% to 2% increase in productivity far outweighed the entire cost of the transformation of Rio Tinto's HR function.[58]

QUESTIONS

1. How did Rio Tinto's revamping of HR help with minimizing the potential problems with the reduction in force? What role would an HRIS (also called a Human Resource information system) have to play in managing an RIF?

2. Without a consistent philosophy, policies, and approaches to reduction in force (or any other disruptions in the future) what would the likely reactions from employees be?

SUPPLEMENTAL CASES

Phillips Furniture

This case describes a small company that has grown large enough to need a full-time HR person. You have been selected to be the HR manager, and you have to decide what HR activities are needed as well as and the role HR is to play. (For the case, go to www.cengage.com/management/mathis.)

Sysco

As a large food services and distribution firm, Sysco had to revise its HR management. Review this case and identify how the Sysco changes modified HR's importance. (For the case, go to www.cengage.com/management/mathis.)

HR, Culture, and Success at Google, Scripps, and UPS

The case describes HR's role in the culture of three different companies. The contribution to organizational success in each case can be identified and further researched. (For the case go to www.cengage.com/management/mathis.)

NOTES

1. Based on "Dow Corning: The Culture with the Right Chemistry," *Workspan*, June 2010, 14–19.
2. Peter Cappelli, "The Restructuring of the Top HR Job," *Human Resource Executive Online*, May 21, 2012, 1–2.
3. "Maintaining Momentum," *Human Resource Executive*, December 2011, 18–20. Karen L. Ferguson and Thomas G. Reid Jr., "Human Resource Management Systems and Firm Performance," *Journal of Management Development*, No. 5, 2010, 471–494.
4. David E. Guest, "Human Resource Management and Performances: Still Searching for Some Answers," *Human Resource Management Journal*, 21, 2011, 3–13.
5. T. Russell Crook, et al., "Does Human Capital Matter? A Meta Analysis of the Relationship between Human Capital and Firm Performance," *Journal of Applied Psychology*, 96, 2011, 443–456. Patrick M. Wright and Gary C. McMahan, "Exploring Human Capital: Putting Human Back into Strategic Human Resource Management," *Human Resource Management Journal*, 21, 2011, 93–104.
6. Y. Gong, et al, "Human Resource Management and Firm Performance," *Journal of Applied Psychology*, 94, 2009, 263–275.

7. Bruce E. Kaufman and Benjamin I. Miller, "The Firm's Choice of HRM Practices: Economics Meets Strategic Human Resource Management," *Industrial and Labor Relations Review*, 64, 2011, 526–557.
8. Rebecca R. Kehoe and Patrick M. Wright, "The Impact of High Performance Human Resource Practices on Employees Attitudes and Behaviors," *Journal of Management*, April 8, 2010, 87–93.
9. James P. Guthrie, et al., "Big Hat, No Cattle? The Relationship between Use of High-Performance Work Systems and Managerial Perceptions of HR Departments," *The International Journal of Human Resource Management*, 62, January 2009, 104–114.
10. Peter Bisson, et al., "The Productivity Imperative," *McKinsey Quarterly*, June 2010, 1–8; Eric Matson and Laurence Prusak, "Boosting the Productivity of Knowledge Workers," *McKinsey Quarterly*, September 2010, 1–6; David Hunt, et al., "Why U.S. Productivity Can Grow without Killing Jobs," *McKinsey Quarterly*, February 2011, 1–6.
11. Christopher Power, "Machines Don't Get Paid Overtime," *Bloomberg Business Week*, August 8, 2010, 17.
12. Chung-Jen Chen and Jing-Wen Huang, "Strategic Human Resource Practices and Innovation Performance," *Journal of Business Research*, 62, January 2009, 104–114.
13. Peter Brown, "The Power of HR Outsourcing," *Strategic HR Review*, 9, 2010, 27–32; Eric Krell, "Focus In to Farm Out," *HR Magazine*, July 2011, 47–49.
14. Jennifer Schramm, "HR's Challenging Next Decade," *HR Magazine*, November 2010, 96.
15. John DeVine, et al., "The Human Factor in Service Design," *McKinsey Quarterly*, January 2012, 1–6.
16. Robert E. Ployhart, et al., "The Consequences of Human Resource Stocks and Flows: A Longitudinal Exam of Unit Service Orientation and Unit Effectiveness," *Academy of Management Journal*, 52, 2007, 996–1015. Katherine Tyler, "Diagnosing Cultural Health," *HR Magazine*, August 2011, 52–53.
17. Carol Morrison, "The Four Ps of High Performance," *Human Resource Executive Online*, June 16, 2011, 1–4. Peter Cappelli, "Creating a Performance Culture," *Human Resource Executive Online*, September 12, 2010.
18. Harry J. Van Buren III, et al., "Strategic Human Resource Management and the Decline of Employee Focus," *Human Resource Management Review*, 21, September 2011, 209–219.
19. Jennifer Schramm, "Under Pressure," *HR Magazine*, April 2011, 104.
20. Based on Diane Brady, "American Airlines Last-Mover Disadvantage," *Bloomberg Business Week*, December 11, 2011, 25–33. Stanley Reed, et al., "On Top of the World-and Out $43 Billion," *Bloomberg Business Week*, November 14, 2011, 27–32.
21. G. S. Oettinger, "The Incidence and Wage Consequences of Home-Based Work in the United States," *Journal of Human Resources*, 46, 2011, 237–260.
22. John Bussey, "Are Companies Responsible for Creating Jobs?" *The Wall Street Journal*, October 28, 2011, B1–B2.
23. Markin Dewhurst, et al., "The Global Company's Challenge," *McKinsey Quarterly*, June 2012, 1–5.
24. Rex Nutting, "Apple's Chinese Labor Problem," *The Denver Post*, February 19, 2012, 4K.
25. Wolfgang Mayrhofer, et al., "Hearing a Different Drummer? Convergence of Human Resource Management in Europe—A Longitudinal Analysis," *Human Resource Management Review*, 21, 2011, 50–67. J. S. Sahadev and M. Demirbag, "Exploring Variations in Employment Practices in the Emerging Economies of Europe," *Human Resource Management Journal*, 21, 2011, 395–414; J. Poor, et al., "Comparative International Human Resource Management in the Light of the Cranet Regional Research Survey," *Employee Relations*, 33, 2011, 428–443.
26. Tom Stamer, "Thinking Globally," *Human Resource Executive Online*, January 1, 2009, 1–4.
27. M. Dewhurst, et al., op cit, 2–5.
28. Peter Cappelli, et al., "The India Way: Lessons for the U.S.," *The*
Academy of Management Perspectives, 24, May 2010, 6–24.
29. Karen V. Beaman, "Going Global," *Human Resource Executive Online*, July 1, 2009, 1–4.
30. Marlene Prost, "When the End Is in Sight," *Human Resource Executive Online*, July 1, 2010, 1–5.
31. Birgit Verworn, et al., "Changing Workforce Demographics: Strategies Derived from the Resource-Based View of HRM," *International Journal of Human Resources Development and Management*, 9, 2009, 149–161.
32. John Dumay and Jim Rooney, "Dealing with an Aging Workforce," *Journal of Human Resource Costing and Accounting*, 15, 2011, 174–195.
33. Michael O'Brien, "A Temp's Perspective," *Human Resource Executive Online*, February 1, 2009, 1.
34. Jennifer Taylor Arnold, "Managing a Nontraditional Workforce," *HR Magazine*, August 2010, 75–77.
35. Bill Kutik, "Lifetimes of Tech Change," *Human Resource Executive Online*, April 3, 2012, 1–2.
36. E. Parry and S. Tyson, "Desired Goals and Actual Outcomes of e-HRM," *Human Resource Management Journal*, 21, 2011, 335–354. Tom Sonde, "Why Isn't Improving HRIS a Management Priority," *Workspan*, June 2011, 51–57.
37. Clinton Wingrove, "Why Automating Bad HR Processes Isn't a Solution," *Workspan*, February 2012, 47–50.
38. Bill Roberts, "The Grand Convergence," *HR Magazine*, October 2011, 39–46.
39. Jeffrey S. Klein, et al., "When Social Networking and the Workplace Collide," *Human Resource Executive Online*, June 16, 2010, 1–4.
40. John F. Birmingham and Jennifer L. Neumann, "Social Media and the Workplace," *Inside Supply Management*, March 2011, 12–14.
41. Jennifer Taylor Arnold, "Twittering and Facebooking While They Work," *HR Magazine*, December 2009, 53–55.
42. Jeanne C. Meister and Karie Willyerd, "Five Myths and Realities about Using Social Media in Your Company," *People and Strategy*, 3, 2010, 4–5.

43. Bill Roberts, "Developing a Social Business Network," *HR Magazine*, October 2010, 54–60.

44. Susan R. Meisinger, "Pinpointing Leadership Qualities," *Human Resource Executive Online*, November 29, 2010, 1–2.

45. David M. Mayer, et al, "Who Displays Ethical Leadership and Why Does It Matter?", *The Academic of Management Journal*, 55, February 2012, 151–171.

46. Ethics Resource Center, www.ethics.org.

47. Based on Michael O'Brien, "'Idol'-izing Ethics," *Human Resource Executive Online*, May 16, 2009.

48. Alexandria Ardichvilli, et al., "Characteristics of Ethical Business Cultures," *Journal of Business Ethics*, 85 (2009), 445–451.

49. Frank Kilmo, "Stricter Ethical Standards Called Key to Global Recovery," February 18, 2009, *HR News*, www.shrm.org.

50. Susan R. Meisinger, "Examining Organizational Ethics," *Human Resource Executive Online*, June 11, 2012, 1–2.

51. To view the code of ethics and its development, go to www.shrm.org.

52. Marja-Liisa Payne, "A Comparative Study of HR Manager's Competencies in Strategic Roles," *International Management Review*, 6, 2010, 5–12.

53. Amanda Benedict, et al., "Leading Now, Leading the Future: What Senior HR Leaders Need to Know," *SHRM Executive Summary*, February 2009, 1–23.

54. Rita Zeidner, "Dave Ulrich: Getting HR Right," *HR Magazine*, August 2009, 21.

55. Dave Zielinski, "Building a Better HR Team," *HR Magazine*, August 2010, 65–67.

56. Jared Shelly, "CFO's Extend Reach into HR," *Human Resource Executive Online*, August 19, 2011, 1–2.

57. Kristen B. Frasch, "The Changing Face of HR," *Human Resource Executive Online*, June 2, 2010, 1–4. Peter Cappelli, "The Last 25 Years Point to the Future," *Human Resource Executive Online*, March 26, 2012, 1–2.

58. Adapted from Andrew Slentz, "Going Global to Last," *HR Magazine*, August 2009, 36–38.

2

Human Resource Strategy and Planning

Learning Objectives

After you have read this chapter, you should be able to:

1 Summarize the organizational strategic planning process.
2 Explain the key differences between good and bad strategy and suggest a way to force strategic asset reallocation.
3 Outline how HR's strategies are merged with organizational strategies and give two examples.
4 Discuss how to forecast for supply and demand of Human Resources.
5 List options for handling a shortage and surplus of employees.
6 Identify how organizations can measure and analyze the effectiveness of HR management practices.

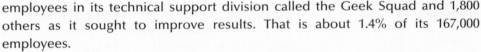

HR HEADLINE

Best Buy Cuts 2,400 Jobs in Turnaround Strategy

B est Buy needed a strategy to combat the "showrooming" of its stores. Showrooming occurs when customers go to a big box's well-stocked stores to see, compare, and demonstrate its products, but then leave and purchase the products at a discount or an online store. The big retailer laid off 600 employees in its technical support division called the Geek Squad and 1,800 others as it sought to improve results. That is about 1.4% of its 167,000 employees.

The company also announced a restructuring that would close 50 of its United States big box stores, cut 400 corporate jobs, and reduce costs by $800 million to be more price competitive. The company plans to open 100 smaller and more profitable Best Buy mobile stores to go with its 1,400 existing locations.

Shortly after the strategy was announced (in an unrelated situation), the CEO of Best Buy abruptly left the company and it was later found that he had had an inappropriate relationship with a female employee. However, the interim CEO reiterated the company's commitment to the strategy of fundamentally changing its operations to improve results. A spokesman said that the layoffs were a part of the company's ongoing turnaround strategy.[1] Best Buy is not the only retailer being affected by showrooming. But given the greater expenses and prices involved in maintaining a well-stocked, fully staffed, full-service store, what strategy can big retailers use to avoid the problem?

Strategy
A plan an organization follows for how to compete successfully, survive, and grow.

The **strategy** an organization follows is its plan for how to compete successfully, survive, and grow. Many organizations have a relatively formal process for developing a written strategy encompassing a three- to five-year period with objectives and goals for each unit.

Organizations seek to achieve and maintain a competitive advantage in the marketplace by delivering high-quality products and services to their customers in a way that competitors cannot duplicate. Strategies to do so might include revising existing products, acquiring new businesses, or developing new products or services using existing capabilities. Other strategic approaches might be to maintain a secure position with a single stable product (like WD-40) or to emphasize a constant stream of new products (like Apple). These are all viable strategies for different businesses, but the strategies chosen will determine the number and capabilities of people needed in the organization. Further, the people already in the organization may limit the strategies that might be successful.

Different companies in the same industry may have different strategies to succeed. Successful strategic management requires accurately analyzing the situation in which the company finds itself deciding what its goals will be, and coming up with actions to achieve those goals. At the end of the day, strategy is about the actions to be taken,[2] as with Best Buy's decision in the chapter opener.

LO1 Summarize the organization's strategic planning process.

2-1 ■ ORGANIZATIONAL STRATEGIC PLANNING

Strategic Planning
The process of defining organizational strategy and allocating resources toward its achievement.

Strategic planning is the process of defining a strategy, or direction, and making decisions on how to allocate the resources of the organization (capital and people) to pursue this strategy. Successful organizations engage in this core business process on an ongoing basis. The strategic plan serves as the road map that provides the organization direction and aligns resources. The process involves several sequential steps that focus on the future of the firm. Figure 2-1 shows the strategic planning process.

2-1a Strategy Formulation

The strategic planning cycle typically covers a three- to five-year time frame, and management considers both internal and external forces when formulating the strategic plan. The guiding force behind the strategic planning process is the **organizational mission,** which is the core reason for the existence of the organization and what makes it unique. The mission statement is usually determined by the organizational founders or leaders and sets the general direction of the organization.

Organizational mission
The core reason for the existence of the organization and what makes it unique.

The planning process begins with an assessment of the current state of the business and the environmental forces that may be important during the planning cycle. Analysis of the strengths, weaknesses, opportunities, and threats (SWOT) is a typical starting point because it allows managers to consider both internal and external conditions. The SWOT analysis helps managers to formulate a strategic plan that considers the organization's ability to deal with the situation at hand. The planning process requires continuous monitoring and responding to environmental changes and competitive conditions.

Managers then determine the objectives for the planning cycle and formulate organization-level strategies to accomplish those objectives. Each function (such as HR)

FIGURE 2-1 Strategic Planning Process for the Organization

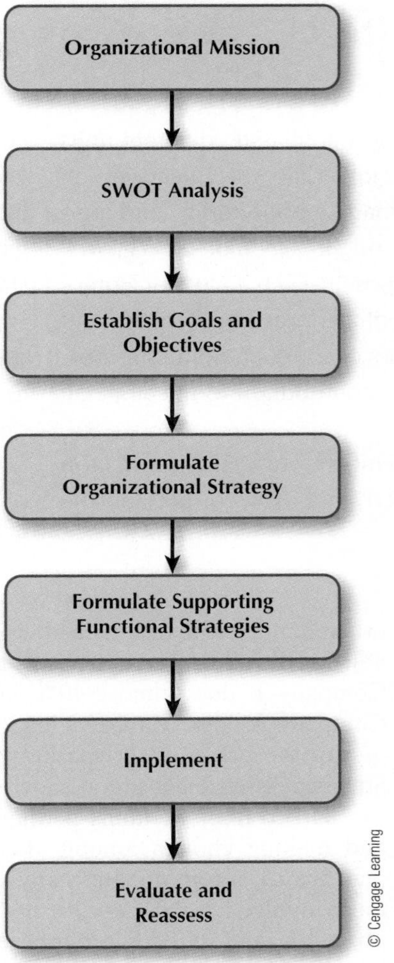

within the organization then formulates strategies that will link to and support the organization-level strategies. The strategic plan is re-evaluated periodically because conditions may change and managers must react to the ever-changing business environment.

LO2 Explain the key differences between good and bad strategy and suggest a way to force strategic asset reallocation.

2-1b Good versus Bad Strategy

Many companies are generating strategies that by their own admission are substandard. In a survey, McKinsey consultants asked 2,000 executives to rate their company's strategies on a set of 10 strategic measures and found that only 35% of the executives felt their company passed more than three of the tests.[3] They concluded that the top management teams need to focus as much time on strategy as they do on operating issues on an ongoing basis if they are to have useful strategy.

Suppose Company A allocates money consistently each year, making only small changes to the allocation of talent, capital, and research dollars. Company B, on the

Forcing Strategic Asset Reallocation

A company may choose to classify different units in the organization into different categories on the basis of their market opportunity and performance. A unit might be labeled "grow," "maintain," or "dispose." Each category comes with clearly differentiated resource investment guidelines. This removes as much politics as possible and focuses on contribution to the strategic goals of each unit.

When Lee Raymond was CEO of Exxon Mobile, he required that 3% to 5% of the company's assets be designated for disposal each year. The divisions could keep these assets *only* if they could show a compelling turnaround program for that unit. The burden to prove the asset should be kept was on the division. The net effect was healthy turnover and an upgrading of units despite the natural desire on the part of executives to keep all the units, including underperforming ones.[5] Such a process can force the reallocation of assets inside the organization and a rethinking of how best to achieve strategic goals.

other hand, evaluates each division's market opportunities and performance and adjusts allocations on the basis of that analysis. Which company performed better? Company B does almost 40% better, although most companies function the way Company A does. Managers in Company A can shift resources to achieve their goals or run the risk that the market will do it for them.[4] The HR Perspective: Forcing Strategic Asset Reallocation shows one way to do this analysis and reallocation.

Bad strategy abounds perhaps because it ignores the difficult path to focusing and making choices among alternatives. Instead of making a choice, a strategy may try to accommodate many conflicting demands and interests. Good strategy must involve an accurate diagnosis of the challenge, an approach to overcome the obstacles, and a focus on coherent actions to make the approach work. It *must* have *focus* and the *choice* of a way to proceed.[6]

However, such focus does not preclude generating ideas for a strategy by opening up the process to stakeholders who might have been previously frozen out of strategic direction setting. For example, 3M, Rite-Solutions, Red Hat, and Wikimedia have all used or experimented with improving their strategy setting through *crowdsourcing*, or opening up the strategy setting process to more people.[7]

L03 Outline how HR's strategies are merged with organizational strategies and give two examples.

2-2 ■ HUMAN RESOURCES AND STRATEGY

Regardless of which specific strategies are adopted for guiding an organization, having the right people will be necessary to make the overall strategies work. If a strategy requires worker skills that are currently not available in the company, it will take time to find and hire people with those skills. Strategic HR management (HRM) provides input for organizational strategic planning and develops specific HR initiatives to help achieve the organizational goals. While it seems important to consider HR in the overall organizational strategy, estimates are that only 30%

of HR professionals are full strategic partners. Their primary role remains one of providing input to top management.[8]

Although administrative and legally mandated tasks are important, HR's strategic contribution can also add value to the organization by improving the performance of the business. Some businesses are highly dependent on human capital for a competitive advantage; others are less so. For example, the productivity of a steel mill depends more on the efficiency of furnaces and quality of raw materials than on human resources. However, every business strategy must be carried out by people, so human capital always has some impact on business success. An important concept covered later in this chapter is the measurement and determination of the value of human capital and HR in a given organization.

Strategic HR management refers to the use of HR management practices to gain or keep a competitive advantage. Talent acquisition, deployment, development, and reward are all strategic HRM approaches that can impact the organization's ability to achieve its strategic objectives.[9]

An important element of strategic HRM is to develop processes in the organization that help align individual employee performance with the organizational strategic objectives.[10] When employees understand the relevant priorities, they can better contribute by applying their skills to advance the strategic goals. Employees who understand the big picture can make decisions that will contribute to achieving the objectives of the firm.[11] HRM practices that facilitate this include talent development and reward systems that channel employee efforts toward the bottom line.

Strategic HR management
Entails providing input into organizational strategic planning and appropriate use of HR management practices to gain competitive advantage.

2-2a Requirements for Human Resource Contribution to Strategy

Specific HR management strategies obviously depend on the strategies and plans of the company.[12] Figure 2-2 highlights some common areas where HR should develop and implement appropriate strategies. To contribute in the strategic planning process, HR professionals provide their perspective and expertise to operating managers by doing the following:

- *Understanding the business*: Knowing the financials and key drivers of business success is important to understanding the need for certain strategies.
- *Focusing on the key business goals*: Programs that have the greatest relevance to business objectives should get priority.
- *Knowing what to measure*: Metrics are a vital part of assessing success, which means picking those measures that directly relate to the business goals.
- *Preparing for the future*: Strategic thinking requires preparing for the future, not focusing on the past—except as a predictor of the future.

For example, when Dunkin' Brands Inc. (the Dunkin' Donuts and Baskin-Robbins parent company) needed to focus on helping Baskin-Robbins franchise owners with recruiting and talent management, HR's strategy had to change to match the organizational strategy. The HR group devised a plan to do so and as a result its mission required a more active role in driving the business, supporting restaurant employees, and delivering a broader array of HR services. This required retraining the HR staff and initiating a wide range of measures to monitor progress.[13] The organization's strategy changed, and HR's strategy had to change too.

FIGURE 2-2 Areas Where HR Can Develop Strategies

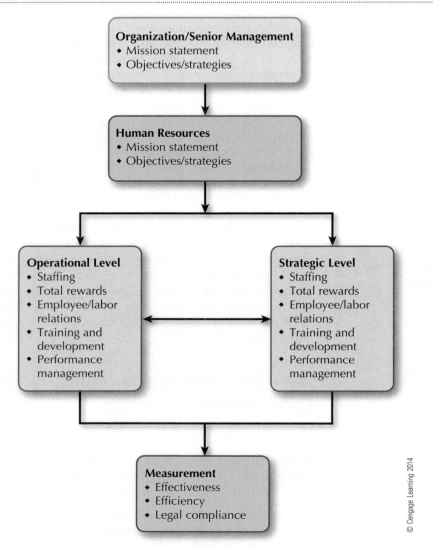

2-2b Human Resources Strategies for Global Competitiveness

The globalization of business means that more organizations now operate across borders with ties to foreign operations, international suppliers, vendors, employees, and other business partners. A global presence can range from importing and exporting to operating as a **multinational corporation (MNC)**. An MNC, sometimes called a "transnational corporation," is an organization that has facilities and other assets in at least one country other than its home country.

Even organizations that operate primarily in the domestic market face pressure from foreign competitors. The supply chain is increasingly internationally dispersed,

GLOBAL

Multinational corporation (MNC)
A corporation that has facilities and other assets in at least one country other than its home country.

and foreign business practices influence operations in the United States. Technology advances have eliminated many barriers to operating on a global scale.

For HR to complement the organization's strategy, it has to consider the route to merging HR's strategies with those of the company. To effectively compete on an international scale, the organization needs expertise to administer all HR activities in a wide range of nations. For example, the firm may decide to standardize talent development and succession planning but permit local managers to establish compensation and labor relations policies. An ideal international strategy strikes a balance between home-country and host-country policies and utilizes the best practices available in each.

Consider two international HR areas that are frequently the basis for HR strategies to support the organizational strategy—offshoring and staffing global operations. Both actions require merging organization's and HR's strategies.

Offshoring Strategies Competitive pressure to lower costs has resulted in many jobs being moved overseas in recent years. **Offshoring** is the relocation of a business process or operation by a company from one country to another. Firms offshore the production of goods as well as the delivery of services to lower-wage countries. Call centers in India are an example of business service offshoring to countries with well-educated, English-speaking workers. Product- and software-development projects are increasingly being offshored because of the lack of science and engineering talent in the United States. Predictions are that offshoring will increase in the future, and few firms have plans to return offshored jobs to the home country.[14]

> **Offshoring**
> The relocation of a business process or operation by a company from one country to another.

These are important decisions that should involve HR.[15] The adoption of a strategy of offshoring should strongly consider two points—reliability and responsiveness[16] Both need HR expertise. *Reliability* has to do with the odds that the offshore vendor (let's say an Indian call center) can deliver and in a consistent manner. Is the turnover rate in the call center so high that the vendor probably *cannot* provide consistent service? *Responsiveness* has to do with the vendor's ability to make changes if necessary. Changes occur regularly in business—so how would the vendor respond if demand for one product falls and the company no longer needs a call center for it? Contracts govern such things but are difficult to make clear on parties' obligations in such a scenario. Offshoring decisions require merging organizational level and HR department level strategies, as does global staffing.

GLOBAL

Global Staffing Strategies Staffing for global operations includes a wide variety of alternatives. The optimal solution is to combine the expertise of local employees with the organization-specific knowledge of employees from the home country (headquarters). Some countries require that the organization employ a certain percentage of workers from the host country. Figure 2-3 shows four strategic HR approaches to international staffing. Each organization will use a staffing model that best fits its culture and strategic goals.

An expatriate is a citizen of one country who is working in a second country and employed by an organization headquartered in the first country. Moving an employee to an overseas assignment for an extended period requires careful selection, training, and planning to make the experience a success. The return of an expatriate (called repatriation) must be well planned and executed for the organization to continue the benefits of the overseas assignment when the employee returns.

Leadership development is especially important for MNCs. It is becoming more important for individuals in top management positions to have international

FIGURE 2-3 Strategic HR Approaches to International Staffing

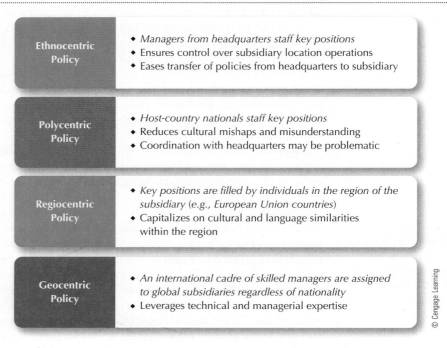

Ethnocentric Policy
- *Managers from headquarters staff key positions*
- Ensures control over subsidiary location operations
- Eases transfer of policies from headquarters to subsidiary

Polycentric Policy
- *Host-country nationals staff key positions*
- Reduces cultural mishaps and misunderstanding
- Coordination with headquarters may be problematic

Regiocentric Policy
- *Key positions are filled by individuals in the region of the subsidiary (e.g., European Union countries)*
- Capitalizes on cultural and language similarities within the region

Geocentric Policy
- *An international cadre of skilled managers are assigned to global subsidiaries regardless of nationality*
- Leverages technical and managerial expertise

© Cengage Learning

experience so that they understand the worldwide marketplace.[17] Effective selection and development processes are needed to ensure that the right individuals are chosen for these roles. Leading across cultures requires specific skills, and organizations should provide formal training along with expatriate assignments to develop leaders who can achieve results in this demanding environment.[18] Again, merging of company and HR strategy is required.

HR planning is frequently a direct consequence of implementing strategies to move the organization forward. HR planning deals with deciding how many people will be needed to execute specific functions of an organization.

2-3 ■ HUMAN RESOURCE PLANNING

Human Resource planning
The process of analyzing and identifying the need for and availability of people so that the organization can meet its strategic objectives.

Human Resource planning is the process of analyzing and identifying the need for and availability of people so that the organization can meet its strategic objectives. The focus of HR planning is to ensure that the organization has the *right number of people* with the *right capabilities*, at the *right times*, and in the *right places*. In HR planning, an organization must consider the availability and allocation of people to jobs over long periods of time, not just for the next month or even the next year.[19]

HR plans can include several approaches. Actions may include shifting employees to other jobs in the organization, laying off employees or otherwise cutting back the number of employees, retraining current employees, and/or increasing the number of employees in certain areas. Factors to consider include the current employees' knowledge, skills, and abilities (KSAs) and the expected vacancies resulting from retirements, promotions, transfers, and discharges. To do this, HR professionals work with executives and managers.[20]

2-3a Human Resources Planning Process

The steps in the HR planning process are shown in Figure 2-4. Notice that the process begins with considering the organizational plans and the environmental analysis that went into developing strategies. The figure includes an environmental analysis to identify the situation in which HR is operating. Strengths, weaknesses, opportunities, and threats are considered. Then the possible *available workforce* is evaluated by identifying both the external and internal workforce.

Once those assessments are complete, forecasts must be developed to determine both the demand for and supply of human resources. Management then formulates HR staffing plans and actions to address imbalances, both short-term and long-term. Specific strategies may be developed to fill vacancies or deal with surplus employees. For example, a strategy might be to fill 50% of expected vacancies by training employees in lower-level jobs and promoting them.

Finally, HR plans are developed to provide specific direction for the management of HR activities related to employee recruiting, selection, and retention. The most telling evidence of successful HR planning is a consistent alignment of the availabilities and capabilities of human resources with the needs of the organization over time.[21]

FIGURE 2-4 HR Planning Process

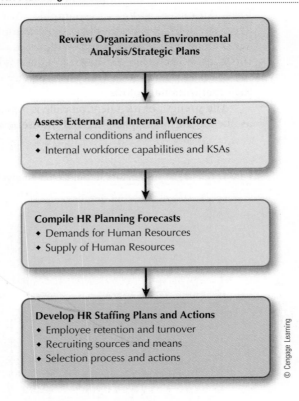

Review Organizations Environmental Analysis/Strategic Plans

Assess External and Internal Workforce
• External conditions and influences
• Internal workforce capabilities and KSAs

Compile HR Planning Forecasts
• Demands for Human Resources
• Supply of Human Resources

Develop HR Staffing Plans and Actions
• Employee retention and turnover
• Recruiting sources and means
• Selection process and actions

© Cengage Learning

2-3b Environmental Analysis

Environmental scanning
The assessment of external and internal environmental conditions that affect the organization.

Before the managers in a company begin strategic planning, they study and assess the dynamics of the environment in which they operate to better understand how these conditions might affect their plans. The process of **environmental scanning** helps to pinpoint strengths, weaknesses, opportunities, and threats that the organization will face during the planning horizon. Whether this is done or not at the organizational level, it should be conducted at the HR planning level.[22]

The external environment includes many economic, political, and competitive forces that will shape the future. For HR the internal environment includes the quality and quantity of talent, the organizational culture, and the talent pipeline and leadership bench strength. Figure 2-5 shows the HR elements of a SWOT analysis that are part of the environmental analysis.

Opportunities and threats emerge from the external environment and can impact the outcomes for the firm. Many of these forces are not within the organization's control, but must be considered in the scanning process because they can affect the business. Dealing with uncertainty in the external environment is an important skill for planners. The external environmental scan includes an assessment of economic conditions, legislative/political influences, demographic changes, and geographic and competitive issues.

Population shifts and demographic changes can affect the organizational strategy. For example, by 2042 non-Hispanic whites will no longer comprise the majority of the U.S. population.[23] Such workforce demographics will affect the labor available to the organization.

Where an organization locates its operations plays a role in how well it will perform. An understanding of geographic advantages and disadvantages can help managers develop appropriate plans. For example, see the HR Perspective: Where Is the Workforce? The strengths and weaknesses of the organization represent internal factors that either create or destroy value. When assessing the internal environment, managers evaluate the quantity and quality of Human Resources, HR practices, and the organizational culture.

The strength of the talent pipeline is a particularly important internal consideration as the organization plans its HR future. Fulfilling strategic objectives is impossible

FIGURE 2-5 HR Factors in the SWOT Analysis

Strengths	Weaknesses
• Intellectual capital • Loyal, committed employees • Innovative, adaptive employees • High-performance practices	• Lack of skilled employees • Lack of leadership pipeline • Outdated talent management practices

Opportunities	Threats
• Market position • Unexplored markets • Global expansion • Technology advances	• Legal mandates and restrictions • Competitor power • Economic uncertainty • Talent shortage

© Cengage Learning

Where Is the Workforce?

Mexico's Sigma Alimentos made a $63 million investment in Oklahoma to make hot dogs and hams but now cannot find the workforce it needs even with high unemployment in the area. The company received millions of dollars in tax incentives to build a factory near downtown Seminole, a small town with many boarded-up and abandoned buildings. With 10% unemployment the community was hungry for jobs, but that hasn't meant that people want to work at Sigma.

Turnover at the plant has topped 100% for its first years. A team leader on the ham line says he has gone through 20 workers in a year and a half on a shift that requires 5 employees. Employees complain about the hours, emphasizing that they want 9-to-5 jobs in an industry that must work shifts that start as early as 4 a.m. to get things done.

Pay is an issue too—nearly a dozen tribal casinos in the area offer $9.50 to $16 an hour for lighter work. Other work is available with a little driving to Oklahoma City to the west. Some do not like working in refrigerated rooms and dealing with the constant smell of animal flesh. Sigma has dealt with its staffing problems in several ways. The company uses overtime and sends recruiters far from town looking for help. Sigma has even considered paying some relocation expenses such as the first month's rent if someone is willing to come to work in Seminole from farther away.

Economists say it is natural that some workers prefer service work with better working conditions. A local economic development group spokesman said he was surprised to see people unwilling to take a $10/hour job at a meat-packing plant. But he would not be surprised to see high turnover, especially if employees once worked at one of the sewing plants that left the area. Job creation and securing a workforce, even in an area with high unemployment, can be challenging.[24]

---

without sufficient skills and talent. Leadership development and succession planning programs ensure that high-quality talent will be available to carry out the strategy. Effective development programs can reduce the high failure rate of people in leadership positions. Selecting individuals with the right talents and teaching them leadership skills can improve the quality of leaders and promote strategic success. **Succession planning** is the process of identifying a plan for the orderly replacement of key employees. The discussion will now turn to how these and other concerns are incorporated into HR planning.

Succession planning
The process of identifying a plan for the orderly replacement of key employees.

2-4 ■ PLANNING FOR EXTERNAL WORKFORCE AVAILABILITY

If a network technology firm plans to double its number of client accounts from 100 to 200 in a three-year period, that firm must also identify how many and what types of new employees will be needed to staff the expanded services, locations, and facilities. Those new employees will probably have to come from outside the current pool of employees. Several specific factors that affect that external pool of potential employees are highlighted next.

2-4a Economic and Governmental Factors

The general economic cycles of recession and boom affect HR planning. Factors such as interest rates, inflation, and economic decline or growth affect the availability of workers and should be considered when organizational and HR plans and objectives are formulated. There is a considerable difference between finding qualified applicants in a 4% unemployment market compared to a 9% unemployment market. As the unemployment rate rises, the number of qualified people looking for work increases, often making it easier to fill some jobs. But those hired may receive lower pay and benefits than in their previous jobs.[25]

A broad array of government regulations affects the labor supply and therefore HR planning. As a result, HR planning must be done by individuals who understand the legal requirements of various government regulations. In the United States and other countries, tax legislation at local, state, and federal levels affects HR planning. Pension provisions and Social Security legislation may change retirement patterns and funding options. Elimination or expansion of tax benefits for job-training expenses might alter some job-training activities associated with workforce expansions. In summary, an organization must consider a wide variety of economics factors and government policies, regulations, and laws during the HR planning process, focusing on specific ones that affect the company.

2-4b Geographic/Competitive Evaluations

When making HR plans, employers must consider a number of geographic and competitive concerns. The *net migration* into a particular region is important. For example, in the past decade, the populations of some U.S. cities in the South, Southwest, and West have grown rapidly and have provided sources of labor. However, areas in the Northeast and Midwest have experienced declining populations or net outmigration. This affects the number of people available to be hired.

Direct competitors are another important external force in HR planning. Failure to consider the competitive labor market and to offer pay scales and benefits comparable with those of organizations in the same general industry and geographic location may cost a company dearly in the long run. Finally, the impact of *international competition* must be considered part of environmental scanning. Global competition for labor intensifies as global competitors shift jobs and workers around the world, as illustrated by the outsourcing of jobs from the United States to countries with cheaper labor.

2-4c Changing Workforce Considerations

Significant changes in the workforce, both in the United States and globally, must be considered when examining the outside workforce for HR planning. Shifts in the composition of the workforce, combined with the use of different work patterns, have created workplaces and organizations that are notably different from those of a decade ago. For example, many organizations face major concerns about having sufficient workers with the necessary capabilities.[26] When scanning the potential and future workforce, it is important to consider a number of variables, including:

- Aging of the workforce
- Growing diversity of workers
- Female workers and work–life balancing concerns
- Availability of contingent workers
- Outsourcing possibilities

When assessing these factors, it is important to analyze how they affect the current and future availability of workers with specific capabilities and experience. For instance, in a number of industries, the median age of highly specialized professionals is over 50 years, and the supply of potential replacements with adequate education and experiences is not sufficient to replace such employees as they retire. Many firms have planned for workforce shortages because of the brain drain created by the retirement of existing older workers.

2-5 ■ PLANNING FOR INTERNAL WORKFORCE AVAILABILITY

Analyzing the jobs that will need to be done and the capabilities of people who are currently available in the organization to do them is the next part of HR planning. The needs of the organization must be compared against the existing labor supply, as well as the potential labor supply available outside the organization.

2-5a Current and Future Jobs Audit

The starting point for evaluating internal workforce strengths and weaknesses is an audit of the jobs that need to be done in the organization. A comprehensive analysis of all current jobs provides a basis for forecasting what jobs will need to be done in the future. Much of the data required for the audit should be available from existing staffing and organizational databases. The following are key questions that are addressed during the internal jobs assessment:

- What jobs exist now and how essential is each job?
- How many individuals are performing each job?
- What are the reporting relationships of jobs?
- What are the vital KSAs (knowledge, skills, and abilities) needed in the jobs?
- What jobs will be needed to implement future organizational strategies?
- What are the characteristics of those anticipated jobs?

2-5b Employee and Organizational Capabilities Inventory

As HR planners gain an understanding of the current and future jobs that will be necessary to carry out organizational plans, they can conduct a detailed audit of current employees and their capabilities. The basic data on employees should be available in the HR records in the organization.

An inventory of organizational skills and capabilities may consider a number of elements. Especially important are:

- Individual employee demographics (age, length of service in the organization, time in present job)
- Individual career progression (jobs held, time in each job, education and training levels, promotions or other job changes, pay rates)
- Individual performance data (work accomplishment, growth in skills, working relationships)

All the details of an individual employee's skills that are stored in an HRIS go into a databank may affect that person's career. Therefore, the data and their use must meet the same standards of job-relatedness and nondiscrimination as those met when the employee was initially hired. Security measures must ensure that sensitive information is available only to those who have a specific use for it.

Managers and HR staff members can gather data on individual employees and aggregate details into a profile of the current organizational workforce. This profile may reveal many of the current strengths and deficiencies of people in the organization. For instance, a skills mismatch may be identified in which some workers are either overqualified or underqualified for their jobs. The profile also may highlight potential future problems. For example, if some specialized expertise, such as advanced technical skills, is lacking in many workers, the organization may find it difficult to take advantage of changing technological opportunities. Or if a large group of experienced employees are all in the same age bracket, their eventual retirements about the same time might lead to future "gaps" in the organization.

LO4 Discuss how to forecast for supply and demand of Human Resources.

Forecasting
Using information from the past and the present to identify expected future conditions.

2-6 ■ FORECASTING HR SUPPLY AND DEMAND

Forecasting uses information from the past and present to predict expected future conditions. When forecasting future HR conditions, the forecast comes from workforce availability and requirements. Projections for the future are, of course, subject to error. Fortunately, experienced people usually are able to forecast with enough accuracy to positively affect long-range organizational planning.

2-6a Forecasting Methods and Periods

Forecasting methods may be either judgmental or mathematical, as Figure 2-6 shows. Methods for forecasting Human Resources range from a manager's best guess to a rigorous and complex computer simulation. Despite the availability of sophisticated judgmental and mathematical models and techniques, forecasting is still a combination of quantitative methods and subjective judgment. The facts must be evaluated and weighed by knowledgeable individuals, who use the mathematical models as tools and make judgments to arrive at decisions.[27]

HR forecasting should be done over three planning periods: short range, intermediate range, and long range. The most commonly used planning period of six months to one year focuses on *short-range* forecasts for the immediate HR needs of an organization. Intermediate- and long-range forecasting are much more difficult processes. *Intermediate-range* plans usually project one to three years into the future, and *long-range* plans extend beyond three years.

2-6b Forecasting the Demand (Need) for Human Resources

The demand for employees can be calculated for an entire organization and/or for individual units in the organization. For example, a forecast might indicate that a firm needs 125 new employees next year, or that it needs 25 new people in sales and customer service, 45 in production, 20 in accounting and information systems, 2 in HR, and 33 in the warehouse. The unit breakdown obviously allows HR planners to better pinpoint the specific skills needed than does the aggregate method.

Demand for Human Resources can be forecast by considering specific openings that are likely to occur. The openings (or demands) are made when new jobs are being created or current jobs are being changed. Additionally, forecasts must consider when employees leave positions because of promotions, transfers, turnovers, and terminations.

FIGURE 2-6 HR Forecasting Methods

Judgmental Methods

- *Estimates* can be either top-down or bottom-up, but essentially people who are in a position to know are asked, "How many people will you need next year?"
- *The rule of thumb* method relies on general guidelines applied to a specific situation within the organization. For example, a guideline of "one operations manager per five reporting supervisors" aids in forecasting the number of supervisors needed in a division. However, it is important to adapt the guideline to recognize widely varying departmental needs.
- *The Delphi technique* uses input from a group of experts whose opinions of forecasted situations are sought. These expert opinions are then combined and returned to the experts for a second anonymous opinion. The process continues through several rounds until the experts essentially agree on a judgment. For example, this approach is used to forecast effects of technology on HR management and staffing needs.
- *Nominal groups*, unlike the Delphi method, require experts to meet face to face. Their ideas maybe cited independently at first, discussed as a group, and then compiled as a report.

Mathematical Methods

- *Statistical regression analysis* makes a statistical comparison of past relationships among various factors. For example, a statistical relationship between gross sales and number of employees in a retail chain may be useful in forecasting the number of employees that will be needed if the retailer's sales increase 15% or decrease 10%.
- *Simulation models* are representations of real situations in abstract form. For example, an econometric model of the growth in software usage would lead to forecasts of the need for software developers. Numerous simulation methods and techniques are available.
- *Productivity ratios* calculate the average number of units produced per employee. These averages can be applied to sales forecasts to determine the number of employees needed. For example, a firm could forecast the number of needed sales representatives using these ratios.
- *Staffing ratios* can be used to estimate indirect labor. For example, if the company usually uses one clerical person for every 25 production employees, that ratio can be used to estimate the need for clerical employees.

© Cengage Learning 2014

An analysis is used to develop decision rules (or "fill rates") for each job or level. For example, a decision rule for a financial institution might state that 50% of branch supervisor openings will be filled through promotions from customer service tellers, 25% through promotions from personal bankers, and 25% from new hires. Forecasters must be aware of multiple effects throughout the organization, because as people are promoted from within, their previous positions become available. Continuing the example, forecasts for the need for customer service tellers and personal bankers would also have to be developed. The overall purpose of the forecast is to identify the needs for Human Resources by number and type for the forecasting period.

2-6c Forecasting the Supply (Availability) of Human Resources

Once HR needs have been forecast, then availability of qualified individuals must be identified. Forecasting availability considers both *external* and *internal* supplies. Although the internal supply may be somewhat easier to calculate, it is important to calculate the external supply as accurately as possible.

External Supply The external supply of potential employees available to the organization can be identified. Government estimates of labor force populations, trends in the industry, and many more complex and interrelated factors must be considered. Such information is often available from state or regional economic development offices. The following items may be included:

- Net migration into and out of the area
- Individuals entering and leaving the workforce
- Individuals graduating from schools and colleges
- Changing workforce composition and patterns
- Economic forecasts for the next few years
- Technological developments and shifts
- Actions of competing employers
- Government regulations and pressures
- Circumstances affecting persons entering and leaving the workforce

Internal Supply Figure 2-7 shows in general terms how the internal supply can be calculated for a specific employer. Estimating internal supply considers the number of external hires and the employees who move from their current jobs into others through promotions, lateral moves, and terminations. It also considers that the internal supply is influenced by training and development programs, transfer and

FIGURE 2-7 Estimating Internal Labor Supply for a Given Unit

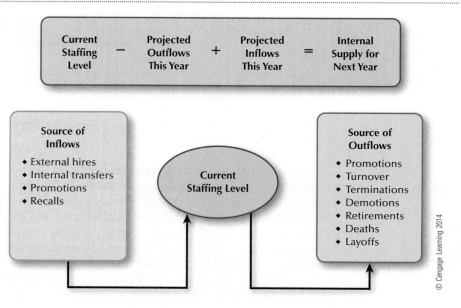

promotion policies, and retirement policies, among other factors. In forecasting the internal supply, data from replacement charts and succession planning efforts are used to project potential personnel changes, identify possible backup candidates, and keep track of attrition (resignations, retirements, etc.) for each department in an organization.

L05 List options for handling a shortage and surplus of employees.

2-7 ■ WORKFORCE SUPPLY ≠ DEMAND

Since the objective of strategic planning is to anticipate and react to future events and conditions, managers should evaluate and revise the strategic plan on a periodic basis. Some have called into question the value of strategic planning in light of economic volatility. However, organizations would fare much worse with no plan in place. Surprises are not good when hiring a workforce, and planning helps reduce surprises.

Attracting and retaining the right talent is an ongoing challenge as the needs of the business change over time. The United States has continued to move from a manufacturing economy to a service economy. This shifting economic base leads to structural mismatches between workers and jobs. Workers with the wrong skills are unable to fill the technical and health service jobs employers need. Ongoing retraining can help overcome some of these problems if strategic planning has identified them. Organizations need to plan for both the quantity and quality of the workforce over the planning horizon. Having sufficient workers with the right qualifications is essential to achieve the strategic plan. If the firm employs too many people for its needs, a talent surplus exists, and if too few, a talent shortage. Because of the rapidly changing conditions, the organization may face a surplus in some parts of the business while facing a shortage in others. Figure 2-8 shows the tactics organizations might use to deal with workforce supply imbalances.

2-7a Managing a Talent Surplus

A talent surplus can be managed within a strategic HR plan in a number of ways. The reasons for the surplus will guide the ultimate steps taken by the organization. If the workforce has the right qualifications but sales revenue has fallen, the primary strategies would involve retaining the best workers while cutting costs. However, if the workforce is not appropriately trained for the jobs needed, the organization may lay off those employees who cannot perform the work. Managers may use various strategies in a progressive fashion to defer workforce reductions until absolutely necessary.

Reduction in Work Hours or Compensation In order to retain qualified employees, managers may institute reduced work hours on a temporary basis. Selected groups of employees may have their workweek reduced or all employees can be asked to take a day or week off without pay. For example, a small family-owned company, asked its 15 full-time workers to take a day off without pay each week to keep all of them on the payroll and avoid layoffs. When the economy improves, these skilled employees will be available to handle the increased workload.

Across-the-board pay cuts can reduce labor costs while retaining some skilled employees. It is important that pay cuts start at the very top of the organization so

FIGURE 2-8 Managing Talent Supply Imbalances

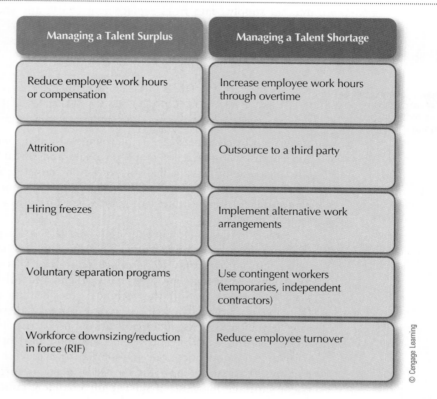

Managing a Talent Surplus	Managing a Talent Shortage
Reduce employee work hours or compensation	Increase employee work hours through overtime
Attrition	Outsource to a third party
Hiring freezes	Implement alternative work arrangements
Voluntary separation programs	Use contingent workers (temporaries, independent contractors)
Workforce downsizing/reduction in force (RIF)	Reduce employee turnover

© Cengage Learning

that employees do not bear all of the hardship. Uniform pay cuts can be felt as a shared sacrifice for the survival of the firm. Organizations may also reduce employee benefits, such as eliminating matching 401K contributions or raising employee health insurance premiums. HR should closely monitor the situation and reinstate pay and benefits levels when the economic outlook improves to maintain employee loyalty and a sense of fairness.

Attrition and Hiring Freezes Attrition occurs when individuals quit, die, or retire and are not replaced. By use of attrition with no additional hiring, no one is cut out of a job, but those who remain must handle the same workload with fewer people. Unless turnover is high, attrition will eliminate only a relatively small number of employees in the short run, but it can be a viable alternative over a longer period of time. Therefore, employers may combine attrition with a freeze on hiring. Employees usually understand this approach better than they do other downsizing methods.

Voluntary Separation Programs Organizations can reduce the workforce while also minimizing legal risks if employees volunteer to leave. Firms often entice employees to volunteer by offering them additional severance, training, and benefits payments. Early retirement buyouts are widely used to encourage more senior workers to leave organizations early. As an incentive, employers may offer expanded health coverage and additional buyout payments to employees so that they will not be penalized economically until their pensions and Social Security benefits take effect. These programs are viewed as a way to accomplish workforce reductions without resorting to layoffs.

Voluntary separation programs appeal to employers because they can reduce payroll costs significantly over time. Although the organization faces some upfront costs, it does not incur as many continuing payroll costs. Using such programs is also viewed as a more humane way to reduce staff than terminating long-service, loyal employees. In addition, as long as buyouts are truly voluntary, an organization offering them is less exposed to age discrimination suits. One drawback is that some employees the company would like to retain might take advantage of a buyout.

Workforce Downsizing It has been given many names, including downsizing, rightsizing, and reduction in force (RIF), but it almost always means cutting employees. Layoffs on a broad scale have occurred with frightening regularity in recent years. Trimming underperforming units or employees as part of a plan that is on the basis of sound organizational strategies may make sense. After a decade of many examples and studies, it is clear that downsizing has worked for some firms.[28] However, it does not increase revenues; it is a short-term cost-cutting measure that can result in a long-term lack of talent. When companies cannibalize the human resources needed to change, restructure, or innovate, disruption follows for some time.[29] Also, downsizing can hurt productivity by leaving "surviving" employees overburdened and demoralized.

Best practices for companies to successfully carry out layoffs include the following:

- Identify the work that is core to sustaining a profitable business.
- Identify the knowledge, skills, and competencies needed to execute the business strategy.
- Protect the bottom line and the corporate brand.
- Constantly communicate with employees.
- Pay attention to the survivors.

A common myth is that those who are still around after downsizing are so grateful to have a job that they pose no problems to the organization. However, some observers draw an analogy between those who survive downsizing and those who survive wartime battles. Bitterness, anger, disbelief, and shock all are common reactions. For those who survive workforce cuts, the culture and image of the firm as a "lifetime" employer often are gone forever.

Severance benefits
Temporary payments made to laid-off employees to ease the financial burden of unemployment.

Severance benefits and outplacement services may be offered by companies to cushion the shock of layoffs and protect the company from litigation. **Severance benefits** are temporary payments made to laid-off employees to ease the financial burden of unemployment. One common strategy is to offer laid-off employees severance benefits that require employees to release the organization from legal claims. Severance benefits are typically based upon length of service with the company, often one or two weeks' pay per year of service. Outplacement services are provided to give displaced employees support and assistance. Outplacement typically includes personal career counseling, résumé-preparation services, interviewing workshops, and referral assistance. Such services are generally provided by outside firms that specialize in outplacement assistance and whose fees usually are paid by the employer. Assisting laid-off workers with gaining new employment can help to alleviate the financial burden on employees and preserve the company image.

2-7b Legal Considerations for Workforce Reductions

HR must be involved during workforce adjustments to ensure that the organization does not violate any of the nondiscrimination or other laws governing workforce reductions. Selection criteria for determining which employees will be laid off must comply with Title VII of the Civil Rights Act as well as the Age Discrimination in Employment Act and the Americans with Disabilities Act. A careful analysis and disparate impact review should be conducted before final decisions are made.

There is no legal requirement to provide severance benefits, and loss of medical benefits is a major problem for laid-off employees. However, under the federal Consolidated Omnibus Budget Reconciliation Act (COBRA), displaced workers can retain their group medical coverage for up to 18 months for themselves, and for up to 36 months for their dependents, if they pay the premiums themselves.

Employers must also comply with the Older Workers Benefit Protection Act (OWBPA) when implementing RIFs. The OWBPA requires employers to disclose the ages of both terminated and retained employees in layoff situations, and a waiver of rights to sue for age discrimination must meet certain requirements. The worker must be given something of value ("consideration") in exchange for the waiver of right to sue, typically severance benefits. When laying off a group of employees, workers over age 40 who are being laid off must be granted 45 days in which to consider accepting severance benefits and waiving their right to sue.

To provide employees with adequate notice of plant closings or mass layoffs, a federal law was passed—the Worker Adjustment and Retraining Notification (WARN) Act. This law requires private or commercial organizations that employ 100 or more full-time workers who have worked more than 6 months in the previous year to give a 60-day notice before implementing a layoff or facility closing that involves more than 50 people. However, workers who have been employed less than 6 months in the prior year, as well as part-time staff members working fewer than 20 hours per week, are not counted toward the total of 50 employees. Despite not being formally counted to determine implementation of the law, these individuals should still be given some form of notice. The WARN Act imposes heavy fines on employers who do not follow the required process and give proper notice.

2-7c Managing a Talent Shortage

Managing a shortage of employees seems simple enough—simply hire more people. However, as mentioned earlier, there can be mismatches between the qualifications needed by employers and the skills possessed by available workers. The list of the 10 hardest jobs to fill in the United States includes engineers, nurses, certain teachers, IT staff, and skilled trades. For these jobs, there may not always be sufficient qualified workers to hire. Companies can use a number of alternative tactics to manage a talent shortage as Figure 2-9 shows.

The existing workers can work overtime. This strategy can work on a short-term basis but is not a solution for a longer-term talent shortage. Workers may appreciate the extra hours and pay for awhile, but eventually fatigue sets in and productivity and quality may drop and injuries and absenteeism may increase.

Outsourcing involves transferring the management and/or routine performance of a business function to an external service provider. Organizations in the United States outsource a wide variety of noncore functions in order to reduce costs or to obtain skills and expertise not available in the organization.

Outsourcing
Transferring the management and performance of a business function to an external service provider.

FIGURE 2-9 Ways to Manage a Talent Shortage

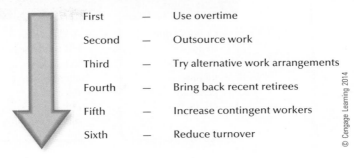

The following are in a common order of usage:

First	—	Use overtime
Second	—	Outsource work
Third	—	Try alternative work arrangements
Fourth	—	Bring back recent retirees
Fifth	—	Increase contingent workers
Sixth	—	Reduce turnover

© Cengage Learning 2014

Alternate work arrangements
Nontraditional schedules that provide flexibility to employees.

Alternate work arrangements are nontraditional schedules that provide flexibility to employees and include job sharing and telecommuting. These are creative solutions to attract and retain skilled employees who want flexibility. Employees can be given more freedom in determining when and how they will perform their jobs. These arrangements are not costly to the organization but do require management support and planning to be effective.[30] Retirees may be rehired on a part-time or temporary basis to fill talent gaps. The advantage is that these individuals are already trained and can be productive immediately. Care must be taken not to interfere with pension payments or other benefits tied to retirement.

The use of contingent employees, who are noncore employees working at a company on a temporary or as-needed basis, can provide short-term help. Professional employer organizations can lease employees to the firm, which is often a good solution for technical talent. Independent contractors can be hired on an as-needed basis to fill talent shortages. The use of independent contractors must be managed closely to ensure compliance with wage and hour, safety, and employee benefit statutes. When using contingent workers, special efforts are needed to assimilate them into the workforce and avoid an "us-and-them" mentality. Contingent workers fill an important need and managers can maximize their contributions through good employee relations practices.

Reducing turnover of qualified employees should be an ongoing effort to maintain a talented workforce. Special attention may be required in times of talent shortages to hold on to skilled employees.

A special instance of HR planning is HR's role in planning for and accomplishing mergers and acquisitions M&A. HR's input can be a key part of mergers and acquisitions.[31]

2-8 ■ HUMAN RESOURCES PLANNING IN MERGERS AND ACQUISITIONS

The purpose of a merger or acquisition is to generate growth by combining two existing companies and creating a more competitive company. Most executives in a recent survey felt M&A is an important strategy for growth through acquiring talent, products, intellectual property, or capabilities.[32] HRM can contribute to the strategic success of mergers and acquisitions. Research has clearly shown

FIGURE 2-10 HR Activities During M&A

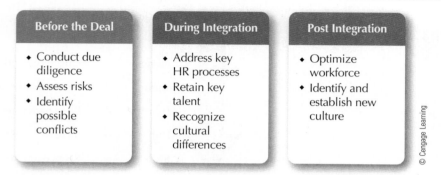

that the majority of M&A fail to deliver on the expected financial, marketing, or product gains, with only about one-third of companies reporting that they achieved their goals.[33] A significant number of failed ventures can trace their roots to HR issues that were not properly addressed such as loss of key staff, culture clashes, and poor communication. To maximize the chances of a successful integration, HR should be involved before, during, and after the deal is completed. Figure 2-10 shows the HR activities and focus during each stage of the merger process.

2-8a Before the Deal

To determine whether or not the two organizations should combine, a rigorous process of due diligence is conducted.[34] **Due diligence** is a comprehensive assessment of all aspects of the business being acquired. Financial, sales and marketing, operations, and Human Resource staffs can all be involved before the final decision is made to merge or acquire the company. Each function determines the assets and liabilities of the target company to ascertain whether there are serious risks to the buyer. HR professionals review issues related to legal compliance, compensation and benefits programs, quality of talent, and labor contract obligations.[35]

Early identification of potential problems such as underfunded pension liabilities or incompatible labor agreements helps management plan for an orderly transition. Due diligence is even more complex when the M&A involves companies in different countries. A thorough, objective analysis of the HR-related issues is critical to make good business decisions. For example, when a North American high-tech company acquired another company to obtain a new technology it found that the cost to maintain the acquired organization's culture was excessive. The attempt to integrate the company lasted five years and required a full-time senior executive to manage interactions and changes to the parent company's policies and systems. Further financial reporting, budgeting, and all cost synergies were affected—negatively. Many companies would have given up. But despite all the problems, the acquisition ultimately proved to be very worthwhile, and the business flourished.[36]

2-8b During Integration

After the deal is closed, the focus of HR activity switches to the orderly transition of basic HR processes such as payroll and benefits migration. During the

Due diligence
A comprehensive assessment of all aspects of the business being acquired.

first 60 days after the acquisition, HR must deliver high-quality administrative and operational support to employees and managers. The immediate concerns are often about basic services needed to run the operations. Frequent communication, employee hotlines, and guidance for managers all contribute to employee retention and loyalty during the chaotic, early days of the transition. During the transition, managers focus on identifying key talent and establishing initiatives to retain these critical employees. Retention bonuses, special assignments, and enhanced severance can be used to keep key talent in place during the integration stage.[37]

Integrating HR information systems is important to provide managers with information about employee capabilities, performance, and potential. The acquiring organization cannot make optimum Human Resource assessments without access to employees' historical information. An inventory of knowledge, skills, and expertise along with performance information provide the data for making suitable assignments for employees from both organizations. Gathering all relevant HR information in a single database helps managers to analyze and compare employee skills and make informed decisions about which employees should be retained.

As the businesses are merged, culture-based conflicts can emerge. For example, when HP and Compaq merged, cultural differences were recognized and addressed. HP had a culture that fostered innovation by giving employees autonomy and opportunities for professional development. Compaq, on the other hand, was a fast-paced company that made decisions quickly. The merger was successful because of the blending of the best parts of the culture in each company. Changing the organizational culture depends upon changing behavior in the organization. Following are four important factors in changing culture:

- *Define the desired behaviors*: Provide behavioral examples of how people are expected to act and tie these behaviors to the performance management system.
- *Deploy role models*: Select leaders who exemplify the desired behaviors and make them visible throughout the organization.
- *Provide meaningful incentives*: Reward the role models with recognition to reinforce their behavior and to signal the rest of the organization.
- *Provide clear and consistent messages*: Align what you say with what you do and reward.

2-8c Post Integration

To realize the expected benefits of a merger, the months following the initial integration are important. Culture changes started in the early days must be maintained. Practical issues regarding talent management and development along with combining compensation systems will solidify the new, united organization. Failure to effectively blend the workforces and move beyond the "us-and-them" mentality can lead to inferior business results, a loss of shareholder value, and the failure of the merger.[38] Continued change efforts are needed to bring all employees to a *one organization* mentality. Breaking down the barriers between the previous practices at each company and implementing the best from both organizations will give employees a sense of value and importance. Ultimately, the outcomes of the deal depend on how HR issues are addressed.

MEASURE

2-9 ■ MEASURING EFFECTIVENESS OF HUMAN RESOURCES AND HUMAN CAPITAL

Effectiveness
The ability to produce a specific desired effect or result that can be measured.

Efficiency
The degree to which operations are done in an economical manner.

Effectiveness for organizations is a measure of the ability of a program, project, or task to produce a specific desired effect or result that can be measured. **Efficiency** is the degree to which operations are carried out in an economical manner. Efficiency can also be thought of as a short-term measure that compares inputs and costs directly against outputs and benefits.

There are many ways of measuring the financial impact of the HR practices in an organization, and many challenges associated with doing so. Return on investment (ROI) is a common measure used by financial professionals to assess the value of an investment. For example, if a firm invests $20,000 for a supervisory training program, what does it gain in lower worker compensation costs, lower legal costs, higher employee productivity, and lower employee turnover? The benefits of HR practices are not always immediately visible, which is what makes measuring HR's impact such a challenge. However, successful efforts can usually be made to assess HR practices.

A long-standing myth perpetuates the notion that one cannot really measure the value of HR practices. That myth has hurt HR's credibility because it suggests that either HR efforts do not add value or they are too far removed from business results to matter. That notion is, of course, untrue. HR, like all other functions, must be evaluated by considering the results of its actions and the value it adds to the organization. Unfortunately, the perceptions of managers and employees in many organizations are mixed because HR has not historically measured and documented its contributions or communicated those results. Further, accounting practices treat expenditures on human capital and talent development as expenses rather than capital investments. This practice encourages top management to view employees as consumers of capital rather than as a long-term investment.

A national working group looked at developing a standard to report human capital value on the Security Exchange Commission (SEC) form 10-K because currently there is no agreed-upon method to account for the value that human capital brings to an organization.[39] However, the effort failed because critics believed that this could fuel acquisitions, talent raiding, or extra competitive pressure.[40]

People-related costs are typically the largest controllable expense in organizations. Effective management of these costs can make a positive difference in the survival of the organization. Collecting and analyzing HR information can pinpoint waste and improper allocation of human resources. It is important that HR managers understand financial and operational measures that drive the business and relate decisions to key performance indicators (KPIs). Metrics, benchmarking, balanced scorecards, and audits can help the organization track HR performance and measure the value of HR practices.[41]

2-9a HR Metrics and Analytics

HR metrics
Specific measures of HR performance indicators.

HR metrics are specific measures of HR practices. They are performance indicators of some element of HR, for example, turnover rate. Metrics are typically used to assess the HR practices and results within the organization over time. A metric can be developed using costs, quantity, quality, timeliness, and other designated goals. Metrics can be developed to track both HR efficiency and

FIGURE 2-11 Key HR Metrics

HR Staff and Expenses	Staffing
• HR-to-employee ratio • Total HR staff • HR expenses per FTE	• Number of positions filled • Time to fill • Cost per hire • Annual turnover rate

Compensation	Training
• Annual wage and salary increases • Payroll as a percentage of operating expenses • Benefit costs as a percentage of payroll	• Hours of training per employee • Total costs for training • Percentage of employees participating in tuition reimbursement program

Retention and Quality	Development
• Average tenure of employees • Percentage of new hires retained for 90 days • Performance quality of employees in first year	• Positions filled internally • Percentage of employees with career plan

© Cengage Learning

effectiveness. A pioneer in developing HR measurements, Jac Fitz-Enz, has identified a wide range of HR metrics. A number of key HR metrics are shown in Figure 2-11.[42]

HR and line managers collect and share the data needed to track performance. Data to track these measures come from several sources within the organization. Financial data are required to determine costs for various HR activities and performance and turnover data can be found in HR and operations records. The real value in using metrics is not in the collection and reporting of the results—it is the analysis and the interpretation of the data that can lead to improvements in human capital utilization.[43] Information and historical data are reviewed and studied to determine the reasons for current performance levels and to learn how to improve these levels in the future.

Metrics and software have been combined to make analysis easier, but it is still an evolving area. *Analytics* can simply be a way to report certain metrics or a sophisticated predictive modeling designed to answer "what if" questions about HR variables.[44] A definition of **HR analytics** that considers both extremes is as follows: HR analytics is an evidence-based approach to making HR decisions on the basis of quantitative tools and models.[45]

Unlike financial reporting, there is not yet a standard for the implementation and reporting of HR measures. Managers choose what and how to report to employees, investors, and other interested parties. For example, see HR Perspective: Using the

HR analytics
An evidence-based approach to making HR decisions on the basis of quantitative tools and models.

Using the *Right* Analytics

When asked which were the most important metrics for valuing HR's contribution to the organization, HR managers rated *retention* and *employee satisfaction* first followed by training and development, recruiting costs, productivity and overall revenue. Certainly, these items are important *but* it is not until you get down the list that you get into factors that the CEO and CFO care most about—costs, open positions, revenue and productivity. Focusing on the wrong issues in analytics can be as costly as doing no analysis at all.

The capability for providing operating managers with the information they want about human capital in the organization is beginning to emerge. HR can stop providing information that no one cares about but HR. Instead, it can provide actionable information, for example, "your turnover rate is X%, here is what it is costing you, and here are some things you can do about it."[46]

For instance, at Superior Energy Services in New Orleans, the HR VP calculated revenue lost for each job type when someone quit. Nearly half the people who quit were skilled operators who had a big impact on revenue. Using predictive modeling to reduce turnover was implemented in that group and turnover dropped significantly.

In another example, executives at PNC Financial in Pittsburgh routinely picked outsiders over inside job candidates. HR used analytics to look at sales performance over several years for external hires versus internal hires and found the internals were significantly more productive in the first year. Later, the outsiders closed the gap but never completely overcame the slow start. Millions of dollars were at stake and PNC changed their hiring practices.[47]

Over time, analytics can help answer some of the questions for which the answers are not entirely clear in every case, such as—does employee engagement relate to financial outcomes?[48]

Right Analytics. This lack of consistency in HR reporting makes it difficult to evaluate an organization and to compare HR practices across organizations. The following characteristics should be considered when developing HR metrics and analytics:

- Accurate data can be collected.
- Measures are linked to strategic and operational objectives.
- Calculations can be clearly understood.
- Measures provide information valued by executives.
- Results can be compared both externally and internally.
- Measurement data drive HR management efforts.

2-9b Human Resources and Benchmarking

Benchmarking
Comparing the business results to industry standards.

Benchmarking is the process of comparing the business metrics and outcomes to an industry standard or best practice. In other words, the organization compares itself to "best-in-class" organizations that demonstrate excellence for a specific process. Benchmarking is focused on external practices that the organization can use to improve its own processes and practices.[49] When implementing benchmarking, managers should be careful to find organizations with similar contexts, cultures, operations, and size.[50] Practices that would work effectively in an organization of

500 employees might not transfer very well to an organization with 5,000 employees. The organization should study and choose benchmarks that will have the greatest impact on the organizational performance.

Many HR professionals report that their organizations collect benchmark data on a planned, periodic basis, while others collect it as needed. Major obstacles to using benchmarks are uncertainty about how to collect the information and what information to collect. Using benchmarking, HR effectiveness is best determined by measures on a year-to-year basis. In that way, the organization can track improvements and results by implementing specific HR practices. While benchmarking helps the firm compare its results to those of other organizations, it does not provide the cause or reason for the relative standing of the organization.[51] So benchmarking is a starting point, not the end point, for improving HR practices.

2-9c Human Resources and the Balanced Scorecard

Balanced scorecard
A framework used to report a diverse set of performance measures.

One effective approach to measuring strategic performance of organizations, including their HR practices, is to use the balanced scorecard. The **balanced scorecard** is a framework organizations use to report on a diverse set of performance measures. Organizations that did not use a balanced scorecard recognized that focusing strictly on financial measures only limited their view.[52] The balanced scorecard balances financial and nonfinancial measures so that managers focus on long-term drivers of performance and organizational sustainability. As shown in Figure 2-12, the balanced scorecard measures performance in four areas:

- *Financial measures*: Traditional financial measures such as profit and loss, operating margins, utilization of capital, return on investment, and return on assets are needed to ensure that the organization manages its bottom line effectively.
- *Internal business processes*: Product and service quality, efficiency and productivity, conformance with standards, and cycle times can be measured to ensure that the operation runs smoothly and efficiently.

FIGURE 2-12 Balanced Scorecard Framework

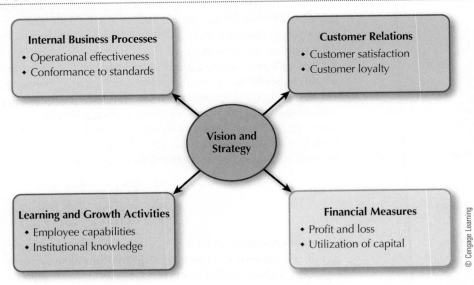

© Cengage Learning

- *Customer relations*: Customer satisfaction, loyalty, and retention are important to ensure that the organization is meeting customer expectations and can depend on repeat business from its customers.
- *Learning and growth activities*: Employee training and development, mentoring programs, succession planning, and knowledge creation and sharing provide the necessary talent and human capital pool to ensure the future of the organization.

Organizational results in each of these areas determine if the organization is progressing toward its strategic objectives. For example, some firms have noticed that when survey results show a decline in employee satisfaction, several months later there are declines in customer loyalty and repeat customer sales. Further, investing money in employee leadership development training can be linked to lower employee turnover and reduced time to hire managers from outside the organization.

A variety of organizations claim to use a balanced scorecard approach. Firms as diverse as Blue Cross, Verizon, and the Mayo Clinic have used this approach to align performance measures with their organizational strategy. Using the balanced scorecard requires spending considerable time and effort to identify the appropriate HR measures in each of the four areas mentioned earlier and how they tie to strategic organizational success. The balanced scorecard should align with company goals and focus on results.[53]

2-9d Human Capital Effectiveness Measures

HR measures outcomes that traditional accounting does not account for. Human capital often provides both the biggest value and the biggest cost to organizations; therefore many metrics reflect people-related *costs*. Measuring the *benefits* of human capital is more challenging but equally important. Assessing the value of human capital demonstrates the importance of effective HR practices that to maintains a high-quality, workforce.[54]

As noted previously, human capital refers to the collective value of the competencies, knowledge, and skills of the employees in the organization. This capital is the renewable source of creativity and innovativeness in the organization but is not reflected in its financial statements.

Revenue per employee is a basic measure of human capital effectiveness. The formula is Revenue/Head Count (full-time employee equivalents). It is a measure of employee productivity and shows the sales revenue generated by each full-time employee. This measure is commonly used in government reporting (see Bureau of Labor Statistics, BLS) as well as by organizations to track productivity over time. If revenues increase but employee head count remains constant, productivity would increase.

Return on investment (ROI)
Calculation showing the value of an investment.

A widely used financial element that can be applied to measure the contribution and cost of HR activities is **return on investment (ROI)**, which is a calculation showing the value of investments in human capital. It can also be used to show how long it will take for the activities to show results. The following formula can be used to calculate the potential ROI for a new HR practice:

$$\text{ROI} = \frac{C}{A + B}$$

where:

A = Operating costs for a new or enhanced system for the time period
B = One-time cost of acquisition and implementation
C = Value of gains from productivity improvements for the time period

Human capital value added (HCVA)
Calculated by subtracting all operating expenses *except* for labor expenses from revenue and dividing by the total full-time head count.

Human capital return on investment (HCROI)
Directly shows the operating profit derived from investments in human capital.

Human economic value added (HEVA)
Wealth created per employee.

ROI is stressed because it is used in most other functions in an organization and is the "language" used by financial staff and top management.[55] It allows managers to choose from among various investment opportunities to determine the best use of funds.

Human capital value added (HCVA) is an adjusted operating profitability figure calculated by subtracting all operating expenses *except* for labor expenses from revenue and dividing by the total full-time head count. It shows the operating profit per full-time employee. Because labor is required to generate revenues, employment costs are added back into operating expense. The formula for HCVA is:

$$\frac{\text{Revenue} - (\text{Operating Expense} - (\text{Compensation} + \text{Benefit Costs}))}{\text{Full-Time Head Count}}$$

Human capital return on investment (HCROI) directly shows the amount of profit derived from investments in labor, the leverage on labor cost. The formula for HCROI uses the same adjusted operating profitability figure as for HCVA, but it is divided by the human capital cost:

$$\frac{\text{Revenue} - (\text{Operating Expense} - (\text{Compensation} + \text{Benefit Costs}))}{(\text{Compensation} + \text{Benefit Costs})}$$

Human economic value added (HEVA) shows the wealth created per employee. It shows how much more valuable the organization has become because of the investment in human capital. Wealth is the net operating profit of a firm after the cost of capital is deducted. Cost of capital is the minimum rate of return demanded by shareholders. When a company is making more than the cost of capital, it is creating wealth for shareholders. An HEVA approach requires that all policies, procedures, measures, and methods use cost of capital as a benchmark against which their return is judged. HR decisions can be subjected to the same analysis. The formula for HEVA is:

$$\frac{\text{Net Profit after Taxes} - \text{Cost of Capital}}{\text{Full-Time Head Count}}$$

Many financial measures can be tracked and reported to show the contribution human capital makes to organizational results.[56] Without such measures, it would be difficult to know what is going on in the organization, identify performance gaps, and provide feedback. Managers should require the same level of rigor in measuring HR practices as they do for other functions in the organization.

Regardless of the time and effort placed on HR measurement and HR metrics, the most important consideration is that HR effectiveness and efficiency must be measured regularly for managers to know how HR practices affects organizational success.[57]

2-9e Human Resources Audit

HR audit
A formal research effort to assess the current state of HR practices.

One means for assessing HR performance is through an HR audit, which is similar to a financial audit. An **HR audit** is a formal research effort to assess the current state of HR practices in an organization. This audit is used to evaluate how well activities in each of the HR areas (staffing, compensation, health and safety, etc.) have been performing, so that management can identify areas for improvement.[58] An HR audit often helps smaller organizations without a formal HR professional to identify issues associated with legal compliance, administrative processes and recordkeeping, employee retention, and other areas.

There are many levels of HR audit. Common levels are as follows:

- *Compliance Audit*: Checks record keeping on state and federal paperwork requirements
- *Benefit Programs Audit*: Reviews regulatory compliance, benefits administration and reporting
- *I-9 Audit*: Reviews compliance with immigration regulations and the I-9 form requirement
- *Specific Program Audit*: Reviews specific HR subareas such as compensation, EEO, or training
- *Full HR Audit*: Reviews all of the above plus any and all other HR functions[59]

Audits frequently use a questionnaire and interviews to collect information, they may be performed by outside entities for more objective data. They can provide assessment about how well HR practices meet established standards and requirements.

SUMMARY

- The strategy an organization follows is its proposition for identifying how to compete successfully and thereby survive and grow.
- HR should be involved in the development and implementation of strategic decisions throughout the organization.
- Strategic planning is a core business process that results in a road map of organizational direction.
- Strategic HRM management refers to the use of practices to gain or keep a competitive advantage by aligning individual employee performance with the organizational strategic objectives.
- Environmental scanning helps to pinpoint strengths, weaknesses, opportunities, and threats that the organization will face during the planning horizon.
- HR functions involve the merging of organizational and HR strategies with offshoring and global staffing strategies.
- HR planning must arrive at the demand for people and the supply of people available.

- Managing a talent surplus may require reducing work hours, downsizing through use of attrition and hiring freezes, voluntary separation programs, and workforce downsizing.
- Managing a talent shortage may be addressed through overtime, reducing turnover, using contingent workers, and outsourcing.
- HR plays a crucial role in mergers and acquisitions, particularly in dealing with integration and organizational culture issues.
- HR effectiveness must be measured using HR metrics that consider both strategic and operational effectiveness.
- Benchmarking allows an organization to compare its practices against "best practices" in different organizations, and HR audits can be used to get a comprehensive overview of HR activities.
- The balanced scorecard can be a useful framework to measure and combine organizational performance measures.
- An HR audit is valuable in providing an overall perspective or in several specific areas.

CRITICAL THINKING CHALLENGES

1. Discuss how globalization has changed jobs in an organization where you have worked. What are some HR responses to those changes?

2. What steps can HR professionals take to ensure that mergers and acquisitions are successful? How can HR help during the integration process?

3. How can an organization maintain its image while dealing with a talent surplus? If layoffs are necessary, what would you recommend managers do to ensure that survivors remain committed and productive?

4. As the HR manager for a multinational corporation, you want to identify HR competencies that are critical for global companies. Visit the website for the World Federation of People Management Association (www.wfpma.com) to research the topic and to identify differences in the body of knowledge in different parts of the world.

5. As the HR Director of a U.S.-based company that is looking at global opportunities in China, you have been asked by the company president to prepare an outline for an HR strategic plan as part of the company's expansion process. You need to develop an HR strategic plan that will integrate the goals, objectives, and strategies of the HR Department with those of the company. The plan also needs to support the objectives of other departments within the company. To get ideas on how to develop an HR strategic plan, go to www.workinfo.com.

   A. What is the process to use for identifying the components of the HR strategic planning process?

   B. What other company strategic objectives must the HR strategic plan integrate and support?

CASE

Analytics at PricewaterhouseCoopers

PricewaterhouseCoopers is a Big Four Accounting firm that was facing high turnover in a key employee segment—senior associates. This is the second stage in a career ladder that starts at the entry level and ends when one becomes a partner in the firm. One possible solution was thought to be deferred compensation, or delaying the salary of some employees so that those who stayed longer would receive more than those who left earlier. The firm could also see that those who stayed longer before they left, were more successful in their careers (such as becoming CFO somewhere else). Would deferred compensation keep people there longer? Would people be convinced to stay longer if they knew it was good for their careers?

A survey collected data from current and former employees who had left. This required finding former employees who had had a relationship with PwC and appealing to their ongoing goodwill toward the firm to get them to respond. The final sample focused on those former employees who had left the firm more recently (in the last 15 years rather than those who had left earlier than 15 years or more). Their response rates were better because they remembered their experiences at the firm better than the group that had left before them. The study specifically looked at career outcomes of those who had left, comparison of work–life balance between current employees and those who had left, and drivers of retention for current employees.

The findings and the actions taken by the firm to deal with what they found had clear and positive impact on the problem. The study showed that adding deferred compensation would have had a *very small* impact on people's willingness to stay. However, work–life balance (avoiding problems of work obligation negatively affecting things at home) and career development/career progression issues did have a *large* influence on the problem of people leaving. Work–life balance solutions are frequently manifested as more flexible work schedules, flexible time off, and even child care and elder care to help the employee manage both work and family obligations better.

The actions the firm took reduced voluntary turnover to the goals it had set. One such action was to provide new tools for managers and Human Resources to deal with the workload balance issues that existed. Another successful action was to strengthen the relationship between partners and the associates. Finally, the company focused on coaching and development including training for the partners in these areas. The analytics study showed that the initially offering defined compensation that was not going to solve the problem, but problems flying below management's radar were causing the high turnover. Management was therefore able to solve the true cause of turnover.[60]

QUESTIONS

1. Why do more companies not use analytics to solve such problems? How would you argue to make the case for analytics in an old-line HR department?

2. What resources could an HR professional consult to begin building expertise in this area of analytics?

SUPPLEMENTAL CASES

Where Do You Find the Bodies?

This case identifies problems associated with HR planning and recruiting in a tight labor market. (For the case, go to www.cengage.com/management/mathis.)

Xerox

This case highlights the challenges of employee retention during stressful and unpredictable times when Xerox was undergoing a significant shift in its strategic focus. (For the case, go to www.cengage.com/management/mathis.)

Pioneers in HR Analytics

HR analytics at four different organizations helped solve several problems and shows how analytics can be used. (For the case, go to www.cengage.com/management/mathis.)

NOTES

1. Based on "Best Buy to Cut 2,400 Jobs in Turnaround Effort," *Casper Star-Tribune*, July 8, 2012, C2.
2. Chris Bradley, "Managing the Strategic Journey," *McKinsey Quarterly*, July 2012, 1–12.
3. Chris Bradley, et al., op cit, 1.
4. Stephen Hall, et al., "How to Put Your Money Where Your Strategy Is," *McKinsey Quarterly*, March 2012, 1–12.
5. Adapted from Stephan Hall, et al., op cit, 9.
6. Richard Rumelt, "The Perils of Bad Strategy," *McKinsey Quarterly*, June 2011, 1–10.
7. Arne Gast and Michele Zanini, "The Social Side of Strategy," *McKinsey Quarterly*, May 2012, 1–10.
8. E. E. Lawler III and J. W. Boudreav, "What Makes HR a Strategic Partner?", CEO (Center for Effective

Organizations) Publication G09-01 (555), 1–23.
9. Katrina Pritchard, "Becoming an HR Strategic Partner: Tales of Transition," *Human Resource Management Journal*, 20, 2010, 175–187.
10. Susan R. Mersinger, "Thinking Strategically," *Human Resource Executive Online*, May 16, 2011, 1–2.
11. Dave Ulrich, et al., "The Role of Strategy Architect in the Strategic HR Organization," *People and Strategy*, 32, 2009, 24–31.
12. Mark L. Legnick-Hall, et al., "Strategic Human Resource Management: The Evolution of the Field," *Human Resource Management Review*, 19, 2009, 64–85.
13. Eric Krell, "Change Within," *HR Magazine*, August 2011, 43–50.
14. Stan Malos, "Regulatory Effects and Strategic Global Staffing Profile:

Beyond Cost Concerns in Evaluating Offshore Location Attractiveness," *Employee Responsibility and Rights Journal*, 22, 2010, 112–131.
15. Aditya Pande, "How to Make Onshoring Work," *Harvard Business Review*, March 2011, reprint F 1103c, 30.
16. Peter Cappelli, "Should You Outsource?", *Human Resource Executive Online*, December 5, 2011, 1–4.
17. Allen Smith, "Offshores Headquarters," *HR Magazine*, November 2009, 49–52.
18. Jeffrey A. Joerres, "Beyond Exports: Better Managers for Emerging Markets," *McKinsey Quarterly*, May 2011, 1–6.
19. Steven Balsam, et al., "The Impact of Firm Strategy on Performance Measures Used in Executive

Compensation," *Journal of Business Research*, 64, 2011, 187–193.

20. Harry J. Van Buren III, et. al., "Strategic HRM and the Decline of Employee Focus," *Human Resource Management Review*, 21, September 2011, 209–219.

21. Paul F. Buller and G. M. McEvoy, "Strategy, HRM, and Performance: Sharpening the Line of Sight," *Human Resource Management Review*, 22, March 2012, 43–56.

22. Don Ruse, et al., "How Strategic Workforce Planning Can Help You Thrive," *Workspan*, December 2009, 26–32.

23. U.S. Census Bureau Population Division, "U. S. Population Projections," www.census.gov.

24. Based on Joel Millman, "Hot Dog Maker, Lured for Its Jobs, Now Can't Fill Them," *The Wall Street Journal*, October 1, 2010, A7 and Carl Bialik, "Sizing Up Private Equity's Job Creation Record," *The Wall Street Journal*, January 21–22, 2012, A2.

25. Peter Cappelli, "Where Are the Jobs?", *Human Resource Executive Online*, January 11, 2011, 1–3.

26. Thomas D. Cairns, "The Supply Side of Labor: HR Must Be Ready to Steer Organizations to the Future," *Employment Relations Today*, 37, Fall 2010, 1–8.

27. Tom Stamer, "A Strategic Workforce Planning Officer?", *Human Resource Executive Online*, June 5, 2012, 1–7.

28. Robert J. Grossman, "Hidden Costs of Layoffs," *HR Magazine*, February 2012, 24–30.

29. John C. Dencker, "Who Do Firms Lay Off and Why?", *Industrial Relations: A Journal of Economy and Society*, 51, 2012, 152–169.

30. Lydell C. Bridgeford, "Bankable Business Case," *Employee Benefit News*, ebn.benefitnews.com, Sept. 1, 2010, 1–7.

31. Linda Tepedino and Muriel Watkins, "Be a Master of Mergers and Acquisitions," *HR Magazine*, June 2010, 53–56.

32. Robert Uhlaner and Andy West, "Organizing for M&A: McKinsey Global Survey Results," *McKinsey Quarterly*, December 2011, 1–9.

33. David Wentworth, "M&A Bounces Back: What Have We Learned?", Institute for Corporate Productivity (i4cp) Trend Watcher No. 476, October 2, 2009.

34. Sharon Birkman Fink, "Address the Human Side of M&A's," *Training*, 46, March/April 2009, 16.

35. LaVerne Shook and Gene Roth, "Downsizing, Mergers, and Acquisitions: Perspectives of HRD Practitioners," *Journal of European Industrial Training*, 35, 2011, 135–153.

36. Ankur Agrawal, et al., "When Big Acquisitions Pay Off," *McKinsey Quarterly*, May 2011, 1–7.

37. Nada Kobeissi, et al., "Managerial Labor Market Discipline and the Characteristics of Merger and Acquisition Transactions," *Journal of Business Research*, 63, July 2010, 721–728.

38. C. Rees and T. Edwards, "Management Strategy and HR in International Mergers," *Human Resource Management Journal*, 19, 2009, 24–39.

39. Jared Shelly, "Reporting HR to Investors," *Human Resource Executive Online*, March 4, 2011, 1–2.

40. Tom Stamer, "Setting Standards," *Human Resource Executive Online*, May 31, 2012, 1–3.

41. Beth Tootell, et al., "Metric: HRM's Holy Grail? A New Zealand Case Study," *Human Resource Management Journal*, 19, 2009, 375–391.

42. "Human Capital Benchmarking Study," *Society for Human Resource Management*, www.shrm.org.

43. Drew Robb, "Creating Metrics for Senior Management," *HR Magazine*, December 2011, 109–111.

44. Allison Rossett, "Metrics Matters," *T & D*, 64, March 2010, 65–69.

45. Laurie Bassi, "Raging Debates in HR Analytics," *People and Strategy*, 34, 2011, 14–18.

46. Andrew R. McIlvaine, "What Lies Ahead," *Human Resource Executive Online*, December 12, 2010, 1–5. Lance Haun, "What HR Is Measuring: Employee Satisfaction and … Retention?", *HR Management, HR News and Trends*, October 27, 2011, 1–3.

47. Bill Roberts, "Analyze This!", *HR Magazine*, October 2009,

35–41. Nora Gardner, et al., "Question for Your HR Chief: Are We Using Our 'People Data' to Create Value?", *McKinsey Quarterly*, March 2011, 1–5.

48. Kathryn Tyler, "Prepare for Impact," *HR Magazine*, March 2011, 53–55.

49. Eric Krell, "Measuring the True Value of Your Services," *HR Magazine*, September 2010, 99–103.

50. Jeremy Shapiro, "Benchmarking the Benchmarks," *HR Magazine*, April 2010, 43–46.

51. Pawan Singh, "The Basics of Benchmarking in the Great Recession," *Workspan*, September 2010, 52–56.

52. Meena Chavan, "The Balanced Scorecard: A New Challenge," *Journal of Management Development*, 28, 2009, 393–406.

53. Robert S. Kaplan, et al., "Managing Alliances with the Balanced Scorecard," *Harvard Business Review*, January-February 2010, 115–126.

54. Stephen Gates and Pascal Langevin, "Human Capital Measures, Strategy, and Performance," *Accounting, Auditing, and Accountability*, 23, 2010, 111–132.

55. Margery Weinstein, "How's Your Human Capital ROI?", *Training*, 47, February 2010, 2. David McGeough, "Measuring ROI," *Training*, 48, March–April 2011, 27.

56. Frank DiBernardino, "The Missing Link: Measuring and Managing Financial Performance of the Human Capital Investment," *People and Strategy*, 34, 2011, 44–47.

57. Alexis A. Fink, "New Trends in Human Capital Research and Analytics," *People and Strategy*, 33, 2010, 14–21.

58. Jody Mousseau and Susan Carter, "How Effective Is Your HR Practice?", *Workspan*, October 2010, 62–66.

59. Eric Krell, "Auditing Your HR Department," *HR Magazine*, September 2011, 101–103.

60. Adapted from Alec Levenson, "Using Targeted Analytics to Improve Talent Decisions," *People and Strategy*, 34, 2011, 34–43.

3

Equal Employment Opportunity

Learning Objectives

After you have read this chapter, you should be able to:

1 Identify the major government agencies that enforce employment discrimination laws.

2 Outline key provisions in the Civil Rights Acts of 1964 and 1991 and compare the two theories of unlawful employment discrimination.

3 Show how women are affected by pay, job assignments, and career issues.

4 Distinguish between the two types of sexual harassment and explain how employers can prevent its occurrence.

5 List key elements of disability discrimination laws.

6 Discuss the legal protections to prevent bias and discrimination based on age, religion, national origin, and other factors.

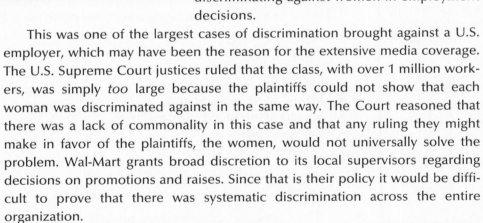

HR HEADLINE

Discrimination at Wal-Mart

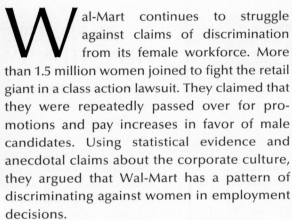

Wal-Mart continues to struggle against claims of discrimination from its female workforce. More than 1.5 million women joined to fight the retail giant in a class action lawsuit. They claimed that they were repeatedly passed over for promotions and pay increases in favor of male candidates. Using statistical evidence and anecdotal claims about the corporate culture, they argued that Wal-Mart has a pattern of discriminating against women in employment decisions.

This was one of the largest cases of discrimination brought against a U.S. employer, which may have been the reason for the extensive media coverage. The U.S. Supreme Court justices ruled that the class, with over 1 million workers, was simply *too* large because the plaintiffs could not show that each woman was discriminated against in the same way. The Court reasoned that there was a lack of commonality in this case and that any ruling they might make in favor of the plaintiffs, the women, would not universally solve the problem. Wal-Mart grants broad discretion to its local supervisors regarding decisions on promotions and raises. Since that is their policy it would be difficult to prove that there was systematic discrimination across the entire organization.

The women involved in the lawsuit, however, are not giving up. They are dividing themselves into smaller groups and filing suits in state courts in California, Texas, and other regions. Their hope is that they can show a pattern of sex discrimination within a smaller region. Faced with the potential for so many future lawsuits, will Wal-Mart revise this local discretion policy in the future?[1]

Basing employment decisions on factors other than worker qualifications is generally illegal in the United States. The costs of litigation, penalties, and harm to the company's reputation can be substantial when violations occur. With the enactment of the Civil Rights Act of 1964 (Title VII), workers in the United States were provided a more level playing field in terms of employment opportunities. Since then, a number of additional laws and Executive Orders have been implemented to prohibit illegal discrimination in the workplace. While the Civil Rights Act stands as the foundation of equal employment laws, it is by no means the only regulation affecting the employer–employee relationship.

Employers have paid (and continue to pay) large amounts for violating EEO laws. This chapter provides an introduction to nondiscrimination requirements and explains how to successfully manage workforce diversity. To provide context, Appendix C lists the major laws governing workplace nondiscrimination.

L01 Identify the major government agencies that enforce employment discrimination laws.

3-1 ■ NATURE OF EQUAL EMPLOYMENT OPPORTUNITY

Civil rights activists in the United States used nonviolent means to protest unequal treatment during the turbulent 1950s, which led to the passage of important nondiscrimination laws and guaranteed an equal opportunity for employment to all.[2] Equal employment opportunity (EEO) means that employment decisions must be made on the basis of job requirements and worker qualifications. Unlawful discrimination occurs when those decisions are made on the basis of **protected characteristics** such as the race, age, sex, disability, or religion of the worker. Under federal, state, and local laws employers are prohibited from considering the following factors in making hiring and other employment decisions:

Protected characteristic
An attribute about an individual that is protected under EEO laws and regulations.

- Age
- Color
- Disability
- Genetic information
- Marital status (some states)
- Military status or experience
- National origin
- Pregnancy
- Race
- Religion
- Sexual orientation (some states and cities)

Equal employment opportunity
Employment that is not affected by illegal discrimination.

These categories are considered protected characteristics under EEO laws and regulations. All workers are provided equal protection; the laws do not favor some groups over others. For example, both men and women can file charges on the basis of alleged sex discrimination.

Equal employment opportunity is a broad-reaching concept that essentially requires employers to make **status-blind** employment decisions. Status blind decisions are made without regard to applicants' personal characteristics (i.e., age, sex, race, and so on). Most employers are required to comply with equal employment opportunity laws. Affirmative action means that an employer takes proactive measures to increase the number of women and minorities in the workforce. The objective of affirmative action plans is to compensate for past patterns of discrimination. Federal contractors are required to implement and maintain affirmative action plans.[3]

Status blind
A concept that emphasizes that differences among people should be ignored and everyone should be treated equally.

3-1a Sources of Regulation and Enforcement

The employment relationship is governed by a wide variety of regulations. All three branches of government have played a role in shaping these laws. Federal statutes enacted by Congress form the backbone of the regulatory environment. State and city governments also enact laws governing activity within their domains. The courts interpret these laws and rule on cases. Case law helps employers to understand how laws are applied and what they must do to comply. Executive Orders are issued by the president of the United States to help government departments and agencies manage their operations.

Government agencies responsible for enforcing laws issue guidelines and rules to provide details on how the law will be implemented. Employers then use these guidelines to meet their obligations in complying with the laws.

The two main enforcement bodies for EEO are the Equal Employment Opportunity Commission (EEOC) and the U.S. Department of Labor (DOL) (in particular, the Office of Federal Contract Compliance Programs [OFCCP]). The EEOC enforces employment laws for employers in both private and public workplaces. The DOL has broad enforcement power and oversees compliance with many employment-related laws. The OFCCP enforces employment requirements set out by Executive Orders for federal contractors and subcontractors. Many states have enforcement agencies to insure compliance with state employment laws. Compliance can become complex for companies that operate in multiple states.

GLOBAL

Multinational companies face a confusing array of nondiscrimination laws in different countries. Many nations in Europe, for example, have laws similar to those in the United States regarding employment discrimination, whereas nations in Asia and other developing economies are less restrictive about workplace practices.[4] Organization leaders determine the best approach to manage their international operations electing to either use the highest standards in all nations or comply with each nation's specific regulations.

Discrimination remains a concern as the U.S. workforce becomes more diverse. Charges filed with the EEOC continue to rise, as shown in Figure 3-1.[5] Over the past 15 years, the total number of charges has increased nearly 24%. While race and sex have historically represented the highest percentages of complaints, in recent years, charges of retaliation have become the most common. Historically, the EEOC has found "no reasonable cause" in about two thirds of those claims. The remaining one third are settled, withdrawn, or pursued by the EEOC. The EEOC has also been held accountable for filing lawsuits against employers without properly investigating charges and has been forced to reimburse the employers' legal costs.[6]

3-2 ■ THEORIES OF UNLAWFUL DISCRIMINATION

Disparate treatment
Occurs when members of a group are treated differently from others.

There are two types of unlawful employment discrimination: disparate treatment and disparate impact.[7] The first type, **disparate treatment**, occurs when either different standards are used to judge individuals or the same standard is used but it is not related to the individuals' jobs. Disparate treatment occurs when individuals with a particular characteristic are treated differently from others. This type of discrimination is typically overt and intentional and often follows a pattern or practice. For example, if female applicants are asked interview questions regarding child-care plans while male applicants are not, then disparate treatment may be occurring.

FIGURE 3-1 Charges Filed with EEOC: 1997, 2011

Charge Basis	Claims Filed 1997 Number, percentage	Claims Filed 2011 Number, percentage
Race	29,199 36%	35,395 35%
Sex	24,728 31%	28,534 29%
National Origin	6,712 8%	11,833 12%
Religion	1,709 2%	4,151 4%
Color	762 1%	2,832 3%
Retaliation	18,198 23%	37,334 37%
Age	15,785 20%	23,465 24%
Disability	18,108 22%	25,742 26%
Equal Pay Act	1,134 1%	919 0.9%
Genetic Information Nondiscrimination Act	Not in force	245 0.2%
Total	80,680	99,947

Note: Total exceed 100% because of multiple charges filed by an individual claimant.

Source: U.S. Equal Employment Opportunity Commission, http://www.eeoc.gov/eeoc/statistics/enforcement/charges.cfm.

The *Ricci v. DeStefano* (2009) case of white firefighters in New Haven, CT, being denied promotion opportunities because of their race demonstrates disparate treatment. A promotion examination administered to eligible firefighters resulted in lower pass rates for black candidates. Fearing a backlash from the black candidates, the city elected to promote no one at all. White firefighters then successfully argued that the decision was based on their race, which was unlawful discrimination.[8]

Disparate impact
Occurs when members of a protected category are substantially underrepresented as a result of employment decisions that work to their disadvantage.

The second type of illegal discrimination, **disparate impact,** occurs when an employment practice that does not appear to be discriminatory has a disproportionally adverse impact on individuals with a particular characteristic. This type of discrimination is often unintentional because identical criteria are used but the results differ for certain groups. For example, using a test for firefighters that requires candidates to carry a 100-pound sack down a ladder is likely to result in more women being eliminated from selection. The same test is used for all candidates with markedly different results on the basis of sex that in this case is job related.

In a landmark case on disparate impact, *Griggs v. Duke Power* (1971),[9] the U.S. Supreme Court ruled that lack of intent is not sufficient for an employer to prove that a practice is lawful. The Court also stated that the employer has the burden to show that a selection practice is directly job related as a business necessity. In the firefighter test where women failed at a higher rate, the test is a true reflection of a job-related duty: carrying a person out of a burning building. Therefore, the test would be lawful even though women would not pass at the same rate as men. A thorough job analysis and a search for alternate selection practices are important steps when disparate impact occurs. The employer must demonstrate that there is no reasonable, nondiscriminatory method available to use. Appendix D explains how disparate impact is defined under the federal government's Uniform Guidelines on Employee Selection Procedures.

Unlawful discrimination can occur in all employment-related decisions, from external hiring to internal promotions, selection for training opportunities, and layoffs and terminations. Job analysis, recordkeeping, and reviewing the results of all employment decisions are important steps to prevent lawsuits on the basis of disparate treatment and disparate impact. Companies can also provide training to managers to increase awareness of discrimination and help to prevent unlawful decisions.[10]

3-2a Equal Employment Opportunity Concepts

Court decisions and administrative rulings have helped to define several basic EEO concepts. The four key concepts discussed next (see Figure 3-2) help to clarify key EEO ideas that lead to fair treatment and nondiscriminatory employment decisions.

Business necessity
A practice necessary for safe and efficient organizational operations.

Business Necessity and Job Relatedness   A **business necessity** is a practice necessary for safe and efficient organizational operations, such as restricting employees from wearing garments that might get caught in machinery although the attire may be required by an employee's religion. Business necessity has been the subject of numerous court cases. Educational requirements are often decided on the basis of business necessity. However, an employer that requires a minimum level of education, such as

FIGURE 3-2 EEO Concepts

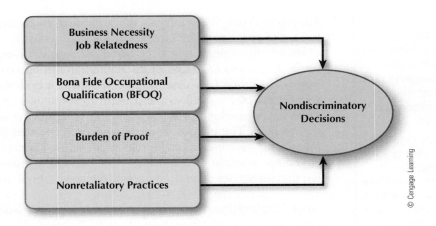

© Cengage Learning

a high school diploma, must be able to defend the requirement as essential to the performance of the job (job related), which may be difficult. For instance, equating a high school diploma with the possession of math or reading abilities is considered questionable.

Employers are expected to use job-related employment practices. The use of criminal background checks and credit reports in the selection process has come under fire because it often results in disparate impact on minority applicants. The EEOC issued guidelines regarding such use of criminal history. Essentially, the EEOC reiterated that the nature of the job sought by the applicant is a major determining factor in whether or not a criminal conviction is job related. Employers seek to find a balance between their obligations to provide a safe working environment and to ensure equal employment opportunity. PepsiCo, Inc. was forced to rescind its rigid policy on criminal background checks because it screened out individuals who were convicted of minor offenses that were irrelevant to the warehouse jobs for which they had applied.[11]

During the last economic recession the credit standing of many individuals was negatively impacted because of job loss. They were further harmed when employers used credit history during the hiring process and denied them employment. A number of states then enacted laws to prevent the use of negative credit reports in hiring decisions unless the job requires handling money or involves spending authority. There is currently no federal law regarding this issue, but the EEOC has spoken out against the practice and the U.S. Congress has considered enacting legislation. The crucial outcome is that hiring criteria must be specifically job related and a matter of business necessity.[12]

Bona Fide Occupational Qualification Employers may discriminate on the basis of sex, religion, or national origin if the characteristic can be justified as a bona fide occupational qualification reasonably necessary to the normal operation of the particular business or enterprise. Thus, a **bona fide occupational qualification (BFOQ)** provides a legitimate reason why an employer can exclude persons on otherwise illegal bases of consideration. The application of a BFOQ is very narrowly determined and an employer seeking to justify hiring on this basis is advised to obtain prior authorization from the EEOC.

What constitutes a BFOQ has been subject to different interpretations in various courts. Legal uses of BFOQs have been found for hiring women as *Playboy* bunnies but not for hiring only female prison guards in a women's prison.[13]

Burden of Proof When a legal issue regarding unlawful discrimination is raised, the **burden of proof** must be satisfied to file suit against an employer and establish that unlawful discrimination has occurred. The plaintiff charging discrimination must establish a *prima facie* case of discrimination through either factual or statistical evidence. The prima facie case means that sufficient evidence is provided to the court to support the case and allow the plaintiff to continue with the claim. The burden then shifts to the employer who must provide a legitimate, nondiscriminatory reason for the decision. The plaintiff then must show either that the employer's reason was a pretext for discrimination or that there is an alternative selection technique that would not result in discrimination. The plaintiff maintains the final burden of proving that an employment decision was the result of unlawful discrimination.[14]

Nonretaliatory Practices Employers are prohibited from retaliating against individuals who file discrimination charges. **Retaliation** occurs when employers take

Bona fide occupational qualification (BFOQ)
Characteristic providing a legitimate reason why an employer can exclude persons on otherwise illegal bases of consideration.

Burden of proof
What individuals who file suit against employers must prove to establish that illegal discrimination has occurred.

Retaliation
Punitive actions taken by employers against individuals who exercise their legal rights.

punitive actions against individuals who exercise their legal rights. For example, a former police officer filed an EEOC charge alleging sex discrimination when she was transferred to a less prestigious job. She later learned that she was receiving less overtime work than her peers and used the department's copier to copy her coworkers' payroll stubs to substantiate her claim. The city's attorney threatened to criminally prosecute her for making the copies on the department's equipment but offered to drop the charges if she withdrew her EEOC complaint. The plaintiff was awarded over $400,000 in damages and costs.[15] Retaliation claims now constitute the highest percentage of charges filed with the EEOC because they can be added to all antidiscrimination charges and a wide range of workplace decisions might be interpreted as retaliatory. An important aspect of retaliation charges is that the charging party may lose the case on the basis of discrimination but still win if the employer took punitive action against him or her, as in the case cited above.

To prevent charges of retaliation, the following actions are recommended for employers:[16]

- Create and disseminate an antiretaliation policy.
- Train supervisors on what retaliation is and what is not appropriate.
- Review all performance evaluation and discipline records to ensure consistency and accuracy.

HR PERSPECTIVE

Retaliation Claimant Prevails

The EEOC won a judgment against Cognis Corporation for taking retaliatory action against Steven Whitlow, a former employee. Cognis implemented a procedure requiring employees to sign a "last-chance" agreement in which each employee forfeited the right to ever file discrimination charges for any alleged violations by the company in exchange for continued employment. In other words, the employee's job depended upon giving up the right to sue the company for any acts of discrimination in the past or the future.

Steven Whitlow had worked at the company for 19 years and he refused to sign this agreement. Cognis, in turn, fired him in retaliation for not signing the agreement. The court ruled in favor of the EEOC and Mr. Whitlow stating that the company acted unlawfully when it violated this fundamental right of employees in the United States. Employees are permitted to file charges or lawsuits when they believe an employer discriminated against them. Employers cannot interfere or take action against an employee (or applicant) for exercising that right. Mr. Whitlow will be compensated for his loss, although the amount is unknown at this time. Here are some tips to avoid this type of incident in the future:

- Consult with the company's legal department before creating any type of binding agreements.
- Make sure that HR staff understand how to approach employees about different types of documents and how those documents should be presented.
- Consult with the company's legal department before approaching any employee who refused to sign the document to understand what options the company has going forward.

Following these tips may help prevent similar lawsuits.[17]

- Conduct a thorough internal investigation of any claims and document the results.
- Take appropriate action when any retaliation occurs.

The HR Perspective: Retaliation Claimant Prevails provides more information about retaliation claims and how to prevent them. Organizations that use a proactive approach may reduce the number of lawsuits and possible fines.

3-3 ■ BROAD-BASED DISCRIMINATION LAWS

L02 Outline key provisions in the Civil Rights Acts of 1964 and 1991 and compare the two theories of unlawful employment discrimination.

Comprehensive equal employment laws provide broad-based protection for applicants and employees. The following sections explain these major laws and compliance requirements.

3-3a Civil Rights Act of 1964, Title VII

Although the very first civil rights act was passed in 1866, it was not until passage of the Civil Rights Act of 1964 that the keystone of antidiscrimination employment legislation was put into place. Title VII, the employment section of the Civil Rights Act of 1964, details the legal protections provided to applicants and employees and defines prohibited employment practices. Title VII is the foundation on which all other workplace nondiscrimination legislation rests.

Title VII of the Civil Rights Act states that it is illegal for an employer to:

- fail or refuse to hire or discharge any individual, or otherwise discriminate against any individual with respect to his compensation, terms, conditions, or privileges of employment because of such individual's race, color, religion, sex, or national origin, or
- limit, segregate, or classify his employees or applicants for employment in any way that would deprive or tend to deprive any individual of employment opportunities or otherwise adversely affect his status as an employee because of such individual's race, color, religion, sex, or national origin.

Title VII Coverage Title VII, as amended by the Equal Employment Opportunity Act of 1972, covers most employers in the United States. Any organization meeting one of the following criteria must comply with rules and regulations that specific government agencies have established to administer the act:

- All private employers of 15 or more employees
- All educational institutions, public and private
- State and local governments
- Public and private employment agencies
- Labor unions with 15 or more members
- Joint labor/management committees for apprenticeships and training

Title VII has been the basis for several extensions of EEO law. For example, in 1980, the EEOC interpreted the law to include sexual harassment. Further, a number of concepts identified in Title VII are the foundation for court decisions, regulations, and other laws discussed elsewhere in this chapter.

3-3b Civil Rights Act of 1991

In response to several Supreme Court decisions during the 1980s, Congress amended the Civil Rights Act of 1964 to strengthen legal protection for employees, provide for jury trials, and allow for damages payable to successful plaintiffs in employment discrimination cases.[18] A key provision of the 1991 act relates to how U.S. EEO laws are applied globally.

The Civil Rights Act of 1991 requires that employers show that an employment practice is job related for the position and consistent with *business necessity*. The Act clarifies that plaintiffs bringing discrimination charges must identify the particular employer practice being challenged and must show only that protected status played *some role in their treatment*. For employers this means that an individual's race, color, religion, sex, or national origin *must play no role* in their employment practices. The Act allows people who have been targets of intentional discrimination based on sex, religion, or disability to receive both compensatory and punitive damages. The penalties are scaled by the size of employer, as shown in Figure 3-3.

While civil rights laws provide protection to employees and applicants on a variety of issues, not all individual differences are covered. The HR Ethics: Should Political Views Be Protected features a story of how political affiliation is not a protected characteristic.

3-3c Executive Orders 11246, 11375, and 11478

Affirmative action
Proactive employment practices to make up for historical discrimination against women and minorities.

Several important executive orders have been issued by the U.S. President that affect the employment practices of federal contractors and subcontractors. The OFCCP in the U.S. Department of Labor is responsible for overseeing federal contractor operations and insuring that unlawful discrimination does not occur. Executive Orders 11246, 11375, and 11478 require federal contractors to take **affirmative action** to compensate for historical discrimination against women, minorities, and handicapped individuals. The concept of affirmative action is not without controversy and some states have passed laws banning the use of such programs.

Supporters offer many reasons why affirmative action is important, while opponents argue firmly against it. Individuals can consider both sides in the debate and compare them with their personal views of affirmative action. The authors of this text believe that whether one supports or opposes affirmative action, it is important to understand why its supporters believe that it is needed and why its opponents believe it should be discontinued.

3-3d Managing Affirmative Action Requirements

Affirmative action program (AAP)
A document reporting on the composition of an employer's workforce, required for federal contractors.

Federal contractors are required to develop and maintain a written **affirmative action program (AAP)** that outlines proactive steps the organization will take to attract and hire members of underrepresented groups. This data-driven program includes analy-

FIGURE 3-3 Penalties under Civil Rights Act of 1991 by Employer Size

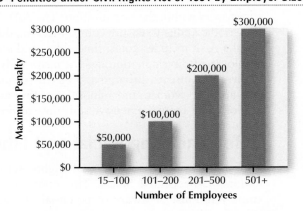

Source: U.S. Equal Employment Opportunity Commission Enforcement Guidance, http://www.eeoc.gov/policy/docs/damages.html.

Should Political Views Be Protected?

Many characteristics about individuals cannot be used in employment matters. Under Title VII of the Civil Rights Act of 1964, employers cannot consider the race, color, sex, national origin, or religion of an applicant or employee when making hiring and other employment decision. Age and disability discrimination laws also restrict employers from considering aspects about people that have little or nothing to do with job performance. However, an individual's political beliefs are not protected under the law. In other words, an employer might use that information to make an employment decision. But, just because it is not illegal, doesn't make it ethical.

Teresa Wagner, a graduate of the University of Iowa's law school, claims that she has been denied employment because of her conservative political beliefs. Ms. Wagner previously taught writing at another law school and was working part-time as a teacher at the University of Iowa. She is opposed to abortion and gay rights and worked passionately to support her views. She

was not hired for a job teaching writing at the university and claims that 46 of the 50 faculty members in the decision process held liberal political views. She believes that she was passed over because of her political beliefs. The university states that she performed poorly in an employment interview, which led to turning her down for the job. The job was given to an individual that had no previous teaching experience.

The case is the first of its kind because Ms. Wagner is arguing that the university's decision was a violation of her First Amendment rights. The case highlights an ethical dilemma in human resource management. Decisions made by organizations may be legal, but may still violate basic human rights. The court will decide if the University of Iowa illegally discriminated against Ms. Wagner. When managers and companies make employment decisions, they are advised to review not only the literal interpretation of laws, but also the moral and ethical code of the organization.[19]

sis of the composition of company's current workforce with a comparison to the availability of workers in the labor market. The overall objective of the AAP is to have the company's workforce demographics reflect as closely as possible the demographics in the labor market from which workers are recruited. The contents of an AAP and the policies flowing from it must be available for review by managers and supervisors within the organization. The AAP is reviewed by the OFCCP and subject to periodic audits to ensure compliance. In addition to an extensive workforce analysis, the AAP includes goals, timetables, and good faith efforts to reduce and prevent employment discrimination against historically disadvantaged groups. Organizations implement outreach programs, targeted recruiting, and training programs to recruit and advance women and minorities. Affirmative action plans vary in length; some are long and require extensive staff time to prepare.

3-3e Managing Racial and Ethnic Discrimination Issues

The original purpose of the Civil Rights Act of 1964 was to address race discrimination in the United States. This concern continues to be important today and employers must be aware of potential HR issues that are based on race, national origin, and citizenship to take appropriate actions.

Charges of racial discrimination continue to make up one-third of all complaints filed with the EEOC. Employment discrimination can occur in numerous ways, from refusal to hire someone because of their race/ethnicity to the questions asked in a selection interview. All employment inquiries and decisions should be based on job related factors and not personal characteristics. See Appendix E for examples of legal and illegal preemployment inquiries. The EEOC found that a trucking delivery company failed to hire qualified black applicants for dockworker positions because of factors unrelated to job performance. The company paid $120,000 to settle the lawsuit.[20]

Sometimes racial discrimination is very subtle. For example, some firms have tapped professional and social networking sites to fill open positions. However, networking sites exclude many people, resulting in disparate impact. Further, the use of employee referral programs can lead to a more homogenous workforce as employees are more likely to refer people of the same demographic background as themselves. One solution is to use *anonymous application procedures* in which names and other identifying characteristics of applicants are deleted from candidate documents. Decision makers in the hiring process are presented only with credentials and job-relevant information. This procedure, while controversial, may level the playing field and reduce the possibility of bias in selection.[21] Under federal law, discriminating against people because of skin color is just as illegal as discriminating because of race. For example, one might be guilty of color discrimination but not racial discrimination if one hired light-skinned African Americans over dark-skinned people.

Racial/Ethnic Harassment Racial/ethnic harassment is such a concern that the EEOC has issued guidelines on it. It is recommended that employers adopt policies against harassment of any type, including ethnic jokes, vulgar epithets, racial slurs, and physical actions. The consequences of not enforcing these policies are seen in a case involving a major transportation company that subjected African American employees to a racially hostile working environment and discriminatory employment conditions. The company was fined $11 million in penalties.

Contrast that case with another that shows the advantage of taking quick remedial action. A black employee filed a lawsuit against a security firm because his supervisor made racially offensive comments. After the company investigated, the white supervisor was disciplined for inappropriate jokes and comments and the complainant was transferred to a different supervisor. The company further conducted in-house diversity training. The court dismissed the lawsuit because the company had taken measures to remedy the harassment. Therefore, prompt investigation and remedial action can protect employers from liability.[22]

LO3 Show how women are affected by pay, job assignments, and career issues.

3-4 ■ SEX/GENDER DISCRIMINATION LAWS AND REGULATIONS

The inclusion of sex as a basis for protected status in Title VII of the 1964 Civil Rights Act has led to additional areas of legal protection and a number of laws and regulations now address discrimination based on sex or gender.

3-4a Pregnancy Discrimination

The Pregnancy Discrimination Act (PDA) of 1978 amended Title VII to require that employers treat maternity leave the same as other personal or medical leaves.

Closely related to the PDA is the Family and Medical Leave Act (FMLA) of 1993, which requires that qualified individuals be given up to 12 weeks of unpaid family leave and also requires that those taking family leave be allowed to return to jobs (see Chapter 13 for details). The FMLA applies to both men and women. Provisions of the Affordable Care Act (2010) allow for break time and a private place for nursing mothers to express breast milk for one year after the birth of a child.[23]

GLOBAL

Women across the globe have experienced discrimination because of pregnancy despite legal protections for childbirth and child rearing. For example, Italian women experience the lowest employment rate in the European Union and Italy ranks below Ghana and Bangladesh in terms of gender equality. Some Italian workers have reported being fired after giving birth.[24]

Discrimination may occur because of employer perceptions of the pregnancy affecting the employee's job performance and attendance, or from questions related to pregnancy or childcare plans asked during an employment interview. A Milwaukee medical-staffing company was fined for firing a woman who had just given birth because the owner made offensive comments about her pregnancy and fired her when she took maternity leave. Discrimination can occur if a pregnant applicant is not hired or is transferred or terminated. Courts have generally ruled that the PDA requires employers to treat pregnant employees the same as nonpregnant employees with similar abilities or inabilities. Employers have a right to maintain performance standards and expectations of pregnant employees but should be cautious to use the same standards for nonpregnant employees and employees with other medical conditions. In *McFee v. Nursing Care Management of America* (2010), terminating a pregnant employee for excessive absenteeism was deemed lawful because the PDA does not require preferential treatment in such cases, only similar treatment to employees with nonpregnancy-related disabilities.[25] A careful review of FMLA policy decisions is important to prevent discrimination claims under the PDA for attendance issues.

Fears about higher health insurance costs and possible birth defects caused by damage sustained during pregnancy lead some employers to reassign women from hazardous jobs to lower-paying, less hazardous jobs. Such reproductive and fetal protection policies have been ruled unlawful.[26]

3-4b Equal Pay and Pay Equity

The Equal Pay Act of 1963 requires employers to pay similar wage rates for similar work without regard to gender. A *common core of tasks* must be similar, but tasks performed only intermittently or infrequently do not make jobs different enough to justify significantly different wages. Differences in pay between men and women in the same jobs are permitted because of:

1. Differences in seniority
2. Differences in performance
3. Differences in quality and/or quantity of production
4. Factors other than sex, such as skill, effort, and working conditions

In response to a procedural issue in pursuit of a fair pay claim, Congress enacted the Lilly Ledbetter Fair Pay Act in 2009, which eliminates the statute of limitations for employees who file pay discrimination claims under the Equal Pay Act. Each paycheck is essentially considered a new act of discrimination. Lawmakers recognized that because pay information is often secret it might take months or even years for an employee to discover the inequity. The successful plaintiff can recover up to two years of back pay.

Pay equity
The idea that pay for jobs requiring comparable levels of knowledge, skill, and ability should be similar, even if actual duties differ significantly.

Pay equity is the idea that pay for jobs requiring comparable levels of knowledge, skill, and ability should be similar, even if actual duties differ significantly. This theory has also been called *comparable worth* in earlier cases. Some state laws mandate pay equity for public-sector employees. However, U.S. federal courts generally have ruled that the existence of pay differences between the different jobs held by women and men is not sufficient to prove that illegal discrimination has occurred.

A major reason for the development of the pay equity idea is the continuing gap between the earnings of women and men. Figure 3-4 shows that across all demographic groups women consistently earn less than men although the difference is shrinking. In 1980, women on average earned 60% of what men earned. By 2010, their earnings had risen to 80% of the average man. Several reasons have been given for this gender pay gap such as the fact that women take more time off during their childbearing years which makes it difficult to remain even with their male counterparts. Persistent, widespread stereotypes, such as the notion that men are more productive than women, may unconsciously influence behavior and manager decisions leading to lower merit increases for women.[27]

FIGURE 3-4 Women's Earnings as Percentage of Men's

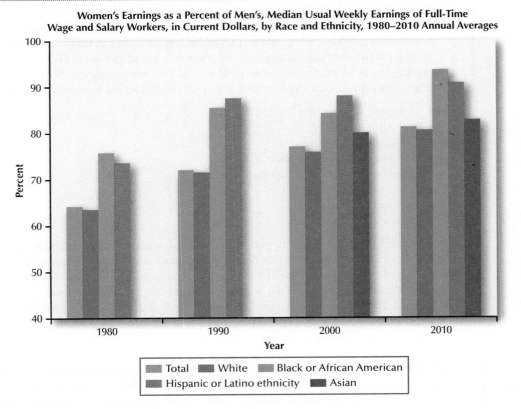

Women's Earnings as a Percent of Men's, Median Usual Weekly Earnings of Full-Time Wage and Salary Workers, in Current Dollars, by Race and Ethnicity, 1980–2010 Annual Averages

Legend: Total, White, Black or African American, Hispanic or Latino ethnicity, Asian

Source: U.S. Department of Labor, Bureau of Labor Statistics, 2010, www.bls.gov.

Employers can take steps to reduce pay inequities.

- Include all benefits and other items that are part of pay to calculate total compensation for the most accurate overall picture.
- Make sure people know how the pay practices work.
- Base pay on the value of jobs and performance.
- Benchmark against local and national markets so that pay structures are competitive.
- Conduct frequent audits to ensure there are no gender-based inequities and that pay is fair internally.

3-4c Managing Sex/Gender Issues

The influx of women into the workforce has had major social, economic, and organizational consequences. The percentage of women in the total U.S. civilian workforce has increased dramatically since 1950, to almost 50% today. During the last economic downturn unemployed workers were more likely to be male because the industries hit hardest in the recession tended to employ more men; construction and manufacturing. Women, on the other hand, are primarily employed in management and professional occupations and less likely to be employed in operations, transportation, or construction occupations.[28]

The growth in the number of women in the workforce has led to more sex/gender issues related to jobs and careers. Since women bear children and traditionally have a primary role in raising children, issues of work–life balance can emerge. Respect for employees' lives outside of the workplace can pay off in terms of attracting and retaining high quality talent. Organizations can offer a range of options to help employees achieve satisfaction in both their work and personal lives. Glassdoor.com reports in its second annual list of the Top 25 Companies for Work–Life Balance that organizations on the list have many of the following features:

- Support from senior leadership
- Flexible hours
- Telecommuting options
- Compressed work weeks
- Family friendly work environments
- Generous paid time off
- On-site cafeteria
- On-site fitness center

Employees at different career stages and with different household structures may seek different elements to help balance work and family obligations. For example, single employees value flexible work arrangements but not a work–family culture, while parents value the work–family culture and supervisors' social support. Organizations considering implementing work–family balance programs have a wide range of choices and benefit most from customizing to their specific culture rather than adopting a one-size-fits-all approach.[29]

Glass ceiling
Discriminatory practices that have prevented women and minorities from advancing to executive-level jobs.

Glass Ceiling For years, women's groups have alleged that women in workplaces encounter a **glass ceiling**, which refers to discriminatory practices that have prevented women and other minority status employees from advancing to executive-level jobs. Despite the fact that organizations with greater gender diversity enjoy better financial performance than those with less diversity, women still hold a small percentage of top leadership jobs in corporations. Only 41 of the Fortune 1000 companies are led by a female CEO. In organizations where diversity is seen as strategically important, a higher percentage of C-level executives are women. There are some differences around the world regarding the importance of diversity. In Asia and developing markets, gender diversity is more important than in Latin America, Europe, and North America.[30]

A related problem is that women have tended to advance to senior management in a limited number of support or staff areas, such as HR and corporate communications. Because executive jobs in these "supporting" areas tend to pay less than jobs in sales, marketing, operations, or finance, the overall impact is to reduce women's career progression and income. Limits that keep women from progressing only in certain fields have been referred to as "glass walls" or "glass elevators." These limitations are seen as being tied to organizational, cultural, and leadership issues.[31]

Breaking the Glass A number of employers have recognized that breaking the glass, whether ceilings, walls, or elevators, is good business for both women and racial minorities. Some of the most common means used to "break the glass" are as follows:

- Establish formal mentoring programs for women and members of racial/ethnic minorities.
- Provide opportunities for career rotation into operations, marketing, and sales for individuals who have shown talent in accounting, HR, and other areas.
- Increase the memberships of top management and boards of directors to include women and individuals of color.
- Establish clear goals for retention and progression of women and minorities and hold managers accountable for achieving these goals.
- Allow for alternative work arrangements for employees, particularly those balancing work/family responsibilities.

3-4d Sexual Orientation

Demographers estimate that about 3% to 5% of Americans identify themselves as being lesbian, gay, bisexual, or transgender (LGBT). That translates to approximately 9 million Americans with alternate sexual orientation. The U.S. Census reports that 650,000 couples reported living with same-sex partners, with 130,000 reporting being married. While there is no federal law prohibiting discrimination on the basis of sexual orientation, 18 states have passed laws to protect applicants and employees from such discrimination.[32] Employers are increasingly offering same-sex employee benefits and accommodating varying lifestyles for their employees; some high-profile CEOs have spoken out in support of rights for LGBT employees.[33]

An issue that some employers have had to address is that of individuals who have had or are undergoing gender transition surgery and therapy. Federal court cases and the EEOC have ruled that sex discrimination under Title VII applies to a person's gender at birth. Thus, it does not apply to the new gender of those who have had sex transformation operations. However, managers and employees are becoming more tolerant of such situations and there is a growing respect for individuals undergoing these procedures. Other issues that arise from sexual orientation or sex-change in workplaces include the reactions of coworkers and manage ensuring that such individuals are evaluated fairly and not discriminated against in work assignments, raises, training, or promotions.[34]

3-4e Nepotism

Nepotism
Practice of allowing relatives to work for the same employer.

Many employers have policies that restrict or prohibit **nepotism**, the practice of allowing relatives to work for the same employer. Other firms require only that relatives not work directly for or with each other or not be placed in positions where collusion or conflict could occur. The policies most frequently cover spouses, siblings, parents, sons, and daughters. Generally, employer antinepotism policies have been upheld by courts, in spite of the concern that these policies tend to discriminate against women more than men (because women tend to be denied employment or leave employers more often as a result of marriage).[35]

3-4f Consensual Relationships and Romance at Work

When work-based friendships lead to romance and off-the-job sexual relationships, managers and employers face a dilemma: Should they "monitor" these relationships to protect the firm from potential legal complaints, thereby "meddling" in employees' private, off-the-job lives? Or do they simply ignore these relationships and the potential problems they present? These concerns are significant given that the employer's response to workplace romance influences employees' and applicants' perceptions of fairness and the degree to which the organization is viewed as a good place to work.[36]

Most executives and HR professionals agree that workplace romances are risky because they have great potential for causing conflict. Dealing with this as a strategic issue means that leaders consider both the costs and the benefits in addition to the legal factors. Adopting practices such as a written policy, ethics code, and performance management system along with training HR leaders can lead to a more balanced approach when dealing with workplace romances.[37]

LO4 Distinguish between the two types of sexual harassment and explain how employers can prevent its occurrence.

3-5 ■ SEXUAL HARASSMENT

Sexual harassment
Actions that are sexually directed, are unwanted, and subject the worker to adverse employment conditions or create a hostile work environment.

Nearly 25% of women report having been harassed at work during their careers. This widespread problem is a form of sex discrimination under Title VII. The Equal Employment Opportunity Commission has issued guidelines designed to curtail sexual harassment. **Sexual harassment** is unwelcome verbal, visual, or physical conduct of a sexual nature that is severe and affects working conditions or creates a hostile work environment. Sexual harassment can occur between a boss and a subordinate, among coworkers, and when nonemployees have business contacts with employees.

Most of the sexual harassment charges filed involve harassment of women by men. However, over 10% of claims were filed by men claiming they were sexually harassed. Interestingly, women almost universally report that they were harassed by a male, while males report an equal percentage of male and female harassers. Most claims of harassment go unreported as victims are reluctant to speak out for fear of retribution. Supervisors are the most frequent harassers, but coworkers and even subordinates have also been involved in these incidents.[38]

3-5a Types of Sexual Harassment

Two basic types of sexual harassment have been defined by EEOC regulations and a number of court cases. Figure 3-5 shows the two types and how they differ. They are defined as follows:

1. **Quid pro quo** is harassment in which employment outcomes are linked to granting sexual favors.
2. **Hostile environment** harassment exists when an individual's work performance or psychological well-being is unreasonably affected by intimidating or offensive working conditions.

Quid pro quo
Sexual harassment in which employment outcomes are linked to the individual granting sexual favors.

Hostile environment
Sexual harassment in which an individual's work performance or psychological well-being is unreasonably affected by intimidating or offensive working conditions.

In quid pro quo harassment, an employee may be promised a promotion, a special raise, or a desirable work assignment, but only if the employee grants some sexual favors to the supervisor. Since supervisors are agents of the company, the company always bears liability for quid pro quo harassment.

The second type, hostile environment harassment, may include actions such as commenting on appearance or attire, telling jokes that are suggestive or sexual in nature, allowing revealing photos and posters to be displayed, or making continual requests to get together after work. These actions can lead to the creation of a hostile work environment. If the employer has taken appropriate steps to prevent sexual harassment, it may be possible to offer an affirmative defense and prevail in a lawsuit.

As mobile phone use and Internet technology have spread, the number of electronic sexual harassment cases has increased.[39] Sexual harassment increasingly occurs via e-mail, social networking sites, and Internet access systems. Cyber sexual harassment may occur when an employee forwards an e-mail joke with sexual content or accesses pornographic websites at work and then shares the content with other employees. Cyber stalking, in which a person continually e-mails an employee requesting dates and sending personal messages, is growing as instant messaging expands. Many employers have policies addressing the inappropriate use of e-mail, company computer systems, and electronic technology usage. Many employers have equipped their computer systems with scanners that screen for inappropriate words and images. Offending employees receive warnings and/or disciplinary actions associated with

FIGURE 3-5 Sexual Harassment Types

Quid pro quo Harassment	Hostile Environment Harassment
• Perpetrated by employee's superior	• Perpetrated by employee's superior, coworkers, and/or third parties
• Employment decisions hinge on whether an employee provides sexual favors	• Pervasive, unwanted sexual comments, pictures, jokes, and/or other derogatory events create a dysfunctional workplace
• Company is liable	• Company may be liable if it cannot offer an affirmative defense

© Cengage Learning 2014

"flagged" items. If an employee uses the company's equipment or computer network, the employer might be liable if the situation is not properly addressed.

3-5b Preventing Sexual Harassment

A proactive prevention approach is the most effective way to reduce sexual harassment in the workplace. If the workplace culture fosters harassment, and if policies and practices do not inhibit harassment, an employer is wise to reevaluate and solve the problem before lawsuits follow.

Companies may avoid liability if they take reasonable care to prohibit sexual harassment, the so-called affirmative defense. Important elements of the affirmative defense include the following:

- Establish a sexual harassment policy.
- Communicate the policy regularly.
- Train employees and managers on avoiding sexual harassment.
- Investigate and take action when complaints are voiced.

Effective training to prevent sexual harassment ideally includes instruction for employees and supervisors on what constitutes sexual harassment and how to handle an incident. Role plays can be especially effective during the training particularly when accompanied by timely feedback and opportunities for practice. Evaluating the effectiveness of the training is important to insure that the training is transferred back to the workplace. Training HR staff in proper investigation techniques is also advised to insure that a prompt, impartial review of all complaints occurs.[40]

3-5c International Context of Harassment

GLOBAL

Fundamental differences regarding power between men and women and a cultural support of sexual harassment lead to very different sexual harassment situations from country to country. According to research, Canada, Denmark, Germany, the Netherlands, Sweden, and the United States are likely to have relatively *less* sexual harassment than countries like East Africa, Hong Kong, Indonesia, Malaysia, Mexico, and Turkey.[41]

L05 List key elements of disability discrimination laws.

3-6 ■ DISABILITY DISCRIMINATION

Several federal laws have been enacted to advance the employment of disabled individuals and to reduce discrimination based on disability. These laws and regulations affect employment matters as well as public accessibility for individuals with disabilities. Despite these attempts to open the workplace to disabled individuals, unemployment among the disabled population has consistently exceeded the overall unemployment rate particularly during economic downturns.[42]

3-6a Rehabilitation Act

The earliest law regarding disabled individuals was passed in 1973 and applied only to federal contractors. The Rehabilitation Act defined many of the terms and concepts incorporated into subsequent laws and provided for equal employment opportunity for disabled workers and applicants. The Act went further and required that federal contractors take affirmative action to employ disabled workers. A section of the contractor's AAP is devoted to steps taken to promote the employment of disabled persons.[43]

3-6b Americans with Disabilities Act

Two decades after passage of the first law prohibiting discrimination against disabled individuals, the Americans with Disabilities Act was enacted in 1990. This Act applies to private employers, employment agencies, and labor unions with 15 or more employees and is enforced by the EEOC. State government employees are not covered by the Americans with Disabilities Act (ADA), which means that they cannot sue in federal courts for relief and damages. However, they may still bring suits under state laws in state courts. Many of the concepts and definitions included in the ADA were based on the Rehabilitation Act.

3-6c ADA Amendments Act

In 2009, Congress passed amendments to the ADA, which overruled several key cases and regulations and reflected the original intent of the ADA. The effect was to significantly broaden the definition of disabled individuals to include anyone with a physical or mental impairment that substantially limits one or more major life activities *without* regard for the ameliorative effects of mitigating measures such as medication, prosthetics, hearing aids, and so on. This establishes a very low threshold for establishing whether an individual is "disabled."

Who Is Disabled? A three-pronged test is used to determine whether or not an individual meets the definition as "disabled." A person must meet one of the following three conditions as stated in the ADA and modified by the Americans with Disabilities Act Amendments Act (ADAAA). A **disabled person** is someone who

1. has a physical or mental impairment that substantially limits that person in some major life activities;
2. who has a record of such an impairment; or
3. who is regarded as having such an impairment.

> **Disabled person**
> Someone who has a physical or mental impairment that substantially limits life activities, who has a record of such an impairment, or who is regarded as having such an impairment.

A person is considered disabled even if any corrective measures are used to reduce the impact of the disability, such as a wheelchair or medication. The only exception is ordinary eyeglasses or contact lenses. Major life activities include not just visible activities like seeing, breathing, and walking but internal bodily functions such as neurological, immune, endocrine, and normal cell growth. The definition of *disabled* no longer rests on the individual's inability to *do* something, but on his or her medical condition, whether or not it limits functioning. This expanded definition of *disabled* now encompasses a much larger percentage of workers, meaning that employers are likely to encounter situations that require action.

The EEOC's final regulations state that some impairments such as autism, blindness, bipolar disorder, cancer, diabetes, HIV infection, major depressive disorder, and so on will be covered disabilities in "virtually all cases." The ADA does not protect current users of illegal drugs and substances, but it does protect those who are recovering addicts.[44]

Mental Disabilities A growing area of concern to employers under the ADA (as amended) is individuals with mental disabilities. A mental disability is defined by the EEOC as "any mental or psychological disorder, such as an intellectual disability, organic brain syndrome, emotional or mental illness, and specific learning disabilities." Employers may find accommodating for mental disabilities is more difficult and that maintaining effective performance standards is a challenge. Mental disabilities may manifest in more unpredictable ways and medications taken to alleviate these conditions can have negative side effects.[45] It is advisable to rely on sound medical information and avoid stereotypes regarding individuals with mental impairment or disabilities.

More ADA complaints are being filed by individuals who have or claim to have mental disabilities. Two of the top seven disabilities most frequently cited in EEOC claims for disability discrimination are mental disabilities: depression, and anxiety disorder. The cases that have been filed have ranged from individuals with a medical history of paranoid schizophrenia or clinical depression to individuals who claim that job stress has affected their marriage or sex life. Regardless of the type of employees' claims, it is important to treat mental disabilities in the same way as physical disabilities. Obtain medical verification of worker limitations and engage in an interactive process to establish a reasonable accommodation.

Employees Who Develop Disabilities For many employers, the impact of the ADA has been the greatest when handling employees who develop disabilities, not when dealing with applicants who already have disabilities. As the workforce ages, it is likely that more employees will develop disabilities. For instance, a warehouse stock worker who suffers a serious leg injury in a motorcycle accident away from work may request reasonable accommodation.

Employers should be prepared to respond to accommodation requests from employees whose contribution to the organization has been satisfactory before they became disabled and who now require accommodations to continue working. Handled inappropriately, these individuals are likely to file either ADA complaints with the EEOC or private lawsuits.

Employees sometimes can be shifted to other jobs where their disabilities do not affect them as much. For instance, the warehouse firm might transfer the injured stock worker to a purchasing inventory job inside so that climbing and lifting are unnecessary. But the problem for employers is what to do with the next worker who develops problems if an alternative job within the organization is not available. Even if the accommodations are just for one employee, the reactions of coworkers must be considered.

3-6d ADA and Job Requirements

Essential job functions
Fundamental job duties.

Reasonable accommodation
A modification to a job or work environment that gives a qualified individual an equal employment opportunity to perform.

Discrimination is prohibited against individuals with disabilities who can perform the **essential job functions**—the fundamental job duties—of the employment positions that those individuals hold or desire. These functions do not include marginal functions of the position. For example, an essential function for the job of cosmetologist is to cut and style hair. A marginal function of that job would be answering the telephone to schedule client appointments. The EEOC provides guidelines to help employers determine which job functions are essential. Figure 3-6 lists the criteria recommended by the EEOC.

For a qualified person with a disability, an employer must make a **reasonable accommodation**, which is a modification to a job or work environment that gives that individual an equal employment opportunity to perform. EEOC guidelines encourage employers and individuals to work together to determine what the

FIGURE 3-6 Determining if a Job Function Is Essential

A Job Function May Be Considered Essential for Any of Several Reasons, Including but Not Limited to the Following:

1. The function may be essential because the reason the position exists is to perform that function.
2. The function may be essential because there is a limited number of employees available who can perform the job function.
3. The function may be highly specialized so that the job incumbent is hired for that expertise or ability to perform the particular function.

Evidence of whether a Particular Function Is Essential Includes, but Is Not Limited to the Following:

1. The employer's judgment as to which functions are essential.
2. Written job descriptions prepared before advertising or interviewing applicants for the job.
3. The amount of time spent on the job performing the function.
4. The consequences of not requiring the incumbent to perform the function.
5. The terms of a collective bargaining agreement.
6. The work experience of past incumbents in the job.
7. The current work experience of incumbents in similar jobs.

Source: Adapted from Part 1630 Regulations to Implement the Equal Employment Provisions of the Americans with Disabilities Act.

appropriate reasonable accommodations are, rather than employers alone making those judgments. Under the ADAAA, the focus has shifted from determining whether or not an individual is disabled to an emphasis on finding ways to accommodate that individual in the workplace. The process of determining a reasonable accommodation is expected to be interactive, with the disabled individual as an active participant in the process. Many options may be considered but in the end the employer has the authority to select the accommodation to be implemented.

Reasonable accommodation is limited to actions that do not place an undue hardship on an employer. An **undue hardship** is a significant difficulty or expense imposed on an employer in making an accommodation for individuals with disabilities. The ADA offers only general guidelines in determining when an accommodation becomes unreasonable and will place undue hardship on an employer. The determination of undue hardship is made on a case-by-case basis. Undue hardship might stem from financial requirements to scheduling options or facilities modifications. What might be reasonable for a large multinational company might be an undue hardship for a smaller firm with fewer resources.

The key to making reasonable accommodations is identifying the essential job functions and then determining which accommodations are reasonable so that the

Undue hardship
Significant difficulty or expense imposed on an employer in making an accommodation for individuals with disabilities.

FIGURE 3-7 Common Means of Reasonable Accommodation

Modified Work Schedules

Special Equipment

Job Restructuring

Job Reassignment

Employer-Provided Assistance

Additional Training Time

Reasonable Accommodation

Source: Adapted from Job Accommodation Network (http://askjan.org/index.html).

individual can perform the core job duties. Common means of reasonable accommodation are shown in Figure 3-7. Architectural barriers should not prohibit disabled individuals' access to work areas or restrooms. Appropriate work tasks must be assigned or modified to allow the individual to perform them effectively. This may mean modifying jobs or work area layouts or providing assistive devices or special equipment. Work hours and break schedules may be adjusted. Fortunately for employers most accommodations needed are relatively inexpensive. Free assistance is readily available from the Job Accommodation Network's online resource center.[46]

Since most organizations are covered, employers under the ADA will likely have a plan in place before an accommodation is requested, which can save time and simplify the process.[47]

The following steps can facilitate this process:

- Define essential functions in advance.
- Handle all requests for accommodation properly.
- Work with the HR staff to explore various options for accommodation.
- Interact with the employee with good faith and documentation.
- Know and follow the reasonable accommodation rules.

Companies are more likely to attract and retain employees with disabilities if they take steps to insure a supportive corporate culture with managers and supervisors who are trained to deal with the special needs of this population. Appropriate screening techniques along with a genuine accommodation process and respectful coworkers can create a workplace where all employees are able to perform at their best, including those with disabilities.[48]

ADA Restrictions and Medical Information The ADA includes restrictions on obtaining and retaining medically related information on applicants and employees. Restrictions include prohibiting employers from rejecting individuals because of a disability and from asking job applicants any question about current or past medical history until a conditional job offer is made. Also, the ADA prohibits the use of pre-employment medical exams, except for drug tests, until a job has been conditionally offered. An additional requirement of the ADA is that all medical information be maintained in files separated from the general personnel files. Medical files must be stored in a secure location and only individuals with a "need-to-know" should be granted access to these files.

3-6e Claims of Discrimination

During the decade prior to the enactment of the ADAA, approximately 16,000 disability discrimination claims were filed with the EEOC each year. In 2010 and 2011, that number skyrocketed to over 25,000 claims per year representing a 17% increase in the historical average. Experts attribute this increase to the changes made in the definition of "disabled" under the ADAA. Prior to the ADAA, employers won 90% of the challenges regarding whether or not an individual was qualified as "disabled." Now that argument is essentially moot and companies no longer aggressively work to disqualify the person from that status.

Claims of discrimination are more common at the lower levels of organizations. However, the CEO of a home furnishings retailer filed charges of disability discrimination claiming that the board of directors perceived her to be disabled based upon a recent diagnosis of breast cancer and terminated her employment. This case shows that *being regarded* as disabled qualifies an individual for protection under the law whether or not the person shows any outward impairment or requests an accommodation. This is an example of the second prong of the definition of "disabled individual" and sends a note of caution that treating someone as if they are disabled does in fact grant them coverage under the law. In fact, "regarded as" claims represent the highest percentage of claims filed in ADA charges.[49] Figure 3-8 shows the most frequent disabilities identified in ADA charges.

3-6f Genetic Bias Regulations

ETHICS

Related to medical disabilities is the emerging area of workplace genetic bias. As medical research has revealed the human genome, medical tests have been developed that can identify an individual's genetic markers for various diseases. Whether these tests should be used and how they are used can raise ethical issues.

Employers that use genetic screening tests do so for two primary reasons. Some use genetic testing to make workers aware of genetic problems that may exist so that medical treatments can begin. Others use genetic testing to terminate employees who may make extensive use of health insurance benefits and thus raise the benefits costs and utilization rates of the employer. A major railroad company, Burlington Northern Santa Fe, had to publicly apologize to employees for secretly testing to determine if they were genetically predisposed to carpal tunnel syndrome.

Genetic Information Nondiscrimination Act Congress passed the Genetic Information Nondiscrimination Act (GINA) in 2009 to limit the use of genetic information by health insurance plans and to prohibit employment discrimination on the basis

FIGURE 3-8 Most Frequent ADA Charges Filed in 2011

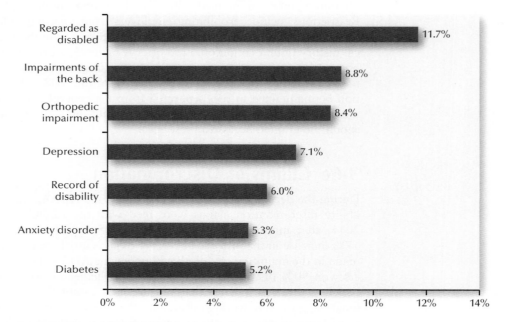

Source: Based on data from U.S. Equal Employment Opportunity Commission, 2011; http://www.eeoc.gov/eeoc/statistics/enforcement/ada-receipts.cfm.

of this information. Employers are prohibited from collecting genetic information or making employment decisions on the basis of genetic information. "Genetic information" includes information about genetic tests of the employee or family members and family medical history. GINA allows exceptions for employees who wish to *voluntarily* participate in a wellness program and when employers need medical certification to determine eligibility for FMLA. Coordinating compliance policies for GINA, ADA, HIPAA, and leave policies can reduce confusion and liability.[50]

L06 Discuss the legal protections to prevent bias and discrimination based on age, religion, national origin, and other factors.

3-7 ■ AGE DISCRIMINATION LAWS

The populations of most developed countries—including Australia, Japan, most European countries, and the United States—are aging.[51] On one hand, these changes mean that as older workers with a lifetime of experiences and skills retire, companies face significant challenges in replacing them with workers with the capabilities and work ethic that characterize the many mature workers in the United States. On the other hand, many older people will remain in the workforce beyond traditional retirement age because of longer life spans, improvements in health, and financial shortfalls in their savings portfolios, leading to a greater possibility of bias and discrimination.[52]

Many countries have enacted laws prohibiting age discrimination. For example, age discrimination regulations within the European Union member nations, Great Britain, Australia, India, Argentina, Canada, and Chile are just a sample of countries that focus on preventing age discrimination in recruitment, promotion, training, and retirement-related actions.[53] In the United States, employment discrimination against individuals age 40 and older is prohibited by the Age Discrimination in Employment Act.

GLOBAL

3-7a Age Discrimination in Employment Act

The Age Discrimination in Employment Act (ADEA) of 1967, amended in 1978 and 1986, prohibits discrimination in terms, conditions, or privileges of employment against all individuals of age 40 or older working for employers having 20 or more workers. However, state employees may not sue state government employers in federal courts because the ADEA is a federal law. Age discrimination charges consistently represent 20% to 25% of all discrimination charges filed with the EEOC. During the last economic downturn employers, fearing lawsuits by older workers, chose instead to lay off younger workers despite their lower salaries.[54]

As with most equal employment issues, a better understanding of what constitutes age discrimination continues to be defined by the courts and the EEOC. Following the Supreme Court decision in *Meacham v. Knolls Atomic Power Laboratory* (2008), the EEOC issued its final rule on disparate impact in age discrimination cases. If an employer asserts that disparate impact is because of "reasonable factors other than age" (RFOA) then the employer must show that its employment practice was reasonably designed to further a legitimate business purpose. Job performance, skills, or employee versatility are examples of reasonable factors other than age in employment decisions. The employer bears the ultimate burden of proof to show that age was not a factor in its actions.[55]

3-7b Older Workers Benefit Protection Act

This law is an amendment to the ADEA and protects employees when they sign liability waivers for age discrimination in exchange for severance packages during reductions in force. Workers over the age of 40 are entitled to receive complete accurate information on the available benefits, a list of all workers impacted in the reduction, and several weeks to decide whether or not to accept severance benefits in exchange for a waiver to sue the employer.[56] This Act ensures that older workers are not compelled or pressured into waiving their rights under the ADEA. Procedures for laying off older workers require legal oversight and a strict protocol to ensure compliance.

3-7c Managing Age Discrimination

One issue that has led to age discrimination charges is labeling older workers as "overqualified" for jobs or promotions. In a number of cases, courts have ruled that the term *overqualified* may have been used as a code word for workers being too old, thus causing them not to be considered for employment. Also, selection and promotion practices must be "age neutral." Older workers face substantial barriers to entry in a number of occupations, especially those requiring significant amounts of training or where new technology has been recently developed. In some cases involving older employees, age-related comments such as "Let's hire a recent college graduate" or "We need younger blood" in conversations were used as evidence of age discrimination.

Stereotypes about older workers are often negative. Many people mistakenly believe that older workers are less productive, resistant to change, more costly to employ and pay, and less trainable. These stereotypes are particularly prevalent in some industries: finance, insurance, retail, and information technology. They persist and often lead to lower ratings in interviews and performance appraisals for older workers.[57]

To counter significant staffing difficulties, some employers recruit older people to return to the workforce through the use of part-time and other attractive scheduling options. During the past decade, the number of older workers holding part-time jobs has increased. It is likely that the number of older workers interested in working part-time will continue to grow.

A strategy used by employers to retain the talents of older workers for a period of time is **phased retirement**, whereby employees gradually reduce their workloads and pay levels. This option is growing in use as a way to allow older workers with significant knowledge and experience to have more personal flexibility, while the organizations retain them for their valuable capabilities. Some firms also rehire their retirees as part-time workers, independent contractors, or consultants. These strategies are intended to help the company retain its institutional knowledge and history.

Phased retirement
Approach in which employees gradually reduce their workloads and pay level.

3-8 ■ RELIGION AND SPIRITUALITY IN THE WORKPLACE

Title VII of the Civil Rights Act prohibits discrimination on the basis of religion. The increasing religious diversity in the workforce has put greater emphasis on religious considerations in workplaces. Faith-based schools and institutions can use religion as a BFOQ for employment practices on a limited scale. Also, employers must make reasonable accommodation efforts regarding an employee's religious beliefs unless they create an undue hardship for the employer.

Religious diversity in the United States is also reflected in the workplace. Figure 3-9 shows the percentage of U.S. adults that practice particular faiths. The wide range of beliefs and practices may evolve as immigrant populations bring with them not only cultural but also religious diversity to the nation and workplaces.

Religious discrimination can take many forms, from hostile remarks to refusal to hire individuals from different faiths. Problems can also arise because of conflicts

FIGURE 3-9 Religious Traditions in the United States

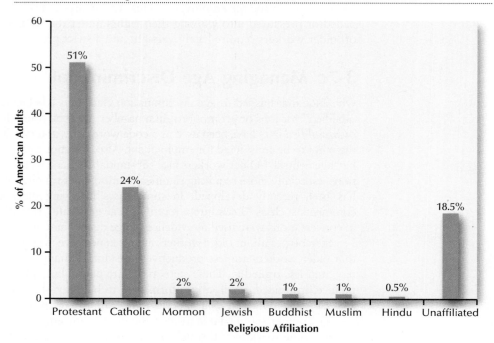

Source: Adapted from Pew Forum on Religion and Public Life (http://religions.pewforum.org/pdf/report-religious-landscape-study-key-findings.pdf).

between employer policies and employee religious practices such as dress and appearance. Some religions have standards about appropriate attire for women or shaving or hair length for men. Generally, employers are encouraged to make exceptions to dress code policies unless public image is so critical that it represents a business necessity. Deferring to customer preferences in making these determinations is risky and may lead to charges of unlawful discrimination. Employers are on firmer ground when worker safety is involved and the employer refuses to modify its dress or appearance policies. For example, a Muslim woman whose religious practice required her to wear a headscarf was not successful in her charge of religious discrimination for being denied employment in a factory with large machines and fast-moving parts. The hazards of the job posed a safety threat and the employer's position was upheld.[58]

Islamaphobia, hatred or fear of Muslims, can impact the work environment and employment experience of both Muslim and non-Muslim employees. There are over 1 million Muslims in the U.S. workforce, many well-educated and financially well-off. Texas Instruments took the lead soon after the September 11, 2001 terror attacks to insure that its Muslim employees were not being subjected to harassment or abuse at work. The company established a Muslim affinity group to provide employees with a forum to offer perspectives on business issues. This type of respect and concern breaks down mistrust and allows all employees to honor their religious beliefs in the workplace.[59]

Islamaphobia
Hatred or fear of Muslims.

3-8a Managing Religious Diversity

The EEOC recommends that employers consider the following reasonable accommodations for employees' religious beliefs and practices:

- Scheduling changes, voluntary substitutes, and shift swaps
- Changing an employee's job tasks or providing a lateral transfer
- Making an exception to dress and grooming rules
- Accommodations relating to payment of union dues or agency fees
- Accommodating prayer, proselytizing, and other forms of religious expression

Another issue concerns religious expression. In the last several years, employees in several cases have sued employers for prohibiting them from expressing their religious beliefs at work. In other cases, employers have had to take action because of the complaints by workers that employees were aggressively "pushing" their religious views at work, thus creating a "hostile environment." Executives and owners of some firms have strong religious beliefs that are carried over into their companies. Some display religious symbols, sponsor study/prayer sessions, and support other religious efforts. But such actions can lead to those with different beliefs feeling discriminated against, thus creating a "hostile environment." Other areas that may need to be considered when dealing with religion at work are food, on-site faith-based groups, office decorations, and religious practices at work.[60]

3-9 ■ MANAGING OTHER DISCRIMINATION ISSUES

A number of other factors, such as national origin/immigration, language, military status, and appearance and weight, might lead to unlawful discrimination.

In addition to the Title VII protections, a number of federal laws have been enacted to address these forms of discrimination. Many of these laws were passed in response to improper decisions by companies that resulted in unfair treatment of applicants or employees.

3-9a Immigration Reform and Control Acts

The United States is home to 40 million foreign-born residents, primarily from Latin America and Asia. This number includes people living in the United States both legally and illegally. Modern-day immigrants are blending in as rapidly as those from previous generations.[61] The influx of immigrants has led to extensive political, social, and employment-related debates. The Immigration Reform and Control Act (IRCA), enacted in 1986, requires employers to verify the employment status of all employees, while not discriminating because of national origin or ethnic background. Employers may not knowingly hire unauthorized aliens for employment in the United States.

Regardless of company size, every employer must comply with the provisions of the Act. High-profile Immigration and Customs Enforcement (ICE) raids on employers since January 2009 have led to audits of 7,500 employers and imposition of $100 million in penalties.[62] Employers ignore these obligations at their own peril. Within the first three days of employment, each employee must complete an Employment Eligibility Verification (commonly called an I-9) form and provide documents proving that they are legally authorized to work in the United States. Figure 3-10 lists the documents accepted in this process. The employer is required to inspect the documents and maintain records for all new hires.[63]

The E-verify federal database instantly verifies the employment eligibility of employees. Federal contractors are required to use the system as are employers in a number of states where it has been mandated. Other employers may use the system to check and verify employees' legal status.[64]

Visa Requirements Various revisions to the IRCA changed some of the restrictions on the entry of immigrants to work in U.S. organizations, particularly organizations with high-technology and other "scarce skill" areas. More immigrants with specific skills have been allowed legal entry, and categories for entry visas were revised.

FIGURE 3-10 Primary Documents to Certify I-9 Compliance

List A	List B	List C
◆ U.S. passport	◆ Driver's license or state-issued ID card	◆ U.S. social security card
◆ Certificate of U.S. citizenship	◆ ID card issued by federal, state, or local government	◆ Certification of birth abroad
◆ Certificate of naturalization	◆ School ID card with photograph	◆ Original or certified copy of birth certificate
◆ Unexpired foreign passport	◆ Voter's registration card	◆ Native American tribal document
◆ Permanent residence card	◆ U.S. military card or draft record	◆ U.S. citizen ID card

© Cengage Learning 2014

Among the most common visas encountered by employers are the B1 for business visitors, H-1B for professional or specialized workers, and L-1 for intracompany transfers.

To discourage hiring immigrants rather than U.S. workers, an employer must file documents with the Labor Department and pay prevailing U.S. wages to the visa holders. Despite these regulations, a number of unions and other entities view such programs as ways to circumvent the limits on hiring foreign workers.

3-9b Language Issues

As the diversity of the workforce increases, more employees have language skills in addition to English. Interestingly, some employers have attempted to restrict the use of foreign languages at work, while other employers have recognized that bilingual employees have valuable skills.

Some employers have policies requiring that employees speak only English at work. These employers contend that the policies are necessary for valid business purposes. The EEOC has issued guidelines clearly stating that employers may require workers to speak only English at certain times or in certain situations, but the business necessity of the requirements must be justified. Teaching, customer service, and telemarketing are examples of positions that may require English skills and voice clarity.

Some employers have found it beneficial to have bilingual employees so that foreign-language customers can contact someone who speaks their language. Bilingual employees are especially needed among police officers, airline flight personnel, hospital interpreters, international sales representatives, and travel guides.

3-9c Military Status Protections

The employment rights of military veterans and reservists have been addressed in several laws. The two most important laws are the Vietnam Era Veterans Readjustment Assistance Act of 1974 and the Uniformed Services Employment and Reemployment Rights Act (USERRA) of 1994. Under the latter, employees are required to notify their employers of military service obligations. Employers must give

FIGURE 3-11 Uniformed Services Employment and Reemployment Rights Act (USERRA) Provisions

Common Issues
- Leaves of absence
- Return to employment rights
- Prompt reemployment on return
- Protection from discharge/retaliation
- Health insurance continuation
- Continued seniority rights

© Cengage Learning

employees serving in the military leaves of absence protections under USERRA, as Figure 3-11 highlights.

With the use of reserves and National Guard troops abroad, the provisions of USERRA have had more impact on employers. This Act does not require employers to pay employees while they are on military leave, but many firms voluntarily provide additional compensation to bridge the gap between military pay and regular pay. Uniformed military personnel are provided up to five years of active duty service leave during which the employer must hold their job. Requirements regarding benefits, disabilities, and reemployment are covered in the Act as well.

3-9d Appearance and Weight Discrimination

Several EEOC cases have been filed concerning the physical appearance of employees. Court decisions consistently have allowed employers to set dress codes and appearance standards as long as they are applied uniformly. For example, establishing a dress code for women but not for men has been ruled discriminatory. Also, employers should be cautious when enforcing dress standards for female employees whose religions prescribe appropriate and inappropriate dress and appearance standards. Some individuals have brought cases of employment discrimination based on height or weight. The crucial factor that employers must consider is that any weight or height requirements must be related to the job, such as when excess weight would hamper an individual's job performance.[65]

Complying with this complex array of regulations requires diligence and careful record keeping. Appendix F provides details on the EEO enforcement process, information about records retention, and the investigation process.

3-10 ■ DIVERSITY TRAINING

Traditional diversity training has a number of different goals. One prevalent goal is to minimize discrimination and harassment lawsuits. Other goals focus on improving acceptance and understanding of people with different backgrounds, experiences, capabilities, and lifestyles. Employees are encouraged to recognize, evaluate, and appreciate differences.

3-10a Components of Traditional Diversity Training

There are often three components to diversity training programs. *Legal awareness* is the first and most common component. Here, the training focuses on the legal implications of discrimination. This limited approach to diversity training focuses only on these legal "do's and don'ts."

Through *cultural awareness* training, organizations hope to build greater understanding of the differences among people. Cultural awareness training helps all participants to see and accept the differences in people with widely varying cultural backgrounds.

The third component of diversity training—*sensitivity training*—is more difficult. The aim here is to "sensitize" people to the differences among them and how their words and behaviors are seen by others. Some diversity training includes exercises containing examples of harassment and other behaviors.

3-10b Mixed Results for Diversity Training

The results of diversity training are viewed as mixed by both organizations and participants. Studies on the effectiveness of diversity training raise some concern that the programs may be interesting or entertaining, but may not produce longer-term changes in people's attitudes and behaviors toward others with characteristics different from their own.[66]

Some argue that traditional diversity training more often than not has failed because it has not reduced discrimination and harassment complaints. Rather than reducing conflict, in a number of situations diversity training has increased hostility and conflict. In some firms, it has produced divisive effects, and has not changed behaviors so that employees can work well together in a diverse workplace.

Negative consequences of diversity training may manifest themselves broadly in a backlash against all diversity efforts. Women and members of racial minorities sometimes see diversity programs as inadequate and nothing but "lip service." Thus, it appears that by establishing diversity programs employers raise expectations but may fail to meet those expectations. On the other side, a number of individuals who are in the majority (primarily white males) interpret the emphasis on diversity as assigning them blame for societal problems. Diversity programs can be perceived as benefiting only women and racial minorities and taking away opportunities for men and nonminorities. This resentment and hostility is usually directed at affirmative action programs that employers have instituted.[67]

3-10c Improving Diversity Training Efforts

Focusing on behavior seems to hold the most promise for making diversity training more effective. For instance, dealing with cultural diversity as part of training efforts for sales representatives and managers has produced positive results. Teaching appropriate behaviors and skills in relationships with others is more likely to produce satisfactory results than focusing just on attitudes and beliefs among diverse employees.[68]

Trainers emphasize that the key to avoiding backlash in diversity efforts is to stress that people can believe whatever they wish, but at work their values are less important than their *behaviors*. Dealing with diversity is not about what people can and cannot *say*; it is about being *respectful* to others.

SUMMARY

- Equal employment is an attempt to level the field of opportunity for all people at work.
- Laws have been enacted to prohibit making employment decisions based on age, color,

disability, national origin, race, religion, and other protected characteristics.

- The Equal Employment Opportunity Commission and Office of Federal Contract Compliance

Programs are the primary enforcement agencies in employment discrimination laws.

- Disparate treatment occurs when individuals are treated differently on the basis of a protected characteristic.
- Disparate impact occurs when employment decisions work to the disadvantage of individuals on the basis of a protected characteristic.
- Employers may be able to defend their management practices using business necessity, job relatedness, and bona fide occupational qualifications (BFOQ).
- Title VII of the 1964 Civil Rights Act was the first significant equal employment law. The Civil Rights Act of 1991 altered and expanded the 1964 provisions.
- Retaliation claims now rank as the most common reason individuals file EEO claims.
- Executive Orders issued by the President govern the relationship between federal contractors and the U.S. government.
- Affirmative action has been intensely litigated, and the debate continues today.
- Several laws on sex/gender discrimination have addressed issues regarding pregnancy discrimination, unequal pay for similar jobs, and sexual harassment.
- As more women have entered the workforce, sex/gender issues in equal employment have included both discrimination through pay inequity and discrimination in jobs and careers.

- The courts have defined two types of sexual harassment—quid pro quo and hostile environment.
- It is vital that employers train all employees on what constitutes sexual harassment, promptly investigate complaints, and take action when sexual harassment is found to have occurred.
- The Americans with Disabilities Act (ADA) requires that most employers identify the essential functions of jobs and make reasonable accommodations for individuals with disabilities unless doing so would result in undue hardship.
- Employment discrimination against persons older than age 40 is illegal according to the Age Discrimination in Employment Act (ADEA).
- Employers are required to make reasonable accommodations for employees with religious beliefs and practices.
- The Immigration Reform and Control Acts (IRCA) regulate the employment of workers from other countries who work in the United States.
- A number of other concerns have been addressed by laws, including discrimination based on religion, military status, and other factors.
- Diversity training has had limited success, possibly because it too often has focused on beliefs rather than behaviors.

CRITICAL THINKING CHALLENGES

1. Discuss some of the protected characteristics covered by Equal Employment Opportunity and why they are important in today's employment setting.

2. You recently learned that two of your key female employees will be taking maternity leave around the same time. What procedures or rules do you need to be aware of based on the Pregnancy Discrimination Act (PDA)?

3. Give an example of sexual harassment you may have witnessed or heard about. How do you think the situation should have been handled if you were the HR manager?

4. Use the U.S. Department of Labor website (www.usdol.gov) to further research a topic discussed in this chapter. Be sure to understand what the particular law (Act) is protecting and what the rules are that companies need to follow to comply with this Act.

HR EXPERIENTIAL PROBLEM SOLVING

Because of a large number of recently retired employees you have been hiring more employees in recent years. The average age of the workforce at your company has changed drastically. The typical age of your employees used to be around 40; however, after many recent additions, it is now 34. The president of the company is worried that the company culture no longer matches up with the needs and values of a younger workforce. As the HR manager you have individually met with every new employee for orientation over recent years, so you feel you have a good idea as to what your workforce is looking for. You have been asked by the company president to suggest a few options to help increase morale and entice employees to stay with the company.

1. List some ideas to help meet the needs and wants of a younger workforce.
2. Going forward, what type of program would you include as part of new employee orientation to help further "sell" the company to your new employees?

CASE

Worker Exploitation at Foxconn/Hon Hai

Foxconn/Hon Hai Precision Ind. Co. Ltd. is a key China-based supplier to several U.S. high-tech companies like Apple, Dell, and HP. Manufacturers have a vested interest in the quality of products from their suppliers and their labor practices. Low-cost labor and a nearly endless supply of employees lead many U.S. companies to deal with suppliers in China. As more U.S. corporations strive for social responsibility, it was only a matter of time before production overseas saw the ripple effect of those decisions. Labor laws in China provide limited protection for workers and therefore the U.S. companies faced an ethical dilemma. Should they monitor labor practices at Foxconn/Hon Hai to ensure that workers were treated respectfully, or should they accept that if Foxconn followed Chinese labor laws it was not their concern?

Hon Hai, the world's largest electronics contract manufacturer, employs over 800,000 workers, who produce parts for iPads, iPhones, and other devices. Workers are housed in a campus with dormitories, a hospital, a bookstore, swimming pools, free bus transportation, and other services. Many of the workers migrated from farm communities to the industrial hubs where Hon Hai's operations are located. Their jobs at Hon Hai's factories are often the first assembly-line jobs they have ever held and they are frequently living far from home and family.

Working conditions at Hon Hai's factories complied with Chinese labor laws but frequently led to what is considered in the U.S. as worker abuse. Workers routinely worked in excess of 40 hours, with most workers averaging 120 hours of overtime per month. That calculates to an average workweek of 70 hours. Many machines were not properly equipped with safety devices leading to injuries. Underage workers were employed. At least 10 employees at the company committed suicide in 2010, which brought labor conditions under great public scrutiny. The company's response was to install safety nets around the dormitories to prevent additional casualties. The uproar from customers and the independent worker-advocacy agency, the Fair Labor Association, led to serious review of working conditions.

Apple had previously questioned labor conditions at Hon Hai. The company sent a team to investigate reports of excessive overtime and other "sweatshop" conditions. After the rash of suicides

'Apple sent a team of executives to China to inspect the factories and meet with Foxconn's CEO. Apple continues to monitor conditions at the supplier that were so bad that the U.S. company could no longer ignore the abhorrent labor practices.

Because of the sheer size of Hon Hai and its importance in the supply chain to electronics manufacturers, discontinuing the relationship would be a very difficult and costly alternative for Apple and others. Hon Hai has implemented a number of improvements for workers that should satisfy its customers and keep its employees safe and healthy. Employees at Hon Hai's factories will now work fewer hours and receive higher pay. For example, there is now a maximum 40-hour work week for each employee, with the option of working up to a maximum of 36 hours of overtime each week. The probation period for entry-level workers was cut in half from six months to three months. The company instituted an Employee Assistance Plan to assist employees with mental health concerns.

Labor laws around the world reflect the priorities of each nation's government and this can lead to great differences between countries. When a U.S.-based company does business with suppliers in other nations, one factor to consider is how workers are treated and what is required by law to insure humane working conditions.[69]

QUESTIONS

1. What obligation does a company like Apple or HP have to insure that suppliers follow the local labor laws? What should Apple do if it discovers that the supplier is not in compliance with those laws?

2. How should a multinational company like Apple reconcile the differences in labor laws around the world? For example, workers in the United States are provided substantial protection from discrimination and unfair treatment. This is not the case in all nations. If a company like Apple is doing business with suppliers around the world, what standard should be used to evaluate labor practices?

3. As someone who might purchase devices made by Apple, Dell, or HP, how does this treatment of workers at a supplier influence your opinion of Apple and other U.S. companies that deal with such suppliers? Does Apple bear any responsibility for these labor problems because of its quest for ever lower costs?

SUPPLEMENTAL CASES

Keep on Trucking

This case illustrates the problems that can be associated with the use of employment tests that have not been validated. (For the case, go to http://www.cengage.com/management/mathis.)

Mitsubishi Believes in EEO—Now

This case shows the problems Mitsubishi had with sexual harassment in the United States. (For the case, go to http://www.cengage.com/management/mathis.)

Religious Accommodation?

This case shows how companies must deal with employees from many cultures and religions. (For the case, go to http://www.cengage.com/management/mathis.)

NOTES

1. Adapted from "Wal-Mart vs. a Million Angry Women," *Bloomberg Businessweek*, November 22–November 28, 2010, 39–40; Rita Pyrillis, "Wal-Mart Ruling Convolutes Class-Action Landscape" *Workforce Management*, July 2012, 10; "Wal-Mart Women Still Seek Justice in Sex Discrimination Case," *Huffington Post*, August 16, 2012.
2. "Civil Rights Movement," August 2012, http://www.history.com/topics/civil-rights-movement.
3. "Office of Federal Contract Compliance Programs: Facts on Executive Order 11246–Affirmative Action," January 2002, http://www.dol.gov/ofccp/regs/compliance/aa.htm.
4. "Global Employment Law: NLRB Ruling Complicates Employers' Internal Investigations," August 2012, http://www.globalemploymentlaw.com/articles.
5. Kevin McGowan, "Retaliation Charges Were Most Common in Record-Breaking FY 2011, BNA Bulletin to Management," January 31, 2012, http://www.bna.com/retaliation-charges-common.
6. Tom Starner, "Bias Claims on the Rise," *Human Resource Executive*, January/February, 2011, 145; Andrew McIlvaine, "It's Pay-Up Time for the EEOC." *Human Resource Executive*, October 16, 2011, 10.
7. Willis Hagen, "Dissection and Analysis of the Recent Cases on Employment Discrimination under Title II of the Civil Rights Act of 1964," *Employee Responsibilities and Rights Journal*, 2011, 171–186; Anne Lindberg, "Disparate Impact or Disparate Treatment: Either Way Leads to Court," *Trend Watcher*, July 10, 2009, 1–5.
8. Kerri Stone, "Ricci Glitch: The Unexpected Appearance of Transferred Intent in Title VII," Loyola Law Review, 2010, 752; *Ricci v. DeStefano*, No. 08-328(E. D.Conn., April 22, 2009).

9. *Griggs v. Duke Power Co.*, 401 U.S. 424, (1971); Mary Birk, "RIFS: Use Statistical Analysis to Avoid Disparate Impact Based on Age," *Legal Report Society for Human Resources Management*, April 2008, 5–8.
10. Jathan Janove, "A Story is Worth a Thousand Lectures." *HR Magazine*, July 2009, 66–68; Roger Achille, "Thorough, Well-Documented Investigation Defeats Discrimination Claim,"*HR Magazine*, March 2012, 93.
11. David Shadovitz, "Questioning Criminal Backgrounds,"*Human Resource Executive*, October 2, 2011, 10; Leslie Silverman, "What HR Professionals Need to Know About the EEOC's New Guidance on Criminal Background Checks," www.shrm.org, 2012; Allen Smith, "Pepsi Settles Dispute Over Criminal Checks for $3 Million,"*HR Magazine*, March 2012, 14.
12. Sara Murray, "Credit Checks on Job Seekers By Employers Attract Scrutiny,"*The Wall Street Journal*, October 21, 2010; SHRM White Paper, "Hiring: Background Checks: Can We Run Credit Reports and Use Them as Part of our Employee Selection Process?", April 28, 2012.
13. *Breiner v. Nevada Dept. of Corrections*, No. 09-15568 (E.D. Nev., July 8, 2010).
14. *Dunlap v. Tennessee Valley Authority*, No. 07-5381 (E.D. Tenn. March 28, 2008); Rowe v. Cleveland Pneumatic Co., 690 F.2d 88 (1982).
15. Amanda Bolliger, "Award of $417,955 Upheld in Retaliation Case," *HR Magazine*, May 2012, 65.
16. Jamie Prenkert, "Handle with Care: Avoiding and Managing Retaliation Claims," *Business Horizons*, May 2012, 1; Lisa Cooney, "Understanding and Preventing Workplace Retaliation," *Massachusetts Law Review*, Volume 88, 2003.
17. Based on *EEOC v. Cognis Corp.*, No. 10-CV-2182 C.D. III (2012); http://www1.eeoc.gov/eeoc/newsroom/release/5-29-12.cfm

18. "U.S. Equal Employment Opportunity Commission: Title I – Federal Civil Rights Remedies, Damages in Cases of International Discrimination," 2012, http://www.eeoc.gov/laws/statutes/cra-1991.cfm.
19. Adapted from Ryan J. Foley, "Teresa Wagner Lawsuit Claims University of Iowa Passed Her Up For Jobs Because of Political Views," *Huff Post College*, October 12, 2012.
20. "U.S. Equal Employment Opportunity Commission: EEOC Race Discrimination Case Against YRC/Yellow Transportation Ends with $11 Million Decree," June 29, 2012, http://www.eeoc.gov/eeoc/newsroom/release/6-29-12a.cfm; "U.S. Equal Employment Opportunity Commission: Caldwell Freight Lines to Pay $120,000 to Settle EEOC Race Discrimination Lawsuit," August 3, 2012, http://www.eeoc.gov/eeoc/newsroom/release/8-3-12.cfm.
21. Olaf Aslund & Oskar Nordstrom Skans, "Do Anonymous Job Application Procedures Level the Playing Field?", *Industrial and Labor Relations Review*, Volume 65, 2012, 82–107.
22. James Hall, Mark Kobata, & Marty Denis, "Legal Briefings: Employer's Prompt Response to Racial Epithets," *Workforce Management*, January 2010, 8.
23. "U.S. Department of Labor, WHD: Break Time for Nursing Mothers," 2010, http://www.dol.gov/whd/nursingmothers.
24. "Italian Women Hoping for Workplace Changes, Protection vs. Discrimination,"*Business World*, August 13, 2012.
25. Mary-Kathryn Zachary, "Pregnancy Discrimination–Avoiding and Defending Lawsuits," Supervision, August 2010, 23–26; Kjersten Whittington, "Mothers of Invention: Gender, Motherhood, and New Dimensions of Productivity in the Science Profession," *Work and Occupations*, August, 2011, 417–456; "Milwaukee Company

Pays for Firing New Mother," *Associated Press*, March 3, 2012; *McFee v. Nursing Care Management of America*, No. 2009-0756 (E.D. Ohio, June 22, 2010).

26. UAW v. Johnson Controls, Inc., 499 US 187 (1991); Mark Valarie, "The Flip Side of Fetal Protection Policies: Compensating Children Injured Through Parental Exposure to Reproductive Hazards in the Workplace," *Golden Gate University Law Review*, Volume 22, 1992, http://digitalcommons.law.ggu.edu/ggulrev/vol22/iss3/4.

27. C. J. Weinberger & P. J. Kuhn, "Changing Levels or Changing Slopes? The Narrowing of the Gender Earnings Gap 1959–1999,"*Industrial and Labor Relations Review*, Volume 63, 2010, 384–406; A. Manning & F. Saidi, "Understanding the Gender Pay Gap: What's Competition Got to do With It?", *Industrial and Labor Relations Review*, 2010, Volume 63, 681–698; Stephen Benard, "Why His Merit Raise is Bigger Than Hers," *Harvard Business Review*, April 2012.

28. "U.S. Department of Labor: Women in the Labor Force in 2010," 2011, http://www.dol.gov/wb/factsheets/Qf-laborforce-10.htm.

29. Jacquelyn Smith, "The Top 25 Companies for Work-Life Balance," Forbes, August 10, 2012; Colette Darcy, Alma McCarthy, Jimmy Hill, & Geraldine Grady, "Work-Life Balance: One Size Fits All? An Exploratory Analysis of the Differential Effects of Career Stage," *European Management Journal*, April 2012, 111–120; Jing Wang & Anil Verma, "Explaining Organizational Responsiveness to Work-Life Balance Issues: The Role of Business Strategy and High-Performance Work Systems," *Human Resource Management*, May/June, 2012, 407–432; Lieke ten Brummelhuis & Tanja van der Lippe, "Effective Work-Life Balance Support for Various Household Structures," *Human Resource Management*, March/April 2010, 173–193.

30. "Catalyst: Women CEOs of the Fortune 1000," July 2012, http://www.catalyst.org/publication/271/women-ceos-of-the-fortune-1000; "Moving Women to the Top: McKinsey Global Survey Results," *McKinsey Quarterly*, October 2010.

31. S. Pichler, P. Simpson, and L. Stroh, "The Glass Ceiling in Human Resources: Exploring the Link Between Women's Representation in Management and the Practices of Strategic HRM and Employee Involvement," *Human Resource Management*, Fall 2008, 463–479; David Johnston & Wang-Sheng Lee, "Climbing the Job Ladder: New Evidence of Gender Inequity," *Industrial Relations: Journal of Economy and Society*, Volume 51, 129–151; P.A. Murray & J. Syed, "Gendered Observations and Experiences in Executive Women's Work," *Human Resource Management Journal*, 2010, Volume 20, 277–293; C. J. Weinberger, "In Search of the Glass Ceiling: Gender and Earnings Growth Among U.S. College Graduates in the 1990s," *Industrial and Labor Relations Review*, 2011, Volume 64, 949–980.

32. "Researcher Estimates 9 Million Americans are Gay or Bisexual," *The Denver Post*, April 7, 2011, 7A; Hope Yen, "Census: 131,729 Gay Couples Report That They're Married," *Casper Star-Tribune*, September 28, 2011, A11.

33. "ACLU: Summary of States Which Prohibit Discrimination Based on Sexual Orientation," June 17, 2005, http://aclu.procon.org/view.background-resource.php?resourceID=1457; Joe Harris, "In the Pink: Corporate Cultures are Reinventing Themselves to Accommodate LGBT Rights," *Florida Agenda*, June 21, 2012.

34. Diane Cadrain, "Accommodating Sex Transformations," *HR Magazine*, October 2009, 59–61.

35. L. Grensing-Pophal, "All in the Family," *HR Magazine*, September 2007, 66–70.

36. Charles Pierce, Katherine Karl, & Eric Brey, "Role of Workplace Romance Policies and Procedures on Job Pursuit Intentions," *Journal of Managerial Psychology*, 2012, Volume 27, 237–263.

37. Charles Pierce & Herman Aquinis, "Moving Beyond a Legal-Centric Approach to Managing Workplace Romances: Organizationally Sensible Recommendations for HR Leaders," *Human Resource Management*, May 2009, 447–464; "The Office Romance," *Bloomberg Businessweek*, September 20–26, 2010, 74–75.

38. Scott Clement, "Quarter of Women Report Being Harassed in Workplace," *The Denver Post*, November 17, 2011, 8A; "Sexual Harassment Statistics in the Workplace," 2012, http://www.sexualharassmentlawfirms.com/Sexual-Harassment-statistics.cfm.

39. Yvette Lee, "Electronic Harassment, Recruiters' Sources, Global Benefits", *HR Magazine*, September 2010, 24; Robyn Berkley & David Kaplan, "Assessing Liability for Sexual Harassment: Reactions of Potential Jurors to Email Versus Face-to-Face Incidents," *Employee Responsibilities and Rights Journal*, 2009, Volume 21, 195–211.

40. "Model Discrimination and Harassment Policy," Ceridian Abstracts, www.hrcompliance.ceridian.com, 1–3; Elissa Perry, Carol Kulik, & Marina Field, "Sexual Harassment Training: Recommendations to Address Gaps Between the Practitioner and Research Literatures," *Human Resource Management*, September/October 2009, Volume 48, 817–837; Christina Stoneburner, "Want an Easy and Cost-Effective Defense to Employment Discrimination Claims: Provide Harassment Training for Your Employees," *Employee Benefit News*, November 22, 2011.

41. Harsh Luther and Uipan Luther, "A Theoretical Framework Explaining Cross-Cultural Sexual Harassment: Integrating Hofsteds and Schwartz," *Journal of Labor Research*, Winter 2007, 169–188.

42. H. Stephen Kaye, "The Impact of the 2007–09 Recession on Workers with Disabilities," *Monthly Labor Review*, October 2010, 19–34.

43. "Fact Sheet: Your Rights Under Section 504 of the Rehabilitation Act," *Department of Health and Human Services*, June 2006.

44. Marlene Prost, "Final ADA Regulations Spell Out Disabilities," *Human Resource Executive Online*, April 8, 2011; James Hall, Mark Kobata, & Marty Denis, "Legal Briefings: Hiring Ban After Failed Drug Test and the ADA," *Workforce Management*, May 2011, 10; James Hall, Mark Kobata, & Marty Denis, "Legal Briefings: EEOC Issues Final Regulations for ADA Amendments Act," *Workforce Management*, June 2011, 12.

45. "ADA Regulations: What is a Mental Impairment?", January 5, 2012, http://hr.blr.com/HR-news/Discrimination/Disabilities-ADA/znt1-ADA-Regulations-What-is-a-Mental-Impairment.

46. Job Accommodation Network, http://askjan.org.

47. Matthew Brodsky, "Disability Flexibility", *Human Resource Executive Online*, September 2, 2011; Jonathan Segal, "ADA Game Changer", *HR Magazine*, June 2010, 121–126.

48. Katie Kuehner-Hebert, "Linking ADA Compliance to Corporate Culture," *Human Resource Executive*, October 16, 2011, 12; Victoria Zellers, "Make a Resolution: ADA Training," *HR Magazine*, January 2009, 81–83.

49. Jared Shelly, "Discrimination Deluge," *Human Resource Executive Online*, April 1, 2011; Jared Shelly, "Disability Discrimination Rises", *Human Resource Executive Online*, February 24, 2011; Joann Lublin & Saabira Chaudhur, "Ex-CEO Says Cancer Led to Her Ouster", *The Wall Street Journal*, August 4/5, 2012.

50. Allen Smith, "Coordinate GINA Compliance with Leave, ADA, and HIPAA Policies", www.shrm.org/legalissues, June 30, 2008; Susan Hauser, "Sincerely Yours, GINA,"

Workforce Management, July 2011, 16–22.

51. "World Population Ageing: 1950–2050," Department of Economic and Social Affairs–Population Division, 2002, http://www.un.org/esa/population/publications/worldageing19502050.

52. MitraToossi, "Labor Force Projections to 2018: Older Workers Staying More Active," *Monthly Labor Review*, November 2009, 30–51; Peter Cappelli & Bill Novelli, "Managing the Older Worker: How to Prepare for the New Organizational Order," Boston, MA: Harvard Business Press, 2010, 8–208.

53. Joanna Lahey, "International Comparison of Age Discrimination Laws," *Research on Aging*, November, 2010, Volume 32(6), 679–697; "Age Discrimination Internationally," 2012, http://www.agediscrimination.info/international/Pages/international.aspx.

54. Dana Mattioli, "With Jobs Scarce, Age Becomes an Issue," *The Wall Street Journal*, May 19, 2009, D4.

55. James Hall, Mark Kobata, & Marty Denis, "Legal Briefings: EEOC Clarifies ADEA Obligations," *Workforce Management*, April 2010, 8; Allen Smith, "Final Rule Issued on Disparate Impact Under ADEA," *HR Magazine*, May 2012, 14.

56. Richard Posthuma & Michael Campion, "Age Stereotypes in the Workplace: Common Stereotypes, Moderators, and Future Research Directions?," *Journal of Management*, February 2009, 158–188.

57. "U.S. EEOC: Understanding Waivers of Discrimination Claims in Employee Severance Agreements," April 2010, http://www.eeoc.gov/policy/docs/qanda_severance-agreements.html.

58. EEOC v. Kelly Services Inc., No. 08-3880 (2010).

59. Robert Grossman, "Muslim Employees: Valuable but Vulnerable," *HR Magazine*, March 2011, 22–27; Stan Malos, "Post-9/11 Backlash in the Workplace: Employer Liability for Discrimina-

tion Against Arab- and Muslim-Americans Based on Religion or National Origin," *Employee Responsibilities and Rights Journal*, Volume 22, 297–310.

60. Robert Grossman, "Religion at Work," *HR Magazine*, December 2008, 27–33.

61. Miriam Jordan, "Immigrants are Still Fitting in," *The Wall Street Journal*, November 14, 2011, A5.

62. Miriam Jordan, "Fresh Raids Target Illegal Hiring," *The Wall Street Journal*, May 3, 2012, A2; Miriam Jordan, "Chipotle Faces Inquiry on Hiring," *The Wall Street Journal*, May 23, 2012, B3.

63. Aliah Wright, "HR Must Be Diligent When It Comes to Verifying Employees," www.shrm.org, March 29, 2010; Hector Chichoni, "I-9 Compliance Crackdowns," *HR Magazine*, February 2011, 63–68.

64. "U.S. Citizenship and Immigration Services," 2012, http://www.uscis.gov/portal/site/uscis; D. Savino, "Immigration Policies and Regulations Continue to Create Uncertainty for Both Employers and Employees," *Employment Relations Today*, Fall 2009, 57–68.

65. R. M. Puhl, T. Andreyeva & K. D. Brownell, "Perceptions of Weight Discrimination: Prevalence and Comparison to Race and Gender Discrimination in America," *International Journal of Obesity*, June 2008, 992–1000; Mark Roehling, Richard Posthuma, and James Dulebohn, "Obesity Related 'Perceived Disability' Claims," *Employee Relations Law Journal*, Spring 2007, 30–51.

66. Katerina Bezrukova, Karen Jehn, & Chester Spell, "Reviewing Diversity Training: Where We Have Been and Where We Should Go," Academy of Management Learning & Education, June 2012, 207–227; Rohini Anand and Mary-Francis Winters, "A Retrospective of Corporate Diversity Training from 1964 to the Present," *Academy of Management Learning and Education*, September 2008, 356–373.

67. Lisa M. Amoroso, Denise L. Loyd, & Jenny M. Hoobler, "The Diversity Education Dilemma: Exposing Status Hierarchies Without Reinforcing Them," *Journal of Management Education*, December, 2010, 795–822.

68. Adapted from Elizabeth Levy Paluck & Donald P. Green, "Prejudice Reduction: What Works? A Review and Assessment of Research and Practice," *Annual Review of Psychology*, January, 2009, 339–367.

69. Based on Jason Dean, "Suicides Spark Inquiries," *Wall Street Journal*, May 27, 2010; Malcolm Moore, "Inside Foxconn's Suicide Factory," *Telegraph UK*, May 27, 2010; Nicholas Kolakowski, "Apple Report Details Response to Foxconn Suicides," eWeek.com, February 15, 2011; Dominic Rushe, "Apple Manufacturer Foxconn Improves on Chinese Workers' Hours and Safety," Guardian.com, August 21, 2012.

Jobs and Labor

4

Workforce, Jobs, and Job Analysis

Learning Objectives

After you have read this chapter, you should be able to:

1 Explain how the workforce is changing in unpredicted ways.
2 Identify components of workflow analysis.
3 Define job design and identify common approaches to job design.
4 Discuss how telework and work flexibility are linked to work–life balancing efforts.
5 Describe job analysis and the stages in the process.
6 List the components of job descriptions.

© Hemera/Thinkstock

Demand for Pilots Will Soar

© Dana Nalbandian/Shutterstock.com

After years of limited job openings for pilots, the airline industry is realizing it will be short of pilots very soon. Aircraft maker Boeing forecasts the need for 466,650 *more* commercial pilots by 2029— about 23,000 annually. Around 97,000 will be needed in North America, but a staggering 185,000 will be needed in the Asia-Pacific market. This demand for pilots is so great that it could turn into a shortage bringing on serious competition around the globe for pilots to fill cockpits.

This surge is brought about by four factors:

- High growth in Asian air travel
- Pilot retirements in the United States
- Increasing air travel in the United States as the economy improves
- Rules changes decreasing pilot flying time

If an airline wanted to start a route from Chicago to Shanghai—that route alone could require 40 additional pilots because of the staffing and equipment requirements for such a long flight. Mandatory retirement age for commercial pilots in the United States is 65, and the wave of pilots hitting that milestone really began in 2012.

Emirates is a Dubai-based airline that already employs 300 Americans as pilots and it is visiting U.S. job fairs because it needs 500 more. The compensation package includes a chauffeur-driven car to and from work, a family education allowance, and profit sharing. The starting salary at a U.S. regional carrier is about $21,000 annually, but a senior captain at a big airline makes more than $186,000 a year. U.S. regional carriers, which are typically the first rung on the career ladder for pilots, are likely to be hit hard as large carriers recruit their pilots.

The pipeline for pilots will have to grow to attract more people. Pilots may even win back some of the benefits they lost in recent years amid restructuring. As one observer notes: "It's going to be a pilot's market."[1]

To understand the workforce and the jobs people in the workforce do, it is important to understand what drives these variables. As discussed in the opening HR Headline, the shortage of pilots has been driven by four changing conditions that together will challenge the airline industry to find enough pilots. Predictions for other elements of the workforce and changing jobs affect all industries in different ways. For example, it has been predicted that the retirement of baby boomers (born 1946–1964) would leave a huge talent gap. But a funny thing happened on the way to retirement—many boomers did not have enough money to retire; health care expenses and other unknowns became a big issue for many, and they did not retire. The wave of retirements has been put off a bit as many older employees choose to continue working (except the pilots who *must* retire at 65).

Another prediction, that of "skills gaps" in certain areas, appears to be on track. Not everyone believed there would be skills shortages in education, health care, and IT while unemployment remains high. But many of the people without jobs do not have the skills needed to fill these well-documented shortages.[2] Generational differences in the workforce have been considered, analyzed, and addressed. Will differences between the generations at work really amount to differences in the way jobs get done, or will the younger workforce adapt?

Historically, part-time positions have not been viewed favorably as people would begrudgingly accept part-time work until they could find a full-time career opportunity. Yet employers want more contingent employees for the flexibility they present, and more employees now want part-time work (also for flexibility).

These changes affect the workforce and show that jobs will continue to change. This chapter explores important workforce issues that affects the jobs employers offer, as well as a technique for determining exactly what people do in their jobs—called job analysis.

L01 Explain how the workforce is changing in unpredicted ways.

4-1 ■ THE WORKFORCE PROFILE

Human Resources deals with that portion of the population that works at a job or is looking for work. An overview of the workforce is a good place to begin an examination of workforce and jobs.

According to the Bureau of Labor Statistics, compared to the labor force of the past, today's workplace force is "older, more racially and ethnically diverse, and composed of more women."[3] It is expected to expand at a slower rate than in previous decades because the U.S. population growth has slowed and there has been a decrease in the labor force participation rate. The **labor force participation rate** is the percentage of the population working or seeking work. Figure 4-1 shows the racial and gender profile of the U.S. workforce in 1990 and projects today's workforce to 2020.

Labor force participation rate
The percentage of the population working or seeking work.

The Census Bureau projects the U.S. population in 2020 to be about 341 million. People aged 55 and older will comprise about 29% of the population. Flows *into* the population include fertility (births) and immigration. Flows out of the population include deaths and outmigration. The fertility (or birth) rate in the United States is roughly at replacement level of 2.1 children per women. Life expectancies for the population continue to increase. Immigration is volatile and difficult to predict because it depends on other countries and economics, but it is estimated that 1.4 million people are annually added to the population by immigration.[4]

FIGURE 4-1 Thumbnail Profile of U.S. Workforce

Group	Number (in thousands)		Percent Distribution		Annual Growth Rate (percent)
	1990	2020	1990	2020	2010–2020
Total, 16 years and older	125,840	164,360	100.0	100.0	0.7
Age, years:					
16–24	22,492	18,330	17.9	11.2	−1.3
25–54	88,322	104,619	70.2	63.7	0.2
55+	15,026	41,411	11.9	25.2	3.3
Gender:					
Men	69,011	87,128	54.8	53.0	0.6
Women	56,829	77,232	45.2	47.0	0.7

Source: U.S. Bureau of Labor Statistics.

The labor force participation rate peaked at 67% before 2000 and has since declined to around 65%. Part of the reason is that older people are still in the population, but are not as likely to be in the workforce as younger people. Put another way, the labor force participation rate for older people is less than that for younger people. Figure 4-2 shows the participation rates by age, gender, and race/ethnicity in 2010 at the last census and projects them to 2020.

4-1a Important Elements of the Workforce Profile

The participation rates help us understand which segments of the population are more likely to be in the labor market in the future. Several variables like age, skills, readiness for work, generational differences, and time worked complete the workforce profile.

Age Youths aged 16–24 are predicted to reduce their participation rates. The younger people in this group are more likely to be students. Workers of ages 25–54 are also projected to reduce their participation rates to 81% in 2020. Workers 55 and older are likely to increase their participation rates in the workforce, at least in part because many do not have enough money to retire.[5]

Older workers coming back to the workforce have a more difficult time finding jobs than their younger counterparts.[6] So, many simply choose not to leave the workforce. Human Resources can plan for an aging workforce by using

FIGURE 4-2 Labor Force Participation Rates

Group	Participation Rate (%)		Percentage-Point Change	Group	Participation Rate (%)		Percentage-Point Change	Group	Participation Rate (%)		Percentage-Point Change
	2010	2020	2010–2020		2010	2020	2010–2020		2010	2020	
Total, 16+ years	64.7	62.5	–2.2	Men, 16+ years	71.2	68.2	–3.0	Women, 16+ years	58.6	57.1	–1.5
16–24	55.2	48.2	–7.0	16–24	56.8	50.6	–6.2	16–24	53.6	45.7	–7.9
25–54	82.2	81.3	–0.9	25–54	89.3	88.4	–1.6	25–54	75.2	74.6	0.6
55+	40.2	43.0	2.8	55+	46.4	47.3	0.9	55+	35.1	39.3	4.2
55–64	64.9	68.8	3.9	55–64	70.0	71.1	1.1	55–64	60.2	66.6	6.4
65+	17.4	22.6	5.2	65+	22.1	26.7	4.6	65+	13.8	19.2	5.4
65–74	25.7	31.0	5.3	65–74	30.4	35.1	4.7	65–74	21.6	27.5	5.9
75–79	10.9	15.2	4.3	75–79	14.5	18.2	3.7	75–79	8.2	13.0	4.8
Race:											
White	65.1	62.8	–2.3								
Men	72.0	69.0	–3.0								
Women	58.5	56.9	–1.6								
Black	62.2	60.3	–1.9								
Men	65.0	63.1	–1.9								
Women	59.9	57.9	–2.0								
Asian	64.7	63.1	–1.6								
Men	73.2	71.0	–2.2								
Women	57.0	56.1	–0.9								
Hispanic origin	67.5	66.2	–1.3								
Men	77.8	75.9	–1.9								
Women	56.6	56.1	–0.4								

Source: U.S. Bureau of Labor Statistics.

demographic models to determine the company's age mix and likely exit rates and then deal with problem areas using such tools as mandatory retirement, early retirement incentives, and so on.[7] While the "Tsunami" of baby boomer retirements has not materialized in many industries yet, the skill gaps resulting as the boomers *do* eventually leave will cause some problems.[8]

Skill Gaps Being able to match talent to what the business and is trying to accomplish is fundamental. For example, lower energy costs, rising wages in China and India, and high international shipping costs may combine to make the United States more attractive to manufacturing again. That means more jobs requiring science, technology, engineering, and math skills (STEM). Yet there is currently a large shortage of those skills in the U.S. workforce.[9] It is not that there are too few high school and college graduates. Rather the problem is the subjects that students are majoring in, and the level and quality of the education received. Figure 4-3 shows the educational attainment at the last census.

High school seniors planning to go to college show declining SAT writing and reading scores. ACT scores suggest that only 25% of the high school graduates that took the test are ready for college.[10] Human Resources can deal with these shortages by planning for the specific skills needed when recruiting and hiring employees and then hiring for those skills.[11] A recent study found that 53% of the HR respondents were indeed planning to conduct a strategic workforce assessment focusing on skill gaps.[12]

Work Ready Credentials "Work ready credentials" are gaining popularity with employers because they measure necessary skills. One certification, the National Work Readiness Credential, is based on a written test of a potential employee's business math skills, oral language skills, and situational judgment. Another work readiness test, the National Career Readiness certificate, is based on American college testing (ACT) work keys system, and gives scores for reading for information, locating information, and applied math.[13] These and other tests like them give an employer an assessment of a person's skills by a professional testing organization. It is no longer necessary to look at a diploma and assume that an individual has certain skills such as ability to read. The skills can be tested and reported to potential employers.

Skills gaps in a company may become an issue when changes in strategy are not matched by the skills of the current workforce. American students are not getting all the "job ready" skills employers need in the people they are hiring.[14]

Generational Differences Much has been written about the expectations of individuals in different age groups and generations. Some common age/generational groups are labeled as follows:

- Mature (born before 1946)
- Baby boomers (born 1946–1964)
- Generation Xers (born 1965–1980)
- Generation Yers (millenials) (born 1981–2000)

Different characteristics have been attributed to generational groups. Those differences are sometimes predicted to be the basis for conflict and turbulence at work.[15] These concerns have generated a great deal of advice on how to deal with the differences.[16]

However, studies and rethinking of the generation differences raise questions as to whether there are really major differences among the generations or just age differences that change as a person grows older. There is little or no evidence that there are generational differences, and apparently none that matter enough to drive important behavior differences.[17]

Part Timers, Contingent, Self-Employed, and Multiple Jobholders A final relevant characteristic of the workforce includes people who are working part time (some

FIGURE 4-3 Education Profile of Workforce

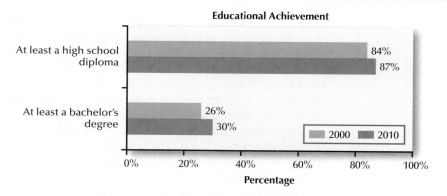

Educational Achievement

At least a high school diploma: 84% (2000), 87% (2010)

At least a bachelor's degree: 26% (2000), 30% (2010)

Legend: 2000, 2010

Percentage

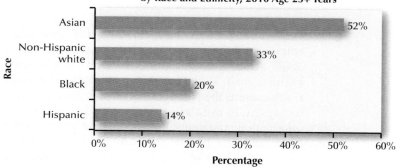

Populations with a Bachelor's Degree by Race and Ethnicity, 2010 Age 25+ Years

Race:
Asian — 52%
Non-Hispanic white — 33%
Black — 20%
Hispanic — 14%

Percentage

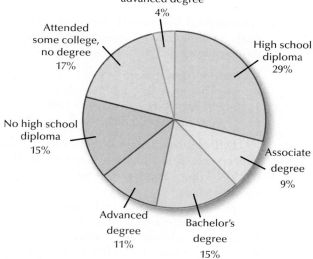

Highest Education Level of Adults Age 25+ Years, 2010

Spent time in graduate school without receiving advanced degree 4%

Attended some college, no degree 17%

High school diploma 29%

No high school diploma 15%

Associate degree 9%

Advanced degree 11%

Bachelor's degree 15%

on purpose), those who work for themselves, and people who have more than one job. The Bureau of Labor Statistics classifies people working less than 35 hours per week as part time, but employers set their own definition of part time as they see fit. Two-thirds of the part-time workforce is female, as mothers may need to lower their hours to provide for child care. But others choose part-time work as well—for example, the number of pediatricians, obstetricians, gynecologists, and pharmacists working part-time has increased markedly. Some companies (around 40%) allow employees to move back and forth between part time and full time status.[18]

Further, some workers move to part time schedules before they retire. Older workers who have retired may agree to come back for part-time work only. Freelancers or independent workers afford flexibility for employers for specific jobs (e.g., a freelance art director might do projects only as needed).[19] The use of contingent workers of whatever label continues to increase because of the resulting flexibility available for both parties.[20]

Self-employment is an important source of work for over 15 million people in the U.S. workforce. Almost 11% of the total workforce is made up of the self-employed.[21] While some people work for themselves, others work for more than one employer. Multiple jobholders constitute about 5% of the workforce with some states showing more multiple jobholders than others.[22] The Dakotas, Minnesota, Vermont, and Iowa have the most multiple jobholders, while Alabama, Louisiana, Florida, and Georgia have the fewest. The HR Skills and Applications box shows some of the issues for the employer of these "moonlighters."

HR SKILLS AND APPLICATIONS

Dealing with a "Moonlighter"

When an employee has more than one job (e.g., a sales executive who doubles as a consultant/speaker), ideally it can benefit both employee and employer. However, moonlighting can cause problems with trade secrets, distracted or unproductive employees, exhaustion, complaints from other employees, and "brand risks" like the high school teacher working as an exotic dancer.

Moonlighting can be advantageous for both parties, as it can help compensate for hard times, develop employee skills, and improve retention. For example, Fujitsu Ltd. in Japan allowed employees to take second jobs after declining sales had reduced employee hours by 33%. This was a win-win situation because productivity was not affected, and the employees remained tied to their primary jobs while avoiding earnings losses.

Employment lawyers and HR managers recommend managing moonlighting by watching job performance and applying conflict of interest policies on a case-by-case basis. An example of such a policy says: "I understand this is my primary job and if another activity conflicts with my duties it may lead to the end of my employment." The statement is included in the employee handbook. Companies may ask employees considering a second job to consult their managers or HR to make sure there is no conflict of interest before taking the other job.[23]

4-2 ■ THE NATURE OF WORK AND JOBS

LO2 Identify components of workflow analysis.

Work
Effort directed toward accomplishing results.

Job
Grouping of tasks, duties, and responsibilities that constitutes the total work assignment for an employee.

One way to visualize an organization is as an entity that takes inputs from the surrounding environment and then, through some kind of "work," turns those inputs into goods or services. **Work** is effort directed toward accomplishing results. The work may be done by humans, machines, or both. The total amount of work to be done in an organization must be divided into jobs so that it can be coordinated in some logical way. A **job** is a grouping of tasks, duties, and responsibilities that constitutes the total work assignment for an employee. These tasks, duties, and responsibilities may change over time and therefore the job may change.

Ideally, when the work to be done in all the jobs in an organization is combined, it should equal the amount of work that the organization needs to have done—no more, no less. The degree to which this ideal is or is not met drives differences in organizational productivity.

Jobs increase in number, evolve, duties change and are combined or eliminated as the needs of the organization change. If this does not happen, the organization is failing to adapt to the changes in its environment and may be becoming outmoded or noncompetitive. Several approaches are used to deal with the common issues surrounding jobs in any organization.

For Southwest Airlines, jobs involve employees working in an enjoyable culture that delivers dependable service at low fares. Southwest employees have a high degree of flexibility in the jobs they perform, even to the point that customer service agents may help clean planes or unload luggage if the workload demands it. Other airlines, such as American and United, have higher fares, more service amenities, and employees with more narrowly defined jobs. The ways the work is done and jobs are designed and performed vary significantly under these two approaches and the differences impact the number of jobs and people needed.

For HR, the way work flows through the organization and how to make that work more efficient is important. Changing the way jobs are done through job redesign may make people more satisfied, and formally reviewing jobs through workflow analysis can help identify what is to be accomplished.

4-2a Workflow Analysis

Workflow analysis
Study of the way work (inputs, activities, and outputs) moves through an organization.

Workflow analysis is the study of the way work moves through an organization. Usually, it begins with an examination of the quantity and quality of the desired and actual *outputs* (goods and services). Next, the *activities* (tasks and jobs) that lead to the outputs are evaluated to see if they are achieving the desired outputs. Finally, the *inputs* (people, material, information, data, equipment, etc.) must be assessed to determine if they make the outputs and activities better and more efficient. Figure 4-4 shows a workflow analysis framework.

An integrating workflow analysis is likely to lead to better employee involvement, greater efficiency, and more customer satisfaction as organizational work is divided into jobs that can be coordinated. For example, at one electric utility company, if a customer called with a service problem, a customer service representative typically took the information and put it into a database. Then, in the operations department, a dispatcher accessed the database to schedule a technician to repair the problem. Then, someone else called to tell the customer when the repair would be done. The technician also received instructions from a supervisor, who got information on workload and locations from the dispatcher.

FIGURE 4-4 Workflow Analysis

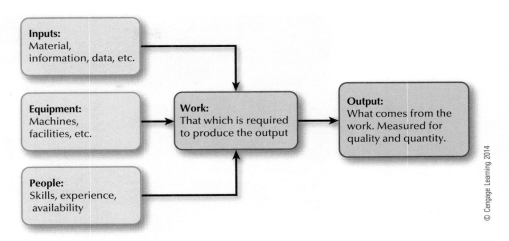

A workflow analysis of this process showed that there were too many steps involving too many jobs. So the utility implemented a new customer service system that combined the dispatching function with customer service. The redesign permitted the customer service representatives to access workload information and schedule the technicians as part of the initial customer phone call, except in unusual situations. The redesign necessitated redefining the tasks, duties, and responsibilities of several jobs. Implementing the new jobs required training the customer service representatives in dispatching, as well as moving dispatchers into the customer service department and training them in all facets of customer service. The result was a more responsive workflow for customers, more efficient scheduling of technicians, and broader jobs for customer service representatives. Ultimately, the company was able to reduce the number of employees involved by 20% through attrition as a result of the workflow analysis. Workflow analysis that focuses on making an organization more effective and efficient is most often used in manufacturing organizations. However, the process can be applied to knowledge work as well.[24]

4-2b Job Design/Job Redesign

L03 Define *job design* and identify common approaches to job design.

Job design
Organizing tasks, duties, responsibilities, and other elements into a productive unit of work.

Job redesign
Taking an existing job and changing it to improve it.

Job design refers to organizing tasks, duties, responsibilities, and other elements into a productive unit of work. **Job redesign** refers to changing an existing job it to improve it. Identifying the components of a given job is an integral part of job design. Job design receives attention for three major reasons:

- Job design can influence *performance* in certain jobs, especially those where employee motivation can make a substantial difference.
- Job design can affect *job satisfaction*. Since people are more satisfied with certain job elements than others, identifying what makes a "good" job becomes critical.[25] Reduced turnover and absenteeism also can be linked to effective job design.
- Job design can impact both *physical* and *mental health*. Problems such as hearing loss, backache, leg pain, stress, high blood pressure, and heart disease sometimes can be traced directly to job design.[26]

FIGURE 4-5 Some Characteristics of Jobs and People

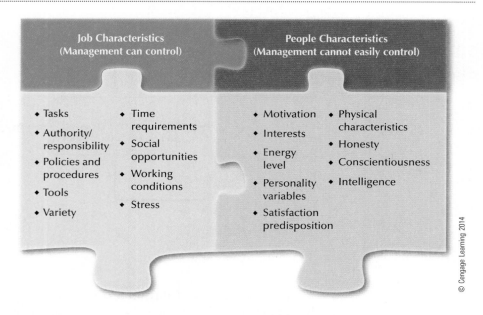

Managers play a significant role in job design because often they are the people who establish jobs and their design components. They must make sure that job expectations are clear, that decision-making responsibilities and the accountability of workers are clarified, and that interactions with other jobs are integrated and appropriate.[27]

The nature and characteristics of both jobs and people should be considered during job design. As Figure 4-5 indicates, managers can influence or control job characteristics, but they usually cannot easily control the basic characteristics of people.

4-2c Using Contingent Workers as Job Design

Organizations employ a variety of workers, and not just full-time workers as we have seen. Depending on economic and competitive factors, the types of workers in one firm may include the following:

- Full-time employees
- Part-time employees
- Independent contractors
- Temporary workers
- Contingent workers

Jobs can be designed to use any of the different types. Although some organizations still use the traditional approach of employing full- and part-time workers, many firms are making significant use of independent, temporary, and contingent workers. These individuals are not employees but generally work at will or on limited contracts, and they may be working for other employers as well. A **contingent worker** is someone who is not a full time employee, but a temporary or part time worker for a specific period of time and type of work.

According to the U.S. Bureau of Labor Statistics, contingent workers are part of a group of "alternative workers" who may be on-call, working through an employment

Contingent worker
Someone who is not an employee, but a temporary or part-time worker for a specific period of time and type of work.

agency, or operating as independent contractors. A number of contingent workers have contracts with employers that establish their pay, hours, job requirements, limitations, and time periods. More employers are using contingent or temporary workers.

Person–Job Fit Not everyone would enjoy being an HR manager, an engineer, a nurse, or a drill-press operator. But some people like and do well at each of these jobs. The **person–job fit** is a simple but important concept of matching characteristics of people with characteristics of jobs.[28]

Person–job fit
Matching characteristics of people with characteristics of jobs.

If a person does not fit a job, theoretically either the person can be changed or replaced or the job can be redesigned. However, though an employer can try to make a "round" person fit a "square" job, it is hard to successfully reshape people. If it is possible to redesign a job, the person-job fit may sometimes be improved more easily.[29] For example, bank tellers talk to people all day; an individual who would rather not talk to others may perform better in a position that does not require so much interaction because that part of the bank teller job likely cannot be changed. Different people will consider some jobs "good" and others "bad." As a result, different people will best fit different kinds of work.[30]

4-2d Common Approaches to Job Design

One way to design or redesign jobs is to simplify the job tasks and responsibilities. Job simplification may be appropriate for jobs that are to be staffed with entry-level employees. However, making jobs too simple may result in boring jobs that appeal to few people, causing high turnover. Several other approaches have also been used as part of job design.

Job Enlargement and Job Enrichment Attempts to alleviate some of the problems encountered in excessive job simplification fall under the general headings of job enlargement and job enrichment. **Job enlargement** involves broadening the scope of a job by expanding the number of different tasks to be performed. **Job enrichment** is increasing the depth of a job by adding, for example, responsibility for planning, organizing, controlling, or evaluating the job. Some examples of job enrichment are as follows:

Job enlargement
Broadening the scope of a job by expanding the number of different tasks to be performed.

Job enrichment
Increasing the depth of a job by adding responsibility for planning, organizing, controlling, or evaluating the job.

- Giving the employee an entire job rather than just a piece of the work.
- Allowing the employee more flexibility to perform the job as needed.
- Increasing the employee's accountability for work by reducing external control.
- Expanding assignments for employees to do new tasks and develop special areas of expertise.
- Directing feedback reports to the employee rather than only to management.

Job Rotation One technique that can break the monotony of an otherwise simple routine job is **job rotation**, which is the process of shifting a person from job to job. There are advantages to job rotation with one being that it develops an employee's capabilities for doing several jobs.[31] For instance, some firms have been successful at using job rotation for employees with disabilities in special assembly lines and different work requirement times. Even people without disabilities can be adaptable and change jobs and careers internally in appropriate ways. Clear policies that identify for employees the nature of job rotations are more likely to make job rotation work.

Job rotation
Process of shifting a person from job to job.

4-2e Characteristics of Jobs to Consider in Design

A model developed by Hackman and Oldham focuses on five important design characteristics of jobs. Figure 4-6 shows that *skill variety*, *task identity*, and *task significance* affect the meaningfulness of work; *autonomy* stimulates responsibility; and *feedback* provides knowledge of results. Each aspect can make a job better for the jobholder to the degree that it is present.

Skill variety
Extent to which the work requires several activities for successful completion.

Task identity
Extent to which the job includes a "whole" identifiable unit of work that is carried out from start to finish and that results in a visible outcome.

Task significance
Impact the job has on other people.

Autonomy
Extent of individual freedom and discretion in the work and its scheduling.

Feedback
The amount of information employees receive about how well or how poorly they have performed.

- **Skill variety** is the extent to which the work requires several activities for successful completion. For example, lower skill variety exists when an assembly-line worker performs the same two tasks repetitively. Skill variety is not to be confused with *multitasking*, which is doing several tasks at the same time with computers, telephones, personal organizers, and other means. The impact of multitasking for an employee may be never getting away from the job which is not an acceptable outcome for everyone.
- **Task identity** is the extent to which the job includes a "whole" identifiable unit of work that is carried out from start to finish and that results in a visible outcome. For example, when a customer calls with a problem, a customer specialist can handle the stages from maintenance to repair in order to resolve the customer's problem.
- **Task significance** is the impact the job has on other people. A job is more meaningful if it is important to other people for some reason. For instance, police officers may experience more fulfillment when dealing with a real threat rather than when merely training to be ready in case a threat arises.[32]
- **Autonomy** is the extent of individual freedom and discretion in the work and its scheduling. More autonomy leads to a greater feeling of personal responsibility for the work.
- **Feedback** is the amount of information employees receive about how well or how poorly they have performed. The advantage of feedback is that it helps employees to understand the effectiveness of their performance and contributes to their overall knowledge about the work.

Motivation, performance and satisfaction can be influenced by the level of each job characteristic. Autonomy and feedback are especially powerful.

FIGURE 4-6 Job Characteristics Model

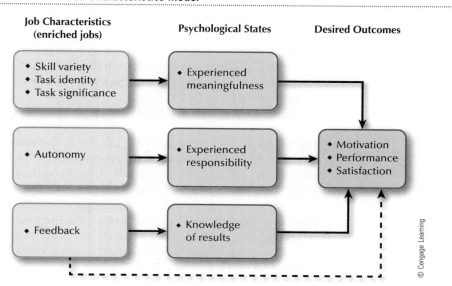

© Cengage Learning

4-2f Using Teams in Job Design

Typically, a job is thought of as something done by one person. However, where appropriate, jobs may be designed for teams to take advantage of the increased productivity and commitment that may follow such a change. Organizations can assign jobs to teams of employees instead of just individuals. Some firms have gone as far as dropping such terms as workers and employees, replacing them with teammates, crew members, associates, and other titles that emphasize teamwork.

As organizations have changed, the types of teams have changed as well. Having global operations with diverse individuals and using technology have affected the nature of teams contributing to organizational projects.

Special-purpose team
Organizational team formed to address specific problems, improve work processes, and enhance the overall quality of products and services.

Self-directed team
Organizational team composed of individuals who are assigned a cluster of tasks, duties, and responsibilities to be accomplished.

Virtual team
Organizational team includes individuals who are separated geographically but who are linked by communications technology.

Special Types of Teams There are several types of teams that may periodically function outside the scope of members' normal jobs.[33] One is the **special-purpose team**, which is formed to address specific problems, improve work processes, and enhance the overall quality of products and services. Often, special-purpose teams are a mixture of employees, supervisors, and managers.

The **self-directed team** is comprised of individuals who are assigned a cluster of tasks, duties, and responsibilities to be accomplished. Unlike special-purpose teams, self-directed work teams become entities that use regular internal decision-making processes. Use of self-directed work teams must be planned well and fit the culture of the organization.

The **virtual team** includes individuals who are separated geographically but who are linked by communications technology. The success of virtual work teams depends on a number of factors, including training of team members, planning and managing virtual tasks and projects, and using technology to enhance teamwork. However, sometimes virtual teams can lead to unresolved problems, less productivity, and miscommunications.[34]

Global Teams Global operations have resulted in an increasing use of virtual teams. Members of these teams seldom or never meet in person. Instead, they "meet" electronically using web based systems. With global teams, it is important for managers and HR to address various issues, including who is to be chosen for the teams, how they are to communicate and collaborate online and in person, and what tasks and work efforts may be done with these teams.

GLOBAL

4-2g Teams and Work Efforts

The use of work teams has been a popular form of job redesign. Improved productivity, increased employee involvement, greater coworker trust, more widespread individual learning, and greater employee use of knowledge diversity are among the potential benefits. In a transition to work teams, it is important to define the areas of work, scope of authority, and goals of the teams. Also, teams must recognize and address dissent, conflict, and other problems.[35]

The role of supervisors and managers changes with use of teams because of the emergence or development of team leaders. Rather than giving orders, often the team leader becomes a facilitator to assist the team, to mediate and resolve conflicts among team members, and to interact with other teams and managers elsewhere.[36]

Teams can be enhanced through task responsibility, discussion structures, and cooperative efforts. Some organizations have noted that teams may underperform requiring managers to define teams expectations clearly, keep them small, and remove individuals who cannot work on the team effectively.[37]

4-3 ■ DESIGNING FLEXIBLE JOBS

Flexibility can be designed into a job by changing *where* the work can be done and *when* the work can be done. These can be taken into consideration in designing jobs as jobs that are more flexible are generally seen as more attractive to employees.

Technology has allowed a "connectedness" between two people on a personal level, but also between an individual employee and others at work. The result can be a much greater ability to vary where and when work can be done. But for all the benefits and the ability to be constantly in communication that technology provides there is a dark side as well—information overload and attention fragmentation. Too much technological flexibility and multiple connectivity without some adaptation can cause problems for some. The need for uninterrupted time to synthesize information, reflect, apply judgment, and make good decisions is an important requirement for certain jobs. Yet it is hard to find such time with the 24/7 on-call world that has developed. Where appropriate, a "focus, filter, and forget" strategy helps some adapt to multiple connectivity.[38] Focus may require disconnecting from the input. Filtering can mean only looking at things that matter, and forgetting means downtime with exercise or relaxation to get away.

The technology that has caused these problems has allowed the ability to work at places other than the usual place of work. Such arrangements are collectively referred to as *telework* or *telecommuting*.

4-3a Place Flexibility—Telework

Individuals who may be working at home or at other places illustrate **telework**, which means that employees work via electronic, telecommunications, and Internet technology. There has been a rapid growth in home-based wage and salary employment recently.[39] Twenty-four percent of Americans report that they work at least some hours at home each week.[40] Employees with higher education levels frequently get more opportunity for telework (see Figure 4-7).

FIGURE 4-7 Education Level and Opportunity for Telework

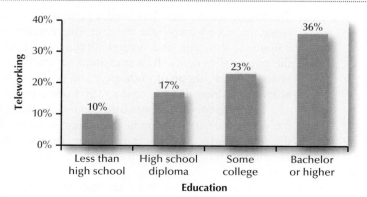

Source: American Time Use Survey, Bureau of Labor Statistics, 2010.

Benefits and Disadvantages The first identified benefits of telework were environmental, dealing with problems caused by traffic and wasted time commuting for employees. Employees may indeed find that they spend less for gasoline, maintenance, lunches, and dry cleaning. Not traveling to work saves employees an average of one extra hour per day.[41] Employers also cite improved productivity and the need for less work space as advantageous. It may be that the ability to telecommute can be a factor in attracting some employees, and reducing turnover for others.

Concerns about telework include the following:

- Teleworkers may work more hours than their office counterparts.
- Lack of "face-time" can hurt careers.
- Employers worry about loss of control.
- Managers must learn to use quality and timeliness of output rather than physical monitoring.
- Some states (such as New York) charge the *employee* income taxes if the *employer* is in that state, regardless of where the employee is located.[42]

Some employers are encouraging one or more days of telework per month. Telecommuting is especially useful during bad weather or widespread health issues such as pandemic flu.

Administering Telework The working relationship with teleworkers should begin with a carefully worded policy. Since managers have less direct supervision of teleworkers a number of issues and employee concerns are raised. Such a policy must consider work time use, evaluation of performance, handling of expenses, and other factors.[43] See HR Skills and Applications: Managing Teleworkers.

Additional issues affect employees and their relationships with coworkers and managers.[44] One is overwork when having to balance home and work requirements.

HR SKILLS AND APPLICATIONS

Managing Teleworkers

More than 17 million full-time employees telework at least one day per month. It appears this interest will continue to grow. To make certain that telework is providing the potential benefits, management training is important for the effective supervision of teleworkers. The following are key areas for training managers.

- *Make sure the job is appropriate for telework.* Not all jobs will work—for example, a receptionist, bank teller, or other job that *requires* face-to-face meeting.
- *Evaluate the employee's abilities.* Can this employee allocate time appropriately? Can he or she work well without direct supervision? Are they self-disciplined?

- *Determine if the teleworker will have appropriate equipment at the alternative worksite.* Will the worker be able to access computer files securely, take phone calls, and can be in touch with the other people necessary?
- *Guidelines for some things can help.* Setting guidelines for such things as forwarding work phones, emphasizing that work time is not for caring for children or elders, and having a quiet work space.
- *Set performance expectations.* Before the telework begins the worker and manager should discuss expectations and what work will be accomplished.[45]

Maintaining employee motivation when individuals are not physically present at company facilities can also be challenging and may increase employee stress. This is a special concern for global employees. Also, the 15-hour time zone difference between the United States and some Asian countries may make it difficult for global employees to participate in conference calls or travel extensively for meetings.

Telework may take one of three forms:

- Regular—employee may spend scheduled days or every day at an office at home.
- Brief occasional—using a home office on weekends or at night to do a project.
- Temporary/Emergency—during bad weather, a natural disaster, or other events causing disruption employees work from home.

4-3b Time Flexibility—Work Scheduling

Different work schedules can be part of designing jobs and have been developed for employees in different occupations and areas. The traditional U.S. work schedule of eight hours a day, five days a week, is in transition. Workers may work less or more than eight hours at a workplace, and may have additional work at home.[46]

The work schedules associated with jobs vary as some jobs must be performed during "normal" daily work hours and on weekdays, while others require employees to work nights, weekends, and extended hours. There are significant differences in the hours worked in different countries as well. Given the global nature of many organizations, HR must adjust to different locations. Organizations are using many work scheduling arrangements based on industry demands, workforce needs, and other factors.[47] These include shift work, the compressed workweek, part-time schedules, job sharing, and flextime.

Shift Work A common work schedule design is shift work. Many organizations need 24-hour coverage and therefore may schedule three eight-hour shifts per day. Most employers provide some form of additional pay, called a *shift differential*, for working the evening or night shifts. Some types of shift work have been known to cause difficulties for some employees, such as weariness, irritability, lack of motivation, and illness. Although shift work is not universally popular, some employers must have 24-hour, 7-day coverage, so shift work is likely to continue to be an option.

Compressed workweek
A workweek in which a full week's work is accomplished in fewer than five 8-hour days.

Compressed Workweek Another type of work schedule design is the **compressed workweek**, in which a full week's work is accomplished in fewer than five 8-hour days. Compression usually results in more work hours each day and fewer workdays each week, such as four 10-hour days, or a 3-day week with 12-hour shifts. Often the workers who shift to 12-hour schedules do not wish to return to 8-hour schedules because they have four days off each week. However, 12-hour schedules can lead to sleep difficulties, fatigue, and an increased number of injuries.

Part-Time Schedules Part-time jobs are used when less than 40 hours per week are required to do a job. Part-time jobs are attractive to those who may not want to work 40 hours per week—older employees, parents of small children, or students. In some cases, professionals may choose part-time work.

Job sharing
Scheduling arrangement in which two employees perform the work of one full-time job.

Job Sharing Another alternative used is **job sharing**, in which two employees perform the work of one full-time job. For instance, a hospital allows two radiological technicians to fill one job, and each individual works every other week. Such arrangements are beneficial for employees who may not want or be able to work full-time because of family, school, or other reasons. The keys to successful job sharing are that both "job sharers" must coordinate effectively together, and each must be competent in meeting the job requirements.[48]

Flextime In flextime, employees work a set number of hours a day but vary starting and ending times. In another variation, employees may work 30 minutes longer Monday through Thursday, take short lunch breaks and leave work at 1 p.m. or 2 p.m. on Friday.

4-3c Managing Flexible Work

Flexible scheduling allows management to relax some of the traditional "time clock" control of employees, while still covering workloads.[49] In some cases, electronic monitoring may be used. For example, in a call-service firm, home-based employees are monitored electronically on their use of phones, breaks, and production.

GLOBAL

4-3d Flexibility and Work–Life Balance

For many employees, balancing their work and personal lives is a significant concern. The quality of an employee's personal and family life is improved by flexibility at work, according to 68% of HR professionals polled.[50] Most employees do not feel they spend enough time with their families, and these problems for expatriates are even more difficult.[51] Figure 4-8 shows the countries that offer the most and the least flexible work situations.

Work–life balance
Employer-sponsored programs designed to help employees balance work and personal life.

    Work–life balance may take the form of employer-sponsored programs designed to help employees balance work and personal life. For example, the University of Kentucky allows flexible work arrangements for its employees, so Randy Hines, who works as a mechanic, can meet his kids at the bus stop around 2:40 every day and walk them home. Hines's work begins at 7:30 a.m. and ends at 4 p.m., but he and his supervisor agreed to a schedule that allows him to come in at 6 a.m. and clock out at 2:30 p.m. It saves Hines $400 per month in child care for which the family does not have to pay.[52]

FIGURE 4-8 Countries with Most/Least Flexible Scheduling

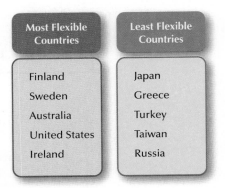

Most Flexible Countries	Least Flexible Countries
Finland	Japan
Sweden	Greece
Australia	Turkey
United States	Taiwan
Ireland	Russia

Source: http://www.grantthornton.com/portal/site/gtcom/menuitem.550794734a67d883a5f2ba40633841ca/?vgnextoid=eb02c0e810360310VgnVCM1000003a8314acRCRD

Work–life balance initiatives can improve recruiting and retention by attracting and keeping people who need the flexibility.[53] However, employees may dismiss such programs as window dressing if they are not applied consistently. It is not uncommon to have such policies identified and available but not actually practiced in some organizations.

L05 Describe job analysis and the stages in the process.

4-4 ■ UNDERSTANDING JOB ANALYSIS

Job analysis
Systematic way of gathering and analyzing information about the content, context, and human requirements of jobs.

Attempts to design and develop jobs that fit effectively into the flow of the organizational work and are interesting to do are called job design. The more narrow focus of job analysis centers on using a formal system to gather information about what people actually do in their jobs. A basic building block of HR management, **job analysis**, is a systematic way of gathering and analyzing information about the content, context, and human requirements of jobs. Job analysis is the basis for all HR practices.

An overview of job analysis is shown in Figure 4-9. The resulting information from job analysis is compiled into *job descriptions* and *job specifications* for use in virtually all HR activities.

FIGURE 4-9 Job Analysis in Perspective

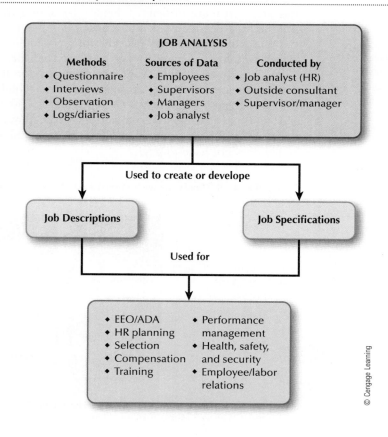

© Cengage Learning

4-4a Purposes of Job Analysis

Job analysis or work analysis has grown in importance as the workforce and jobs have changed.[54] To be effective, HR planning, recruiting, and selection all should be based on job requirements and the capabilities of individuals that are identified by job analysis. In equal employment opportunity (EEO) matters, accurate details on job requirements are needed because the credentials in job descriptions can affect court decisions. Additionally, compensation, training, and employee performance appraisals should all be based on the specific identified needs of the jobs. Job analysis is also useful in identifying job factors and duties that may contribute to workplace health/safety and employee/labor relations issues. Information from job analyses can be helpful in making a distinction among jobs includes the following:

- Work activities and behaviors
- Interactions with others
- Performance standards
- Financial and budgeting impact
- Machines and equipment used
- Working conditions
- Supervision given and received
- Knowledge, skills, and abilities needed

Job analysis is widely used in the United States but is only emerging as an HR tool in some non-Western countries.[55]

4-4b Job Analysis Responsibilities

Job analysis requires a high degree of coordination and cooperation between the HR unit and operating managers. The assignment of responsibility for job analysis depends on who can best perform various parts of the process. In large companies, the HR unit supervises the process to maintain its integrity and writes the job descriptions and specifications for uniformity. The managers review the efforts of the HR unit to ensure accuracy and completeness. They also may request new job analyses when jobs change significantly. In small organizations, managers may perform all job analysis responsibilities. Figure 4-10 shows a typical division of job analysis responsibilities in organizations between the HR unit and managers.

FIGURE 4-10 Typical Division of HR Responsibilities: Job Analysis

HR Unit	Managers
• Coordinates job analysis • Writes job descriptions and specifications for review by managers • Periodically reviews job descriptions and specifications • Reviews managerial input to ensure accuracy • May seek assistance from outside experts for difficult or unusual analyses	• Complete or help complete job analysis information • Review job descriptions and specifications and maintain their accuracy • Request new analyses as jobs change • Use job analysis information to identify performance standards • Provide information to outside experts

© Cengage Learning

Different types of job analysis can be used. The most traditionally and widely used method is task-based job analysis. Yet some organizations have emphasized the need for competency-based job analysis. Both types of job analysis are discussed next.

4-4c Task-Based Job Analysis

Task
Distinct, identifiable work activity composed of motions.

Duty
Work segment composed of several tasks that are performed by an individual.

Responsibilities
Obligations to perform certain tasks and duties.

Competencies
Individual capabilities that can be linked to enhanced performance by individuals or teams.

Task-based job analysis is the most common form and focuses on the tasks, duties, and responsibilities performed in a job. A **task** is a distinct, identifiable work activity composed of motions, whereas a **duty** is a larger work segment composed of several tasks that are performed by an individual. Since both tasks and duties describe activities, it is not always easy or necessary to distinguish between the two. For example, if one of the employment supervisor's duties is to interview applicants, one task associated with that duty would be asking job-related questions. **Responsibilities** are obligations to perform certain tasks and duties. Task-based job analysis seeks to identify all the tasks, duties, and responsibilities that are part of a job.

4-4d Competency-Based Job Analysis

Unlike the traditional task-based approach to analyzing jobs, the competency approach considers how knowledge and skills are used. **Competencies** are individual capabilities that can be linked to performance by individuals or teams.

The concept of competencies varies widely from organization to organization. The term *technical competencies* is often used to refer to specific knowledge and skills of employees. A different set of competencies are *behavioral competencies*. The following have been identified as *behavioral competencies*:

- Customer focus
- Team orientation
- Technical expertise
- Results orientation
- Communication effectiveness
- Leadership
- Conflict resolution
- Innovation
- Adaptability
- Decisiveness

The competency approach attempts to identify the competencies that have been shown to drive employee performance.[56] For instance, many supervisors talk about employees' attitudes, but they have difficulty identifying exactly what they mean by *attitude*. A variety of methodologies are used to help supervisors articulate examples of competencies and how those factors affect performance.[57]

Unlike the traditional task-based job analysis, one purpose of the competency approach is to influence individual and organizational behaviors in the future. The competency approach may be more broadly focused on behaviors, rather than just on tasks, duties, and responsibilities. Some of the more comprehensive competency-based job analysis components may extensively include knowledge, skills, abilities, and personality characteristics.[58]

Integrating Technology and Competency-Based Job Analysis As jobs continue to change, technology expands, and workers become more diverse, there may be a more integrated use of both job analysis approaches.[59] Another factor that will contribute to the use of both types of job analysis is that strategic competencies are identified for some jobs, not just performing job tasks and duties.[60] In the future, people doing jobs are more likely to need integrated job analysis, rather than just one approach. The decision about whether to use a task-based or competency-based approach to job analysis is affected by the nature of jobs; however, task-based analysis is likely to remain more widely used as it is the most defensible legally,[61] and it is the primary focus of the remainder of this chapter.

4-5 ■ IMPLEMENTING JOB ANALYSIS

The process of job analysis must be conducted in a logical manner, following appropriate management and professional psychometric practices.[62] Analysts usually follow a multistage process, regardless of the specific job analysis methods used. The stages for a typical job analysis, as outlined in Figure 4-11, may vary somewhat with the number of jobs included.

F I G U R E   4 - 1 1   Stages in the Job Analysis Process

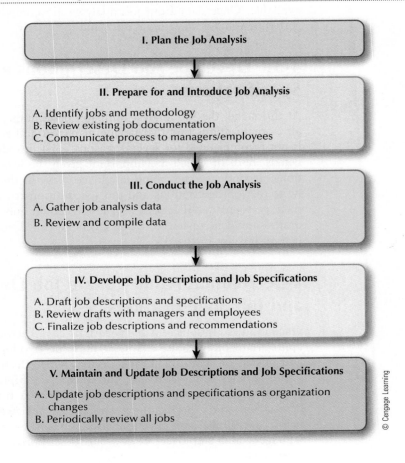

I. Plan the Job Analysis

II. Prepare for and Introduce Job Analysis

A. Identify jobs and methodology
B. Review existing job documentation
C. Communicate process to managers/employees

III. Conduct the Job Analysis

A. Gather job analysis data
B. Review and compile data

IV. Develope Job Descriptions and Job Specifications

A. Draft job descriptions and specifications
B. Review drafts with managers and employees
C. Finalize job descriptions and recommendations

V. Maintain and Update Job Descriptions and Job Specifications

A. Update job descriptions and specifications as organization changes
B. Periodically review all jobs

© Cengage Learning

4-5a Plan the Job Analysis

Prior to the job analysis process itself is the planning done to gather information about jobs from managers and employees. Probably the most important consideration is to identify the objectives of the job analysis, which might be as simple as updating job descriptions or as comprehensive as revising the compensation programs in the organization. Whatever the purpose identified, the effort needs the support of top management.

4-5b Prepare for and Introduce the Job Analysis

Preparation for job analysis includes identification of the jobs to be analyzed. Next review organization charts, existing job descriptions, previous job analysis information, and other resources. This includes identifying those who will be involved in conducting the job analysis and the methods to be used. A key part is identifying and communicating the process to appropriate managers, affected employees, and others.

4-5c Conduct the Job Analysis

Data about jobs are collected using various methods, based on time and resources available. Once data from job analyses are compiled, the information should be sorted by job, organizational unit, and job family.

4-5d Develope Job Descriptions and Job Specifications

At this stage, the job analyst draft job descriptions and job specifications. Generally, organizations find that having managers and employees write job descriptions is not recommended for several reasons. First, it reduces consistency in format and details, both of which are important given the legal consequences of job descriptions. Second, managers and employees vary in their writing skills and they may write the job descriptions and job specifications to reflect what they do and what their personal qualifications are, not what the job requires. However, completed drafts should be reviewed by managers and supervisors, and then with employees, before they are finalized.

4-5e Maintain and Update Job Descriptions and Job Specifications

Once job descriptions and specifications have been completed and reviewed by all appropriate individuals, a system must be developed for keeping them current and posted on a firm's intranet source. One effective way to ensure that appropriate reviews occur is to use current job descriptions and job specifications as part of other HR activities. For example, each time a vacancy occurs, the job description and specifications should be reviewed and revised as necessary before recruiting and selection efforts begin. Similarly, in some organizations, managers and employees review job descriptions during performance appraisal interviews.

4-6 ■ JOB ANALYSIS METHODS

Job analysis information about what people are doing in their jobs can be gathered in a variety of ways. Traditionally, the most common methods have been (1) observation, (2) interviewing, and (3) questionnaires. However, the expansion of technology has led to computerization and web-based job analysis information resources. Sometimes a combination of these approaches is used depending on the situation and the organization.

4-6a Observation

With the observation method, a manager, job analyst, or industrial engineer watches an employee performing the job and takes notes to describe the tasks and duties performed. Use of the observation method is limited because many jobs do not have complete and easily observed job duties or job cycles. Thus, observation may be more useful for repetitive jobs and in conjunction with other methods or as a way to verify information.

Work Sampling One type of observation, work sampling, does not require attention to each detailed action throughout an entire work cycle. This method allows a job analyst to determine the content and pace of a typical workday through statistical sampling of certain actions rather than through continuous observation and timing of all actions. Work sampling is particularly useful for routine and repetitive jobs.

Employee Diary/Log Another observation method requires employees to "observe" their own performance by keeping a diary/log of their job duties, noting how frequently those duties are performed and the time required for each one. Although this approach can generate useful information, it may be burdensome for employees to compile an accurate log. The logging approach can be technology-based, reducing some of the problems.

4-6b Interviewing

The interview method requires a manager, job analyst, or an HR specialist to talk with the employees performing each job. A standardized interview form is used most often to record the information. Both the employee and the employee's supervisor must be interviewed to obtain complete details on the job.

Sometimes, group or panel interviews are used. A team of subject matter experts (SMEs) who have varying insights about a group of jobs is assembled to provide job analysis information. This option may be particularly useful for highly technical or complex jobs. Since the interview method alone can be quite time consuming, combining it with one of the other methods is common.

4-6c Questionnaires

The questionnaire is a widely used method of gathering data on jobs. A survey instrument is developed and given to employees and managers to complete. The typical job questionnaire often covers the areas shown in Figure 4-12.

FIGURE 4-12 Typical Areas Covered in a Job Analysis Questionnaire

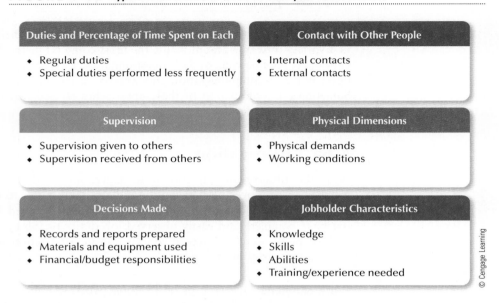

Duties and Percentage of Time Spent on Each
- Regular duties
- Special duties performed less frequently

Contact with Other People
- Internal contacts
- External contacts

Supervision
- Supervision given to others
- Supervision received from others

Physical Dimensions
- Physical demands
- Working conditions

Decisions Made
- Records and reports prepared
- Materials and equipment used
- Financial/budget responsibilities

Jobholder Characteristics
- Knowledge
- Skills
- Abilities
- Training/experience needed

© Cengage Learning

The questionnaire method offers a major advantage in that information about a large number of jobs can be collected inexpensively in a relatively short period of time. However, the questionnaire method assumes that employees can accurately analyze and communicate information about their jobs. Using interviewing and observation in combination with the questionnaire method allows analysts to clarify and verify the information gathered in questionnaires.

Managerial Job Analysis Questionnaire Since managerial jobs often differ from jobs with more clearly observable routines and procedures, some specialized job analysis methods exist for management jobs. One well-known method is the Management Position Description Questionnaire (MPDQ). Comprised of more than 200 statements, the MPDQ examines a variety of managerial dimensions, including decision making and supervising.

4-6d Job Analysis and O*Net

A variety of resources to help with job analysis are available from the U.S. Department of Labor (DOL). These resources have been developed and used over many years by a variety of entities. *Functional job analysis* uses a competency approach to job analysis. A functional definition of what is done in a job can be generated by examining the three components of *data*, *people*, and *things*. The levels of these components traditionally have been used to identify and compare important elements of more than 120 jobs in the *Dictionary of Occupational Titles (DOT)*. O*Net is currently the main DOL resource available and provides employers with a wide range of useful items.

The O*Net database now contains data on more than 800 occupations, classified by industry. Included in the occupational categories are the following:

- Task statements of importance, relevance, and frequency
- Abilities (work activities, knowledge, skills, and work content)
- Training, work experiences, and education
- Interests and work values, work styles, and job zones

O*Net can be used in different ways. For example, one way is to see what abilities will be needed in certain jobs. More than 50 abilities are listed, including arm-hand steadiness, fluency of ideas, time sharing, visualization, written and oral comprehension, and speech clarity. Employers can use the abilities and the other components to generate data for some parts of job analysis and for developing job descriptions.

O*Net also now contains the *Dictionary of Occupational Titles (DOT)* and has hundreds of jobs descriptions already written and available. For example, on HR jobs, the DOT and O*Net have listed details on occupations such as Employee Relations Specialist and Human Resource Advisor. For these and all other types of jobs, an extensive list of tasks and detailed work activities is provided. A Spanish version is available. The details provided give supervisors, managers, and HR professionals a valuable resource as they develop or revise job descriptions, compare recruiting advertisements, develop training components, and perform other HR activities. In summary, O*Net is a database of worker attributes and job characteristics to describe jobs and the skills workers will need to perform them.[63] It can be accessed at www.onetcenter.org.

4-7 ■ BEHAVIORAL AND LEGAL ASPECTS OF JOB ANALYSIS

Job analysis involves determining what the core job is. A detailed examination of jobs, although necessary, sometimes can be a demanding and disruptive experience for both managers and employees, in part because job analysis can identify the difference between what currently is being performed in a job and what should be done. This is a major issue about job analysis for some employees, but it is not the only concern. Other behavioral factors can affect job analysis.

4-7a Current Incumbent Emphasis

A job analysis and the resulting job description and job specifications should not just describe what the person currently in the job does and that person's qualifications. The incumbent may have unique capabilities and the ability to expand the scope of the job to assume more responsibilities, but the employer might have difficulty finding someone exactly like that employee if the person were to leave. Consequently, it is useful to focus on core duties and necessary knowledge, skills, and abilities by determining what the job would be if the incumbent were to quit or be moved to a different job. Focus should be on the *job* and not the incumbent working in the job.[64]

4-7b "Inflation" of Jobs and Job Titles

People have a tendency to inflate the importance and significance of their jobs. Since job analysis information is used for compensation purposes, both managers and employees hope that "puffing up" jobs will result in higher pay levels, greater "status" for résumés, and more promotional opportunities.

Inflated job titles also can be used to enhance employees' images without making major job changes or pay adjustments. For instance, banking and financial institutions often use officer designations to enhance status. In one small Midwestern bank, an employee who had three years' experience as a teller was "promoted" with no pay increase to Second Vice President of Customer Service. In effect, she became the lead teller when her supervisor was out of the bank, and now could sign more customer account forms, but her duties and compensation were basically the same.

An additional concern is the use of offbeat titles. For example, what is a "group idea management director," "chief transformation officer," or "marketing evangelist"? What does a "human character manager" really do? These examples illustrate how job titles may be misleading, both inside and outside the place of employment. Titles should convey a clear picture of what a job involves.

4-7c Employee and Managerial Anxieties

Both employees and managers have concerns about job analysis. The resulting job description is supposed to identify what is done in a job. However, it is difficult to capture all facets of a job in which employees perform a variety of duties and operate with a high degree of independence.

Employee Fears One concern that employees may have involves the purpose of a detailed investigation of their jobs. Some employees fear that an analysis of their jobs will limit their creativity and flexibility by formalizing their duties. They are also concerned about pay deduction or even layoff as a result of job analysis. However, having accurate, well-communicated job descriptions can assist employees by clarifying their roles and the expectations within those roles. One effective way to handle anxieties is to involve the employees in the revision process.

The content of a job may often reflect the desires and skills of the incumbent employee. For example, in one firm, an employee promoted to customer service supervisor continued to spend considerable time answering customer calls, rather than supervising employees taking the calls. As part of job analysis discussions, the operations manager discussed the need for the supervisor to train the employees on handling special customer requests and to delegate more routine duties to others.

Managerial Straitjacket Another concern of managers and supervisors is that the job analysis and job descriptions will unrealistically limit managerial flexibility. Since workloads and demands change rapidly, managers and supervisors may elect to move duties to other employees, cross-train employees, and have flexible means available to accomplish work. If job descriptions are written or used restrictively, employees may argue that a change or omission to a job description should limit management's flexibility to require that work. In organizations with unionized workforces, some very restrictive job descriptions may exist.

Because of such difficulties, the final statement in many job descriptions is a miscellaneous clause that consists of a phrase similar to "Performs other duties as needed upon request by immediate supervisor." This statement covers unusual situations in an employee's job. However, duties covered by this phrase cannot be considered essential functions under legal provisions including the Americans with Disabilities Act, as discussed next.

4-7d Legal Aspects of Job Analysis

The *Uniform Guidelines on Employee Selection Procedures* (in Appendix D) make it clear that HR requirements must be tied to specific job-related factors if employers are to defend their actions as a business necessity. Job descriptions are frequently the link to these job-related factors.

Job Analysis and the Americans with Disabilities Act One result of the Americans with Disabilities Act (ADA) is increased emphasis by employers on conducting job analyses, as well as developing and maintaining current and accurate job descriptions and job specifications.

The ADA requires that organizations identify the *essential job functions*, which are the fundamental duties of a job. These do not include the marginal functions of the positions. **Marginal job functions** are duties that are part of a job but are incidental or ancillary to the purpose and nature of the job. As covered in Chapter 3, the three major considerations used in determining essential functions and marginal functions are the following:

Marginal job functions
Duties that are part of a job but are incidental or ancillary to the purpose and nature of the job.

- Percentage of time spent on tasks
- Frequency of tasks done
- Importance of tasks performed

Job analysis should also identify the physical demands of jobs. For example, the important physical skills and capabilities used on the job of a nursing representative could include being able to hear well enough to aid clients and doctors. However, hearing might be less essential for a heavy equipment operator working in a quarry.

Job Analysis and Wage/Hour Regulations As will be explained in Chapter 11, the federal Fair Labor Standards Act (FLSA) and most state wage/hour laws indicate that the percentage of time employees spend on manual, routine, or clerical duties affects whether they must be paid overtime for hours worked in excess of 40 hours a week. To be exempt from overtime, the employees must perform their primary duties as executive, administrative, professional, or outside sales employees. Primary has been interpreted to mean occurring at least 50% of the time.

Other legal-compliance efforts, such as those involving workplace safety and health, can also be aided through the data provided by job analysis and job descriptions. It is difficult for an employer to have a legal staffing system without performing job analysis. Truly, job analysis is the most basic HR activity and the foundation for most other HR efforts.

HR SKILLS AND APPLICATIONS

Writing Job Descriptions

Although not the most exciting part of HR management, developing and maintaining current job descriptions are important activities. Some key suggestions for writing a job description that includes the essential functions and duties of a job are:

- *Compose specific duty statements*:
  1. A precise action verb and its object
  2. The frequency of the duties and the expected outcomes
  3. The tools, equipment, aids, and processes to be used
- *Be logical*: If the job is repetitive, describe the tasks as they occur in the work cycle. For varied jobs, list the major tasks first and follow those with the less frequent and/or less important tasks in order.
- *Use proper details*: Make sure the description covers all the meaningful duties of the job, but avoids too many details.

- *Be specific*: For example, instead of saying "Lifts heavy packages," say "Frequently lifts heavy packages weighing up to 50 pounds."
- *Use the active voice*: Start each statement with a functional verb in the present tense (third-person singular)—for instance, "Compiles," "Approves," or "Analyzes." Avoid terms like *handles*, *maintains*, and *processes*.
- *Describe, do not prescribe*: Say "Operates electronic imaging machine," not "Must know how to operate electronic image machine." (The latter is a job specification, not a job description.)
- *Be consistent*: Define terms like *may*, *occasionally*, and *periodically*.
- *Prepare a miscellaneous clause*: This clause provides flexibility and may be phrased as follows: "Performs other related duties as assigned by supervisory personnel."

LO6 List the components of job descriptions.

4-8 ■ JOB DESCRIPTIONS AND JOB SPECIFICATIONS

The output from analysis of a job is used to develop a job description and its job specifications. Together, these two documents summarize job analysis information in a readable format and provide the basis for defensible job-related actions.

4-8a Job Descriptions

Job description
Identification of the tasks, duties, and responsibilities of a job.

In most cases, the job description and job specifications are combined into one document that contains several sections. A **job description** identifies the tasks, duties, and responsibilities of a job. It describes what is done, why it is done, where it is done, and, briefly, how it is done. The HR Skills and Applications: Writing Job Descriptions shows suggestions for writing job descriptions.

4-8b Job Specifications

Job specifications
The knowledge, skills, and abilities (KSAs) an individual needs to perform a job satisfactorily.

While the job description describes activities to be done, the **job specifications** list the knowledge, skills, and abilities (KSAs) an individual needs to perform a job satisfactorily. KSAs might include the education, experience, work skill requirements, personal abilities, and mental and physical requirements a person needs to do the job, not necessarily the current employee's qualifications.[65]

4-8c Performance Standards

Performance standards
Indicators of what the job accomplishes and how performance is measured in key areas of the job description.

Performance standards flow directly from a job description and indicate what the job accomplishes and how performance is measured in key areas of the job description. If employees know what is expected and how performance is to be measured, they have a much better chance of performing satisfactorily. Unfortunately, performance standards are often not developed as supplemental items in job descriptions. Even if performance standards have been identified and matched to job descriptions, they must be communicated to employees if the job descriptions are to be effective tools.

4-8d Job Description Components

A typical job description contains several major parts. The following content text presents an overview of the most common components. Each organization will format job descriptions in a way best suited to its culture and management practices. Consistency of information and formatting across all organizational jobs insures uniformity.

Identification The first part of the job description is the identification section which includes the job title, department, reporting relationships, location, and date of analysis. It is advisable to note other information that is useful in tracking jobs and employees through HR systems. Additional items commonly noted in the identification section are job code, pay grade, exempt/nonexempt status under the Fair Labor Standards Act (FLSA), and the EEOC classification (from the EEO-1 form).

General Summary The general summary is a concise statement of the general responsibilities and components that make the job different from others. One HR specialist has characterized the general summary statement as follows: "In thirty words or less, describe the essence of the job." Often, the summary is written after all other sections are completed so that a more complete overview is prepared.

Essential Job Functions and Duties Essential functions and duties, are generally listed in order of importance. It contains clear, precise statements on the major tasks, duties, and responsibilities performed. Writing this section is the most time-consuming aspect of preparing job descriptions.

Job Specifications The qualifications needed to perform the job satisfactorily are identified in the job specifications section. The job specifications typically are stated as: (1) knowledge, skills, and abilities; (2) education and experience; and (3) physical requirements and/or working conditions. The components of the job specifications provide information necessary to determine what accommodations might and might not be possible under the Americans with Disabilities Act.

FIGURE 4-13 Sample Job Description

Identification Section

Position Title: Customer Service Supervisor

Department: Marketing/Customer Service   EEOC Class: O/M
Reports To: Marketing Director   FLSA Status: Exempt

General Summary

Supervises, coordinates, and assigns work of employees to ensure customer service department goals and customer needs are met.

Essential Job Functions

1. Supervises the work of customer service representatives to enhance performance by coordinating duties, advising on issues or problems, and checking work. (55%)
2. Provides customer service training for company employees in all departments. (15%)
3. Creates and reviews reports for service orders for new and existing customers. (10%)
4. Performs employee performance evaluations, training, and discipline. (10%)
5. Follows up with customer complaints and issues and provides resolutions. (10%)
6. Conducts other duties as needed guided by marketing director and executives.

Knowledge, Skills, and Abilities

- Knowledge of company products, services, policies, and procedures.
- Knowledge of marketing and customer programs, data, and results.
- Knowledge of supervisory requirements and practices.
- Skill in completing multiple tasks at once.
- Skill in identifying and resolving customer problems.
- Skill in oral and written communication, including Spanish communications.
- Skill in coaching, training, and performance evaluating employees.
- Skill in operating office and technological equipment and software.
- Ability to communicate professionally with coworkers, customers and vendors.
- Ability to work independently and meet managerial goals.
- Ability to follow oral and written instructions.
- Ability to organize daily activities of self and others and to work as a team player.

Education and Experience

Bachelor's degree in business or marketing, plus 3–5 years of industry experience. Supervisory, marketing, and customer service experience helpful.

Physical Requirements	Percentage of Work Time Spent on Activity			
	0–24	25–49	50–74	75–100
Seeing: Must be able to see well enough to read reports.				X
Hearing: Must be able to hear well enough to communicate with customers, vendors, and employees.				X
Standing/Walking: Must be able to move about department.			X	
Climbing/Stooping/Kneeling: Must be able to stoop or kneel to pick up paper products or directories.	X			
Lifting/Pulling/Pushing: Must be able to lift up to 50 pounds.	X			
Fingering/Grasping/Feeling: Must be able to type and use technical sources.				X

Working Conditions: Normal working conditions absent extreme factors.

Note: *The statements herein are intended to describe the general nature and level of work being performed, but are not to be seen as a complete list of responsibilities, duties, and skills required of personnel so classified. Also, they do not establish a contract for employment and are subject to change at the discretion of the employer.*

Disclaimers and Approvals Many job descriptions include approval signatures by appropriate managers and a legal disclaimer. This disclaimer allows employers to change employees' job duties or to request employees to perform duties not listed, so that the job description is not viewed as a contract between the employer and the employee.[66] Figure 4-13 contains a sample job description and job specifications for a customer service supervisor. Also, Appendix G has sample HR-related job descriptions.

SUMMARY

- The workforce is changing but not entirely in the predicted ways.
- The workforce participation rate has declined reducing the percentage of people in certain groups who are in the workforce.
- Work-ready credentials are ways to determine skills rather than assume that a degree grants specific skills to all who hold it.
- Work in an organization is divided into jobs and workflow analysis shows how work flows through the organization.
- Job design involves developing jobs that people can do well. It may include simplification, enlargement, enrichment, or rotation.
- Designing jobs so that they incorporate skill variety, task identity and significance, autonomy, and feedback can improve jobs for employees.
- Work teams can be used in designing jobs.
- Jobs can be designed for place or time flexibility.
- Telework is leading to more place flexibility and can be regular, brief occasional, or temporary/emergency.

- Shift work, compressed work week, part time, job sharing, and flextime can provide time/schedule flexibility.
- Job analysis is a systematic investigation of the content, context, and human requirements of a job.
- Task-based job analysis focuses on the tasks, duties, and responsibilities associated with jobs.
- Competency-based job analysis focuses on basic characteristics of performance such as technical and behavioral competencies.
- A number of methods of job analysis are used, with interviews and questionnaires being the most popular.
- The behavioral reactions of employees and managers and legal-compliance issues must be considered as part of job analysis.
- The end products of job analysis are job descriptions, which identify the tasks, duties, and responsibilities of jobs, and job specifications, which list the knowledge, skills, and abilities needed to perform a job satisfactorily.

CRITICAL THINKING CHALLENGES

1. Describe how changes in the workforce have been impacting organizations, including organizations for which you have worked recently.

2. For many individuals, the nature of work and jobs is changing. Describe these changes, some reasons for them, and how they are affecting both HR management and individuals.

3. Explain how you would conduct a job analysis in a company that has never had job descriptions. Utilize the O*Net as a resource for your information.

4. You have recently assumed the role of HR Manager in your company. In reviewing the company records, you note that the job descriptions were last updated five years ago. The Company President has taken the position that there is no need to update the job descriptions. However, you also note that the company has grown by 50% during the last five years, resulting in many changes, including some in job functions. You want to build a business case to convince the Company President of the need to update the job descriptions. To help you build your case, use the information on the purpose of job descriptions at www.hrtools.com.

A. How can job descriptions be used as a management tool?

B. What role do job descriptions have in helping companies comply with various legal issues?

CASE

Bon Secours Health Care

Health care has used flexible work arrangements for years as managers try to provide round the clock care for patients. Recently it has become even more difficult as shortages in the health care workforce have required creativity to attract and keep people.

Bon Secours Richmond Health Systems uses a variety of flexible scheduling innovations for hard-to-fill evening and weekend shifts at its hospitals. Employees can choose from compressed work weeks (four 10 hour shifts or three 12 hour shifts), weekends only with extra pay, four- or eight-hour shifts, and seven days on followed by seven days off.

Women make up 85% of the workforce, and flexible schedules work well for them. Depending on life stage, employees may make different choices. A new employee just out of college may prefer working full time with a rotating schedule, but workers with children may need a fixed schedule that doesn't rotate. Some employees with several children may want to work part time. Part time is made attractive by providing full benefits and employer-assisted housing for those scheduled for as little as 16 hours per week.

Bon Secours' flexible work arrangements are credited with lowering first year employee turnover rates from 50% to 10% in four years. The national benchmark average is 28%. Employee engagement scores have risen from 3.6 to 4.55 on a 5-point scale, and employees can read success stories in the employee newsletter that may provide solutions to any dilemmas they may have with regard to scheduling. In small lunches with the CEO, employees have confirmed that they value having more control over their time.

Eight-five percent of Bon Secours employees use a flexible schedule either formally or informally. Forty-five percent use a compressed work week and 10% job share. Twenty-five percent work a temporary or part-time work schedule, and 3% do telework.[67]

QUESTIONS

1. How well could this level of flexible scheduling work in another industry? For example, consider scheduling in a steel mill.

2. Identify other potential flexible work ideas that Bon Secours might use.

3. Flexible scheduling is common in health care. What would be the likely result without flexible scheduling?

SUPPLEMENTAL CASES

The Reluctant Receptionist

This case illustrates how incomplete job analysis and job descriptions create both managerial and employee problems. (For the case, go to www.cengage.com/management/mathis.)

Jobs and Work at R. R. Donnelley

This case describes how a printing firm had to increase productivity and redesign jobs. (For the case, go to www.cengage.com/management/mathis.)

Flexible Work and Success at Best Buy

This case illustrates flexible scheduling at Best Buy. (For the case, go to www.cengage.com/management/mathis.)

NOTES

1. Adapted from Charisse Jones, "Demand for Pilots Is Set to Soar," *USA Today*, June 21, 2011, 1–2.
2. Adrienne Fox, "At Work in 2020," *HR Magazine*, January 2010, 18–23.
3. Mitra Toossi, "Labor Force Projections to 2020: A More Slowly Growing Workforce," *Monthly Labor Review*, January 2012, 43–64.
4. Toosi, *op cit.*, 46.
5. Kent E. Allison, "Will Your Employees Ever Be Able to Retire?", *Workspan*, October 2011, 67–69.
6. Peter Cappelli, "Older Workers and the Job Market," *Human Resource Executive Online*, October 11, 2010, 1–4.
7. Robert L. Clark and Linda S. Ghent, "Strategic HR Management with an Aging Workforce: Using Demographic Models to Determine Optimal Employment Policies," *Population Research and Policy Review*, May 27, 2009, 1–17.
8. Thomas D. Cairns, "The Supply Side of Labor: HR Must Be Ready to Steer Organizations to the Future," *Employment Relations Today*, 37, Autumn 2010, 1–8.
9. Susan R. Meisinger, "The Good News and the Bad News," *Human Resource Executive Online*, May 14, 2012, 1–2.
10. Stephanie Banchero, "SAT Reading, Writing Scores Hit Low," *The Wall Street Journal*, September 15, 2011, A2.
11. Aaron Sorenson and Don Ruse, "Workforce Planning," *Workspan*, December, 2010, 58–63.
12. Jennnifer Schramm, "Planning for Population Shifts," *HR Magazine*, February 2011, 80.
13. Diane Cadrain, "Work Readiness Credentials Gain Popularity with Employers," *2010 HR Trendbook*, 31.
14. Pat Galagan, "Bridging the Skills Gap," *T + D*, 64, February 2010, 47. McKinsey Global Institute, "The Growing U.S. Jobs Challenge," *McKinsey Quarterly*, June 2011, 2.
15. Elissa Tucker and Rachelle Williams, "Generational Turbulence," *Workspan*, December 2011, 38–43.
16. Tamara J. Erickson, "Generation Y in the Workforce," *Harvard Business Review*, February 2009, 43–49.
17. Peter Cappelli, "Enough with the Generational Studies!", *Human Resource Executive Online*, November 8, 2010, 1–2. Kenneth P. De Muse and Kevin J. Miodzik, "A Second Look at Generational Differences in the Workforce," *People and Strategy*, 33, Issue 2, 2010, 50–58.
18. "Part Timers Make People Strategy Whole," *HR Magazine*, August 2011, 28–30.
19. Emily Glazer, "Freelancers Get the Perks of a Full Timer," *The Wall Street Journal*, February 19, 2011, 4K.
20. "Temporary Help Wanted," *Human Resource Executive*, March 2012, 13.
21. Steven F. Hipple, "Self Employment in the United States," *Monthly Labor Review Online*, September 2010, 1–2.
22. Jim Campbell, "Multiple Jobholding in States in 2010, *Monthly Labor Review*, September 2011, 32.
23. Adapted from Eric Krell, "Second Jobs: Blessing or Curses?", *HR Magazine*, March 2010, 57–59.
24. Bradley R. Staats and David M. Upton, "Lean Knowledge Work," *Harvard Business Review*, October 2011, 100–110.
25. H. Rao, "What 17th Century Pirates Can Teach Us about Job Design," *Harvard Business Review*, October 2010, 44.
26. R. Iles, et al., "Psychological and Physiological Reactions to High Workloads," *Psychology*, 63, 2010, 407–436.
27. D. Holman, et al., "Work Design Variation and Outcomes in Call Centers, *Industrial and Labor Relations Review*, 62, 2009, 510–532.
28. James B. Avery, et al., "The Additive Value of Positive Psychological Capital in Predicting Work Attitudes and

Behavior," *Journal of Management*, 2010, 47–62.

29. Rosanna Miguel and Suzanne Miklos, "Individual Executive Assessment: Sufficient Science, Standards and Principles," *Industrial and Organizational Psychology*, 2011, 330–333.

30. Corine Boon, et al., "The Relationship Between Perception of HR Practices and Employee Outcomes: Examining the Role of Person-Organization and Person-Job Fit," *The International Journal of Human Resource Management*, 22, 2011, 138–162.

31. Steve Tuckey, "Job Rotation Not Without Risk," *Human Resource Executive Online*, August 18, 2011, 1–3.

32. Teresa Amabile and Steven Kramer, "How Leaders Kill Meaning at Work," *McKinsey Quarterly*, January 2012, 1–8.

33. Jessica L. Wildman, "Task Types and Team Level/Attributes: Synthesis of Team Classification Literature," *Human Resource Development Review*, 11, 2012, 97–129.

34. Michael Boyer O'Leary and Mark Mortensen, "Go Con (Figure): Subgroups, Imbalance and Isolates in Geographically Dispersed Teams," *Organization Sciences*, 21, Jan–Feb 2010, 115–131.

35. The Wharton School, "The Dark Side of Teamwork," *Human Resource Executive Online*, April 13, 2012, 1–2.

36. Steven E. Humphrey, et al., "Developing a Theory of the Strategic Core of Teams," *Journal of Applied Psychology*, 94, January 2009, 48–61.

37. Diane Coutu, "Why Teams Don't Work," *Harvard Business Review*, 87, May 2009, 98–105.

38. Derek Dean and Caroline Webb, "Recovering from Information Overload," *McKinsey Quarterly*, January 2011, 1–8.

39. G. S. Oettinger, "The Incidence and Wage Consequences of Home-Based Work in the United States," *Journal of Human Resources*, 46, 2011, 237–260.

40. Marg C. Noonan and Jennifer L. Glass, "The Hard Truth about Telecommuting," *Monthly Labor Review Online*, 135, June 2012, 1.

41. Cecily Raiborn and Janet B. Butler, "A New Look at Telecommuting and Telework," *Journal of Corporate Accounting and Finance*, 20, July/August 2009, 31–39.

42. Ibid.

43. Dori Meinert, "Make Telecommuting Pay Off," *HR Magazine*, June 2011, 33–37. Evan H. Offstein, et al., "Making Telework Work," *Strategic HR Review*, 9, 2010, 32–37.

44. James E. Hutton and Carolyn Strand Norman, "The Impact of Alternative Telework Arrangements on Organizational Commitment," *Journal of Information Systems*, 24, Spring 2010, 67–90. David Shadovitz, "Telework Hits a Roadblock," *Human Resource Executive Online*, July 14, 2011, 1–2.

45. Rose Stanley, "Effective Ways to Manage Teleworkers," *Workspan*, January 2010, 83.

46. Harriet B. Presser and Brian W. Ward, "Nonstandard Work Schedules over the Life Course: A First Look," *Monthly Labor Review*, July 2011, 3–16.

47. Lonnie Golden, "Flexible Daily Work Schedules in U.S. Jobs: Formal Introductions Needed?", *Industrial Relations*, 48, January 2009, 27–54.

48. Timothy R. Hinkin and J. Bruce Tracey, "What Makes It So Great?", *Cornell Hospitality Quarterly*, 51, March 8, 2010, 158–170.

49. Jim Fickness, "Build Your Company's Flexibility Muscles Now," *Workspan*, May 2011, 72–77. Sayed Sadjady, "Find the Right Balance with Flexibility," *Workspan*, June 2012, 62–66.

50. Stephan Miller, "Flexible Hours in the Ranks," *2010 HR Trendbook*, 16–17.

51. Heather S. McMillan, "Constructs of the Work/Life Interface," *Human Resource Development Review*, 10, 2011, 6–25. Julie Cook Ramrrey, "Finding Balance Abroad," *Human Resource Executive Online*, August 1, 2009, 1–4.

52. Michael O'Brien, "Balancing Work/Life by the Hour," *Human Resource Executive Online*, July 11, 2011, 1–4.

53. F. Brisco, et al., "Memberships Has Its Privileges? Contracting and Access to Jobs that Accommodate Work-Life Needs," *Industrial and Labor Relations Review*, 64, 2011, 258–282.

54. Frederick P. Morgeson and Erich C. Dierdorff, "Work Analysis: From Technique to Theory," *APA Handbook of Industrial and Organizational Psychology*, 2, 2011, 3–41.

55. Rehman Safdar, et al., "Impact of Job Analysis on Job Performance," *Journal of Diversity Management*, 5, 2010, 17–25.

56. Juan I. Sanchez and Edward L. Levine, "What Is (or Should Be) the Difference Between Competency Modeling and Traditional Job Analysis?", *Human Resource Management Review*, 19, 2009, 53–63.

57. Michael M. Campion, et al., "Doing Competencies Well: Best Practices in Competency Modeling," *Personnel Psychology*, 64, 2011, 225–262.

58. Klas Eric Soderquist, et al., "From Task Based to Competency Based," *Personnel Review*, 39, 2010, 325–346. Sal Ranade, "Reframe Jobs, Reap Rewards," *People and Strategy*, 33, 2010, 33–40. H. Aguinis, et al., "Using Web Based Frame-of-Reference Training to Decrease Biases in Personality Based Job Analysis," *Personnel Psychology*, 62, 2009, 405–438.

59. T. A. Stetz et al., "New Tricks for an Old Dog: Visualizing Job Analysis Results," *Public Personnel Management*, 31, 2009, 91–100.

60. Veronika Kucharova, "Comparison of Job Analysis Traditional and Process Approach," *Human Resource Management and Ergonomics*, 4, February 2010, 1–16.

61. Michael M. McDaniel, et al., "The Uniform Guidelines Are a Detriment to the Field of Personnel Selection," *Industrial and Organizational Psychology*, 4, December 2011, 494–514.

62. R. B. Briner and D. M. Rousseau, "Evidence-Based 1-0 Psychology:

Not There Yet," *Industrial and Organizational Psychology*, 4, March 2011, 3–22.

63. Morgeson and Dierdorff, *op cit*, 15.

64. Deb Levine and Lesa Albright, "How Do I Conduct Job Analysis?", *HR Magazine*, November 2010, 21.

65. Chad H. Van Iddekinge, et al., "An Examination of the Validity and Incremental Value of Needed-at-Entry Ratings," *Applied Psychology: An International Review*, 60, 2011, 24–45.

66. Kathy Pennell, "The Role of Flexible Job Descriptions in Succession Management," *Library Management*, 31, 2010, 279–290.

67. Based on Dori Meinert, "The Gift of Time," *HR Magazine*, November 2011, 39.

5

Individual/ Organization Relations and Retention

Learning Objectives

After you have read this chapter, you should be able to:

1 Discuss four different views of motivation at work.

2 Explain the nature of the psychological contract.

3 Define the difference between job satisfaction and engagement.

4 Identify a system for controlling absenteeism.

5 Describe different kinds of turnover and how turnover can be measured.

6 Summarize various ways to manage retention.

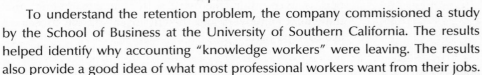

Why Are the Accountants Leaving?

PricewaterhouseCoopers was faced with runaway turnover, poor employee engagement, and a drop in service quality associated with not being able to retain its top talent. Their $28 billion in revenue came from 155,000 employees in 153 countries. In the United States, about 29,000 employees at 70 locations constituted the accounting firm's human capital.

To understand the retention problem, the company commissioned a study by the School of Business at the University of Southern California. The results helped identify why accounting "knowledge workers" were leaving. The results also provide a good idea of what most professional workers want from their jobs.

- The employees want development and coaching on the job, not simply training courses. Challenging work and assistance with the development of knowledge and skills to position them for career growth in the future are important.
- Lower worklife balance, pay, and job satisfaction were evident among employees who intended to leave.
- Only 20% of new hires joined the company intending to build a long-term career at the firm.
- The ability to keep employees who were promoted to managers as they became more valuable in the marketplace was a challenge.

The company had to recognize that knowledge workers want to have a portfolio of experiences that provide marketable skills. Further, every staff member had personal interests that were different depending on their stage of life and career. A senior manager noted that the key to strengthening retention was understanding employee goals and providing coaching, connection, and experiences that would challenge them.

Changes made included increasing feedback, using teams, mentoring, career coaching, setting specific performance expectations, managing the workload, and offering flexible work arrangements and sabbaticals. Over several years, turnover dropped from 26% to less than 10% annually, and the company was listed as #58 in *Fortune*'s "100 Best Places to Work."[1]

Work organizations are comprised of employees who potentially can keep the company successfully moving forward. However, the value of a given employee depends on the level of his or her performance on the job. That performance depends on the effort put into the work, ability, and support from the employer. Effort is a result of motivation and worthy of some consideration here. The relationship an employee feels with the employer has many elements that might affect his or her performance.[2] Expectations, job satisfaction, commitment, engagement, and loyalty are some of those elements.

The relationship between employees and their company can also affect two very expensive HR issues—absenteeism and turnover.[3] Both represent withdrawal from the organization. Understanding why people stay with an organization (called retention) or choose to withdraw requires understanding several aspects of the relationship. These include rewards, opportunity for development, reasonableness of HR policies, job and worklife issues, relationships with other people at work including the boss, and a general perception that the employing organization is well-managed. Chapter 10 deals with managing and appraising performance. But the basics for understanding the relationship between individual employees and the employer and the consequences of that relationship are covered here.

5-1 ■ INDIVIDUALS AT WORK

The relationship between the individual and his or her employing organization helps explain why people might choose to leave a job or stay. For an employer to want to keep an employee, that individual must be performing well.[4] Several factors affect the performance of individual employees—their abilities, effort expended, and the organizational support they receive. The HR unit in an organization exists in part to analyze and address those areas. Exactly what the role of the HR unit in an organization "should be" depends upon what upper management expects. As with any management function, HR management activities should be developed, evaluated, and changed as necessary so that they can contribute to the performance of the organization and individuals at work.

5-1a Individual Performance Factors

The three major factors that affect how a given individual performs are illustrated in Figure 5-1. They are (1) individual ability to do the work, (2) effort expended,

FIGURE 5-1 Components of Individual Performance

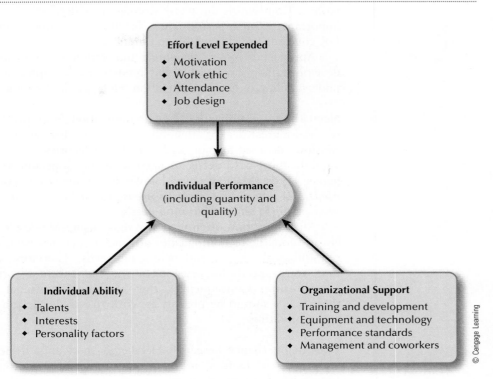

© Cengage Learning

and (3) organizational support. The relationship of those factors is broadly defined in management literature as follows:

$$\text{Performance } (P) = \text{Ability } (A) \times \text{Effort } (E) \times \text{Support } (S)$$

Individual performance is enhanced to the degree that all three components are present within an individual employee. However, performance is diminished if any of these factors are reduced or absent. For instance, assume that several production workers have the ability to do their jobs and work hard, but the organization provides outmoded equipment or the supervisors' management style causes negative reactions among the workers so performance suffers.

Take another example of a customer service representative in a call center who has both the abilities and excellent support. But the individual hates "being tied to a telephone cord" all day and is frequently absent because of dislike of the job even though it pays well. In both cases, individual performance is likely to be lower than in situations where all three components are present. Individual motivation is often a predictor of effort expended. A brief overview of motivation as it affects performance is presented next.

Motivation
The desire within a person causing that person to act.

5-1b Individual Motivation

Motivation is the desire within a person causing that person to act. People usually act for one reason: to reach a goal. Thus, motivation is a goal-directed drive, and it seldom occurs in a void. The words *need, want, desire,* and *drive* are all similar to *motive,* from which the word *motivation* is derived. Understanding motivation is important because performance, reaction to compensation, turnover, and other HR concerns are affected by and influence it.

Approaches to understanding motivation vary because many theorists have developed their own views and models. Each approach has contributed to the understanding of human motivation. Here we briefly look at four approaches.

Need Theory The theory of human motivation developed by Abraham Maslow has received a great deal of attention. He assumes that only unsatisfied needs motivate. Maslow classified human needs into five categories that ascend in a definite order. Until the more basic needs are adequately met, a person will not fully strive to meet higher needs. Maslow's well-known hierarchy is composed of (1) *physiological needs,* (2) *safety and security needs,* (3) *belonging and love needs,* (4) *esteem needs,* and (5) *self-actualization needs.*

An assumption often made by those using Maslow's hierarchy is that workers in modern, technologically advanced societies basically have satisfied their physiological, safety, and belonging needs. Therefore, they will be motivated first by the needs for self-esteem and the esteem of others, and then by self-actualization. Consequently, this reasoning continues; conditions to satisfy these needs should be present at work to enable the job itself to be meaningful and motivating.

Two-Factor Theory Frederick Herzberg's motivation/hygiene theory assumes that one group of factors, *motivators,* accounts for motivation. *Hygiene factors* can cause dissatisfaction with work if not adequately addressed but do not motivate.

Motivators
- Achievement
- Recognition
- Work itself
- Responsibility
- Advancement

Hygiene Factors
- Interpersonal relationships
- Company policy/administration
- Supervision
- Salary
- Working conditions

The implication of Herzberg's research for management and HR practices is that even when managers carefully consider and address hygiene factors to avoid employee dissatisfaction, employees may not be motivated to work harder. The two factor theory suggests that only motivators cause employees to exert more effort and thereby enhance employee performance. Subsequent research has questioned whether the two groups of factors are really as distinct as Herzberg thought. Figure 5-2 shows a comparison of needs theory and two-factor theory.

Equity
The perceived fairness of what the person does compared with what the person receives.

Equity Theory People want to be treated fairly at work. **Equity** is defined as the perceived fairness of what the person does compared with what the person receives for doing it. *Inputs* are what a person brings to the organization, including educational level, age, experience, productivity, and other skills or efforts. The items received by a person, or the *outcomes,* are the rewards obtained in exchange for inputs. Outcomes include pay, benefits, recognition of achievement, prestige, and any other rewards received. Note that an outcome can be either

FIGURE 5-2 **Need Theory and Two Factor Theory Compared**

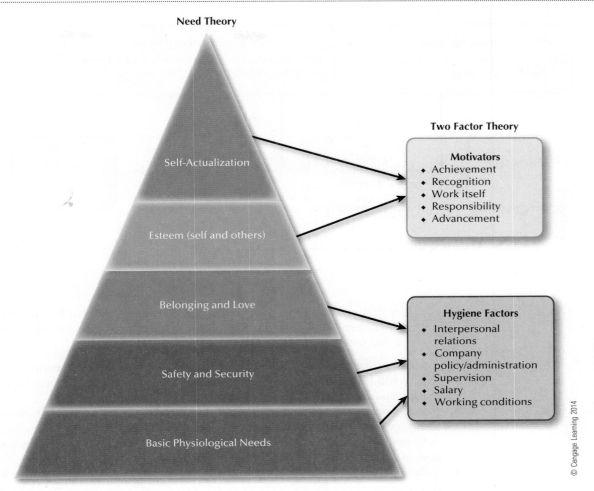

tangible (economic benefits such as money) or intangible (such as recognition or achievement).

The employee's view of fair value is critical to the relationship between performance and job satisfaction because one's sense of equity is an exchange and comparison process. Assume an employee is an information technology (IT) specialist who exchanges talents and efforts (inputs) for the tangible and intangible rewards (outputs) the employer provides. To determine perceived equity the employee compares her talents, skills, and efforts to those of other IT specialists both internally and at other firms. That perception—correct or incorrect—significantly affects that person's evaluation of the inputs and outcomes. A sense of inequity occurs when the comparison process results in an imbalance between inputs and outcomes.

Expectancy Theory Lyman Porter and E. E. Lawler suggest that motivation is also influenced by what people expect. If expectations are not met, people may feel that they have been unfairly treated and consequently become dissatisfied. This theory states that individuals base decisions about their behaviors on their

FIGURE 5-3 Simplified Expectancy Model of Motivation

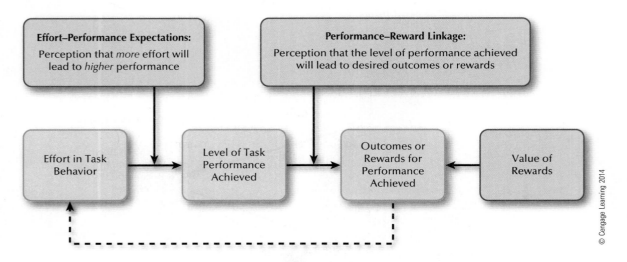

© Cengage Learning 2014

expectations that one or another alternate behavior is more likely to lead to desired outcomes. As Figure 5-3 shows, the three aspects of the behavior-outcome relationships are as follows:

- *Effort–Performance Expectations* refer to employees' beliefs that working harder will lead to high performance. If people do not believe that working harder leads to performance, then their efforts may diminish.
- *Performance–Reward Linkage* considers individuals' expectations that high performance will actually lead to rewards. The performance–reward relationship indicates how instrumental or important effective performance is in producing desired results.
- *Value of Rewards* refers to how valuable the rewards are to the employee. One determinant of employees' willingness to exert effort is the degree to which they value the rewards offered by the organization.

This model of motivation suggests that employees' levels of effort (motivation) are not simply a function of rewards. Employees must believe that they have the *ability to perform the tasks well*; they must expect that *high performance will result in receiving rewards*; and they must *value those rewards*. If all three conditions are met, employees will be motivated to exert greater effort.[5]

5-1c Management Implications for Motivating Individual Performance

There is a motivating effect associated with making successful progress in meaningful work. Some would argue that this is the most powerful basis for motivation. Managers can undermine the meaningfulness of a person's work and therefore motivation by dismissing its importance, moving people off work before they finish it, shifting goals constantly, or neglecting to keep people updated on changing priorities. All these can diminish the motivation associated with meaningful work.[6]

Motivation provides the effort necessary for an individual to work on his or her own as a self-starter. It also provides the necessary effort for teamwork and collaboration with others. If it values teamwork and collaboration, the organization's culture is a good motivation lever for managers to use for this purpose.[7]

Financial rewards are often mentioned as motivators, and indeed for some people in some circumstances they can be.[8] A financial reward system must differentiate among good, average, and poor performers and the financial rewards must be given for good performance if it is to be effective as a motivator. Performance management can contribute to motivation only if the process is viewed as accurate, transparent, and fair (equitable).[9] Other key motivators are praise (when deserved), recognition, being trusted, and autonomy to do one's job. Performance by individuals depends on the relationship between individuals and the ways in which the organization has structured these motivators.

Many organizations spend considerable money to "motivate" their employees by using a wide range of tactics. For example, some firms have motivational speakers to inspire employees. Other employers give T-shirts, mugs, books, and videos to employees as motivators. However, the effectiveness of these expenditures has been questioned, particularly given the short-term nature of many of these programs and rewards.

In summary, answering the question often asked by managers, "How do I motivate my employees?" requires diagnosing of employees' efforts, abilities, and expectations, as well of those of the organization.

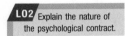
L02 Explain the nature of the psychological contract.

5-2 ■ INDIVIDUAL WORKERS AND ORGANIZATIONAL RELATIONSHIPS

The relationship between an individual and his or her employer can be affected by HR practices and can vary widely from favorable to unfavorable. Understanding the relationships between individuals and organizations is more than just academically interesting. The economic health of most organizations depends on the efforts of employees with the ability and motivation to do their jobs well. The relationship between an employee and an employer affects both of them. Important elements of these relationships include the psychological contract, job satisfaction, commitment, engagement, and loyalty (see Figure 5-4).

5-2a Psychological Contract

Psychological contract
The unwritten expectations employees and employers have about the nature of their work relationships.

A concept that has been useful in understanding individuals' relationships with their employers is that of a **psychological contract**, which refers to the unwritten expectations employees and employers have about the nature of their work relationships. The psychological contract can create either a positive or a negative relationship between an employer and an individual.[10] It is based on trust and commitment that leads to meeting both the employer's and employee's expectations and needs.

Unwritten psychological contracts between employers and employees encompass expectations about both tangible items (e.g., wages, benefits, employee productivity, and attendance) and intangible items (e.g., loyalty, fair treatment, and job security).[11] Employers may attempt to detail their expectations through employee handbooks and policy manuals, but those materials are only part of the total "contractual" relationship.

FIGURE 5-4 The Individual/Organizational Relationship

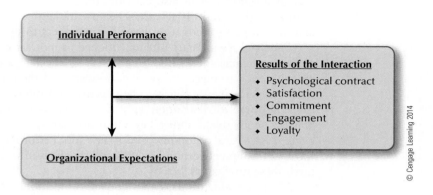

© Cengage Learning 2014

The Changing Psychological Contract Traditionally, employees expected to exchange their efforts and capabilities for secure jobs that offered competitive pay, a solid range of benefits, and career progression within an organization, among other factors.[12] But as some organizations have changed economically, they have addressed various organizational crises by downsizing and eliminating workers who had given long and loyal service. Consequently, in these firms, a number of remaining employees question whether they should remain loyal to and stay with their employers. The contract has been altered.

When individuals feel that the psychological contract provides them some control and perceived rights in the organization, they are more likely to be committed to the organization and utilize their knowledge, skills, and abilities to accomplish performance results.[13] A psychological contract usually recognizes at least the following expectations:

Employers Will Provide
- Competitive compensation and benefits
- Flexibility to balance work and home life
- Career development opportunities

Employees Will Contribute
- Continuous skill improvement and increased productivity
- Reasonable length of service
- Extra efforts and results when needed

ETHICS

Psychological contracts can be strengthened and employee commitment enhanced when the organization is involved in a cause that is important to the employee. Conversely, psychological contracts can be violated, not only by personal mistreatment, but from a perception that the organization has abandoned an important principle or cause. For instance, when unethical or illegal behavior occurs in upper management, the psychological contract is violated, and employees may feel anger, distrust, reduced loyalty and commitment, and increased willingness to leave.

GLOBAL

Global Psychological Contract Concerns With many organizations having global operations, the psychological contract becomes more complicated. Employees in foreign countries and expatriate employees from the United States have varying psychological contract expectations. For expatriates, if the organizational expectations are not made clear prior to their relocation, there is a greater chance that the assignment will be cut short or the employee will quit upon returning home.[14]

An additional concern for multinational firms is to meet the different psychological contract expectations of individuals in different cultures and countries. Consider the number of jobs that have been shifted from the United States and Europe to China, India, Romania, Mexico, the Philippines, Brazil, and other countries with different cultures. Being aware of varying psychological contract issues with foreign employees is important if global HR efforts are to be successful.

L03 Define the difference between job satisfaction and engagement.

Job satisfaction
A positive emotional state resulting from evaluating one's job experiences.

5-2b Job Satisfaction and Commitment

In its most basic sense, **job satisfaction** is a positive emotional state resulting from evaluating one's job experiences. Job *dissatisfaction* occurs when one's expectations are not met. For example, if an employee expects clean and safe working conditions, that employee is likely to be dissatisfied if the workplace is dirty and dangerous.

Sometimes job satisfaction is called *morale*, a term usually used to describe the job satisfaction of a group or organization. For an example see the HR Perspective: Organizational Redesign and Morale. Frequently cited reasons for decline in morale include more demanding and stressful work, less contact with management, and less confidence in compensation and other rewards. Satisfied workers are less likely to leave the organization than their less-satisfied counterparts.[15]

HR PERSPECTIVE

Organizational Redesign and Morale

Organizations sometimes need to redesign themselves, but clearly not all redesigns are successful. In fact, a recent survey by McKinsey & Company of executives who had taken their companies through a redesign showed that only 8% felt the changes (1) added value, (2) were completed on time, and (3) fully met the business objectives set for the redesign.

The more successful redesigns focused on individual issues, including changing mindsets, providing clear communications, and making certain the support systems reflected the changes. Good company redesigns were more likely to be described as improving morale or job satisfaction in the company than the less successful ones. In fact, the successful efforts overcame employee distraction and demoralization—two of the most common challenges to successful redesign.

Successful changes were more likely to involve set detailed goals for the timing of the changes as well. The best were reported by executives who set time frames under 3 months or over 18 months. Because of these tactics, employee discomfort leading to poor morale was briefer or minimized by the length of time taken for the changes. Morale is often a casualty when redesigns are poorly implemented. Morale is commonly hurt in the short run in every change, but the most widespread damage is relatively short lived if the change is done well. In the McKinsey study, 47% said job satisfaction was adversely impacted, but that dropped to 28% six months after implementation was finished. However, for the time that it persisted, employee demoralization and resulting poor morale had the most negative impact on reaching the goals that the change was designed to foster.

While morale may suffer from a reorganization, explaining how it will work, making sure it does work, changing mind-sets, and doing it relatively quickly all seem to minimize negative effects.[16]

Attitude survey
A survey that focuses on employees' feelings and beliefs about their jobs and the organization.

Organizational commitment
The degree to which employees believe in and accept organizational goals and desire to remain with the organization.

One way employers address job satisfaction, and ultimately retention, is by regularly surveying employees. One specific type of survey used by many organizations is an **attitude survey**, which focuses on employees' feelings and beliefs about their jobs and the organization. Management can respond to the results after they are compiled. If the employer takes responsive actions, employees may view the employer more positively; however, if management ignores the survey results, their inaction can lead to lower job satisfaction.

The degree to which employees believe in and accept organizational goals and want to remain with the organization is called **organizational commitment**. Job satisfaction influences organizational commitment, which in turn affects employee retention and turnover. Thus, it is the interaction of the individual and job that determines levels of job satisfaction and organizational commitment.

Many organizations and researchers study job satisfaction. At any one time the number of people dissatisfied with their jobs nationally varies from 15% to 40% of people are dissatisfied with their jobs. Higher unemployment rates usually mean more dissatisfied workers in the workforce since it is more difficult to change jobs, and people stay longer with jobs they do not like. Individual managers have an impact on job satisfaction, and younger employees tend to have lower job satisfaction than older employees.[17] Currently, younger employees are affected by older employees delaying retirement for financial reasons; this affects their advancement opportunities, which in turn affects their job satisfaction.[18]

Figure 5-5 shows some of the most commonly recognized components of job satisfaction.

FIGURE 5-5 Components of Job Satisfaction

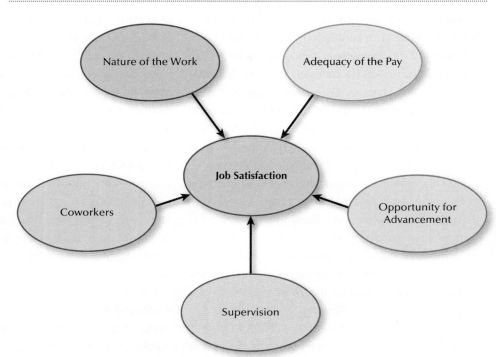

5-2c Employee Engagement and Loyalty

Employee engagement
The extent to which an employee's thoughts and behaviors are focused on the employer's success.

Employee engagement is a term that has received much attention in the HR practitioner literature but less academic attention.[19] Engagement can include satisfaction, support from management, using effort beyond a minimum, intention to stay, and other concepts.[20] It is a combination of several ideas often measured separately. Descriptions of "engaged employees" and "disengaged employees" are shown in Figure 5-6.

Although the concept of engagement is still evolving, a working definition might be the extent to which an employee's thoughts and behaviors are focused on the employer's success. Surveys suggest that perhaps 30% of workers are engaged in their jobs, half are not engaged, and about 20% are actively disengaged.[21] The concept of employee engagement is seductive because it suggests that workers could contribute much more to organizational results if there were realistic ways to better engage the workforce.[22]

Loyalty Many employees still want security, stability, a supervisor they respect, competitive pay and benefits, and the opportunity to advance. But competition and increasing costs of doing business have led companies to trim payrolls and to no longer offer the employment opportunities listed above. As a result, the era of company loyalty is thought to have passed, and that people are more inclined to move between companies.[23]

Loyalty
Being faithful to an institution or employer.

Loyalty can be defined as being faithful to an institution or employer. Loyalty is a reciprocal exchange—employees' loyalty to a company depends on their perceptions of the company's loyalty to them. The trend toward having employees bear more of the risk in their pensions, health insurance, and career development has sent a clear message that the employee must control his or her own future as the employer is not loyal.[24]

A logical extension of organizational engagement focuses specifically on *continuance commitment* factors. These are the factors that influence decisions to remain with or leave an organization, and ultimately they are reflected in employee retention and turnover statistics. The relationships among satisfaction, commitment, and turnover are similar across cultures, full- and part-time workers, genders, and occupations.[25] Employee engagement and loyalty partially explaining performance. Individuals who are not as satisfied with their jobs or

FIGURE 5-6 Engaged and Disengaged Employees

Engaged Employees	Disengaged Employees
◆ Put in extra effort	◆ Simply put in time
◆ Are highly involved in their jobs	◆ Do not do best work
◆ Employ both effort and thought	◆ Are "checked out"/apathetic
◆ Are active/busy	◆ Do only their basic jobs
◆ Are fully invested in their jobs	◆ React only to pay

© Cengage Learning 2014

who are not as committed to the organization are more likely to withdraw from the organization. Disengaged and disloyal employees seem unlikely to perform well.

One kind of "withdrawal" is to leave the organization—that is, turnover. Another kind of withdrawal is absenteeism, which is simply not reporting to work on time on a regular basis. Absenteeism is covered in the next section.

LO4 Identify a system for controlling absenteeism.

Absenteeism
Any failure by an employee to report for work as scheduled or to stay at work when scheduled.

5-3 ■ EMPLOYEE ABSENTEEISM

A major issue in the relationship between employee and employer relates to employees who are absent from their work and job responsibilities. **Absenteeism** is any failure by an employee to report for work as scheduled or to stay at work when scheduled. Being absent from work may seem like an insignificant matter to an employee. But if a manager needs 12 people in a unit to get the work done, and 4 of the 12 are frequently absent, either the output of the unit will decrease or additional workers will have to be hired to meet needs. Productivity losses due to absenteeism for some employers can be very expensive. The average daily cost is 1.3 times the wages of the absent worker.[26] Some people are also not concerned about arriving at work on time. Tardiness can be closely related to absenteeism, as the HR Skills and Applications: Controlling Tardiness describes.

Concern over uncontrolled absenteeism must be weighed against the problem of "presenteeism," which occurs when people are sick and should stay home to avoid spreading illness but come to work anyway. This may occur for many reasons including the belief that no one else can do the job, role models who come to work sick, or overly stringent absenteeism controls.[27] Effective absence management involves striking a balance between supporting employees who are legitimately unable to work and meeting operational needs.

5-3a Types of Absenteeism

Employees can be absent from work or tardy for several reasons. Clearly, some absenteeism is inevitable because of illness, death in the family, and other personal reasons. Though absences such as those that are health related are unavoidable and understandable, they are still very costly. Many employers have sick leave policies that allow employees a certain number of paid days each year for *involuntary* absences. However, much absenteeism is avoidable, or *voluntary*. Absence can also be planned (the least disruptive), unplanned, incidental (less than a week), or extended (lasting beyond a week).

Many employees see no real concern about being absent or late to work because they feel that they are "entitled" to some absenteeism. In many firms, a relatively small number of individuals are responsible for a large share of the total absenteeism in the organization. Regardless of the reason, employers need to know if someone is going to be absent so they can make adjustments. Organizations have developed different ways for employees to report their absences. Wal-Mart and others have established an automated system in which their employees who will be absent call a special phone number. Others use special electronic notification e-mail accounts.

The British supply chain firm, Wincanton, experienced considerable health-related absence problems, but got good results using an outside company to help.

HR SKILLS AND APPLICATIONS

Controlling Tardiness

Tardiness, in which individuals report to work late, is a part of the issue of absenteeism. Whether an employee is a few minutes or a few hours late, tardiness means time away from work and frequently affects the work of others in a negative way. About 16% of workers come to work late once a week and 8% are late at least twice a week.[28]

Some tardiness may not be controllable by employees, such as that caused by traffic problems, public transportation delays, road construction, and traffic accidents. However, many employees are late to work for personal, family, or other reasons. For instance, employees are sometimes tardy because of lack of sleep the night before. Lateness might also be related to family issues, such as getting children to school or aiding an elderly or sick relative. Other people simply may not want to be at an early work meeting and come in late to avoid it.

Regardless of the reason, tardiness becomes a more serious problem when it is chronic and amounts to absenteeism. When this occurs, managers may use the following:

- Establish and consistently communicate policies on lateness.
- Remind individuals of the consequences of tardiness, especially if it is frequent.
- Have specific discussions with tardy employees on the reasons for their lateness, and then document those reasons as part of their personnel records.
- If appropriate, consider individual flexible work scheduling, focusing on the number of hours worked without having a specific set work time.
- Implement disciplinary actions for employees who are repeatedly or frequently tardy, especially for those who are tardy for reasons that are personal and controllable.
- Establish a good model through personal behavior.
- Be realistic—someone who routinely works late should not be disciplined for occasional tardiness.

Instead of calling their manager, employees call "Active Health Partners" and speak to a nurse. Medical advice is given along with an anticipated return to work date. The employee's manager is then given an e-mail or text with the information. Relevant information is given as an online report to Wincanton periodically. The process reduced total absenteeism by 50% at some sites and absence duration from seven days to four. Ninety percent of the employees felt their calls had been dealt with politely and appropriately by the nurses.[29]

5-3b Controlling Absenteeism

Voluntary absenteeism is best controlled if managers understand its causes, costs, and believe absenteeism *can be* controlled.[30] Once it is understood, they can use a variety of approaches to reduce it. Figure 5-7 shows sources of direct and indirect costs. Organizational policies on absenteeism should be stated clearly in an employee handbook and emphasized by supervisors and managers.

FIGURE 5-7 Sources of Direct and Indirect Costs of Absenteeism

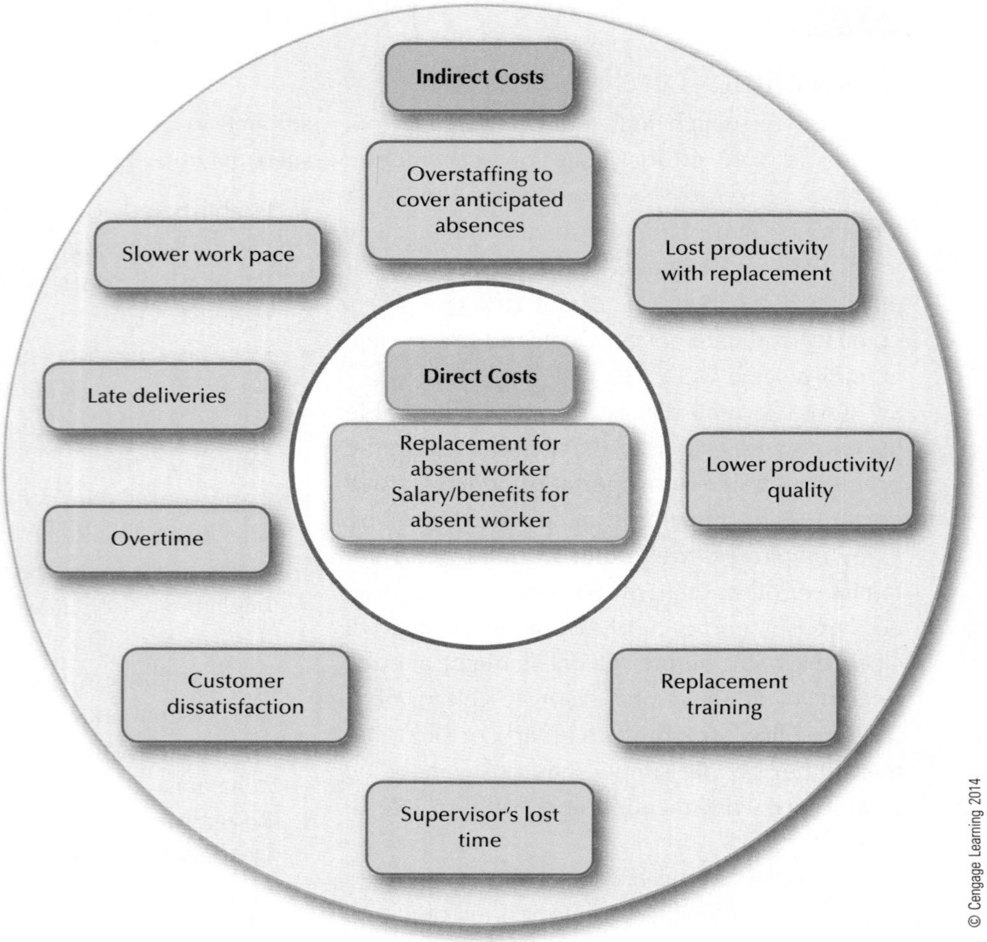

© Cengage Learning 2014

Employers use methods such as the following to address absenteeism:

- *Disciplinary approach*: Many employers use this approach. People who are absent the first time receive an verbal warning, and subsequent absences result in written warnings, suspension, and finally dismissal.
- *Positive reinforcement*: Positive reinforcement includes actions such as giving employees cash, recognition, time off, and other rewards for meeting attendance standards. Offering rewards for consistent attendance, giving bonuses for missing fewer than a certain number of days, and "buying back" unused sick leave are all positive reinforcement methods of reducing absenteeism.
- *Combination approach*: A combination approach ideally rewards desired behaviors and punishes undesired behaviors. This carrot-and-stick approach uses policies and discipline to punish offenders and various programs and rewards to recognize employees with outstanding attendance. For instance, employees with perfect attendance may receive incentives of travel and other rewards. Those with excessive absenteeism would be terminated.

- *No-fault policy*: With a no-fault policy, the reasons for absences do not matter, and the employees must manage their own attendance unless they abuse that freedom. Once absenteeism exceeds normal limits, then disciplinary action up to and including termination of employment can occur. The advantages of the no-fault approach are that there is uniformity in the ways absence is handled, and supervisors and HR staff do not have to judge whether absences count as excused or unexcused.
- *Paid-time-off (PTO) programs*: Some employers have paid-time-off programs, in which vacation time, holidays, and sick leave for each employee are combined into a paid-time-off (PTO) account. Employees use days from their accounts at their discretion for illness, personal time, or vacation. If employees run out of days in their accounts, they are not paid for any additional days missed. PTO programs generally reduce absenteeism, particularly one-day absences, but they often increase overall time away from work because employees use all of "their" time off by taking unused days as vacation days.

5-3c Measuring Absenteeism

MEASURE

Labor Department estimates of the percentage of employees absent at any given time run from 3% to 5% and in some firms/industries as high as 8%.[31] A major step in reducing absenteeism is to decide how the organization is going to record absences and what calculations are necessary to maintain, and then benchmark those rates. Controlling or reducing absenteeism must begin with continuous monitoring of the absenteeism statistics in work units. Such monitoring helps managers pinpoint employees who are frequently absent and departments that have excessive absenteeism. Common information to be calculated includes the following:

- How many people are absent
- How many days of work are lost per month
- What are the compensation totals for absent workers
- Which units/jobs have attendance problems[32]

Various methods of measuring or computing absenteeism exist. One formula suggested by the U.S. Department of Labor is as follows:

$$\frac{\text{Number of person-days lost through job absence during period}}{(\text{Average number of employees}) \times (\text{Number of workdays})} \times 100$$

The absenteeism rate can also be based on number of hours instead of number of days.

One set of metrics that can be calculated is the rate of absenteeism, which can be based on annual, monthly, quarterly, or other periods of time. Other useful measures of absenteeism might include the following:

- *Incidence rate*: The number of absences per 100 employees each day
- *Inactivity rate*: The percentage of time lost to absenteeism
- *Severity rate*: The average time lost per absent employee during a specified period of time (a month or a year)

Additional information can be gained by separating absenteeism data into short-term and long-term categories. Different problems are caused by employees who are absent for one day 10 times during a year, and employees who are absent one time for 10 days.

Turnover
The process in which employees leave an organization and have to be replaced.

5-4 ■ EMPLOYEE TURNOVER

Turnover occurs when employees leave an organization and have to be replaced. Many organizations have found that turnover is a very costly problem. For instance, health care firms in one state experienced over 30% turnover annually. The turnover cost in the state for nursing jobs alone was more than $125 million per year, with individual nurse turnover costs being $32,000 per person who left.[33]

The extent to which employers face high turnover rates and costs varies by organization and industry. For example, the Society for Human Resource Management (SHRM) calculates that the average for all industries is 15% annual turnover. But companies in service industries such as restaurants have an average 35% annual rate. Entertainment and recreation has 27% turnover and retail 22%. Health care and social assistance are at 20% annual turnover.[34]

High turnover rates have a negative impact on several dimensions of organizational performance especially safety, productivity, and financial performance.[35] Turnover typically goes up as unemployment rates drop and dissatisfied employees can find other jobs.[36] Research shows that morale (or job satisfaction), the labor market (opportunity to leave), and intention to quit or stay have major impacts on turnover.[37] Further, a history of poor attempts at organizational change lead to higher turnover intentions.[38] However, human resources systems designed to reduce turnover can indeed succeed.[39] See the HR Perspective: Reducing Turnover at Boys & Girls Clubs of America for an example of managing turnover.

HR PERSPECTIVE

Reducing Turnover at Boys & Girls Clubs of America

The Boys & Girls Clubs of America in Atlanta has about 370 corporate employees. They have typically tracked voluntary turnover, and take out of the calculations those people who retire and those who leave headquarters to go to work for a local boys and girls club. Most turnover occurs among people who have been there one to three years. Through exit interviews the organization determined that the most frequent reasons people left were a bad job fit, or that the job did not meet original expectation.

As a result of its analysis, the HR department implemented a "more high touch" recruiting system to reduce the number of poor hires. This included multiple interviews on-site. Further, recruiters changed how they measure recruiting success to include finding a *good* candidate, rather than just any candidate. They used to look at time-to-fill-vacancy, but now they focus on quality of hire. Supervisors evaluate quality of hire, and HR looks at performance reviews of new hires as well.

Among 82 new hires, the organization kept 93% in the first two years of the new approach, and overall turnover rate dropped from 11% to 9%. The Director of Organizational Development says, "That number would scare us if it applied to our high-performers" but the organization is in the range of 90+ percent retention rates for high performers. The organization tracks top performers and those with high potential who leave the organization separately. Only about half of companies of various sizes track turnover among top performers according to a recent study.[40]

5-4a Types of Employee Turnover

Turnover is classified in many ways. One classification uses the following categories, although the two types are not mutually exclusive:

- **Involuntary Turnover**
  Employees are terminated for poor performance, work rule violations or through layoffs

- **Voluntary Turnover**
  Employees leave by choice

Involuntary turnover is triggered at all levels by employers terminating workers because of organizational policies and work rule violations, excessive absenteeism, performance standards that are not met by employees, and other issues. Voluntary turnover can be caused by many factors, some of which are not employer controlled. Common voluntary turnover causes include job dissatisfaction, pay and benefits levels, supervision, geography, and personal/family reasons. Career opportunities in other firms, when employees receive unsolicited contacts, may lead to turnover for individuals, especially those in highly specialized jobs such as IT. Voluntary turnover may increase with the size of the organization, most likely because larger firms are less effective in preventing turnover.

Another view of turnover classifies it on the basis of whether it is good or bad for the organization:

- **Functional Turnover**
  Lower-performing or disruptive employees leave

- **Dysfunctional Turnover**
  Key individuals and high performers leave

Not all turnover in organizations is negative. On the contrary, functional turnover represents a positive change. Some workforce losses are desirable, especially if those who leave are lower-performing, less reliable, and/or disruptive individuals. Of course, dysfunctional turnover also occurs. That happens when key individuals leave, often at crucial times. For example, a software project leader leaves in the middle of a system upgrade to take a promotion at another firm. His departure causes the timeline to slip because of the difficulty of replacing him. Further, other software specialists in the firm begin to seek out and accept jobs at competitive firms because he left. This is truly dysfunctional turnover.

Employees quit for many reasons, only some of which can be controlled by the organization. Another classification uses the following terms to differentiate types of turnover:

- **Uncontrollable Turnover**
  Employees leave for reasons outside the control of the employer

- **Controllable Turnover**
  Employees leave for reasons that could be influenced by the employer

Some examples of reasons for turnover the employer cannot control include: (1) the employee moves out of the geographic area, (2) the employee decides to stay home with young children or an elder relative, (3) the employee's spouse is transferred, or (4) the employee is a student worker who graduates from college. Even though some turnover is inevitable, employers recognize that reducing turnover saves money, and that they must address turnover that is controllable. Organizations are better able to keep employees if they address the concerns of those individuals that might lead to controllable turnover.

Churn
Hiring new workers while laying off others.

Turnover and "Churn" Hiring new workers while laying off others is called **churn**. This practice raises a paradox in which employers sometimes complain about not being able to find workers with the right skills while they are laying off other employees.

As organizations face economic and financial problems that result in layoffs, the remaining employees are more likely to consider jobs at other firms. In this situation, turnover is more likely to occur, and efforts are needed to keep existing employees. HR actions such as information sharing, opportunities for more training/learning, and emphasis on job significance can be helpful in lowering turnover intentions of individuals.

5-4b Measuring Employee Turnover

The U.S. Department of Labor estimates that the cost of replacing an employee ranges from one-half to five times the person's annual salary depending on the position.[41] The turnover rate for an organization can be computed on a monthly or yearly basis. The following formula, in which *separations* means departures from the organization, is widely used:

$$\frac{\text{Number of employee separations during the year}}{\text{Total number of employees at midyear}} \times 100$$

Common turnover rates range from almost 0% to more than 100% a year and vary among industries. As a part of HR management information, turnover data can be gathered and analyzed in many ways, including the following categories:

- Job and job level
- Department, unit, and location
- Reason for leaving
- Length of service
- Demographic characteristics
- Education and training
- Knowledge, skills, and abilities
- Performance ratings/levels

Two examples illustrate why detailed analyses of turnover are important. A manufacturing organization had a companywide turnover rate that was not severe, but 80% of the turnover occurred within one department. Specific actions such as training supervisors, and revising pay levels were needed to resolve problems in that unit. In a different organization, a global shipping/delivery firm identified reasons for turnover of sales and service employees and was able to focus on those reasons and reduce turnover in that group. The actions reduced turnover significantly, which contributed to an annual savings of several million dollars in direct and indirect costs. In both of these examples, the targeted turnover rates declined as a result of employer actions taken in response to the turnover analyses that were done.

5-5 ■ HR METRICS: DETERMINING TURNOVER COSTS

A major step in reducing the expense of turnover is to decide how the organization is going to record employee departures and what calculations are necessary to maintain and benchmark the turnover rates. Determining turnover costs can be

FIGURE 5-8 Model for Costing Lost Productivity

Job Title: _____

A. Typical annual pay for this job
B. Percentage of pay for benefits multiplied by annual pay
C. Total employee annual cost (A + B)
D. Number of employees who voluntarily quit the job in the past
   12 months
E. Number of months it takes for one employee to become fully productive
F. Per person turnover cost ([E ÷ 12] × C × 50%)*
G. Annual turnover cost for this job (F × D)

*Assumes 50% productivity throughout the learning period (E).

© Cengage Learning

relatively simple or very complex, depending on the nature of the efforts made and the data used.

Figure 5-8 shows a model for calculating the cost of productivity lost to turnover. Of course, this is only one cost associated with turnover. But it is one that is more difficult to conceptualize. If a job pays (A) $20,000 and benefits cost (B) 40%, then the total annual cost for one employee (C) is $28,000. Assuming that 20 employees have quit in the previous year (D) and that it takes three months for one employee to be fully productive (E), the calculation results in a per person turnover cost (F) of $3,500. Overall, the annual lost productivity (G) would be $70,000 for the 20 individuals who have left. In spite of the conservative and simple nature of this model, it easily makes the point that productivity lost to turnover is costly. As another example, if 150 tellers in a large bank corporation leave in a year, calculations done according to this model produce turnover costs of more than $500,000 a year.

MEASURE

5-5a Detailing Turnover Cost

Other areas in addition to lost productivity to be included in calculating detailed turnover costs include the following:

- *Separation costs*: HR staff and supervisory time, pay rates to prevent separations, exit interview time, unemployment expenses, legal fees for separations challenged, accrued vacation expenditures, continued health benefits, and others.
- *Vacancy costs*: Temporary help, contract and consulting firm usage, existing employee overtime, and other costs until the person is replaced.
- *Replacement costs*: Recruiting and advertising expenses, search fees, HR interviewer and staff time and salaries, employee referral fees, relocation and moving costs, supervisor and managerial time and salaries, employment testing costs, reference checking fees, pre-employment medical expenses, relocation costs, and others.
- *Training costs for the new person*: Paid orientation time, training staff time and pay, costs of training materials, supervisor and manager time and salaries, coworker "coaching" time and pay, and others.

- *Hidden/indirect costs*: Costs that are less obvious, such as reduced productivity (calculated above), decreased customer service, lower quality, additional unexpected employee turnover, missed project deadlines, and others.

Turnover metrics illustrate that turnover is an expensive HR and managerial issue that must be constantly evaluated and addressed. Figure 5-9 summarizes the costs of turnover.

As noted, not all turnover is negative. Losing low performers should be considered positive. There may be an "optimal" amount of useful turnover necessary to replace low performers and add part-time or contract workers with special capabilities to improve workforce performance.

MEASURE

5-5b Optimal Turnover

Turnover costs and benefits can be calculated separately for various organizational segments. HR frequently strives to minimize all turnover but in some cases more turnover may be better. For example, reducing turnover makes sense when it is very expensive, when those leaving are more valuable than their replacements, or when there may not be suitable replacements. However, more turnover in certain segments of the organization may make sense if it costs very little, those leaving are less valuable than their replacements, or there is certainty that good replacements are available.[42] Sometimes turnover is good, other times it clearly is not. A more sophisticated view tries to optimize the impact of turnover for the organization.[43] The solution is to calculate the financial impact of different types of turnover and attach a dollar cost to it to determine the optimum level.[44]

FIGURE 5-9 Components of Turnover Cost

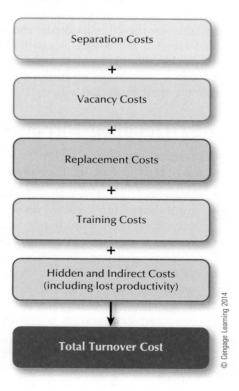

© Cengage Learning 2014

5-6 ■ RETENTION OF HUMAN RESOURCES

In one sense retention is the opposite of turnover. However, the reasons key people choose to stay with an employer may not be the opposite of those that compel others to quit. Retaining top talent is a concern for many employers, and understanding retention is the key to keeping more of those top performers.

5-6a Myths and Realities about Retention

Keeping good employees is a challenge for all organizations and becomes even more difficult as labor markets change. Unfortunately, some myths have arisen about what it takes to retain employees. Some of the most prevalent myths and realities that exist are as follows:

1. *Money is the main reason people leave.* Money is certainly a powerful recruiting tool, and if people feel they are being paid inadequately, they may be more likely to leave. But if they are paid close to the competitive level they expect, other parts of the job become more important than the pay they receive.
2. *Hiring has little to do with retention.* This is not true. Recruiting and selecting the people who fit the jobs and who are less likely to leave in the first place, and then orienting them to the company, can greatly increase retention. It is important to select for retention. Do not hire people with a history of high turnover.
3. *If you train people, you are only training them for another employer.* Developing skills in employees may indeed make them more marketable, but it also tends to improve retention. When an employer provides employees with training and development assistance, job satisfaction may increase and employees may be more likely to stay, particularly if they see more future opportunities internally.
4. *Do not be concerned about retention during organizational change.* The time when organizational change takes place is exactly when employees worry about leaving. Although some people's jobs may have to be cut because of organizational factors, the remaining employees that the company *would like to keep* may have the most opportunity and reason to leave voluntarily. For example, during a merger or acquisition, most workers are concerned about job security and their employer's future. If they are not made to feel a part of the new organization early on, many may leave or evaluate other alternatives.
5. *If high performers want to leave, the company cannot hold them.* Employees are "free agents," who can indeed leave when they choose. The key to keeping high performing employees is to create an environment in which they want to stay and grow.

5-6b Drivers of Retention

Since both people and jobs are so varied, managers and HR professionals need to realize that individuals may remain or leave their employment for both job-related and personal reasons.[45] For instance, if employees choose to leave an organization for family reasons (e.g., because a spouse is transferring or to raise children), there may be a limited number of actions the employer can take to keep them on the job. However, there are significant actions that an employer can take to retain employees in many other circumstances. Figure 5-10 illustrates some of these "drivers" of retention, or areas in which employers can take action to strengthen the possibility of keeping employees.

The actual reasons that people stay or leave may vary by job, industry and organizational issues, geography, and other factors. For instance, a survey of executives by Robert Half International found that the most common factors that caused satisfactory employees to quit their jobs were unhappiness with management, limited career advancements and recognition, insufficient pay and benefits, and job boredom.[46] This survey illustrates that many of the factors involved in retention drivers are factors within the employer's control, as shown in Figure 5-10.

Organizational and Management Factors Many organizational/management factors influence individuals' job satisfaction and their decisions to stay with or leave their employers. Organizations that have clearly established goals and hold managers and employees accountable for accomplishing results are viewed as better places to work, especially by individuals wishing to progress both financially and career-wise. Further, effective management provides the resources necessary for employees to perform their jobs well.

Other organizational components that affect employee retention are related to the management of the organization. In some organizations external events are seen as threatening, whereas in others they are seen as challenges requiring responses. The latter approach can be a source of competitive advantage, especially if an organization is in a growing, dynamic industry. Another organizational factor that can affect employee job performance and potential turnover intentions is "organizational politics." This can include managerial favoritism, having to be involved in undesirable activities, taking credit for what others do, and other actions that occur in many departments and organizational settings.

A final factor affecting how employees view their organizations is the quality of organizational leadership. If a firm is not effectively managed, then employees may be disappointed by the ineffective responses and inefficiencies they deal with in their jobs and may want to leave.[47] A study in China found that even workers with low pay and poor working conditions showed greater commitment to their jobs when

FIGURE 5-10 Drivers of Retention

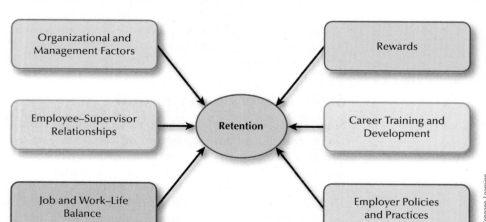

good management was present (including good HR practices and well-managed production operations) despite the pay and working conditions.[48]

Employee/Supervisor Relationships Work relationships that affect employee retention include *supervisory/management support* and *coworker relations*. A supervisor or manager builds positive relationships and aids retention by being fair and nondiscriminatory, allowing work flexibility and work-family balancing, giving feedback that recognizes employee efforts and performance, and supporting career planning and development.

Additionally, many individuals build close relationships with coworkers. Such work-related friendships do not appear on employee records, but these relationships can be an important signal that a workplace is positive. Overall, what this means is that it is not just *where* people work but also with *whom* they work that affects employee retention. If individuals are not linked with or do not relate well to their coworkers, there is greater likelihood for turnover to occur.[49]

Job and Work–Life Balance Many individuals have seen a decline in job security during the past decades. All the downsizings, layoffs, mergers and acquisitions, and organizational restructurings have affected employee commitment, loyalty, and retention. As coworkers experience layoffs and job reductions, the anxiety levels of the remaining employees rise. Consequently, employees start thinking about leaving before they also get laid off. Organizations in which job continuity and security are high tend to have higher retention rates.[50]

Some jobs are considered "good" and others are thought to be "bad," but not all people agree on which jobs are which. As mentioned previously, the design of jobs and peoples' preferences can vary significantly. Job design factors that can impact retention include the following:

- A knowledge, skills, and abilities mismatch, either through overqualification or underqualification, can lead to turnover.
- Job accomplishments and workload demands that are dissatisfying or excessively stressful may impact performance and lead to turnover.
- Both timing of work schedules and geographic locations may contribute to burnout in some individuals but not others.
- The ability of employees to balance work and life requirements affects their job performance and retention.[51]

Rewards The tangible rewards that people receive for working come in the form of pay, incentives, and benefits. Employees often cite better pay or benefits as the reason for leaving one employer for another. Employers do best with retention if they offer *competitive pay and benefits*, which means they must be close to what other employers are providing and what individuals believe to be consistent with their capabilities, experience, and performance. If compensation is not close to market, often defined as within 10% to 15% of the "market" rate, turnover is likely to be higher.

However, the reality of compensation is a bit more complex than it seems at first glance. Studies typically show a modest positive relationship between pay level and satisfaction with a job. However, there is a great deal of variance across employees—some value money more than others and for different reasons. Employee preferences are outside the control of employers.[52]

Another part of reward is that individuals need to be satisfied with both the actual levels of pay and the processes used to determine pay. That is why the performance management and performance appraisal processes must be designed so they are linked to compensation increases. To strengthen links between organizational and individual performance, private-sector firms are increasingly using variable pay and incentive programs.[53]

Another reward is *employee recognition*, which can be both tangible and intangible. Tangible recognition comes in many forms, such as "employee of the month" plaques and perfect-attendance certificates. Intangible and psychological recognition includes feedback from managers and supervisors acknowledging extra effort and performance, even if monetary rewards are not given. Other kinds of rewards include perks of different types—usually used to retain employees with skill sets in short supply. For examples, see the HR Perspective: Using Perks to Help Retention.

Career Training and Development Many employees in all types of jobs consistently indicate that organizational efforts to aid their career training and development can significantly affect employee retention. *Opportunities for personal growth* lead the list of reasons why individuals took their current jobs and why they stay there. Personal growth might include personal rebooting as well for software developers. A software firm developed a "paid, paid vacation." Employees get $7,500 extra pay to take their paid vacations. The only catch is that they must unplug and actually go on vacation. The company received 2,500 applications for eight positions since the "paid, paid vacation" idea went viral. The CEO says the perk was driven by competitive demand for software developers but he had no idea the reaction would be so strong.

HR PERSPECTIVE

Using Perks to Help Retention

Aspenware, a software developer in Denver, goes beyond free lunches and days off for skiing. It offers employees free time to pursue projects that have potential as a startup, subsidiary, or a new line of business. Janet McIllece recently spent 10 to 20 hours per week for six months trying to find ways to explain complex data on the health of a stream to nontechnical audiences. Aspenware freed her to work on the project with her brother, a biologist with the U.S. Fish and Wildlife Service. They also paid for a three-day visit to Spokane for the project. Financing would have been available had the project turned into a business, with ownership stakes for McIllece but that did not occur.

The market for software developers is very tight, making employers come up with ways to treat their employees even better to retain them. Some notable perks include pet-sitting services, in-house chefs, and a lifetime supply of Pabst Blue Ribbon beer. But the in-house incubation program at Aspenware goes beyond that, allowing employees to discover their entrepreneurial and creative nature. The company carves out time and provides financing for ideas that may lead to a new line of business or a spinoff start-up.

Aspenware's founder stated: "Any of our people can get a job anywhere given their talent … " "There are lots of things we have to try to make sure this is an environment people want to be in."[54]

Training and development efforts can be designed to indicate that employers are committed to keeping employees' knowledge, skills, and abilities current. Also, training and development can help underused employees attain new capabilities. Such a program has been very successful at Southwest Airlines.

Organizations address training and development in many ways. Tuition aid programs, typically offered as a benefit by many employers, allow employees to pursue additional educational and training opportunities. These programs may contribute to higher employee retention rates because the employees' new knowledge and capabilities can aid the employer. Also, through formal career planning efforts, employees and their managers discuss career opportunities in the organization and career development activities that will help them to grow.

Career development and planning efforts may include formal mentoring programs. For instance, information technology (IT) organizations are using career development programs so that IT individuals can expand their skills outside of technical areas. Programs in some firms cover communication and negotiation tactics, which gives the employees additional capabilities that are needed in managerial and other jobs. Companies can help reduce attrition by showing employees that they are serious about career advancement opportunities.[55]

ETHICS

Employer Policies and Practices Other factors found to affect retention are the employer policies. For instance, the reasonableness of HR policies, the fairness of disciplinary actions, and the means used to decide work assignments and opportunities all affect employee retention. If individuals feel that policies are unreasonably restrictive, unethical, or are applied inconsistently, they may be more likely to look at jobs offered by other employers.

The increasing demographic diversity of U.S. workplaces makes the *nondiscriminatory treatment* of employees important, regardless of gender, age, and other characteristics. The organizational commitment and job satisfaction of ethnically diverse individuals are affected by perceived discriminatory treatment. Many firms have recognized that proactive management of diversity issues affects individuals of all backgrounds.

5-6c Retention of Top Performers

Organizations that cannot consistently retain their top performers have a less qualified workforce, and perhaps are understaffed as well. Do high performers differ from other employees on the things that are likely to keep them with the firm? A study of 24,829 employees suggests the answer is "yes."[56] The top performers mentioned *job satisfaction* most frequently as a reason they were staying. This was followed by *extrinsic rewards*, *work relationships*, and *commitment to the organization*. Figure 5-11 shows comments made by high performers when asked why they stay with their company. Low performers were more likely to stay because of pay and benefits than because of positive attitudes toward the job, company, or coworkers.

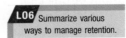

L06 Summarize various ways to manage retention.

5-7 ■ MANAGING RETENTION

The foregoing sections have summarized the results of many studies and popular HR practices to identify factors that can affect retention. Retention is important because turnover can cause poor performance in otherwise productive units. The focus now turns toward the keys to managing retention as part of effective HR management.

FIGURE 5-11 **Comments from High Performers as to Why They Stay with Their Employer**

Individual/Organization Relations	Comments
Job Satisfaction	• I am happy in my current position and enjoy the work I do here. • I still enjoy coming to work every day.
Rewards	• The benefits are among the best in the industry. • I believe the pay, benefits and bonus incentives are competitive compared to other companies.
Work Relationships	• The people I have come to know here prevent me from wanting to leave. • My supervisor is a great role model.
Commitment	• I believe in loyalty to the company that hired me. • I am proud to work here.

Source: Adapted from John P. Hausknecht, et al., "Targeted Employee Retention: Performance Based and Job-related Differences in Reported Reasons for Staying," *Human Resource Management*, 48, March–April 2009, pp. 269–288.

MEASURE

5-7a Retention Assessment and Metrics

Calculating both turnover and retention provides a more complete view of worker movement. By definition, the retention rate is the percentage of employees at the beginning of a period who remain at the end.[57]

To ensure that appropriate actions are taken to enhance retention, management decisions require data and analyses rather than subjective impressions, anecdotes of selected individual situations, or panic reactions to the loss of key people. Examples of a process for managing retention are highlighted in Figure 5-12.

Analysis of turnover data is an attempt to get at the cause of retention problems. Managers should recognize that turnover is only a symptom of other factors that may be causing problems. When the causes are treated, the symptoms may be eliminated. Some of the first areas to consider when analyzing data about retention include the work, pay/benefits, supervision, occupations, departments, and demographics of those leaving and staying. Common methods of obtaining useful perspectives are employee surveys, exit interviews, and first-year turnover evaluations.

FIGURE 5-12 Process for Managing Retention

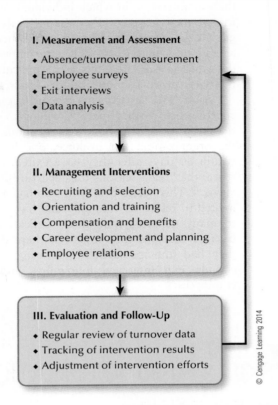

I. **Measurement and Assessment**

- Absence/turnover measurement
- Employee surveys
- Exit interviews
- Data analysis

II. **Management Interventions**

- Recruiting and selection
- Orientation and training
- Compensation and benefits
- Career development and planning
- Employee relations

III. **Evaluation and Follow-Up**

- Regular review of turnover data
- Tracking of intervention results
- Adjustment of intervention efforts

© Cengage Learning 2014

Employee Surveys Employee surveys can be used to diagnose specific problem areas, identify employee needs or preferences, and reveal areas in which HR activities are well received or viewed negatively. Whether the surveys cover general employee attitudes, job satisfaction, or specific issues, the survey results must be examined as part of retention measurement efforts. For example, a growing number of "mini-surveys" on specific topics are being sent via e-mail questionnaires, blogs, and other means.

Regardless of the topics in a survey, employee input provides data on the "retention climate" in an organization. By obtaining data on how employees view their jobs, their coworkers, their supervisors, and organizational policies and practices, these surveys can be starting points for reducing turnover and increasing the length of time that employees are retained. Some employers conduct attitude surveys yearly, while others do so intermittently.

By asking employees to respond candidly to an attitude survey, management is building employees' expectations that actions will be taken on the concerns identified. Therefore, a crucial part of conducting an attitude survey is providing feedback to those who participated in it. It is especially important that even negative survey results be communicated to avoid fostering the appearance of hiding the results or placing blame.

Exit interview
An interview in which individuals who are leaving an organization are asked to give their reasons.

Exit Interviews One widely used means for assisting retention assessment efforts is the **exit interview,** in which individuals who are leaving the organization are asked to give their reasons. HR must regularly summarize and analyze the data by category (e.g., reasons for leaving, department, length of service, etc.) to provide managers and supervisors with information for improving company efforts.[58] As described in the HR Skills and Applications: Conducting Exit Interviews, the exit interview process should include certain elements.

Many HR departments regularly contact former employees who were valuable contributors, as they may be willing to provide more information on email questionnaires or in telephone conversations conducted some time after they have left the organization. For instance, one health care firm contacts former employees within 60 days after they have exited. Many times these follow-up conversations reveal the "real" reasons for departures, other than what was said in the exit interviews.[59] This health care firm also has a program through which ex-employees are invited to return as "alumni" and have lunch with former coworkers. This has led to many departed individuals indicating they would like to return to the firm because the jobs they took elsewhere did not turn out to be as "promising" as they had anticipated. Thus, rehiring can be aided by ongoing efforts such as e-mails, exit interview follow-ups, and continuing contacts with good former employees.[60]

HR SKILLS AND APPLICATIONS

Conducting Exit Interviews

Departing employees may be reluctant to divulge their real reasons for leaving. A skilled HR interviewer may be able to gain useful information that departing employees do not wish to share with managers and supervisors. The following suggestions may be useful when conducting exit interviews:

- Decide who will conduct the exit interview and when the discussion will occur. Often these interviews occur on the last day or so of a departing individual's employment.
- Emphasize that the information provided by the departing employee will be treated confidentially and used to make improvements.
- Utilize a checklist or a set of standard questions so that the information can be summarized. Typical areas covered include reasons for leaving, supervision, pay, training, liked and disliked aspects of the job, and details on

the organization to which the employee is moving.

When doing the actual exit interview, numerous questions can be asked. Those typically asked include the following:

[Q]: Why are you leaving?
[Q]: What have you liked and disliked about your job and managers?
[Q]: What company actions have made you and other employees more or less positive?
[Q]: What would or would not lead you to recommend the employer to future possible hires?
[Q]: Did you receive adequate training and support?
[Q]: Did the job match your expectations when you were hired?
[Q]: What was frustrating about working here?
[Q]: What suggestions do you have to improve working conditions?

First-Year Turnover Evaluations A special type of retention assessment focuses on first-year employees. It is not unusual for turnover to be high among employees during their first year. Sometimes the cause of departure is voluntary; for example, individuals may identify a mismatch between what they expected in their jobs and managers and what actually occurs, or between their perceptions of the new job and its reality. Other times individuals are involuntarily removed for poor performance in the first year. Some causes can be excessive absenteeism and mismatches with job requirements, or conflicts with other employees and managers. If these situations occur too often, HR may need to reevaluate recruiting and selection processes, as well as its job previews to make sure they are realistic.

Overall, focus on first-year retention and turnover is useful because individuals who stay for a year are more likely to extend their employment and have greater retention beyond the first year. Also, effective first-year efforts may lead to future career development, higher performance, and other positive retention factors.

5-7b Retention Evaluation and Follow-Up

Management can take numerous actions to deal with retention issues. The choice of a particular action depends on the analysis of the turnover and retention problems in a particular organization and should be custom-tailored for that organization.

Tracking of intervention results and *adjustment of intervention efforts* should be part of retention evaluation and follow-up. Some firms use pilot programs to see how changes affect retention before extending them to the entire organization. For instance, to test the effect of flextime scheduling on employee turnover, a firm might try flexible scheduling in one department. If the turnover rate in that department drops in comparison to the turnover rates in other departments still working with set schedules, the firm might extend the use of flexible scheduling to other departments.

SUMMARY

- Individual performance is captured by the formula Performance = Ability × Effort × Support.
- Motivation is explained by many theories—some of the most commonly used are needs theory, two factor theory, equity theory, and expectancy theory.
- Psychological contracts are unwritten expectations that employees and employers have about the nature of their work relationships.
- The interaction between individuals and their jobs affects both job satisfaction and organizational commitment. The extent to which employees feel linked to organizational success can affect employee engagement and loyalty.
- Employee engagement is the extent to which an employee's thoughts and behaviors are focused on the employer's success.

- Loyalty to an employer depends on the employee's perception that the employer is loyal in return.
- Absenteeism and tardiness are related and both require analysis and management.
- Absenteeism has both direct and indirect costs that add up to an expensive problem.
- Getting accurate measures on absenteeism is the beginning of solving the problem.
- Turnover occurs when employees leave an organization and must be replaced. It can be classified in many ways, but it should be measured and its costs determined.
- There is an optimum level of turnover that is likely *not* zero.
- Drivers of retention include organizational, managerial, and job factors that may affect employees' worklife balance, compensation and

other rewards, career training and development, and employer policies and practices.

- Retention of employees is a major focus of HR management efforts in organizations.

- It is assisted by the use of retention measures, including employee surveys and exit interviews.
- Managing retention should include evaluation and tracking of both retention actions and turnover follow-up.

CRITICAL THINKING CHALLENGES

1. Describe your expectations for a job. How well does your employer meet the expectations you bring to the psychological contract?

2. If you became the new manager at a restaurant with high employee turnover, what actions would you take to increase retention of employees?

3. As the HR manager, you must provide the senior management team with turnover costs for the following high-turnover position. Use websites such as www.talentkeepers.com and www.keepemployees.com, to calculate turnover and analyze the variables involved. Also identify any other data that might be relevant, and then discuss how you would reduce the turnover.
   Position: Machine operator
   Number of employees: 250
   Number of turnovers: 85
   Average wage: $11.50/hour
   Cost of benefits: 35% of payroll

4. Your company has reaped the benefits of having long-term, tenured employees, but many of them are now approaching retirement. It is anticipated that approximately 20% of the company's workforce will retire in the next three to five years. In reviewing the remaining workforce through HR planning efforts, you have become aware of work–life balance issues that need to be reviewed and addressed. The company president has requested that you prepare a retention plan outlining these issues as well as ways to address them. Resources to help you address the issues in the retention plan can be found at www.workfamily.com.

A. What steps will you take to identify key priorities in the work–life balance issues?

B. How will you present a business case to gain management support for addressing those issues to help retain existing workers and to fill the positions vacated by retiring employees?

CASE

Reducing Turnover at Rosemont Center

Rosemont Center Inc., in Columbus, Ohio, is a mental health and social services agency providing services to youths and low-income families. The services provided include outpatient therapy, foster care, day treatment, and mental health services.

Annual employee turnover reached 72%. The 62 employees included therapists, counselors, and social workers. At its peak the staff numbered 150 but funding cuts led to elimination of some programs. During the ensuing layoffs, voluntary turnover jumped. Low morale and motivation became a problem for the survivors, and the quality of services was affected.

The HR Director checked the accuracy of the turnover metrics to verify their validity and then put together a task force to identify causes. They identified the following causes:

- Demanding work
- Work–life balance—night work and weekends
- Low salaries
- On-call responsibilities without compensation

Exit interviews and employee satisfaction surveys were reviewed, and managers of similar agencies in Ohio were interviewed. These interviews were performed to hopefully find solutions that could improve employee satisfaction and reduce turnover.

Recommendations to the board for change from the task force included:

- *Career development*—internal job bidding for promotions and transfers to allow employees to apply for positions at Rosemont even before they were vacant and make an internal list of people who would consider jobs at the center.
- *Rewards*—a salary study to make sure salaries were competitive.
- *Management and organization*—develop a system of support for directors and supervisors to reduce recruiting costs and orientation costs for new employees. Encourage openness in communication so employees felt free to make suggestions or express concerns.
- *Work–life balance*—promote employee assistance programs and provide training on work–life balance.

With backing from the board of directors, the resulting program reduced turnover to 48%. The job bidding was a key element in that success.

Compensation was increased as a result of the salary study, and employees were given more choices of benefits. Rosemont generated a list of candidates who wanted to work there. When a position opened, there were several candidates from which to choose. Formal training for management personnel had a positive effect on staff, who began to feel more supported by their supervisors. The company developed a training agenda which received funding. Finally, quarterly all-staff meetings and other events began fostering a more open culture.

The improved turnover rate with attendant reduced costs and better morale impressed the board members, and resulted in improved service as well.[61]

QUESTIONS

1. Did the social services nature of this organization make the turnover situation any different that in a private company? Why or why not?

2. Have you seen similar efforts occur in places where you have worked? Describe them and comment on their success in that context. What could have been done differently?

SUPPLEMENTAL CASES

The Clothing Store

This case describes the approach of one firm to improving employee retention. (For the case, go to http://www.cengage.com/management/mathis.)

Accenture—Retaining for Itself

This case describes what a large consulting company does to help retain a virtual workforce. (For the case go to http://www.cengage.com/management/mathis.)

Alegent Health

This case discusses how Alegent, a large nonprofit health care system, improved employee retention and reduced turnover. (For the case, go to http://www.cengage.com/management/mathis.)

NOTES

1. Adapted from Michael J. Fention and Susan A. Mohrman, "Where Counting Counts," *HR Magazine*, January 2010, 31–35.

2. Peter Cappelli, "Checking in with the Next Generation," *Human Resource Executive-Online*, December 6, 2010, 1–2.

3. Cyril Tuohy, "The Employer-Employee Bond Frays Further," *Human Resource Executive-Online*, July 21, 2011, 1–2.

4. John C. Dencker, "Who Do Firms Lay Off and Why?", *Industrial Relations: A Journal of Economy and Society*, 51, 2012, 152–169.
5. Denny Strigl, "Results Drive Happiness," *HR Magazine*, October 2011, 113.
6. Teresa Amabile and Steen Kramer, "How Leaders Kill Meaning at Work," *McKinsey Quarterly*, January 2012, 1–8.
7. Nitin Notria, et al., "Employee Motivation a Powerful New Model," *Harvard Business Review*, July–August 2008, 1–8.
8. "Motivation in Today's Workplace: The Link to Performance," *SHRM Research Quarterly*, Second Quarter, 2010, 1–9.
9. Jake G. Messersmith, et al., "Unlocking the Black Box: Exploring the Link Between High Performance Work Systems and Performance," *Journal of Applied Psychology*, 96, 2011, 1105–1118.
10. T. H. Ng, et al., "Psychological Contract Breaches, Organizational Commitment, and Innovation-related Behaviors," *Journal of Applied Psychology*, 94, 2010, 744–751.
11. S. D. Montes and D. Zeig, "Do Promises Matter? An Exploration of the Role of Promises in Psychological Contract Breach," *Journal of Applied Psychology*, 95, 2009, 1243–1260.
12. S. Tietze and S. Nardin, "The Psychological Contract and the Transition from Office-based to Home-based Work," 21, 2011, 318–334.
13. S. Svensson and Lars-Erik Wolven, "Temporary Agency Workers and Their Psychological Contracts," *Employee Relations*, 32, 2010, 184–199.
14. J. W. Beck and P. T. Walmshey, "Selection Ratio and Employee Retention as Antecedents of Competitive Advantage," *Industrial and Organizational Psychology*, 2012, 92–95.
15. Edel Conway and Kathy Monks, "Unraveling the Complexity of High Commitment: An Employee Level Analysis," *Human Resource Management Journal*, 19, 2009, 140–148.
16. Giancarlo Ghislanzoni, et al., "Taking Organizational Redesigns from Plan to Practice: McKinsey Global Survey Results," *McKinsey Quarterly*, December 2010, 1–9.
17. Paola Spagnoli, et al., "Satisfaction with Job Aspects: Do Patterns Change Over Time?", *Journal of Business Research*, 65, 2012, 609–616.
18. Lin Grensing-Pophal, "Holding Pattern," *HR Magazine*, March 2009, 64–68.
19. Brad Shuck, "Integrative Literature Review: Four Emerging Perspectives of Employee Engagement," *Human Resource Development Review*, 10, 2011, 304–328.
20. Brad Shuck and Karen Wollard, "Employee Engagement and HRD: A Seminal Review of the Foundations," *Human Resource Development Review*, 9, 2010, 89–110.
21. Adrienne Fox, "Raising Engagement," *HR Magazine*, May 2010, 35–40.
22. Kristen B. Frasch, "The 'Virtuous Cycle' of Engagement and Productivity," *Human Resource Executive Online*, August 22, 2011, 1–2; Lynn Gresham, "SHRM Survey Finds Engagement, Retention Top HR Concerns," *Employee Benefit News*, July 6, 2011, 1–4; Andrew R. McIlvaine, "The Human Risk Factor," *Human Resource Executive Online*, February 6, 2012, 1–5.
23. Bob Pike, "Who Else Values Loyalty?", *Training*, November/December 2011, 69.
24. The Wharton School, "Declining Employee Loyalty: A Casualty of the New Workplace," *Human Resource Executive Online*, July 16, 2012, 1–5.
25. F. Pilchler and C. Wallace, "What Are the Reasons for Differences in Job Satisfaction Across Europe?", *European Sociological Review*, 25, 2009, 535–549; T. W. H. Ng, et al., "Does the Job Satisfaction—Job Performance Relationship Vary Across Cultures?", *Journal of Cross Cultural Psychology*, 40, 2009, 761–796.
26. Michael Klachefsky, "Health Related Cost Productivity: The Full Cost of Absence," *Productivity Insight #2*, Standard Insurance Company, August 2012, 1.
27. Denise Baker-McClearn, et al., "Absence Management and Presenteeism: The Pressures on Employees to Attend Work and the Impact of Attendance on Performance," *Human Resource Management Journal*, 20, 2010, 311–328.
28. Kathy Gurchiek, "Worker Punctuality Improves Slightly," *HR Magazine*, May 2010, 24.
29. Carol Madden, "Wincanton Reduces Sickness Absences by 10,000 Days," *Human Resource Management International Digest*, 17, 2009, 35–37.
30. Vivienne Walker and David Barnford, "An Empirical Investigation into Health Sector Absenteeism," *Health Services Management Research*, 24, August 2011, 142–150.
31. Robert J. Grossman, "Gone But Not Forgotten," *HR Magazine*, September 2011, 34–46.
32. *Ibid.* 44.
33. "Estimating Turnover Costs," www.workforce.com.
34. Eric Krell, "5 Ways to Manage High Turnover," *HR Magazine*, April 2012, 63–65.
35. Jason D. Shaw, "Turnover Rates and Organizational Performance," *Organizational Psychology Review*, 1, August 2011, 187–213.
36. David Shadovitz, "Talent Turnover Going Up … Again," *Human Resource Executive*, July/August 2012, 10.
37. Robert P. Steel and John W. Lounsbury, "Turnover Process Models: Review and Synthesis of a Conceptual Literature," *Human Resource Management Review*, 19, 2009, 271–282.
38. Prashant Bordia, "Haunted by the Past: Effects of Poor Change Management History on Employee Attitudes and Turnover," *Group and Organization Management*, 36, April 2011, 191–222.
39. Rosemary Batt and Alexander J. S. Colvin, "An Employment Systems Approach to Turnover: HR Practices, Quits, Dismissals, and Performance," *The Academy of Management Journal*, 54, August 2011, 695–718; I. Y. Haines, et al., "The Influence of HR Management Practices on Employee Voluntary Turnover Rates in the Canadian Non Government Sector," *Industrial and Labor Relation Review*, 63, 2010, 228–246.
40. Adrienne Fox, "Drive Turnover Down," *HR Magazine*, July 2012, 23–27.

41. For details on industries, types of jobs, and other components, go to www.dol.gov.

42. Wayne F. Cascio, "Be a Ringmaster of Risk," *HR Magazine*, April 2012, 38–43.

43. W. Stanley Siebert and Nikolay Zubanov, "Searching for the Optimal Level for Employee Turnover," *Academy of Management Journal*, 52, 2009, 294–313.

44. Gary Kranz, "Keeping the Keepers," *Workforce Management*, April 2012, 34–37.

45. David G. Allen, et al., "Retaining Talent: Replacing Misconceptions with Evidence-Based Strategies," *Academy of Management Perspectives*, 24, May 2010, 48–64.

46. "Unhappiness with Management, Limited Advancement Cited as Top Reasons Employees Quit," *WorldatWork Study*, January 21, 2009, www.worldatwork.org.

47. Adrienne Fox, "Avoiding Furlough Fallout," *HR Magazine*, September 2009, 37–40.

48. David C. Wyld, "China's Turnover Syndrome: Does Good Management Trump Job Conditions for Factory Workers?", *Academy of Management Perspective*, 23, November 2009, 93–94.

49. Will Felps, et al., "Turnover Contagion: How Coworker's Job Embeddedness and Job Search Behaviors Influence Quitting," *Academy of Management Journal*, 52, June 2009, 545–561.

50. Gilad Chen, et al., "The Power of Momentum: A New Model of Dynamic Relationships between Job Satisfaction Change and Turnover Intentions," *Academy of Management Journal*, 54, February 2011, 159–181.

51. SHRM Online Staff, "Flexible Work Plans Key to Retention," *HR Magazine*, December 2010, 105.

52. David C. Wyld, "Does Money Buy More Happiness on the Job?", *Academy of Management Perspectives*, 25, February 2011, 101–102.

53. Caroline Yang, "Maximize Employee Retention Through Total Rewards Programs," *Workspan*, June 2011, 25–28; Lani P. Barovick, "Sharing the Rain," *HR Magazine*, November 2010, 51–54.

54. Andy Vuong, "Ideas Unleashed," *Denver Post*, July 22, 2012, Section K, 1.

55. Michael O'Brien, "Extending the Honeymoon," *Human Resource Executive*, December 2011, 40–42.

56. John P. Hausknecht, et al., "Targeted Employee Retention: Performance Based and Job-Related Differences in Reported Reasons for Staying," *Human Resource Management*, 48, March–April 2009, 269–288.

57. Margaret Fiester, "How Do I Calculate Retention," *HR Magazine*, May 2009, 34.

58. Robert A. Giacalone, "Researching Exit Interviews," *Human Resource Executive Online*, March 1, 2012, 1–3.

59. M. Sureesh Baabu, et al., "Exit Interviews and their Empanelment," *SRM Management Digest*, 2011, 315–319.

60. Joyce L. Gioia, "Meaningful Exit Interviews Help One Bank Cut Turnover and Save," *Global Business and Organizational Excellence*, January/February 2011, 36–43.

61. Adapted from Sonya M. Latta, "Save your Staff, Improve your Business," *HR Magazine*, January 2012, 30–32.

6

Recruiting and Labor Markets

Learning Objectives

After you have read this chapter, you should be able to:

1 List different ways in which labor markets can be identified and approached.

2 Discuss the strategic decisions covering recruiting image, outsourcing, and other related areas.

3 Explain why Internet recruiting has grown and how it affects recruiting efforts done by employers.

4 Highlight five external recruiting sources.

5 Identify three internal sources for recruiting and issues associated with their use.

6 Describe three factors to consider when using recruiting measurement and metrics.

HR HEADLINE

Getting Creative to Recruit College Students

Some employers are developing creative strategies to attract talent coming out of college. Graduates are interested in a more interactive recruiting experience, in which they receive extensive information about the workplace and discuss available opportunities with employees who work for the company. They prefer employers who provide opportunities for workers to make a difference in the lives of other people and the communities in which they live. Companies that present these opportunities when recruiting have a distinct advantage when it comes to hiring younger employees. Making the recruiting experience dynamic and entertaining can apparently go a long way when hiring individuals in the Generation Y group.

Several organizations stand out with students by using creative recruiting approaches. For instance, the accounting firm Deloitte developed a program called Maximum Impact that gives undergraduate students a chance to volunteer time over their spring break to help communities in need. Students also get to participate in various networking sessions, and Deloitte professionals offer employment information during a career night. Maximum Impact has been an excellent tool for attracting and hiring good talent.

Ernst & Young, another certified professional accounting (CPA) firm, has developed a similar volunteer program that encourages students to submit community-project proposals, and participants compete for $10,000 in funding to help support these ideas. They also stay connected to some of the firm's advisors and executives, and such networking opens the door for future employment opportunities. Finally, Harrah's Entertainment Inc., offers a program called the MBA World Series of Poker that is held at Caesar's Palace Hotel and Casino in Las Vegas, Nevada. In addition to playing games and having fun, students can participate in recruiting sessions that provide information about careers in the organization.[1]

The staffing process used by an employer depends on HR planning and retention and must include both successful recruiting and selection efforts. However, as the HR Headline: Getting Creative to Recruit College Students illustrates, new approaches are constantly evolving. Without significant attention and measurement, recruiting and selection can become just a set of necessary administrative functions: coordinating internal openings, handling the flow of candidate data, dealing with regulatory reporting, and moving candidates through the system. Consequently, companies must be innovative in their approach to recruiting so that they can get the best employees.

Recruiting
Process of generating a pool of qualified applicants for organizational jobs.

This chapter examines recruiting, and the next chapter examines selection. **Recruiting** is the process of generating a pool of qualified applicants for organizational jobs. If the number of available candidates equals the number of people to be hired, no real selection is required—the choice has already been made. The organization must either leave some openings unfilled or take all the candidates. One survey of employers found that almost half of the hiring managers cited less-qualified applicants as the biggest recruiting and hiring challenge.[2] Given these concerns, it is important to view recruiting broadly as a key part of staffing, and not just as a collection of administrative and operational activities.

6-1 ◼ RECRUITING

Recruiting is becoming more important as labor markets evolve. Although recruiting can be expensive, an offsetting issue that must be considered is the cost of unfilled jobs. For example, consider a company in which three operations-related jobs are vacant. Assume these three vacancies cost the company $300 for each business day the jobs remain vacant. If the jobs are not filled for four months, the cost of this failure to recruit in a timely fashion will be about $26,000.

Although cost is certainly an issue, and some employers are quite concerned about cost per hire and the cost of vacancies, *quality* of recruits is an equally important consideration. For example, if an organizational strategy focuses on quality as a competitive advantage, a company might choose to hire only from the top 15% of candidates for critical jobs, and from the top 30% of candidates for all other positions. Though this approach may raise the cost per hire, it will improve workforce quality.

These examples illustrate that recruiting should not be seen only as an expense but also as an important part of overall HR planning and strategy. To be effective, recruiters need to integrate efforts involving labor markets, recruiting responsibilities and goals, business strategies, and recruiting sources. Figure 6-1 highlights these integral components for effective recruiting.

6-1a Strategic Recruiting and Human Resources Planning

It is important that recruiting be treated as a part of strategic HR planning because it is a key mechanism for filling the positions necessary to produce the organization's goods and services. Recruiting requires an employer to

- know the industry and where to successfully recruit qualified employees;
- identify keys to success in the labor market, including competitors' recruiting efforts;
- cultivate relationships with sources of prospective employees;

FIGURE 6-1 Integral Components for Effective Recruiting

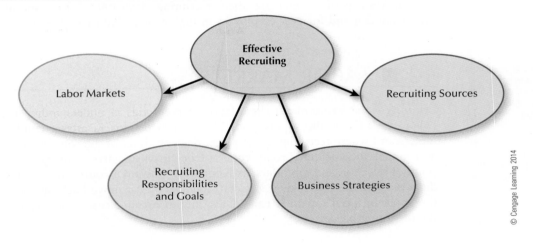

© Cengage Learning 2014

- promote the company brand so that the employer is known as a good place to work; and
- use recruiting metrics to measure the effectiveness of recruiting efforts.

Recruiting decisions can identify not only the kinds and numbers of applicants but also how difficult recruiting efforts may be depending on the type of jobs. In addition, effective recruiting focuses on discovering talent before it is needed.

6-1b Training of Recruiters/Managers and Outsourcing

ETHICS

Regardless of the methods used, an important consideration is the training of recruiters and managers. Training on recruiting-related activities, communications skills, and job details is common. Those involved in recruiting should learn the actions that might violate equal employment opportunity (EEO) regulations and how to handle diversity issues with applicants. Such training issues often include appropriate language to use with applicants so that racist, sexist, and other inappropriate remarks do not hurt the image of the employer and result in legal complaints.

Training may also include the importance of employer representatives engaging in ethical behaviors during recruiting efforts. One way to evaluate such training efforts is through follow-up activities. For instance, to assess ethical behavior when recruiting college graduates, some employers send follow-up surveys to interviewees asking about the effectiveness of the recruiters and the image the candidates have of the employers as a result of the recruiting contacts.[3]

A firm must also decide whether to outsource the recruiting function. Farming out various HR activities can help companies focus on other important strategic competencies. A recent study determined that line managers believed that HR was more effective when recruiting efforts were outsourced.[4] Given that many companies downsized their recruiting staffs during the recent recession, some are finding that outsourcing is necessary because competent recruiters are difficult to find. However, many recognize the importance of retaining a good in-house recruiting team, even during the lean times, to more effectively connect with job candidates.

Companies such as BASF have done just that.[5] BASF and other companies such as Sodexo USA plan to increase their recruiting departments to respond to the increasing demand for new employees in high-growth industries.[6]

6-2 ■ LABOR MARKETS

L01 List different ways in which labor markets can be identified and approached.

Labor markets
The supply pool from which employers attract employees.

Learning some basics about these labor markets aids in understanding recruiting. **Labor markets** are the supply pool from which employers attract employees. To understand where recruiting takes place, one can think of the sources of employees as a funnel, in which the broad scope of labor markets narrows progressively to the point of selection and job offers, as Figure 6-2 shows. Of course, if the selected candidates reject the offers, then HR staff members must move back up the funnel to the applicant pool for other candidates, and in extreme cases may need to reopen the recruiting process.

6-2a Labor Market Components

Labor force population
All individuals who are available for selection if all possible recruitment strategies are used.

Several means of identifying labor markets exist. One useful approach is to take a broad view of the labor markets and then narrow them down to specific recruiting sources. The broadest labor market component and measure is the **labor force population**, which is made up of all individuals who are available for selection if all possible recruitment strategies are used. For firms with operations in multiple countries, the labor force population can be much larger than that of a business operating in only one country. For example, some U.S.-based airlines have customer service centers located in the Philippines, India, and other countries as well as the United States. The labor force population for such businesses is much broader than that of a business operating in only one of these countries.

FIGURE 6-2 Labor Market Components

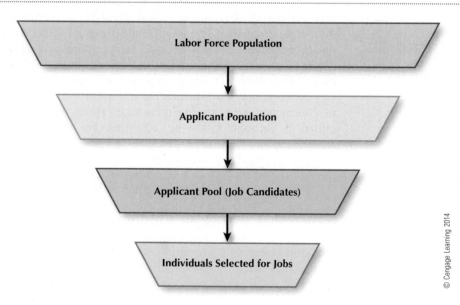

© Cengage Learning 2014

Applicant population
A subset of the labor force population that is available for selection using a particular recruiting approach.

The **applicant population** is a subset of the labor force population that is available for selection if a particular recruiting approach is used. This population can be broad or narrow depending on the jobs needing to be filled and the approaches used by the employer. For example, if a firm is recruiting highly specialized engineers for multiple geographic locations, the recruiting methods may involve a broad range of approaches and sources, such as contacting professional associations, attending conventions, utilizing general and specialized websites, using recruiting consulting firms, and offering recruitment incentives to existing employees.

However, a smaller firm in a limited geographic location might limit its recruiting for management trainees to MBA graduates from major universities in the area. This recruiting method would result in a different group of applicants from those who might apply if the employer were to advertise the openings for management trainees on a local radio station, post a listing on an Internet jobs board, or encourage current employee referrals and applications. Figure 6-3 illustrates some common considerations for determining applicant populations.

Applicant pool
All persons who are actually evaluated for selection.

The **applicant pool** consists of all persons who are actually evaluated for selection. Many factors can affect the size of the applicant pool, including the reputation of the organization and industry as a place to work, the screening efforts of the organization, the job specifications, and the information available. It is useful to develop an *applicant tracking system* when considering the applicant pool. Using such a system can make the recruiting process more effective.[7] For example, when the size of the applicant pool increases recruiters can identify the most effective future employees for several jobs, and not just fill current jobs because of a larger supply.[8]

Unemployment Rates and Labor Markets When the unemployment rate is high in a given market, many people are looking for jobs. When the unemployment rate is low, there are fewer applicants. Unemployment rates vary with business cycles and present very different challenges for recruiting at different times. The number of individuals looking for work in the United States has increased considerably over the last several years because of the recent recession and a persistently high unemployment rate. Some sources suggest there will be a slow recovery with slightly more corporate hiring, and other sources claim that the chances of getting hired will not improve in the future.[9] Some companies are taking their time to fill open positions and are being more selective in the hiring process because of decreased consumer spending and increased business competition so that hiring decisions are effective. When individuals are hired, they are expected to contribute effectively

FIGURE 6-3 Considerations for Determining Applicant Populations

Considerations for Determining Applicant Populations

- Number and type of recruits needed to fill jobs
- Timing of recruiting to ensure effective placement in organization
- External and internal messages on the details of jobs to be filled
- Qualifications of applicants to be considered by recruiters
- Sources for obtaining qualified applicants for jobs to be filled
- Outside and inside recruiting means to be used by recruiters
- Administrative recruiting and application review activities
- Consideration of organization's strategies to determine recruiting goals

© Cengage Learning 2014

from day one.[10] Further, recent investments in technology by companies such as Google and Boston Scientific could further dampen the incentive to hire new employees in the short-term as technology replaces employees.[11]

6-2b Different Labor Markets and Recruiting

The supply of workers in various labor markets differs substantially and affects staffing. Organizations recruit in many labor markets, including industry-specific markets and occupational, educational and technical, and geographic markets. Labor markets can be viewed in several ways to provide information that is useful for recruiting. These labor markets can include both internal and external sources.

Industry and Occupational Labor Markets Labor markets can be classified by industry and occupation. For example, the biggest increases in U.S. jobs until the year 2016 are going to be in the positions of registered nurses, retail sales and customer service representatives, home health aides, and postsecondary teachers.[12] These jobs represent the health care, retail, and education industries. Surveys illustrate that filling these jobs will be more difficult during the next few years. Trucking and welding jobs are also expected to present significant recruiting difficulties.[13]

Recruiting for smaller firms can also be challenging. For instance, a small CPA firm had to work extensively to identify which CPA professionals would prefer working in a small firm rather than a large one. One key to this firm's recruiting efforts was to clearly identify the unique characteristics of working in a smaller firm, which included greater assignment variety, more work flexibility, and better career possibilities.[14] Those characteristics would appeal to some but not all who might apply.

Educational and Technical Labor Markets Another way to look at labor markets is by considering the educational and technical qualifications that define the people being recruited. Employers may need individuals with specific licenses, certifications, or educational backgrounds. For instance, recruiting physician leaders for a medical organization led to the establishment of a special search committee to set goals for the organization. Then, as part of recruiting and selection, the top candidates were asked to develop departmental vision statements and three-year goals. That information made the recruiting and selection process more effective.[15] Business schools are also taking active steps to make sure that MBA students get the kinds of experiences that make them attractive to organizations by networking extensively with executives and recruiters.[16]

Another special labor market is suppliers and contractors for U.S. military forces. Firms such as Cintas Corporation, with more than 34,000 employees, and Raytheon, with 77,000 employees, serve as federal government defense contractors. The need to recruit for specialty jobs in engineering and technology by such firms illustrates why considering different types of technical labor markets is necessary.[17]

A prominent labor market that is expected to be in high demand over the next decade is bilingual/multilingual employees, particularly those individuals who can speak Spanish or Chinese. With some research showing a lack of motivation among workers to learn these languages, this educational/technical area should be in high demand with good work opportunities. Similarly, third-culture children, or individuals who have spent considerable time in geographic/cultural regions different from those of their parents, will also be in demand because of their knowledge of diverse cultural environments and flexibility.[18]

Geographic Labor Markets One common way to classify labor markets is based on geographic location. Markets can be local, area or regional, national, or international. Local and area labor markets vary significantly in terms of workforce availability and quality, and changes in a geographic labor market may force changes in recruiting efforts. For instance, if a new major employer locates in a regional labor market, other existing area employers may see a decline in their numbers of applicants.

Geographic markets require different recruiting considerations. For example, attempting to recruit locally for a job market that is a national competitive market will likely result in disappointing applicant rates. A catalog retailer that tries to recruit a senior merchandising manager from the small town where the firm is located may encounter difficulties, although it may not need to recruit nationally for workers to fill administrative support jobs. Varying geographic labor markets must be evaluated as part of recruiting. It is often a function of how much the jobs pay in addition to the quantity of available talent.

GLOBAL

Global Labor Markets Employers in the United States are tapping global labor markets when necessary and offshoring when doing so is advantageous. Firms in different industries are expanding in India, China, Indonesia, Romania, Poland, and other countries. This expansion has caused an increase in the number of host country nationals hired to fill positions in foreign offices.

The migration of U.S. work overseas has been controversial. While many decry the loss of American jobs, some employers respond that they cannot be competitive in a global market if they fail to take advantage of labor savings. For example, at some operations in India and China, U.S. employers pay less than half of what they would pay for comparable jobs to be performed in U.S. facilities. A significant number of U.S. and European firms have farmed out software development and back-office work to India and other countries with lower wages. However, advancements in American worker productivity have made it possible to have fewer U.S. employees to produce certain items, resulting in cost savings, even at higher wage rates. Hence, those jobs are not being exported to other countries. In addition, companies may experience recruiting challenges as they begin hiring local talent because job candidates, might not be adequately prepared for employment, as is the case sometimes in India.[19]

The use of the Internet has resulted in recruiting in more varied geographic regions. But recruiting employees for global assignments may present problems that require different approaches from those used in the home country. The recruiting processes must account for variations in culture, laws, and language, as well as the individual preferences of potential workers. Dealing with foreign labor markets can also be challenging because recruiting can be regulated and require the approval of local personnel or labor authorities. Hiring foreign employees in the United States is subject to certain legal requirements, including visa requirements, and organizations must be concerned about hiring illegal immigrants.

L02 Discuss the strategic decisions covering recruiting image, outsourcing, and other related areas.

6-3 ■ STRATEGIC RECRUITING DECISIONS

When there are economic declines in certain geographic areas and occupations, many talented individuals become available, and recruiting costs can be lower.[20] But whether recruits are plentiful or scarce, employers must decide on several basic recruiting issues.

6-3a Recruiting Presence and Image

Recruiting efforts may be viewed as either continuous or intensive. Continuous efforts to recruit offer the advantage of keeping the employer in the recruiting market. For example, with college recruiting, some organizations may find it advantageous to have a recruiter on a given campus each year. Employers who visit a campus only occasionally are less likely to build a following at that school over time. Also, continuous recruiting may lead to constant Internet job postings, contact with recruiting consultants, and other favorable market-related actions.

Intensive recruiting may take the form of a vigorous recruiting campaign aimed at hiring a given number of employees, usually within a short period of time. Sometimes such efforts are the result of unforeseeable changes in external factors, but they also can result from a failure in the HR planning system to identify needs in advance or to anticipate drastic changes in workforce needs.

Employment brand
Image of the organization that is held by both employees and outsiders.

Employment Branding and Image The **employment brand** or image of an organization is the view both employees and outsiders have of it. Organizations that are seen as desirable employers are better able to attract qualified applicants than are those with poor reputations. For example, a successful company might offer excellent opportunities for advancement to employees, which can greatly enhance the corporate brand image. However, if the workplace is consistently stressful, and employees must work long hours to be considered for these advancement opportunities, the resulting employer brands can cause high turnover and fewer applicants interested in working for the company. See the HR Perspective: Recruiting Employees at McDonald's with Positive Branding for discussion of these issues.

HR PERSPECTIVE

Recruiting Employees at McDonald's with Positive Branding

Successful companies often use branding to improve the perceptions people have about their organizations. Besides influencing what people think, positive branding can enhance the ability of companies to recruit and retain outstanding employees by increasing the number of candidates who apply for jobs and decreasing the possibility that existing employees quit. According to research, much of this employment branding revolves around creating good rewards for employees, such as good pay, providing desirable workplace opportunities, and creating positive job characteristics.

McDonald's recently determined that a vast majority of its current employees thought that the company provided good rewards, but findings also showed that customers had a far less positive impression of the organization. In an effort to improve these perceptions, McDonald's surveyed employees to determine the firm's most valued rewards, which were identified as friendly coworkers, a flexible work environment, and good career potential. In order to communicate these strengths to potential workers, the company used presentations, speeches, and Internet-based messages to spread positive employment information through the ranks, ultimately reaching many key stakeholders.

Growing evidence suggests that these employment branding efforts are working for McDonald's. The company is experiencing lower employee turnover and appears on the Best Multinational Companies to Work For list. In addition, McDonald's recently hired more than 60,000 employees in one day, which demonstrates the popularity of the company as a potential employer.[21]

Companies can spend considerable effort and money establishing brand images for their products. The same attention must be spent on developing employer brands on the basis of the many opportunities afforded to employees. These brands convey to potential job candidates the benefits of working for particular organizations, and research indeed suggests that individuals evaluate employer brands when looking for work. The positive perceptions generated by these brands should also be based on a positive Employee Value Proposition, which is developed by highlighting a company's commitment to employee excellence and development.[22] The company brand can help generate more recruits through applicant self-selection because it affects whether individuals ever consider a firm and submit applications. Recruiting and employer branding should be seen as part of organizational marketing efforts and linked to the overall image and reputation of the organization and its industry.

6-3b Organization-Based versus Outsourced Recruiting

A basic decision that needs to be made is whether the recruiting will be done by the employer or outsourced to a third party. This decision need not be an either/or situation entirely. In most organizations, HR staff members handle many of the recruiting efforts. However, because recruiting can be a time-consuming process and HR staff and managers in organizations have many other responsibilities, outsourcing is a way to decrease the number of staff needed for recruiting and free some of their time for other responsibilities.

Recruitment process outsourcing (RPO) can be done to improve the number and quality of candidates, as well as to reduce recruiting costs.[23] Estimates are that RPO is expected to grow significantly in the near future. Both large and small employers in different industries outsource functions such as placement of advertisements, initial screening of résumés, and initial telephone contacts with potential applicants.

Professional Employer Organizations and Employee Leasing A specific type of outsourcing is professional employer organizations (PEOs) and the employee leasing process. The employee leasing process is simple: An employer signs an agreement with the PEO, after which the employer's staff is hired by the leasing firm and leased back to the company for a fee. In turn, the leasing firm writes the paychecks, pays taxes, prepares and implements HR policies, keeps all the required HR records for the employer, and bears legal liability.

One advantage of leasing companies for employees is that they may receive better benefits than they otherwise would get in many of the small businesses. But all this service comes at a cost to employers. Leasing companies often charge employers between 4% and 6% of employees' monthly salaries. Thus, while leasing may save employers money on benefits and HR administration, it also may increase total payroll costs.

A PEO and an employment agency are different types of entities. A PEO has its own workforce, which it supplies by contract to employers with jobs. However, an employment agency provides a "work-finding" service for job seekers and supplies employers with applicants whom they may then hire.

6-3c Regular versus Flexible Staffing

Another strategic decision involves how much recruiting will be done to fill staffing needs with regular full-time or part-time employees. Decisions as to who should be recruited hinge on whether to seek regular employees or to use more flexible approaches, which might include temporaries or independent contractors. Many employers have decided that the cost of keeping a regular workforce has become excessive and is growing worse because of economic, competitive, and governmental requirements. However, not just money is at issue. The large number of employment regulations also constrains the employment relationship, making many employers reluctant to hire new regular full-time employees.

Flexible staffing involves workers who are not traditional employees. Using flexible staffing arrangements allows an employer to avoid some of the cost of full-time benefits such as vacation pay, health care, and pension plans. Flexible staffing may lead to recruiting in different markets, since it includes the use of temporary workers and independent contractors. Despite the many benefits, there are also many challenges associated with using flexible staffing, including low motivation, performance, and increased costs. Many of the pros and cons associated with flexible staffing are presented in Figure 6-4.[24]

Temporary Workers Employers that use temporary employees can hire their own temporary staff members or contract with agencies supplying temporary workers on an hourly, daily, or weekly rate. Originally developed to provide clerical and office workers to employers, temporary workers in professional, technical, and even managerial jobs are becoming more common. This reality is driven by the many benefits that these workers provide organizations.

Some employers hire temporary workers as a way to screen individuals to move into full-time, regular employment. Better-performing workers may move to regular positions when these positions become available. This "try before you buy" approach is potentially beneficial to both employers and employees. In addition, companies hire temporary workers because matching the firm's needs with the right workers can be easier, the costs associated with benefits can be avoided, and staffing flexibility is often greatly enhanced. For example, Harley-Davidson recently

FIGURE 6-4 Pros and Cons of Utilizing Flexible Staffing

Pros	Cons
• Enables organizations to hire workers without incurring high costs.	• Flexible workers can sometimes exhibit poor job performance in the workplace.
• Reduces time spent on recruiting efforts, including efforts spent on the screening and initial training of workers.	• Low motivation might occur because of a lack of opportunity for long-term employment and job advancement.
• Facilitates a flexible workplace model in some organizations.	• Time limits on temporary work contracts prevent significant enhancements in individual skills and knowledge.
• Companies can avoid litigation associated with the termination of permanent workers.	• Companies might have to offer premium wages to attract individuals working in more advanced fields.
• Severance benefits not usually provided to individuals when work ends.	

agreed to a new union contract that enables the company to hire and utilize temporary workers on an as needed basis without providing guaranteed hours or benefits.[25] However, if individuals come through temporary service firms, those firms typically bill client companies a placement charge if a temporary worker is hired full-time. Also, employing temporary workers as opposed to full-time workers can have implications in regard to federal laws such as the Family Medical Leave Act, the Fair Labor Standards Act, and others.[26]

Independent Contractors Some firms employ independent contractors as workers who perform specific services on a contract basis. These workers must be truly independent as determined by regulations used by the U.S. Internal Revenue Service and the U.S. Department of Labor. This information is discussed further in Chapter 11. Independent contractors are used in many areas, including building maintenance, security, advertising, and others. One major reason for the use of independent contractors is that some employers experience significant savings because benefits are not provided to those individuals. From an independent contractor perspective, a recent study also found that the motivation to enter such an agreement appears to be higher among highly skilled individuals who are either beginning their careers or fully experienced in their professions. At least for men, the motivation to perform contract work decreases as responsibilities to family become more prominent.[27]

6-3d Recruiting and EEO: Diversity Considerations

Recruiting strategies take into account a number of EEO and diversity considerations. Figure 6-5 shows the major issues companies face when proactively addressing a diverse applicant pool.

EEO and Recruiting Efforts Recruiting is a key employment-related activity and is subject to various considerations, especially equal employment laws and regulations.

FIGURE 6-5 Recruiting and Diversity Considerations

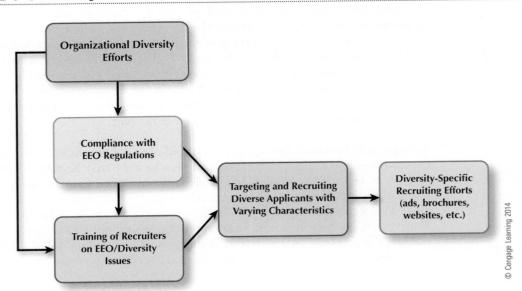

As part of legal compliance in the recruiting process, organizations may work to reduce disparate impact, or underrepresentation of protected-class members compared to the labor markets utilized by the employer. If disparate impact exists, then the employer may need to make special efforts to persuade protected-class individuals to apply for jobs. For employers with affirmative action programs (AAPs), special ways to reduce disparate impact can be identified as goals listed in those plans. Also, many employers who emphasize internal recruiting should take steps to attract minority applicants externally if disparate impact exists in the current workforce.

EEOC guidelines state that no direct or indirect statements of gender or age are permitted. These guidelines affect interviews, advertisements, and other recruiting activities. Some examples of impermissible terminology are *young and enthusiastic*, *Christian values*, and *journeyman lineman*. Also, advertisements should contain wording about being an equal opportunity employer, or even more specific designations such as EEO/M-F/AA/ADA. Employers demonstrate inclusive recruiting by having diverse individuals represented in company materials, in advertisements, and as recruiters.

Recruiting Diversity A broad range of factors can be considered when recruiting for diversity. Many employers have expanded efforts to recruit workers from what, for some, are nontraditional labor pools. Nontraditional diverse recruitees for certain jobs may include the following:

- Persons with different racial/ethnic backgrounds
- Workers over 40 years of age; particularly retirees
- Single parents
- Workers with disabilities
- Welfare-to-work workers
- Homeless/substance abuse workers

The growth in racial/ethnic workforce diversity means that a wider range of potential employment sources should be utilized. Changes in diversity also need to be monitored and evaluated to ensure that the workplace, through properly managed recruiting strategies, is representative of these population demographics. For example, the growth in Hispanics in the United States means that specialized recruiting programs might be needed to identify qualified individuals from this group for employment. Other potential employees may include older workers and retirees who are interested in seeking new employment opportunities. Single parents may be attracted to a family-friendly employer that offers flexibility, including part-time work, because it is frequently difficult to balance job and family life. Some firms also recruit stay-at-home parents by using flexibility and work-at-home technology. Finally, individuals with disabilities are another group of potential human resources, a group that has been overlooked in the past.

Realistic Job Previews Providing a balanced view of the advantages, demands, expectations, and challenges in an organization or a job may help attract employees with more realistic expectations and reduce the number of employees who quit a few months after being hired because the "reality" they discover does not match what they expected. See the HR Skills and Applications: Realistic Job Previews Showcase Work for examples of this approach. Recruiting efforts can benefit from *realistic job previews (RJPs)*, but their usage must be monitored. RJPs will be further discussed in the next chapter as part of the selection process.[28]

HR SKILLS AND APPLICATIONS

Realistic Job Previews Showcase Work

Many employers utilize realistic job previews as a basis to more effectively recruit good employees. Companies that utilize such previews provide a better snapshot of the jobs being staffed, which ultimately enhances retention, mainly because individuals feel more informed about the expectations associated with work. Even though companies have been using such approaches for the last 50 years, the process is becoming popular again because of high turnover rates experienced in some organizations. In fact, realistic job previews can reduce the expenses associated with recruiting because candidates can be more effectively matched with important job expectations, thereby ensuring that there is a stronger bond between work and worker. Realistic job previews work particularly well with employees who have limited job experiences in a profession, and individual turnover in the earlier stages of employment can be reduced by ensuring that there is a proper match.

Many companies have used realistic job previews to good effect. The recruitment of housekeeping staff in the franchised properties of Hilton and Aloft BWI Airport has been greatly enhanced by using different worker exercises that determine good job fit. The convenience store chain Sheetz uses a series of video-based job presentations to convey to candidates the basic expectations of different positions in the organization. The Idaho State Police also uses realistic job previews to reduce turnover on the force, requiring candidates to ride with current police officers and to participate in a walk-through of work areas.[29]

6-3e Recruiting Source Choices: Internal versus External

Most employers combine the use of internal and external recruiting sources. Both promoting from within the organization (internal recruitment) and hiring from outside the organization (external recruitment) come with advantages and disadvantages.

Organizations that face rapidly changing competitive environments and conditions may need to place a heavier emphasis on external sources in addition to developing internal sources. A possible strategy might be to promote from within if a qualified applicant exists and to go to external sources if not. However, for organizations operating in environments that change slowly, emphasis on promotion from within may be more suitable. Recent evidence suggests that internal recruiting might produce the best results overall because existing employees who are given new work opportunities tend to perform considerably better than external hires, at least in the first three years of employment in a new job.[30] Once the various recruiting policy decisions have been addressed, the actual recruiting methods can be identified and used for both internal and external recruiting.

L03 Explain why Internet recruiting has grown and how it affects recruiting efforts done by employers.

6-4 ■ INTERNET RECRUITING

The Internet has become the primary means for many employers to search for job candidates and for applicants to look for jobs. The growth in Internet use is a key reason that the following employer actions occur:

- Adjusting general employer recruiting systems to use new approaches
- Identifying new types of recruiting for specific jobs
- Training managers and HR professionals on technical recruiting sources, skills, and responsibilities

6-4a E-Recruiting Media or Methods

The growth in the Internet has led both employers and employees to use Internet recruiting tools. Internet links, Web 2.0 sites, blogs, tweets, and other types of Internet/Web-based applications have become viable parts of recruiting. One survey of e-recruiting software providers identified numerous firms as e-recruiting clients, and some of them serve more than 1,000 employers.[31] Of the many recruiting sites using special software, the most common ones are Internet job boards, professional/career websites, and employer websites.

Internet Job Boards Many Internet job boards, such as Monster, Yahoo!, and HotJobs, provide places for employers to post jobs or search for candidates. Job boards offer access to numerous candidates. Recruiters can use a single website, such as MyJobHunter.com, to obtain search links to many other major job sites. Applicants can also use these websites to do one match and then send résumés to all jobs in which they are interested.[32] However, many of the individuals accessing these sites are "job lookers" who are not serious about changing jobs, but are checking out compensation levels and job availability in their areas of interest. Despite such concerns, HR recruiters find general job boards useful for generating applicant responses.

Professional/Career Websites Many professional associations have employment links on their websites. As illustration, for HR jobs, see the Society for Human Resource Management site, www.shrm.org, or WorldatWork, www.worldatwork .org. SHRM has established a job posting center that recruiters and employers can use to post a wide range of HR openings.[33] Many private corporations maintain specialized career or industry websites to focus on IT, telecommunications, engineering, medicine, and other areas. Use of these targeted websites may slightly limit recruiters' search time and efforts. Also, posting jobs on such websites is likely to target applicants specifically interested in the job field and may reduce the number of applications from less-qualified applicants.

Employer Websites Despite the popularity of job boards and association job sites, many employers have learned that their own company websites can be very effective and efficient when recruiting candidates and reinforcing the employer brand. Employers include employment and career information on their websites under headings such as "Employment" or "Careers." This is the place where recruiting (both internal and external) is often conducted. On many of these sites, job seekers are encouraged to e-mail résumés or complete online applications.

Since a website can be an effective tool for marketing the company, the formatting of the employment section of an organization's website must be creative and attractive enough to market jobs and careers effectively. A company website should present a favorable image of the employer by outlining information on the organization, including its products and services, organizational and industry growth potential, and organizational operations. In addition, a recent study determined that including positive employee testimonials on recruiting websites made the employer more desirable and credible to job candidates; so HR departments and other hiring managers should consider incorporating such statements into the online-recruiting process.[34]

6-4b Recruiting and Internet Social Networking

The Internet has led to social networking of individuals on blogs, tweets, and a range of websites. Many people initially use social media more than job board sites to look for a job.[35] Internet contacts often include people who work together as well as past personal contacts and friends. Evidence suggests that many graduates are using social media and the Internet to locate work opportunities, and many companies are utilizing technology to more extensively identify and attract talent. HR professionals in a variety of organizations such as UnitedHealth Group and DeVry University are utilizing some form of social networking to enhance the recruitment of employees. In addition, UPS is using Web 2.0 and other technology to better communicate with potential hires by posting employment announcements and video messages about work in the company and offering smartphone job application opportunities. Further, AT&T and Hewitt Associates have developed similar mobile recruiting strategies, whereby cell phones are used to better communicate with job candidates.[36]

The informal use of the Web and mobile devices presents some interesting recruiting advantages and disadvantages for both employers and employees. Social networking sites allow job seekers to connect with employees of potential hirers. For instance, some sites include posts on what it is like to work for a specific boss, and job hunters can contact the posters and ask questions. An example is LinkedIn, which has a job-search engine that allows people to search for contacts who work for employers with posted job openings.

Firms and employers are now engaging in social collaboration by joining and accessing social technology networks such as Facebook and others. Posting job openings on these sites means that millions of website users can see the openings and can make contact online. Often those doing recruiting can send individuals to the company website and then process candidates using electronic résumés or completed online applications.[37] See the HR Skills and Applications: Social Networking Enhances Recruiting Efforts.

Job Applicants and Social Network Sites Many individuals see social media and networking websites as a key part of online recruiting. A study of 200 users of one such website indicated that the individuals who were job seeking were doing so for proactive reasons such as career opportunities, job inquiries, and others. Relatively few of them were passive job seekers who were just looking at website information.[38]

Almost half of surveyed employers indicated that instead of using general job boards, they were changing to social networking and niche job sites for recruiting workers with specific skills. However, employers who use social networking sites for recruiting must have plans and well-defined recruiting tools to take full advantage of these sites.[39]

HR SKILLS AND APPLICATIONS

Social Networking Enhances Recruiting Efforts

HR professionals are utilizing social networking websites as a cost-effective tool for identifying quality talent. Social networking sites have the capacity to link a multitude of online communities and users so that people can exchange a variety of information. Membership within these online websites is typically free, and the networks are extensive, so interest among both potential employees and companies is high given that communication is greatly enhanced. In fact, many companies are creating career "microsites" and other online interactive communities to more readily share employment information and opportunities with potential employees. These efforts position companies much more competitively with recruiting, and demonstrate to candidates a belief in using the latest technology to improve communication. Social networking can enhance recruiting in the following ways:

- The use of social networking websites creates more standardization in the résumés included online, and information can be assessed by recruiters much more easily.

- The technology enables companies to identify and possibly attract passive talent, or those individuals who are qualified for work in other companies, but who are not currently looking to change jobs (and do not have an updated résumé).

Companies should also consider some key challenges associated with social networking recruitment:

- HR professionals should not rely exclusively on social networking websites to recruit new employees because not everyone utilizes these websites; doing so might hurt a company's ability to hire the most qualified individuals for jobs.
- Recruiting through social networking websites must align with current staffing strategies utilized by the organization, and the recruiting experiences of candidates should be consistent across the different types of technology used to identify talent (i.e., social networking vs. e-mail, social networking vs. website, etc.).[40]

6-4c Recruiting Using Special Technology Means

For many years, the Internet has been used by people globally. Several special Internet tools that can be used as part of recruiting efforts are blogs, e-videos, and tweets.

Blogs and Recruiting Both employers and individuals have used blogs as part of recruiting to fill jobs. Firms such as Best Buy, Microsoft, Honeywell, and Manpower have used blogs on which individuals could read and provide content. For instance, describing job openings and recruiting needs on the Best Buy blog has resulted in individuals responding to job ads in areas such as finance, marketing, HR, and other specialties. Numerous other employers have used blogs to generate recruiting interest as well.[41]

E-Video and Recruiting With video capabilities of all types available, employers are using videos in several ways. Some firms use videos to describe their company characteristics, job opportunities, and recruiting means. Suppliers such as Monster.com,

CareerTV, and others have worked with employer clients to produce online recruitment videos.[42] UPS also uses video messages about the company to attract new employees, and this approach, as well as others, have dramatically enhanced the firm's ability to effectively hire employees.[43]

Recruiting through Twitter Twitter can be used for many purposes, including personal, social, legal, and employment-related messages. More than 7 million people have joined Twitter.com to become "tweeters." One professional sent a tweet in January, and by June of that year more than 20,000 people had responded by contacting JobAngels with tweets.[44]

The Twitter system limits messages to 140 specific characters, but even so tweeting has rapidly become a social network recruiting method. Recruiters send tweet messages to both active and passive job candidates, and then follow up with longer e-mails to computers, personal contacts, and other actions to facilitate recruiting. Since Twitter is a relatively new service, the process of how exactly it will be best used for recruiting is still evolving.[45]

ETHICS

6-4d Legal Issues in Internet Recruiting

With Internet recruiting expanding, new and different concerns have arisen. Several of these issues have ethical and moral as well as legal implications. The following examples illustrate some of these concerns:

- When companies use screening software to avoid looking at the thousands of résumés they receive, are rejections really based on the qualifications needed for the job?
- How can data about an individual's protected characteristics be collected and analyzed for reports?
- Are too many individuals being excluded from the later phases of the Internet-recruiting process based on unlawful information?
- Which applicants really want jobs? If someone has accessed a job board and sent an e-mail asking an employer about a job opening, does the person actually want to be an applicant?
- What are the implications of Internet recruiting in terms of confidentiality and privacy?

Loss of privacy is a potential disadvantage with Internet recruiting. Sharing information gleaned from people who apply to job boards or even company websites has become common. As a company receives résumés from applicants, it is required to track those applicants and file its EEO report. But the personal information that can be seen by employers on websites such as Facebook, LinkedIn, and others may be inappropriate and can possibly violate legal provisions. Also, blogging creates enough possible legal concerns that regulations may be implemented by the U.S. Federal Trade Commission (FTC).[46]

Employment lawyers are issuing warnings to employers about using remarks posted on LinkedIn, Facebook, and Twitter in the hiring process. According to one survey of employers, about three-fourths of hiring managers in various-sized companies checked persons' credentials on LinkedIn, about half used Facebook, and approximately one-fourth used Twitter.[47] Some of the concerns raised have included postings of confidential details about an employee's termination, racial/ethnic background or gender, and the making of discriminatory comments. All of these actions could lead to wrongful termination or discrimination lawsuits. Since

The Ethics of Hiring through Social Media

The use of social media such as You Tube, Facebook, and Twitter, and other online groups to recruit employees has become commonplace in organizations. Even though social networking can be a useful approach for identifying good talent, there are some inherent risks and ethical issues related to such a recruiting strategy. Indeed, many companies have not developed specific policies about how online information should be used in recruiting efforts, which raises legal concerns. For instance, when social media is used to obtain information about applicants, individuals might be able to claim they have been discriminated against on the basis of criteria unrelated to the job itself (i.e., race, ethnicity, gender, etc.). Making matters worse, individuals can be screened out early in the application process when demographic factors can be used in a biased and unethical way. Further, other information that should not be used in the decision to grant employment can be obtained, such as religious affiliation, lifestyle, and medical concerns. The following list provides a summary of several key guidelines that should be considered when using social media as a tool for hiring good employees:

- HR professionals should conduct social media Internet searches rather than hiring managers so that these background checks are conducted in an unbiased manner.
- Social media background information should be considered only after an individual has been interviewed for a position, which better ensures EEO compliance.
- Social media checks should be conducted at the same point in the application process for all candidates.
- Document what information was used from social media to take a candidate out of the applicant pool.[48]

Internet usage has legal implications for recruiting, HR employment-related policies, training, and enforcement should be based on legal advice. In addition to various legal challenges, there are many ethical concerns related to social media hiring, and the HR Ethics: The Ethics of Hiring through Social Media discusses some of these challenges.

6-4e Advantages of Internet Recruiting

Employers have found many advantages to using Internet recruiting. Compared to other recruiting methods such as newspaper advertising, employment agencies, and search firms Internet recruiting can save the company money. Another major advantage is that, by reaching out to so many people potentially representing diverse backgrounds and regions, a very large pool of applicants can be generated using Internet recruiting.

Internet recruiting can also save time. Applicants can respond quickly to job postings by sending electronic responses, rather than using snail mail. Recruiters can respond more rapidly to qualified candidates to obtain additional applicant information, request additional candidate details, and establish times for further communication, including interviews.[49]

A good website and useful Internet resources can also help recruiters reach "passive" job seekers—those who have a good job and are not really looking to change jobs but who might consider it if a better opportunity were presented. These individuals often do not list themselves on job boards, but they might visit a company website for other reasons and check out the careers or employment section. A well-designed corporate website can help stimulate interest in some passive job seekers, as well as other potential candidates.

6-4f Disadvantages of Internet Recruiting

The positive things associated with Internet recruiting should be balanced against disadvantages, some of which have already been suggested. Because of broader exposure, Internet recruiting often creates additional work for HR staff members and others internally. More online job postings must be sent; many more résumés must be reviewed; more e-mails, blogs, and tweets need to be dealt with; and expensive specialized software may be needed to track the increased number of applicants resulting from Internet-recruiting efforts. In addition, many of the online applicants might not be qualified for open jobs, and some companies are shying away from Internet boards in favor of social networking websites that provide better leads. Further, while different social networking websites such as LinkedIn and Twitter can be viable sources of leads, there is reason to believe that some individuals don't like to be bothered with work-related information on their Facebook accounts, and that a sufficient return on investment is not generated.[50]

Another issue with Internet recruiting is that some applicants may have limited Internet access, especially individuals from lower socioeconomic groups and from certain racial/ethnic groups, raising issues of fairness in hiring. Indeed, a recent study determined that individuals perceived greater fairness in more traditional (offline) application approaches compared to online approaches.[51] In addition, it is easy to access Internet-recruiting sources, but not all who do so are actively looking for new jobs. However, they require much employer time to process.

Internet recruiting is only one approach to recruiting, but its use has been expanding. Also, how well the Internet recruiting resources perform must be compared to the effectiveness of other external and internal recruiting sources.

LO4 Highlight five external recruiting sources.

6-5 ◼ OTHER EXTERNAL RECRUITING SOURCES

External recruiting is part of effective HR staffing. Regardless of the methods used, external recruiting involves some common advantages and disadvantages, which are highlighted in Figure 6-6. Some of the prominent traditional and evolving recruiting methods are highlighted next.

6-5a Media Sources

Media sources such as newspapers, magazines, television, radio, and billboards have typically been widely used in external recruiting. Some firms have sent direct mail using purchased lists of individuals in certain fields or industries. Internet usage has led to media sources being available online, including postings, ads,

FIGURE 6-6 Advantages and Disadvantages of External Recruiting

Advantages	Disadvantages
• New employees bring new perspectives that can be applied to business opportunities and challenges. • Training new hires may be cheaper and faster because of prior external experience. • New hires are likely to have fewer internal political issues/challenges in the firm. • New hires may bring new industry insights and expertise. • Potentially larger applicant pool generated by search efforts.	• The firm may not select someone who will fit well with the job and the organization. • The process may cause morale problems for internal candidates not selected. • New employees may require longer adjustment periods and orientation efforts. • The recruiting process may take more time and resources. • Recruiters often must evaluate more applications.

© Cengage Learning 2014

videos, Webinars, and many other expanding media services. In some cities and towns, newspaper ads are still very prominent, though they may trigger job searchers to go to an Internet source for more details.

Recruiting patterns differ depending on company and location; for instance, filling jobs at community banks in rural areas might involve different types of recruiting from filling jobs in larger banks in urban areas.[52] Whatever medium is used, it should be tied to the relevant labor market, the job, the company, and should provide sufficient, easy-to-understand information. Figure 6-7 shows the information a good recruiting ad contains.

Effectiveness of Evaluating Media Ads HR recruiters should measure the responses that different ads generate to evaluate the effectiveness of various sources. The easiest way to track responses to ads is to use different contact names, e-mail addresses, or phone number codes in each ad, so the employer can identify which advertisement has prompted each applicant response that is received.

Although the total number of responses to each ad should be tracked, judging the success of an ad only by this number is a mistake. For example, it is better to have 10 responses with two qualified applicants than 30 responses with only one qualified applicant. Therefore, after individuals are hired, follow-up should be done to see which sources produced the employees who stay longer and perform better.

6-5b Competitive Recruiting Sources

Other sources for recruiting include professional and trade associations, trade publications, and competitors. Many professional societies and trade associations publish newsletters or magazines and have websites containing job ads. Such sources may be useful for recruiting the specialized professionals needed in an industry.

Some employers have extended recruiting to customers. Retailers such as Wal-Mart and Best Buy have aggressive programs to recruit customers to become employees in stores. While in the store, customers at these firms can pick up applications, apply online using kiosks, and even schedule interviews with managers or

FIGURE 6-7 What to Include in an Effective Recruiting Ad

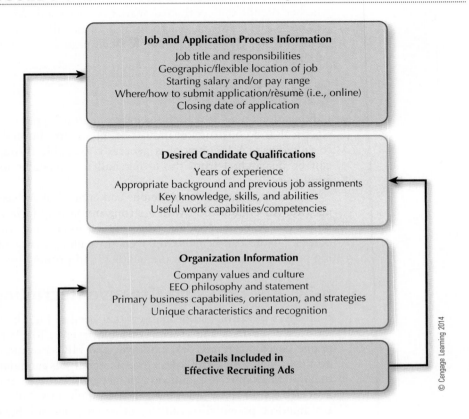

Job and Application Process Information

Job title and responsibilities
Geographic/flexible location of job
Starting salary and/or pay range
Where/how to submit application/rèsumè (i.e., online)
Closing date of application

Desired Candidate Qualifications

Years of experience
Appropriate background and previous job assignments
Key knowledge, skills, and abilities
Useful work capabilities/competencies

Organization Information

Company values and culture
EEO philosophy and statement
Primary business capabilities, orientation, and strategies
Unique characteristics and recognition

**Details Included in
Effective Recruiting Ads**

© Cengage Learning 2014

HR staff members. Other firms have included employment announcements when sending out customer bills or newsletters.

6-5c Employment Agencies

Employment agencies, both public and private, are a recruiting source. Every state in the United States has its own state-sponsored employment agency. These agencies operate branch offices in cities throughout the states and do not charge fees to applicants or employers. They also have websites that potential applicants can use without having to go to the offices.

Private employment agencies operate in most cities. For a fee collected from either the employee or the employer, these agencies do some preliminary screening and put employers in touch with applicants. Private employment agencies differ considerably in the levels of service, costs, policies, and types of applicants they provide.

Headhunters
Employment agencies that focus their efforts on executive, managerial, and professional positions.

Headhunters The size of the fees and the aggressiveness with which some firms pursue candidates for executive and other openings have led to such firms being called **headhunters**. These employment agencies focus their efforts on executive, managerial, and professional positions. The executive search firms are split into two groups: (1) *contingency firms* that charge a fee only after a candidate has been hired by a client company, and (2) *retainer firms* that charge a client a set fee whether or not the contracted search is successful. Most larger firms work on a retainer basis. However, search firms are generally ethically bound not to approach employees of client companies in their search for job candidates for another employer.[53]

6-5d Labor Unions

Labor unions may be a useful source of certain types of workers. For example, in electrical and construction industries, unions traditionally have supplied workers to employers. A labor pool is generally available through a union, and workers can be dispatched from the hiring hall to particular jobs to meet the needs of employers.

In some instances, labor unions can control or influence recruiting and staffing activity. An organization with a strong union may have less flexibility than a non-union company in deciding who will be hired and where those people will be placed. Unions can benefit employers through apprenticeship and cooperative staffing programs, as they do in the building and printing industries.

6-5e Job Fairs and Creative Recruiting

Employers in various labor markets that need to fill a large number of jobs quickly have used job fairs and special recruiting events. Job fairs have been held by economic development entities, employer and HR associations, and other community groups to help bring employers and potential job candidates together. For instance, the SHRM chapter in a midwestern metropolitan area annually sponsors a job fair at which 75 to 100 employers can meet applicants. Publicity in the city draws several hundred potential recruits for different types of jobs. However, two cautionary notes are in order: (1) Some employers at job fairs may see attendees who are currently their employees "shopping" for jobs with other employers; and (2) "general" job fairs are likely to attract many people, including attendees who are not only unemployed but also unemployable. Industry- or skill-specific events usually offer more satisfactory candidates. Such job fairs can also attract employed candidates who are casually looking around but may not put their résumés on the Internet.

Virtual job fairs with Web-based links have been used by the federal government and others for recruiting. Drive-through job fairs at shopping malls have been used by employers in many communities. At one such event, interested persons could drive up to a tent outside the mall, pick up applications from a "menu board" of employers, and then park and interview in the tent with recruiters if time allowed. Such creative recruiting methods can sometimes be used to generate a pool of qualified applicants quickly so that jobs can be filled in a timely manner.

6-5f Educational Institutions and Recruiting

College and university students are a significant source of entry-level professional and technical employees. Most universities maintain career placement offices in which employers and applicants can meet. Many considerations affect an employer's choice of colleges and universities at which to conduct interviews, as Figure 6-8 indicates.

Since college/university recruiting can be expensive and require significant time and effort, employers need to determine whether current and future jobs require

FIGURE 6-8 College Recruiting: Considerations for Employers

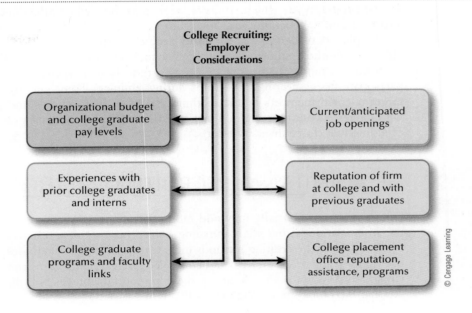

individuals with college degrees in specific fields. Despite economic changes in many industries and among employers, a majority of organizations that were surveyed still plan to have more than half of their hires be college graduates.[54]

Numerous factors determine success in college recruiting. Some employers actively build continuing relationships with individual faculty members and career staff at designated colleges and universities. Maintaining a presence on campus by providing guest speakers to classes and student groups increases the contacts for an employer. Employers with a continuing presence and support on a campus are more likely to see positive college recruiting results.

Desirable Attributes of College Recruits For many employers, a desirable grade point average (GPA) is a key criterion for evaluating job candidates during on-campus interviews. Attending elite universities can also enhance the attractiveness of a candidate for some, but evidence suggests that, in the long run, there is little difference in success between individuals who attend more prestigious schools and those who do not.[55] In addition, employers are also more likely to hire college candidates with related employment experience, which is why internships are very important to employers, candidates, and college/university efforts. Internships give college students the opportunity to work for different companies and gain important experience. These work arrangements often lead to full-time employment after graduation, benefiting both the intern and the hiring organization. A recent study found that both interns and companies use different impression management and interactive strategies to enhance the likelihood that a positive hiring decision will be prompted by the internship.[56]

School Recruiting High schools and vocational/technical schools may be valuable sources of new employees for some organizations. Many schools have a centralized guidance or placement office. Participating in career days and giving company tours to school groups are ways of maintaining good contact with school sources. Cooperative programs, in which students work part-time while attending school, may also be useful in generating qualified future applicants for full-time positions.

Employers recognize that they may need to begin attracting students with capabilities while those students are in high school. For example, GE, IBM, and other corporations fund programs to encourage students with science and math skills to participate in engineering internships during summers. Some employers specifically target talented members of racial/ethnic groups in high schools and provide them with career encouragement, summer internships, and mentoring programs as part of aiding workforce diversity efforts.

6-6 ■ INTERNAL RECRUITING METHODS

L05 Identify three internal sources for recruiting and issues associated with their use.

Filling openings internally may add motivation for employees to stay and grow in the organization rather than pursuing career opportunities elsewhere. The most common internal recruiting methods include organizational databases, job postings, promotions and transfers, current-employee referrals, and re-recruiting of former employees and applicants. Some of the common advantages and disadvantages of internal recruiting are highlighted in Figure 6-9.

6-6a Internal Recruiting Databases and Internet-Related Sources

HR information technology systems allow HR staff to maintain background and knowledge, skills, and abilities (KSA) information on existing employees. As openings arise, HR can access databases by entering job requirements and then get a listing of current employees meeting those requirements. Software can sort employee data by occupational fields, education, areas of career interests, previous work histories, and other variables. For instance, if a firm has an opening for someone with

FIGURE 6-9 Advantages and Disadvantages of Internal Recruiting

Advantages	Disadvantages
• The morale of a promotee is usually high.	• "Inbreeding" of employees may result in a less diverse workforce, as well as a lack of new ideas.
• The firm can better assess a candidate's abilities on the basis of prior work performance.	• Individuals not promoted may experience morale problems.
• Recruiting costs are lower for some jobs.	• Employees may engage in "political" infighting for promotions.
• The process is a motivator for good performances by employees.	• A development program often is needed to transfer employees into supervisory and management jobs.
• The process can aid succession planning, future promotions, and career development.	• Some managers may resist having employees promoted into their departments.

© Cengage Learning 2014

an MBA and marketing experience, the key words *MBA* and *marketing* can be entered in a search field, and the program displays a list of all current employees with these two items identified in their employee profiles. Online and electronic talent profiles can also be developed to identify good talent. Companies such as Hoover's Inc., and New Balance Athletic Shoe Inc., are using such innovative approaches to be more effective at filling jobs.[57]

The advantage of such databases is that they can be linked to other HR activities. Opportunities for career development and advancement are major reasons why individuals stay at or leave their employers. With employee databases, internal opportunities for individuals can be identified. Employee profiles are continually updated to include items such as additional training and education completed, special projects handled, and career plans and desires noted during performance appraisals and career-mentoring discussions.

6-6b Job Posting

Job posting
System in which the employer provides notices of job openings and employees respond by applying for specific openings.

The major means for recruiting current employees for other jobs within the organization is **job posting,** a system in which the employer provides notices of job openings and employees respond by applying for specific openings. Without some sort of job posting system, it is difficult for many employees to find out what jobs are open elsewhere in the organization. In many unionized organizations, job posting and bidding can be quite formal because the procedures are often spelled out in labor agreements. Seniority lists may be used by organizations that make promotions based strictly on seniority.

Regardless of the means used, the purpose of the job posting system is to provide employees with more opportunities to move within the organization. When establishing and managing a job posting system, some questions can be addressed:

- What happens if no qualified candidates respond to postings?
- Must employees inform their supervisors that they are applying for another job?
- Are there restrictions on how long an employee must stay in a job before applying for another internal one?
- What types of or levels of jobs will not be posted?

Internet/Web-Based Job Posting While many employers historically have had some kind of job posting system in place for internal jobs, many companies are using proactive efforts to get employees to apply through Web-based systems. Kenexa, Oracle, Softscape, LinkedIn, ResumePal, Facebook, and JobFox are just some of the vendors that provide internal recruiting website job posting. The complexity of using such job posting methods varies according to the employer and the technology capabilities and systems available.[58] Employees can log onto a company intranet and create personal profiles, including career objectives, education, skill sets, and pay expectations. They may also attach a résumé. When a job opens, the placement program automatically mines the database for matches. Candidates are then notified by e-mail and go through the regular hiring cycle.

Effective Job Posting For job posting efforts to be effective, especially with better-performing employees, posting wording must be relevant and accurate. Also, the posting should be based on the important characteristics needed. People are more likely to respond because of the job's reputation, coworkers and bosses, and the possibility of more important and interesting work.[59]

Jobs generally are posted internally before any external recruiting is done. The organization must allow a reasonable period of time for present employees to check notices of available jobs before it considers external applicants. Employees whose bids are turned down should discuss with their supervisors or someone in the HR department what knowledge, skills, and abilities are needed to improve their opportunities in the future.

Promotions and Transfers Many organizations choose to fill vacancies through promotions or transfers from within whenever possible. Firms such as Verizon Communications, Dow Chemical, Microsoft, and IBM have established systems to encourage employees to learn about current and future career needs and opportunities. Some advantages of these programs are reducing employee turnover, enhancing individuals' skills and talent, and improving productivity.[60]

Although often successful, internal transfer and promotion of employees within the company may have some drawbacks. For instance, a person's performance on one job may not be a good predictor of performance on another, because different skills may be required on the new job. Also, as employees transfer or are promoted to other jobs, individuals must be recruited to fill the vacated jobs. Planning on how to fill those openings should occur before the job transfers or promotions, not afterward.

6-6c Employee-Focused Recruiting

One reliable source of potential recruits is suggestions from current or former employees. Because current and former employees are familiar with the employer, most of them will not refer individuals who are likely to be unqualified or who will make them look bad for giving the referral. Also, follow-up with former employees is likely to be done only with individuals who were solid employees previously. Companies are also staying in touch with former employees through online networking websites so that they may be encouraged to work for the organization again.[61]

Current-Employee Referrals A reliable source of people to fill vacancies is composed of acquaintances, friends, and family members of current employees, which is discussed in the HR Perspective: College Alumni Provide Important Recruiting Leads. Current employees can acquaint potential applicants with the advantages of a job with the company, furnish e-mails and other means of introduction, and encourage candidates to apply. Word-of-mouth referrals and discussions can positively aid organizational attractiveness and lead to more application decisions by those referred.[62] However, using only word-of-mouth or current-employee referrals can violate equal employment regulations if diverse applicants are underrepresented in the current organizational workforce. Therefore, some external recruiting might be necessary to avoid legal problems in this area.

Employers in many geographic areas and occupational fields have established employee referral incentive programs. Midsized and larger employers are more likely to use employee referral bonuses. Some referral programs provide different bonus amounts for hard-to-fill jobs compared with common openings; in these situations, appropriate legal concerns should be met.[63]

College Alumni Provide Important Recruiting Leads

Companies are finding out that current employees who attended college can sometimes be relied on to help get good talent into the organization. These individuals are often aware of other qualified students and graduates affiliated with their colleges who would like to find work. Such candidates can be identified during conversations among alumni who are currently employed in the company, or they can be considered when alumni hear about job opportunities in the firm and consider individuals they already know from their college days.

Relying on alumni can be very helpful to the recruiting function because HR professionals can get in touch with potential employees who might not have considered working for the company on their own. Employees from a particular school make the workplace more appealing to students who are currently enrolled at the same college. In this sense, alumni networking that effectively build relationships with college students can help an organization build a more positive corporate brand image. Alumni organizations at universities are also helpful when recruiters would like to identify potential job candidates who have already graduated from school. Finally, companies can send alumni to career fairs that are held on college campuses to more readily connect with current students, or alumni can visit campuses to communicate with students and evaluate their résumés.[64]

Rerecruiting
Seeking out former employees and recruiting them again to work for an organization.

Rerecruiting of Former Employees and Applicants Former employees and applicants represent another source for recruitment. Both groups offer a time-saving advantage because something is already known about them. Seeking them out as candidates is known as **rerecruiting** because they were recruited previously. Former employees are considered an internal source in the sense that they have ties to the employer; sometimes they are called "boomerangers" because they left and came back.

Individuals who have left for other jobs sometimes are willing to return because the other jobs and employers turned out to be less attractive than initially thought. For example, at Qualcomm, a California-based telecommunications firm, about 70% of former Qualcomm individuals who left voluntarily indicated that they would return if requested.[65] The discussion of exit interviews in a previous chapter illustrated that rerecruiting can be a key recruiting contribution.

To enhance such efforts, some firms have established "alumni reunions" to keep in contact with individuals who have left, and also to allow the companies to rerecruit individuals as appropriate openings arise. Key issues in the decision to rerecruit someone include the reasons why the individual left originally and whether the individual's performance and capabilities were good.

Another potential source consists of former applicants. Although they are not entirely an internal source, information about them can be found in the organizational files or an applicant database. Recontacting those who have previously applied for jobs and had good qualifications can be a quick and inexpensive way to fill unexpected openings. For instance, one firm that needed two cost accountants immediately contacted qualified previous applicants and was able to hire two individuals who were disenchanted with their current jobs at other companies.

LO6 Describe three factors to consider when using recruiting measurement and metrics.

MEASURE

6-7 ■ RECRUITING EVALUATION AND METRICS

To determine the effectiveness of various recruiting sources and methods have been, it is important to evaluate recruiting efforts. The primary way to find out whether recruiting efforts are financially effective is to conduct formal analyses as part of recruiting evaluation. An evaluation done by a consulting firm found that higher shareholder value occurred when time required for successful recruiting was used as a metric. If recruiting was completed within two weeks, the study noted that the total return to shareholders was about 60%, compared to about 10% for companies that needed more than seven weeks to fill job openings. Also, greater use of employee referrals produced a much higher return to shareholders than use of other recruiting means.[66]

Various other factors can be measured when evaluating recruiting. Figure 6-10 indicates many key recruiting measurement areas in which employers frequently conduct evaluations.

6-7a Evaluating Recruiting Quantity and Quality

Organizations evaluate recruiting effectiveness to see how their recruiting efforts compare with past patterns and with the recruiting performance of other organizations. Measures of recruiting effectiveness can be used to see whether sufficient numbers of targeted population groups are being attracted.

For example, one area of concern in recruiting might be attracting diverse applicants. In Chicago, a network-based recruiting firm received only 16 black and 4 Hispanic applicants out of 276 individuals for a customer service job. Yet Chicago has 37% blacks and 26% Hispanics in its population. Clearly, the efforts to increase recruiting in these racial/ethnic groups needed major attention.[67]

Information about job performance, absenteeism, cost of training, and turnover by recruiting source also helps adjust future recruiting efforts. For example, some companies find that recruiting at certain colleges or universities furnishes stable,

FIGURE 6-10 Recruiting Measurement Areas

Recruiting Measurement Metric Areas

Recruits:
- Quantity/Quality
- Recruitment satisfaction analyses
- Time to fill openings
- Cost per recruiting method
- Process metrics
- Yield ratios
- Selection rates
- Acceptance rates
- Success base rates

© Cengage Learning

high performers, whereas recruiting at other schools provides employees who are more prone to leave the organization. General metrics for evaluating recruiting include quantity and quality of applicants.

Quantity of Applicants Because the goal of a good recruiting program is to generate a large pool of applicants from which to choose, *quantity* is a natural place to begin evaluation. The basic measure here considers whether the quantity of recruits is sufficient to fill job vacancies. A related question is: Does recruiting at this source provide enough qualified applicants with an appropriate mix of diverse individuals?

Quality of Applicants In addition to quantity, a key issue is whether or not the qualifications of the applicants are sufficient to fill the job openings. Do the applicants meet job specifications, and do they perform the jobs well after hire? What is the failure rate for new hires for each recruiter? Measures that can be used include items such as performance appraisal scores, months until promotion, production quantity, and sales volume for each hire.

6-7b Evaluating Recruiting Satisfaction

The satisfaction of two groups is useful in evaluating recruiting. Certainly the views of managers with openings to fill are important, because they are HR "customers" in a very real sense. But the applicants (those hired and those not hired) are also an important part of the process and can provide useful input.

Managers can respond to questions about the quality of the applicant pool, the recruiter's service, the timeliness of the process, and any problems that they experienced. Applicants might provide input on how they were treated, their perceptions of the company, and the length of the recruiting process and other aspects.

6-7c Evaluating the Time Required to Fill Openings

Looking at the length of time it takes to fill openings is a common means of evaluating recruiting efforts.[68] If openings are not filled quickly with qualified candidates, the work and productivity of the organization are likely to suffer. If it takes 45 days to fill vacant positions, managers who need those employees will be unhappy. Also, as noted earlier, unfilled positions cost money.

Generally, it is useful to calculate the average amount of time it takes from contact to hire for each source of applicants, because some sources may produce recruits faster than others. For example, one firm calculated the following averages for nonexempt, warehouse and manufacturing jobs:

Source	Average Time from Contact to Hire (days)
Internet applicants	32
Employment agencies	25
Walk-in candidates	17
Employee referrals	12

These data revealed that, at least for this firm, the Internet methods and use of employment agencies took significantly longer to fill the openings than did relying on walk-in candidates and employee referrals. Matching the use of sources to the time available showed that employee referrals resulted in the fastest recruiting results for that particular group of jobs. However, different results might occur when filling executive jobs or highly skilled network technician jobs. Overall, analyses need to be made both organization-wide and by different types of jobs.

6-7d Evaluating the Cost of Recruiting

Different formulas can be used to evaluate recruiting costs. The calculation most often used to measure such costs is to divide total recruiting expenses for the year by the number of hires for the year:

$$\frac{\text{Total recruiting expenses}}{\text{Number of recruits hired}}$$

The problem with this approach is accurate identification of details that should be included in the recruiting expenses. Should expenses for testing, background checks, relocations, or signing bonuses be included, or are they more properly excluded?

Once those questions are answered, the costs can be allocated to various sources to determine how much each hire from each source costs. It is logical that employers should evaluate the cost of recruiting as a primary metric. Recruiting costs might include costs for employment agencies, advertising, internal sources, external means, and others.[69] The costs can also be sorted by type of job—costs for hiring managers, administrative assistants, bookkeepers, and sales personnel will all be different.

Certainly, cost is an issue, and some employers are quite concerned about cost per hire, but quality might be the trade-off. For example, if an organizational HR strategy focuses on quality as a competitive advantage, a company might choose to hire only from the top 15% of candidates for critical jobs.

6-7e General Recruiting Process Metrics

Because recruiting activities are important, the costs and benefits associated with them should be analyzed. A cost/benefit analysis of recruiting efforts may include both direct costs (advertising, recruiters' salaries, travel, agency fees, etc.) and indirect costs (involvement of operating managers, public relations, image, etc.). Cost/benefit information on each recruiting source can be calculated. Comparing the length of time that applicants hired from each source stay in the organization with the cost of hiring from that source also offers a useful perspective.

Yield ratio
Comparison of the number of applicants at one stage of the recruiting process with the number at the next stage.

Yield Ratios One means for evaluating recruiting efforts is **yield ratios**, which compare the number of applicants at one stage of the recruiting process with the number at another stage. The result is a tool for approximating the required size of the initial applicant pool. It is useful to visualize yield ratios as a pyramid in which the employer starts with a broad base of applicants that progressively narrows. As Figure 6-11 depicts, to end up with five hires for the job in question, the example company must begin with 100 applicants in the pool, as long as yield ratios remain as shown.

A different approach to using yield ratios suggests that over the length of time, organizations can develop ranges for crucial ratios. When a given indicator ratio

FIGURE 6-11 Sample Recruiting Evaluation Pyramid

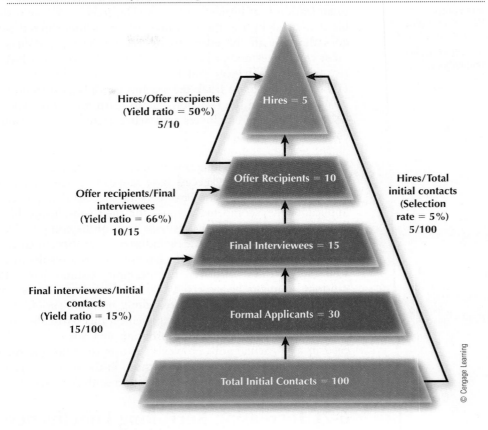

© Cengage Learning

falls outside that range, it may indicate problems in the recruiting process. As an example, in college recruiting the following ratios might be useful:

$$\frac{\text{College seniors given second interviews}}{\text{Total number of seniors interviewed}} = \text{Range of } 30\% - 50\%$$

$$\frac{\text{Number who accept offer}}{\text{Number invited to the company to visit}} = \text{Range of } 50\% - 70\%$$

$$\frac{\text{Number hired}}{\text{Number offered a job}} = \text{Range of } 70\% - 80\%$$

$$\frac{\text{Number finally hired}}{\text{Total number interviewed on campus}} = \text{Range of } 10\% - 20\%$$

Selection rate
Percentage hired from
a given group of
candidates.

Selection Rate   Another useful calculation is the **selection rate,** which is the percentage hired from a given group of candidates. It equals the number hired divided by the number of applicants; for example, a rate of 30% indicates that 3 out of 10 applicants were hired. The selection rate is also affected by the validity of the selection process. A relatively unsophisticated selection program might pick 8 out of 10 applicants for the job. Four of those might turn out to be good employees. A more valid selection process might pick 5 out of 10 applicants but 4 of 5 perform well. Selection rate measures not just recruiting but selection issues as well. So do acceptance rate and success base rate.

Acceptance Rate Calculating the acceptance rate helps identify how successful the organization is at hiring candidates. The **acceptance rate** is the percent of applicants hired divided by the total number of applicants offered jobs. After the company goes through all the effort to screen, interview, and make job offers, hopefully most candidates accept job offers. If they do not, then HR might want to look at reasons why managers and HR staff cannot "close the deal." It is common for HR staff members to track the reasons candidates turn down job offers. That analysis helps explain the rejection rate to learn how competitive the employer is compared with other employers and what factors are causing candidates to choose employment elsewhere.

Success Base Rate A longer-term measure of recruiting effectiveness is the success rate of applicants. The success base rate can be determined by comparing the number of past applicants who have become successful employees against the number of applicants they competed against for their jobs, using historical data within the organization. Also, the success base rate can be compared with the success rates of other employers in the area or industry using benchmarking data. This rate indicates whether the quality of the employees hired results in employees who perform well and have low turnover. For example, assume that if 10 people were hired at random, it might be expected that 4 of them would be satisfactorily performing employees. Thus, a successful recruiting program should be aimed at attracting the 4 in 10 who are capable of doing well on this particular job.

Realistically, no recruiting program will attract only the people who will succeed in a particular job. However, efforts to make the recruiting program attract the largest proportion possible of those in the base rate group can make recruiting efforts more productive in both the short and long term.

6-7f Increasing Recruiting Effectiveness

Consideration of the following recruiting activities should be done to make recruiting more effective:

- *Résumé mining*—a software approach to getting the best résumés for a fit from a big database
- *Applicant tracking*—an approach that takes an applicant all the way from a job listing to performance appraisal results
- *Employer career website*—a convenient recruiting place on an employer's website where applicants can see what jobs are available and apply
- *Internal mobility*—a system that tracks prospects in the company and matches them with jobs as they come open
- *Realistic job previews*—a process that individuals can use to get details on the employer and the jobs
- *Responsive recruitment*—whereby applicants receive timely responses

Recruiting effectiveness can be increased by using the evaluation data to target different applicant pools, tap broader labor markets, change recruiting methods, improve internal handling and interviewing of applicants, and train recruiters and managers.

Another key way to increase recruiting effectiveness rests with the recruiters themselves. Those involved in the recruiting process can either turn off recruits or create excitement. For instance, recruiters who emphasize positive aspects about the jobs and their employers can enhance recruiting effectiveness. Thus, it is important that recruiters communicate well with applicants and treat them fairly and professionally. Effective recruiting is crucial for every company, as it leads to the opportunity to select individuals for employment who will enhance organizational success.

SUMMARY

- Recruiting is the process of generating a pool of qualified applicants for organizational jobs through a series of activities.
- Recruiting must be viewed strategically as tied to HR planning, and discussions should be held about the relevant labor markets in which to recruit.
- The components of labor markets are labor force population, applicant population, and the applicant pool.
- Labor markets can be categorized by geographic area, industry, occupation, qualifications, and other characteristics.
- Employers must make decisions about organization-based versus outsourced recruiting, regular versus flexible staffing, and other aspects of recruiting.
- Efforts should be made to recruit a diverse workforce, including older workers, individuals with disabilities, women, and members of racial/ethnic groups.
- Internet recruiting has grown in use through job boards, various websites, social networking, and special technology methods.

- While Internet recruiting may be able to save costs and time, it can also generate more unqualified applicants and may not reach certain groups of potential applicants.
- The decision to use internal or external recruiting sources should consider both the advantages and disadvantages of each source.
- The most common external recruiting sources are media sources, competitive sources, labor unions, employment agencies, job fairs and special events, and educational institutions.
- The most common methods of internal recruiting include organizational databases, job postings, promotions and transfers, current-employee referrals, and rerecruiting of former employees and applicants.
- Recruiting efforts should be evaluated as part of utilizing HR measurement to assess the effectiveness of the methods and approaches.
- Recruiting evaluation using recruiting metrics typically includes evaluating recruiting quantity and quality, tracking the time to fill openings, examining the costs and benefits of various recruiting sources, and determining recruiting satisfaction.

CRITICAL THINKING CHALLENGES

1. What labor markets should be considered when recruiting to fill an opening for a sales representative for a pharmaceutical manufacturer?
2. Discuss ways a regional bank could use the Internet effectively to recruit loan officer professionals.
3. Describe how a local firm might be able to utilize college/university interns to generate future applicants for jobs planned within the next one to two years.
4. Assume you are going to look for a current job of interest to you. Utilize broad websites such as www.Job.com, Yahoo! HotJobs, Monster,

Taleo, and others to learn about job possibilities for yourself.
5. Your small marketing company of about 50 workers has traditionally recruited employees using newspaper print advertisements. Due to diminished recruiting effects from your ads, the company is interested in using more Internet and social media recruiting. The company president has requested that you, as HR manager, prepare an overview of how Internet recruiting efforts will be different from the traditional methods used by the company. You will need to make a case for why the company should transition to

Internet recruiting and identify the benefits for doing so. To prepare an overview, review the resources found at http://www.recruitersnetwork.com/.

A. What will your company need to do differently to actively use Internet recruiting as

you compete with other employers for qualified applicants?

B. As you recruit marketing professionals, identify the niche websites that you recommend be used for your Internet postings and the reasons for your recommendations.

CASE

FedEx's Independent Contractors: Is the Company Really Recruiting Employees?

The use of independent contractors by package delivery companies appears to be a good idea. The arrangement requires a contractor to purchase the appropriate vehicles, contract with a company that specializes in the delivery of packages, and complete delivery schedules on the basis of sound management approaches. The relationship ideally benefits both the delivery firm and the independent contractor because the company gets packages delivery without having to invest in and maintain the vehicles, while the contractor gets to run his or her organization based on individual preferences.

Unfortunately, one or both parties can end up feeling slighted in this arrangement because of various control and monetary frustrations. By definition, independent contractors are not covered by certain employment laws and do not receive some benefits, but the loss of such protections are usually acceptable because the independent contractor operates as a separate business entity. However, when a delivery company starts to directly supervise an independent contractor's work, the lines between "contractor" and "employee" become blurred. It is easy to understand why an independent contractor would want to be considered an employee, and be entitled to important benefits and protections if control of the contractor's business is effectively being surrendered to the delivery company.

FedEx has for some time utilized a multitude of independent contractors, many of which are single-driver/single-vehicle outfits, to augment its delivery services, and the company has enjoyed many successes using this business model. Contractors must

pass basic pre-employment tests (physical/drug screenings), be good drivers with acceptable records, and possess an appropriate vehicle for deliveries. Drivers must also sign a nonnegotiable contract that specifies the nature of the working relationship with FedEx. The agreement sets forth fairly strict standards with regard to appearance and vehicle maintenance/operation (i.e., drivers cannot use vehicles for personal use with the FedEx logo displayed), but the company does not specify how the deliveries are completed (i.e., routes, hours of operation, etc.). Contractors are generally expected to work Tuesdays through Saturdays, and up to 60 hours within a typical workweek, and drivers must complete a training program that includes both classroom instruction and practical driving exercises. Drivers are assigned a delivery area or region, which can be changed with sufficient notice, and provisions are specified in the contract about support for delivery volume (too much and too little). Pay is provided on factors such as delivery numbers, types of deliveries, and safety record.

Given these requirements, as well as the stringent working conditions that independent contractors must endure working with FedEx, drivers have looked for support from unions and lawyers, or have established drivers groups, in an effort to get recognized as legitimate employees of the company. These concerns have also led to many lawsuits directed at FedEx. Based on these problems, it may be that FedEx needs to revise its agreement so that independent contractors don't feel like they are employees of the company.[70]

QUESTIONS

1. Describe why FedEx's delivery agreement blurs the line between being an employee of the company and being an independent contractor for the company.

2. How should the company address the interpretative problems associated with its delivery agreement with independent contractors?

SUPPLEMENTAL CASES

Recruiting at Kia

This case highlights how the car manufacturer utilized an extensive recruiting process to hire good employees at a facility located in Georgia. (For the case, go to www.cengage.com/management/mathis.)

Northwest State College

This case shows how recruiting policies can work against successful recruiting when a tight labor market exists. (For the case, go to www.cengage.com/management/mathis.)

Enterprise Recruiting

This case highlights how a large car rental firm uses a range of recruiting approaches successfully. (For the case, go to www.cengage.com/management/mathis.)

NOTES

1. Based on Julie C. Ramirez, "Recruiting with Class," *Human Resource Executive Online*, June 2, 2010, www.hreonline.com.
2. Rick Be, "Employment Doldrums May Be Easing, Survey Notes," *Workforce Management Online*, August 25, 2009, www.workforce.com.
3. "Ethics as Recruiting Tool," *Journal of Accountancy*, January 2009, 21.
4. Hsi-An Shih and Yun-Hwa Chiang, "Exploring the Effectiveness of Outsourcing Recruiting and Training Activities, and the Prospector Strategy's Moderating Effect," *The International Journal of Human Resource Management*, 22 (2011), 163–180.
5. Scott Flander, "Recruiting's New Era," *Human Resource Executive Online*, September 2, 2010, http://www.hreonline.com.
6. Joe Light, "Firms Enlist More Recruiters," *The Wall Street Journal*, December 20, 2010, B6.
7. "What SmBs Should Look for in an Applicant Tracking System," September 25, 2009, www.taleo.com.
8. John Yuva, "Round Up the Recruits," *Inside Supply Management*, July 2008, 23–25; Auren Hoffman, "Why Hiring Is Paradoxically Harder in a Downturn," *HR Leaders*, July 14, 2009, www.hrleaders.org.
9. Julie Bennett, "Surveys Point to an Improving Job Market," *The Wall Street Journal*, February 14, 2011, B9; Ben Casselman and Conor Dougherty, "Indicators Signal Recovery's Fragility," *The Wall Street Journal*, September 16, 2011, A4; Edward Lazear, "The Jobs Picture is Still Far From Rosy," *The Wall Street Journal*, January 20, 2012, A13.
10. Scott Flander, "Recessionary Assessments," *Human Resource Executive Online*, June 16, 2009, www.hreonline.com; Mark Whitehouse, "Unfilled Openings Frustrate the Jobless," *The Wall Street Journal*, October 11, 2010, A4.
11. David L. Lynch, "Did That Robot Take My Job?" *Bloomberg BusinessWeek*, January 9–15, 2012, 15–16.
12. U.S. Bureau of Labor Statistics, www.bls.gov.
13. Joe Barrett, "Manufacturers Get Top Talent for Hard-to-Fill Jobs," *The Wall Street Journal*, May 30, 2009, A5.
14. "Recruiting for Small Firms," *Journal of Accountancy*, December 2008, 40.
15. Kurt Scott, "The Search for Effective Physician Leaders," *Physician Executive*, March/April 2009, 44–48.
16. Diana Middleton, "Schools Give Firms Say Amid Tough Job Market," *The Wall Street Journal*, January 6, 2011, B9.
17. Theresa Minton-Eversole, "Mission: Recruitment," *HR Magazine*, January 2009, 43–45.
18. Julie C. Ramirez, "Courting Chameleons," *Human Resource Executive Online*, June 16, 2009, www.hreonline.com; Joe Light, "Help Wanted: Multilingual Employees," *The Wall Street Journal*, January 18, 2011, B7.
19. Geeta Anand, "India Graduates Millions, but Too Few Are Fit to

Hire," *The Wall Street Journal*, April 5, 2011, A12.

20. John Sullivan, "Countercyclical Hiring: The Greatest Recruiting Opportunities in the Last 25 Years," *Electronic Resource Exchange*, August 24, 2009, www.ere.net.

21. Based on Jerry M. Newman, Richard Floersch, and Mike Balaka, "Employment Branding at Branding at McDonald's: Leveraging Rewards for Positive Outcomes," *Workspan*, March 2012, 20–24.

22. Ralf Wilden, Siegfried Gudergan, and Ian Lings, "Employer Branding: Strategic Implications for Staff Recruitment," *Journal of Marketing Management*, 26 (2010), 56–73; Ron Thomas, "What to Ask as You Start 2012: Why Would Somebody Work for You?" HR Updates, January 3, 2012, peter.reis@me.com.

23. "What Is Recruitment Process Outsourcing?" *Recruitment Process Outsourcing Association*, June 2009, www.RPOassociation.org.

24. Adapted from Yukako Ono, "Why Do Firms Use Temporary Workers?" *Chicago Fed Letter* (published by Federal Reserve Bank of Chicago), March 2009.

25. Sudeep Reddy, "Employers Increasingly Rely on Temps, Part-Timers," *The Wall Street Journal*, October 11, 2010, A4; Robert Grossman, "Strategic Temptations," *HR Magazine*, March 2012, 24–32.

26. Keisha-Ann G. Gray, "Dividing Lines," *Human Resource Executive Online*, September 8, 2009, www.hreonline.com.

27. Matthew J. Bidwell and Forrest Briscoe, "Who Contracts? Determinants of the Decision to Work as an Independent Contractor among Information Technology Workers," *Academy of Management Journal*, 52 (2009), 1148–1168.

28. Brendan J. Morse and Paula M. Popovich, "Realistic Recruitment Practices in Organizations," *Human Resource Management Review*, 19 (2009), 1–8; William Gardner, et al., "Attraction to Organizational Culture Profiles: Effects of Realistic Recruiting ...," *Management Communication Quarterly*, 22 (2009), 437–472.

29. Based on Michael A. Tucker, "Show and Tell," *HR Magazine*, January 2012, 51–53.

30. Peter Cappelli, "Do Outside Hires Perform Better?" *Human Resource Executive Online*, April 23, 2012, www.hreonline.com.

31. "E-Recruiting Software Providers," *Workforce Management*, June 22, 2009, 14.

32. "New Job Search Engine Makes Finding a Job Easier," *The Career News*, September 21, 2009, www.thecareernews.com.

33. For details, go to www.shrm.org/jpc.

34. H. Jack Walker, Hubert S. Field, William F. Giles, Achilles A. Armenakis, and Jeremy B. Bernerth, "Displaying Employee Testimonials on Recruiting Websites: Effects of Communication Media, Employee Race, and Job Seeker Race on Organization Attraction and Information Credibility," *Journal of Applied Psychology*, 94 (2009), 1354–1364.

35. Dan Schaubel, "Skip Job Boards and Use Social Media Instead," *BusinessWeek Online*, July 29, 2009, 14.

36. Jennifer T. Arnold, "Recruiting on the Run," *HR Magazine*, February 2010, 65–67; Maura C. Ciccarelli, "It's Personal," *Human Resource Executive Online*, September 16, 2010, www.hreonline.com; Laura Petrecca, "More Grads Use Social Media to Job Hunt," *The Wall Street Journal*, April 15, 2011, B1.

37. Chris Tratar, "Recruiting by Relationship to Fill the Candidate Pipeline," *Workforce Management*, July 20, 2009, S5.

38. Vangie Sison, "Social Media: Attracting Talent in the Age of Web 2.0," *Workspan*, May 2009, 45–49; Sam De Kay, "Are Business-Oriented Social Networking Websites Useful Resources for Locating Passive Job Seekers?" *Business Communications Quarterly*, March 2009, 101–104.

39. Gonzalo Hernandez and Ed Frauenheim, "Logging Off of Job Boards," *Workforce Management*, June 22, 2009, 25–28.

40. Based on Richard Doherty, "Getting Social with Recruitment," *Strategic HR Review*, 9 (2010), 11–15.

41. Juki Hasson, "Blogging for Talent," *HR Magazine*, October 2007, 65–68.

42. Andrew R. McIlvaine, "Lights, Camera, Interview," *Human Resource Executive*, September 16, 2009, 22–25; Rita Zeidner, "Companies Tell Their Stories in Recruit-

ment Videos," *HR Trendbook*, 2008, 28.

43. Laura Petrecca, "More Grads Use Social Media to Job Hunt," *The Wall Street Journal*, April 15, 2011, B1.

44. Adrienne Fox, "Newest Social Medium Has Recruiters All-a-Twitter," *HR Disciplines*, June 24, 2009, www.shrm.org/hrdisciplines.

45. Tracy Cote and Traci Armstrong, "Why Tweeting Has Become an Ad Agency's Main Job Posting Strategy ....?" *Workforce Management Online*, May 2009, www.workforce.com.

46. For details and current status, go to www.ftc.gov. Also see Ed Fraurnheim and Rich Bell, "A Tighter Rein on HR Blogging?" *Workforce Management Online*, September 2009, www.workforce.com.

47. Tresa Baldas, "Lawyers Warn Employers Against Giving Glowing Reviews on LinkedIn," *National Law Journal*, July 6, 2009, www.nlj.com.

48. Based on Jonathan A. Segal, "Dancing on the Edge of a Volcano," *HR Magazine*, April 2011, 83–86.

49. Gary Crispin, "The Future of Recruiting," *Human Resource Executive*, September 16, 2009, 32–35.

50. Joe Light, "Recruiters Rethink Online Playbook," *The Wall Street Journal*, January 18, 2011, B7; Andrew R. McIlvaine, "Do Friends Let Friends Recruit via Facebook," *Human Resource Executive Online*, July 25, 2011, www.hreonline.com; Anonymous, "The State of Social Media in the Workplace: Uses and Measurement," *T+D*, December 2011, 21.

51. Meinald T. Thielsch Lisa Traumer, and Leoni Pytlik, "E-Recruiting and Fairness: The Applicant's Point of View," *Information Technology Management*, published online April 4, 2012.

52. Eric Robbins and Forest Myers, "The Staffing Challenges Lie Ahead for Community Banks," *RMA Journal*, April 2009, 18–23.

53. Stephenie Overman, "Searching for the Top," *HR Magazine*, January 2008, 47–52.

54. Theresa Minton-Eversole, "Companies Plan Modest Hiring of 2009 College Graduates," *HR Disciplines*, April 17, 2009, www.shrm.org/hrdisciplines.

55. Peter Cappelli, "The Values of Elite Colleges," *Human Resource Executive Online*, January 3, 2012, www.hreonline.com.

56. Julie C. Ramirez, "Taking Them Seriously," *Human Resource Executive Online*, July 1, 2010, www.hreonline.com; Hao Zhao and Robert C. Liden, "Internship: A Recruitment and Selection Perspective," *Journal of Applied Psychology*, 96 (2011), 221–229.

57. Drew Robb, "Sizing Up Talent," *HR Magazine*, April 2011, 77–79.

58. Bill Kutik, "Still Trying to Get Recruiting Right," *Human Resource Executive Online*, April 6, 2009, www.hreonline.com/HRE.

59. Peter Weddle, "The Really Big Impact of a Small Number of Sentient Specifics," *Dice Review*, July 2009, http://marketing.dice.com.

60. Sarah E. Needleman, "New Career, Same Employer," *The Wall Street Journal*, April 21, 2008, B9.

61. Michael A. Tucker, "Don't Say Goodbye," *HR Magazine*, August 2011, 71–73.

62. Greet Van Hoye and Filip Lievens, "Tapping the Grapevine: A Closer Look at Word-of-Mouth as a Recruitment Source," *Journal of Applied Psychology*, 94 (2009), 341–352.

63. "What Issue Should We Consider in Implementing Employee Referral Program?" *HRCompliance*, August 15, 2009, www.hrcompliance.cerdian.com.

64. Based on Steve Taylor, "Capitalizing on College Ties," *HR Magazine*, December 2009, 48–51.

65. Michael O'Brien, "Gone, But Not Forgotten," *Human Resource Executive*, September 2, 2009, 30–33.

66. Ed Emerman, "Effective Recruiting Tied to Strong Financial Performance," *Watson-Wyatt Worldwide*, 2009, www.watsonwyatt.com/news.

67. Fay Hansen, "Sourcing Disappears as Applications Pile Up for Overwhelmed Recruiters," *Workforce Management Online*, July 23, 2009, www.workforce.com.

68. "Building Championship Recruiting Teams," *Staffing Exclusives*, April 14, 2009, www.StaffingInstitute.org.

69. Alice Snell, "Focus on Process to Reduce Your Recruiting Costs," *Best Practices in Recruitment*, 2009, www.workforce.com, S5.

70. Based on Todd D. Saveland, "FedEx's New 'Employees': Their Disgruntled Independent Contractors," *Transportation Law Journal*, 36 (2009), 95–119.

7

Selecting Human Resources

Learning Objectives

After you have read this chapter, you should be able to:

1 Understand selection and placement, as well as the associated theory and application of these practices.

2 Discuss the steps of a typical selection process.

3 Identify three types of selection tests and legal concerns about their uses.

4 Contrast several types of selection interviews and some key considerations in conducting these interviews.

5 Specify how legal concerns affect background investigations of applicants and use of medical examinations in the selection process.

6 Describe the major issues to be considered when selecting candidates for global assignments.

Selecting a Proper Ethics Officer

Organizations such as Allstate are finding out the importance of selecting a good ethics officer to help manage the company's overall approach to business ethics. Demand for ethics officers has been steadily increasing as a result of the Enron, Tyco, WorldCom, and Bernie Madoff scandals, and recent SHRM findings suggest that many firms are developing these specialized positions to tackle ethical challenges in the workplace. Ethics officers are expected to be the key administrators of an organization's compliance efforts and help institutionalize values that encourage employees to act ethically.

In the past, HR departments were expected to carry the ethics torch by ensuring that ethical standards and codes were developed and effectively communicated to employees. HR professionals should continue to play an important role in the development of organizational ethics in the future. Despite the new emphasis on ethics officers, HR managers must be involved in the creation of ethics training that prepares them for the challenges they face on the job. They must also develop valid selection approaches to hire ethical employees. Finally, HR professionals need to be actively involved in the development of an organizational culture that prompts ethical reasoning among employees.

Given the importance of the ethics officer, as both a creator and coordinator of ethics policy, what should companies consider when filling this position? First, the HR director and other key leaders should be included in the selection process because there should be a good match between the goals of HR and the organization and those of the ethics officer. Benchmarking can also be used to determine how other companies are hiring and utilizing ethics officers to manage corporate ethics. HR can also more effectively select the "right" ethics officer by referencing the company's current climate of ethics, including past transgressions and triumphs, to get a better idea of what personal characteristics will be needed in the position.[1]

Selection is one of the most important areas of human resources in organizations because getting the right people in the proper places at the correct times is critical for business success. Certainly for a business which depends on good people and good performance to succeed the process of selection is very important. For an organization that is failing, improvement may need to come from many sources, but it is difficult to imagine appropriate changes coming without some new and competent people to carry out those changes. In athletic organizations that are not doing well, it is the selection of new coaches and players that prompts improvements, and the continued selection of good athletes and coaches that allows ongoing success. The same is true of other organizations.

7-1 ■ SELECTION AND PLACEMENT

LO1 Understand selection and placement, as well as the associated theory and application of these practices.

Selection
The process of choosing individuals with the correct qualifications needed to fill jobs in an organization.

Selection is the process of choosing individuals with the correct qualifications to fill jobs in an organization. Without these qualified employees, an organization is far less likely to succeed. A useful perspective on selection and placement comes from two observations that underscore the importance of effective staffing:

- *Hire hard, manage easy.* The investment of time and effort in selecting the right people for jobs will make managing them as employees much less difficult because many problems are eliminated.
- *Good training will not make up for bad selection.* When people without the appropriate aptitudes are selected, employers will have difficulty training them to do those jobs that they do not fit.[2]

7-1a Placement

Placement
Fitting a person to the right job.

The ultimate purpose of selection is **placement**, or fitting a person to the right job. Placement of people should be seen primarily as a matching process. How well an employee is matched to a job can affect the amount and quality of the employee's work, as well as the training and operating costs required to prepare the individual to do the work. Further, employee morale is an issue because good fit encourages individuals to be positive about their jobs and what they accomplish.[3]

Selection and placement activities typically focus on applicants' knowledge, skills, and abilities (KSAs), but they should also focus on the degree to which job candidates generally match the situations experienced both on the job and in the company. Psychologists label this *person–environment fit*. In HR it is usually called **person/job fit**. Fit is related not only to work satisfaction, but also to company commitment and the desire to quit work.

Person/job fit
Matching the KSAs of individuals with the characteristics of jobs.

Lack of fit between a person's KSAs and job requirements can be classified as a *mismatch*. A mismatch results from poor pairing of a person's needs, interests, abilities, personality, and expectations with characteristics of the job, rewards, and the organization in which the job is located. What makes placement difficult and complex is the need to match people and jobs on multiple dimensions.[4]

People already working in jobs can help identify the most important KSAs for success as part of job analysis. The fit between the individual and job characteristics is particularly important when dealing with overseas assignments because employees must have the proper personalities, skills, and interpersonal abilities to be effective in the international environment.

Person/organization fit
The congruence between individuals and organizational factors.

Attraction-selection-attrition (ASA) theory
Job candidates are attracted to and selected by firms where similar types of individuals are employed and individuals who are different quit their jobs to work elsewhere.

In addition to the match between people and jobs, employers are concerned about the congruence between people and companies, or the **person/organization fit**.[5] Person/organization fit is important from a *values* perspective, with many organizations trying to positively link a person's principles to the values of the company. Organizations tend to favor job applicants who effectively blend into how business is conducted. As a result, the **attraction-selection-attrition (ASA) theory** is often used to better understand the concept of fit in companies. The ASA theory proposes that job candidates are attracted to and selected by firms where similar types of individuals are employed, and that individuals who are very different quit their jobs to work elsewhere.[6] Based on these ideas, it is easy to see why person/organization fit is important for long-term selection and placement strategies. If positive fit is established, organizations should have a more motivated and committed workforce that is more likely to stay and perform.

Other ideas about fit have been proposed. For instance, *compilational fit* occurs when several lower-level factors such as similar work group personalities or worksite teamwork prompt an increase in higher-level consequences, including organizational performance and productivity. For example, positive fit and workplace characteristics experienced by waiters in a hotel restaurant will encourage them to work harder to satisfy customers, thus increasing the hotel's overall financial performance. *Compositional fit* occurs when the people involved in creating fit are doing so at different levels of a firm (i.e., what top managers do can affect perceived fit among line employees). Other factors influencing fit include *spillover*, a situation in which perceptions of good or bad fit in one area of work spills over into beliefs about fit in other areas of the organization, and *spiraling*, which involves positive or negative perceptions about fit, impacting other feelings (good or bad) about the workplace.[7]

7-1b Selection, Criteria, Predictors, and Job Performance

Regardless of whether an employer uses specific KSAs or a more general approach, effective selection of employees involves using selection criteria and predictors of these criteria. At the heart of an effective selection system must be the knowledge of what constitutes good job performance. Knowing what good performance looks like in a particular job helps identify what it takes for the employee to achieve successful performance. These are called selection criteria. A **selection criterion** is a characteristic that a person must possess to successfully perform work. Figure 7-1 shows that ability, motivation, intelligence, conscientiousness, appropriate risk, and permanence might be selection criteria for many jobs. Selection criteria that might be more specific to managerial jobs include leading and deciding, supporting and cooperating, organizing and executing, and enterprising and performing.[8]

Selection criterion
Characteristic that a person must possess to successfully perform work.

Predictors of selection criteria
Measurable or visible indicators of selection criteria.

To determine whether candidates might possess certain selection criteria (such as ability and motivation), employers try to identify **predictors of selection criteria**, which are measurable or visible indicators of those positive characteristics (or criteria). Figure 7-1 shows how job performance, selection criteria, and predictors are interrelated. If a candidate possesses appropriate amounts of any or all of these predictors, it might be assumed that the person would stay on the job longer than someone without those predictors.[9] In addition, the information gathered about an applicant using the individual predictors included in application forms, tests, and interviews should focus on the likelihood that the person will execute

FIGURE 7-1 Job Performance, Selection Criteria, and Predictors

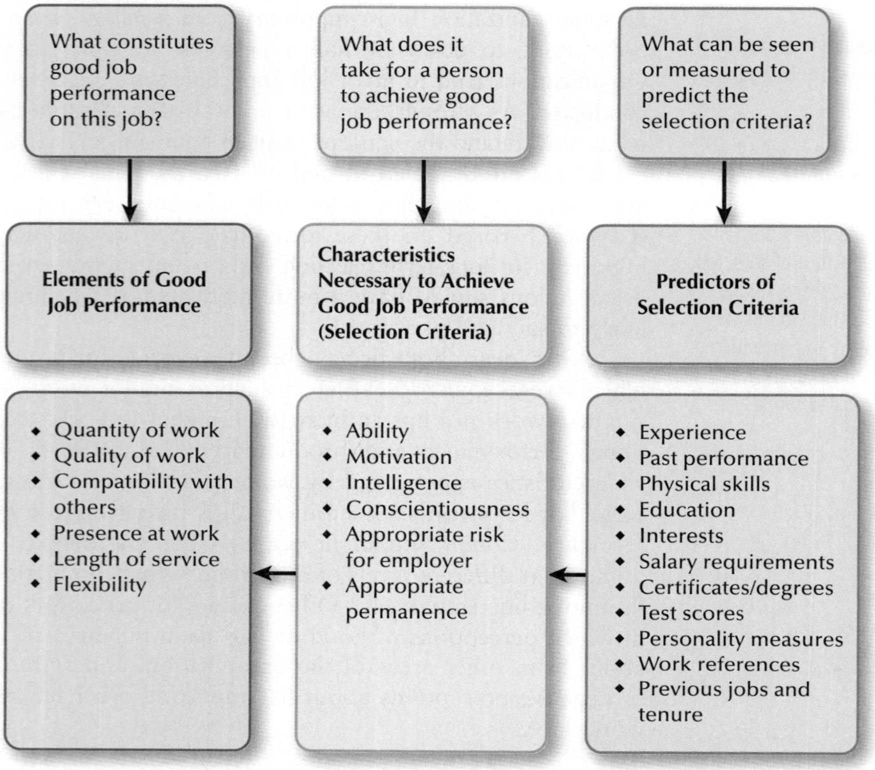

What constitutes good job performance on this job?

What does it take for a person to achieve good job performance?

What can be seen or measured to predict the selection criteria?

Elements of Good Job Performance

Characteristics Necessary to Achieve Good Job Performance (Selection Criteria)

Predictors of Selection Criteria

- Quantity of work
- Quality of work
- Compatibility with others
- Presence at work
- Length of service
- Flexibility

- Ability
- Motivation
- Intelligence
- Conscientiousness
- Appropriate risk for employer
- Appropriate permanence

- Experience
- Past performance
- Physical skills
- Education
- Interests
- Salary requirements
- Certificates/degrees
- Test scores
- Personality measures
- Work references
- Previous jobs and tenure

© Cengage Learning

the job competently once hired, so the factors need to be valid for the purposes of selection.[10]

7-1c Validity and Reliability

In selection, validity is the correlation between a predictor and job performance. In other words, validity occurs to the extent that the predictor actually predicts what it is supposed to predict. Several types of validity are used in selection. Most validity decisions use a **correlation coefficient**, an index number that gives the relationship between a predictor variable and a criterion (or dependent) variable. Correlations range from -1.0 to $+1.0$, with larger absolute scores suggesting stronger relationships.

Concurrent validity is one method for establishing the validity associated with a predictor. Concurrent validity uses current employees to validate a predictor or "test." As shown in Figure 7-2, concurrent validity is measured when an employer tests current employees and correlates the scores with their performance ratings on appraisals.

A disadvantage of the concurrent validity approach is that employees who have not performed satisfactorily at work are probably no longer with the firm and therefore cannot be tested. Also, extremely good employees may have been promoted or may have left the company for better work situations. Any learning on the job also might confound test scores.

Correlation coefficient
Index number that gives the relationship between a predictor variable and a criterion variable.

Concurrent validity
Measured when an employer tests current employees and correlates the scores with their performance ratings.

FIGURE 7-2 Concurrent and Predictive Validity

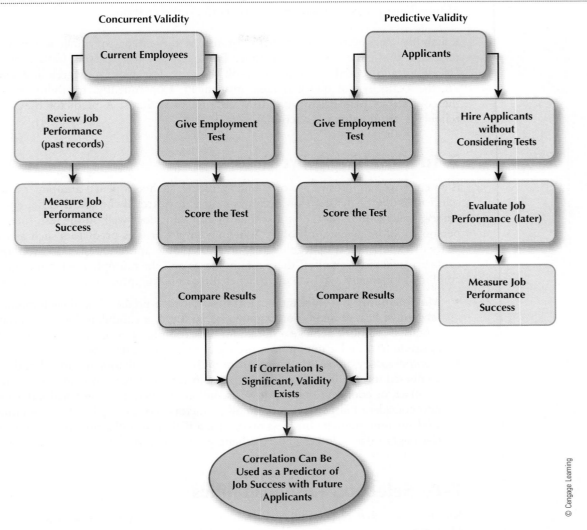

Predictive validity
Measured when test results of applicants are compared with subsequent job performance.

Another method for establishing criterion-related validity is predictive validity. To calculate **predictive validity**, test results of applicants are compared with their subsequent job performance (see Figure 7-2). Job success is measured by assessing factors such as absenteeism, accidents, errors, and performance appraisal ratings. For example, if the employees who had one year of experience at the time of hire demonstrate better performance than those without such experience, then the experience requirement can be considered a valid predictor of job performance. In addition, individual experience may be used as an important selection criterion when making future staffing decisions.

The Equal Employment Opportunity Commission (EEOC) has favored predictive validity because it includes the full range of performance and test scores. However, establishing predictive validity can be challenging for HR managers because a large sample of individuals is needed (usually at least 30) and a significant amount of time must transpire (perhaps one year) to do the analysis.

Reliability Reliability of a predictor or test is the extent to which it repeatedly produces the same results over time. For example, if a person took a test in December and scored 75, and then took the same test again in March and scored 76, the exam is probably a reliable instrument. Consequently, reliability involves the consistency of predictors used in selection procedures. A predictor that is not reliable is of no value in selection.

7-1d Combining Predictors

If an employer chooses to use only one predictor, such as a pencil-and-paper test, to select individuals, the decision becomes straightforward. If the test is valid, encompasses a major dimension of a job, and an applicant does well on the test, then that person could be given a job offer. When an employer uses predictors such as three years of experience, a college degree, and acceptable aptitude test score, job applicants are evaluated on all of these requirements and the multiple predictors must be combined in some way. Two approaches for combining predictors are as follows:

- *Multiple hurdles*: A minimum cutoff is set on each predictor, and each minimum level must be "passed." For example, to be hired, a candidate for a sales representative job must achieve a minimum education level, a certain score on a sales aptitude test, and a minimum score on a structured interview.
- *Compensatory approach*: Scores from individual predictors are added and combined into an overall score, thereby allowing a higher score on one predictor to offset, or compensate for, a lower score on another. The combined index takes into consideration performance on all predictors. For example, when admitting students into graduate business programs, a higher overall score on an admissions test might offset a lower undergraduate grade point average.

7-1e Selection Responsibilities

Selection is a key responsibility for all managers and supervisors in a company. However, organizations vary in how they allocate selection responsibilities between HR specialists and operating managers. The need to meet EEOC requirements and the inherent strategic implications of the staffing function have caused many companies to place greater emphasis on hiring procedures and techniques and to centralize selection in the HR department. In other companies, each department (or its management team) screens and hires its own personnel. Managers, especially those working in smaller firms, often select their own employees because these individuals directly impact their work. But the validity and effectiveness of this approach may be questionable because many managers lack training in selection procedures and regulations.

Another approach is one in which HR professionals initially screen the job candidates, and the managers or supervisors make the final selection decisions from the qualified applicant pool. Generally, the higher the positions being filled, the greater the likelihood that the ultimate hiring decisions will be made by operating managers rather than HR professionals.

Selection responsibilities are affected by the existence of a central employment office, which is usually housed within a Human Resources department. In smaller organizations, a full-time employment specialist or group is impractical. But for larger firms, centralizing activities in an employment office might be appropriate.

The employment function in any organization may be concerned with some or all of the following activities: (1) receiving applications, (2) interviewing the applicants, (3) administering tests to applicants, (4) conducting background investigations, (5) arranging for physical examinations, (6) placing and assigning new employees, (7) coordinating follow-up evaluations of these employees, (8) conducting exit interviews with departing employees, and (9) maintaining appropriate records and reports.

L02 Discuss the parts of a typical selection process.

7-2 ■ THE SELECTION PROCESS

Most organizations follow a series of consistent steps to process and select applicants for jobs. Company size, job characteristics, the number of people needed, the use of electronic technology, and other factors cause variations on the basic process. Selection can take place in a day or over a much longer period of time, and certain phases of the process may be omitted or the order changed, depending on the employer and the job being filled. If the applicant is processed in one day, the employer usually checks credentials/previous employment after selection. Figure 7-3 shows steps in a typical selection process.

7-2a Applicant Job Interest

Individuals seeking employment can indicate interest in many ways. Traditionally, individuals have submitted résumés by mail or fax, or applied in person at an employer's location. But with the growth in Internet recruiting, many individuals complete applications online or submit résumés electronically.

Regardless of how individuals express interest in employment, the selection process has an important public relations dimension. Discriminatory hiring practices, impolite interviewers, unnecessarily long waits, unreturned telephone inquiries, inappropriate testing procedures, and lack of follow-up responses can produce unfavorable impressions of an employer. Job applicants' perceptions of the organization will be influenced by how they are treated.

Realistic job preview
Process through which a job applicant receives an accurate picture of a job.

Realistic Job Previews Many individuals know little about companies before applying for employment. Consequently, when deciding whether to accept a job, they pay particularly close attention to the information received during the selection process, including compensation data, work characteristics, job location, and promotion opportunities. Unfortunately, some employers make jobs appear better than they really are. **Realistic job previews** provide potential employees with an accurate introduction to a job so that they can better evaluate the employment situation. Indeed, a realistic job preview can directly identify necessary training and clarify a job role. Also, in global assignments, the use of realistic job previews increases individual confidence and improves decision making about an expatriate position.

A company should consider several strategies when developing a recruiting brand and conveying it to potential employees via realistic job previews. The brand of the

FIGURE 7-3 Selection Process Flowchart

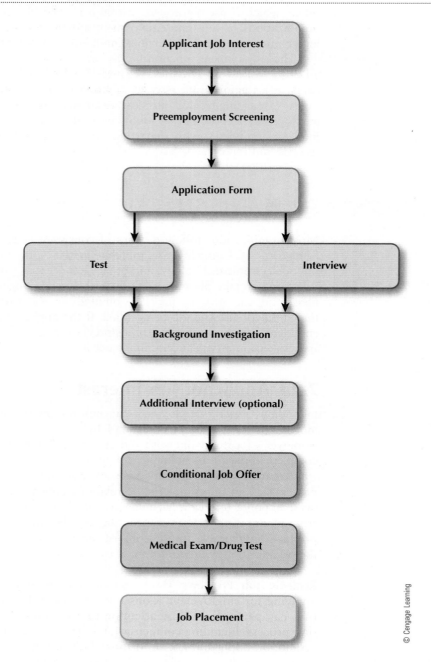

© Cengage Learning

company should establish in the minds of recruits the company's overall purpose for being in business, and it should honestly portray the jobs that are performed by individuals already employed in the firm. A project director of a recruiting firm suggests that a firm should evaluate its own strengths and develop a list of employment benefits that would make the company appear attractive to potential employees. These points may include building human capital, good compensation, and ethics and social responsibility. At the same time, a company needs to convey the less attractive aspects of work, such as difficult work schedules or extensive travel. However, any negative job attributes can be outweighed by the positive factors already covered.

Truth-in-Hiring Lawsuits Recruiters may exaggerate promotional opportunities, pay, or even the company's financial position in an attempt to hire a candidate. However, a candidate who leaves a good job to accept a position and later discovers such exaggerations may choose to sue the company for misrepresenting the job. It is important for hiring managers to be truthful in their descriptions of jobs so that candidates understand the positives and negatives associated with work in a particular company.

7-2b Preemployment Screening

Many employers conduct preemployment screening to determine if applicants meet the minimum qualifications for open jobs before they have the applicants fill out an application.

Electronic Assessment Screening The use of electronic preemployment screening or assessment has grown. Much of this screening utilizes computer software to review the many résumés and application forms received during the recruiting and application process. Large companies often use different types of software to receive, evaluate, and track the applications of many potential employees.

When a job posting generates 1,000 or more applications (which is not unusual with large companies or in difficult economic times), responding to each would be a full-time job. Electronic screening can speed up the process, and this approach may take several forms: disqualification questions; screening questions to get at KSAs and experience; valid assessment tests; and background, drug, and financial screening. Some of the assessments might include auditions for the job that are conducted on the basis of simulations of specific job-related tasks. For example, in a call center, branch-manager candidates are given virtual customers with service problems, and they demonstrate their ability to foster relationships with the virtual clients and to make quick personnel decisions with virtual employees.[11] A good strategy is to use simple electronic assessment early to reduce the number of applicants before requiring applications or interviews, which leaves a much more qualified list of remaining applicants with which to work.[12]

7-2c Application Forms

Some employers do not use preemployment screening prior to having applicants fill out an application form. Instead, they have every interested individual complete an application first. These completed application forms then become the basis for pre-screening information. But collecting, storing, and tracking these forms can create unnecessary and significant work for HR staff members.

Application forms, which are used universally, can take on different formats. Properly prepared, the application form serves four purposes:

1. It is a record of the applicant's desire to obtain a position.
2. It provides the interviewer with an applicant profile that can be addressed during the interview.

3. It is a basic employee record for applicants who are hired.
4. It can be used for research on the effectiveness of the selection process.

Many employers use only one application form for all jobs, but others use several forms depending on the position. For example, a hotel might use one form for management and supervisory staff and another for line employees.

Application Disclaimers Application forms should contain disclaimers and notices so that appropriate legal protections are clearly stated. These recommended disclosures include the following:

- *Employment-at-will*: Indicates the right of the employer or the applicant to terminate employment at any time with or without notice or cause (where applicable by state law)
- *Reference contacts*: Requests permission to contact previous employers listed by the applicant on the application form or résumé
- *Employment testing*: Notifies applicants of required drug tests, pencil-and-paper tests, physical exams, or electronic or other tests that will be used in the employment decision
- *Application time limit*: Indicates how long application forms are active (typically six months), and that persons must reapply or reactivate their applications after that period
- *Information falsification*: Conveys to an applicant that falsification of application information can be grounds for serious reprimand or termination

EEOC Considerations and Application Forms An organization should retain all applications and hiring-related documents and records for three years. Guidelines from the EEOC and court decisions require that the data requested on application forms must be job related. Though frequently found on application forms, questions that ask for the following information are illegal. (See Appendix D for review.)

- Marital status
- Height/weight
- Number and ages of dependents
- Information on spouse
- Date of high school graduation
- Contact in case of emergency

Most of the litigation surrounding application forms has involved questions regarding the gender and age of a potential employee, so special consideration should be dedicated to removing any items that relate to these personal characteristics. Concerns about inappropriate questions stem from their potential to elicit information that should not be used in hiring decisions. Figure 7-4 shows a sample application form containing questions that generally are legal.

Résumés as Applications Applicants commonly provide background information through résumés. When the situation arises, EEOC standards require that an employer treats a résumé as an application form. If an applicant voluntarily furnishes some information on a resume that cannot be legally obtained, the employer should not use that information during the selection process. Some employers require those who submit résumés to complete an application form as well so there is consistent information on every applicant.

FIGURE 7-4 **Sample Application Form**

Application for Employment
An Equal Opportunity Employer* Today's Date _____

PERSONAL INFORMATION Please Print or Type

| Name | (Last) | (First) | (Full middle name) |

| Current address | City | State | Zip code | Phone number ( ) |

| What position are you applying for? | Date available for employment? | E-mail address |

| Are you willing to relocate? ☐ Yes ☐ No | Are you willing to travel if required? ☐ Yes ☐ No |

| Have you ever been employed by this Company or any of its subsidiaries before? ☐ Yes ☐ No | Indicate location and dates |

| Can you, after employment, submit verification of your legal right to work in the United States? ☐ Yes ☐ No | Have you ever been convicted of a felony? ☐ Yes ☐ No | *Convictions will not automatically disqualify job candidates. The seriousness of the crime and the date of conviction will be considered.* |

PERFORMANCE OF JOB FUNCTIONS

Are you able to perform all the functions of the job for which you are applying, with or without accommodation?

☐ Yes, without accommodation   ☐ Yes, with accommodation   ☐ No

If you indicated you can perform all the functions with an accommodation, please explain how you would perform the tasks and with what accommodation.

EDUCATION

School level	School name and address	No. of years attended	Did you graduate?	Course of study
High school				
Vo-tech, business, or trade school				
College				
Graduate school				

PERSONAL DRIVING RECORD

This section is to be completed ONLY if the operation of a motor vehicle will be required in the course of the applicant's employment.

| How long have you been a licensed driver? | Driver's license number | Expiration date | Issuing State |

List any other state(s) in which you have had a driver's license(s) in the past:

| Within the past five years, have you had a vehicle accident? ☐ Yes ☐ No | Been convicted of reckless If yes, give dates: or drunken driving? ☐ Yes ☐ No | Been cited for moving violations? If yes, give dates: ☐ Yes ☐ No |

| Has your driver's license ever been revoked or suspended? ☐ Yes ☐ No   If yes, explain: | Is your driver's license restricted?   If yes, explain: ☐ Yes ☐ No |

*We are an Equal Opportunity Employer. We do not discriminate on the basis of race, religion, color, gender, age, national origin, or disability.

Regardless of how the background information is collected, there are several issues that should be considered when screening applications. For instance, companies should be dutiful about checking the truthfulness of the information presented on résumés and application forms. Research suggests that a noteworthy percentage of applicants knowingly embellish their past work experiences. Companies also have to be careful about rejecting applicants who appear to be "overqualified" for jobs because evidence suggests that these individuals can exhibit high levels of work productivity when given opportunities on the job.[13] Somewhat related to overqualified candidates are the many "silver-collar" applicants today who continue to work at retirement age because of good health. These individuals help retention, motivation, collegiality, and role-modeling good work behaviors (e.g., exhibiting good attendance and positive customer service).[14]

7-2d Security Concerns and Immigration Verification

Businesses need to be proactive about verifying the identities and credentials of job applicants. Part of these efforts rest on the careful examination of the accuracy of the details included on résumés, which evidence suggests are often embellished and/or fabricated for professional gain.[15] Businesses are required to review and record identity documents, such as Social Security cards, passports, and visas, and to determine if they appear to be genuine because it is illegal to knowingly hire employees who are not in the country legally. A recent study found that identity thieves can sometimes predict individual Social Security numbers on the basis of birth information, so extra caution should be exercised in some cases.[16] If HR personnel know they are working with fraudulent documents, corporate liability exists, and seizure of assets and criminal liability for top management can occur. U.S. Immigration and Customs Enforcement (ICE) can also audit the records of a business to make certain there has been compliance with employment eligibility laws and rules. Such audits may come from employer filings of government labor documents, disgruntled employees, identity theft complaints, or suspicious patterns of activity.[17]

Employers must use the revised form I-9 for each employee hired and must determine within 72 hours whether an applicant is a U.S. citizen, registered alien, or illegal alien. A government program called E-Verify is run by the Department of Homeland Security to help with this process. The use of E-Verify is mandatory for government contractors or subcontractors.[18] A recent report determined that some individuals are utilizing false identities to obtain clearance to work through E-Verify, so greater security measures will be needed in the future.[19]

An employer should have a policy to comply with immigration requirements and to avoid knowingly hiring or retaining illegal workers. I-9s should be completed, updated, and audited. Some companies are even using paperless I-9 systems to better manage employment eligibility verification because electronic processing reduces errors, incompleteness, and illegibility and improves the overall management of documentation.[20]

7-3 ■ SELECTION TESTING

LO3 Identify three types of selection tests and legal concerns about their uses.

Many kinds of tests can be used to help select qualified employees. Literacy tests, skill-based tests, personality tests, and honesty tests can be used to assess various individual factors that are important for the work to be performed. These useful employment tests allow companies to predict which applicants will likely be the most successful before being hired.

However, selection tests must be evaluated extensively before being utilized as a recruiting tool. The development of the test items should be linked to a thorough job analysis, which is covered in Chapter 4. Also, initial testing of the items should include an evaluation by knowledge experts, and statistical and validity assessments of the items should be conducted. Furthermore, adequate security of the testing instruments should be coordinated, and the monetary value of these tests to the firm should be determined. For example, Gerber Products Company was found to be using preemployment selection tests for entry-level positions that did not have sufficient evidence of validity. The tests were negatively impacting minority applicants. Gerber paid 1,912 minority and female applicants $900,000 in back pay and interest.[21] Figure 7-5 provides a summary of the specific issues that need to be documented when creating preemployment tests, in the context of these many challenges. For instance, the research used to create a test, the accuracy and consistency of an instrument, and details about administration and analysis are important considerations that should be documented. It is also important to consider that multiple testing approaches should be used when evaluating job applicants.[22]

7-3a Ability Tests

Cognitive ability tests
Tests that measure an individual's thinking, memory, reasoning, verbal, and mathematical abilities.

Tests that assess an individual's ability to perform in a specific manner are grouped as ability tests. These are sometimes further differentiated into *aptitude tests* and *achievement tests*. **Cognitive ability tests** measure an individual's thinking, memory, reasoning, verbal, and mathematical abilities. Valid tests such as the Wonderlic Personnel Test and the General Aptitude Test Battery (GATB) can be used to determine applicants' basic knowledge of terminology and concepts, word fluency, spatial orientation, comprehension and retention span, general and mental ability, and conceptual reasoning.

FIGURE 7-5 Issues to Document when Creating Preemployment Tests

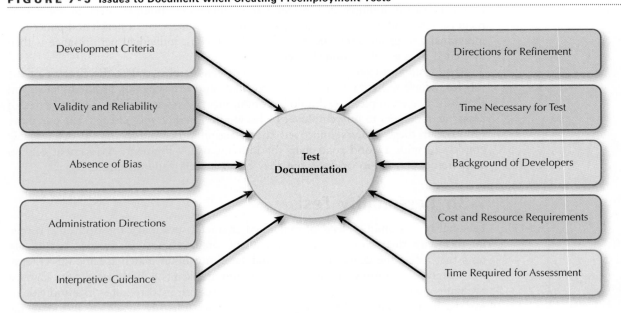

Source: Adapted from Theresa Minton-Eversole, "Avoiding Bias in Pre-Employment Testing," *HR Magazine*, December 2010, 77–80.

Physical ability tests
Tests that measure an individual's abilities such as strength, endurance, and muscular movement.

Psychomotor tests
Tests that measure dexterity, hand–eye coordination, arm–hand steadiness, and other factors.

Work sample tests
Tests that require an applicant to perform a simulated task that is a specified part of the target job.

Situational judgment tests
Tests that measure a person's judgment in work settings.

Physical ability tests measure an individual's abilities such as strength, endurance, and muscular movement. At an electric utility, line workers must regularly lift and carry equipment, climb ladders, and perform other physical tasks; therefore, testing of applicants' mobility, strength, and other physical attributes is job related. Some physical ability tests measure factors like range of motion, strength and posture, and cardiovascular fitness. Some companies are even using the Body Mass Index (BMI) measure as part of physical exams to determine generalized fitness for duty. However, using BMI to determine fitness can violate requirements of the 2008 ADA Amendments Act, which treats obesity as a protected characteristic.[23] Care should also be taken to limit physical ability testing until after a conditional job offer is made to avoid violating provisions of the Americans with Disabilities Act (ADA).

Various skill-based tests can be used, including **psychomotor tests**, which measure a person's dexterity, hand–eye coordination, arm–hand steadiness, and other factors. Tests such as the MacQuarie Test for Mechanical Ability can measure manual dexterity for assembly-line workers and others using psychomotor skills regularly.

Many organizations use situational tests, or **work sample tests**, which require an applicant to perform a simulated task that is a specified part of the target job. Requiring an applicant for an administrative assistant's job to type a business letter as quickly as possible would be one such test. An "in-basket" test is a work sample test in which a job candidate is asked to respond to memos in a hypothetical in-basket that are typical of the problems experienced in that job. Once again, these tests should assess criteria that are embedded in the job that is to be staffed.

Situational judgment tests are designed to measure a person's judgment in work settings. The candidate is given a situation and a list of possible solutions to the problem. The candidate then has to make judgments about how to deal with the situation. Situational judgment tests are a form of job simulation.[24]

Assessment Centers An assessment center is not a place but an assessment exercise composed of a series of evaluative tests used for selection and development. Most often used in the selection process when filling managerial openings, assessment centers consist of multiple exercises and are evaluated by multiple raters. In one assessment center, candidates go through a comprehensive interview, a pencil-and-paper test, individual and group simulations, and work exercises. Individual performance is then evaluated by a panel of trained raters.

The tests and exercises in an assessment center must reflect the content of the job for which individuals are being screened, and the types of problems faced on that job. For example, a technology communications organization used a series of assessment centers to hire employees who would interact with clients. The company found that these centers improved the selection process and also provided new employees with a good road map for individual development. Assessment centers are often expensive to operate, but they result in very little disparate impact.

7-3b Personality Tests

Personality is a unique blend of individual characteristics that can affect how people interact with their work environment. Many organizations use various personality tests that assess the degree to which candidates' attributes match specific job criteria. For instance, a sporting goods chain offers job applicants a Web-based test. The test evaluates their personal tendencies, and test scores are used to categorize individuals for the hiring decision. Many types of personality tests are available, including the Myers-Briggs test.

FIGURE 7-6   Big Five Personality Characteristics

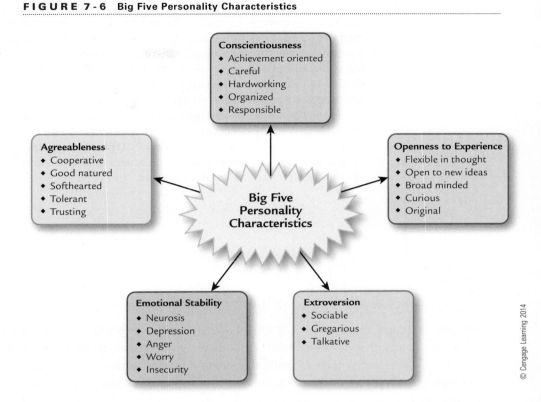

Although many personality characteristics exist, some experts believe that there is a relatively small number of underlying major traits. The most widely accepted approach to studying these underlying personality traits (although not the only one) is the "Big Five" personality framework. The Big Five traits are generally considered to be useful predictors of various types of job performance in different occupations. The factors are shown in Figure 7-6. Several of the Big Five traits are related to dimensions such as burnout and accident involvement in both work and nonwork contexts.

Faking Personality Tests Faking is a major concern for employers using personality tests. Many test publishers admit that test profiles can be falsified, and they try to reduce faking by including questions that can be used to compute a social desirability or "lie" score. Researchers also favor the use of "corrections" based on components of the test to account for faking—a preference that also constitutes a strong argument for professional scoring of personality tests.[25] Another possibility is use of a fake warning, which instructs applicants that faking can be detected and can result in a negative hiring impression.

7-3c Honesty/Integrity Tests

Companies are utilizing different tests to assess the honesty and integrity of applicants and employees. Employers use these tests as a screening mechanism to prevent the hiring of dishonest employees, to reduce the frequency of lying and theft on the job, to communicate to applicants and employees alike that dishonesty will not be tolerated, and to reduce accidents. Honesty/integrity tests can be valid as broad screening devices for organizations if used properly, and the HR Skills and Applications section discusses some of the benefits. Research also indicates that, even though honesty tests can be expensive to administer, much of these costs were justified by savings in workers' compensation claims.[26]

However, these instruments have limitations. For instance, socially desirable responding is a key concern, and some questions can be considered overly invasive, insulting, and not job related. Sometimes false-positives are generated (or an honest person is scored as "dishonest"). Test scores might be affected by individual demographic factors such as gender and race.

HR PERSPECTIVE

Using Integrity Tests Gets Better Employees

Integrity tests are among the assessment tools used by companies to help with candidate screening. These instruments measure the extent to which employees are willing to act unethically or dishonestly on the job, including lying to others, stealing resources, abusing drugs and alcohol, and harming coworkers. Use of these tests has continued to rise given that preemployment lie detector evaluations were deemed inappropriate for most jobs by the 1988 Employee Polygraph Protection Act. Integrity tests are usually placed into one of two categories, including *overt* assessments that directly indicate what is being measured, and *covert* forms that don't convey the traits and tendencies being assessed.

More recently, many companies are starting to use generalized personality inventories to better ascertain candidate fit with the organization. These instruments tap a variety of individual dimensions, with ethics being one part of the analysis. However, sectors such as retail, law enforcement, childcare, and utilities are still actively utilizing honesty tests to evaluate job candidates. AT&T incorporates integrity and personality assessments into its hiring processes to ensure good person-job fit, as well as to screen out individuals who might misuse or steal corporate resources. The Indianapolis firm hhgregg Inc., also utilizes a personality instrument that includes some questions about ethics and integrity to make good hiring decisions. Hospitality Management Corp. of Dallas found that the use of integrity tests in the properties it oversees reduced workers' compensation claims, mainly because of the more honest employees that were hired.

One of the advantages of integrity tests is that they are often considered to be a more valid selection approach compared to other preemployment screening methods such as generalized background, credit, and criminal checks. This is because honesty tests tend to be more valid predictors of how employees will act in the future, rather than focusing on what they did in the past. In fact, research shows that integrity tests are the best predictors of counterproductive actions, and evidence indicates that companies using them are hiring better employees who stay longer and perform at higher levels.[27]

Polygraphs The polygraph, more generally and incorrectly referred to as a lie detector, is a mechanical device that measures a person's galvanic skin response, heart rate, and breathing rate. The idea behind the polygraph is that if a person answers a question deliberately incorrectly, the body's physiological responses will "reveal" the falsification through the recording mechanisms of the polygraph. As a result of concerns about polygraph validity, Congress passed the Employee Polygraph Protection Act, which prohibits most employers from the use of polygraphs for pre-employment screening purposes. Federal, state, and local government agencies are exempt from the act. Also exempt are certain private-sector employers such as security companies and pharmaceutical companies. The act does allow employers to use polygraphs as part of internal investigations of thefts or losses. But in those situations, the polygraph test should be taken voluntarily, and the employee should be allowed to end the test at any time.

7-3d Controversies in Selection Testing

Two areas in selection testing generate controversies and disagreements. One is the appropriateness of general mental ability testing, and the other is the validity of personality testing for selection.

General mental ability testing is well established as a valid selection tool for many jobs, but since some minority groups tend to score lower on such exams, there is considerable controversy over whether such tests *ought* to be used.[28] When these tests are used, the case for business necessity must be made, and the instrument used should be validated for the organization using it.

Personality testing for selection flourished during the 1950s. More than 60% of large companies at one time used it for selection.[29] Sears, Standard Oil, and Procter and Gamble used such testing extensively. But in the 1960s researchers concluded that personality assessment is not a good tool for selection, and the use of these tests dropped drastically. In the 1990s, interest in research on personality as a selection tool resurfaced and vendors began selling personality-oriented selection tests. But an important research article appearing in *Personnel Psychology* concluded that personality explains so little about actual job outcomes that we should think very carefully about using it *at all* for employment decisions.[30]

7-3e Selection Interviewing

LO4 Contrast several types of selection interviews and some key considerations in conducting these interviews.

Interviewing of job applicants is done both to obtain additional information and to clarify information gathered throughout the selection process. Interviews are commonly conducted at two levels: first, as an initial screening interview to determine if the person has met minimum qualifications, and then later, as an in-depth interview with HR staff members and/or operating managers to determine if the person will fit into the designated job. Before the in-depth interview, information from all available sources is pooled so that the interviewers can reconcile conflicting information that may have emerged from tests, application forms, and references.

Some companies have excessive interview time requirements. For example, one company requires applicants to bring their lunch and spend hours on simulated work tasks, several with tight deadlines.[31] However, a court case in California held that temporary employees were owed overtime pay for time spent in job placement interviews.[32] Although this case dealt with staffing firm employees, the message is that there may be a limit on how long the employment interviewing process can

Virtual Interviews Help Hiring

Virtual interviewing is becoming a more common way to enhance the selection process in organizations, with many believing that this approach is beneficial. Virtual interviewing involves utilizing real-time interactive technology to conduct live discussion sessions with job candidates and interviewers while they are not physically present in the same room. The most common technologies that are used to conduct these interviews include video conferencing facilities and communication services offered over the Internet. There are also many vendors that offer extensive support and guidance to facilitate the process, including HireVue, and Greenjobinterview.com, and ooVoo. Experiences in organizations such as the University of California-Los Angeles and CDW suggest that both job candidates and hiring managers generally have positive views about virtual interviewing.

Regardless of the specific method used, virtual interviewing has many key advantages. For instance, candidates can attend interview sessions without having to leave where they live, and participating managers often don't have to leave their work sites to attend interview meetings. If candidates are located in their offices while being interviewed, hiring managers can also get a glimpse into how they organize their work areas. Since travel is not needed with virtual interviews, the time to screen and select job candidates can be greatly reduced. All of these advantages point to reduced total costs associated with selection.

Despite these positives, there are several disadvantages that should be considered by HR professionals. For example, some technologies used to enhance live communication (i.e., video conferencing) can be expensive and complicated to set up. In addition, some job candidates might not be comfortable with virtual interviews because the experience can be less personal than that with face-to-face interviews. Further, they might not be familiar with how to use the technology effectively, resulting in poor performance during the interview and removal from consideration. Virtual interviewing also counts on all job candidates having relatively equal access to the appropriate Internet connections and technologies, which is often not the case.[33]

reasonably go on. Other companies utilize technology to help the interview process, and virtual interviews are becoming more common in the workplace today. The HR Skills and Applications: Virtual Interviews Help Hiring explores this new trend in employee selection.

7-3f Inter-Rater Reliability and Validity

Interviews must be reliable and allow interviewers, despite their limitations, to pick the same applicant capabilities again and again. High *intra*-rater reliability (within the same interviewer) can be demonstrated, but only moderate-to-low *inter*-rater reliability (across different interviewers) is generally shown. Inter-rater reliability becomes important when each of several interviewers is selecting employees from a pool of applicants, or if the employer uses team or panel interviews with multiple interviewers.

FIGURE 7-7 Validity and Structure in Selection Interviews

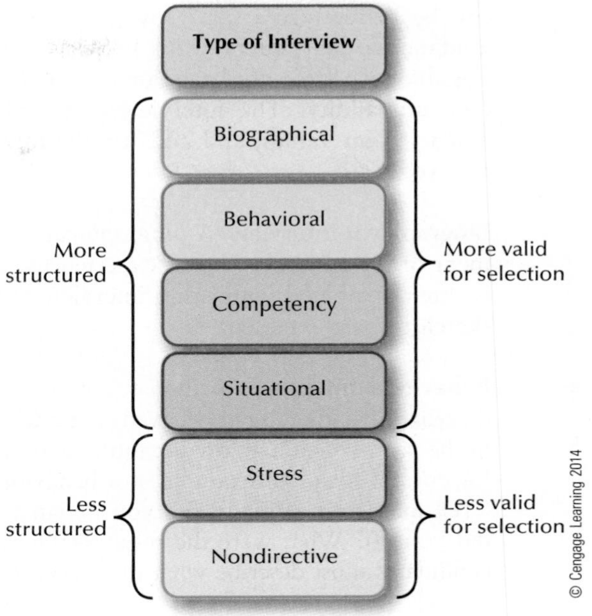

However, interviews must also be valid for the purposes of useful selection, and validity can vary depending on the degree of structure that is utilized in an interview format. Basically, an unstructured interview does not usually provide much actual validity, causing a growth in the popularity of structured interviews. As Figure 7-7 shows, various types of selection interviews are used. They range from structured to unstructured, and they vary in terms of validity.

7-3g Structured Interviews

Structured interview
Interview that uses a set of prepared, job-related questions that are asked of all applicants.

A **structured interview** involves a set of prepared, job-related questions that are asked of all applicants so that comparisons can be made more easily, resulting in better selection decisions. The structured interview is useful in the initial screening process because many applicants can be effectively evaluated and compared. However, the structured interview does not have to be rigid. The predetermined questions should be asked in a logical manner but should not be read word for word. The applicants should be allowed adequate opportunity to explain their answers, and interviewers should probe with additional questions until they fully understand the responses. This process can make the structured interview more reliable and valid than other interview approaches.[34]

Structured interviews—in any of several forms, including biographical, behavioral, competency, and situational—are useful when making selection decisions. The structured format ensures that a given interviewer has similar information on each candidate. It also ensures that when several interviewers ask the same questions of applicants, there is greater consistency in the subsequent evaluation of those candidates. In fact, it has been recommended that structured interviews be utilized in selection efforts for federal jobs because individual work performance can be better forecasted. However, companies might have to provide additional guidance to help interviewers implement this approach.[35] Interview questions and possible responses are based on job analysis and checked by job experts to ensure content validity. The interviewer typically codes the suitability of the answer, assigns point values, and adds up the total number of points each interviewee has received.

Biographical Interview A *biographical interview* focuses on a chronological assessment of the candidate's past experiences. This type of interview is widely used and is often combined with other interview techniques. Overall, the process provides a sketch of past experiences.

Behavioral interview
Interview in which applicants give specific examples of how they have performed a certain task or handled a problem in the past.

Behavioral Interview In the **behavioral interview** technique, applicants are asked to describe how they have behaved or performed a certain task or handled a problem in the past, which may predict future actions and show how applicants are best suited for current jobs. An example of a behavioral interview line of questioning might be: "Tell me about a time when you initiated a project. What was the situation? What did you do? What were the results?" Questions such as these can be useful because candidates must describe what they have done to complete job requirements.

Competency Interview The *competency interview* is similar to the behavioral interview except that the questions are designed to provide the interviewer with a benchmark against which to measure the applicant's response. A *competency profile* for the position is often utilized, which includes a list of competencies necessary to do that particular job. Using competencies as a benchmark to predict job candidate success is useful because interviewers can identify the factors needed in specific jobs.

Situational interview
Structured interview that contains questions about how applicants might handle specific job situations.

Situational Interview The **situational interview** contains questions about how applicants might handle specific job situations. A variation is termed the *case study interview*, which requires a job candidate to diagnose and correct organizational challenges during the interview. Situational interviews assess what the interviewee would consider to be the best option, not necessarily what they did in a similar situation.[36]

7-3h Less-Structured Interviews

Some interviews are done unplanned and are not structured at all. Such interviewing techniques may be appropriate for fact finding, or for counseling interviews. However, they are not best for selection interviewing. These interviews may be conducted by operating managers or supervisors who have had little interview training. An *unstructured interview* occurs when the interviewer improvises by asking questions that are not predetermined. A *semistructured interview* is a guided conversation in which broad questions are asked and new questions arise as a result of the discussion. For example, What would you do differently if you could start over again?

Stress interview
Interview designed to create anxiety and put pressure on applicants to see how they respond.

Stress Interview A **stress interview** is designed to create anxiety and put pressure on applicants to see how they respond. In a stress interview, the interviewer assumes an extremely aggressive and insulting posture. Firms using this approach often justify doing so because employees will encounter high degrees of job stress. For example, stress interview might be appropriate in selecting FBI agents or people for high-stress, high-pressure customer complaint positions, but it is not appropriate for most positions. The stress interview can be a high-risk approach for an employer because an applicant is probably already anxious, and the stress interview can easily generate a poor image of the interviewer and the employer. Consequently, an applicant the organization wishes to hire might turn down the job offer.

Nondirective interview
Interview that uses questions developed from the answers to previous questions.

A **nondirective interview** uses questions that are developed from the answers to previous questions. The interviewer asks general questions designed to prompt applicants to describe themselves. The interviewer then uses applicants' responses to shape the next question. With a nondirective interview, as with any less-structured interview, difficulties for selection decisions include keeping the conversation job related and obtaining comparable data on various applicants. Many nondirective interviews are only partly organized; as a result, a combination of general and specific questions is asked in no set order, and different questions are asked of different applicants for the same job. Comparing and ranking candidates is thus more open to subjective judgments and legal challenges, so they are best used for selection sparingly, if at all.

7-3i Who Conducts Interviews?

Job interviews can be conducted by an individual, by several individuals sequentially, or by panels or teams. For some jobs, such as entry-level positions requiring fewer skills, applicants might be interviewed solely by a human resource professional. For other jobs, employers screen applicants by using multiple interviews, beginning with a human resource professional and followed by the appropriate supervisors and managers. Then a selection decision is made collectively. Managers need to ensure that multiple interviews are not redundant.

Panel interview
Interview in which several interviewers meet with candidate at the same time.

Team interview
Interview in which applicants are interviewed by the team members with whom they will work.

Other interview formats are also utilized. In a **panel interview**, several interviewers meet with the candidate at the same time so that the same responses are heard by all. Panel interviews may be combined with individual interviews. In a **team interview**, applicants are interviewed by the team members with whom they will work. However, without proper planning, an unstructured interview can occur during these group sessions, and applicants are sometimes uncomfortable with the format.

7-3j Effective Interviewing

Many people think that the ability to interview is an innate talent, but this contention is difficult to support. Just being personable and liking to talk is no guarantee that someone will be an effective interviewer. In fact, there are many factors related to interviewers that can influence how well interviewees perform, including the ability to prompt good social interaction, personality, and the design and structure of the interview itself.[37] Even the questions that are asked of individuals can arguably affect the quality of interview sessions, and Figure 7-8 provides a variety of questions commonly used in selection interviews and what they are attempting to predict.

Interviewing skills are developed through training. Suggestions for making interviewing more effective are as follows:

- *Plan the interview.* Interviewers should review all information before the interview, and then identify specific areas for questioning.[38]
- *Control the interview.* This includes knowing in advance what information must be collected, systematically collecting it during the interview, and stopping when

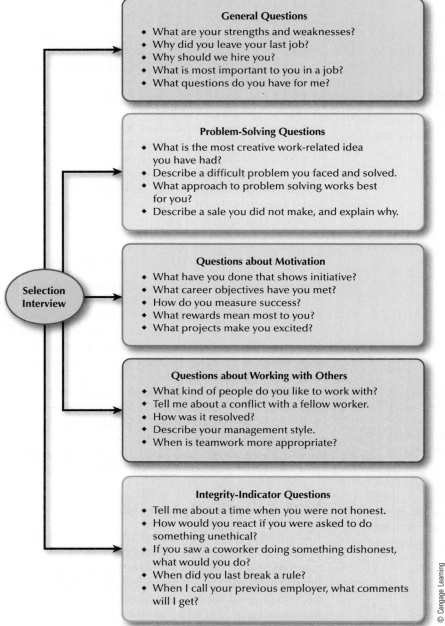

FIGURE 7-8 Questions Commonly Asked in Selection Interviews

General Questions
- What are your strengths and weaknesses?
- Why did you leave your last job?
- Why should we hire you?
- What is most important to you in a job?
- What questions do you have for me?

Problem-Solving Questions
- What is the most creative work-related idea you have had?
- Describe a difficult problem you faced and solved.
- What approach to problem solving works best for you?
- Describe a sale you did not make, and explain why.

Questions about Motivation
- What have you done that shows initiative?
- What career objectives have you met?
- How do you measure success?
- What rewards mean most to you?
- What projects make you excited?

Questions about Working with Others
- What kind of people do you like to work with?
- Tell me about a conflict with a fellow worker.
- How was it resolved?
- Describe your management style.
- When is teamwork more appropriate?

Integrity-Indicator Questions
- Tell me about a time when you were not honest.
- How would you react if you were asked to do something unethical?
- If you saw a coworker doing something dishonest, what would you do?
- When did you last break a rule?
- When I call your previous employer, what comments will I get?

Selection Interview

© Cengage Learning

that information has been collected. An interviewer should not monopolize the conversation.
- *Use effective questioning techniques.* Use questions that will produce full and complete answers that can be evaluated on the basis of job relatedness.
- *Get a balanced view.* Interviews should consider both the positive and negative attributes of job candidates to make an informed hiring decision.

Questions to Avoid The following are kinds of questions that should be avoide, selection interviews:

- *Yes/no questions*: Unless verifying specific information, the interviewer should avoid questions that can be answered "yes" or "no." For example, "Did you have good attendance on your last job?" will probably be answered simply "yes."
- *Obvious questions*: An obvious question is one for which the interviewer already has the answer and the applicant knows it.
- *Questions that rarely produce a true answer*: Avoid questions that prompt a less-than-honest response. An example is "How did you get along with your coworkers?" The likely answer is "Just fine."
- *Leading questions*: A leading question is one to which the answer is obvious from the way the question is asked. For example, "How do you like working with other people?" suggests the answer "I like it."
- *Illegal/inappropriate questions*: Questions that involve information such as race, age, gender, national origin, marital status, number of children, and other family-related issues are illegal.[39] They are just as inappropriate in the interview as on the application form.
- *Questions that are not job related*: All questions should be directly job related.

Listening Responses to Avoid Effective interviewers avoid listening responses such as nodding, pausing, making casual remarks, echoing, and mirroring. The applicant might try to please the interviewers by examining the feedback provided. However, giving no response to an applicant's answers may imply boredom or inattention. Therefore, interviewers should use friendly but neutral comments when acknowledging the applicant's responses.

7-3k Problems in the Interview

Operating managers and supervisors are more likely than HR personnel to use poor interviewing techniques because they do not interview often or lack training. Several problems anyone may exhibit include the following:

- *Snap judgments*: Some interviewers decide whether an applicant is suitable within the first two to four minutes of the interview, and spend the rest of the time looking for evidence to support their judgment.
- *Negative emphasis*: When evaluating suitability, unfavorable information about an applicant is often emphasized more than favorable information.
- *Halo effect*: The *halo effect* occurs when an interviewer allows a positive characteristic, such as agreeableness, to overshadow other evidence. The phrase *devil's horns* describes the reverse of the halo effect; this occurs when a negative characteristic, such as inappropriate dress, overshadows other traits.
- *Biases and stereotyping*: "Similarity" bias occurs when interviewers favor or select people whom they believe to be like themselves on the basis of a variety of personal factors. Interviewers should also avoid any personal tendencies to stereotype individuals because of demographic characteristics and differences.
- *Cultural noise*: Interviewers must learn to recognize and handle cultural noise, which stems from what applicants believe is socially acceptable rather than what is factual.

L05 Specify how legal concerns affect background investigations of applicants and use of medical examinations in the selection process.

7-4 ■ BACKGROUND INVESTIGATIONS

The need for background checking can be found in a wide range of positions: school teachers, janitors, bank tellers, and so on.[40] Background information can be obtained from many sources. Some of these sources include past job records, credit history, testing records, educational and certification records, drug tests, Social Security numbers, sex offender lists, motor vehicle records, and military records.

Failure to check the backgrounds of people who are hired can lead to embarrassment and legal liability. Hiring workers who commit violent acts on the job is one example. For jobs in certain industries, such as those that provide services to children, vulnerable adults, security, in-home services, and financial services, background checks are mandated in some states. Nationally background checks are required for people with commercial drivers' licenses who drive tractor-trailer rigs and buses interstate.

7-4a Negligent Hiring and Retention

Negligent hiring
Occurs when an employer fails to check an employee's background and the employee injures someone on the job.

Negligent retention
Occurs when an employer becomes aware that an employee may be unfit for work but continues to employ the person, and the person injures someone.

Lawyers say that an employer's liability hinges on how well it investigates an applicant's background. Consequently, details provided on the application form should be investigated extensively, and these efforts should be documented.

Negligent hiring occurs when an employer fails to check an employee's background and the employee later injures or harms someone while performing job duties. There is a potential negligent hiring problem when an employer hires an unfit employee, a background check is insufficient, or an employer does not research potential risk factors that would prevent a positive hire decision.[41] Similarly, **negligent retention** occurs when an employer becomes aware that an employee may be unfit for employment but continues to employ the person, and the person injures someone. Negligent hiring and retention have become noteworthy issues in the trucking/shipping industry where brokers are being held liable for the accidents of contractors when safety records are not adequately considered.[42]

Many organizations use outside vendors that specialize in conducting background checks because these firms can provide these services much more efficiently and effectively. Background checks can raise the concern that the information reported might be inaccurate or outdated. For instance, a woman was denied employment by a company because a background report provided by an outside firm contained adverse information. However, after getting the report corrected, she was hired by the company. Consequently, the information provided in criminal record checks should be used judiciously and with caution. Despite the frequency of criminal background checks, some companies do hire ex-offenders, which is discussed in the HR Perspective: Should a Company Consider Hiring Ex-Offenders? However, companies need to consider the potential negative problems associated with negligent hiring claims in some jobs when hiring ex-offenders.[43]

Some employers are using personal websites and the Internet to perform background checks on employees. Many believe that websites provide extra insight into a job candidate's individual characteristics, regardless of the information that has been submitted to the company through the application form or résumé. Online network sites such as Facebook are also used to obtain a variety of personal information. There is some debate about the appropriateness of requesting user passwords for social networking websites, especially if they are not being used for screening.[44]

ETHICS

Should a Company Consider Hiring Ex-Offenders?

The hiring of ex-offenders is likely to be much more common since a noteworthy portion of the population has been convicted of a crime. These individuals face many challenges when it comes to finding good jobs. Organizations that have hired ex-offenders have experienced some positive benefits from workers who appreciate the chance to work despite their past histories, and of course some negative ones too. Some organizations equate these opportunities to corporate social responsibility because providing employment to ex-offenders can help the communities in which companies operate.

In the future, it might also be more difficult to deny these individuals employment because doing so might cause disparate impact for some job seekers. Companies will also have to be more proactive about providing sound evidence that supports a business necessity argument. There are industries such as insurance, finance, and firearms retailing that routinely evaluate the criminal histories of job candidates. Others such as aviation and child care require certain specific types of background assessments. Some HR professionals avoid taking into consideration past offenses associated with violence, fraud, or sex on the basis of EEOC provisions. However, there are some measures companies can take to better manage the employment of ex-offenders:

- Be aware of all state and federal laws related to fair employment and background checks to avoid the ever increasing potential for lawsuits.
- Check the language used in job announcements to make sure that ads comply with EEOC standards.
- Background checks should be conducted in the later stages of recruitment and selection, and profiles for individual jobs can be developed that specify which specific types of background checks need to be conducted.
- Work with parole officers and prisoners to become comfortable discussing the kinds of issues that affect ex-offenders, and hire individuals who are willing to take responsibility for past actions.[45]

In addition, much of the information on personal Web pages appears to be difficult to erase or alter, so some candidates and employees just have to live with less-than-flattering content once it is posted. Also, damaging information can be posted about individuals by anyone on the Internet, further complicating the process of performing fair and legitimate background checks if this information is utilized in job selection.

7-4b Legal Constraints on Background Investigations

Various federal and state laws protect the rights of individuals whose backgrounds may be investigated during preemployment screening. One important step when conducting a background investigation is to obtain a signed release from the applicant giving the employer permission to conduct the investigation. Another requirement is making sure that background investigations are relevant to the jobs being performed and part of business necessity.[46]

Credit History and Criminal Background Checks Many employers check applicants' credit histories. The logic is that poor credit histories may signal, either correctly or incorrectly, a certain level of responsibility. Firms that check applicants' credit records must comply with the federal Fair Credit Reporting Act. This act basically requires disclosing that a credit check is being conducted, obtaining written consent from the person being checked, and furnishing the applicant with a copy of the report. Some state laws also prohibit employers from obtaining certain credit information. Credit history should be checked on applicants for jobs in which use of, access to, or management of money is an essential job function. For example, financial institutions have a vested interest in checking the credit histories for its employees who handle money, and retailers might conduct credit checks on cashiers and managerial staff who also deal directly with money.

Mismanaged credit checks might violate the Fair Credit Reporting Act and prompt complaints to the EEOC. Companies use these assessments only when needed, such as hiring for a job that involves financial responsibility.[47] A recent study also found that the utilization of credit checks for hiring employees was not viewed in a favorable manner among participating students.[48] Further, states are exploring legislation that might limit the use of credit history checks for the purposes of employment screening.[49]

Employers conduct criminal background checks to prevent negligent hiring lawsuits. However, they must make sure that these checks are performed consistently and fairly across different employees applying for similar types of positions.[50] For example, PepsiCo recently had to revise its criminal background check approach and pay a significant fine because it unfairly took into consideration individual offenses that were not related to performance in the job being staffed.[51] Figure 7-9 provides some practical advice for using criminal and credit history background checks.

7-4c Medical Examinations and Inquiries

Medical information on applicants may be used to determine their physical and mental capabilities for performing jobs. Physical standards for jobs should be realistic, justifiable, and linked to essential job requirements. Even though workers with disabilities can competently perform many jobs, they may sometimes be rejected because of their physical or mental limitations.[52]

FIGURE 7-9 Practical Advice for Criminal and Credit History Checks

Key Considerations
• Questions about arrests are avoided on application forms and during interviews.
• Checks might not be performed until an offer is ready to be extended.
• Determine which jobs require criminal/credit checks and which ones don't.
• Past criminal history or poor credit do not necessarily prevent a positive hiring decision.
• HR should determine whether a person is employable when challenges are identified.

Source: Adapted from Bill Roberts, "Close-Up on Screening," *HR Magazine*, February 2011, 23–29.

ADA and Medical Inquiries The ADA prohibits the use of preemployment medical exams, except for drug tests, until a job has been conditionally offered. Also, the ADA prohibits a company from rejecting an individual because of a disability and from asking job applicants any question related to current or past medical history until a conditional job offer has been made. Once a conditional offer of employment has been made, then some organizations ask the applicant to complete a pre-employment health checklist or the employer pays for a physical examination of the applicant.[53] It should be made clear that the applicant who has been offered the job is not really hired until successful completion of the physical inquiry.

Drug Testing Drug testing, a widely used selection tool, may be conducted as part of a medical exam, or it may be done separately. If drug tests are used, employers should remember that the accuracy of tests varies according to the type of test used, the drug tested, and the quality of the laboratory where the test samples are sent. Because of the potential impact of prescription drugs on test results, applicants should complete a detailed questionnaire on this matter before the testing. If an individual tests positive for drug use, then an independent medical laboratory should administer a second, more detailed analysis. Whether urine, blood, saliva, or hair samples are used, the process of obtaining, labeling, and transferring the samples to the testing lab should be outlined clearly and definite policies and procedures should be established and followed.[54]

7-4d Previous Employment Checks/Personal References

Work-related references from previous employers and supervisors can provide a valuable snapshot of a candidate's background and characteristics. Previous employment checks protect the company from negligent hiring claims, provide an overview of job candidates' past performance and honesty, and verify work credentials. Figure 7-10 outlines some of the important reasons for contacting applicant references.[55]

With regard to personal references, recommendations provided by job candidates can sometimes be of limited predictive value because individuals knowingly pick references of people who will speak highly of them.[56] Previous supervisors and employers can often provide more useful information that can be utilized to more effectively evaluate job candidates. Good questions to ask previous supervisors or employers include the following:

- What were the dates of employment?
- What was the position held?
- What were the job duties?
- What strengths/weaknesses did you observe?
- Were there any problems?
- Would you rehire?

There are many ways to conduct employment checks, and one of the most common methods involves using the telephone to get information. Managers should consider using an approach that attempts to verify the factual information given by the applicant. Some organizations send preprinted reference forms to individuals who are giving references for applicants. These forms often contain a release statement signed by the applicant, so that those providing references can see that they

FIGURE 7-10 Reasons for Previous Employment Checks

Why Check Applicant References?

- To Prevent Negligent Hiring
- To Verify Individual Credentials/History
- To Evaluate Past Work/Future Potential
- To Evaluate Applicant's Character
- To Prevent Unethical Work Conduct
- To Enhance Workplace Safety
- To Follow State and Federal Regulations

ETHICS

have been released from liability on the information they furnish. Figure 7-11 provides a helpful checklist of recommendations for handling references during the selection process.[57] Another challenge that that HR professionals need to recognize are the challenges related to fake references, and the HR Ethics: Fake References A New Trend Hurting Selection discusses this issue.

7-4e Making the Job Offer

The final step of the selection process involves extending an offer. Offers are made to job candidates after they have met the minimum job requirements and are comparatively more qualified than other applicants. A threshold selection approach that evaluates job candidates across different tests and evaluative procedures on the basis of clear benchmarks can be an effective tool for identifying top individuals for job offers.[58]

Job offers are often given over the telephone. Many companies then formalize the offer in a letter that is sent to the applicant. Some believe that the offer document should be reviewed by legal counsel and that the terms and conditions of employment be clearly identified. Care should be taken to avoid vague, general statements and promises about bonuses, work schedules, or other matters that might change later. These documents should also provide for the selected candidate to sign an acceptance of the offer and return it to the employer, who should place it in the candidate's personnel files.

FIGURE 7-11 Checklist for Handling Applicant References

> ✔ Create and follow specific guidelines for work checks/references.
>
> ✔ Specify that only well-trained HR/hiring managers perform checks.
>
> ✔ Require candidates to provide a list of previous supervisors.
>
> ✔ Get written consent to communicate with former employers.
>
> ✔ Communicate by telephone or e-mail with previous work sources.
>
> ✔ Document details about employment contacts and opinions.

HR ETHICS

Fake References: A New Trend Hurting Selection

HR professionals need to be aware of the ethical challenges associated with performing background checks on applicants for the purposes of selection. For instance, evidence indicates that job candidates often include inaccurate and/or misleading information on their resumes, and a poor job market might encourage individuals to further exaggerate their educational and professional experiences. Slowdowns in the economy also cause some job seekers to provide fake references in order to appear more marketable to companies.

Web-based organizations exist, such as www.careerexcise.com and www.fakeresume.com, that provide fake reference services, including false verbal references over the telephone, fabricated letters of recommendation, and documentation outlining "made-up" work experiences. Some job candidates have even resorted to providing their own names as references by pretending to be legitimate recommenders.

Given these challenges, the following list provides a summary of several key guidelines that should be considered so that good selection decisions can be made:

- Individuals performing reference checks should never rely on phone numbers such as those from cell phones that cannot be appropriately confirmed.
- When a candidate's résumé has discrepancies, or references appear suspicious, hiring managers must make the extra effort to find sources that verify the information provided. These due diligence efforts could include searching the Internet for more information or making phone calls to other knowledgeable parties.
- If it is suspected that a job candidate is fabricating previous work experiences, exaggerating previous salary, or is describing companies that might not exist, then HR professionals should ask for a copy of the W-2 form.[59]

L06 Describe the major issues to be considered when selecting candidates for global assignments.

GLOBAL

7-5 ■ GLOBAL STAFFING ISSUES

Staffing global assignments involves making selection decisions that impact (or take place in) other countries. When staffing global assignments, cost is a major consideration because establishing a business professional in another country can run as high as $1 million for a three-year job assignment. Further, if a business professional quits an international assignment prematurely or wants to transfer home, associated costs can be even greater. Failure rates for global assignments can run as high as 50% of those sent overseas.

7-5a Types of Global Employees

As noted earlier, global organizations can be staffed in many ways, including with expatriates, host-country nationals, and third-country nationals. Each staffing option presents some unique HR management challenges.[60] For instance, when staffing with citizens of different countries, different tax laws and other factors apply. HR professionals need to be knowledgeable about the laws and customs of each country represented in their workforce.[61] Experienced expatriates can provide a pool of talent that can be used as the firm expands operations into other countries.

7-5b Selection Process for Global Assignments

The selection process for an international assignment should provide a realistic picture of the life, work, and culture to which the employee may be sent. HR managers start by preparing a comprehensive description of the job to be done such as typical responsibilities and work duties. Figure 7-12 shows many key competencies for successful global employees, which include the following:

- *Cultural adjustment*: Individuals who accept foreign job assignments need to be able to successfully adjust to cultural differences.
- *Personal characteristics*: The experiences of many global firms demonstrate that the best employees in the home country may not be the best employees in a global assignment, primarily because of personal characteristics of individuals.
- *Organizational requirements*: Many global employers find that knowledge of the organization and how it operates is important.
- *Communication skills*: Expatriate employees should be able to communicate in the host-country language both verbally and in writing.
- *Personal/family concerns*: The preferences and attitudes of spouses and other family members can influence the success of expatriate assignments.

There are many issues that organizations face when making global selection decisions. A growing issue for U.S. firms that hire individuals to fill jobs in other countries is the need for adequate background checks. Global companies want to ensure that their employees have acceptable work histories and personal characteristics. To satisfy this demand, many firms have begun to specialize in preemployment screening of global employees. Some countries have government-controlled employment processes that require foreign employers to obtain government approval in order to hire local employees. Many countries such as the United States and Australia require foreign workers to obtain work permits or visas.

FIGURE 7-12 Selection Factors for Global Employees

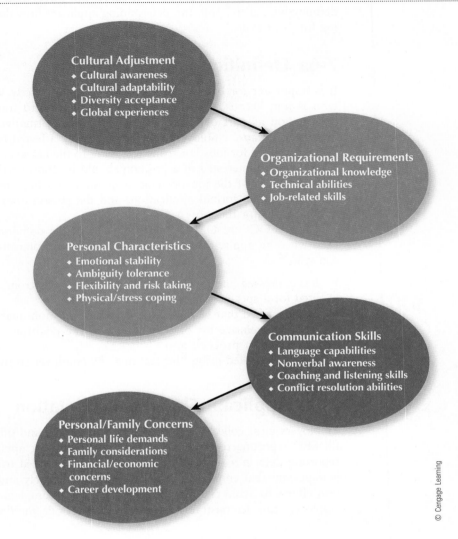

Cultural Adjustment
- ◆ Cultural awareness
- ◆ Cultural adaptability
- ◆ Diversity acceptance
- ◆ Global experiences

Organizational Requirements
- ◆ Organizational knowledge
- ◆ Technical abilities
- ◆ Job-related skills

Personal Characteristics
- ◆ Emotional stability
- ◆ Ambiguity tolerance
- ◆ Flexibility and risk taking
- ◆ Physical/stress coping

Communication Skills
- ◆ Language capabilities
- ◆ Nonverbal awareness
- ◆ Coaching and listening skills
- ◆ Conflict resolution abilities

Personal/Family Concerns
- ◆ Personal life demands
- ◆ Family considerations
- ◆ Financial/economic concerns
- ◆ Career development

© Cengage Learning

For U.S.-based firms, the assignment of women and members of racial/ethnic minorities to international posts involves complying with U.S. EEOC regulations and laws. Also, most U.S. EEOC regulations and laws apply to foreign-owned firms operating in the United States.

7-6 ■ LEGAL CONCERNS IN THE SELECTION PROCESS

Selection is subject to many regulations, especially the EEO regulations and laws discussed previously. All steps in the selection process, application forms, interviews, tests, background investigations, and any other selection activities must be conducted in a nondiscriminatory manner. But three areas deserve special mention: defining who is an applicant, determining applicant flow documentation, and selecting for "soft skills."

7-6a Definition of an Applicant

It is important for employers to carefully define exactly who is an applicant and who is not, because many employers are required to track and report applicant information as part of equal employment and affirmative action plans. It is also important because employers may be negatively affected by individuals who claim to have applied for jobs but really just want to file lawsuits. Any minimally-qualified person who is interested in a position should be considered an applicant even if no formal posting of the job opening in question has been made, the person has not filed any sort of formal application, and the person does not meet the minimum qualifications for the job.

The EEOC and OFCCP have agreed on this definition of "applicant" to be used when an application has been submitted electronically. An applicant is a person who[62]

- has expressed interest through the Internet or electronically and is being considered for a specific position by the employer;
- has identified that he or she has the basic position qualifications;
- does not remove his or her interest in the position at anytime during the selection process; and
- has been ranked using "hit features" by employer software.

7-6b Applicant Flow Documentation

Employers must collect applicant data on race, sex, and other demographics to fulfill EEO reporting requirements. Many employers ask applicants to provide EEOC reporting data in a separate form that may be attached to the application form. It is important that employers review this form separately and not use it in any selection efforts to avoid claims of impropriety. Since completing the form is voluntary, employers can demonstrate that they tried to obtain the data.

7-6c "Soft Skills" and Selection

Selection in its "scientific" form is about finding valid predictors of what will be needed on a job and picking people who score high on those predictors. These "hard skills" include cognitive skills, the acquiring of knowledge through education, and technical skills. Alternatively, "soft skills," which include interpersonal, human behavior, and leadership skills, often complement other characteristics and prompt outstanding individual job performance.[63] Even though these skills can be challenging to identify, there is interest in the assessment and development of "emotional intelligence," or individual self-awareness and self-regulation that enhances one's ability to work well with others, as a mechanism for cultivating soft skills. Companies might consider using one of the available measurement tools to assess that important dimension.[64]

SUMMARY

- Selection is the process that matches individuals and their qualifications to jobs in an organization.
- Placement of people should consider both person/job fit and person/organization fit.
- Mismatches in fit can occur because of skills, geography, time required, earning expectations, and work/family issues.
- Predictors linked to criteria are used to identify the applicants who are most likely to perform jobs successfully.
- The selection process—from applicant interest through preemployment screening, application, testing, interviewing, and background investigation—must be handled by trained, knowledgeable individuals.
- Truth-in-hiring lawsuits may arise from overselling a job.
- Employers are using electronic preemployment screening to cut down applicant pools.
- Application forms must meet EEO guidelines and must ask only for job-related information.
- Selection tests include ability tests, assessment centers, personality tests, and honesty/integrity tests. Some are controversial.
- Structured interviews, including behavioral and situational ones, are more effective and face

- fewer EEO compliance concerns than do unstructured interviews and nondirective interviews.
- Interviews can be conducted individually, by multiple individuals, or by technology. Regardless of the method, effective interviewing questioning techniques should be used.
- Background investigation can be conducted in a variety of areas. Both when requesting and when giving reference information, employers must take care to avoid potential legal concerns such as negligent hiring and negligent retention.
- Global organizations can be staffed by individuals who are expatriates, host-country nationals, or third-country nationals.
- Selection factors for global employees include cultural adjustment, personal characteristics, communication skills, personal/family concerns, and organizational requirements.
- Selection decisions must be based on job-related criteria in order to comply with various legal requirements.
- HR professionals must be careful to properly identify, track, and document applicants.
- Selecting for "soft skills" must follow the model used for more visible skills.

CRITICAL THINKING CHALLENGES

1. Develop a set of soft skills necessary for a college professor's job.
2. Put together a structured interview for hiring assistant managers at a large retail store.
3. How would you do a complete background investigation on applicants to minimize concerns about negligent hiring?
4. Your accounting manager has decided that a behavioral interview to select accountants will solve many hiring problems. What can you tell the manager about this type of interview and whether it is likely to be effective? Check www.job-interview.net and other sources to gather information.

5. Your insurance company recently entered into a business contract with a company in the financial industry that requires extensive background checks for all your existing employees and future applicants who will be doing work associated with the contract. Previously your company conducted only employment verification checks in the hiring process. The management team discussions have raised questions and concerns about issues that need to be considered as the company develops and implements a more extensive background screening protocol. Resources to help you identify issues, best practices, and requirements can be found at

www.hire-safe.com/Employment_Background_
Check_Guidelines.pdf.

A. What concerns does your company need to
consider in following background check
guidelines?

B. Discuss with the management team the
steps your company needs to take to ensure
that it complies with the Fair Credit
Reporting Act.

CASE

Using Data to Enhance Hiring Decisions

Many organizations struggle with selection because
predicting how employees will perform once hired
is difficult. Hiring decisions are frequently made
even more difficult because of a lack of awareness
of the key employee knowledge and skills that are
needed to function effectively in a job, as well as
the lack of good selection instruments and tests
that enables hiring managers to identify the best
job candidates. These challenges can lead to
improper selection decisions, poor employee job
attitudes and job fit, and high turnover, so HR
professionals have a vested interest in determining
better ways of identifying good talent for their
companies.

One approach that has been used extensively in
other functions, and that is being utilized more frequently in HR, involves the use of primary data to
facilitate good decision-making. Using data to drive
selection decisions provides hiring managers the
right information needed to identify the kinds of
characteristics individuals should ideally have to
successfully perform work. Information is usually
collected directly from employees working in a particular position, often times with a questionnaire,
and this information is correlated with performance
data in an effort to determine which characteristics
are significantly related to the kinds of positive
work outcomes that the company expects from its
employees (i.e., low turnover, high productivity,
etc.). After identifying a list of positive characteristics, HR professionals can develop selection tests
and other evaluation tools that can be used to
make more appropriate hiring decisions.

One organization that has successfully relied on
data to enhance decisions related to employee selection is Bon-Ton stores Inc., a retail organization
with several hundred stores located in 23 states.

The company was experiencing high turnover,
specifically among its cosmetic salespersons, and
wanted to take proper steps to bring these numbers
down to more acceptable levels. The selection test
used by the company was apparently not identifying
the proper talent needed in this particular job, Bon-
Ton turned to the outside recruitment firm Kenexa
for assistance with hiring.

A study was conducted to identify the employee
characteristics that predicted high job performance in
the sales position, and information was collected
from several hundred cosmetic associates using a
250-item questionnaire. Performance data were also
compiled from Bon-Ton's productivity archives. The
analysis enabled the company to isolate the factors
that led to job success, and an assessment test and
standardized interview questions were developed to
make better hiring decisions in the company.

The results have been very positive for Bon-
Ton. For instance, turnover statistics for the cosmetics sales associates had decreased dramatically.
In addition, sales performance has increased in the
cosmetics group, further highlighting the validity of
the program. The company is now planning to use
this selection approach in other areas of the firm to
enhance hiring decisions for other jobs.[65]

QUESTIONS

1. Discuss how using a data-driven approach to
hiring can enhance selection in companies.

2. What other methods besides surveying might be
used to collect important selection data from
employees?

3. What types of skills will HR professionals need
to develop a data-driven approach to selection in
companies?

SUPPLEMENTAL CASES

Full Disclosure on Sex Offenders?

This case investigates how Megan's Law, which specifies that all states are required to have all convicted sex offenders register so that residents are aware of their presence in a neighborhood, generates implications about the use of criminal registries in hiring and employee management. (For the case, go to www.cengage.com/management/mathis.)

Strategic Selection: A Review of Two Companies

This case shows how Hallmark and United Health Group use selection as part of their strategic approach to HR. (For the case, go to www.cengage.com/management/mathis.)

Selecting a Programmer

This case demonstrates how using a test after a pool of candidates has already been interviewed can present some difficulties. (For the case, go to www.cengage.com/management/mathis.)

NOTES

1. Based on Mark McGraw, "The HR-Ethics Alliance," *Human Resource Executive Online*, June 16, 2011, www.hreonline.com.

2. Alan Krueger and David Schkade, "Sorting in the Labor Market," *Journal of Human Resources*, 43 (2008), No. 4, 859–883.

3. Melanie Wanzek, "On Second Thought," *Sunday World Herald*, May 10, 2009, CR1.

4. Metin Celik, I. Deha Er, and Y. Ilker Topcu, "Computer-Based Systematic Executive Model of HRM in Maritime Transportation Industry: The Case of Master Selection for Embarking on Board Merchant Ships," *Expect Systems with Applications*, 36 (2009), 1048–1060.

5. Robert Grossman, "Hiring to Fit the Culture," *HR Magazine*, February 2009, 41–50.

6. Jon Billsberry, Danielle L. Talbot, Patrick C. Nelson, Julian A. Edwards, Steven G. Godrich, Ross A. G. Davidson, and Christopher J. P. Carter, Book review of *The People Make the Place: Dynamic Linkages Between Individuals and Organizations* by D. Brent Smith (editor). *Personnel Psychology*, 63 (2010), 483–487.

7. Jon Billsberry, Julian A. Edwards, Danielle L. Talbot, Patrick C. Nelson, Ross A. G. Davidson, Steven G. Godrich, and Philip J. G. Marsh, book review of *Perspectives on Organizational Fit* by Cheri Ostroff and Timothy A. Judge. *Personnel Psychology*, 62 (2009), 880–883.

8. Dave Bartram, "The Great Eight Competencies: A Criterion-Centric Approach to Validation," *Journal of Applied Psychology*, 90 (2005), 1185–1203.

9. Murray Barrick and Ryan Zimmerman, "Hiring for Retention and Performance," *Human Resource Management*, March–April 2009, 183–206.

10. Peter Cappelli, "The Impact of a High School Diploma," *HR Executive Online*, August 18, 2008, www.hreonline.com, 1–3.

11. Aldo Sualdi, "Job Seekers Put Résumé Responders in a Frazzle," *The Denver Post*, November 8, 2009, K1; Gina Ruiz, "Job Candidate Assessment Tests Go Virtual," *Workforce Management Online*, January 2008, 1–4.

12. Adrienne Hedger, "3 Ways to Improve Your Employee Screening," *Workforce Management*, March 16, 2009, 26–30.

13. Andrew O'Connell, "The Myth of the Overqualified Worker," *Harvard Business Review*, December 2010, 30; Lorri Freifeld, "Hiring the Overqualified," *Training*, March/April 2011, 8.

14. Wendy Webb, "Work is the New Retirement," *Training*, March/April 2009, 44–45.

15. Lin Grensing-Pophal, "Tackling the Issue of Employee Identity," *Human Resource Executive Online*, September 23, 2011, www.hreonline.com.

16. Alessandro Acquisti and Ralph Gross, "Predicting Social Security Numbers from Public Data," *Proceedings of the National Academy of Sciences*, 106 (2009), 10975–10980.

17. Allison Balvs (ed.), "Employers Beware: ICE Crackdown Target 652 Businesses Nationwide," *Baird Holm Labor and Employment Law Update*, August 2009, 1–2.

18. "Federal Contractors Required to Use E-Verify Beginning Sept. 8, 2009," *Ceridian Abstracts*, www.hrcompliance.ceridian.com, 1.

19. Bill Leonard, "Researchers: Stolen Identities Often Slip Through E-Verify," *HR Magazine*, April 2010, 11.

20. Dave Zielinski, "Automating I-9 Verification," *HR Magazine*, May 2011, 57–60.

21. "Gerber Agrees to Pay $900,000 to Minorities and Females for Hiring Discrimination," *Ceridian Abstracts*, August 26, 2009, www.hrcompliance.ceridian.com, 1.

22. Theresa Minton-Eversole, "Avoiding Bias in Pre-Employment Testing," *HR Magazine*, December 2010, 77–80.

23. Andrew R. Mcllvaine, "BMI: An Imperfect Recruiting Tool," *Human Resource Executive Online*, January 20, 2011, www.hreonline.com.

24. Deborah L. Whetzel and Michael A. McDonald, "Situational Judgment Tests: An Overview of Current Research," 19 (2009), 188–202.

25. Louis Greenstein, "Web of Deceit," *Human Resource Executive*, June 16, 2008, 57–60.

26. Michael C. Sturman and David Sherwyn, "The Utility of Integrity Testing for Controlling Workers' Compensation Costs," *Cornell Hospitality Quarterly*, 50 (2009), 432–445; Celina Oliver, Maggie Shafiro, Peter Bullard, and Jay C. Thomas, "Use of Integrity Tests May Reduce Workers' Compensation Losses," *Journal of Business Psychology*, 27 (2012), 115–122.

27. Based on Bill Roberts, "Your Cheating Heart," *HR Magazine*, June 2011, 55–60.

28. Frank Schmidt, et al., "General Mental Ability, Job Performance, and Red Herrings: Responses to Osterman, Hauser, and Schmitt," *Academy of Management Perspectives*, November 2007, 64–76.

29. David Autor and David Scarborough, "Does Job Testing Harm Minority Workers? Evidence from Retail Establishments," *Quarterly Journal of Economics*, February 2008, 219–277; Peter Cappelli, "Assessing Personality," *Human Resource Executive Online*, www.hreonline.com.

30. Frederick Morgeson, et al., "Reconsidering the Use of Personality Tests in Personnel Selection Contexts," *Personnel Psychology*, 60, 2007, 683–729.

31. Joann Lublin, "What Won't You Do for a Job?" *The Wall Street Journal*, June 2, 2009, B1.

32. Mark McGraw, "Costly Job Interviews," *Human Resource Executive Online*, November 4, 2009, www.hreonline.com, 1–2.

33. Based on Michael O'Brien, "The Future of Recruiting," *Human Resource Executive Online*, September 16, 2009, www.hreonline.com; Andrew R. Mcllvaine, "Lights, Camera...Interview," *Human Resource Executive Online*, September 16, 2009, www.hreonline.com.

34. Therese Macan, "The Employment Interview: A Review of Current Studies and Directions for Future Research," *Human Resource Management Review*, 19 (2009), 203–218; Denis Morin and Pascale L. Denis, book review of *The Structured Interview: Enhancing Staff Selection* by Normand Pettersen and Andre Durivage, *Personnel Psychology*, 63 (2010), 250–255.

35. Therese Macan, "The Employment Interview: A Review of Current Studies and Directions for Future Research," *Human Resources Management Review*, 19 (2009), 203–218.

36. Alexandra Lopez-Pacheco, "How Do I Recruit Great Employees?" *National Post* (Canada), June 8, 2009, FP8; Laura Quinn, and Maxine Dalton, "Leading for Sustainability Implementing the Tasks of Leadership," *Corporate Governance*, 9, 2009, 21–38.

37. Allen I. Huffcutt, Chad H. Van Iddekinge, and Philip L. Roth, "Understanding Applicant Behavior in Employment Interviews: A Theoretical Model of Interviewee Performance," *Human Resource Management Review*, 21 (2011), 353–367.

38. "Failing the Interview," *DDI*, www.ddiworld.com.

39. Jonathan A. Segal, "Hiring Days Are Here Again," *HR Magazine*, July 2011, 58–60.

40. Cheryl Thompson, "Background Checks for Experiential Education Could Get Centralized," *American Journal of Health System Pharmacy*, September 2009, 1603–1604.

41. Julia Levashina and Michael A. Campion, "Expected Practices in Background Checking: Review of the Human Resource Management Literature," *Employee Responsibilities and Rights Journal*, 21 (2009), 231–249.

42. Jonathan S. Reiskin, "Jury Finds Freight Broker Liable for 23.8 Million Fatality Award," *Transportation Topics Online*, April 6, 2009, www.ttnews.com.

43. Stacy A. Hickox, "Employer Liability for Negligent Hiring of Ex-Offenders," *Saint Louis University Law Journal*, 55 (2011), 1001–1046.

44. Bill Leonard, "Few Employers Use Social Media to Screen Applicants" *HR Magazine*, October 2011, 16; "Nothing to Like in Facebook Prying," *The Denver Post*, April 1, 2012, 3D.

45. Based on Eric Krell, "Criminal Background," *HR Magazine*, February 2012, 45–54.

46. Richard G. Brody, "Beyond the Basic Background Check: Hiring the 'Right' Employees," *Management Research Review*, 33 (2010), 210–223.

47. Bill Roberts, "Close-Up on Screening," *HR Magazine*, February 2011, 23–29.

48. Marsha L. Nielson and Kristin M. Kuhn, "Late Payments and Leery Applicants: Credit Checks as a Selection Test," *Employee Responsibilities and Rights Journal*, 21 (2009), 115–130.

49. David Migoya, "Employers See Their Worth; Job Seekers the Woe," The Denver Post, February 8, 2012, A1.

50. Bill Roberts, 2011.

51. Allen Smith, "Pepsi Settles Dispute Over Criminal Checks for $3 Million," *HR Magazine*, March 2012, 14.

52. "Ruling Complicates Return-to-Work Tests," *Business Insurance*, October 5, 2009, 8.

53. "General Communication Guidelines," *Ceridian Abstracts*, April 8, 2009, www.hrcompliance.ceridian.com.

54. "The Legal Side of Workplace Drug-Free Policies," *Safety Compliance Letter 2487*, 2008, 7–13; Jo Douglas, "Green Light for Drugs and Alcoholic Testing," *NZ Business*, 22, No. 4, 2008, 84.

55. Dori Meinert, "Seeing Behind the Mask," *HR Magazine*, February 2011, 31–37.

56. JoAnn Lublin, "Bulletproofing Your References in the Hunt for a New

Job," *The Wall Street Journal*, April 7, 2009, B9.

57. Dori Meinert, "Seeing Behind the Mask," *HR Magazine*, February 2011, 31–37.

58. Mike Noon, "Simply the Best? The Case for Using Threshold Selection in Hiring Decisions," *Human Resource Management Journal*, 22 (2012), 76–88.

59. Based on Bill Leonard, "Fake Job Reference Services Add New Wrinkle to Screening," *HR Magazine*, January 2010, 9; Michael O' Brien, "Risky References," *Human Resource Executive Online*, April 1, 2010, www.hreonline.com.

60. Mary Siegfried, "A New Approach to Global Staffing," *Inside Supply Management*, March 2008, 30–32.

61. Ann Marie Ryan, et al., "Going Global: Cultural Values and Perceptions of Selection Procedures," *Applied Psychology: An International Review*, 2008, 1–37.

62. Allen Smith, "OFCCP Updates Guidance on Internet Applicant," *HR News*, November 17, 2006, www.shrm.org/news.

63. Melvin R. Weber, Dori A. Finley, Alleah Crawford, David Rivera, Jr., "An Exploratory Study Identifying Soft Skill Competencies in Entry-Level Managers," *Tourism and Hospitality Research*, 9 (2009), 353–361; Deborah H. Stevenson and Jo Ann Starkweather, "PM Critical Competency Index: IT Execs Prefer Soft Skills," *International Journal of Project Management*, 28 (2010), 663–671.

64. James A. Penny, book review of Assessing Emotional Intelligence: A Competency Framework for the Development of Standards for Soft Skills by Peter Carblis, *Personnel Psychology*, 63 (2010), 490; Golnaz Sadri, "Emotional Intelligence: Can It Be Taught?" *T+D*, September 2011, 65.

65. Based on Bill Roberts, "Hire Intelligence," *HR Magazine*, May 2011, 63–67.

Training, Development, and Performance

8

Training Human Resources

Learning Objectives

After you have read this chapter, you should be able to:

1 Define training and discuss why a strategic approach is important.

2 Identify three types of analyses used to determine training needs.

3 Specify how to design and evaluate an orientation program.

4 Explain different means of internal and external training delivery.

5 Describe the importance of e-learning as part of current training efforts.

6 Provide an example for each of the four levels of training evaluation.

© vm/iStockphoto.com

HR HEADLINE

Tuition Reimbursement for New Skills Training

Amazon.com started a program that allows full-time employees to enroll in college courses of their choice. The policy, called the Amazon Career Course Program, was developed to enhance workers' skills and provide individuals the opportunity to study in academic areas that suit their personal preferences. The company pays for 95% of tuition, textbooks, and associated fees up-front for enrollment in accredited programs that provide occupational certificates and associate degrees. Amazon will pay for both traditional on-campus classes and online distance courses, but individuals must be employed by Amazon on an hourly basis in the United States and have worked a total of three consecutive years to sign up for tuition reimbursement.

In addition, Amazon will only provide financial support to individuals who enroll in courses that prepare them to work in high-demand, well-compensated fields such as medical technology, computer design, and aircraft repair. Paying for expenses up-front opens doors for Amazon workers who cannot afford the tuition, books, and fees associated with getting an education.

The motivation to provide such a program is driven by the notion that Amazon can help employees plan and train for their future professional pursuits. Amazon also wanted to provide an innovative program to employees when many other companies were scaling back on benefits, thus enhancing the firm's ability to effectively recruit and keep good talent. Indeed, career advancement is a key concern of employees and has a place in both attraction and retention.

The program can also foster the idea that Amazon cares about employee well-being because individuals get to choose the job skills they would like to acquire or develop. However, companies should also consider the costs associated with tuition reimbursement and the possible resulting turnover and make sure such a program will work for them.[1]

Businesses must change if they are to survive because the environment in which they must compete changes. For this reason, employee training is an ongoing process for most organizations. In the United States more than $126 billion is spent on training annually, or more than $1,000 per employee on average.[2]

Training
Process whereby people acquire capabilities to perform jobs.

Training is the process whereby people acquire capabilities to perform jobs. Training provides employees with specific, identifiable knowledge and skills for use in their present jobs. Organizational training may include "hard" skills, such as teaching sales representatives how to use intranet resources, showing a branch manager how to review an income statement, or helping a machinist apprentice how to set up a drill press. "Soft" skills are critical in many instances and can be taught as well. These skills may include communicating, mentoring, managing a meeting, and working as part of a team.

Some companies are using social media to aid in the training process. Verizon, for example, uses three social media approaches to train. Device Blog is used to support new wireless device launches. It is modeled after tech blogs and provides general information, how-to videos, and trouble-shooting tips. Device Forums uses learning from peers for retail employees by asking questions, posting tips, and serving as a crosscheck. Learning Communities allow employees to complete online device training modules and discover "do's and don'ts" in dealing with a new device. Topics mirror the customer's experience.[3]

LO1 Define training and discuss why a strategic approach is important.

8-1 ■ TRAINING AND HUMAN RESOURCES

What kinds of activities usually require training? Common training topics include safety, customer service, computer skills, quality initiatives, dealing with sexual harassment, and communication. Benefits of well-done training for individuals include enhanced skills, greater ability to adapt and innovate, better self-management, and performance improvement. For organizations, training can bring improvements in effectiveness and productivity, more profitability and reduced costs, improved quality, and increased human capital.

8-1a Training Categories

Training can be designed to meet many objectives and can be classified in various ways. As Figure 8-1 shows, some common groupings of training include the following:

- *Required and regular training*: Complies with various mandated legal requirements (e.g., OSHA and EEO) and is given to all employees (e.g., new employee orientation)
- *Interpersonal and problem-solving training*: Addresses both operational and interpersonal problems and seeks to improve organizational working relationships (e.g., interpersonal communication, managerial/supervisory skills, and conflict resolution)[4]
- *Job and technical training*: Enables employees to perform their jobs better (e.g., product knowledge, technical processes and procedures, customer relations)
- *Developmental and career training*: Provides longer-term focus to enhance individual and organizational capabilities for the future (e.g., business practices, executive development, organizational change, and leadership)

It is common for a distinction to be drawn between *training* and *development*, with development being broader in scope and focusing on individuals' gaining new capabilities useful for both present and especially future jobs. Development is discussed in Chapter 9. Training is the focus of this chapter.

FIGURE 8-1 Types of Training

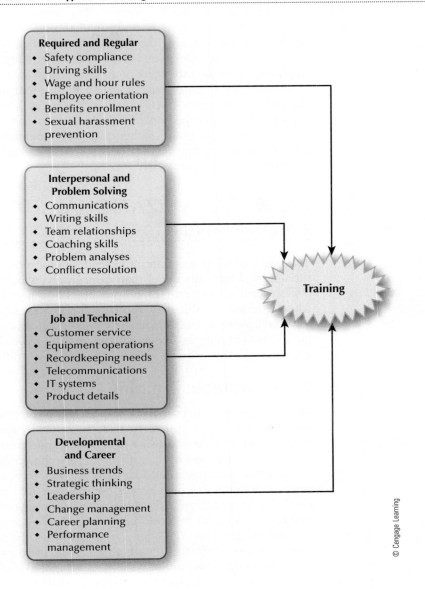

© Cengage Learning

8-1b Legal Issues and Training

Some legal issues must be considered when designing and delivering training. One concern centers on the criteria and practices used to select individuals for inclusion in training programs. Organizations need to make sure these factors are job related and do not result in disparate impact because training can be an opportunity to advance in the organization. Also, failure to accommodate the participation of individuals with disabilities in training can expose organizations to EEO lawsuits. Using psychological assessments, to identify soft skills like emotional intelligence falls under the uniform guidelines and must be validated.[5]

Another legal issue involves requiring employees to sign *training contracts* to protect the costs and time invested in specialized employee training. For instance, a telecommunications firm paid $17,000 each to train four network technicians and certify them in specialized equipment. The firm required that each technician sign a training contract whereby one-fourth of the cost would be forgiven each year the employee stayed following the training. A technician who left sooner would be liable to the firm for the unforgiven balance. Health care organizations, IT firms, and other employers often use training contracts, especially for expensive external training.

Finally, the Department of Labor has ruled that nonexempt employees who are training outside normal working hours (e.g., at home by completing Web-based classes) must be compensated for their time. In one situation, a company required employees to spend about 10 hours at home completing a Web-based class. In this case, the company had to pay the employees for their 10 hours of training under the Fair Labor Standards Act.[6]

8-2 ■ ORGANIZATIONAL STRATEGY AND TRAINING

Training represents a significant expenditure for most employers. However, it is too often viewed tactically rather than strategically, which means that training is seen as a short-term activity rather than one that has longer-term effects on organizational success. However, this may be changing. For example, during the last recession, some companies chose to maintain training that was necessary for long-term strategic goals. Training is frequently supported by words from management, but is among the first expenses to be cut when times get difficult.[7]

8-2a Strategic Training

Training can indeed help the organization accomplish its goals. For example, if sales increases are a critical part of the company's strategy, appropriate training would identify what is causing lower sales and recommend a solution. For maximum impact HR and training professionals should get involved with the business and partner with operating managers to help solve their problems. Additionally, strategic training can help reduce the mind-set that training alone can solve most employee or organizational problems. It is not uncommon for operating managers and trainers to react to most important performance problems by saying, "I need a training program on X." With a strategic focus, the organization is more likely to assess whether training can actually address these issues and what else might be done. Training alone cannot fix all organizational problems.

The value of training can be seen at Walt Disney World where the company has established specific training plans. The implementation of those training plans results in a distinct competitive advantage for the organization. For example, at the Disney Institute, employees (called "cast members") get training experience from their guests' perspectives. As a part of their training, individuals taking hotel reservations stay at a resort as guests to gain greater understanding of what they are selling and to experience the services themselves. The training is so effective the company markets the training program.

However, not *all* training is effective. Only one-quarter of respondents to a McKinsey survey said their training programs measurably improved business performance, and most companies don't measure training effectiveness. Most simply ask whether participants liked the training or not.[8] To be a strategic investment training must align with company goals and provide something of value.

8-2b Organizational Competitiveness and Training

General Electric, Dell, Motorola, Marriott, Cisco, FedEx, and Texas Instruments all emphasize the importance of training employees and managers. These companies and others recognize that training efforts can be integral to business success. For these companies, training is similar to the "continuous improvement" practiced by some manufacturing firms.

The nature of technological innovation and change is such that if employees are not trained all the time, they may fall behind and the company could become less competitive. Without continual training, organizations may not have staff members with the knowledge, skills, and abilities (KSAs) needed to compete effectively.[9]

Training also can affect organizational competitiveness by aiding in the retention of employees. One reason why many individuals may stay or leave organizations is the availability of career training and development opportunities. Employers who invest in training and developing their employees may enhance retention efforts.[10] Figure 8-2 shows how training may help accomplish certain organizational strategies.

Knowledge Management For much of history, competitive advantage among organizations was measured in terms of physical capital. However, as the information age has evolved, "intelligence" has become the raw material that many organizations make and sell through their "knowledge workers."[11] **Knowledge management** is the way an organization identifies and leverages knowledge to be competitive.[12] It is the art of creating value by using intellectual capital, which is what the organization (or, more exactly, the people in the organization) knows. Knowledge management is a conscious effort to get the right knowledge to the right people at the right time so that it can be shared and put into action.[13]

> **Knowledge management**
> The way an organization identifies and leverages knowledge to be competitive.

FIGURE 8-2 Linking Strategies and Training

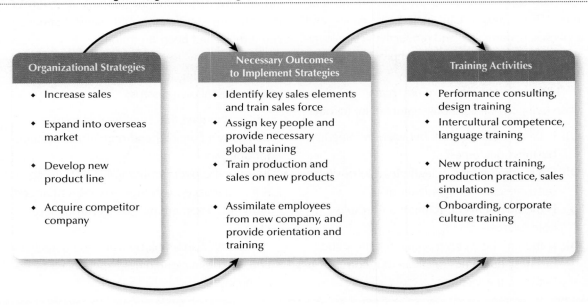

Organizational Strategies	Necessary Outcomes to Implement Strategies	Training Activities
• Increase sales	• Identify key sales elements and train sales force	• Performance consulting, design training
• Expand into overseas market	• Assign key people and provide necessary global training	• Intercultural competence, language training
• Develop new product line	• Train production and sales on new products	• New product training, production practice, sales simulations
• Acquire competitor company	• Assimilate employees from new company, and provide orientation and training	• Onboarding, corporate culture training

© Cengage Learning

Training as a Revenue Source and Other Positive Outcomes Some organizations have identified that training can be a source of business revenue, as well as other positive outcomes. For instance, Microsoft, Ceridian, Cisco, Hewlett-Packard, and other technology firms bundle customer training with products and services they sell. Also, manufacturers of industrial equipment offer customers training on machine upgrades and new features. Customers of many of these firms pay for additional training either by course, by participant, or as part of equipment or software purchases. Not only are the costs of the trainers' salaries, travel, and other expenses covered, but the suppliers also make a profit on the training through the fees paid by customers. As a side benefit, customer satisfaction and loyalty increase if customers know how to use the products and services purchased. Thus, customer training can aid customer retention and enhances future sales revenues. The HR Skills and Applications: Building Support for Training discusses how HR professionals can increase support for training.

HR SKILLS AND APPLICATIONS

Building Support for Training

Some executives are not very interested in training and see such efforts as a serious cost to businesses. Consequently, HR professionals need to make a strong case for training by showing how individual learning can enhance the bottom line. In particular, they must effectively communicate to top leaders how training activities prompt positive *results* in the organization, especially if they want to generate sustained support for these programs in the long term. These results can include revenues and expenses, performance and productivity, employee and customer attitudes, quality improvement, turnover, and many other metrics.

HR managers can explore many questions when trying to build a strong argument for training:

[Q]: Is there a definite link between training and business outcomes?

[Q]: Do training efforts actually lead to positive outcomes in the organization?

[Q]: Is the link between training and results coincidental?

[Q]: Is the link between training activities and business outcomes because of a correlation between the factors?

The answers to these questions can be difficult to determine in practice because so many factors influence cause-and-effect relationships. For instance, it can seem impossible at times to isolate one factor from many variables that can contribute to a positive organizational outcome. Sometimes, the positive business result is purely coincidence because it would have occurred without any help from the training function of the company, and it would have happened even if there had been no training.

The best way for HR professionals to build support for training inside the organization is to consider the following steps:

- Utilize the data that is generated from a company's financial and operational systems for analysis.
- Identify the overarching goals of training (i.e., increased customer service, enhanced work attitudes, greater job performance, etc.).
- Try to establish a link between the objectives and the positive outcomes experienced by the company.[14]

Integration of Performance with Training Job performance, training, and employee learning must be integrated to be effective. Organizations find that training experiences that use real business problems to advance employee learning are better than approaches that do not. Rather than separating the training experience from the context of actual job performance, trainers can incorporate everyday business issues as learning examples, thus increasing the realism of training exercises and scenarios. For example, as part of management training at General Electric, managers are given actual business problems to solve, and they must present their solutions to business leaders. Using real situations for practice is yet another way of merging the lines between training, learning, and job performance.

Sales Training Organizational competitiveness in many industries hinges on the success of the sales function. Innovative products or services do not magically find customers—they require well-prepared professional salespeople to inform the appropriate audience. A key element in sales force success is often the training opportunities available. While slightly over one-third of firms can directly connect sales training to improved sales or ROI, 85% do track such measures as increase in closes, improved client relationships, and reduction in cost per sale as a result of sales training.[15]

Organizations frequently focus their primary sales training efforts on large annual or biannual events. This is an expensive method of training because of travel costs, instruction costs, and reduced sales hours during training. Salespersons are often social beings and an event that provides for sharing experiences with peers is usually well received. However, a mix of other approaches can cut costs and can also be effective. Simulations, Web conferences, e-learning, self-paced learning, and virtual coaching can all be used to leverage sales training. Using such advances presents some challenges to the trainers who must develop them but presents flexibility and opportunity if done well.[16]

Sales training can cover a wide variety of skills: call execution, presentation skills, negotiation skills, strategy development, and other skills that lend themselves well to simulation of the sales situation.[17] Sales simulations are one logical training tool that can help the sales force be more competitive and successful.

GLOBAL

8-2c Global Competitiveness and Training

For a global firm, the most brilliant strategies ever devised will not serve to improve competitiveness unless the company has well-trained employees throughout the world to carry them out. A global look at training is important as firms establish and expand operations worldwide. For U.S. employers, the challenge has increased because of the decline in specialized skilled and technical workers. Considering the number of global employees with international assignments, training is part of global competitive success.

Global Assignment Training The orientation and training that expatriates and their families receive before departure significantly affect the success of an overseas assignment. When these programs are offered, most expatriates participate in them, usually producing a positive effect on cross-cultural adjustment. Also, training helps expatriates and their families adjust to and deal with host-country counterparts. A recent survey showed that companies recognize that their expatriates often are well-trained in skills and technical capabilities but much less well prepared for the host country culture.[18]

A related issue is the promotion and transfer of foreign citizens to positions in the United States. For example, many Japanese firms operating in the United States conduct training programs to prepare Japanese employees and their families for the food, customs, labor and HR practices, and other facets of working and living in the United States. As more global organizations start or expand U.S. operations, more cross-cultural training will be necessary for international employees relocated to the United States.[19]

Intercultural Competence Training Global employers are providing intercultural competence training for their global employees. Intercultural competence incorporates a wide range of human social skills and personality characteristics. As noted in Figure 8-3, three components of intercultural competence require attention when training expatriates for global assignments:

- *Cognitive*: What does the person know about other cultures?
- *Emotional*: How does the person view other cultures, and how sensitive is the person to cultural customs and issues?
- *Behavioral*: How does the person act in intercultural situations?

Increasingly, global employers are using training methods that allow individuals to behave in international situations and then receive feedback. One method is the Culture Assimilator. Used worldwide, especially by European-based firms, the Culture Assimilator is a programmed training and learning method consisting of short case studies and critical incidents. The case studies describe intercultural interactions and potential misunderstandings involving expatriates and host-country nationals.

In China, intercultural competence training takes a slightly different turn. Companies in China face a big challenge in finding, training, and keeping skilled employees who can thrive in Western-style multinational corporations (MNCs). China has a workforce of 800 million, but only a small percentage is considered skilled enough to work in MNCs. The Chinese educational system does not teach the range of needed skills, so companies are educating and training workers.

Chinese culture encourages learning and growth. A Chinese proverb says, "If you want 100 years of prosperity, grow people," so Chinese employees

FIGURE 8-3 Intercultural Competence Training

Component	Possible Training
Cognitive	◆ Culture-specific training (traditions, history, cultural customs, etc.) ◆ Language course
Emotional	◆ *Uneasiness*: Social skills training focusing on new, unclear, and intercultural situations ◆ *Prejudices*: Coaching may be clarifying ◆ *Sensitivity*: Communication skills course (active listening, verbal/nonverbal cues, empathy)
Behavioral	◆ Culture Assimilator method ◆ International projects ◆ Social skills training focusing on intercultural situations

Source: Developed by Andrea Graf, PhD, and Robert L. Mathis, PhD, SPHR.

usually value the opportunity to be trained. In fact, if they see companies bring in expatriates or non-Chinese workers, they view those companies as having only a short-term investment in China and to be less likely to offer career growth. Available training is a retention tool that Chinese employees are apparently demanding.[20]

8-3 ■ PLANNING FOR TRAINING

Whether global, national, or local in scope, training efforts benefit from careful planning before it is provided. Planning includes looking at the big picture in which the training takes place, as well as specifics for the design of a particular training effort. For example, the needs for skills have changed over time and soft skills like adaptability, problem solving, and professionalism have increased in value in some firms. Planning that recognizes and includes changes such as these may make for a more effective training program.

Another training planning issue for some companies is knowledge retention for the firm. When retirees leave, they take everything they have learned during a career. Perhaps a retiree is the only one in the company who knows how to operate a piece of machinery or mix a certain chemical solution. In some areas, technology changes so fast that even young people leaving a company may take with them information that cannot easily be replicated. Companies are responding to the need for knowledge retention in various ways, including identifying critical employees, having existing critical employees train and mentor others, producing white papers, and keeping former employees on call for a period of time after their departure.

Training plans allow organizations to identify what is needed for employee performance *before* training begins so that there is better alignment between training and strategic needs. Effective training planning efforts consider the following questions:

- Is there really a need for the training?
- Who needs to be trained?
- Who will do the training?
- What form will the training take?
- How will knowledge be transferred to the job?
- How will the training be evaluated?

8-3a Planning for New Employees: Orientation/Onboarding

A good example of one kind of training that requires planning is orientation. Also called *onboarding*, orientation is the most important and widely conducted type of regular training done for new employees.

Orientation
Planned introduction of new employees to their jobs, coworkers, and the organization.

Orientation, which is the planned introduction of new employees to their jobs, coworkers, and the organization, is offered by most employers. It requires cooperation between individuals in the HR unit and operating managers and supervisors.[21] In a small organization without an HR department, the new employee's supervisor or manager usually assumes most of the responsibility for orientation.[22] In large organizations, managers and supervisors, as well as the HR department, often work as a team to orient new employees. Unfortunately, without good planning, new employee orientation sessions can come across as boring, irrelevant, and a waste of time to both new employees and their department supervisors and managers. But orientation which can also be thought of as institutionalized socialization tactics can be very effective—if done well.

Among the decisions to be made when planning for new employee orientation are *what* to present and *when* to present it. Too much information on the first day leads to perceptions of ineffective onboarding. Several shorter sessions over a longer period of time, bringing in information as it is needed, are more effective. Effective orientation achieves several key purposes:

- Establishes a favorable employee impression of the organization and the job
- Provides organization and job information
- Enhances interpersonal acceptance by coworkers

HR PERSPECTIVE

Satisfying the Millennial Generation with Innovative Onboarding

Effective employee onboarding requires careful planning and preparation, but the orientation process also needs to be innovative enough to get employees excited about working for the company. Fox Filmed Entertainment has designed such an onboarding program to better connect with its tech-oriented and motivated workforce, which is staffed with many individuals from the millennial generation. To make orientation more entertaining and show younger workers that the company understands their generational preferences and icons, the Bart Simpson character from the television show *The Simpsons* appears in the orientation video shown to new hires.

The natural-gas pipeline firm El Paso Corp. headquartered in Houston, TX also developed an innovative onboarding process geared to better resonate with technology-driven younger employees. Onboarding at the company is now all automated, which greatly reduces the amount of time needed to complete the process. This

change has led to significant cost savings in the millions of dollars for the organization, and it shows employees that the firm can be technology-oriented.

There is strong reason to believe that other companies would benefit from considering these trends. A recent KRC Research study sponsored by Microsoft and Insurity found that younger individuals employed in the insurance field prefer more innovation and technology in the office environment such as virtual communication, social networking media, and real-time messaging. These findings underscore the fact that younger staff members are more interconnected from a technology perspective, and they often seek these experiences in the workplace. Onboarding and orientation programs can be linked to these preferences by including in them more automation and technology. Companies can also make onboarding more entertaining by better matching the company's brand with individuals' employment experiences.[23]

- Accelerates socialization and integration of the new employee into the organization
- Ensures that employee performance and productivity begin more quickly

Electronic Orientation Resources One way of improving the efficiency of orientation is to use electronic resources. Most employers have implemented some kind of electronic onboarding activities to improve their employee orientation efforts.[24] Employers can place general employee orientation information on company intranets or corporate websites. New employees log on and review much of the general material on organizational history, structure, products and services, mission, and other background, instead of sitting in a classroom where the information is delivered in person or by video. Specific questions and concerns can be addressed by HR staff and others after employees have reviewed the web-based information.

Other companies may use electronic resources a bit differently. For example, at one company, when candidates accept an offer, they get an e-mail with a link to a password-protected website that welcomes them. They fill out their I-9, W-2, and other forms on that website from home. Before reporting to work, they get daily e-mails explaining where to park, where to get uniforms, and where to drop off their dry cleaning. Assigning a desk, getting a computer and security clearance, and many other orientation tasks are all done before the first day on the job by electronic onboarding. The HR Perspective: Satisfying Millennial Generation shows other examples.

MEASURE

8-3b Orientation: Evaluation and Metrics

Although orientation is important and can provide many advantages for both the organization and the new employee, it is not always done well.[25] To determine the effectiveness of an orientation training program, evaluation using specific metrics is appropriate. Measurement should be made of the success of both the orientation program *and* the new hires themselves. Suggested metrics include the following:[26]

• *Tenure turnover rate*	What percentage of new hires left the organization in 6 months or less?
• *New hires failure factor*	What percentage of the total annual turnover was new hires?
• *Employee upgrade rate*	What percentage of new employees received a high performance rating?
• *Development program participation rate*	What percentage of new employees have moved on to training for or promotion to higher jobs?

Successfully integrating new hires is important, and measuring the degree of success allows the orientation program to be managed well. The way in which a firm plans, organizes, and structures its training affects the way employees experience the training, which in turn influences the effectiveness of the training. After good planning, effective training requires the use of a systematic training process. Figure 8-4 shows the four phases of a systematic approach: assessment, design, delivery, and evaluation. Using such a process reduces the likelihood that unplanned, uncoordinated, and haphazard training efforts will occur.

FIGURE 8-4 Systematic Training Process

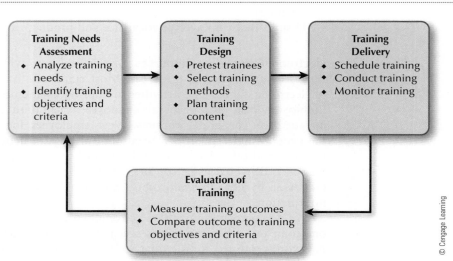

© Cengage Learning

L02 Identify three types of analyses used to determine training needs.

8-4 ■ TRAINING NEEDS ASSESSMENT

Assessing organizational training needs is the diagnostic phase of a training plan. This assessment includes issues related to employee and organizational performance to determine if training can help. Needs assessment measures the competencies of a company, a group, or an individual as they relate to what is required. It is necessary to find out what is happening and what should be happening before deciding if training will help, and if so what kind of training is needed. For instance, suppose that in looking at the performance of clerks in a billing department, a manager identifies problems that employees have with their data-entry and keyboarding abilities, and she decides that they would benefit from instruction in these areas. As part of assessing the training needs, the manager has the clerks take a data-entry test to measure their current keyboarding skills. Then the manager establishes an objective of increasing the clerks' keyboarding speed to 60 words per minute without errors. The number of words per minute without errors is the criterion against which training success can be measured, and it represents the way in which the objective is made specific.

8-4a Analysis of Training Needs

The first step in assessing training needs is analyzing what training might be necessary. Figure 8-5 shows the three sources used to analyze training needs.

Organizational Analysis Training needs can be diagnosed by analyzing organizational outcomes and looking at future organizational needs. A part of planning for training is the identification of the KSAs that will be needed now and in the future as both jobs and the organization change. Both internal and external forces will influence training and must be considered when doing organizational analysis. For instance, the problems posed by the technical obsolescence of current employees

FIGURE 8-5 Sources of Information for Needs Assessment

Organization Analysis
- Grievances
- Accidents
- Waste/scrap
- Training observations
- Observations
- Customer complaints
- Exit interviews
- Equipment use
- Attitude surveys

Job/Task Analysis
- Employee KSAs
- Benchmarks
- Effectiveness
- Job specifications
- Efficiency data
- Employees surveys

Individual Analysis
- Performance appraisals
- Tests
- Records
- Assessment centers
- Questionnaires
- Surveys
- Job knowledge tools

© Cengage Learning 2014

and an insufficiently educated labor pool from which to draw new workers should be confronted and incorporated in the training design.

Organizational analysis comes from various measures of organizational performance. Departments or areas with high turnover, customer complaints, high grievance rates, high absenteeism, low performance, and other deficiencies can be pinpointed. Following the identification of problems, objectives can be developed if training is a solution. During organizational analysis, focus groups of managers can be used to evaluate changes and performance that might require training.

Job/Task Analysis A second level of analyzing training needs is to review the jobs involved and the tasks performed. By comparing the requirements of jobs with the KSAs of employees, training needs can be identified.[27] For example, at a manufacturing firm, analysis identified the tasks performed by engineers who served as technical instructors for other employees. By listing the tasks required of a technical instructor, HR established a program to teach specific instructional skills and the engineers were able to become more successful instructors.

Another way to pinpoint training gaps in the job or task being done is to survey employees, and have them anonymously evaluate the current skill levels of themselves and their peers. This not only identifies job needs but also heightens employees' awareness of their own learning needs. A training needs survey can take the form of questionnaires or interviews with supervisors and employees individually or in groups. Web-based surveys, requests, and other inputs from managers and employees can be used to identify training needs or jobs.

A good example of needs assessment for a particular job occurred in the construction industry where there was a rash of accidents among Spanish-speaking construction workers. Construction companies recognized the need for training in English as a second language for many people. Restaurants, hospitals, and hotels have faced the same issue for certain jobs.

Individual Analysis The third means of diagnosing training needs focuses on individuals and how they perform their jobs.

The most common approach for making individual analysis is to use performance appraisal data. In some instances, a good HR information system can be used to identify individuals who require training in specific areas to be eligible for promotion. To assess training needs through the performance appraisal process, a supervisor first determines an employee's performance strengths and inadequacies in a formal review. Then the supervisor can design training to help the employee overcome the weaknesses and enhance the strengths.

Another way of assessing individual training needs is to use both managerial and nonmanagerial (or peer) input about the kind of training that is needed. Individuals can also identify their own training needs.[28] Obtaining this kind of input can be useful in building support for the training from those who will be trained, as they help to identify training needs.

Tests can be a good means of individual-level analysis. For example, a police officer might take a qualification test with his or her service pistol every six months to indicate the officer's current skill level. If an officer cannot qualify, training would certainly be necessary.

8-4b Establishing Training Objectives and Priorities

Once training requirements have been identified using needs analyses, training objectives and priorities can be established by a "gap analysis," which indicates the distance between where an organization is with its employee capabilities and where it needs to be. Training objectives and priorities are then determined to close the gap.[29] Three possible areas for training objectives can be:

- *Attitude*: Creating interest in and awareness of the importance of something (e.g., sexual harassment training)
- *Knowledge*: Imparting cognitive information and details to trainees (e.g., understanding how a new product works)
- *Skill*: Developing behavioral changes in how jobs and various task requirements are performed (e.g., improving speed on an installation)

The success of training should be measured in terms of the objectives that were set for it. Useful objectives are measurable. For example, an objective for a new sales clerk might be to *demonstrate the ability to explain the function of each product in the department within two weeks*. This objective checks *internalization*, that is, whether the person really learned the training content and is able to use the training.

Since training seldom is an unlimited budget item and because organizations have multiple training needs, prioritization is necessary. Ideally, management looks at training needs in relation to strategic plans and as part of the organizational change process. Then the training needs can be prioritized on the basis of objectives. Conducting the training most needed to improve organizational performance will produce visible results more quickly.

8-5 ■ TRAINING DESIGN

LO3 Specify how to design and evaluate an orientation program.

Once training objectives have been determined, training design can start. Whether job-specific or broader in nature, training must be designed to address the specific objectives. Effective training design considers the learners and instructional strategies, as well as how to maximize the transfer of training from class to the job site.

Working in organizations should be a continual learning process. Different approaches are possible because learning is a complex psychological process. Each of the elements shown in Figure 8-6 must be considered for the training design to be effective and produce learning.

FIGURE 8-6 Training Design Elements

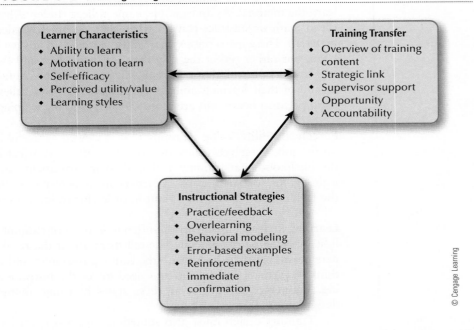

8-5a Learner Characteristics

For training to be successful, learners must be ready and able to learn. Learner readiness means that individuals have the ability to learn. However, individuals also must have the motivation to learn, have high confidence, see value in learning, and have a learning style that fits the training.

Ability to Learn Learners must possess basic skills, such as fundamental reading or math proficiency, and sufficient cognitive abilities. Companies may discover that some workers lack the cognitive ability to comprehend their training. Some have found that a significant number of job applicants and current employees lack the reading, writing, and math skills needed to learn the jobs. Employers might deal with the lack of basic employee skills in several ways:

- Offer remedial training to existing employees who need it.
- Test and hire workers who already have the necessary skills.
- Work with local schools to help better educate potential hires for jobs.

Motivation A person's desire to learn training content, referred to as *motivation to learn*, is influenced by multiple factors. For example, differences in gender and ethnicity and the resulting experiences may affect the motivation of adult learners. The student's motivational level may also be influenced by the instructor's motivation and ability, friends' encouragement to do well, classmates' motivational levels, the classroom's physical environment, and the training methods used. Regardless of what motivates without that motivation, the student will not learn the material.

Self-efficacy
People's belief that they can successfully learn the training program content.

Self-Efficacy Learners must possess **self-efficacy**, which refers to people's belief that they can successfully learn the training program content. For learners to be ready for and receptive to the training content, they must believe that it is possible for them to learn the material. As an example, some college students' levels of self-efficacy diminish in math or statistics courses when they do not feel adequately able to grasp the material. These perceptions may have nothing to do with their actual ability to learn, but rather reflect the way they see themselves and their abilities.[30] Instructors and trainers must find appropriate ways to boost the confidence of trainees who are unsure of their learning abilities because people who believe strongly that they can learn perform better and are more satisfied with the training they receive.

Perceived Utility/Value Training that is viewed as useful is more likely to be tried on the job. Perceived utility or value of training is affected by a need to improve, the likelihood that training will lead to improvement, and the practicality of the training for use on the job. Learners must perceive a close relationship between the training and things they want in order for training to be used on the job.

Learning Styles People learn in different ways. For example, *auditory* learners learn best by listening to someone else tell them about the training content. *Tactile* learners must "get their hands on" the training resources and use them. *Visual* learners think in pictures and figures and need to see the purpose and process of the training. Trainers who address all these styles by using multiple training methods can design more effective training.

Training design must also sometimes address special issues presented by **adult learning**. Certainly, the training design must consider that all the trainees are adults, but adults come with widely varying learning styles, experiences, and personal goals. For example, training older adults in technology may require greater attention to explaining the need for changes and enhancing the older trainees' confidence and abilities when learning new technologies. In contrast, younger adults are more likely to be familiar with new technology because of their earlier exposure to computers and technology, but less able to work alone to learn skills.

Malcolm Knowles's classic work on adult learning suggests five principles for designing training for adults.[31] According to that work and subsequent work by others, adults

- have the need to know why they are learning something;
- have a need to be self-directed;
- bring more work-related experiences into the learning process;
- enter into a learning experience with a problem-centered approach to learning; and
- are motivated to learn by *both* extrinsic and intrinsic factors.

8-5b Instructional Strategies

An important part of designing training is to select the right mix of teaching strategies to fit learner characteristics. Practice/feedback, overlearning, behavioral modeling, error-based examples, and reinforcement/immediate confirmation are some of the prominent strategies available in designing the training experience.

Practice/Feedback For some training, it is important that learners practice what they have learned and get feedback on how they have done so they can improve. **Active practice** occurs when trainees perform job-related tasks and duties during training. It is more effective than simply reading or passively listening. For instance, assume a person is being trained as a customer service representative. After being

---

Adult learning
Ways in which adults learn differently than younger people.

Active practice
Performance of job-related tasks and duties by trainees during training.

given some basic selling instructions and product details, the trainee calls a customer and uses the knowledge received.

Active practice can be structured in two ways. The first, **spaced practice**, occurs when several practice sessions are spaced over a period of hours or days. The second, **massed practice**, occurs when a person performs all the practice at once.[32] Spaced practice works better for some types of skills and for physical learning that requires "muscle memory," whereas massed practice is usually more effective for other kinds of learning, such as memorizing tasks. Imagine the difficulty of trying to memorize the lists of options for 20 dishwasher models if memorized at a rate of one model a day for 20 days. By the time the appliance salespeople had learned the last option, they likely would have forgotten the first one.

Overlearning Overlearning is repeated practice even after a learner has mastered the performance. It may be best used to instill "muscle memory" for a physical activity to reduce the amount of thinking necessary and make responses automatic. But overlearning also produces improvement in learner retention. Even with overlearning, refreshers are still sometimes necessary to maintain proficiency.

Behavioral Modeling The most elementary way in which people learn and one of the best is through **behavioral modeling**, which involves copying someone else's behavior. The use of behavioral modeling is particularly appropriate for skill training in which the trainees must use both knowledge and practice. It can aid in the transfer of skills and the usage of those skills by those who are trained. For example, a new supervisor can receive training and mentoring on how to handle disciplinary discussions with employees by observing as the HR director or department manager deals with such problems.

Behavioral modeling is used extensively as the primary means for training supervisors and managers in interpersonal skills.[33] Fortunately or unfortunately, many supervisors and managers end up modeling behaviors they see their bosses exhibit. For that reason, supervisor training should include good role models to show learners how to properly handle interpersonal interactions with employees.

Error-Based Examples The error-based examples method involves sharing with learners what can go wrong when they do not use the training properly. A good example is sharing with pilots what can happen when they are not aware of a situation they and their aircraft are encountering. Situational awareness training that includes error-based examples improves air crew situational awareness. Error-based examples have been incorporated in military, firefighting, police, and aviation training and have wide potential uses in other situations. Case studies showing the negative consequences of errors are a good tool for communicating error-based examples.[34]

Reinforcement and Immediate Confirmation The concept of **reinforcement** is based on the *law of effect*, which states that people tend to repeat responses that give them a positive reward and to avoid actions associated with negative consequences. Positively reinforcing correct learned responses while providing negative consequences at some point for wrong responses can change behavior.[35] Closely related is an instructional strategy called **immediate confirmation**, which is based on the idea that people learn best if reinforcement and feedback are given as soon as possible after exhibiting a response. Immediate confirmation corrects errors that, if made and not corrected throughout the training, might establish an undesirable pattern that would need to be unlearned. It also aids with the transfer of training to the job.

Spaced practice
Practice performed in several sessions spaced over a period of hours or days.

Massed practice
Practice performed all at once.

Behavioral modeling
Copying someone else's behavior.

Reinforcement
Based on the idea that people tend to repeat responses that give them some type of positive reward and to avoid actions associated with negative consequences.

Immediate confirmation
Based on the idea that people learn best if reinforcement and feedback are given as soon as possible after training.

8-5c Training Transfer

Finally, trainers should design training for the best possible transfer from the classroom to the job. Transfer occurs when trainees actually use on the job what knowledge and information they learned in training. The amount of training that effectively gets transferred to the job is estimated to be relatively low, especially given all the time and money spent on training. Not all employees apply training to their jobs immediately after training. Among those who do not use the training immediately, the likelihood of it being used decreases over time.[36]

Effective transfer of training meets two conditions. First, the trainees can take the material learned in training and apply it to the job context in which they work. Second, employees maintain their use of the learned material over time. Many things can increase the transfer of training.[37] Offering trainees an *overview of the training content* and *how it links to the strategy* of the organization seems to help with both short-term and longer-term training transfer. Another helpful approach is to ensure that the *training mirrors the job* context as much as possible. For example, training managers to be better selection interviewers could include role-playing with "applicants" who respond in the same way that real applicants would.

One of the most consistent factors in training transfer is the *support* new trainees receive *from their supervisors* to use their new skills when they return to the job.[38] Supervisor support of the training, feedback from the supervisor, and supervisor involvement in training are powerful influences in transfer. *Opportunity to use the training* is also important. To be trained on something but never to have the opportunity to use it obviously limits transfer. Learners need the opportunity to use new skills on the job if the skills are to remain.

Finally, *accountability* helps transfer training from class to job. Accountability is the extent to which someone expects the learner to use the new skills on the job and holds them responsible for doing so.[39] It may require supervisory praise for doing the task correctly and sanctions for not showing proper trained behavior, but making people accountable for their own trained behavior is effective.

8-6 ■ TRAINING DELIVERY

Once training has been designed, the actual delivery of training can begin. Regardless of the type of training done, many approaches and methods can be used to deliver it. The growth of training technology continues to expand the available choices, as shown in Figure 8-7.

Whatever the approach used, a variety of considerations must be balanced when selecting training delivery methods. The common variables considered are the following:

- Nature of training
- Subject matter
- Number of trainees
- Individual versus team
- Self-paced versus guided
- Training resources/costs
- E-learning versus traditional learning
- Geographic locations involved
- Time allotted
- Completion timeline

FIGURE 8-7 Training Delivery Options

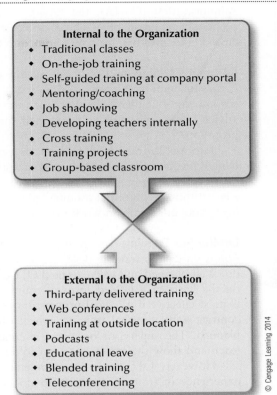

Internal to the Organization
- Traditional classes
- On-the-job training
- Self-guided training at company portal
- Mentoring/coaching
- Job shadowing
- Developing teachers internally
- Cross training
- Training projects
- Group-based classroom

External to the Organization
- Third-party delivered training
- Web conferences
- Training at outside location
- Podcasts
- Educational leave
- Blended training
- Teleconferencing

© Cengage Learning 2014

To illustrate, a large firm with many new hires may be able to conduct employee orientation using the Internet, videos, and specific HR staff members, while a small firm with few new hires may have an HR staff member meet individually with the new hires for several hours. A medium-sized company with three locations in a geographic area may bring supervisors together for a two-day training workshop once a quarter. However, a large, global firm may use Web-based courses to reach supervisors throughout the world, with content available in several languages. Frequently, training is conducted internally to the organization, but some types of training use external resources.

Further, training can be formal or informal.[40] Formal training is very visible because it consists of planned learning activities. Informal training takes place when learning may not even be the primary focus, but it occurs anyway. Informal learning may be the result of self-initiated effort or simply serendipitous, but it often occurs as needed.[41]

8-6a Internal Training

Internal training generally applies very specifically to the organization and its jobs. Such training is popular because it saves the cost of sending employees away and often avoids the cost of outside instructors. Skills-based technical training is frequently conducted inside organizations. Training materials are often created internally as well. Because of rapid changes in technology, building and updating technical skills may become crucial internal training needs. Basic technical skills training is also being mandated by federal regulations in areas where the Occupational Safety and Health Administration (OSHA), the Environmental Protection Agency (EPA), and other agencies have jurisdiction. Three specific types of internal delivery options will be discussed here: informal training, on-the-job training, and cross training.

Informal training
Training that occurs through interactions and feedback among employees.

Informal Training As noted one source of instruction is **informal training**, which occurs through interactions and feedback among employees. Much of what employees know about their jobs they learn informally from asking questions and getting advice from other employees and their supervisors, rather than from formal training programs.

Informal learning tends to occur as a result of a need in the context of working.[42] It may involve group problem solving, job shadowing, coaching, or mentoring; or it may evolve from employees seeking out other people who have the needed knowledge. Although "informal training" may seem to be a misnomer, a great deal of learning occurs informally in work organizations, and some of it happens by design.

On-the-job training
The most common training because it is flexible and relevant.

On-the-Job Training The most common type of training at all levels in an organization is **on-the-job training** (OJT) because it is flexible and relevant to what employees do. Well-planned and well-executed OJT can be very effective. OJT, which is designed on the basis of a guided form of training known as job instruction training (JIT), is most effective if a logical progression of stages is used, as shown in Figure 8-8. In contrast with informal training, which often occurs spontaneously, OJT should be planned. The supervisor or manager conducting the training must be able to both teach and show the employees what to do.

However, OJT has some problems. Those doing the training may have no experience in training, no time to do it, or no desire to participate in it. Under such conditions, learners essentially are on their own, and training likely will not be effective. Another problem is that OJT can disrupt regular work. Unfortunately, OJT can amount to no training at all sometimes, especially if the trainers simply allow the trainees to learn the job on their own. Bad habits or incorrect information from the supervisor or manager can also be transferred to the trainees.

Cross training
Training people to do more than one job.

Cross Training **Cross training** occurs when people are trained to do more than one job—theirs and someone else's. For the employer, the advantages of cross training are flexibility and development.[43] Even though cross training is attractive to the

FIGURE 8-8 Stages for On-the-Job Training

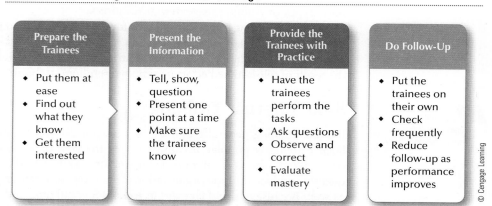

© Cengage Learning

employer, it is not always appreciated by employees, who may feel that it requires them to do more work for the same pay. To counteract such responses and to make it more appealing to employees, learning "bonuses" can be awarded for successfully completing cross training.

In some organizations, the culture may be such that people seek cross-training assignments to grow or prepare for a promotion, but that is not the case in all organizations.[44] Unions typically are not in favor of cross training because it threatens job jurisdiction and broadens jobs. Cross training may require scheduling work differently during training, and temporary decreases in productivity may result from it as people learn. Overall, an effective cross-training program can overcome the concerns mentioned and has the potential to be good for both employer and employee.

8-6b External Training

External training, or training that takes place outside the employing organization, is used extensively by organizations of all sizes. Organizations use external training if they lack the capability to train people internally or when many people need to be trained quickly. External training may be the best option for training in smaller firms because of limitations in the size of their training staffs and in the number of employees who need various types of specialized training. Whatever the size of the organization, external training provides these advantages:

- It may be less expensive for an employer to have an outside trainer conduct training in areas where internal training resources are limited.
- The organization may have insufficient time to develop internal training materials.
- The staff may not have the necessary level of expertise for the subject matter in which training is needed.
- There are advantages to having employees interact with managers and peers in other companies during external training programs.

Outsourcing of Training Many employers of all sizes outsource training to external training firms, consultants, and other entities. Perhaps one-third of training expenditures go to outside training sources. The reasons more outside training is not used may be cost concerns, and a greater emphasis on internal linking of training to organizational strategies.

A popular route for employers is to use vendors and suppliers to train employees.[45] Several computer software vendors offer employees technical certifications on their software. For example, being a Microsoft Certified Product Specialist gives employees credentials that show their level of technical expertise. Such certifications provide employees with items to put on their résumés should they decide to change jobs. These certifications also benefit employers, who can use them as job specifications for hiring and promotion.

Many suppliers host users' conferences, where employees from different firms receive detailed training on using products, services, and features that are new to the employees. Some vendors will conduct the training inside an organization as well if sufficient numbers of employees need training.

Government-Supported Job Training Federal, state, and local governments provide a wide range of external training assistance and funding.[46] The Workforce Investment Act (WIA) provides states with block grant programs that target adult education, disadvantaged youth, and training employees. Employers hiring and training individuals who meet the WIA criteria receive tax credits and other assistance for six months or more, depending on the program regulations.

At state and local levels, employers who add to their workforces can take advantage of programs that provide funding assistance to offset training costs. As an example, many states offer workforce training assistance for employers. Quick Start (Georgia), Smart Jobs (Texas), and Partnership (Alabama) are three well-known training support efforts. Such programs are often linked to two-year and four-year colleges throughout the state.[47]

Educational Assistance Programs Some employers pay for additional education for their employees. Typically, the employee pays for a course that applies to a college degree and is reimbursed upon successful completion of the course. The amounts paid by the employer are considered nontaxable income for the employee up to amounts set by federal laws.

Lifelong Learning Accounts (LiLA) programs can be offered by employers. These accounts are like 401(K) plans—employers and employees contribute to a fund for adult education. The employee owns the plan and keeps it even if the employee leaves the company. It can be used to further one's education, perhaps to move to a different job in the company.

One concern about traditional forms of employee educational programs is that they may pose risks for the employer. Upon completion of the degree, the employee may choose to take the new skills and go elsewhere. Employers must plan to use the new skills immediately following employee graduation to improve retention.

8-6c Combination Training Approaches

Whether training is delivered internally or externally, appropriate training must be chosen. The following section identifies two common training approaches that often integrate internal and external means. Some are used more for job-based training, while others are used more for development.

Cooperative/Apprentice Training Cooperative training approaches mix classroom training and on-the-job experiences. This training can take several forms. One form, generally referred to as *school-to-work transition*, helps individuals move into jobs while still in school or upon completion of formal schooling. Such efforts may be arranged with high schools, community colleges, or some universities.

Another form of cooperative training used by employers, trade unions, and government agencies is *apprentice training*. An apprenticeship program provides an employee with on-the-job experience under the guidance of a skilled and certified worker. Certain requirements for training, equipment, time length, and proficiency levels may be monitored by a unit of the U.S. Department of Labor. Figure 8-9 indicates the most common areas that use apprenticeships to train people for jobs. Apprenticeships usually last two to five years, depending on the occupation. During this time, the apprentice usually receives lower wages than the certified individual.

A form of cooperative training called *internship* usually combines job training with classroom instruction from schools, colleges, and universities.[48] Internships benefit both employers and interns. Interns get real-world exposure, a line on their résumés, and a chance to closely examine a possible employer. Employers get a cost-effective source of labor and a chance to see the intern work before making a final hiring decision.

FIGURE 8-9 **Most Common Apprenticeship Occupations**

- Electrician (construction)
- Carpenter
- Plumber
- Pipe fitter
- Sheet metal worker

- Structural-steel worker
- Elevator constructor
- Roofer
- Sprinkler fitter
- Bricklayer

© Cengage Learning

ETHICS

L05 Describe the importance of e-learning as part of current training efforts.

8-6d E-Learning: Online Training

E-learning is use of a Web-based technology to conduct training online. E-learning is popular with employers. The major reasons are cost savings and access to more employees. Training conducted with some kind of learning technology is likely to continue to increase. Almost 30% of learning hours today are totally technology based, according to an ASTD report, and e-learning is preferred by workers under the age of 30.[49]

Financial service companies and technology companies were among the first to use Internet training; other industries such as retailing have been slower to use e-learning with only about 20% of retailers using technology for training.[50] Other sectors such as the hospitality industry has successfully used e-learning to enhance training.[51]

CISCO Systems shows how the technology companies (as one would expect) embrace the use of technology in learning when they redid their ethics training. The ethics training, while important, was by their admission "dry as the desert." "We were just cramming ethics and compliance down the employees' throats," noted one manager. However, the new version of that training uses American Idol, the television singing contest as a model. Employees can view four cartoon "contestants" each telling a 3½-minute tale of a challenging ethical situation. Three judges then make a decision on their stories. After viewing, employees vote on which judge they think gave the most appropriate response, and can see instantly how their vote matched up with the company-wide vote. The ethics office then gives the correct answer. The new approach is viewed as interesting, engaging, and fun. Positive responses from the toughest critics of all (CISCO Systems engineers) suggest the project has been a success.[52]

CISCO System's application of e-learning has a game orientation that uses technology. However, a survey shows that such an innovative approach is still in the minority of e-learning applications. Most companies use the technology for testing skills and knowledge or as part of classroom instruction (called blended learning).[53]

Distance Training/Learning Many college and university classes use some form of Internet-based course support. Hundreds of college professors use various packages to make their lecture content available to students. These packages enable virtual chat and electronic file exchange among course participants and enhance instructor–student contact.

Many large employers similarly use interactive two-way television to present classes. The medium allows an instructor in one place to see and respond to a "class" in any number of other locations. With a fully configured system, employees can take courses from anywhere in the world. Webinars are a type of web-based training that has reached a level of popularity both as company training and as a source of profit for the organization.[54]

Simulations and Games Computer-based training involves a wide array of multi-media technologies—including sound, motion (video and animation), graphics, and hypertext—to tap multiple learner senses. Computer-supported simulations within e-learning can replicate the psychological and behavioral requirements of a task, often in addition to providing some physical resemblance to the trainee's work environment.

Simulations and games are not the same although the distinction gets fuzzy at times. **Simulations** seek to reproduce parts of the real world so they can be experienced, manipulated, and learning can occur. **Games** are exercises that entertain and engage. They may or may not resemble the real world of work but can sometimes be used to illustrate points in training. For example, games are success-fully used in team building, communication, leadership, and time management training.[55]

From highly complicated systems that replicate difficult landing scenarios for pilots to programs that help medical trainees learn to sew sutures, simulations allow for safe training when the risks associated with failure are high. For example, sanitation workers can get practice driving on slick roads and down tight alleys without damaging anything. A $450,000 computer simulation uses videos, move-ment, and sound to simulate driving a dump truck. Accidents from poor truck han-dling skills include damage to fences, posts, and buildings. The safety training simulation reduces such accidents.

Certain industries are on the cutting edge of simulation for training such as avi-ation, military, and health care. Flight simulators allow a fledgling pilot to practice without crashing an expensive plane and killing themselves. Military simulations allow use of large weapons systems without killing anyone. Mannequins that are really "computerized patients" allow physicians to learn skills without practicing on a live patient.[56] The nuclear energy industry is another place where simulations are used for training.

Good games are fundamentally different from simulations.[57] Their goal is to provide fun and engagement.[58] Angry birds, football, and chess inspire some to spend a great deal of time enjoying the game. Yet games can be designed to teach to certain learning goals too.[59] See HR Perspective: Using Games to Stimulate Learning in Organizations for insight.

Mobile Learning Predictions have been that training will incorporate more use of mobile devices such as smartphones, tablets, or netbooks, the potential uses seem endless.[60] However, barriers to mobile learning include budget restrictions, integrat-ing this technology with existing training, and security concerns.[61] But while the physical classroom, Webinars, and formal e-learning courses are not going away, mobile learning is on the rise.[62] Some current ways mobile devices can be used in training include the following. Employees can use mobile devices to access instruc-tion manuals for hardware and software. In class, courses can be augmented with five-minute videos accessible from mobile devices, turning classrooms into blended learning.[63] Some organizations like Verizon have created YouTube like repositories or enterprise networks where employees post videos created for knowledge-sharing.[64] It may be that learners like this technology as it creates more learner control over the learning process.[65]

Simulations
Reproduce parts of the real world so they can be experienced, manipu-lated, and learning can occur.

Games
Exercises that entertain and engage.

Using Games to Stimulate Learning in Organizations

Unfortunately, individual learning in a training seminar can be viewed by some as a boring activity. Whether the process involves listening to someone lecture about unfamiliar concepts, or whether it involves reading through information on a computer and taking basic quizzes over the material, learning in these traditional ways can harm employees' motivation to learn. This is why the use of games as learning tools has become a popular approach to create more interest in training activities. Indeed, games stimulate learning because realistic situations can be presented to employees that require immediate decision making and action, and games typically provide prompt feedback about individual performance.

Games can be created to present players with the same challenges they will face on the job. Rules of engagement, player interactivity, and communication can be used to manage outcomes that can be quantified. An advantage with games is that the activities can be conducted either in an online environment with computer-generated characters and contexts or in a

real-time, face-to-face situation where trainees interact directly. Research shows that the versatility and interaction found in games lead to high levels of learning and engagement. The downside to games is that they are difficult to create and take time and money to develop. Additionally, the rules, actions, and playing environments of games all require considerable attention to detail, and the actual time that needs to be invested in playing games can be significant.

There are several approaches that can be utilized to enjoy the advantages of gaming and avoid the disadvantages. For instance, elements of gaming such as decision making can be incorporated into the training environment without creating a full-scale game. Games that allow participants to fail may cause individuals to feel compelled to experiment and learn how to complete work more effectively. Finally, it is important to develop a story (or context) around a game so that trainees feel more engaged with the material and activities, and consistent feedback should be provided to reinforce learning.[66]

Blended Learning Generally, technology is moving from center stage to becoming embedded in the learning and training processes. As learning and work merge even more closely in the future, technology is likely to integrate seamlessly into the work environment of more employees.

Blended learning
Learning approach that combines methods, such as short, fast-paced, interactive computer-based lessons and teleconferencing with traditional classroom instruction and simulation.

However, e-learning does not work well as the sole method of training, according to employers. A solution seems to be **blended learning**, which might combine short, fast-paced, interactive computer-based lessons and teleconferencing with traditional classroom instruction and simulation. Deciding which training is best handled by which medium is important.[67] A blended learning approach can use e-learning for building knowledge of certain basics, a Web-based virtual classroom for building skills, and significant in-person, traditional, instructor-led training sessions and courses. Use of blended learning provides greater flexibility in the use of multiple training means and enhances the appeal of training activities to different types of employees.[68]

Advantages and Disadvantages of E-Learning The rapid growth of e-learning makes the Internet or an intranet a viable means for delivering training content. But

FIGURE 8-10 Advantages and Disadvantages of E-Learning

Advantages	Disadvantages
• Is self-paced; trainees can proceed on their own time • Is interactive, tapping multiple trainee senses • Enables scoring of exercises/assessments and the appropriate feedback • Incorporates built-in guidance and help for trainees to use when needed • Allows trainers to update content relatively easily • Can enhance instructor-led training • Is good for presenting simple facts and concepts • Can be paired with simulation	• May cause trainee anxiety • Some trainees may not be interested in how it is used • Requires easy and uninterrupted access to computers • Is not appropriate for some training (leadership, cultural change, etc.) • Requires significant upfront investment both in time and costs • Requires significant support from top management to be successful • Some choose not to do it even if it is available

© Cengage Learning

e-learning has both advantages and disadvantages that must be considered. In addition to being concerned about employee access to e-learning and the desire to use it, some employers worry that trainees will use e-learning to complete courses quickly but will not retain and use much of what they have learned on the job. Taking existing training materials, putting them on the Internet, and cutting the training budget is not the way to succeed with e-learning. An important question to ask is, Can this material be learned as well online as through conventional methods? In some cases, the answer is "no"; in others the answer is "yes."[69]

Figure 8-10 presents a listing of the most commonly cited advantages and disadvantages of e-learning.

8-7 ■ TRAINING EVALUATION

L06 Give an example for each of the four levels of training evaluation.

Evaluation of training compares the post-training results to the pre-training objectives of managers, trainers, and trainees. Too often, training is conducted with little thought of measuring and evaluating it later to see how well it worked. Since training is both time consuming and costly, it should be evaluated.[70]

8-7a Levels of Evaluation

It is best to consider how training is to be evaluated before it begins. Donald L. Kirkpatrick identified four levels at which training can be evaluated.[71] They are reaction, learning, behaviors, and results.

Reaction Organizations evaluate the reaction levels of trainees by conducting interviews with or administering questionnaires to the trainees. Assume that 30 managers attend a two-day workshop on effective interviewing skills. A reaction-level measure could be gathered by having the managers complete a survey that asked them to rate the value of the training, the style of the instructors, and the usefulness of the training to them.

Learning Learning levels can be evaluated by measuring how well trainees have learned facts, ideas, concepts, theories, and attitudes. Tests on the training material are commonly used for evaluating learning, and they can be given both before and after training to provide scores that can be compared. If test scores indicate learning problems, then instructors get feedback and courses can be redesigned so that the content can be delivered more effectively. Of course, learning enough to pass a test does not guarantee that trainees will remember the training content months later or that it will change job behaviors.

Behaviors Evaluating training at the behavioral level means measuring the effect of training on job performance through observing job performance. For instance, the managers who participated in an interviewing workshop might be observed conducting actual interviews of applicants for jobs in their departments. If the managers asked questions as they had been trained to and used appropriate follow-up questions, then behavioral indicators of the effectiveness of the interviewing training exist.

Results Employers evaluate results by measuring the effect of training on the achievement of organizational objectives. Since results such as productivity, turnover, quality, time, sales, and costs are relatively concrete, this type of evaluation can be done by comparing records before and after training. For the managers who attended interviewing training, evaluators could gather records of the number of individuals hired compared with the number of employment offers made before and after the training.

The difficulty with measuring results is pinpointing whether changes were actually the result of training or of other major factors. For example, the managers who completed the interviewing training program can be measured on employee turnover before and after the training, but turnover also depends on the current economic situation, the demand for workers, and many other variables.

8-7b Training Evaluation Metrics

Training is expensive, and it is an HR function that requires measurement and monitoring. Cost–benefit analysis and return-on-investment (ROI) analysis are commonly used to measure training results, as are various benchmarking approaches.

MEASURE

Cost–Benefit Analysis Comparison of costs and benefits associated with training.

Cost–Benefit Analysis Training results can be examined through **cost–benefit analysis**, which is comparison of costs and benefits associated with training. There are four stages in calculating training costs and benefits:

1. *Determine training costs.* Consider direct costs such as design, trainer fees, materials, facilities, and other administration activities.
2. *Identify potential savings results.* Consider employee retention, better customer service, fewer work errors, quicker equipment production, and other productivity factors.
3. *Compute potential savings.* Gather data on the performance results and assign dollar costs to each of them.
4. *Conduct costs and savings benefits comparisons.* Evaluate the costs per participant, the savings per participant, and how the costs and benefits relate to business performance numbers.

FIGURE 8-11 Possible Costs and Benefits in Training

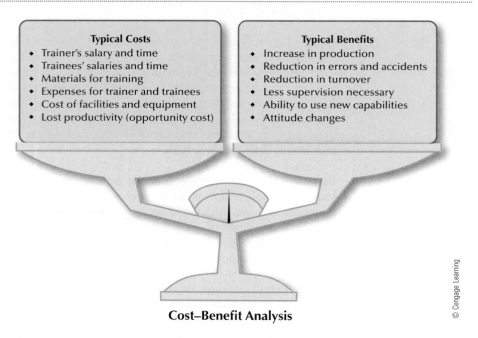

Typical Costs
- Trainer's salary and time
- Trainees' salaries and time
- Materials for training
- Expenses for trainer and trainees
- Cost of facilities and equipment
- Lost productivity (opportunity cost)

Typical Benefits
- Increase in production
- Reduction in errors and accidents
- Reduction in turnover
- Less supervision necessary
- Ability to use new capabilities
- Attitude changes

Cost–Benefit Analysis

© Cengage Learning

Figure 8-11 shows some typical costs and benefits that may result from training. Even though some benefits (such as attitude changes) are hard to quantify, comparisons of costs and benefits associated with training remains a way to determine whether training is cost-effective. For example, one firm evaluated a traditional safety training program and found that the program did not lead to a reduction in accidents. Therefore, the safety training was redesigned, and better safety practices resulted. E-learning should be evaluated as well.[72]

Return-on-Investment Analysis and Benchmarking In organizations, training is often expected to produce an ROI. Still, too often, training is justified because someone liked it, rather than on the basis of resource accountability.[73] ROI simply divides the return produced because of the training by the cost (or investment) of the training.

In addition to evaluating training internally, some organizations use benchmark measures to compare it with training done in other organizations. To do benchmarking, HR professionals gather data on training in their organization and compare them with data on training at other organizations in the same industry and in companies of a similar size. Comparison data are available through the American Society for Training and Development and its Benchmarking Service. This service has training-related data from more than 1,000 participating employers who complete detailed questionnaires annually. Training can also be benchmarked against data from the American Productivity & Quality Center and the Saratoga Institute.

8-7c Training Evaluation Designs

With or without benchmarking data, internal evaluations of training programs can be designed in many ways. The rigor of the three designs discussed next increases with each level.

Post-Measure The most obvious way to evaluate training effectiveness is to determine after the training whether the employees can perform the way management wants them to perform. Assume that a customer service manager has 20 representatives who need to improve their data-entry speeds. After a one-day training session, they take a test to measure their speeds. If the representatives can all type the required speed after training, was the training beneficial? It is difficult to say—perhaps most of them could have done as well before training. Tests after training do not always clearly indicate whether a performance is a result of the training or could have been achieved without the training.

Pre-/Post-Measure By differently designing the evaluation just discussed, the issue of pretest skill levels can be considered. If the data-entry speed is measured before and after training, then it will indicate whether the training made any difference. However, a question would remain: Was any increase in speed a response to the training, or did these employees simply work faster because they knew they were being tested? People often perform better when they know their efforts are being evaluated.

Pre-/Post-Measure with a Control Group Another evaluation design can address the preceding problem. In addition to testing the 20 representatives who will be trained, the manager can test another group of representatives who will not be trained, to see if they do as well as those who are to be trained. This second group is called a control group. After training, if the trained representatives work significantly faster than those who were not trained, the manager can be reasonably sure that the training was effective.

SUMMARY

- Training is the process that provides people with the capabilities they need to do their jobs.
- Four types of training are regular/required, job/technical, interpersonal/problem solving, and developmental/career.
- A strategic approach to training links organizational strategies and HR planning to various training efforts.
- Training affects factors such as organizational competitiveness, knowledge management, revenue, and performance.
- Global strategies must consider training as a key component, including intercultural competence training to prepare employees to respond more appropriately to situations encountered during global assignments.
- The training process consists of four phases: assessment, design, delivery, and evaluation.
- Training needs can be assessed using organizational, job/task, and individual analyses, and

then training objectives can be set to help the organization meet those needs.

- Training design must consider learner readiness, learning styles, and learning transfer.
- Training can be delivered internally (e.g., OJT training) or through external means, and formally (e.g., through classes) or informally.
- Common training approaches include cooperative training and classroom/conference training.
- Orientation is a form of onboarding designed to help new employees learn about their jobs.
- E-learning is training conducted using the Internet or an intranet, and both its advantages and its disadvantages must be considered in its development.
- Various organizations are taking advantage of training that uses technology, such as Web-based multimedia, video streaming, simulation, and virtual reality.
- Training can be evaluated at four levels: reaction, learning, behavior, and results.

- Training evaluation metrics may include cost–benefit analysis, ROI analysis, and benchmarking.

- A pre-/post-measure with a control group is the most rigorous design for training evaluation; other, less rigorous designs can be used as well.

CRITICAL THINKING CHALLENGES

1. Identify training needs for a group of new salespeople in a high-end jewelry store.

2. Why is evaluating training an important part of strategic training?

3. Develop an orientation checklist on the basis of one first-day session and a second session of four hours 30 days later.

4. Make a briefing for division managers showing the advantages and disadvantages of e-learning and how to "blend" it with other teaching techniques. Use websites, including www.ASTD. org.

5. Because of rapid growth of your technology company, the executive team has asked HR to develop an internal training program. The purpose of the program is to help employees recently promoted to supervisory positions develop the leadership skill sets they need to be successful as supervisors. This will be the first formal training program for your small company. As part of the process, you want to consider the learning styles of the new supervisors. To assist you in developing a successful, results-oriented program, review various training websites, including www.agelesslearner.com.

A. To meet the needs of the varied learning styles and maximize the learning potential of the participants, what training techniques should be implemented?

B. Identify the content topics that you will recommend be included in the program to ensure the development of successful leaders.

CASE

Using Performance Support to Improve Learning

The training done in most companies is based on the formal learning that takes place in planned exercises and classroom activities. Despite this reality, some learning groups that have done well despite the uncertainty of the business climate have moved beyond this traditional model to a more employee-centered learning framework. Such a model is based on the idea that learning must be enabled and consistently supported by training professionals, and employees should to some extent self-direct their own training endeavors and learn how to apply the information on the job.

Informal learning can be created and managed internally in a company through a process called "Performance Support". Performance Support involves giving employees informational assistance that addresses the issues they currently face while performing their work to increase job performance. When managed properly by (1) clearly establishing how Performance Support will help the organization and (2) getting the firm's leaders and IT professionals to support its implementation, the process can lead to an increase in overall organizational effectiveness.

The home and furniture design firm Herman Miller set out to implement Performance Support as part of an effort to enhance employees' performance of their jobs. Herman Miller faced many challenges and opportunities that precipitated the move toward self-learning, including employees' low interest in formal training, an increase in calls to an understaffed help desk, and the unveiling of six new products. In addition, the company highlighted many new competencies that individuals were expected to integrate into their daily functioning as employees. The Performance Support frameworks were launched in a way that did not intimidate workers, and additional models were slowly introduced as employees showed some success.

Companies can consider piloting the introduction and application of Performance Support systems as a way to make the learning occur in a more fluid fashion. The system should be managed so that the appropriate information is available to employees based on the history of queries that have occurred in the past. Additionally, access to the Performance Support networks should be made readily available on mobile devices so that information can be accessed anywhere and on the fly.

The use of Performance Support was much higher than typical classes being offered at Herman Miller, reducing expenses significantly for the organization. Competencies were also being cultivated in the workplace through the use of the Performance Support network. The company's IT Support Center, sales and marketing managers, and executive panel that developed the competencies were all strong champions of the program and were instrumental in developing subsequent awareness and support throughout the ranks.[74]

QUESTIONS

1. The case introduces a rather complex information-based approach to encourage learning on the job. How is this approach different from traditional training? Are there any similarities?

2. How would you implement a Performance Support system?

3. What are the challenges and opportunities associated with a Performance Support informational network with regard to individual learning?

SUPPLEMENTAL CASES

Training Crucial for Hotels

This case illustrates the increased role training is playing in large U.S. hotel chains. (For the case, go to www.cengage.com/management/mathis.)

New Payroll Clerk

This case shows the frustration that often accompanies the first day at work, and why orientation is important in reducing turnover. (For the case, go to www.cengage.com/management/mathis.)

Twenty-First Century Onboarding

This case outlines orientation efforts of Sun Microsystems, El Paso Corporation, and Zimmerman Advertising. (For this case, go to www.cengage .com/management/mathis.)

NOTES

1. Based on Jeffrey S. Eisenberg, "A New Direction in Skills Training?", *Human Resource Executive – Online*, August 9, 2012, 1–2.

2. Herman Aguinis and Kurt Kraiger, "Benefits of Training and Development for Individuals and Teams, Organizations and Society," *Annual Review of Psychology*, 60 (2009), 451–474.

3. Margery Weinstein, "Verizon Connects to Success," *Training*, January/February 2011, 40–42.

4. Kristen B. Frasch, "Calling All White Men (to diversity training)," *Human Resource Executive*, October 2012, 11.

5. Gabrielle Wirth and Gary Gansle, "Jump toward Emotional Intelligence," *HR Magazine*, October 2012, 87–90.

6. James Hall and Marty Denis, "Compensability of Job Related Training," *Workplace Management*, April 6, 2009, 10.

7. Jennifer Schramm, "Undereducated," *HR Magazine*, September 2011, 136.

8. Aaron DeSmet, et al., "Getting More from your Training Programs," *McKinsey Quarterly*, October 2010, 1–6.

9. Vichet Sum, "Integrating Training in Business Strategies Means Greater Impact of Training on the Firm's Competitiveness," *Research in Business and Economics Journal*, 2011, 4, 1–19.

10. Andrea Davis, "Back to School," *Employee Benefit News*, September 15, 2012, 26–28.

11. Neal Goodman, "After You Train, Retain," *Training*, September/October 2011, 46.

12. Mary Key et al., "Knowledge Management," *People and Strategy*, 2009, 32, 42–47.

13. Steve Trautman, "Focusing Knowledge Retention on Millennials," *Workforce Management*," August 2010, 6.

14. Adapted from John Castaldi, "Constructing a Business Case for Training: Cause, Coincidence, or Correlation?", *T+D*, June 2012, 32–34.

15. Stanley Harris, "Driving Growth: Effective Sales Training," *Brandon Hall Group*, April 2012, 1–9.

16. Ann Pace, "Sales Training for the Virtual Interaction," *T+D*, June 2012, 18.

17. Steve Gielda, "Simulations Give Sales Training a Dose of Reality," *T+D*, November 2011, 53–55.

18. Ann Tace, "Training for the Leap Overseas," *T+D*, August 2009, 18.

19. Andrea Edmundson, "Culturally Accessible E-Learning," *T+D*, April 2009, 41–45.

20. Jan Selmer, "Expatriate Cross-Cultural Training for China: Views and Experience of 'China Hands'," *Management Research Review*, 2009, 33, 41–53.

21. "Benefits of Onboarding", *Training*, July/August 2011, 7.

22. Donald L. Caruth, et al., "Getting Off to a Good Start," *Industrial Management*, March/April 2010, 1–4.

23. Based on Tom Starner, "Bringing Them on Board," *Human Resource Executive Online*, November 1. 2009, 1–4; Kate Day and Lisa Maria Fedele, "Learning at the Speed of Life," *T+D*, June 2012, 61–63.

24. Jennifer Taylor Arnold, "Ramping Up Onboarding," *HR Magazine*, May 2010, 75–78.

25. George Brandt, "Onboarding: An Act of Transformational Leadership," *People and Strategy*, 2010, 33, 4–5.

26. Bill Gilmyers and Amir Assadi, "What Your New Hires Are Telling You," *Workspan*, July 2009, 30–38.

27. Holly Dolezalek, "Best Practices Deconstructed," *Training*, June 2009, 46, 50–52.

28. Marty Buck and Mary Martin, "Leaders Teaching Leaders," *HR Magazine*, September 2012, 60–62.

29. "Soft Skills: A Case for Higher Education and Workplace Training," *T+D*, November 2011, 65, 16.

30. Yaping Gong, et al., "Employee Learning Orientation, Transformational Leadership, and Employee Creativity: The Mediating Role of Employee Creative Self-Efficacy," *The Academy of Management Journal*, August 2009, 52, 765–778.

31. Malcolm S. Knowles, Elwood F. Holton III, and Richard A. Swanson, *The Adult Learner*, 6th ed. (New York: Elsevier, 2005).

32. Simone Kauffeld and Nale Lehmann-Willenbrock, "Sales Training: Effects of Spaced Practice on training Transfer," *Journal of European Industrial Training*, 2010, 34, 23–37.

33. "Best Practices and Outstanding Initiatives," *Training*, January/February 2011, 96.

34. Tal Katz-Navon, et al., "Active Learning: When Is More Better? The Case of Resident Physician's Medical Errors," *Journal of Applied Psychology*, 2009, 94, 1200–1209.

35. Kendra Lee, "Reinforce Training," *Training*, May/June 2011, 24.

36. Harry J. Martin, "Improving Training Impact through Effective Follow-up," *Journal of Management Development*, 2010, 29, 520–534.

37. Brian D. Blume, et al., "Transfer of Training: A Meta-Analytic Review," *Journal of Management*, 2010, 36, 1065–1102.

38. Harry J. Martin, "Workplace Climate and Peer Support as Determinants of Training Transfer," *Human Resource Development Quarterly*, Spring 2010, 21, 87–104.

39. Lisa M. Burke and Alan M. Saks, "Accountability in Training Transfer," *Human Resource Development Review*, 2009, 8, 382–402.

40. Nancy J. Lewis, "Informal Learning: Style vs. Substance" *Training*, January/February 2011, 18–19.

41. Ronald Jacobs and Yoonhe Park, "A Proposed Conceptual Framework of Workplace Learning," *Human Resource Development Review*, 8 (2009), 133–150.

42. Jacobs and Park, op. cit., 140–141.

43. Yvette Lee, "Job Swapping, I-9 Forms, Travel Pay," *HR Magazine*, April 2011, 24.

44. J. A. C. Bokhorst, "The Impact of the Amount of Work in Process on the Use of Cross Training," *International Journal of Production Research*, 2011, 49, 3171–3190.

45. "Tips to Outsource Training," *Training*, September/October 2010, 7.

46. Kathryn Tyler, "Mining for Training Treasure," *HR Magazine*, September 2009, 99–102.

47. Patricia Claghorn, "Certainly Not Half Baked: A True Community College and Business Partnership," *T+D*, July 2011, 65, 20.

48. Andrew R. McIlvaine, "Labor Abuse – or a Golden Opportunity?", *Human Resource Executive Online*, April 12, 2012, 1–2.

49. American Society of Training and Development, www.astd.org.

50. Greg Wright, "Retailers Buy Into E-Learning," *HR Magazine*, December 2010, 87–90.

51. "Motel 6/Studio 6 Revamp Training Efforts," *Training*, September/October 2011, 7.

52. Michael O'Brian, "Idolizing Ethics," *Human Resource Executive Online*, May 16, 2009, 1–3.

53. Allison Rossett, and James Marshall, "E-learning: What's Old Is New Again," *T+D*, January 2010, 64, 34–38.

54. Kenedra Lee, "Ensure Webinar-Based Training Success," *Training*, November/December 2010, 14.

55. Swati Karve, "Facilitation Skills: Using Training Games," *T+D*, July 2011, 67, 30–31.

56. Matt Bolch, "Focus on Games and Simulations," *Training*, October/November 2009, 53–56.

57. Margery Weinstein, "Sizing Up Simulation," *Training*, December 2010, 46–47.

58. Clark Aldrich, "Because You Can't Learn to Ride a Bicycle from a Book," *T+D*, December 2009, 24–26; Greg Greunke, "Training Game Changer," *HR Magazine*, September 2012, 67–72.

59. Joseph P. Giunta, "Designing Games that Really Teach," *T+D*, June 2010, 76–77; Drew Robb, "Let the Games Begin," *HR Magazine*, September 2012, 93–97; T. Sitzmann, "A Meta-Analytic Examination of the Instructional Effectiveness of Computer-Based Simulation Games," *Personnel Psychology*, 2011, 64, 489–528.

60. Kristie Donnelly, "Learning on the Move," *Development and Learning in Organizations*, 2009, 23, 8–11.

61. Lorrie Lykins, "Creating a Viable Mobile Learning Strategy Remains a Challenge," *T+D*, June 2012, 26.

62. Bill Roberts, "From E-Learning to Mobile Learning," *HR Magazine*, August 2012, 61–65.

63. Ibid, p. 62.

64. Dave Zielinski, "Group Learning," *SHRM.org*, May 1, 2012, 3.

65. K. A. Orvis, "Power to the People: Using Learner Control to Improve Trainee Reactions and Learning in Web-based Instructional Environments," *Journal of Applied Psychology*, 2009, 94, 960–971.

66. Adapted from Jeanne Meister and Karie Willyerd, "Looking Ahead at Social Learning: 10 Predictions," *T+D*, July 2010, 64, 34–41.

67. Jennifer Hofmann, "Top 10 Challenges of Blended Learning," *Training*, March/April 2011, 12–13.

68. P. J. Elkeles, "A Flexible Approach to Developing Leadership," *Workforce Management*, May 2010, 28.

69. Peter Cappelli, "Does Online Instruction Work?", *Human Resource Executive Online*, July 15, 2010, 1–3.

70. Jenny Cermak and Monica McGurk, "Putting a Value on Training," *McKinsey Quarterly*, July 2010, 1–6.

71. Donald Kirkpatrick, "The Four Levels Are Still Relevant," *T+D*, 64, September 2010, 16.

72. Sateve Yacovelli, "How to Effectively Evaluate E-Learning," *T+D*, July 2012, 52–57.

73. Kendra Lee, "Create a Simple Plan for ROI," *Training*, July/August 2011, 14, Phaedra Brotherton, "Organizations Lag Behind in Measuring Learning's Value," *T+D*, February 2011, 65, 16–17.

74. Adapted from Bob Mosher and Jeremy Smith, "The Case for Performance Support," *Training*, November/December 2011, 12–13.

9

Talent, Careers, and Development

Learning Objectives

After you have read this chapter, you should be able to:

1 Identify the importance of talent management and discuss two reasons it may be difficult.

2 Explain what succession planning is and its steps.

3 Differentiate between organization-centered and individual-centered career planning.

4 List options for development needs analyses.

5 Discuss three career issues that organizations and employees must address.

6 Identify several management development methods.

HR HEADLINE

Talent Management Should Be Solutions-Driven

© Tupungato/Shutterstock.com

HR professionals propose policies that they think will help employees develop in the long run, thus helping the organization succeed. However, many of these policies often don't address the current problems that line managers face as they interact with their workers' careers. Line managers do not always get excited about talent management initiatives because they might not relate directly to the challenges that they currently experience. As a result, insufficient management buy-in is a common problem, with talent management, and the newly developed HR initiatives may not be very successful. Organizations such as Sysco Corporation and Deloitte are trying to develop talent management programs that are perceived to be more relevant and effective.

HR professionals diagnose line managers' day-to-day problems and develop policies that address their concerns regarding talent management and employee development. HR leaders must think diagnostically in a manner similar to medical doctors and provide initiatives from the HR department that truly help the talent-related problems that managers experience. By doing so, they won't have to try too hard to sell these ideas because the solutions will sell themselves.

Houston-based food supplier Sysco Corporation is one company that used such an approach. After conducting research and determining that job tenure was related to leader effectiveness, the company created a developmental program that prepared people for positions of authority. HR managers were able to sell the program because it addressed important business needs and did not require employees to miss much work.

Talent management can be linked with solid metrics that support the policies. Ideally, these metrics should show how the implementation of these efforts will increase performance and the company's bottom line. Some managers at companies like Deloitte also believe that HR professionals should be rotated into line-level jobs to get a better idea of the problems that exist in the different operational areas of a firm. By functioning as involved diagnosticians and problem solvers, HR managers can provide line managers with sound HR policies that enhance both talent and career management.[1]

Workforce planning is based on having the correct number of employees as they are needed by the organization and its managers. Workforce planning works with talent management, which focuses on having the right individuals ready for the jobs when needed. A significant part of talent management involves developing a pipeline of talented people. Additionally, talent management focuses on key positions and job families that will be required, skills that will be needed, and competency models, talent pools, and assessments of employees.

This chapter focuses on talent management as a strategy to build company performance. Much of this approach involves having a plan that effectively deals with employees' careers and provides for their developmental needs. In addition, talent management includes programs that cultivate important capabilities and competencies.

LO1 Identify the importance of talent management and discuss two reasons it may be difficult.

9-1 ■ TALENT MANAGEMENT AS STRATEGY

Strategic talent management
The process of identifying the most important jobs in a company that provide a long-term competitive advantage, and then creating appropriate HR policies to develop employees so that they can effectively work in these jobs.

Successful talent management is strategic because the development of employees should be linked to what the organization is trying to do. Organizations must respond quickly to changes in environmental demands, and having the right talent helps those responses. **Strategic talent management** is the process of identifying the most important jobs in a company that provide a long-term advantage, and then developing employees so that they can effectively work in these jobs.[2] Both talent and strategy are among the most important drivers of success in some organizations including research and development labs.[3] This suggests that companies should consider talent management when developing their business strategies. Chief Human Resource Management Officers may work in advisory roles related to business strategy, which requires them to establish important relational networks with key decision makers.[4]

Talent management policies that develop employee's careers—should be viewed as a strategic tool rather than as a cost.[5] This can provide employees who create a competitive advantage for the firm through individual competencies and appropriate roles.[6] Evidence suggests that many organizations in the United States are using talent management, but some have not fully integrated it into decision-making processes or allowed the approach to be driven by business needs. Greater emphasis on building competencies can establish a system that works well.[7] The major components in the employment life cycle (i.e., training/development, performance and succession management, etc.) should be integrated as one unit.[8]

Companies can reduce risks and increase the rewards of talent management by adopting an approach that relies on (1) the development of current employees and hiring outside talent, (2) the creation of talent pools and broad competencies in employees, (3) the use of short-term talent forecasts that are likely more reliable, and (4) establishing a balance between employees' and companies' ownership of career development.[9] SunTrust adopted a slightly different approach by developing several key business values, which included a focus on teamwork, client relationships, and strong growth through profits, and then aligning strategies to these principles.[10] There is also growing interest in the creation of community-based talent networks that provide developmental opportunities for individuals from K–12 through college, and well into their careers as working professionals.[11]

9-2 ■ TALENT MANAGEMENT IN PERSPECTIVE

The idea that human capital can be a source of competitive advantage for organizations is gaining ground, but many firms are not designed or managed to optimize talent performance.[12] Choices for dealing successfully with talent needs are to (1) emphasize stability in employment and develop talent internally, (2) develop agility as an organization and buy talent as needed, or (3) use some combination of (1) and (2). So the nature of the business and the environment in which it operates to some extent define appropriate strategies for talent management.

Talent management can be challenging because of the nature of "talent" itself. For example, a "deep bench" of talent can be thought of as inventory. But unlike boxes full of empty bottles, talent does not necessarily remain available until needed—people will leave the company to work in more desirable employment situations.[13] The shelf life of promising managers and specialists is short if they do not have opportunities in their current place of work.

Job candidates indicate that they are most attracted to opportunities to learn and grow. In fact, career development ranks higher than work–life balance and compensation/benefits for most job seekers.[14] This makes the need for a successful talent management program even greater. Attracting and retaining talent is only part of the equation—companies must keep people engaged by looking for individual characteristics that lead to job success, providing good development opportunities for high-performing employees, and having a management team that builds confidence in the company's future prospects.[15]

One way to think of talent management is as a process that goes beyond simply recruiting and selection to meeting the needs of the organization with talent. Along the way, all the elements of talent management are encountered: training, succession planning, career planning, development, and performance management. Figure 9-1 shows the process. Training and performance management are covered in other chapters but succession planning, career planning, and development are covered in this chapter.

FIGURE 9-1 Talent Management Process

© Cengage Learning 2014

9-2a Talent Management Information Systems

Talent management seems to lend itself to the use of various software-based systems that purport to integrate all the pieces of talent management into one manageable whole. For example, one company used a talent management system to:

- document new employee orientation and training;
- track classroom training and certifications completed by all store employees;
- automate registration of participants for training and development activities;
- report on completions of training certifications for employees; and
- compile and report the training and development history of individuals for use with career planning and development.

However, according to one survey, although many companies are planning to use talent management technology, about half still use a manual rather than automated approach.[16]

One reason for the demand for automated talent management systems is the situation that arose during the last recession. Many talented people were cut from the workforce, and some companies cut more of them than was necessary. Some employers view automated information as a way to avoid this problem in the future.[17] As an example of the potential in automated systems, Comcast Corporation can run a search across the entire organization to find people with certain qualifications who are strong in specific skills. If a person is needed for a business development position with strong customer communication and strategic skills, a search of the system will perhaps locate a dozen people in the company with these skills and excellent performance reviews during the last year.[18]

The drive to automate talent management also comes in part from the desire to pull together HR, finance, and operations data to get insights on talent that are otherwise difficult to obtain. Whether current systems do this in a way that deals appropriately with the key issues is still unclear. However, regardless of the current state of the art, the potential for automated talent management systems in the future is great as a tool to aid decision making, but these systems are certainly not the entire solution to talent management challenges.

9-2b Scope of Talent Management

As talent management has evolved, a variety of approaches and tools have also developed. The following sections describe the approaches that define talent management.

Target Jobs The first issue is to identify the types of jobs that will be the focus of talent management efforts. In some organizations, talent management focuses on the CEO and other executive jobs, rather than focusing more broadly. Other organizations target senior management, mid-level managers, and other key jobs. However, those groups only represent about one-third of the total workforce, which raises the question of whether talent management efforts would be more useful if they were more widely implemented within the workforce.

High-pos
Individuals who show high promise for advancement in the organization.

High-Potential Individuals Some organizations focus talent management efforts primarily on "high-potential" individuals, often referred to as **high-pos**. Attracting, retaining, and developing high-pos have become the main emphases for some talent management efforts. Firms may classify individuals as being in the top 10% and limit participation in intensive talent management efforts to that group. Other organizations view talent management more broadly. Targeting primarily high-pos may lead to many other employees seeing their career opportunities as being limited. Talent management may need to include more than the top 10% in some cases. Unfortunately, evidence suggests that many companies do not effectively find high-pos among the ranks of existing employees.[19]

Yet, identifying top performers may not be as difficult as trying to keep such individuals satisfied and engaged at work. When dealing with high-pos, employers sometimes utilize incorrect assumptions and approaches, such as:

- believing that they are fully engaged in the workplace;
- thinking they are willing and able to become leaders;
- failing to get top leaders involved in their development;
- not giving them opportunities to build needed competencies;
- lacking reward and recognition for them; and
- not informing them of future plans.[20]

Further, many companies do not provide useful feedback to high performers using proper assessment and measurement instruments, and leaders are often not involved in or held accountable for the management of these individuals.[21]

However, many prominent companies such as General Electric, Unilever North America, and IBM have established programs that effectively identify and cultivate talent in high-pos by linking corporate strategy to the development of leaders and providing learning opportunities that grow the business and the individual.[22] Indeed, the management of high-pos requires several key best practices such as deciding what kinds of employees are needed given the strategy, properly identifying talent, making varied job experiences available, and promptly disseminating performance feedback.[23] Other important approaches that can keep top performers engaged include recognizing their talents, including them in an ongoing development process (rather than short-term), providing substantive, yet flexible opportunities for them to gain additional responsibility and visibility in the firm, and partnering them with good mentors.[24]

Competency Models What does a person who is ready to be moved up look like? What competencies should the person have? Competency models show knowledge, skills, and abilities (KSAs) for various jobs. An employer must ask, "What talent do we need to achieve this?" The answer can be found in a competency model. Competency models help to identify talent and gaps. Some companies maintain libraries of competency models. One has more than 900 such models for different jobs.[25] These libraries create a clear path for talent planning. Competency models might be created for executives, managers, supervisors, salespeople, technical professionals, and other key jobs. An example of such a competency is problem solving, which involves addressing complex organizational problems and developing solutions.

Talent Pools   Talent pools are a way to reduce the risk that the company may not need a certain specialty after developing it. The idea is to avoid developing for a narrow specialized job and instead develop a group or pool of talented people with broad general competencies that could fit a wide range of jobs. Once developed, they can be allocated to specific vacancies. Just-in-time training and coaching can make the fit work.[26]

Career Tracks   Career tracks are a series of steps that one follows to become ready to move up. For example, a potential branch manager in a bank might take rotational assignments in customer sales, teller supervisor, credit cards, and other positions before being considered ready to handle the branch manager's job. Firms such as Costco and Xerox Europe have successfully utilized career tracks that move individuals to new jobs calling for higher-level capabilities as tools for increasing employee motivation and reducing turnover.[27]

Assessment   Assessment most often involves tests of one sort or another. Tests for IQ, personality, aptitude, and other factors can be used. A portfolio of tests and other assessments to help predict a person's potential for a job is called an "assessment center," which will be discussed in more detail later in this chapter.

Development Risk Sharing   The employer always runs a risk in developing talent in that an employee who has been developed will choose to leave with the valuable skills gained. A way to reduce this risk is to have promising employees volunteer for development on their own time. Executive MBA programs that can be attended on evenings or weekends, extra projects outside a person's current assignment, volunteer projects with nonprofit organizations, and other paths can be used. The employer might contribute through tuition reimbursement or some selected time away from the job, but the risk is at least partly shared by the employee because they have invested their time in the process.

9-3 ■ SUCCESSION PLANNING

LO2 Explain what succession planning is and its steps.

Succession planning
Preparing for the inevitable movements of personnel that creates holes in the hierarchy that need to be filled by other qualified individuals.

The basis for a company dealing successfully with staffing changes such as retirements, transfers, promotions, and turnover is succession planning. **Succession planning** encourages an organization to prepare for the inevitable movements of personnel that create holes in the hierarchy that need to be filled by other qualified individuals. "Bench strength" and the leadership pipeline are metaphors for ways to prevent the void by having replacements ready.

However, succession planning involves more than simply replacement planning. Replacement planning usually involves creating a list of temporary replacements for important jobs, especially during crisis situations.[28] Succession planning should include a well-designed development system for employees.[29] The process should be able to place the right people in the right positions.[30] Succession planning can be the process of farming a plan for the orderly replacement of key employees. This was the case at Xerox when a methodical plan was put into place to have Ursula Burns replace Anne Mulcahy as CEO using various on-the-job developmental experiences that systematically prepared her for the job.[31]

Some organizations have unfortunately moved away from succession planning because of the layoffs, employee departures, and budgetary setbacks caused by the last recession. But firms must still focus on business needs by identifying the key jobs that will satisfy these needs and the proper talent to work in these positions, as well as create appropriate development activities. HR will still need to demonstrate that succession planning can be an important part of talent management.[32]

9-3a Succession Planning Process

Whether in small or large firms, succession planning is linked to strategic planning through the process shown in Figure 9-2. The process consists of first defining positions that are critical to the strategy,[33] and then making certain top management is involved personally with talent identification, mentoring, and coaching. It may be appropriate to tie some level of incentive to executive success in the process. The next step is to assess the talent available in the organization and determine who has the potential, who is ready now for promotion, and who needs additional development. The development practices can vary but should be aimed at specific needs in specific individuals. Finally, evaluating the success of the process is important, and appropriate measures are necessary to do so.[34]

All the work involved in the succession planning process should result in two products: (1) identification of potential emergency replacements for critical positions and (2) other successors who will be ready with some additional development. The development necessary should be made clear to the people involved, along with a plan for achieving the development.[35]

Role of HR in Succession Planning Often HR has the primary responsibility for succession planning organization-wide. However, for CEO and senior management succession efforts, top executives and board members often have major involvement. In this case, HR commonly performs the following actions:[36]

- Functioning as an objective voice and measuring effectiveness of the program
- Interpreting data collected about employees who might fill future positions
- Being available for job candidates who seek counseling
- Enhancing the development opportunities in the firm
- Helping track and evaluate individual development efforts

GLOBAL

Global Succession Planning Succession planning is not just an issue in the U.S. In fact, the percentage of older employees who will leave the workforce is even higher in countries such as Japan, Germany, Italy, and England. In those countries, as well as the United States, the growth of immigrants has added to the population, which also means that employers are facing both legal and workforce diversity issues. Even in countries with growing native workforces, such as China and India, succession planning is important. Having younger workers with international experiences and contacts who can replace senior managers is a growing concern faced worldwide by employers of different sizes and industries.[37]

FIGURE 9-2 Succession Planning Process

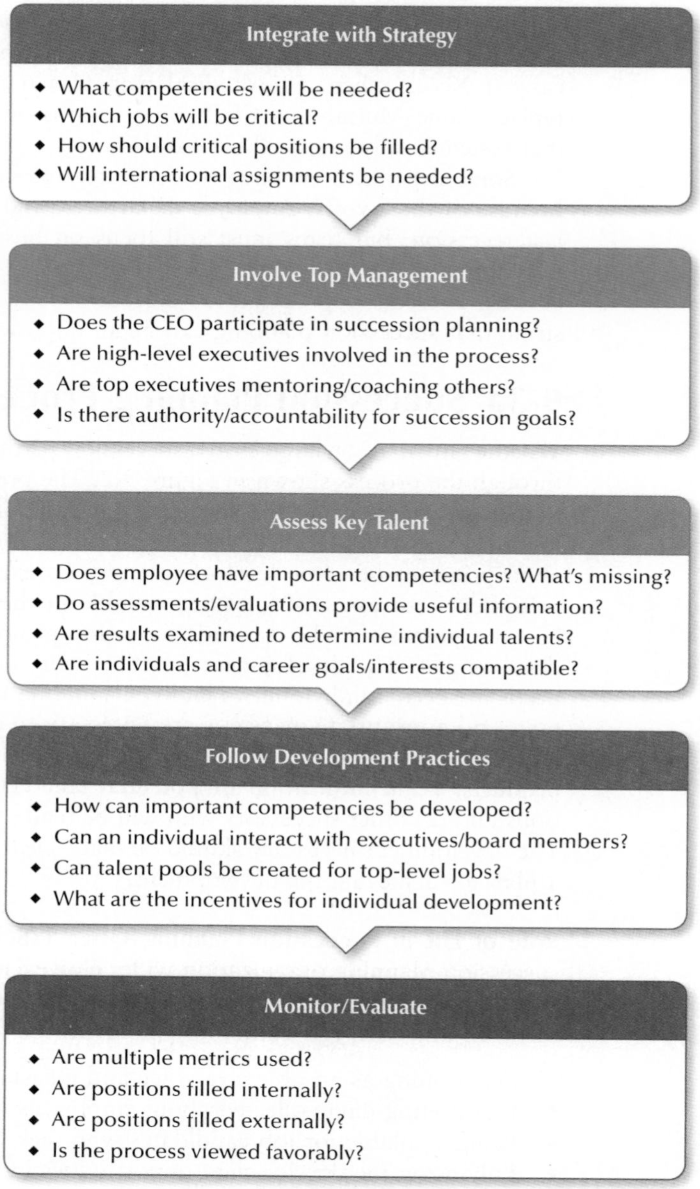

Integrate with Strategy

- ◆ What competencies will be needed?
- ◆ Which jobs will be critical?
- ◆ How should critical positions be filled?
- ◆ Will international assignments be needed?

Involve Top Management

- ◆ Does the CEO participate in succession planning?
- ◆ Are high-level executives involved in the process?
- ◆ Are top executives mentoring/coaching others?
- ◆ Is there authority/accountability for succession goals?

Assess Key Talent

- ◆ Does employee have important competencies? What's missing?
- ◆ Do assessments/evaluations provide useful information?
- ◆ Are results examined to determine individual talents?
- ◆ Are individuals and career goals/interests compatible?

Follow Development Practices

- ◆ How can important competencies be developed?
- ◆ Can an individual interact with executives/board members?
- ◆ Can talent pools be created for top-level jobs?
- ◆ What are the incentives for individual development?

Monitor/Evaluate

- ◆ Are multiple metrics used?
- ◆ Are positions filled internally?
- ◆ Are positions filled externally?
- ◆ Is the process viewed favorably?

© Cengage Learning 2014

Succession in Small and Closely Held Organizations Succession planning can be especially important in small and medium-sized firms, but few of these firms formalize succession plans. In fact, the lack of succession planning is frequently viewed as one of the biggest threats facing small businesses. Even if many CEOs plan to pass the business leadership on to a family member, most of these firms would benefit from planning for orderly succession, particularly if nonfamily members or owners are involved. Addressing the development needs of the successor also helps to avoid a host of potential problems for both the organization and family-member relationships.

9-3b Succession Planning Decisions

Several areas require decisions as part of succession planning. These decisions require the following analysis: How can you identify and classify current talent? Should you "make" or "buy" talent? How can you measure system success?

Identifying Current Talent Companies can be proactive in identifying the right managers and employees needed for successful succession planning. Managers determine if individuals are ready, willing, and able to perform duties at a higher level in the organization. Developmental "growth factors" such as conceptual understanding, learning motivation, social astuteness, and emotional stability indicate someone is ready for managerial roles.[38] Leaders should also take a current inventory of the talent that is already employed in the organization. Figure 9-3 illustrates one approach that can be employed to facilitate such a talent inventory.[39] Since focusing only on potential or performance may be too narrow when developing succession plans for jobs and identifying candidates, a two-dimensional grid can

FIGURE 9-3 Talent Inventory Grid

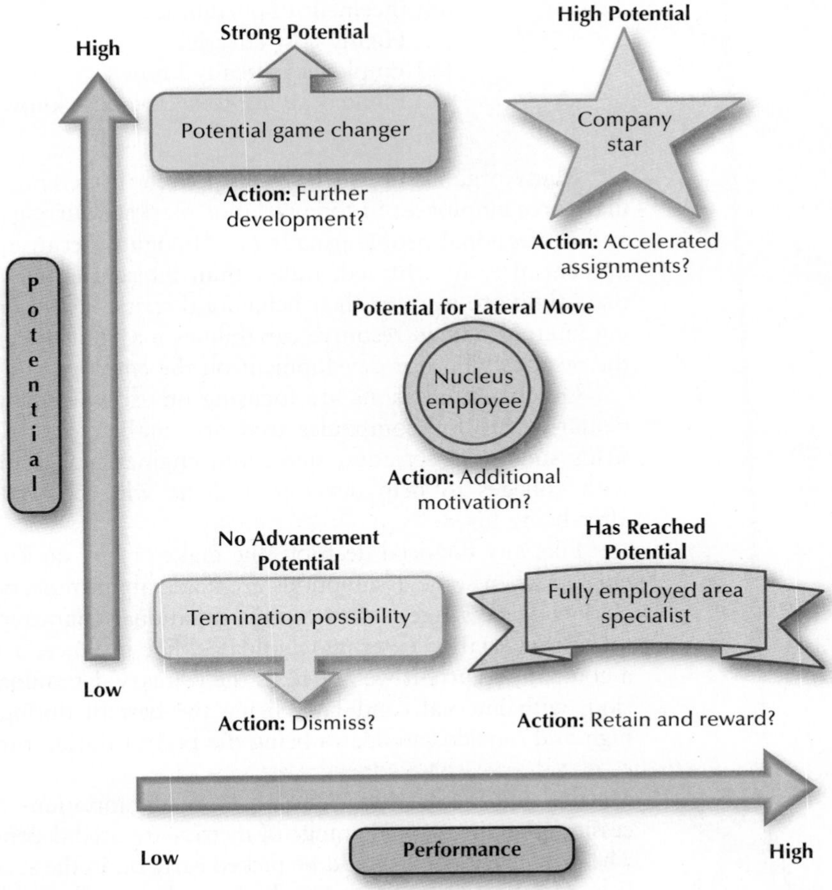

be specified outlining individuals' potential to be promoted on one axis, and current job performance on the other axis.

Such a talent inventory grid is particularly helpful in jobs that tend to be more complex. For example, assume that succession planning is being conducted for a General Manager of a large luxury hotel. The position needs candidates who have extensive experience, industry contacts, community involvement, leadership and management capabilities, and other important competencies that suggest high potential. These considerations are especially important if the current General Manager has these qualities and is a high-performer. To combine potential and performance, a two-dimensional grid like the one shown in Figure 9-3 can be used.

Make-or-buy
Develop competitive Human Resources or hire individuals who are already developed from somewhere else.

"Make-or-Buy" Talent? Employers face a **"make-or-buy"** choice: develop ("make") competitive human resources, or hire ("buy") individuals who are already developed from somewhere else. There are a number of advantages and disadvantages associated with each particular approach.[40]

Buy talent:	(+) Company can tap into new knowledge/perspectives
	(+) Obtain needed skills that will help the company
	(−) Can be a costly strategy
	(−) Risk associated with hiring unproven employees
Make talent:	(+) Company can provide employees required competencies and advancement opportunities
	(+) Highly cost effective
	(+) Employees already known
	(−) Limited ability to secure new knowledge/perspectives
	(−) May take longer

Many organizations show an apparent preference for buying rather than making scarce employees in today's labor market. Current trends indicate that technical and professional people usually are "bought" because of the amount of skill development already achieved, rather than internal employees being picked because of their ability to learn or their behavioral traits. However, hiring rather than developing internal human resource capabilities may not fit certain environments, and puts the responsibility for development on the employee.

Other organizations are focusing on growing their own leaders.[41] This is particularly true for companies that are unable to find qualified job candidates in fields such as the trades, sales, and engineering. Some firms are even partnering with colleges to help develop students who can make significant contributions after being hired.[42]

Like any financial decision, the make-or-buy decision can be quantified and calculated when some assumptions are made about time, costs, availability, and quality. Yet, evidence suggests that certain situational characteristics should dictate whether to hire internal or external candidates. For instance, a recent study determined that a company's current well-being is the primary determinant of successful CEO succession, with internal candidates being the best fit during times when performance is high and outside candidates being the best fit during times of crisis.[43]

Metrics and Succession Planning Some organizations measure the impact is of succession planning. A wide range of metrics are used depending on the company's plans. The proper metric(s) should be picked early on in the succession decision process. One key measure a company might consider involves identifying the reduced costs of turnover, which is related to employee retention. Another factor to explore is how

MEASURE

succession planning and its follow-up may lead to higher performance and organizational profitability. Organizations might also track how job vacancies are filled, the availability of candidates, and success rates of succession decisions.

Computerized Succession Planning Models The expansion of information technology capabilities has resulted in employers being able to have succession planning components available electronically to staff members. Skills tracking systems, performance appraisals, and other databases can be linked to succession plans. As employees complete training and development activities, their data can be updated and viewed as career openings become available in the company. Via intranet systems, employees can access and update their data, review job and career opportunities, and complete skill and career interest self-surveys.

9-3c Benefits of Formal Succession Planning

Succession planning can be done formally and informally. As companies become larger, the benefits of formal succession planning become greater, and for these larger companies, formal planning is recommended. Key benefits include the following:

- Having a supply of highly qualified individuals ready for future job openings
- Providing career opportunities and plans for individuals, which helps retention and performance motivation
- Providing a basis for the continual review of staffing requirements as organizational changes occur over time
- Enhancing the "brand" of the company and establishing the organization as a desirable place to work

Common Succession Planning Mistakes CEO succession should be a focus of the boards of directors, not solely HR. One reason why boards have increased the priority of CEO succession is that the Sarbanes-Oxley Act provisions demand that boards do CEO succession planning.

But focusing only on CEO and top management succession is one of the most common mistakes made. Other mistakes include the following:

- Starting too late, when openings are already occurring
- Not linking well to strategic plans
- Allowing the CEO to direct the planning and make all succession decisions
- Looking only internally for succession candidates

All of these mistakes are indicative of poor succession planning.[44] An example of the importance of succession planning is seen in the banking industry. Regulatory provisions and auditors are requiring banks to have succession plans identified for top management jobs. Also, law firms are recognizing the importance of succession planning as more senior partners retire.

Longer-term succession planning should include mid-level and lower-level managers, as well as other key nonmanagement employees. Some firms target key technical, professional, and sales employees as part of succession planning. Others include customer service representatives, warehouse specialists, and additional hourly employees who may be able to move up into other jobs or departments.

Actions such as the planning of careers and development follow from succession planning efforts. The HR Perspective: Staffing Top Positions with Positive Succession Planning describes how one organization performs succession planning.

Staffing Top Positions with Positive Succession Planning

Community Health Systems Professional Services Corp., a Tennessee-based health care consulting and managerial services firm, has developed a unique homegrown approach to the management of succession in the independent hospitals that rely on the company's support. This succession model is based primarily on the development of individual talent so that appropriate and qualified personnel are given high-level job assignments after they have received the necessary work experiences that prepare them for promotion opportunities. Some of these job assignments involve working under top leaders in "assistant" positions to gain important job experiences that can be applied in the future, while other situations call for the promotion of individuals directly into CEO-level assignments. Evidence suggests that the firm's executive recruiting group, focusing on a blend of internal and external talent, has done a good job placing people in hospitals that are affiliated with Community Health Systems Professional Services Corp.

Several factors directly contribute to these successes. The company uses many screening tools to identify the right individuals for top-level jobs, and these tools have enabled the organization to get good candidates for over 75% of these open positions without the assistance of outside recruiting firms. In addition, the company keeps an active dialogue going with top leaders after they are hired, and training and development opportunities are provided to enhance career management. Some noteworthy approaches that company uses include the following:

- Using the Internet, social networking websites, and external/internal referrals to develop stronger relationships with potential job candidates.
- Requiring job candidates to complete an online evaluation that identifies their skills and traits, and then benchmarking these characteristics to the qualities held by high performing employees in the company. These assessments provide a snapshot of individuals' strengths and weaknesses that can be explored during the interview process.
- Providing viable candidates the opportunity to demonstrate their competencies by using scenario-based interview sessions that are shaped by the information identified in the profile data.
- Developing assistant C-level positions that give emerging talent the opportunity to learn from senior managers.[45]

Career
Series of work-related positions a person occupies throughout life.

9-4 ■ CAREERS AND CAREER PLANNING

A **career** is the series of work-related positions a person occupies throughout life. People pursue careers to satisfy their individual needs. Careers are an important part of talent management, but individuals and organizations view careers in distinctly different ways.[46] Changes in employer approaches to planning for replacement managers based upon a less predictable business environment have put much of the responsibility for a career on the shoulders of individual employees. However, companies need to take some responsibility in the career planning process by helping employees make good decisions and by providing positive work opportunities.

When a company attempts to manage careers internally, there may be typical career paths that are identified for employees.

9-4a Changing Nature of Careers

The old model of a career in which a person worked up the ladder in one organization is becoming rarer. In a few industries, changing jobs and companies every few years is becoming more common. Many U.S. workers in high-demand jobs, such as information technologists and pharmacists, can dictate their own circumstances to some extent. The average 30- to 35-year-old in the United States may have already worked for up to seven different firms. Physicians, teachers, economists, and electricians do not change jobs as frequently on average, however, even in some of these professions valuable employees who are given offers to switch jobs do so at a higher rate than in the past.

Different Views of Careers Various signs indicate that the patterns of individuals' work lives are changing in many areas: more freelancing, more working at home, more frequent job changes, and more job opportunities but less security. Rather than letting jobs define their lives, more people set goals for the type of lives they want and then use jobs to meet those goals. However, for dual-career couples and working mothers, balancing work demands with personal and family responsibilities can be difficult to do.

Labels for several views of careers include the following:[47]

- *Protean career*: assumes individuals will drive their careers and define goals to fit their lives; individuals adapt to career demands by shaping their own KSAs.
- *Career without boundaries*: views a manager as having many possible trajectories for a career, and many are across organizational boundaries; careers can span many companies or industries.
- *Postcorporate career*: individual leaves the large company and builds a career working in smaller businesses or starting entrepreneurial ventures.
- *Kaleidoscope career*: building a career by focusing on important employment factors such as authenticity, work–life balance, and challenge.
- *Hybrid career*: a career that is defined by both protean and career without boundaries viewpoints.

All these different views of careers have merit for different individuals, but they all show that any organization-centered career planning effort will have to consider the unique needs of the individual employee.

9-4b Organization-Centered Career Planning

Since careers are different than in the past, managing them puts a premium on career development by both employers and employees. Effective career planning considers both organization-centered and individual-centered perspectives. Figure 9-4 summarizes the organizational and individual approaches to career planning.

Organization-centered career planning frequently focuses on identifying career paths that provide for the logical progression of people between jobs in an organization. Individuals follow these paths as they advance in organizations. For example, the right person might enter the sales department as a sales representative, then be promoted to account director, to district sales manager, and finally to vice president of sales.

A good career planning program includes the elements of talent management, performance appraisals, development activities, transfer and promotion opportunities,

Organization-centered career planning
Career planning that focuses on identifying career paths that provide for the logical progression of people between jobs in an organization.

FIGURE 9-4 Organizational and Individual Career Planning Perspectives

Organizational Perspective
- Identify future staffing needs
- Plan career ladders
- Assess individual potential and needs
- Match organizational needs to individual KSAs
- Develop/audit career system for success

A Person's Career

Individual Perspective
- Identify personal KSAs and interests
- Plan life/career goals
- Assess alternative career paths inside and outside organization
- Note personal changes through life/career progressions

© Cengage Learning 2014

and succession planning. To communicate with employees about opportunities and help with planning, employers frequently use career workshops, a career "center," newsletter, and career counseling. Individual managers often play the role of coach and counselor in their direct contact with individual employees and within an HR-designed career management system.

The approach used by organizations to enhance careers should provide opportunities for individual growth and development. For example, companies now favor using career lattices comprised of multidirectional job changes and lateral moves as mechanisms for providing employees important career experiences.[48] Another system for managing individual careers is the career path, or "map," which is created and shared with employees.

Career Paths Employees need to know their strengths and weakness, and they often discover those through company-sponsored assessments. Then, career paths to develop the weak areas and fine-tune the strengths are developed. **Career paths** represent employees' movements through opportunities over time. Although most career paths are thought of as leading upward, good opportunities also exist in cross-functional or horizontal directions.

Career paths
Represent employees' movements through opportunities over time.

Working with employees to develop career paths has aided employers in retaining key employees. For example, CDM, the operations, engineering, construction, and consulting company based in Cambridge, Massachusetts, developed career paths based on input collected from key stakeholders including top leaders, scientists, and engineers. These career paths reflected the most important competencies needed to accomplishment company objectives, and proficiency levels and progression maps were established to guide how employees would move to jobs within and between career paths. The entire process was linked to the talent management and development programs that existed in the company.[49]

Employer Websites and Career Planning Many employers have careers sections on their websites to list open jobs. An employer's website is a link to the external world, but should also be seen as a link to existing employee development. Sites can also be used for career assessment, information, and instruction. When designing websites, firms should consider the usefulness of the careers section for development as well as recruitment.

Accommodating Individual Career Needs As noted earlier, not everyone views a career the same way. These perceptions can be driven by employees' varying career stages, which are often defined by different individual preferences regarding work and home. Providing opportunities for appropriate work–life balance is one way that companies can accommodate the changing needs that employees have as they progress through their career stages. Permitting telecommuting for fast-track employees unwilling or unable to relocate is another way to keep talent in the succession pipeline by accommodating individual needs. Such flexibility is often the difference between continuing a career at a firm and moving on.

9-4c Individual-Centered Career Planning

Organizational changes have altered career plans for many people. Individuals have had to face "career transitions"—in other words they have had to find new jobs. These transitions have emphasized the importance of **individual-centered career planning**, which focuses on an individual's responsibility for a career rather than on organizational needs.

Individual-centered career planning
Career planning that focuses on an individual's responsibility for a career rather than on organizational needs.

Individual Actions for Career Planning Individuals who successfully manage their own careers perform several activities:

- *Self-assessment*: Individuals need to think about what interests them, what they do not like, what they do well, and their strengths and weaknesses. Career advisors use many tools to help people understand themselves. Common professional tests include the Strong Interest Inventory to determine preferences among vocational occupations, and the Allport-Vernon-Lindzey Study of Values to identify a person's dominant values.
- *Feedback on reality*: Employees need feedback on how well they are doing, how their bosses see their capabilities, and where they fit in organizational plans for the future. One source of this information is through performance appraisal feedback and career development discussions.
- *Setting of career goals*: Deciding on a desired path, setting timetables, and writing these items down all set the stage for a person to pursue the career of choice. These career goals are supported by short-term plans for the individual to get the experience or training necessary to move forward toward the goals.[50]

Individual Career Choices Four general individual characteristics affect how people make career choices:

- *Interests and values*: People tend to pursue careers that they believe match their interests and values. But over time, interests change for many people, and career decisions eventually are made on the basis of special skills, abilities, and career paths that are realistic for the individual.
- *Self-image*: A career is an extension of a person's self-image, as well as a molder of it. People follow careers they can "see" themselves in and avoid those that do not fit with their perceptions of their talents, motives, and values.
- *Personality*: An employee's personality includes that individual's personal orientation (e.g., extraversion, openness to experience, and conscientiousness) and

personal needs (including affiliation, power, and achievement needs). Individuals with certain personality types gravitate to different clusters of occupations.

- *Social backgrounds*: Socioeconomic status and the educational levels and occupations of a person's parents are included in an individual's social background. Children of a physician or a welder know from a parent what that job is like and may either seek or reject it on the basis of how they view the parent's job.

Less is known about how and why people choose specific organizations than about why they choose specific careers. One obvious factor is timing—the availability of a job when the person is looking for work. The amount of information available about alternatives is an important factor as well. Beyond these issues, people seem to pick an organization on the basis of a "fit" of the climate of the organization as they view it and their own personal characteristics, interests, and needs.

9-4d Career Progression Considerations

The typical career for individuals today includes more positions, transitions, and organizations than in the past, when employees were less mobile and organizations were more stable as long-term employers. But there remain general patterns in people's lives that affect their careers.

Theorists in adult development describe the first half of life as the young adult's quest for competence and for a way to make a mark in the world. According to this view, a person attains happiness during this time primarily through achievement and the acquisition of capabilities. The second half of life is different. Once the adult starts to measure time to the expected end of life rather than from the beginning, the need for competence and acquisition changes to the need for integrity, values, and well-being. For many people, internal values take precedence over external scorecards or accomplishments such as wealth and job title status. In addition, mature adults already possess certain skills, so their focus may shift to interests other than skills acquisition. Career-ending concerns, such as life after retirement, reflect additional shifts. Figure 9-5 shows a model that identifies general career and life periods.

Representative of this life pattern is the idea that careers and lives are not predictably linear but cyclical. Individuals experience periods of high stability followed by transition periods of less stability, and by inevitable discoveries, disappointments, and triumphs. These cycles of structure and transition occur throughout individuals' lives

FIGURE 9-5 General Career Periods

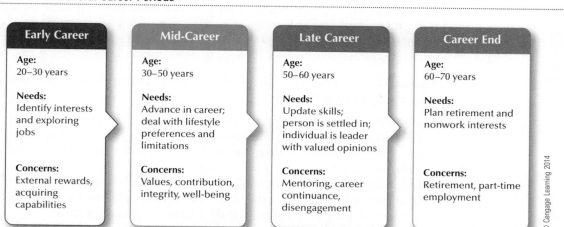

Early Career	Mid-Career	Late Career	Career End
Age: 20–30 years	**Age:** 30–50 years	**Age:** 50–60 years	**Age:** 60–70 years
Needs: Identify interests and exploring jobs	**Needs:** Advance in career; deal with lifestyle preferences and limitations	**Needs:** Update skills; person is settled in; individual is leader with valued opinions	**Needs:** Plan retirement and nonwork interests
Concerns: External rewards, acquiring capabilities	**Concerns:** Values, contribution, integrity, well-being	**Concerns:** Mentoring, career continuance, disengagement	**Concerns:** Retirement, part-time employment

© Cengage Learning 2014

and careers. This cyclical view may be an especially useful perspective for individuals affected by downsizing or early career plateaus in large organizations. Such a perspective underscores the importance of flexibility in an individual's career. It also emphasizes the importance of individuals' continuing to acquire more and diverse KSAs.

Early Career Issues Early career needs include finding interests, developing capabilities, and exploring jobs. Some organizations do a better job than others of providing those opportunities. Offering programs that satisfy the needs of individuals who are just starting their careers such as flexible work situations, alternative workplace arrangements, development activities, and opportunities to make additional income are some approaches employers use to make jobs more attractive.

However, individuals in the early stages of their work in a profession need to take greater responsibility in career planning. Such effort establishes greater ownership over individual development and facilitates empowerment. Being proactive about career planning also decreases the likelihood of sitting back and letting someone (or something) else manage the process.

Career Plateaus Those who do not change jobs may face another problem: career plateaus. Many workers define career success in terms of upward mobility. As the opportunities to move up decrease, some employers try to convince employees they can find job satisfaction in lateral movement. Such moves can be reasonable if employees learn new skills that increase individual marketability in case of future layoffs, termination, or organizational restructurings.

One strategy for individuals to move beyond career plateaus is to take seminars and university courses. This approach may reveal new opportunities for plateaued employees. Rotating workers to other departments is another way to deal with career plateaus. A computer chip manufacturer instituted a formal "poaching" program that encouraged managers to recruit employees from other departments, thereby giving employees greater opportunities to experience new challenges without having to leave the employer.

Some plateaued individuals change careers and go into other lines of work altogether. Figure 9-6 shows a "portable" career path that one might encounter under those career situations. In summary, plateaued employees present a particular challenge for employers. They can affect morale if they become negative, but they may also represent valuable resources that are not being used appropriately.

9-4e Career Transitions

Career transitions can be stressful for individuals who change employers and jobs. Three career transitions are of special interest to HR: organizational entry, job loss, and retirement.[51]

Career Entry and Job Loss Starting as a new employee can be overwhelming. "Entry shock" is especially difficult for younger new hires who find the work world very different from school.[52] Entry shock includes the following concerns:

- *Supervisors*: The boss–employee relationship is different from the student–teacher relationship.
- *Feedback*: In school, feedback is frequent and measurable, but that is not true of most jobs.
- *Time*: School has short (quarter/semester) time cycles, whereas time horizons are longer at work.
- *The work*: Problems are more tightly defined at school; at work, the logistical and political aspects of solving work problems are less certain.

FIGURE 9-6 Portable Career Path

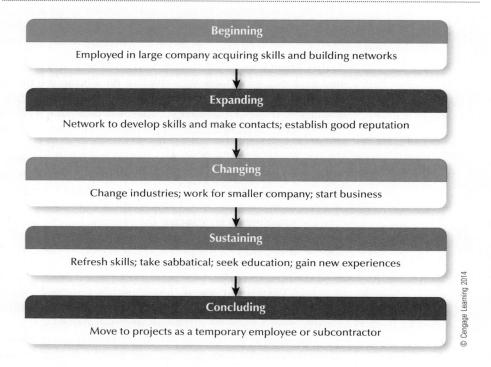

Job loss as a career transition has been most associated with downsizing, mergers, and acquisitions. Losing a job is a stressful event in one's career, frequently causing depression, anxiety, and nervousness. The financial implications and the effects on family can be extreme as well. Yet the potential for job loss continues for many individuals, and effectively addressing their concerns should be considered in career transition decision making.

Retirement Issues The process of retirement can be seen in many ways. For instance, retirement represents a decision-making situation whereby an individual chooses to leave the workplace to pursue personal interests. Retirement can also be understood as an adjustment away from the demands of the workplace to greater psychological well-being achieved outside the job. Still another view of retirement is centered on a protean-based philosophy that explores how well individuals manage their growth and employment opportunities after leaving a career. Finally, retirement can be thought of as a component of HRM because companies provide incentives, training, and other programs that influence retirement decisions.[53]

Whether retirement comes at age 50 or age 70, it can require a major adjustment for many people. Some areas of adjustment faced by retirees include self-direction, a need to belong, satisfying achievement needs, personal space, and goals. To help address concerns over these issues, as well as anxieties about finances, some employers offer preretirement planning seminars for employees.

Career development for people at the end of their careers may be managed in many ways. Phased-in retirement, consulting arrangements, and callback of some retirees as needed all act as means for gradual disengagement between the organization and the individual. However, phased-in retirement (which is widely seen as a good situation for all involved) faces major obstacles in current pension laws.

Under many pension plans, employees who are working may not receive pension benefits until they reach a "normal" retirement age.[54]

Early retirement often occurs as a result of downsizings and organizational restructurings. These events have required many managers and professionals to determine what is important to them while still active and healthy, with some deciding to remain employed in extended or second careers, and others electing to leave the workforce to enjoy leisure time and the pursuit of personal interests. To successfully encourage early retirement, management must avoid several legal issues, such as forced early retirement and pressuring older workers to resign.

9-5 ■ COMMON INDIVIDUAL CAREER PROBLEMS

Four career issues are sufficiently common as to need individual treatment. These are problems with technical and professional workers, women, dual-career couples, and individuals with global careers.

9-5a Technical and Professional Workers

Technical and professional workers, such as engineers, scientists, and IT systems experts, present a special challenge for organizations. Many of these individuals want to stay in their technical areas rather than enter management, yet advancement in many organizations requires a move into management. Most of these people like the idea of the responsibility and opportunity associated with advancement, but they do not want to leave the professional and technical activities at which they excel. Further, the skills required in management roles are very difficult than those needed in technical jobs.

Dual-career ladder
System that allows a person to advance up either a management or a technical/professional ladder.

An attempt to solve this problem is the **dual-career ladder**, a system that allows a person to advance through either a management or a technical/professional ladder. Dual-career ladders are now used at many firms, most commonly in technology-driven industries such as pharmaceuticals, chemicals, computers, and electronics. For instance, a telecommunications firm created a dual-career ladder in its IT department to reward talented technical people who do not want to move into management. Different tracks, each with attractive job titles and pay opportunities, are provided. Some health care organizations are using "master" titles for senior experienced specialists such as radiologists and neonatal nurses who do not want to be managers. The masters are often mentors and trainers for younger specialists. Unfortunately, the technical/professional ladder may be viewed as "second-class citizenship" within some organizations.

9-5b Women and Careers

The percentage of working women has increased over the last several decades, with women making up about half the workforce. Women are employed in all occupations and jobs, but their careers may have a different element than those of men. Since women bear children and are often the primary caregiver, their career planning and advancement may be disrupted.

Work, Family, and Careers A career approach for women frequently is to work hard before children arrive, plateau or step off the career track when children are younger, and go back to career-focused jobs that allow flexibility when the children are older. This approach is referred to as sequencing. But some women who sequence are concerned that the job market will not welcome them when they return, or that the time away will hurt their advancement chances.

The interaction and conflicts among home, family, and career often affect women differently than they do men. By the time men and women have been out of school for six years, on average women have worked much less time than men. These and other career differences provide challenges for many females. Employers can tap into the female labor market by offering child-care assistance, flexible work policies, and a general willingness to be accommodating. A recent study determined that women are indeed using such flexible employment situations to better manage their careers.[55]

Other approaches have been developed in companies to better utilize women's talents in the workplace. The HR Skills and Applications: Women Develop Holistic Mentoring Program explores mentoring as a positive career management strategy. In particular, partnering women with senior executives, rather than less influential managers, can be useful because these individuals can function as strong advocates for competent female leaders.[56] Connecting women with the proper mentors who are willing to act as sponsors in getting them better, more high-profile positions is the key.[57]

HR PERSPECTIVE

Women Develop Holistic Mentoring Program

In effort to provide women better career opportunities at Qualcomm Inc., 15 women executives representing different organizational levels and functional areas of the firm voluntarily met to discuss the factors that had benefitted their job experiences while working for the company. They found that positive workplace relationships made the biggest difference in their ability to successfully take advantage of opportunities and tackle challenges on the job. They also decided that a more programmatic approach was needed to help women in the company, and this approach would eventually take shape in the form of a new piloted mentorship program.

A pilot program was designed to accomplish many objectives, including the selection and accomplishment of career aspirations, the enhancement of women's KSAs, the creation of diverse employment partnerships, and the development of a corporate philosophy that supports mentoring in the workplace. The program included a total of 40 women who worked with high-level

mentors representing different functional areas of Qualcomm. Mentees were given one-on-one opportunities to develop using the advice provided by mentors. Supplemental learning was provided through professional development training and panel sessions covering topics such as presentation skills and tips for career success. Mentors and mentees were matched by comparing responses provided on an online career questionnaire, and participants attended an informal follow-up meeting to get to know each other better.

The mentoring process itself was holistic in nature, meaning that it encompassed a wide variety of important work characteristics. More specifically, a "Five Mys" framework was developed to guide the identification of career improvement areas, which included the components "My Style," "My Career," "My World," "My Craft," and "My Life." Follow up surveys and focus groups facilitated the evaluation of the program, and after careful consideration of the initial findings, the mentoring approach was considered a success.[58]

Glass ceiling
Situation in which women fail to progress into top and senior management positions.

Glass Ceiling Another concern specifically affecting women is the **glass ceiling**. This issue describes the situation in which women fail to progress into top and senior management positions. Nationally, women hold about half of managerial/professional positions but only 10% to 15% of corporate officer positions.[59] Evidence also suggests that women may not be placed as effectively after graduation as men, and that they do not perform as well when returning to the corporate arena from employment in educational, nonprofit, or government entities.[60] Inflexible beliefs about women's roles and placement in the workplace are some of the possible causes of these disparities.[61]

Some organizations provide leaves of absence, often under Family and Medical Leave Act (FMLA) provisions, but proactively keep women involved in the company during time off. Some have used e-mentoring for women temporarily off their jobs. Other firms use "phased returns," whereby women employees return to work part-time and then gradually return to full-time schedules. Consequently, in the United States, women are making slow but steady strides into senior management and executive positions. A recent study determined that women might break the glass ceiling with a phenomenon called the "glass cliff," a situation where a male-led firm in "crisis mode" may turn to women to help turn the business around.[62]

9-5c Dual-Career Couples

As the number of women in the workforce continues to increase, particularly in professional careers, so does the number of dual-career couples. The U.S. Bureau of Labor Statistics estimates that more than 80% of all couples are dual-career couples. Marriages in which both mates are managers, professionals, or technicians have doubled over the past two decades.[63] Problem areas for dual-career couples include family issues and job transfers that require relocations.

Family–Career Issues For dual-career couples with children, family issues may conflict with career progression. It is important that such career development problems be recognized as early as possible. Whenever possible, involving both partners in planning, even when one is not employed by the company, may enhance the success of such efforts.

Relocation of Dual-Career Couples Traditionally, employees accepted transfers as part of upward mobility in organizations. However, both employees and companies often find relocations undesirable because individuals must move away from friends/family, the process is expensive, housing is a challenge, and decreasing numbers who are willing to move suggest that relocations are on the decline as a favored career development strategy.[64]

For some dual-career couples, the mobility required because of one partner's transfer often interferes with the other's career. In addition to having two careers, dual-career couples often have established support networks of coworkers, friends, and business contacts to cope with both their careers and their personal lives. Relocating one partner in a dual-career couple may mean upsetting this carefully constructed network for the other person or creating a "commuting" relationship. Recruiting a member of a dual-career couple to a new location may require HR assistance in finding an equally attractive job for the candidate's partner at the new location through assistance for the nonemployee partner.[65]

GLOBAL

9-5d Global Career Concerns

Global career management can be even more perplexing than managing domestic talent. The movement of managers and employees can be challenging because the corporate policies and cultural characteristics in different countries are often dissimilar, and individual expectations about the success of global assignments can vary greatly, thus affecting motivation and commitment. Successful companies develop a culture that champions the movement of talent globally. Further, they create sound mobility programs and processes that organize assignee information, effectively evaluate candidates, and provide coaching support during global assignments and repatriation efforts.[66] Evidence suggests that providing such career support can decrease employees' intentions to quit and improve their beliefs about career prospects in multinational firms.[67]

Many global employees experience anxiety about their continued career progression. Indeed, while individuals may indicate a willingness to relocate, likely driven by recessionary pressures, workers in the United States and United Kingdom are less interested in global relocation opportunities.[68] Therefore, the international experiences of expatriates must offer benefits both to the employer and to the expatriates in terms of career management.[69] Firms sometimes address this issue by bringing expatriates back to the home country for development programs and interaction with other company managers and professionals during the assignment. Another potentially useful approach is to establish a mentoring system that matches an expatriate with a corporate executive at the headquarters.

Repatriation
Planning, training, and reassignment of global employees back to their home countries.

Repatriation The issue of **repatriation** involves planning, training, and reassignment of global employees back to their home countries. After expatriates return home, they often no longer receive special compensation packages available to them during their assignments. The result is that they may feel a net decrease in total income, even if they receive promotions and pay increases. In addition to dealing with concerns about personal finances, returning expatriates often must re-acclimate to U.S. lifestyles, transportation, and other cultural circumstances, especially if they have been living in less-developed countries.

Many expatriates have had a greater degree of flexibility, autonomy, and independent decision making while living overseas than their counterparts in the United States. Back in the home organization, repatriated employees must readjust to closer working and reporting relationships with other corporate staff.

Another major concern focuses on the organizational status of expatriates upon return. Many expatriates wonder what jobs they will have, whether their international experiences will be valued, and how they will be accepted back into the organization. Unfortunately, many global employers do a poor job of repatriation. To counter this problem, companies should consider providing expatriates assistance through flexible assignments, mentoring efforts, meetings with key managers, and guarantees of temporary employment after the early completion of foreign assignments.[70] Organizations should also provide career support to expatriates by ensuring that there is good communication during assignments and that proper repatriation training is provided.[71]

Global Development Global managers are more expensive than home-country managers, and more problematic as well.[72] Most global firms have learned that it is often a mistake to staff foreign operations with only personnel from headquarters, and they quickly hire local nationals to work in a country. For this reason, global management development must focus on developing local managers as well as global executives. Global competencies should also be developed earlier within careers, instead of assigning senior, domestic-based executives to international positions.[73] Development areas can include activities such as promoting cultural issues, running an international business, enhancing leadership/management skills, handling problematic people, and building personal qualities. Organizations might also recruit foreign graduate students into fast-track development programs to staff global positions, offer international assignments to leaders to improve their work experience, and utilize social networking to enhance training and development.[74]

LO4 List options for development needs analyses.

Development
Efforts to improve employees' abilities to handle a variety of assignments and to cultivate employees' capabilities beyond those required by the current job.

9-6 ■ DEVELOPING HUMAN RESOURCES

Development represents efforts to improve employees' abilities to handle a variety of assignments and to cultivate employees' capabilities beyond those required by the current job. Development can benefit both organizations and employees. Employees and managers with appropriate experiences and abilities may enhance organizational competitiveness and the ability to adapt to a changing environment. In the development process, individuals' careers may also evolve and shift to new or different focuses. For instance, Panda Express utilizes many employee physical development programs that focus on weight management, exercise, and personal well-being.[75] Similarly, Hilton utilized a developmental program for executives that required them to work in various areas of different hotels to better understand how top-level business decisions influence the firm's properties.[76]

Development differs from training. It is possible to train people to answer customer service questions, drive a truck, enter data in a computer system, set up a drill press, or assemble a television. However, development in areas such as judgment, responsibility, decision making, and communication presents a bigger challenge. These areas may or may not develop through ordinary life experiences of individuals. A planned system of development experiences for all employees, not just managers, can help expand the overall level of capabilities in an organization. Figure 9-7 profiles development and compares it with training.

FIGURE 9-7 Development versus Training

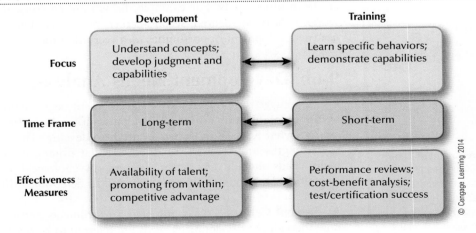

© Cengage Learning 2014

9-6a Possible Development Focuses

Some important and common management capabilities that may require development include an action orientation, quality decision-making skills, ethical values, and technical skills. Abilities to build teams, develop subordinates, direct others, and deal with uncertainty are equally important but much less commonly developed capabilities for successful managers. For some tech specialties (tech support, database administration, network design, etc.), certain nontechnical abilities must be developed as well, such as the ability to work under pressure, work independently, solve problems quickly, and use past knowledge in a new situation.

One point about development is clear: In numerous studies that asked employees what they want out of their jobs, training and development ranked at or near the top. The primary assets that individuals have are their knowledge, skills, and abilities (KSAs), and many people view the development of their KSAs as an important part of their jobs.

Lifelong Learning Learning and development are closely linked. For most people, lifelong learning and development are necessary and desirable. For many professionals, lifelong learning may mean meeting continuing education requirements to retain certificates. For example, lawyers, CPAs, teachers, dentists, and nurses must complete continuing education requirements in most states to keep their licenses to practice. For other employees, learning and development may involve training to expand existing skills and to prepare for different jobs, for promotions, or even for new jobs after retirement.

Assistance from employers needed for lifelong development typically comes through programs at work, including tuition reimbursement programs. However, much of lifelong learning is voluntary, takes place outside work hours, and is not always formal. Although it may have no immediate relevance to a person's current job, learning often enhances an individual's confidence, ideas, and enthusiasm.

Redevelopment Whether due to a desire for career change or because the employer needs different capabilities, people may shift jobs in midlife or mid-career. Redeveloping people in the capabilities they need is logical and important. In the last decade, the number of college enrollees over the age of 35 has increased dramatically. But helping employees go back to college is only one way of redeveloping them. Some companies offer redevelopment programs to recruit experienced workers from other fields. For example, firms needing truck drivers, reporters, and IT workers have sponsored second-career programs. Public-sector employers have used redevelopment opportunities as a recruiting tool.

9-6b Development Needs Analyses

Like employee training, employee development begins with analyses of the needs of both the organization and the individuals. Either the company or the individual can analyze what KSAs a given person needs to develop. The goal, of course, is to identify strengths and weaknesses. Methods that organizations use to assess development needs include assessment centers, psychological testing, and performance appraisals. Development metrics are used to determine effectiveness.

Assessment Centers Collections of test instruments and exercises designed to diagnose individuals' development needs are referred to as **assessment centers**. Companies

Assessment centers
Collections of instruments and exercises designed to diagnose individuals' development needs.

can use assessment centers for both developing and selecting managers. Employers use assessment centers for a wide variety of jobs.

In a typical assessment-center experience, an individual spends two or three days away from the job performing many assessment activities. These activities might include role-playing, tests, cases, leaderless-group discussions, computer-based simulations, and peer evaluations. Frequently, they also include in-basket exercises, in which the individual handles typical work and management problems. For the most part, the exercises represent situations that require the use of individual skills and behaviors. During the exercises, several specially trained judges observe the participants and later share their observations with the candidates.

Assessment centers provide an excellent means for determining individual potential.[77] Management and participants often praise them because they are likely to overcome many of the biases inherent in interview situations, supervisor ratings, and written tests. Experience shows that key variables such as leadership, initiative, and supervisory skills cannot be measured with tests alone. Assessment centers also offer the advantage of helping to identify employees with potential in large organizations. Supervisors may nominate people for the assessment center, or employees may volunteer. For talented people, the opportunity to volunteer is invaluable because supervisors may not otherwise recognize their potential interests and capabilities.

Assessment centers can also raise concerns. Some managers may use the assessment center to avoid making difficult promotion decisions. Suppose a plant supervisor has personally decided that an employee is not qualified for promotion. Rather than being straightforward and informing the employee, the supervisor sends the employee to the assessment center, hoping the report will show that the employee is unqualified for promotion. Problems between the employee and the supervisor may worsen if the employee earns a positive report, highlighting the potential for supervisor bias. Having HR oversee the results of assessment centers can mitigate such concerns.

Psychological Testing Psychological tests have been used for years to determine employees' developmental potential and needs. Intelligence tests, verbal and mathematical reasoning tests, and personality tests are often given. Psychological testing can furnish useful information on individuals about such factors as motivation, reasoning abilities, leadership style, interpersonal response traits, and job preferences.

The biggest problem with psychological testing lies in interpretation, because untrained managers, supervisors, and workers usually cannot accurately interpret test results. After a professional scores the tests and reports the values to others in the organization, untrained managers may attach their own meanings to the findings. Also, some psychological tests are of limited validity, and test takers may fake desirable responses. Thus, psychological testing is appropriate only when the testing and feedback processes are closely handled by a qualified professional.

Performance Appraisals Well-done performance appraisals can be a source of development information. Performance data on productivity, employee relations, job knowledge, and other relevant dimensions can be gathered in such assessments. In this context, appraisals designed for development purposes (discussed in more detail in Chapter 10) may be different and more useful in aiding individual employee development than appraisals designed strictly for administrative purposes.

Development Metrics Organizations can use metrics to determine employees' developmental needs as well as measure development success. For example, assessments that target the proper skills needed to perform work can be used to identify the content that should be included in development programs.[78] The effectiveness of development programs can also be ascertained by using metrics. For instance, Harrah's Entertainment utilized metrics to determine how effective its efforts have been in developing greater engagement among workers.[79]

9-7 ■ HUMAN RESOURCES DEVELOPMENT APPROACHES

Common development approaches can be categorized under three major headings, as Figure 9-8 depicts. Investing in human intellectual capital can occur on or off the job and in "learning organizations." Development becomes imperative as "knowledge work," such as research skills and specialized technology expertise, increases for almost all employers. But identifying the right mix of approaches for development needs requires analyses and planning.

9-7a Job-Site Development Approaches

All too often, unplanned and perhaps useless activities pass as development on the job. To ensure that the desired development actually occurs, managers must plan and coordinate their development efforts. Managers can choose from various job-site development methods.[80]

Coaching
Observation with suggestion.

Coaching The oldest on-the-job development technique is **coaching**, which involves observation and feedback given to employees by immediate supervisors. Coaching is the continual process of learning by doing. For coaching to be effective, employees and their managers must have a healthy and open relationship.

The success of coaching is being seen in companies throughout the world. One type of coaching that is growing is team coaching. This approach focuses on coaching groups of employees on how to work more effectively as parts of workforce

FIGURE 9-8 HR Development Approaches

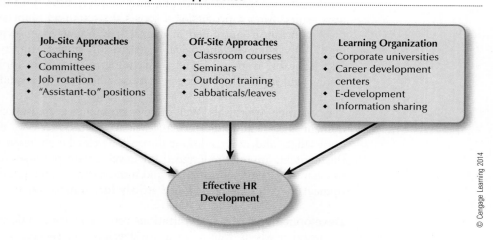

© Cengage Learning 2014

teams. Such team efforts may utilize outside consultants and cover many areas. Group coaching on leadership may help create high-performance teams.

Unfortunately, organizations may be tempted to implement coaching without sufficient planning. Even someone who is good at a job will not necessarily be able to coach someone else to do it well. "Coaches" can easily fall short in guiding learners systematically, even if they know which experiences are best.[81] The coach's job responsibilities may take priority over learning and coaching of subordinates. Also, the intellectual component of many capabilities might be better learned from a book or a course before coaching occurs. Outside consultants may be used as coaches at the executive level.

Committee Assignments Assigning promising employees to important committees may broaden their experiences and help them understand the personalities, issues, and processes governing the organization. For instance, employees on a safety committee can gain a greater understanding of safety problems and management, which would help them to become supervisors. They may also experience the problems involved in maintaining employee safety awareness. However, managers need to guard against committee assignments that turn into time-wasting activities.

Job rotation
Process of moving a person from job to job.

Job Rotation The process of moving a person from job to job is called **job rotation**, and it is widely used as a development technique. For example, a promising young manager may spend three months in a plant, three months in corporate planning, and three months in purchasing. When properly handled, such job rotation fosters a greater understanding of the organization and aids with employee retention by making individuals more versatile, strengthening their skills, and reducing boredom. When opportunities for promotion within a smaller or medium-sized organization are scarce, job rotation through lateral transfers may help rekindle enthusiasm and develop employees' talents. A disadvantage of job rotation is that it can be expensive because a substantial amount of time is required to acquaint trainees with the different people and techniques in each new unit.

Assistant to Positions Some firms create assistant to positions, which are staff positions immediately under a manager (e.g., Assistant to HR Director). Through such jobs, trainees can work with outstanding managers they might not otherwise have met. Some organizations set up "junior boards of directors" or "management cabinets" to which trainees may be appointed. These assignments provide useful experiences if they present challenging or interesting tasks to trainees.

9-7b Off-Site Development Approaches

Off-the-job development techniques give individuals opportunities to get away from their jobs and concentrate solely on what is to be learned. Contact with others who are concerned with slightly different problems and come from different organizations may provide employees with new and different perspectives. Various off-site methods can be used.

Classroom Courses and Seminars Most off-the-job development programs include some classroom instruction. People are familiar with classroom training, which gives it the advantage of being widely accepted. But the lecture system sometimes used in classroom instruction encourages passive listening and reduced learner participation, which is a distinct disadvantage. Sometimes trainees have little opportunity to question, clarify, and discuss the lecture material. The effectiveness of classroom instruction depends on multiple factors: group size, trainees' abilities, instructors' capabilities and styles, and subject matter.

Organizations often send employees to externally sponsored seminars or professional courses, such as those offered by numerous professional and consulting entities. Organizations also encourage continuing education by reimbursing employees for the costs of college courses. Tuition reimbursement programs provide incentives for employees to study for advanced degrees through evening and weekend classes that are given outside of their regular workdays and hours.

Outdoor Development Experiences Some organizations send executives and managers to experiences held outdoors, called *outdoor training* or outdoor development. The rationale for using these wilderness excursions, which can last one day or a week (or longer), is that such experiences can increase self-confidence and help individuals reevaluate personal goals and efforts. For individuals in work groups or teams, shared risks and challenges outside the office environment can create a sense of teamwork. The challenges may include rock climbing in the California desert, whitewater rafting on a river, backpacking in the Rocky Mountains, or handling a longboat off the coast of Maine.

Survival-type management development courses may have more impact than many other management seminars. But companies must consider the inherent perils. Some participants have been unable to handle the physical and emotional challenges associated with rappelling down a cliff or climbing a 40-foot tower. The decision to sponsor such programs should depend on the capabilities of the employees involved and the learning objectives.

Sabbatical
Time off the job to develop and rejuvenate oneself.

Sabbaticals and Leaves of Absence A **sabbatical** is an opportunity provided by some companies for employees to take time off the job to develop and rejuvenate, as well as to participate in activities that help others. Some employers provide paid sabbaticals, while others allow employees to take unpaid sabbaticals. The length of time taken off from work varies greatly.

Companies that offer sabbaticals speak well of the results. Positive reasons for sabbaticals are to help prevent employee burnout, offer advantages in recruiting and retention, and boost individual employee morale. Female employees have made use of sabbaticals or leaves for family care reasons. The value of this time off to employees is seen in better retention of key women, who also often return more energized and enthusiastic about their work–life balancing act. The nature of the learning experience generally falls outside the control of the organization, leaving it somewhat to chance. The HR ethics: Sabbaticals Reinvigorate Employees discusses the use of sabbaticals in organizations as a career development tool.

9-7c Learning Organizations and Development

As talent management becomes more important, employers may wish to encourage *learning organizations*. Learning organizations do their best to teach employees how to be effective through formal learning processes such as seminars, job experiences, and sound leadership, as well as through informal mechanisms such as social learning, behavioral norms, and information sharing. Such a learning environment can be difficult to introduce into an organization where it has not grown on its own. But in situations where it already exists, a learning organization offers a

Sabbaticals Reinvigorate Employees

Some organizations have developed sabbatical programs to help reduce individual burnout and turnover, and to increase worker engagement and motivation, particularly for those employees who work in jobs that are highly stressful. Popular for many years in the academic world, sabbaticals are starting to become more common in the business community, especially among firms ranked in *Fortune* magazine's 100 Best Companies to Work For. Sabbaticals give employees the ability to take time off from work to do things such as regaining their energy, working on developmental activities to enhance their careers, and/or participating in enrichment projects that help communities outside the company. In this sense, sabbaticals can be considered visible symbols of ethics and social responsibility because employees and stakeholders benefit from the company's concern about their well-being.

Sabbaticals are beneficial for both employees and employers. The individuals taking the sabbatical get the opportunity to "recharge their batteries" and pursue interests that help them develop as business professionals. However, the workers who are not on sabbatical also benefit because they get a chance to cover for the absent em-

ployees and perform new job duties. Evidence suggests that these opportunities are strongly related to employee attraction and retention because (1) job candidates like sabbaticals and (2) the programs are usually tied to employment longevity. Further, sabbaticals are not typically costly to companies because other employees usually cover the workload of individuals who are gone, making the program resource-neutral. For instance, Kimpton Hotels & Restaurants started giving managers one month off from work after they had been employed with the company for seven years. The sabbaticals were offered to give aspiring leaders a chance to gain valuable work experience while individuals were away. The program was a success because it helped with succession planning and empowered participants.

The characteristics and administration of sabbaticals vary among companies, such as who is eligible to participate (i.e., some companies only allow top leaders to take the time off), but these programs tend to share some common characteristics in practice. Sabbaticals usually last one to two months and often involve paid time off. Further, sabbaticals are often taken within a specific time after the eligibility threshold has been met by employees.[82]

significant opportunity to develop employees. Figure 9-9 depicts some possible means for developing employees in a learning organization.

Knowledge-based organizations that deal primarily with ideas and information must have employees who are experts at one or more conceptual tasks. These employees continuously learn and solve problems in their areas of expertise. Developing such employees requires an "organizational learning capacity" based on solving problems and learning new ways not previously used. Encouraging them to pass their knowledge on to others is the basis for a learning organization.

Corporate Universities and Career Development Centers Large organizations may use corporate universities to develop managers and other employees. For instance, for over 50 years McDonald's has used Hamburger University to deliver accredited courses that prepare its managers for the challenges and opportunities associated with

FIGURE 9-9 Characteristics of a Learning Organization

Characteristics of a Learning Organization
- Informal development
- Formal development
- Team sharing
- Coaching or mentoring
- Observation
- Individual development plans
- Job rotation

Result

Individual learning and development

© Cengage Learning

managing the company.[83] Sometimes regarded as little more than fancy packaging for company training, such classes may not provide a degree, accreditation, or graduation in the traditional sense. To make corporate universities more effective, these programs need to focus on the creation of important individual skills that help organizations accomplish goals, and the effectiveness of corporate universities needs to be assessed. A related alternative, partnerships between companies and traditional universities, can occur where the universities design and teach specific courses for employers.[84]

Career development centers can also be set up to coordinate in-house programs and programs provided by third parties. They may include assessment data for individuals, career goals and strategies, coaching, seminars, and online approaches.

E-Development The rapid growth in technology has led to more use of e-development. Online development can take many forms, such as video conferencing, live chat rooms, document sharing, video and audio streaming, and Web-based courses. HR staff members can facilitate online development by providing a *learning portal*, which is a centralized website for news, information, course listings, business games, simulations, and other materials.

Online development allows participation in courses previously out of reach due to geographic or cost considerations. It allows costs to be spread over a larger number of people, and it can be combined with virtual reality and other technological tools to make presentations more interesting. It can eliminate travel costs as well. When properly used, e-development is a valuable HR tool. However, lack of realism can diminish the learning experience. The focus must be learning, not just "using the technology."

LO6 Identify the several management development methods.

9-8 ■ MANAGEMENT DEVELOPMENT

Although development is important for all employees, it is essential for managers. Without appropriate development, managers may lack the capabilities to best deploy and manage resources (including employees) throughout the organization. While classroom training can be helpful, experience often contributes more to the development of senior managers because much of it occurs in varying real-life, on-the-job situations.

However, in many organizations it is difficult to find managers for middle-level jobs that provide important work experience. Some individuals refuse to take middle-management jobs, feeling that they are caught between upper management and supervisors. Similarly, not all companies take the time to develop their own senior-level managers. Instead, senior managers and executives are often hired from outside, leaving the company's middle managers behind. Figure 9-10 shows experience-based sources of managers' learning and lists some important lessons for supervisors, middle managers, and senior-level executives that should be provided by development activities.

Numerous approaches are used to mold and enhance the experiences that managers need to be effective.[85] The most widely used methods are supervisor development, leadership development, management modeling, management coaching, management mentoring, and executive education.

9-8a Supervisor Development

The beginning level for managerial development is the first-line supervisory job. It is often difficult to go from being a member of the work group to being the boss. Therefore, the new supervisors who are used to functioning as individual contributors often require new skills and mind-sets to be successful supervisors.

Employers may conduct *presupervisor training*. This is done to provide realistic job previews of what supervisors will face and to convey to individuals that they cannot just rely on their current job skills and experience in their new positions. Development for supervisors may vary but usually includes some common elements.

FIGURE 9-10 Management Lessons Learned from Job Experience

SOURCES OF MANAGERS' LEARNING

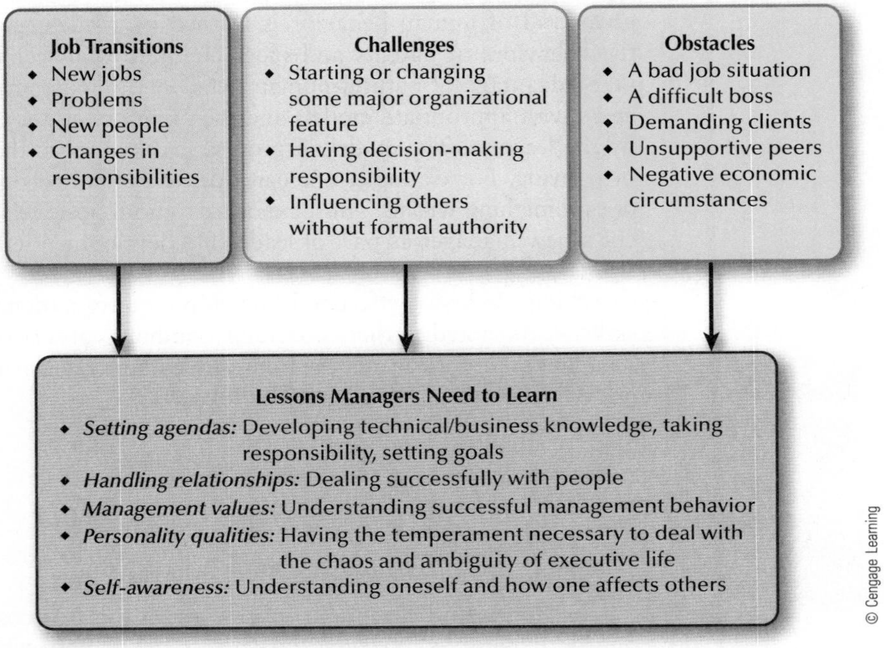

The usual contents for supervisor training and development includes several topics, such as basic management responsibilities, time management, and human relations.

Human relations training helps to prepare supervisors to deal with "people problems" associated with overseeing employees. The training focuses on the development of the human relations skills a person needs to work well with others. Most human relations programs are aimed at new or relatively inexperienced first-line supervisors and middle managers. They cover motivation, leadership, employee communication, conflict resolution, team building, and other behavioral topics.

The most common reason employees fail after being promoted to a supervisors's job is poor teamwork with subordinates and peers. Other common reasons for management failure include not understanding expectations, failure to meet goals, difficulty adjusting to management responsibilities, and inability to balance work and home lives.

9-8b Leadership Development

Organizations are aware that effective leaders create positive change and are important for organizational success. Firms such as Johnson & Johnson, General Electric, and 3M Company are among the top firms in leadership development. Leadership development is expanding a person's capacity to be effective in leadership roles. This development occurs in many ways: classroom programs, assessments, modeling, coaching, job assignments, mentoring, and executive education.

While universities may produce smart, ambitious graduates with good technical skills, many face a very steep learning curve when making the change from school into leadership positions.[86] Common ways to help individuals transition successfully into leadership roles include modeling, coaching, mentoring, and executive education.

Modeling A common adage in management development says that managers tend to manage as they were managed. In other words, managers learn by behavior modeling, or copying someone else's behavior. This tendency is not surprising, because a great deal of human behavior is learned by modeling. Children learn by modeling the behaviors of parents and older children. Management development efforts can take advantage of natural human behavior by matching young or developing managers with appropriate models and then reinforcing the desirable behaviors exhibited by the learners. The modeling process involves more than straightforward imitation or copying. For example, one can learn what not to do by observing a model who does something wrong. Thus, exposure to both positive and negative models can benefit a new manager as part of leadership development efforts.

Coaching Coaching effective leadership requires patience and good communication skills.[87] As noted earlier, coaching combines observation with suggestions. Like modeling, it complements the natural way humans learn. An outline of good coaching pointers will often include the following:

- Explain appropriate behaviors.
- Make clear why actions were taken.
- Accurately state observations.
- Provide possible alternatives/suggestions.
- Follow up and reinforce positive behaviors used.

Leadership coaching is a specific application of coaching. Companies may use outside experts as executive coaches to help managers improve leadership skills.

Sometimes these experts are used to help deal with problematic management styles. Consultants serving as executive coaches predominantly come from a psychology or counseling background and can serve many roles for a client by providing key questions and general directions. Sometimes they meet with employees in person, but many do their coaching by phone or electronically. Research on the effectiveness of leadership coaching suggests that coaching can be beneficial in dealing with chronic stress, psychological difficulties, and even physiological problems faced by executives and managers.

Management
mentoring

A relationship in which experienced managers aid individuals in the earlier stages of their careers.

Management Mentoring A method called **management mentoring** is a relationship in which experienced managers aid individuals in the earlier stages of their careers.[88] Such a relationship provides an environment for conveying technical, interpersonal, and organizational skills from a more-experienced person to a designated less-experienced person. Not only does the inexperienced employee benefit, but the mentor also may enjoy having the opportunity and challenge of sharing wisdom.[89]

Fortunately, many individuals have a series of advisors or mentors during their careers and may find advantages in learning from the different mentors. Additionally, those being mentored may find previous mentors to be useful sources for networking. Figure 9-11 describes the four stages in most successful mentoring relationships.

In many countries around the world, the proportion of women holding management jobs is lower than the proportion of men holding such jobs. Similarly, the number of racial and ethnic minorities who fill senior management positions is also low. Company mentoring programs that focus specifically on women and individuals of different racial/ethnic backgrounds have been successful in some larger firms. On the basis of various narratives of successful women executives, breaking the glass ceiling requires developing political sophistication, building credibility, and refining management styles aided by mentoring.

FIGURE 9-11 **Stages in Management Mentoring Relationships**

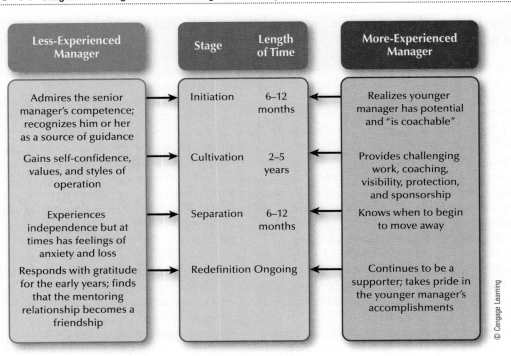

© Cengage Learning

Executive Education Executives in an organization often face difficult jobs because of changing and unknown circumstances. Churning at the top of organizations and the stresses of executive jobs contribute to increased turnover in these positions. In an effort to decrease turnover and increase management development capabilities, organizations are using specialized education for executives. This type of training includes executive education traditionally offered by university business schools and adds strategy formulation, financial models, logistics, alliances, and global issues. Enrollment in Executive Masters of Business Administration (EMBA) degree programs is also popular.

9-8c Problems with Management Development Efforts

Management development efforts are subject to certain common mistakes and problems. Many of the problems have resulted from inadequate HR planning and a lack of coordination of HR development efforts. Common problems include the following:

- Failing to conduct adequate needs analysis
- Trying out fad programs or training methods
- Substituting training for selecting qualified individuals

Another common management development problem is *encapsulated development*, which occurs when an individual learns new methods and ideas, but returns to a work unit that is still bound by old attitudes and methods. The development was "encapsulated" in the classroom and is essentially not used on the job. Consequently, individuals who participate in development programs paid for by their employers may become discouraged and move to new employers who allow them to use their newly developed capabilities more effectively.

SUMMARY

- Talent management is important because it is concerned with the attraction, development, and retention of human resources.
- Training, succession planning, career planning, and performance management are crucial parts of talent management.
- Succession planning is the process that identifies how key employees are to be replaced, including deciding whether to make or buy talent and how to use electronic and Web-based succession planning programs.
- Mistakes can occur in succession planning, including focusing only on CEO and senior management succession.
- The nature of careers is changing because retention of employees and work–life balance have become more important.
- Career planning may focus on organizational needs, individual needs, or both; and career

- paths and employer websites are part of career planning.
- A person chooses a career according to interests, self-image, personality, social background, and other factors.
- Several special individual career issues must be addressed, including those related to technical and professional workers.
- Career issues for women may include work–family balancing and glass ceiling concerns, as well as being part of dual-career couples.
- Global career development has special challenges, including relocations of dual-career couples, global development, and repatriation.
- Development differs from training because it focuses on less tangible aspects of performance, such as attitudes and values.
- Developing specific competencies may require life-long learning and redevelopment of employees.

- Needs analyses for development may include assessment centers, psychological testing, and performance appraisals.
- HR development approaches can involve job-site, off-site, and learning organization activities.
- On-the-job development methods include coaching, committee assignments, job rotation, and "assistant-to" positions.
- Off-site development means often include classroom courses, seminars, and degrees; outdoor experiences; and sabbaticals and leaves of absences.

- Learning organization development efforts reflect knowledge-based means, such as corporate universities and centers and e-development efforts.
- Management development is a special focus in many organizations, including supervisor development and leadership development.
- Management modeling, coaching, and mentoring are valuable parts of management development efforts.

CRITICAL THINKING CHALLENGES

1. Discuss what talent management is and why it is a consideration addressed by a growing number of employers.
2. Describe the broad range of talent management efforts that use software applications by going to www.learn.com. Then give some examples of firms that have successfully used these applications.
3. How has the increase in uncertainty in business affected the "make-or-buy" decision, and is this trend likely to change?
4. Design a management development program for first-level supervisors in an electric utility company. What courses and experiences do they need?
5. You are the HR Director of a large manufacturing company that is approximately 50 years old. The company has reaped the benefits of a mostly tenured workforce, and many

of the key workers are now approaching retirement age. It is anticipated that approximately 20% of the company's workforce will retire in the next three to five years. You are also planning to retire within that period of time. To assist the company with the retirement transition process, you want to present a business case to the President for a succession plan for several key positions, including the Chief Financial Officer and Director of Operations.

A. Which outside company advisors should be included in the succession planning process?
B. The successor employee for the replacement of the Chief Financial Officer and Director of Operations positions should have an advanced level of work experience in what key essential functions? How can the company help candidates get these experiences?

CASE

Walgreens Scores Victory with Volunteers

In an effort to better utilize the talent level of its human resources, Walgreens created an innovative talent management program for its finance division, which involved getting input from current employees who volunteered their time to help the firm. A key component of this career development plan was the use of HR business partners throughout the

organization who worked with operational leaders to create skills-based training programs for employees. By focusing on the development of important skills, current workers would ideally be better prepared for the challenges and opportunities that existed in Walgreens. What made this program particularly unique is its reliance on volunteers to identify important skill sets and create the kinds of initiatives that would help employees gain the most relevant competencies.

The creation of this training and career development effort was a detailed process that required extensive teamwork, coordination, and strategic planning. The primary components of the program were also based on several key themes and institutional approaches:

1. Walgreens initially advertised and promoted the program in the company's newsletter and in various meetings. Employee volunteers were told that their commitment to the program would ultimately help all workers enhance their long-term career opportunities at Walgreens. This strategy generated great interest among employees, and the company quickly identified the appropriate number of volunteers to kickoff the initiative.

2. Developmental blueprints were developed by employees so that individuals could better control their own career prospects at Walgreens. These blueprints helped
   - identify possible employment paths that operated through a variety of career tracks;
   - provide the proper training activities and enhancement opportunities that facilitate the accomplishment of career goals; and
   - position the company as a desirable employer.

3. A multistep phase-in of the program was initiated, which involved placing employees on teams that supervised different functional components of the blueprint model. These components included training and development, managerial succession, reward systems, technology utilization, metric identification and scorecards (using an employee survey), and many others.

4. Online educational videos and multimedia content was offered to employees to enhance their career development in the firm.

While the program has improved talent management at Walgreens, another big change has occurred because finance and accounting professionals were trained to better manage human resources, broadening the discipline's appeal across professional boundaries.[90]

QUESTIONS

1. Why was it good for Walgreens to get input from volunteers?

2. Why was it necessary to rely on employee blueprints to enhance career management in the company?

3. Why was it important to familiarize individuals in other business functions of the organization? How should this approach help Walgreens?

SUPPLEMENTAL CASES

Leadership Leverage

The case demonstrates how a healthcare company utilized talent group to better management the development of employees. (For the case, go to www.cengage.com/management/mathis.)

Equipping for the Future

This case shows how one company in the oil industry started a succession planning program. (For the case, go to www.cengage.com/management/mathis.)

Developed Today, Gone Tomorrow

This case illustrates a serious concern some employers have about developing employees only to have them leave. (For the case, go to www.cengage.com/management/mathis.)

NOTES

1. Based on Grae Yohe, "The Talent Solution," *Human Resource Executive Online*, June 2, 2009, www.hreonline.com.
2. David G. Collings and Kamel Mellahi, "Strategic Talent Management: A Review and Research Agenda," *Human Resource Management Review*, 19 (2009), 304–313.
3. Wouter Aghina, Marc de Jong, and Daniel Simon, "How the Best Labs Manage Talent," *McKinsey Quarterly*, May 2011, www.mckinsey-quarterly.com.
4. Maura C. Ciccarelli, "Trust at the Top," *Human Resource Executive Online*, November 1, 2011, www.hreonline.com.
5. Jack Berry, "Transforming HRD into an Economic Value Add," *T + D*, September 2011, 66–69.
6. Nancy Smith, "A Strategic Approach to Role-Based Talent Management," *Training*, July/August 2011, 10–12, www.trainingmag.com.
7. Karen O'Leonard, "Talent Management Facebook 2010," Bersin & Associates Research Report, 1–13.
8. Adrienne Fox, "Achieving Integration," *HR Magazine*, April 2011, 43–51.
9. Peter Cappelli, "A Supply Chain Model for Talent Management," *People & Strategy*, 32 (2009), Issue 3, 4–7.
10. Mary Slaughter, "Success at Suntrust Begins and Ends with Talent," *T + D*, November 2011, 38–42.
11. Edward E. Gordon, "Refocusing Strategic Talent Management," *Training*, January/February 2011, 14–15, www.trainingmag.com.
12. Edward Lawler, *Talent: Making People Your Competitive Advantage* (Jossey-Bass, 2008).
13. P. Cappelli, 2009, 5.
14. Helene Cavalli, "Development Opportunities Most Important to Job Seekers," *LinkedIn*, December 1, 2009, 1–3.
15. Andrew R. McIlvaine, "The Human Risk Factor," *Human Resource Executive*, February 2012, 1, 14–18.
16. "Talent Management Continues to Go High Tech," *HR Focus*, October 2009, 8–9.
17. Ed Frauenheim, "Special Report on HR Technology—Talent Planning for the Times," *Workforce Management*, October 19, 2009, 37–43.
18. Grae Yohe, 2009, www.hreonline.com.
19. Anonymous, "High Potentials May Be Slipping Through the Cracks" *T + D*, October 2011, 15.
20. Jean Martin and Conrad Schmidt, "How to Keep Your Top Talent," *Harvard Business Review*, 88 (2010), Issue 5, 54–61.
21. Margery Weinstein, "Hi-Po to Go," *Training*, February 2009, 8, www.trainingmag.com.
22. Maura C. Ciccarelli, "Perfecting the Hi-Po Process," *Human Resource Executive Online*, April 2, 2012, www.hreonline.com.
23. Boris Groysberg and Nitin Nohria, "How to Hang on to Your High Potentials," *Harvard Business Review*, 89 (2011), Issue 10, 76–83.
24. Robert J. Grossman, "The Care and Feeding of High-Potential Employees," *HR Magazine*, August 2011, 34–39.
25. Adrienne Hedger, "How to Improve Talent Management?" *Workforce Management*, September 8, 2008, 54; Jon Younger, et al., "Developing Your Organization's Brand as a Talent Developer," *Human Resource Planning*, 30 (2007), 23.
26. P. Cappelli, 2009, 6.
27. Stephenie Overman, "On the Right Track," *HR Magazine*, April, 2011, 73–75.
28. William J. Rothwell, "Replacement Planning: A Starting Point for Succession Planning and Talent Management," *International Journal of Training and Development*, 15 (2011), Issue 1, 87–99.
29. Gail Dutton, "Succession Success," *Training*, May 2009, 44–45, www.trainingmag.com.
30. William J. Rothwell, "The Future of Succession Planning," *T + D*, September 2010, 51–54.
31. Anne Mulcahy, "Xerox's Former CEO on Why Succession Shouldn't Be a Horse Race," *Harvard Business Review*, 88 (2010), Issue 10, 47–51.
32. Robert J. Grossman, "Rough Road to Success," *HR Magazine*, June 2011, 47–51.
33. Stephan Miles and Theodore Dysart, "Road Map for Successful Succession Planning," *Directors and Boards*, First Quarter 2008, 57–59.
34. Dan Dalton and Catherine Dalton, "CEO Succession: Best Practices in a Changing Environment," *Journals of Business Strategy*, 28 (2007), 11–13.
35. Charles Greer and Meghna Virick, "Diverse Succession Planning Lessons from the Industry Leaders," *Human Resource Management* (2009), 351–367.
36. Aaron Sorenson and Deb Jacobs, "A Practitioner's Guide to Succession Planning," *Workspan*, March 2011, 19–25.
37. Jennifer Robison, "Scientific, Systematic Succession Planning," *Gallup Management Journal*, June 2, 2009, 1–6.
38. "Potential—for What?" Hay Group consulting firm publication, January 2008.
39. Adapted from Kathryn Tyler, "On the Grid," *HR Magazine*, August 2011, 67–69.
40. Angela Hills, "Succession Planning – or Smart Talent Management?" *Industrial and Commercial Training*, 41 (2009), 3–8.
41. Matt Boyle, "The Art of Succession," *BusinessWeek*, May 11, 2009, 30–32.
42. Andrew McIlvaine, "Finding Talent: Buy It or Make It?" *Human Resource Executive Online*, June 14, 2011, www.hreonline.com.
43. James M. Citrin and Dayton Ogden, "Succeeding at Succession," *Harvard Business Review*, 88 (2010), Issue 11, 29–31.
44. Paula Ketter, "Sounding Succession Alarms," *T + D*, January 2009, 20.
45. Based on Amy Andrews-Emery, "Finding Top People for the Top

Spots," *HR Magazine*, August 2010, 42–44.

46. Traci McCready and Chris Hatcher, "How to Align Career Development and Succession Planning," *Workspan*, March 2009, 61–63.

47. Sherry E. Sullivan and Yehuda Baruch, "Advances in Career Theory and Research: A Critical Review and Agenda for Future Exploration," *Journal of Management*, 35 (2009), No. 6, 1542–1572.

48. Maura Ciccarelli, "Lattice vs. Ladder," *Human Resource Executive Online*, November 1, 2010, www. hreonline.com.

49. Bob Campbell, Scott Cohen, Charlene P. Allen, and Susan Cromidas, "One Company's Approach to Career Path Success," *Workspan*, May 2010, 65–71.

50. Yongho Park and William Rothwell, "The Effects of Organizational Learning Climate, Career Enhancing Strategy, and Work Orientation on the Protean Career," *Human Resource Development International*, 8 (2009), 387–405.

51. Nancy Wendlandt and Aaron Rochler, "Addressing the College to Work Transition," *Journal of Career Development*, 35 (2008), 151–165.

52. Thomas Ng and Daniel Feldman, "The School to Work Transition: A Role Identity Perspective," *Journal of Vocational Behavior*, 71 (2007), 114–134.

53. Mo Wang and Kenneth S. Shultz, "Employee Retirement: A Review and Recommendations for Future Investigation," *Journal of Management*, 36 (2010), No. 1, 172–206.

54. Collin Barr, "Pension Tension on the Rise," *Fortune CNN Money*, November 30, 2009, 1–3.

55. Mary Shapiro, Cynthia Ingols, Regina O'Neill, and Stacy Blake-Bead, "Making Sense of Women as Career Self-Agents: Implications for Human Resource Development," *Human Resource Development Quarterly*, 20 (2009), No. 4, 477–501.

56. Ilene H. Lang, "Co-Opt the Old Boy's Club: Make It Work for Women," *Harvard Business Review*, 89 (2011), Issue 11, 44.

57. Herminia Ibarra, Nancy M. Carter, and Christine Silva, "Why Men Still Get More Promotions than Women," *Harvard Business Review*, 88 (2010), Issue 9, 80–126.

58. Adapted from Shannon Sullivan, "Developing Women Leaders Through Grassroots Mentorship," *Workspan*, November 2010, 52–56.

59. Jessica Marquez, "Gender Discrimination Begins Much Earlier than Exec Levels, Report Shows," *Workforce Management*, May 12, 2009, 1–3.

60. Nancy M. Carter and Christine Silva, "Women in Management: Delusions of Progress," *Harvard Business Review*, 88 (2010), Issue 3, 19–21.

61. "How Women Can Contribute More to the US Economy," *McKinsey Quarterly*, April 2011, www. mckinseyquarterly.com.

62. Susanne Bruckmuller and Nyla R. Branscombe, "How Women End up on the Glass Cliff," *Harvard Business Review*, 89 (2011), Issue 1/2, 26.

63. Cathy Arnst, "Women Want Careers Just as Much as Men," *BusinessWeek*, March 27, 2009, 1.

64. Bill Roberts, "Lowdown on Relo," *HR Magazine*, August 2009, 49–51.

65. Michael Harvey, et al., "Global Dual-Career Exploration and the Role of Hope and Curiosity," *Journal of Management Psychology*, 24 (2009), 178–197; Theresa Minton-Eversole, "Easing the Travails of Trailing Spouses," *HR Magazine*, November 2011, 43–46.

66. Eileen Mullaney, "Talent Mobility," *Workspan*, February 2012, 32–36.

67. Johannes A. V. van der Heijden, Marloes L. van Engen, and Jaap Paauwe, Expatriate Career Support: Predicting Expatriate Turnover and Performance," *International Journal of Human Resource Management*, 20 (2009), Issue 4, 831–845.

68. Ann Pace, "Work Relocation Trends Shifting," *T + D*, August 2011, 24.

69. Jean-Luc Cerdin and Marie Le Pargneux, "Career and International Assignment Fit," *Human Resource Management*, January–February 2009, 5–25.

70. Vadim Kostovski, "Repatriation Considerations in a Cost Aware Economy," *Workspan*, August 2009, 34–39.

71. Alice Andors, "Happy Returns," *HR Magazine*, March 2010, 61–63.

72. Bill Leisy and N. S. Rajan, "Global Talent Management," *Workspan*, March 2009, 39–45.

73. Kristen B. Frasch, "Defining Global Leadership Competencies," *Human Resource Executive Online*, August 5, 2011, www.hreonline.com.

74. Neal Goodman, "Talent Development in a Global Economy," *Training*, July/August 2011, 42, www. trainingmag.com.

75. Karl Taro Greenfeld, "The Sharin' Huggin' Lovin' Carin' Chinese Food Money Machine," *Bloomberg Businessweek*, November 22–November 28, 2010.

76. Dori Meinert, "In the Trenches," *HR Magazine*, August 2011, 28.

77. Jayson Saba, et al., "Assessments in Talent Management," *Aberdeen Group*, 2009, www.aberdeen.com, 1–23.

78. Kendra Lee, "Use Diagnostic Skills Assessments," *Training*, February 2010, 22, www.trainingmag.com.

79. Thomas H. Davenport, Jeanne Harris, and Jeremy Shapiro, "Competing on Talent Analytics," *Harvard Business Review*, 88 (2010), Issue 10, 52–58.

80. Alina Dizik, "Training Without a Campus," *The Wall Street Journal*, April 15, 2009, D4.

81. "What Is a Coaching Culture?" *Coaching Conundrum 2009 Global Executive Summary*, Blessing White, 2009, 5–23.

82. Based on Kathryn Tyler, "Sabbaticals Pay Off," *HR Magazine*, December 2011, 38–42.

83. Pat Galagan and Jeanne Meister, "90,000 Served Hamburger University Turns 50," *T + D*, April 2011, 46.

84. Jessica Li and Amy Lui, "Prioritizing + Maximizing the Impact of Corporate Universities," *T + D*, May 2011, 54.

85. Lisa Dragoni, et al., "Understanding Management Development," *Academy of Management Journal*, 52 (2009), 731–743.

86. E. Norman, "Develop Leadership Talent During a Recession," *Workspan*, May 2009, 35–42.

87. Robert Hooijberg and Nancy Lane, "Using Multisource Feedback Coaching Effectively in Executive Education," *Academy of Management Learning and Education*, 8 (2009), 483–493.

88. Lillian Eby, et al., "Does Mentoring Matter?" *Journal of Vocational Behavior*, 72 (2008), 254–267.

89. Susan Wells, "Tending Talent," *HR Magazine*, May 2009, 53–56.

90. Based on Tara Shawel, "Homegrown Career Development," *HR Magazine*, April 2011, 36–38.

10

CHAPTER

Performance Management and Appraisal

Learning Objectives

After you have read this chapter, you should be able to:

1 Identify why performance management is necessary.

2 Distinguish among three types of performance information.

3 Explain the differences between administrative and developmental uses of performance appraisal.

4 Describe the advantages and disadvantages of multisource (360-degree) appraisals.

5 Discuss the importance of training managers and employees on performance appraisal, and give examples of rater errors.

6 Identify several concerns about appraisal feedback and ways to make it more effective.

© Hemera/Thinkstock

Performance Management at Intuit

© David Paul Morris/Bloomberg/Getty Images

Performance management, if it is done correctly, sends clear messages to employees about what matters to the company and its managers. Intuit Inc. is a provider of financial management tools to accountants and financial institutions. The company sets growth plans annually and translates those into "stretch goals" for employers and teams. The intent is to reward aggressive innovation, even if a project fails. Overall business impact is the key concern, not just the completion of goals. The company feels that a goal-oriented culture can become frustrating if it allows employees to set objectives that are easy to reach.

Intuit believes that identifying peoples' contributions is essential to a performance culture, and the firm uses the following performance labels: *top performers*, *solid contributors*, *trailing performers*, and *continually low performers*. The evaluation given to top performers signals they have contributed beyond most others, and Intuit insists that managers make full use of all available rewards to reinforce top performance including compensation, recognition, and opportunity. These can also include merit raises, bonuses, equity awards, spot awards, development opportunities, and growth assignments.

The company tests its performance management system by asking, "Would we put our performance management system on our recruitment website as a way to attract good candidates?" Intuit feels that transparency, trust, and accountability will help performance management maintain its key role in a high-performance culture.[1]

Individual job performance is of interest to both organizations and managers. Good performance creates success for the organization and poor performance threatens that success.[2] All managers want employees who perform their jobs well, but that does not happen automatically. Well-designed performance management practices greatly increase the likelihood that good performance will follow, and for some poor performance will be identified and dealt with.

Performance management identifies the necessary work an individual is to do. It should also encourage, measure, and evaluate that performance. And finally it seeks to communicate, improve, and reward performance.[3] Even well-intentioned employees do not always know exactly what is expected or how to improve their performance. This guarantees that performance management will be necessary. Further, if dismissal becomes necessary the employer must be able to show that the employee was advised of the problems and the consequences of failing to improve. Dismissal without these necessary steps can risk a negative legal outcome.[4]

10-1 ■ THE NATURE OF PERFORMANCE MANAGEMENT

The performance management process starts by identifying the goals an organization needs to accomplish to remain competitive and profitable. Managers then identify how they and their employees can support those objectives by successfully completing work. Of course, the sum of the work completed in all jobs should be what is necessary to advance the strategic plan.

As Figure 10-1 shows, performance management links strategy to results. However, just having a strategic plan does not guarantee that results will be achieved. Strategies must be translated into department- or unit-level actions. Then these actions must be assigned to individuals who are then held accountable for their accomplishment.

Performance management is often confused with one of its key components—performance appraisal. **Performance management** is a series of activities designed to ensure that the organization gets the performance it needs from its employees. **Performance appraisal** is the process of determining how well employees do their jobs relative to a standard and communicating that information to them. Performance appraisal is a part of performance management rather than its entirety.[5]

At a minimum, a performance management system should do the following:

- Make clear what the organization expects.
- Document performance for personnel records.
- Identify areas of success and needed development.
- Provide performance information to employees.

Performance management
Series of activities designed to ensure that the organization gets the performance it needs from its employees.

Performance appraisal
Process of determining how well employees do their jobs relative to a standard and communicating that information to them.

A successful performance management system allows managers to better prepare employees for their work responsibilities by focusing on the most important components of these activities.[6] For example, in one company employees are rated on standardized job criteria by their supervisor, but they also complete self-evaluations. They are given the supervisor's completed evaluation forms several days ahead of appraisal meetings to consider the ratings. "Performance agreements" that follow explicitly connect the individual actions to corporate goals,

FIGURE 10-1 Performance Management Linkage

```
                    ┌──────────────────────────────────────┐
                    │        Organizational Strategies       │
                    └──────────────────────────────────────┘
                                      │
                                      ▼
                    ┌──────────────────────────────────────┐
                    │         Performance Management          │
                    │  ◆ Identify expected performance levels │
                    │  ◆ Encourage high levels of performance │
                    │  ◆ Measure individual performance; then evaluate │
                    │  ◆ Provide feedback on individual performance │
                    │  ◆ Provide assistance as needed         │
                    │  ◆ Reward or discipline depending on performance │
                    └──────────────────────────────────────┘
                                      │
                                      ▼
                    ┌──────────────────────────────────────┐
                    │          Employee Performance           │
                    └──────────────────────────────────────┘
                                      │
                                      ▼
                    ┌──────────────────────────────────────┐
                    │     Performance Management Outcomes     │
                    │  ◆ Pay increases                        │
                    │  ◆ Incentive rewards                    │
                    │  ◆ Promotions/advancement               │
                    │  ◆ Training and development             │
                    │  ◆ Career planning                      │
                    │  ◆ Disciplinary actions                 │
                    └──────────────────────────────────────┘
                                      │
                                      ▼
                    ┌──────────────────────────────────────┐
                    │          Organizational Results         │
                    │  ◆ Goals met or not met                 │
                    │  ◆ Employee satisfaction or dissatisfaction │
                    │  ◆ Correspondence between performance and pay │
                    └──────────────────────────────────────┘
```

© Cengage Learning

and the communication involved in forging those agreements ensures that managers and employees understand important performance issues.

GLOBAL

10-1a Global Cultural Differences in Performance Management

Performance management and appraisals are very common in the United States and some other countries. However, it can be challenging to institute U.S. practices in countries that have dissimilar cultures.

In some countries and cultures, it is uncommon for managers to rate employees or to give direct feedback, particularly if some points are negative. For instance, in several countries, including China and Japan, there is great respect for authority and age. Consequently, expecting younger subordinates to engage in joint discussions with their managers through a performance appraisal process is uncommon. Use of programs such as multisource/360-degree feedback (discussed later in this chapter) would also be culturally unusual.[7]

In some other cultures, employees may view criticism from superiors as personally devastating rather than as useful feedback that highlights individual training and development needs. Therefore, many managers do not provide feedback, and employees do not expect it. "Cultural customs" associated with formal meetings may need to be observed. For example, in some Eastern European countries, it is common to have coffee and pastries or an alcoholic drink before beginning any formal discussion. These examples illustrate that performance management processes may need to be adapted or changed in different global settings.[8]

10-1b Performance-Focused Organizational Cultures

Organizational cultures can vary on many dimensions, and one of these differences involves the degree to which performance is emphasized. Some corporate cultures are based on an *entitlement* approach, meaning that *adequate* performance and stability dominate the organization. Employee rewards vary little from person to person and have little to do with individual performance differences. As a result, performance appraisal activities are viewed as having few ties to performance and being primarily a "bureaucratic exercise."

At the other end of the spectrum is a *performance-driven* organizational culture focused on results and contributions. In this context, performance evaluations link results to employee compensation and development.[9] This approach is particularly important when evaluating CEO performance because companies should hold top leaders accountable for corporate outcomes and motivate them to improve operational and financial results.

There are benefits to developing a performance-focused culture throughout the organization. Firms with performance-focused cultures have more positive performance than do those with a maintenance-orientation culture.[10] Figure 10-2 shows the components of a successful performance-focused culture, which usually means pay depends on performance. However, a pay-for-performance approach can present several challenges to organizations. For example, in educational institutions which usually have an entitlement philosophy teacher pay-for-performance plans are seen as creating inequity, if some teachers get bonuses and others receive no extra compensation. Tying bonuses to criteria such as students' performance on tests/achievement, teaching evaluations, and professional growth has been met with harsh criticism.

Despite these issues, it appears that a performance-based-pay culture is desirable. It is sometimes argued that companies are not doing enough about poor performers, and that failure to deal with poor performance is unfair to those who work hard. In one financial services company, a new CEO instituted a performance system that gave star performers raises as high as 20% and poor performers nothing. The tougher performance system encouraged poor performers to leave the company voluntarily, increased the performance of many other employees, and enhanced company profitability. Successfully managing performance can change behavior for the better.[11]

FIGURE 10-2 Components of a Performance-Focused Culture

Clear Expectations, Goals, and Deadlines

Detailed Appraisal of Employee Performance

Clear Feedback on Performance

Manager and Employee Training as Needed

Consequences for Performance

© Cengage Learning

10-2 ■ IDENTIFYING AND MEASURING EMPLOYEE PERFORMANCE

Performance criteria vary from job to job, but common employee performance measures include the following:

- Quantity of output
- Quality of output
- Timeliness of output
- Presence/attendance on the job
- Efficiency of work completed
- Effectiveness of work completed

Job duties
Identify the important elements in a given job.

Specific **job duties** from a job description should identify the important elements in a given job. It is useful for managers and employees to discuss job duties and agree on their relative importance although such agreement is not always emphasized.[12] Job duties define what the organization pays employees to do. Therefore, the performance of individuals on their job duties should be measured and compared against appropriate standards, and the results should be communicated to the employee.

Multiple job duties are the rule rather than the exception in most jobs. An individual might demonstrate better performance on some duties than others, and some duties might be more important than others to the organization. For example, professors are broadly required to conduct research, teach classes, and provide service to important university stakeholders. Some professors may focus heavily on one area of work over the others, which can cause performance management issues if their universities value all parts of the job equally.

Weights can be used to show the relative importance of different duties in a job. For example, in a management job at a company that wants to improve customer feedback, control operational costs, and encourage quality improvements, weights might be assigned as follows:

Weighting of Management Duties at Sample Firm	Weight
Improve customer feedback	50%
Control operational costs	30%
Encourage quality improvements	20%
Total Management Performance	**100%**

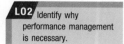

10-2a Types of Performance Information

Managers can use three different types of information about employee performance, as Figure 10-3 shows. *Trait-based information* identifies a character trait of the employee, such as attitude, initiative, or creativity, and may or may not be job related. For example, conscientiousness is often found to be a trait that is an important determinant of job performance. Yet traits tend to be ambiguous, and biases of raters can affect how traits are viewed, so court decisions generally have held that trait-based performance appraisals are too vague to use when making HR decisions such as promotions or terminations. Also, focusing too much on trait characteristics such as "potential" can lead managers to ignore important behaviors and outcomes.

Behavior-based information focuses on specific behaviors that lead to job success. For a waitperson, the behavior "menu up-selling" can be observed and used as

FIGURE 10-3 Types of Performance Information

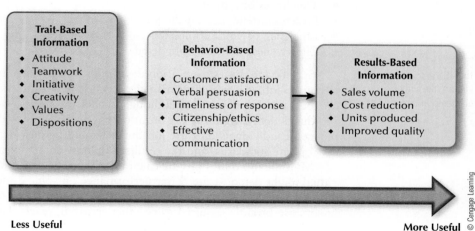

performance information. Additionally, an HR Director who institutes an "open-door policy" behaves in a manner that may increase communication with employees. Behavioral information can specify the behaviors management expects employees to exhibit. A potential problem arises when any of several behaviors can lead to successful performance, and employees rely on different behaviors to complete work. For example, one salesperson might successfully use one verbal persuasion strategy with customers, while another salesperson might use another successfully because no one approach can be utilized effectively by all individuals.

Results-based information considers employee accomplishments. For jobs in which measurement is easy and obvious, a results-based approach works well. For instance, a professor might receive extra compensation for securing grants or publishing papers in certain academic journals, or a salesperson in a retail outlet might receive extra commission pay based on how many products are sold. However, in this approach, that which is measured tends to be emphasized, which may leave out equally important but difficult-to-measure parts of work.[13] For example, a car salesperson who gets paid *only* for sales may be unwilling to do paperwork and other work not directly related to selling cars. Further, ethical or legal issues may arise when only results are emphasized, and *how* the results were achieved is not considered, so care should be taken to balance the different types of information.[14]

Performance measures can be viewed as objective or subjective. The *objective measures* can be observed—for example, the number of cars sold or the number of invoices processed can be counted. *Subjective measures* require judgment on the part of the evaluator and are more difficult to determine. One example of a subjective measure is a supervisor's ratings of an employee's "attitude," which typically cannot be viewed directly. Consequently, subjective measures should be used carefully.[15]

10-2b Performance Standards

Performance standards
Define the expected levels of employee performance.

Performance standards define the expected levels of employee performance. Sometimes they are labeled *benchmarks*, *goals*, or *targets*—depending on the approach taken. Realistic, measurable, clearly understood performance standards benefit both organizations and employees. Performance standards define how satisfactory job performance is defined, so performance standards should be established *before* work is performed. Well-defined standards ensure that everyone involved knows the performance expectations.

Both numerical and nonnumerical standards can be established. Sales quotas and production output are familiar numerical performance standards. A standard of performance can also be based on nonnumerical criteria. Assessing whether someone has met a performance standard, especially a nonnumerical one, can be difficult, but can be done. For example, how would you measure someone's ability to speak a foreign language before the person is sent overseas? Figure 10-4 lists performance standards that facilitate such measurement and make assessing a person's performance level, even though this is nonnumerical performance, much more accurate.

To make sure performance standards are applied uniformly, many organizations "calibrate" performances. Calibrating is often a group review conducted by managers to discuss the reasons behind each employee's rating. Ratings can be adjusted up or down by the group to ensure the ratings reflect similar performance standards.[16] This process can increase inter-rates reliability.

FIGURE 10-4 ACTFL Performance Standards for Speaking Proficiency

Performance Level	Demonstrated Ability
Superior	• Participated fully in conversations relating to needs and professional interests • Discusses topics both concretely and abstractly • Can deal effectively with unfamiliar speaking situations
Intermediate	• Can participate in simple conversations on predictable topics • Can satisfy simple needs to survive in the language's culture • Can ask and answer questions
Novice	• Can respond to simple questions • Can convey minimal meaning by using isolated words or memorized phrases • Can satisfy a limited number of immediate needs

© Cengage Learning

MEASURE

10-2c Performance Metrics in Service Businesses

Measuring service performance is difficult because services are often very individualized for customers, there is typically great variation in the services that can be offered, and quality is somewhat subjective. Yet the performance of people in service jobs is commonly evaluated with the basic productivity measures used in the industry. Some of the most useful sources of performance differences among managers in service businesses are as follows:

- Regional differences in labor costs
- Service agreement differences
- Equipment/infrastructure differences
- Work volume

On an individual level, common measures might include cost per employee, incidents per employee per day, number of calls per product, cost per call, sources of demand for services, and service calls per day. Once managers have determined appropriate measures of the service variance in their company, they can deal with waste and service delivery. *Performance that is measured can be managed.*[17]

10-3 ■ PERFORMANCE APPRAISALS

Performance appraisals are used to assess an employee's performance and provide a platform for feedback about past, current, and future performance expectations. Several terms can be used when referring to performance appraisals. These include *employee rating, employee evaluation, performance review, performance evaluation,* or *results appraisal.*

Performance appraisals are widely used for administering wages and salaries and identifying individual employee strengths and weaknesses. Most U.S. employers use performance appraisals for office, professional, technical, supervisory, middle management, and nonunion production workers, and there are many reasons for this widespread use. Performance appraisals can provide answers to a wide array of work-related questions, and by communicating a road map for success, poor performance can sometimes be improved. Even after a positive appraisal, employees benefit if the feedback helped them to determine how to improve job performance. In addition, even though an employer may not need a reason to terminate an employee, appraisals can provide justification for such actions should that become necessary.

But a gap may exist between actual job performance and the way it is rated. Poorly done performance appraisals lead to disappointing results for all concerned, and there is reason to believe that evaluations can cause bad feelings and damaged relationships if not managed well.[18] Some believe that performance evaluations are an unnecessary part of work because of vague rating standards, self-interest, and/or deception on the part of rating managers.[19] Indeed, performance reviews can be politically oriented and highly subjective in nature, which will adversely impact the relationships between managers and their employees. However, having no formal performance appraisal can weaken discipline and harm an employee's ability to improve, and well done appraisals are entirely possible. See the HR Perspective: Making Appraisals Work at Hilton Worldwide.

HR PERSPECTIVE

Making Appraisals Work at Hilton Worldwide

The new chief HR officer at Hilton Worldwide found he had to create a performance management system from scratch when he arrived. Performance appraisals varied greatly, if they existed at all. In many companies (including Hilton), the performance management process is needlessly complex, is not connected to business goals, and is hated by managers and employees alike.

The fundamentals of performance management should be simple, reflected Matt Schuyler, the new CHRO at Hilton. Employees agree to goals at the start of the year, supervisors assess their progress at the end of the cycle, a good conversation is had on how the employee is doing, and rewards are based on whether the goals were met. Fixing the overly complex process involves going back to the basics.

At Hilton, managers and employees now set objectives at the beginning of the year and check mid-way to see how things are going. The system documents individual accomplishments so there are no surprises during the evaluation. The "mid-year check in" is designed to encourage continuous feedback over the rating period. The idea of keeping things simple, focusing on the conversation, and emphasizing two-way communication has been positive because satisfaction with the performance management process increased by 37% in an employee survey. "The goal of performance management is to give you feedback so you can get better, not to damage you or make you feel bad," says Schuyler.[20]

ETHICS

10-3a Performance Appraisals and Ethics

Performance appraisals may or may not focus on the ethics with which a manager performs his or her job. Managers may be expected to take an active role in managing ethics in their area of responsibility but often do not understand the process. Many companies do not have a program to develop awareness of ethics and some have no policies at all regarding ethical behavior. Yet discussing ethics in performance appraisals is one way to emphasize it. Codes of conduct can provide useful company guidelines on ethical behavior, training can teach important workplace ethical values, and communication of ethical approaches to reoccurring workplace problems can help promote an ethical culture. But rewarding ethical behavior and punishing undesirable behavior are also reasonable approaches for improving ethical practices in an organization. Doing so requires including ethics in performance measurement.

A recent study of the relationship between ethics and performance appraisals found that the amount of time spent doing performance appraisals affected the incidence of ethical issues in the process.[21] More time spent means a greater likelihood that ethical issues would be discussed. Managers doing performance appraisals should have objectives for the evaluations and be held accountable to make sure they dedicate enough time to do the appraisals well. Training managers on performance appraisal and the ethical components of the process are most likely to be successful in improving the problems. HR can monitor the process for specific results.

10-3b Uses of Performance Appraisals

LO3 Explain the differences between administrative and developmental uses of performance appraisal.

Organizations generally use performance appraisals in two potentially conflicting ways. One use is to provide a measure of performance for consideration in making pay or other administrative decisions about employees. This *administrative* role often creates stress for managers doing the appraisals and the employees being evaluated because the rater is placed in the role of judge. The other use focuses on the *development* of individuals.[22] In this role, the manager acts more as a counselor and coach than as a judge. The developmental performance appraisal emphasizes current training and development needs, as well as planning employees' future opportunities and career directions. Whether a performance appraisal is to be used in an administrative capacity or as a developmental tool affects several aspects of the process.[23] Figure 10-5 shows both uses for performance appraisals.

Administrative Uses of Appraisals Three administrative uses of appraisal impact managers and employees the most: (1) determining pay adjustments; (2) making job placement decisions on promotions, transfers, and demotions; and (3) choosing employee disciplinary actions up to and including termination of employment.

A performance appraisal system is often the link between employee job performance and the additional pay and rewards that they can receive. Performance-based compensation affirms the idea that pay raises are given for performance accomplishments rather than for length of service (seniority), or granted automatically to all employees at the same percentage levels. In pay-for-performance compensation systems, managers have evaluated the performance of individuals and have made compensation recommendations. If any part of the appraisal process fails, better-performing employees may not receive larger pay increases, and the result is perceived inequity in compensation.

FIGURE 10-5 Uses for Performance Appraisals

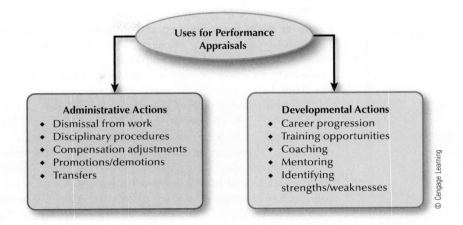

Many U.S. workers say that they see little connection between their performance and the size of their pay increases due to flaws in performance appraisals. Consequently, people argue that performance appraisals and pay discussions should be done separately. Two realities support this view. One is that employees often focus more on the pay received than on the developmental appraisal feedback. The other is that managers sometimes manipulate ratings to justify the pay they wish to give individuals. As a result, many employees view the appraisal process as a game because compensation increases have been predetermined before the appraisal is completed.

To address these issues, managers can first conduct performance appraisals and discuss the results with employees, and then several weeks later hold a shorter meeting to discuss pay issues. For example, one company created different performance appraisal and compensation forms that are considered separately at different times. By adopting such an approach, the results of the performance appraisal can be considered before the amount of the pay adjustment is determined. Also, the performance appraisal discussions between managers and employees can focus on issues for improvement—not just pay raises.

Employers are obviously interested in the administrative uses of performance appraisals such as decisions about promotions, terminations, layoffs, and transfer assignments. Promotions and demotions based on performance must be documented through performance appraisals; otherwise, legal problems can occur.[24]

Developmental Uses of Appraisals For employees, a performance appraisal can be a primary source of information and feedback. By identifying employee strengths, weaknesses, potentials, and training needs through performance appraisal feedback, supervisors can inform employees about their progress, discuss areas in which additional training may be beneficial, and outline future developmental plans.[25]

It is clear that employees do not always know where and how to perform better, and managers should not expect improvement if they are unwilling to provide developmental feedback. Many firms, such as the diesel engine parts distributor Cummins Mid-South LLC, are combining performance management and learning management processes with technological support programs that prompt more effective evaluations, increased employee development, and reduced turnover.[26]

The purpose of giving feedback on performance is to both reinforce satisfactory employee performance and to address performance deficiencies. The developmental function of performance appraisal can also identify areas in which the employee might wish to grow. For example, in a performance appraisal interview targeted exclusively to development, an employee found out that the only factor keeping her from being considered for a management job in her firm was the lack of a working knowledge of cost accounting. Her supervisor suggested that she consider taking some night courses at the local college.

The use of teams provides a different set of circumstances for developmental appraisals. The manager may not see all of an employee's work, but the employee's team members do. Team members can provide important feedback. However, whether teams can handle administrative appraisals is still subject to debate; clearly some cannot. When teams are allowed to design appraisal systems, they tend to "get rid of judgment" and avoid differential rewards. Thus, group appraisal may be best suited for developmental rather than administrative purposes.

10-3c Decisions about the Performance Appraisal Process

A number of decisions must be made when designing performance appraisal systems. Some important ones involve identifying the appraisal responsibilities of the HR unit and of the operating managers, selecting the type of appraisal system to use, and establishing the timing of appraisals.

Appraisal Responsibilities If done properly, the appraisal process can benefit both the organization and the employees. As Figure 10-6 shows, the HR unit typically designs a performance appraisal system. Managers then appraise employees using the appraisal system. During development of the formal appraisal system, managers usually offer input about how the final system will work.

It is important for managers to understand that appraisals are *their* responsibility. Through the appraisal process, good employee performance can be made even better, poor employee performance can be improved, and poor performers can be removed from the organization. Performance appraisal must not simply be an HR requirement but should also be an important management process because guiding employees' performance is among the most important responsibilities a manager has.

FIGURE 10-6 Typical Division of HR Responsibilities: Performance Appraisal

HR Unit	Managers
• Design and maintains appraisal system	• Typically rate performance of employees
• Trains raters	• Prepare formal appraisal documents
• Track timely receipt of appraisals	• Review appraisals with employees
• Review completed appraisals for consistency	• Identify development areas

Type of Appraisals: Informal versus Systematic Performance appraisals can occur in two ways: informally and/or systematically. A supervisor conducts an *informal appraisal* whenever necessary. The day-to-day working relationship between a manager and an employee offers an opportunity for the evaluation of individual performance. A manager communicates this evaluation through various conversations on or off the job, or by on-the-spot discussion of a specific occurrence. Although such informal feedback is useful and necessary, it should not replace formal appraisal.

Frequent informal feedback to employees can prevent surprises during a formal performance review. However, informal appraisal can become *too* informal. For example, a senior executive at a large firm so dreaded face-to-face evaluations that he delivered one manager's review while both sat in adjoining stalls in the men's room.

A *systematic appraisal* is used when the contact between a manager and employee is more formal, and a system is in place to report managerial impressions and observations on employee performance. This approach to appraisals is quite common. Systematic appraisals feature a regular time interval, which distinguishes them from informal appraisals. Both employees and managers know that performance will be reviewed on a regular basis, and they can plan for performance discussions.

Timing of Appraisals Most companies require managers to conduct appraisals once or twice a year, most often annually. Employees commonly receive an appraisal 60 to 90 days after hiring, again at 6 months, and annually thereafter. *Probationary* or *introductory employees*, who are new and in a trial period, should be informally evaluated often—perhaps weekly for the first month, and monthly thereafter until the end of the introductory period. After that, annual reviews are typical. For employees in high demand, some employers use accelerated appraisals—every six months instead of every year. This is done to retain those employees since more feedback can be given and pay raises may occur more often. Meeting more frequently with employees may enhance individual performance. For instance, one company requires managers to meet with employees on a quarterly basis, but because some employees wanted even more feedback, managers scheduled meetings every few weeks.

10-3d Legal Concerns and Performance Appraisals

Since appraisals are supposed to measure how well employees are doing their jobs, it may seem unnecessary to emphasize that performance appraisals must be job related. However, it is important for evaluations to adequately reflect the nature of work performed. Companies need to have appraisal systems that satisfy the courts, as well as performance management needs. The HR Skills and Applications: Elements of a Legal Performance Appraisal System shows the elements to consider.

10-4 ■ WHO CONDUCTS APPRAISALS?

Performance appraisals can be conducted by anyone familiar with the performance of individual employees. Possible rating situations include the following:

- Supervisors rating their employees
- Employees rating their superiors
- Team members rating each other
- Employees rating themselves
- Outside sources rating employees
- A variety of parties providing multisource, or 360-degree, feedback

HR SKILLS AND APPLICATIONS

Elements of a Legal Performance Appraisal System

The elements of a performance appraisal system that can survive court tests can be determined from existing case law. It is generally agreed that a legally defensible performance appraisal should include the following:

- Performance appraisal criteria based on job analysis
- Absence of disparate impact
- Formal evaluation criteria that limit managerial discretion
- A rating instrument linked to job duties and responsibilities
- Documentation of the appraisal activities
- Personal knowledge of and contact with each appraised individual
- Training of supervisors in conducting appraisals
- A review process that prevents one manager, acting alone, from controlling an employee's career
- Counseling to help poor performers improve

Of course, having all these components is no guarantee against lawsuits. However, including them does improve the chance of winning lawsuits that might be filed.

10-4a Supervisory Rating of Subordinates

The most widely used means of rating employees is based on the assumption that the immediate supervisor is the person most qualified to evaluate an employee's performance realistically and fairly. To help provide accurate evaluations, some supervisors keep records of employees performance so that they can reference these notes when rating performance. For instance, a sales manager might periodically observe a salesperson's interactions with clients and make notes so that constructive performance feedback can be provided at a later date. Training supervisors to do observation and evaluation well improves the process.[27]

10-4b Employee Rating of Managers

A number of organizations ask employees to rate the performance of their immediate managers. A variation of this type of rating takes place in colleges and universities, where students evaluate the teaching effectiveness of professors in the classroom. Another example is an Indian firm, which requires employees to rate their bosses as part of a multisource review process. All evaluations are then posted on the company's intranet. These performance appraisal ratings are generally used for management development purposes.

Having employees rate managers provides three primary advantages. First, in critical manager–employee relationships, employee ratings can be quite useful for identifying competent managers. The rating of leaders by combat soldiers is one example of such a use. Second, this type of rating program can help make a manager more responsive to employees. This advantage can quickly become a disadvantage if the manager focuses on being "nice" rather than on managing; people who are pleasant, but have no other qualifications may not be good managers in many situations. Finally, employee appraisals can contribute to career development efforts for managers by identifying areas for growth.

A major disadvantage of having employees rate managers is the negative reaction many have to being evaluated by employees. Also, the fear of reprisals may be too great for employees to give realistic ratings. This may prompt workers to rate their managers based solely on the way they are treated rather than on critical job requirements. The problems associated with this appraisal approach limit its usefulness to certain situations, including managerial development and improvement efforts.[28]

10-4c Team/Peer Rating

Having employees and team members rate each other is another type of appraisal with the potential to both help and hurt. Peer and team ratings are especially useful when supervisors do not have the opportunity to observe each employee's performance, but work group members do. For instance, some of the advanced training programs in the U.S. military use peer ratings to provide candidates extensive feedback about their leadership qualities and accomplishments. Peer evaluations are also common in collegiate schools of business where professors commonly require students to conduct peer evaluations after the completion of group-based projects. One challenge of this approach is obtaining ratings for virtual or global teams, in which the individuals work primarily through technology, not in person (i.e., an online college class). Another challenge is obtaining ratings from and for individuals who are on many special project teams throughout the year.

It is possible that any performance appraisal, including team/peer ratings, can negatively affect teamwork and participative management efforts. Although team members have good information on one another's performance, they may not choose to share it in the interest of sparing feelings; alternatively, they may unfairly attack other group members. Some organizations attempt to overcome such problems by using anonymous appraisals and/or having a consultant or HR manager interpret team/peer ratings.

10-4d Self-Rating

Self-appraisal works in certain situations.[29] As a self-development tool, it requires employees to think about their strengths and weaknesses and set goals for improvement.[30] Employees working in isolation or possessing unique skills may be particularly suited for self-ratings because they are the only ones qualified to rate themselves. Overall, the use of self-appraisals in organizations has increased. For instance, one organization successfully incorporated self-ratings into a traditional rating approach that did not generate enough dialogue and direction for individual development; reactions from both workers and supervisors were favorable.

However, employees may use quite different standards and not rate themselves in the same manner as supervisors. Research exploring whether people might be more lenient or more demanding when rating themselves is mixed, with self-ratings being frequently higher than supervisory ratings. Still, employee self-ratings can be a useful source of performance information for development.[31]

10-4e Outsider Rating

People outside the immediate work group may be asked to participate in performance reviews. This "field review" approach can include someone from the HR department as a reviewer, or completely independent reviewers from outside the organization. Examples include a review team evaluating a college president or a panel of division managers evaluating a supervisor's potential for advancement in the company. A disadvantage of this approach is that outsiders may not know the important demands within the work group or organization.

The customers or clients of an organization are good sources for outside appraisals. For sales and service jobs, customers may provide useful input on the performance behaviors of employees. For instance, many hospitality organizations such as restaurants and hotels use customer comments cards or secret shoppers to gather feedback about the service provided by customer contact personnel, and this information is commonly used for job development purposes.

LO4 Describe the advantages and disadvantages of multisource (360-degree) appraisals.

10-4f Multisource/360-Degree Rating

Multisource rating, or 360-degree feedback, has grown in popularity. Multisource feedback recognizes that for many jobs, employee performance is multidimensional and crosses departmental, organizational, and even national boundaries. Therefore, information needs to be collected from many sources to adequately and fairly evaluate an incumbent's performance in one of these jobs.[32]

The major purpose of 360-degree feedback is *not* to increase uniformity by soliciting like-minded views. Instead, it is designed to capture evaluations of the employee's different roles to provide richer feedback during an evaluation. Figure 10-7 shows some of the parties who can be involved in 360-degree feedback. For example, an HR manager for an insurance firm deals with seven regional sales managers, HR

FIGURE 10-7 Multisource Appraisal

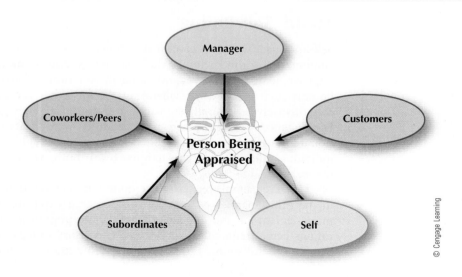

© Cengage Learning

administrators in five claims centers, and various corporate executives in finance, legal, and information technology. The Vice President of HR uses 360-degree feedback to gather data on all facets of the HR manager's job before completing a performance appraisal on the individual. Similar examples can be cited in numerous managerial, professional, technical, operational, and administrative jobs.

Significant administrative time and paperwork are required to request, obtain, and summarize feedback from multiple raters. Using electronic systems for the information can greatly reduce the administrative demands of multisource ratings and increase the effectiveness (i.e., privacy and expediency) of the process.

Developmental Use of Multisource Feedback As originally designed and used, multisource feedback focuses on the use of appraisals for the development of individuals. Conflict resolution skills, decision-making abilities, team effectiveness, communication skills, managerial styles, and technical capabilities are just some of the developmental areas that can be evaluated. It is widely believed that 360-degree feedback is more useful in a personal growth system than in an administrative system, although more use is appearing in administrative systems.[33]

Administrative Use of Multisource Feedback The popularity of 360-degree feedback systems has led to the results being used for compensation, promotion, termination, and other administrative decisions. When using 360-degree feedback for administrative purposes, managers must anticipate the potential problems.[34] Differences among raters can present a challenge, especially when using 360-degree ratings for discipline or pay decisions. Bias can just as easily be rooted in customers, subordinates, and peers as in a boss, and the lack of accountability of those sources can affect the ratings. "Inflation" of ratings is common when the sources know that their input will affect someone's pay or career. At one manufacturing firm, the apparent back scratching associated with multisource reviews led the company to drop the program. Also, issues of confidentiality and anonymity have led to lawsuits. Even though multisource approaches offer possible solutions to some of the well-documented dissatisfaction associated with performance appraisals, a number of other questions have arisen as multisource appraisals have become more common.

Evaluating Multisource Feedback Research on multisource/360-degree feedback has revealed both positives and negatives. More variability than expected may be seen in the ratings given by the different sources. Thus, supervisor ratings may need to carry more weight than peer or subordinate input to resolve the differences. One concern is that those peers who rate poor-performing coworkers tend to inflate the ratings so that the peers themselves can get higher overall evaluation results in return.

Another concern is whether 360-degree appraisals improve the process or simply multiply the number of problems by the number of raters.[35] Also, some wonder whether multisource appraisals really create sufficiently better decisions to offset the additional time and investment required. These issues appear to be less threatening when the 360-degree feedback is used *only for development*, so companies should consider using multisource feedback primarily as a developmental tool to enhance future job performance while minimizing the use of multisource appraisals as an administrative tool.

10-5 ■ TOOLS FOR APPRAISING PERFORMANCE

Performance can be appraised by a number of methods. Some employers use one method for all jobs and employees, some use different methods for different groups of employees, and others use a combination of methods.[36] The following discussion highlights different tools that can be used, as well as some of the advantages and disadvantages of each approach.

10-5a Category Scaling Methods

The simplest methods for appraising performance are category scaling methods, which require a manager to mark an employee's level of performance on a specific form divided into categories of performance. A *checklist* uses a list of statements or words from which raters check statements that are most representative of the characteristics and performance of employees. Often, a scale indicating perceived level of accomplishment on each statement is included with the checklist, which then becomes a type of graphic rating scale.

10-5b Graphic Rating Scales

Graphic rating scale
Scale that allows the rater to mark an employee's performance on a continuum.

The **graphic rating scale** allows the rater to mark an employee's performance on a continuum indicating low to high levels of a particular characteristic. Because of the straightforwardness of the process, graphic rating scales are common in performance evaluations. Figure 10-8 shows a sample appraisal form that combines graphic rating scales with essays. Three aspects of performance can be appraised using graphic rating scales: *descriptive categories* (such as quantity of work, attendance, and dependability), *job duties* (taken from the job description), and *behavioral dimensions* (such as decision making, employee development, and communication effectiveness).

Each of these types can be used for different jobs. How well employees meet established standards is often expressed either numerically (e.g., 5, 4, 3, 2, 1) or verbally (e.g., "outstanding," "meets standards," "below standards"). If two or more people are involved in the rating, they may find it difficult to agree on the exact level of performance achieved relative to the standard in evaluating employee performance. Notice that each level specifies performance standards or expectations to reduce variation in interpretations of the standards by different supervisors and employees.

Concerns with Graphic Rating Scales Graphic rating scales in many forms are widely used because they are easy to develop and provide a uniform set of criteria to evaluate the job performance of different employees. However, the use of scales can cause rater error because the form might not accurately reflect the relative importance of certain job characteristics, and some factors might need to be added to the ratings for one employee, while others might need to be dropped. If they fit the person and the job, the scales work well. However, if they fit poorly, managers and employees who must use them might complain about "the rating form."

Another concern is that regardless of the scales used, the focus should be on the job duties and responsibilities identified in job descriptions. The closer the link between the scales and what people actually do, as identified in current and complete job descriptions, the stronger the relationship between the ratings

FIGURE 10-8 Sample Performance Appraisal Form

Date sent: 4/19/14   Return by: 5/01/2014

Name: Joe Hernandez   Job title: Receiving Clerk

Department: Receiving   Supervisor: Marian Williams

Employment status (check one): Full-time ___X___ Part-time _____   Date of hire: 5/12/02

Rating period: From: 4/30/13   To: 4/30/14

Reason for appraisal (check one): Regular interval _X_   Introductory ____   Counseling only ____   Discharge ____

Using the following definitions, rate the performance as I, M, or E.

I—Performance is below job requirements and **improvement is needed.**

M—Performance **meets** job requirements and standards.

E—Performance **exceeds** job requirements and standards **most** of the time.

SPECIFIC JOB RESPONSIBILITIES: List the prinicipal activities from the job summary, rate the performance on each job duty by placing an X on the rating scale at the appropriate location, and make appropriate comments to explain the rating.

I ———————————————— M ———————————— E

Job Duty #1: Inventory receiving and checking
Explanation: _____
_____

I ———————————————— M ———————————— E

Job Duty #2: Accurate record keeping
Explanation: _____
_____

I ———————————————— M ———————————— E

Attendance (including absences and tardies):   Number of absences ____   Number of tardies ____
Explanation: _____
_____

Overall rating: In the box provided, place the letter—**I, M, or E**—that best describes the employee's overall performance.

Explanation: _____
_____

and the job, as viewed by employees and managers. Also, should the performance appraisal results be challenged legally, the closer performance appraisals measure what people actually do, the more likely employers are to prevail in a lawsuit.

An additional drawback to graphic rating scales is that separate traits or factors are often grouped, and the rater is given only one box to check. For example, *dependability* could refer to meeting deadlines for reports, or it could refer to attendance and tardiness. If a supervisor gives an employee a rating of 3, which aspect of dependability is being rated? One supervisor might rate employees on meeting deadlines, while another rates employees on attendance.

Another drawback is that the descriptive words sometimes used in scales may have different meanings to different raters. Terms such as *initiative* and *cooperation* are subject to many interpretations, especially if used in conjunction with words such as *outstanding*, *average*, and *poor*. As Figure 10-9 shows, scale points can be defined carefully to minimize misinterpretation.

Behavioral Rating Scales In an attempt to overcome some of the concerns with graphic rating scales, employers may use behavioral rating scales designed to assess individual actions instead of personal attributes and characteristics. Different approaches are used, but all describe specific examples of employee job behaviors. In a **behaviorally anchored rating scale** (BARS), these examples are "anchored" or measured against a scale of performance levels.

When creating a BARS system, identifying important *job dimensions*, which are the most important performance factors in a job description, is done first. Short statements describe both desirable and undesirable behaviors (anchors). These are then "translated," or assigned, to one of the job dimensions. Anchor statements are usually developed by a group of people familiar with the job. The group then assigns each anchor a number that represents how effective or ineffective the behavior is, and the anchors are fitted to a scale. Figure 10-10 contains an example that rates customer service skills for individuals taking orders for a national catalog retailer. Spelling out the behaviors associated with each level of performance helps minimize some of the problems related to graphic rating scales.

Several problems are associated with the behavioral approach. First, creating and maintaining behaviorally anchored rating scales requires extensive time and

Behaviorally Anchored Rating Scale
Scales describe specific examples of job behavior, which are then measured against a performance scale.

FIGURE 10-9 Sample Terms for Defining Standards

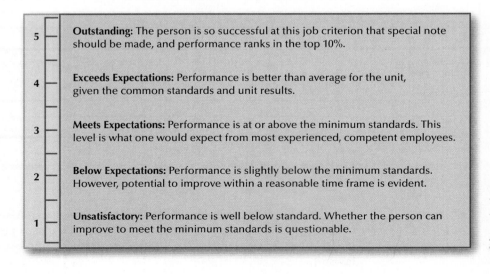

5 — **Outstanding:** The person is so successful at this job criterion that special note should be made, and performance ranks in the top 10%.

4 — **Exceeds Expectations:** Performance is better than average for the unit, given the common standards and unit results.

3 — **Meets Expectations:** Performance is at or above the minimum standards. This level is what one would expect from most experienced, competent employees.

2 — **Below Expectations:** Performance is slightly below the minimum standards. However, potential to improve within a reasonable time frame is evident.

1 — **Unsatisfactory:** Performance is well below standard. Whether the person can improve to meet the minimum standards is questionable.

© Cengage Learning

FIGURE 10-10 Behaviorally Anchored Rating Scale for Customer Service Skills

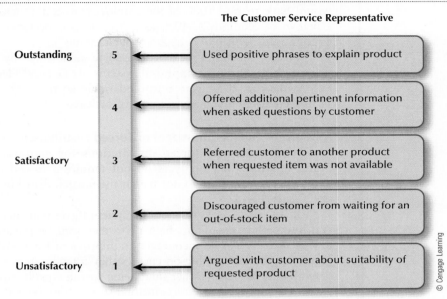

The Customer Service Representative

Outstanding	5	Used positive phrases to explain product
	4	Offered additional pertinent information when asked questions by customer
Satisfactory	3	Referred customer to another product when requested item was not available
	2	Discouraged customer from waiting for an out-of-stock item
Unsatisfactory	1	Argued with customer about suitability of requested product

© Cengage Learning

effort. In addition, many appraisal forms are needed to accommodate different types of jobs in an organization. For instance, because nurses, dietitians, and admissions clerks in a hospital all have distinct job descriptions, a separate BARS form needs to be developed for each position.

10-5c Comparative Methods

Comparative methods require that managers directly compare the performance levels of their employees against one another, and these comparisons can provide useful information for performance management. An example of this process would be an information systems supervisor comparing the performance of one programmer with that of other programmers. Comparative techniques include ranking and forced distribution.

Ranking
Performance appraisal method in which all employees are listed from highest to lowest in performance.

Ranking The **ranking** method lists the individuals being rated from highest to lowest based on their performance levels and relative contributions. One disadvantage of this process is that the sizes of the performance differences between employees are often not clearly indicated. For example, the job performance of individuals ranked second and third may differ little, while the performance of those ranked third and fourth differ a great deal. This limitation can be mitigated to some extent by assigning points to indicate performance differences. Ranking also means someone must be last, which ignores the possibility that the last-ranked individual in one group might be equal to the top-ranked employee in a different group. Further, the ranking task becomes unwieldy if the group of employees to be ranked is large.

Forced distribution
Performance appraisal method in which ratings of employees' performance levels are distributed along a bell-shaped curve.

Forced Distribution Forced distribution is a technique for distributing ratings that are generated with any of the other appraisal methods and comparing the ratings of people in a work group. With the **forced distribution** method, the ratings of employees' performance may be distributed along a bell-shaped curve.[37]

For example, a medical clinic administrator ranking employees on a 5-point scale would have to rate 10% of the employees as a 1 ("unsatisfactory"), 20% as a 2 ("below expectations"), 40% as a 3 ("meets expectations"), 20% as a 4 ("above expectations"), and 10% as a 5 ("outstanding").

Forced distribution has been used in some form by an estimated 30% of all firms with performance appraisal systems. At General Electric, the managers identified as the top 20% were rewarded richly so that few would leave. The bottom 10% were given a chance to improve or leave.

Advantages and Disadvantages of Forced Distribution One reason why firms have mandated the use of forced distributions for appraisal ratings is to deal with "rater inflation."If employers do not require a forced distribution, performance appraisal ratings often do not match the normal distribution of a bell-shaped curve (see Figure 10-11).

The use of a forced distribution system forces managers to identify high, average, and low performers. Thus, high performers can be rewarded and developed, while low performers can be encouraged to improve or leave. Advocates of forced ranking argue that forced distribution ensures that compensation increases truly are differentiated by performance rather than being spread equally among all employees.

But the forced distribution method suffers from several drawbacks.[38] Perhaps in a truly exceptional group of employees there is not 10% who are unsatisfactory. Another one problem is that a supervisor may resist placing any individual in the lowest (or the highest) group. Difficulties also arise when the rater must explain to an employee why he or she was placed in one group while others were placed in higher groups. In some cases, the manager may make false distinctions between employees. By comparing people against each other, rather than against a standard of job performance, supervisors trying to fill the percentages may end up giving employees

FIGURE 10-11 **Forced Distribution on a Bell-Shaped Curve**

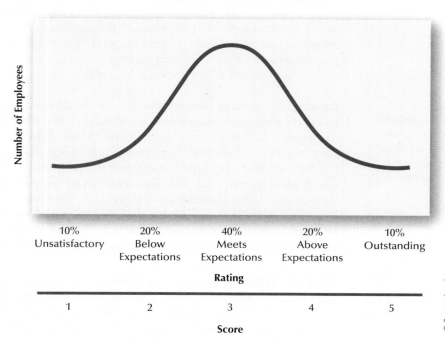

very subjective ratings.[39] Finally, forced ranking structures can increase anxiety in employees, promote conformity, and encourage gaming of the system. Consequently, a number of firms have been involved in lawsuits about forced distribution performance appraisal processes.

10-5d Narrative Methods

Managers may be required to provide written appraisal narratives. Some appraisal methods are entirely written, rather than using predetermined rating scales or ranking structures. Documentation and descriptive text are the basic components of the critical incident and essay methods.

Critical Incident In the critical incident method, the manager keeps a written record of both favorable and unfavorable actions performed by an employee during the entire rating period. When a critical incident involving an employee occurs, the manager writes it down. For instance, when a sales clerk at a clothing store spends considerable time with a customer helping him purchase a new suit, a manager might document this exceptional service for later review during an annual evaluation. The critical incident method can be used with other approaches to document the reasons why an employee was given a certain rating.

Essay The essay method requires a manager to write a short essay describing each employee's performance during the rating period. Some free-form essays are without guidelines; others are more structured, using prepared questions that must be answered. The rater usually categorizes comments under a few general headings. The essay method allows the rater more flexibility than other methods do, sometimes too much. As a result, appraisers often combine the essay with other methods.

The effectiveness of the essay approach often depends on a supervisor's writing and observation skills. Some supervisors do not express themselves well in writing and as a result produce poor descriptions of employee performance, whereas others have excellent writing skills and can create highly positive impressions of their employees. If well composed, essays can provide highly detailed and useful information about an employees' job performance.[40]

10-5e Management by Objectives

Management by objectives (MBO)
Performance appraisal method that specifies the performance goals that an individual and manager identify together.

Management by objectives (MBO) specifies the performance goals that an individual and manager identify together. Goal setting has been extensively researched.[41] Each manager sets objectives derived from the overall goals and objectives of the organization; however, MBO should not be a disguised means for a superior to dictate the objectives of individual managers or employees. Other names for MBO include *appraisal by results*, *target coaching*, *work planning and review*, *performance objective setting*, and *mutual goal setting*.

MBO Process Implementing a guided self-appraisal system using MBO is a four-stage process. The stages are as follows:

1. *Job review and agreement*: The employee and the superior review the job description and the key activities that constitute the employee's job. The idea is to agree on the exact makeup of the job.
2. *Development of performance standards*: Together, the employee and his or her superior develop specific standards of performance and determine a satisfactory

level of performance that is specific and measurable. For example, a quota of selling five cars a month may be an appropriate performance standard for a salesperson.

3. *Setting of objectives*: Together, the employee and the superior establish objectives that are realistically attainable.

4. *Continuing performance discussions*: The employee and the superior use the objectives as a basis for continuing discussions about the employee's performance. Although a formal review session may be scheduled, the employee and the supervisor do not necessarily wait until the appointed time to discuss performance. Objectives can be mutually modified as warranted.

The MBO process seems to be most useful with managerial personnel and employees who have a fairly wide range of flexibility and control over their jobs. When imposed on a rigid and autocratic management system, MBO will often fail. Emphasizing penalties for not meeting objectives defeats the development and participative nature of MBO.

10-5f Combinations of Methods

No single appraisal method is best for all situations, so a performance measurement system that uses a combination of methods may be sensible. Using combinations may offset some of the advantages and disadvantages of individual methods. Category scaling methods are easy to develop, but they usually do little to measure strategic accomplishments. Further, they may make inter-rater reliability problems worse. Comparative approaches help reduce leniency and other errors, which makes them useful for administrative decisions such as determining pay raises. But comparative approaches do a poor job of linking performance to organizational goals, and by themselves do not provide feedback for improvement as well as other methods do.

Narrative methods work well for development because they potentially generate more feedback information. However, without good definitions of performance criteria or standards, they can be so unstructured as to be of little value for administrative uses. The MBO approach works well to link performance to organizational goals, but it can require much effort and time for defining objectives and explaining the process to employees. Narrative and MBO approaches may not work as well for lower-level jobs as for positions with more varied duties and responsibilities.

When managers can articulate what they want a performance appraisal system to accomplish, they can choose and mix methods to realize advantages of each approach. For example, one combination might include a graphic rating scale of performance on major job criteria, a narrative for developmental needs, and an overall ranking of employees in a department. Different categories of employees (e.g., salaried exempt, salaried nonexempt, maintenance, etc.) might require different combinations of methods.

LO5 Discuss the importance of training managers and employees on performance appraisal, and give examples of rater errors.

10-6 ■ TRAINING MANAGERS AND EMPLOYEES IN PERFORMANCE APPRAISAL

Court decisions on the legality of performance appraisals and research on appraisal effectiveness both stress the importance of training managers and employees on performance management and conducting evaluations.

For employees, performance appraisal training focuses on the purposes of appraisal, the appraisal process and timing, and how performance criteria and standards are linked to job duties and responsibilities. Most systems can be improved by training supervisors in how to do performance appraisals. Since conducting the appraisals is important, training should center around minimizing rater errors and providing raters with details on documenting performance information. Training is essential for those who have recently been promoted to managerial jobs and conducting performance appraisals is a new experience for them. Managers with informed positive views of the performance appraisal system are more likely to use the system effectively. Unfortunately, such training occurs only sporadically or not at all in many organizations.

Without training, managers and supervisors often "repeat the past," meaning that they appraise others much as they have been appraised in the past. The following list is not comprehensive, but it does identify some topics to be covered in appraisal training for managers:

- Appraisal process and timing
- Performance criteria and job standards that should be considered
- How to communicate positive and negative feedback
- When and how to discuss training and development goals
- Conducting and discussing the compensation review
- How to avoid common rating errors

10-6a Rater Errors

There are many possible sources of error in the performance appraisal process. One of the major sources is the rater. Although completely eliminating errors is impossible, making raters aware of potential errors and biases helps.

Varying Standards When appraising employees, a manager should avoid applying different standards and expectations to employees performing the same or similar jobs. Such problems often result from the use of ambiguous criteria and subjective weightings by supervisors.

Recency and Primacy Effects The **recency effect** occurs when a rater gives greater weight to recent events when appraising an individual's performance. Examples include giving a student a course grade on the basis of only the student's performance in the last week of class or giving a drill press operator a high rating even though the operator made the assigned quota only in the last two weeks of the rating period. Another time related issue is the **primacy effect**, which occurs when a rater gives greater weight to information received first when appraising an individual's performance.

Central Tendency, Leniency, and Strictness Errors Ask students, and they will tell you which professors tend to grade easier or harder. A manager may develop a similar *rating pattern*. Appraisers who rate all employees within a narrow range in the middle of the scale (i.e., rate everyone as "average") commit a **central tendency error**, giving even outstanding and poor performers an "average" rating.[42]

Rating patterns also may exhibit leniency or strictness. The **leniency error** occurs when ratings of all employees fall at the high end of the scale. To avoid conflict, managers often rate employees higher than they should. This "ratings boost" is especially likely when no manager or HR representative reviews the completed appraisals. The **strictness error** occurs when a manager uses only the lower part of the scale to rate employees.

Recency effect
Occurs when a rater gives greater weight to recent events when appraising an individual's performance.

Primacy effect
Occurs when a rater gives greater weight to information received first when appraising an individual's performance.

Central tendency error
Occurs when a rater gives all employees a score within a narrow range in the middle of the scale.

Leniency error
Occurs when ratings of all employees fall at the high end of the scale.

Strictness error
Occurs when ratings of all employees fall at the low end of the scale.

Rater bias
Occurs when a rater's values or prejudices distort the rating.

Rater Bias When a rater's values or prejudices distort the rating, **rater bias** occurs. Such bias may be unconscious or quite intentional. For example, a manager's dislike of certain ethnic groups may cause distortion in appraisal information for some people. Use of age, religion, seniority, sex, appearance, or other "classifications" may also skew appraisal ratings if the appraisal process is not properly designed. A review of appraisal ratings by higher-level managers may help correct this problem.

Halo effect
Occurs when a rater scores an employee high on all job criteria because of performance in one area.

Horns effect
Occurs when a low rating on one characteristic leads to an overall low rating.

Halo and Horns Effects The **halo effect** occurs when a rater scores an employee high on all job criteria because of performance in one area.[43] For example, if a worker has few absences, the supervisor might give the worker a high rating in all other areas of work, including quantity and quality of output, without really thinking about the employee's other characteristics separately. The opposite is the **horns effect**, which occurs when a low rating on one characteristic leads to an overall low rating.

Contrast error
Tendency to rate people relative to others rather than against performance standards.

Contrast Error Rating should be done using established standards. One problem is the **contrast error**, which is the tendency to rate people relative to one another rather than against performance standards. For example, if everyone else performs at a mediocre level, then a person performing only slightly better may be rated as "excellent" because of the contrast effect. But in a group where many employees are performing well, the same person might receive a lower rating. Although it may be appropriate to compare people at times, the performance rating usually should reflect comparison against performance standards, not against other people.

Similar-to-Me/Different-from-Me Errors Sometimes, raters are influenced by whether people show characteristics that are the same as or different from their own.[44] For example, a manager with an MBA degree might give subordinates with MBAs higher appraisals than those with only bachelor's degrees. The error comes in measuring an individual against another person rather than measuring how well the individual fulfills the expectations of the job.

Sampling Error If the rater has seen only a small sample of the person's work, an appraisal may be subject to sampling error. For example, assume that 95% of the reports prepared by an employee have been satisfactory, but a manager has seen only the 5% that had errors. If the supervisor rates the person's performance as "poor," then a sampling error has occurred. Ideally, the work being rated should be a broad and representative sample of all the work completed by the employee.

LO6 Identify several concerns about appraisal feedback and ways to make it more effective.

10-7 ■ APPRAISAL FEEDBACK

After completing appraisals, managers need to communicate results to give employees a clear understanding of how they compare to performance standards and organizations expectations. Organizations commonly require managers to discuss appraisals with employees. The appraisal feedback interview provides an opportunity to clear up any misunderstandings on both sides. In this interview, the manager should focus on coaching and development as well, and not just tell the employee, "Here is how you rate and why."[45]

10-7a The Appraisal Interview

The appraisal interview presents both an opportunity and a challenge. It can be an emotional experience for the manager and the employee because the manager must communicate both praise and constructive criticism. A major concern for managers is how to emphasize the positive aspects of the employee's performance while still discussing ways to make needed improvements. If the interview is handled poorly, the employee may feel resentment, which could lead to future performance problems. Consequently, a manager should identify how employees add value to the organization and show appreciation when employees make valuable contributions.[46] When poor performance must be discussed, managers might consider using a "self-auditing" approach that relies on questions that encourage employees to identify their own performance deficiencies.

Employees usually approach an appraisal interview with some concern. They may feel that discussions about performance are both personal and important to their continued job success. At the same time, they want to know how their managers view their performance. Figure 10-12 summarizes hints for an effective appraisal interview for supervisors and managers.

10-7b Reactions of Managers and Employees

Managers who must complete evaluations of their employees often resist the appraisal process.[47] Many feel that their role requires them to assist, encourage, coach, and counsel employees to improve their performance. However, being a judge on the one hand and a coach and a counselor on the other hand may cause internal conflict.

Knowing that appraisals may affect employees' future careers may also cause altered or biased ratings. This problem is even more likely when managers know that they will have to communicate and defend their ratings to the employees, their bosses, or HR specialists. Managers can simply make the employee's ratings positive and avoid unpleasantness. But avoidance helps no one. A manager *owes* an employee a well-done appraisal, no matter how difficult an employee is, or how difficult the conversation about performance might be.

FIGURE 10-12 Appraisal Interview Hints for Appraisers

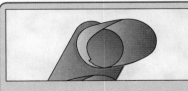

DO	DO NOT
◆ Prepare before interview	◆ Talk too much
◆ Focus on objective performance	◆ Berate or lecture the employee
◆ Be specific about ratings and feedback	◆ Focus entirely on negative job performance
◆ Develop a future improvement plan	◆ Think that the employee always has to agree
◆ Reinforce employee successes	◆ Compare the employee with others

© Cengage Learning

Employees may well see the appraisal process as a threat and feel that the only way for them to get a higher rating is for someone else to receive a low rating. This win–lose perception is encouraged by comparative methods of rating. Emphasis on the self-improvement and developmental aspects of appraisal appears to be the most effective way to reduce this reaction.[48]

Another common employee reaction resembles students' response to tests. A professor may prepare a test that she perceives to be fair, but students may see it differently. Likewise, employees being appraised may not necessarily agree with the manager doing the appraising. However, in most cases, employees will view appraisals done well as what they are meant to be—constructive feedback. Many employees want appraisals, but some may find it difficult to get honest feedback.[49]

10-7c Effective Performance Management

Regardless of the approach used, managers must understand the intended outcome of performance management.[50] When performance management is genuinely used to develop employees as resources, it usually works. When a key part of performance management, the performance appraisal, is used to punish employees, performance management is less effective. In its simplest form performance appraisal is the observation: "Here are your strengths and weaknesses, and here is a way to develop for the future."

Done well, performance management can lead to higher employee motivation and satisfaction. To be effective, a performance management system, including the performance appraisal processes, should be:

- beneficial as a development tool
- useful as an administrative tool
- legal and job related
- viewed as generally fair by employees
- effective in documenting employee performance
- Clear about who are high, average, and low performers

SUMMARY

- Performance management systems attempt to identify, measure, communicate, develop, and reward employee performance.
- Performance management has a broad organizational focus, whereas performance appraisals are the processes used to evaluate how employees perform their jobs and then communicate that information to employees.
- Effective performance management has a number of components, beginning with a performance-focused organizational culture.
- Job criteria identify important elements of a job, and affect the establishment of performance standards.
- Federal employment guidelines and court decisions influence the performance appraisal process.

- Appraising employee performance serves both administrative and developmental purposes.
- Performance appraisals can be done either informally or systematically.
- Appraisals can be conducted by superiors, employees (rating superiors or themselves), teams, outsiders, or other sources.
- Appraisal methods include category scaling, graphic rating scales, comparative, narrative, and management by objectives.
- Graphic rating scales and behavioral rating scales are widely used.
- Comparative methods include ranking and forced distribution, both of which raise methodological and legal concerns.

- Narrative methods include the critical incident technique and the essay approach.
- Training managers and employees on how to conduct performance appraisals can contribute to the effectiveness of a performance management system.

- Many performance appraisal problems are caused by a number of different rater errors.
- The appraisal feedback interview is a vital part of any appraisal system, and the reactions of both managers and employees must be considered when evaluating the system.

CRITICAL THINKING CHALLENGES

1. Describe how an organizational culture and the use of performance criteria and standards affect the remaining components of a performance management system.

2. Suppose you are a supervisor. What errors might you make when preparing the performance appraisal on a clerical employee? How might you avoid those errors?

3. Based on your experiences, as well as the chapter information, what are some good "rules of thumb" for conducting successful performance appraisal interviews?

4. Review the performance appraisal process and appraisal form used by a current or former employer, and compare them with those provided by other students. Also review other appraisal issues by going to www.workforce .com and searching for articles on *performance appraisals*. Develop a report suggesting changes to make the performance

appraisal form and process you reviewed more effective.

5. As the new HR Director of a company in the behavioral health industry, you have the responsibility to develop a performance management system. You need to present a business case to senior executives that the performance management system does not stand alone and must be integrated into the company's strategic plan, business needs, and measurements. For information on performance management best practices, review various publications in the articles tab at www.insala.com.

A. Given several key practices for a successful performance management system, which ones should be implemented first?

B. Identify key measurements to transition the company from the current system of looking at personality factors to a new system of looking at performance factors.

CASE

Performance Management at Netflix

Netflix has a unique approach to the performance of its employees. It employs a culture with few rules and no tolerance for average or poor performers. Workers can earn top-of-the-market pay but no bonuses, development, training, or career planning. Vacation is at the discretion of the employee. The focus is on what people get done, not how many hours or days they worked. Netflix officials maintain that when employee discretion rules, employees can be trusted to do the right things. Reed Hastings, the CEO, says "We are more focused on the absence

of procedure—managing through talented people rather than a rule book."

There is no policy on vacation time. Workers decide, for example, how much vacation and sick leave to take. The only rules are being out sick for more than five days requires a doctor's excuse, and time-off beyond 30 days per year requires HR approval. The HR Director interviewed an applicant who expressed surprise at the vacation time approach. He said, "I am a workaholic and never take time off. I need someone to make sure I take my time or I won't use it." He was told, "We hire adults and if you do not know how to manage your vacations you won't fit in."

If someone does something wrong, they are told it was wrong. After that they either "get it" or they are gone. The CEO says, "We try to be fair, but the length of an employee's Netflix career is not our primary concern. If someone is not extraordinary we let them go." If a person is rated as average or mediocre during the performance review process, he or she is dismissed. The HR officer notes that really good workers get frustrated at working with average performers. They feel it is important to get rid of those who do not perform even though other companies often do not.

Annual 360-degree reviews provide "direct and honest feedback." Another HR official notes, "In many companies when I want you to leave, my job is to prove you're incompetent. Here I write a check. We exchange severance for a release." The company does not "coddle" employees and does not ask how someone

"feels." When they are dismissed people usually find new jobs quickly and to date no one has sued.

The culture is designed to initiate and maintain creativity. If efficiency was the goal, more structure and rules would be needed, the CEO notes. As the company gets bigger, it may be more difficult to allow the same amount of freedom. As one observer noted, 'Good people can do things and can be relied on to police themselves." The lack of rules coupled with a serious performance culture makes Netflix an interesting place to work.[51]

QUESTIONS

1. Would you find working at Netflix exciting or frightening? Why?

2. Can everyone in a company be above average? If so, how can you tell if someone is truly above average?

3. Are performance evaluations important in this culture?

SUPPLEMENTAL CASES

Performance Management Improvements for Bristol-Myers Squibb

This case identifies how performance management systems might be redesigned. (For the case, go to www.cengage.com/management/mathis.)

Building Performance through Employee Participation

The case outlines what was done at Jewelers Mutual Insurance in allowing employees to have a say in

performance management. (For the case, go to www.cengage.com/management/mathis.)

Unequal/Equal Supervisors

This case identifies the consequences of giving appraisal ratings that may not be accurate. (For the case, go to www.cengage.com/management/mathis.)

NOTES

1. Adapted from Bob Campbell, et al., "Performance Management: Rewired for Recovery," *Workspan*, 07/2010, 42–48.

2. Paul Falcone, "Held Hostage by Underperformers," *HR Magazine*, October 2012, 92–93.

3. Andrew R. McIlvaine, "There's Got to Be a Better Way," *Human Resource Executive*, July/August 2012, 13–15. Samuel A. Culbert, "The Case for Killing Performance Reviews," *Human Resource Executive Online*, July 16, 2012, 1–2.

4. Jonathan A. Segal, "Performance Management Blunders," *HR Magazine*, November 2010, 75–77.

5. Jamie A. Gruman and Alan M. Saks, "Performance Management and Employee Engagement," *Human*

Resource Management Review, (2011), 21, 123–136.

6. Michael Cohn, "6 Steps to Manager Performance," *Employee Benefit News,* October 2011, 12–13.

7. Hao-Chieh Lin and Sheng-Tsung Hov, "Managerial Lessons from the East," *The Academy of Management Perspectives,* November 2010, 24, 6–16.

8. Giovanni Azzone and Tommaso Palermo, "Adopting Performance Appraisal and Reward Systems," *Journal of Organizational Change Management,* 2011, 24, 90–111.

9. Jake C. Messersmith et al., "Unlocking the Black Box: Exploring the Link Between High Performance Work Systems and Performance," *Journal of Applied Psychology,* 2011, 96, 1105–1118.

10. Y. Gong, et al., "Human Resource Management and Firm Performance," *Journal of Applied Psychology,* 2009, 94, 263–275.

11. Angelo S. Denisi, "Managing Performance to Change Behavior," *Journal of Organizational Behavior Management,* 2011, 31, 262–276.

12. Angela R. Connell and Satoris S. Culbertson, "Eye of the Beholder: Does What Is Important about a Job Depend on Who Is Asked?", The Academy of Management Perspectives, May 2010, 24, 83–84.

13. Dan Ariely, "You Are What You Measure," *Harvard Business Review,* June 2010, 38.

14. James Broadbent and Richard Laughlin, "Performance Management Systems: A Conceptual Model," *Management Accounting Research,* 2009, 20, 283–295.

15. Stephanie Banchero, "Illinois Attempts to Link Teacher Tenure to Results," *The Wall Street Journal,* January 4, 2011, A3.

16. Rebecca R. Hastings, "Most Large Companies Calibrate Performance Pool Finds," *HR Magazine,* February 2012, 87.

17. Andrew Likierman, "The 5 Traps of Performance Measurement," *Harvard Business Review,* October 2009, 96–101.

18. Michelle Brown, et al., "Consequences of the Performance Appraisal Experience," *Personnel Review,* 2010, 39, 375–396.

19. Jeffrey Spence and Lisa Keeping, "Conscious Rating Distortion in Performance Appraisal," *Human Resource Management Review,* June 2011, 21, 85–95.

20. Based on Andrew McIlvaine, "There's Got to Be a Better Way," *Human Resource Executive,* July/August 2012, 14–18.

21. G. P. Sillup and R. Klimberg, "Assessing the Ethics of Implementing Performance Appraisal Systems," *The Journal of Management Development,* 2010, 29, 38–55.

22. Marie-Helene Budworth and Sara Mann, "Performance Management Where Do We Go From Here?", *Human Resource Management Review,* 2011, 21, 81–84.

23. Jochen Reb and Gary J. Greguras, "Understanding Performance Ratings: Dynamic Performance, Attributions, and Rating Purpose," *Journal of Applied Psychology,* 2010, 95, 213–220.

24. Dana Mattioli, et. al., "Bad Call: How Not to Fire a Worker," *The Wall Street Journal,* September 9, 2011, B1. Jathan Janove, "Reviews – Good for Anything?", *HR Magazine,* June 2011, 121–126.

25. Ann Pace, "A New Era in Performance Management," *T + D,* October 2011, 65, 10.

26. Jennifer Taylor Arnold, "Two Needs, One Solution," *HR Magazine,* May 2009, 75–77.

27. Stephanie C. Payne, et al., "Comparison of Online and Traditional Performance Appraisal Systems," *Journal of Management Psychology,* 2009, 24, 526–544.

28. Paul Rowson and Kip Kipley, "Tips to Help Managers Optimize Performance Appraisals," *Workspan,* October 2010, 28–33.

29. Barbara M. Moskal, "Self-Assessments: What Are their Valid Uses?", *Academy of Management Learning and Education,* June 2010, 9, 314–320.

30. Lawrence C. Bassett, "No Such Things as Perfect Performance Management," *Human Resource Executive,* September 16, 2012, 26, 6.

31. John W. Fleenor, et al., "Self-Other Ratings Agreement in Leadership: A Review," *The Leadership Quarterly,* 2010, 21, 1005–1034.

32. Dean Stamoulis, *Senior Executive Assessment* (West Sussex, UK, Wiley-Blackwell) 2009 and R. Lepsinger and A. D. Lucia, *The Art and Science of 360° Feedback,* 2nd Ed. (San Francisco, Pfeiffer) 2009.

33. Rainer Hensel, et al., "360° Feedback: How Many Raters Are Needed for Reliable Ratings?", *The International Journal of Human Resource Management,* 2010, 21, 2813–2830.

34. Tracy Maylett, "360 Degree Feedback Revisited: The Transition from Development to Appraisal," *Compensation and Benefits Review,* 2009, 1–8.

35. B. J. Hoffman and D. J. Woehr, "Disentangling the Meaning of Multisource Performance Ratings Source and Dimension Factors," *Personnel Psychology,* 2009, 62, 735–765.

36. James Smither and Manuel London (editors), *Performance Management: Putting Research Into Action* (San Francisco: Jossey-Bass) 20089, 297–328.

37. Dori Meinert, "A Crack in the Bell Curve," *HR Magazine,* April 2012, 22.

38. Deidra J. Schleicher et al., "Rater Reactions to Forced Distribution Rating Systems," *Journal of Management,* August 2009, 35, 899–927.

39. Susan M. Steward, "Forced Distribution Performance Evaluation Systems: Advantages, Disadvantages, and Keys to Implementation," *e Content Management,* March 2010, 16, 168–179. E. O'Boyle Jr. and J. Arguinis, "The Best and the Rest: Revisiting the Norm of Normality of Individual Performance," *Personnel Psychology,* 2012, 65, 79–119.

40. Stéphane Brutus, "Words versus Numbers: A Theoretical Exploration of Giving and Receiving Narrative Comments in Performance Appraisal," *Human Resource Management Review,* 2010, 20, 144–157.

41. Lisa D. Ordóñez, et al., "Goals Gone Wild: The Systematic Side Effects of Overprescribing Goal Setting," *Academy of Management Perspectives,* February 2009, 23, 6–16. E. A. Locke and Gary P. Latham, "Has Goal Setting Gone Wild or

Have Its Attackers Abandoned Good Scholarship?", *Academy of Management Perspectives*, February 2009, 23, 17–23. Osnat Bouskila-Yam and Avraham N. Kluger, "Strength Based Performance Appraisal and Goal Setting," *Human Resource Management Review*, 2011, 21, 1370–147. A. Kleingeld et al., "The Effect of Goal Setting on Group Performance: a Meta Analysis," *Journal of Applied Psychology*, 2011, 96, 1289–1304.

42. Jasmijn C. Bol, "The Determinants and Performance Effects of Managers' Performance Evaluation Biases," *Accounting Review*, September 2011, 86, 1549–1575.

43. K. NG, et al, "Rating Leniency and Halo in Multisource Feedback Ratings," *Journal of Applied Psychology*, 2011, 96, 1033–1044.

44. Peter A. Heslin and Don Vandervalle, "Performance Appraisal Procedural Justice," *Journal of Management*, November 2011, 37, 1694–1718.

45. Michael E. Gordon and Lea P. Stewart, "Conversing about Performance," *Management Communication Quarterly*, February 2009, 22, 473–501.

46. Adrienne Fox, "Curing What Ails Performance Reviews," *HR Magazine*, January 2009, 52–56.

47. Michael Rosenthal, "Performance Review 201," *Training*, July/August 2010, 44.

48. E. M. Mone and Manuel London, *Employee Engagement Through Effective Performance Management* (New York, NY, Taylor and Francis Group) 2009.

49. Robert S. Kaplan, "Top Executives Need Feedback: Here's How They Can Get It," *McKinsey Quarterly*, September 2011, 1–8.

50. Steve Browne, "HR Roundtable: Should Performance Reviews Live or Die?", *HR Roundtable*, November 17, 2011. Sbrowne@larosas.com

51. Based on Robert J. Grossman, "Tough Love at Netflix," *HR Magazine*, April 2010, 37–41.

© Hemera/Thinkstock

Compensation

11

Total Rewards and Compensation

Learning Objectives

After you have read this chapter, you should be able to:

1 Identify the three general components of total rewards and give examples of each.

2 Explain the major laws governing employee compensation.

3 Outline strategic compensation decisions.

4 Understand the challenges of managing global compensation systems.

5 Illustrate the steps in developing a base pay system.

6 Describe how individual pay rates are set.

HR HEADLINE

No Poaching Rules Leave High-Tech Employees Out in the Cold

Most Americans have voluntarily placed their names on a "Do Not Call" list to prevent unsolicited telemarketing calls. But a conspiracy among high-tech employers in Silicon Valley led to software engineers being placed on a "Do Not Cold Call" list without their knowledge, a situation that could hold down their compensation. The list didn't prevent telemarketers from calling; it prevented recruiters from calling to solicit them for potentially better jobs in the industry. It seems that many prominent high-tech companies (like Apple, Google, Pixar, and Intel) had agreed to restrict poaching from each other to stabilize compensation and limit turnover of highly skilled employees. The companies shared the names of their employees with each other and placed them on the restricted list. Some agreements went so far as to ban hiring employees who had, on their own, applied for work at a rival firm.

These secret agreements were widely instituted to eliminate salary "bidding wars" among the companies. Employees receiving job offers from a rival tech firm could use that as leverage to request a pay increase with the current employer. And rivals might be able to learn about another company's pay practices by interviewing employees from the firm.

The courts view this practice as a violation of antitrust legislation and a restraint of trade. Top level managers have been implicated in the agreements. The companies involved were connected with each other because many executives had overlapping board seats on other defendants' boards and worked closely with each other. While antitrust lawsuits usually involve the pricing and sale of products or services, the labor market and compensation are also governed by these regulations.

Decisions on the lawsuits have not been handed down. However companies are forewarned that limiting employee mobility, pay, and opportunity to freely move in the job market can be a dangerous and costly way to retain talented workers.[1]

Total rewards
Monetary and nonmonetary rewards provided by companies to attract, motivate, and retain employees.

To attract and retain high-quality talent, companies design reward packages that will appeal to a variety of people. Companies address pay and benefits with a **total rewards** philosophy. The total rewards package includes all forms of compensation, the monetary and nonmonetary rewards provided by a company to attract, motivate, and retain employees as shown in Figure 11-1. The effectiveness of the reward system depends on linking compensation to organizational objectives and strategies so that employees are encouraged to work in a manner that benefits the company and its stakeholders. For example, General Motors recently tied a portion of salaried employees' bonus pay to customer loyalty ratings in new car sales and after-sales transactions. The company has focused on retaining customers and building on repeat business and is rewarding engineers, vehicle designers, field representatives, and other workers for improving this organizational metric.[2]

An effective total rewards approach balances the interests and costs of the company with the needs and expectations of employees. This can be a difficult process. On one hand, compensation related costs represent one of the largest portions of total operating expenses in most companies. On the other hand, employees want

FIGURE 11-1 Total Rewards Components

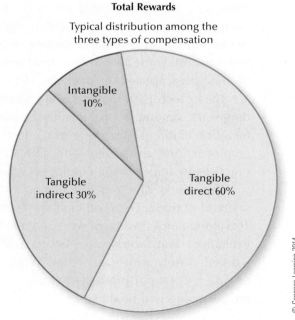

Total Rewards

Typical distribution among the three types of compensation

Intangible 10%

Tangible indirect 30%

Tangible direct 60%

© Cengage Learning 2014

to be compensated fairly and have their individual needs met. Employees continually make choices between spending more time at work or engaging in leisure activities. If compensation for working is not valued as highly as free time to pursue enjoyable activities, people will decide to work less and play more.[3] The challenge for the firm is to achieve an optimal relationship between costs and employee impact while considering many financial and operational factors.[4]

The concept of total rewards requires a much broader understanding of pay or compensation than has traditionally been the case in business organizations. A total rewards philosophy emphasizes how a company can use *both* tangible and intangible rewards to strengthen employee motivation and commitment, especially in challenging economic times.[5] Indeed, a lagging economy will likely require employers to make difficult but necessary adjustments to total rewards to reflect new business conditions. Broadly defining compensation should also help companies develop creative policies that keep employees motivated. Examples of creative compensation include concierge services at USAA, on-site child care at Yum! Brands, defensive driving classes for employees' dependents at Webb-Stiles Company, and paid sabbaticals at Intel.[6]

11-1 ■ NATURE OF TOTAL REWARDS AND COMPENSATION

LO1 Identify the three general components of total rewards and give examples of each.

Since labor represents such a major cost item to companies, top management and HR executives work toward aligning total rewards systems and components with the objectives of the organization.[7] Several strategic decisions guide the design of compensation practices:

- Legal compliance with all applicable laws and regulations
- Cost-effectiveness for the organization
- Internal and external equity for employees
- Optimal mix of compensation components
- Performance enhancement for the organization
- Performance recognition and talent management for employees
- Enhanced recruitment, involvement, and retention of employees

Employers strive to maintain their costs at a level that rewards employees fairly for their knowledge, skills, abilities, and performance accomplishments while allowing the firm to remain competitive and successful. WorldatWork is a leading professional association that focuses on compensation. The organization has developed a well-respected model of total rewards that includes tangible direct, tangible indirect, and intangible rewards.[8] Figure 11-2 identifies elements of three primary components of the total rewards package. It shows that total rewards can be broadly defined and also indicates that intangible rewards are an important aspect of the package.

Determining which rewards are valued by employees and applicants and finding affordable ways to provide those rewards can be challenging. Total reward programs should be evaluated on an ongoing basis to ensure that employees find them satisfying and that they are cost-effective and sustainable for the organization.[9] The organizational culture and pay policy should be complementary and consistent. For example, if the culture is a team-focused environment, total rewards might emphasize team/group rewards rather than individual rewards.

FIGURE 11-2 Elements of Total Rewards

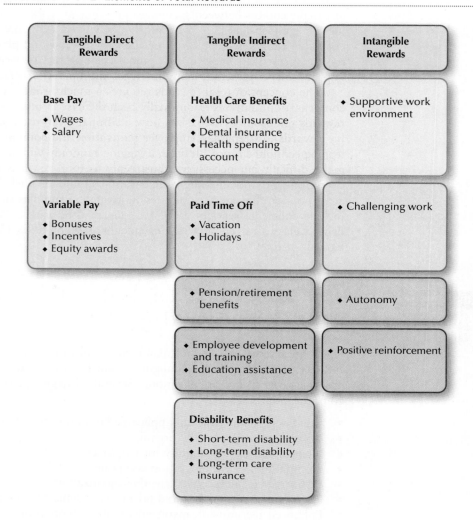

Tangible Direct Rewards	Tangible Indirect Rewards	Intangible Rewards
Base Pay ♦ Wages ♦ Salary	**Health Care Benefits** ♦ Medical insurance ♦ Dental insurance ♦ Health spending account	♦ Supportive work environment
Variable Pay ♦ Bonuses ♦ Incentives ♦ Equity awards	**Paid Time Off** ♦ Vacation ♦ Holidays	♦ Challenging work
	♦ Pension/retirement benefits	♦ Autonomy
	♦ Employee development and training ♦ Education assistance	♦ Positive reinforcement
	Disability Benefits ♦ Short-term disability ♦ Long-term disability ♦ Long-term care insurance	

Source: Adapted from *WorldatWork* (http://www.worldatwork.org).

11-1a Components of Compensation

Tangible rewards
Elements of compensation that can be quantitatively measured and compared between organizations.

Intangible rewards
Elements of compensation that cannot be as easily measured or calculated.

Tangible rewards can be measured, and it is possible to calculate the monetary value of each reward. Employees can easily compare the tangible rewards offered by various organizations. Alternatively, **intangible rewards** cannot be as easily measured or quantified. How would an employee put a dollar value on having decision-making authority or working in a supportive work environment? The perceived value of such intangible rewards can differ among employees, making the total rewards approach complex. Recent research shows that work–life balance programs and employee well-being efforts make a significant difference to workers and in some cases can outweigh the tangible rewards offered by a company.[10]

One tangible component of a compensation program is *direct compensation*, the monetary rewards for work done and performance results achieved. *Base pay*

Base pay
Basic compensation that an employee receives, usually as a wage or salary.

Wages
Payments calculated directly from the amount of time worked by employees.

Salary
Consistent payments made each period regardless of the number of hours worked.

Variable pay
Compensation linked directly to individual, team, or organizational performance.

Benefit
Indirect reward given to an employee or group of employees as part of membership in the organization.

and *variable pay* are the most common forms of direct compensation. The most common indirect compensation is employee *benefits*.

Base Pay The basic compensation that an employee receives, usually provided as an hourly wage or a salary, is called **base pay**. Many organizations use two base pay categories, hourly and salaried, which are identified according to the way pay is determined and the nature of the jobs. Hourly pay is most common and is based on time. Employees paid by the hour receive **wages** which are payments calculated on the basis of the time worked. In contrast, employees paid a **salary** receive the same payment each period regardless of the number of hours worked.

Variable Pay Another type of direct pay is **variable pay**, compensation linked directly to individual, team, or organizational performance. The most common types of variable pay are bonuses, incentive program payments, equity awards, and commissions. Hay Group found that companies are increasing the use of variable pay as a means of aligning compensation with changing business strategies and improving performance.[11] Variable pay, including executive compensation, is discussed in Chapter 12.

Benefits Many organizations provide indirect rewards in the form of employee benefits. With indirect compensation, employees receive financial rewards without receiving actual cash. A **benefit** is an indirect reward given to an employee or a group of employees for organizational membership, regardless of performance. Examples of benefits are health insurance, vacation pay, and retirement pensions. Benefits are discussed in Chapter 13.

11-2 ■ LAWS GOVERNING COMPENSATION

LO2 Explain the major laws governing employee compensation.

Pay practices are regulated by several key laws that address issues such as overtime pay, minimum wage standards, hours of work, and pay equity. The following discussion examines the laws and regulations affecting base compensation. Laws and regulations affecting incentives and benefits are examined in Chapters 12 and 13.

11-2a Fair Labor Standards Act (FLSA)

The primary federal law affecting compensation is the Fair Labor Standards Act (FLSA), which was passed in 1938. Compliance with FLSA provisions is enforced by the Wage and Hour Division of the U.S. Department of Labor (DoL). Penalties for wage and hour violations often include awards of up to two years of back pay for affected current and former employees along with a monetary penalty. Willful violations may be penalized by up to three years of back pay. For example, Wal-Mart was assessed over $5 million in back wages and penalties for overtime violations resulting from improperly classifying employees as exempt from overtime and Staples Inc., was fined over $42 million to settle similar claims.[12] The DoL launched a public service campaign called We Can Help, an outreach program to encourage low-wage and immigrant workers to report pay complaints.[13] The provisions of both the original act and subsequent revisions focus on the following major areas:

- Minimum wage
- Limits on the use of child labor
- Exempt and nonexempt status (overtime provisions)

Minimum Wage The FLSA sets a minimum wage to be paid to a broad spectrum of covered employees. Congressional action is the only way the minimum wage can be changed. A lower minimum wage is set for "tipped" employees, such as restaurant servers, but their compensation must equal or exceed the minimum wage when average tips are included. The current minimum wage of $7.25 an hour was set as part of the Fair Minimum Wage Act of 2007. Eight states raised their minimum wage levels by an average of 32 cents per hour. If a state's minimum wage is higher than the federal minimum wage, employers must pay this higher wage. Employers that operate in multiple states must monitor legislation that might affect their operations. Some research suggests that minimum wage increases lead to a reduction in employment or working hours for entry-level workers, while other studies show that there is no impact on employment.[14]

Child Labor Provisions The child labor provisions of the FLSA set the minimum age for employment with unlimited hours at 16 years. For hazardous occupations, the minimum is 18 years of age. Individuals 14 to 15 years old may work outside school hours with certain limitations. Many employers require age certificates for employees because the FLSA makes the employer responsible for determining an individual's age. Age certificates are supplied by high schools.

Exempt and Nonexempt Statuses Under the FLSA, employees are classified as exempt or nonexempt. **Exempt employees** hold positions for which employers are not required to pay overtime. **Nonexempt employees** must be paid overtime. The current FLSA regulations used to establish whether or not a job qualifies for exempt status classify jobs into five categories as shown in Figure 11-3. The regulations identify several factors to be considered when determining exempt status. The regulations are complex and a thorough review of each job is recommended to ensure proper classification and prevent misclassifying employees. Job duties can change over time, and it is wise to periodically review all jobs in the organization.[15] To review the details for each exemption, go to the U.S. DoL's website at *www.dol.gov*.

Exempt employees
Employees who are not paid overtime.

Nonexempt employees
Employees who must be paid overtime.

FIGURE 11-3 Determining Exempt Status under the FLSA

Categories for Exempt Status	Major Criteria for Exempt Status

• Executive
• Administrative
• Professional (learned and creative)
• Computer employee
• Outside sales (including pharmaceutical sales)
	• Pay level per week—minimum of $455/week
	• Paid on a salary basis
	• Job duties and responsibilities
	  ◇ Primary duties of managing
	  ◇ Decision discretion/judgment
	  ◇ Requires advanced knowledge and/or training/education
	  ◇ Pursue artistic or creative endeavors

Source: Adapted from the dol.gov website.

When designing base pay, employers often categorize jobs into groupings that tie the FLSA status with the method of payment. Employers are required to pay overtime for *hourly* jobs to comply with the FLSA. Employees in positions classified as *salaried nonexempt* are also entitled to overtime pay. Salaried nonexempt positions sometimes include secretarial, clerical, and salaried blue-collar positions (like shift supervisor). A common mistake made by employers is to avoid paying overtime to all salaried employees, even though some may qualify for nonexempt status. Exempt status is not necessarily granted to all salaried jobs; each job must be evaluated on a case by case basis. The FLSA does not require employers to pay overtime for *salaried exempt* jobs.

Overtime The FLSA established overtime pay requirements at one and one-half times the regular pay rate for all hours worked over 40 in a week, except for exempt employees. There are other exceptions to the overtime requirements, such as farm workers, but these exceptions are rare.

The workweek is defined as a consecutive period of 168 hours (24 hours × 7 days), which does not have to be a calendar week. Hospitals and nursing homes are allowed a special definition of the workweek to accommodate their 24/7 scheduling demands. No daily number of hours requiring overtime is set, except for special provisions relating to hospitals and other specially designated organizations. Thus, if a manufacturing firm operates on a 4-day/10-hour schedule, no overtime pay is required by the act until the worker exceeds 40 hours worked.

Common Overtime Issues For individuals who are nonexempt employers must consider many issues. These include the following:

- *Compensatory time off*: "Comp" hours are earned by public-sector nonexempt employees in lieu of payment for extra time worked at the rate of one and one-half times the number of hours over 40 that are worked in a week. Comp time is prohibited in the private sector and cannot be legally offered to employees working for private organizations.
- *Incentives for nonexempt employees*: Employers must add the amount of direct work-related incentives to an employee's base pay and then calculate overtime pay as one and one-half times the higher (adjusted) rate of pay.
- *Training time*: Time spent in training must be counted as time worked by nonexempt employees unless it is voluntary or not directly job-related.
- *Travel time*: Travel time must be counted as work time if it occurs during normal work hours for the benefit of the employer. Travel to and from work is not considered compensable travel time.
- *Donning and doffing time*: Some jobs require employees to change clothes or to spend a significant amount of time donning protective equipment before they report for duty. Regulations regarding putting on and taking off such clothing and gear are complex. Questions regarding specific cases should be researched with the DoL.

The FLSA does not require employers to provide breaks, lunch periods, or to pay double-time for any hours worked. State laws vary on these topics and employers should research compliance requirements in all states in which they operate. The complexity of overtime determination and related matters can be confusing for managers, employees, and HR professionals. The DoL has many informative publications on its website that clarify these issues.

11-2b Pay Equity Laws

Title VII of the Civil Rights Act of 1964 prohibits discrimination based on race, color, sex, religion, or national origin. However, prior to its passage, pay discrimination on the basis of sex was outlawed under the Equal Pay Act of 1963. Since then, additional laws have been enacted to counter wage discrimination on the basis of sex.

Equal Pay Act of 1963 The act prohibits companies from using different wage scales for men and women performing substantially the same jobs. Pay differences can be justified on the basis of merit, seniority, quantity or quality of work, experience, or factors other than gender. Similar pay must be given for jobs requiring equal skills, equal responsibilities, equal efforts, or jobs done under similar working conditions.

Lilly Ledbetter Fair Pay Act This law was enacted in 2008 in response to a Supreme Court decision restricting the statute of limitations allowed under the Equal Pay Act for claiming pay discrimination based on sex. Under the Equal Pay Act, an employee alleging discrimination had up to 300 days to file a claim. The Fair Pay Act essentially treats each paycheck as a new act of discrimination. Pay discrimination need not be intentional to be unlawful. Pay practices resulting in disparate impact are also actionable. Steps to reduce liability include conducting a periodic disparate impact analysis of compensation plans, properly documenting all compensation decisions, retaining complete pay records for an appropriate duration, and limiting discretion in pay decisions to higher levels in the organization.[16]

11-2c Independent Contractor Regulations

The growing use of contingent workers by many organizations has drawn the attention of several enforcement agencies such as the Internal Revenue Service (IRS), DoL, U.S. Treasury Department, and state taxing authorities. When workers are improperly classified as independent contractors, payroll tax revenues are lost and workers are not insured for unemployment or work-related injuries.[17] According to some estimates, 3.4 million employees are misclassified as independent contractors, costing the United States $54 billion in underpaid employment taxes and $15 billion in unpaid FICA and unemployment taxes.[18]

For an employer, classifying someone as an independent contractor rather than an employee offers major advantages. The employer does not have to pay Social Security, unemployment, or workers' compensation costs. These additional payroll levies may add 10% or more to the costs of hiring the individual as an employee. The misclassification of employees as independent contractors has become such a serious problem that the IRS launched an amnesty program to allow employers to report misclassifications and pay for past payroll tax obligations. The hope was that through the Voluntary Classification Settlement Program, employers would come forward rather than wait for an audit, which is likely to be much more costly and time-consuming.[19]

Most federal and state entities rely on the criteria for independent contractor status established by the Internal Revenue Service (IRS). Figure 11-4 lists the factors used by the IRS to determine whether or not an individual can be classified as an independent contractor. A worker does not have to meet all 20 criteria and no single factor is decisive in establishing the worker's status. Each case is analyzed and the weight of evidence is used to make the final determination.[20] Key differences between an

FIGURE 11-4 IRS Guidelines for Independent Contractor Status

Behavioral Control/Instructions/Training That the Business Gives to the Worker

- When and where to do the work
- What tools and equipment to use
- What workers to hire or to assist with the work
- Where to purchase supplies and services
- What work must be performed by a specified individual
- What order or sequence to follow
- How work results are achieved

Financial Control

- Extent of the worker's investment
- Extent to which worker makes services available to a relevant market
- How the business pays the worker
- Whether or not the business reimburses travel expenses
- The extent to which the workers can realize a profit or loss

Type of Relationship

- Written contracts
- Whether the business provides employee-type benefits to the worker
- Permanency of the relationship
- Extent to which services provided by the worker are a key aspect of the regular business of the company

Source: IRS, Publication 15A, 2012.

employee and an independent contractor are evaluated by reviewing behavioral control, financial control, and relationship-type factors.

11-2d Additional Laws Affecting Compensation

Prevailing wage
An hourly wage determined by a formula that considers the rate paid for a job by a majority of the employers in the appropriate geographic area.

Several compensation-related laws apply to firms that have contracts with the U.S. government. These laws require that federal contractors pay a **prevailing wage,** which is determined by a formula that considers the rate paid for a job by a majority of the employers in the appropriate geographic area. The Davis-Bacon Act of 1931, the Walsh-Healy Public Contracts Act, and the McNamara-O'Hara Service Contract Act include prevailing wage clauses that apply to firms engaged in federal construction projects or that work directly on federal government contracts.

Garnishment
A court order that directs an employer to set aside a portion of an employee's wages to pay a debt owed to a creditor.

Garnishment occurs when a creditor obtains a court order that directs an employer to set aside a portion of an employee's wages to pay a debt owed to the creditor. Regulations passed as a part of the Consumer Credit Protection Act limit the amount of wages that can be garnished. The act also restricts the right of employers to terminate employees whose pay is subject to a single garnishment order. All 50 states have laws applying to wage garnishments.

L03 Outline strategic compensation decisions.

11-3 ■ STRATEGIC COMPENSATION DECISIONS

Managers often address the compensation philosophy, communication approach, and administrative responsibilities of a company's compensation approach. These decisions relate to how total reward programs are designed and shared with employees.

11-3a Compensation Philosophies

Managers establish a guiding philosophy regarding total rewards and communicate this approach to motivate employees and direct their efforts toward organizational objectives. Employee satisfaction with compensation is affected by how closely their personal beliefs mesh with the company's philosophy and how closely the company's actions follow its stated philosophy.[21] There are two basic compensation philosophies that are situated at opposite ends of a continuum, as shown in Figure 11-5. At one end of the continuum is the *entitlement* philosophy, and at the other end is the *performance* philosophy. Most compensation systems fall somewhere in between these two extremes.

Entitlement philosophy
Assumes that individuals who have worked another year are entitled to pay increases, with little regard for performance differences.

Entitlement Philosophy The **entitlement philosophy** assumes that individuals who have worked another year are entitled to pay increases with little regard for performance differences. When organizations give automatic increases to their employees every year, they are using the entitlement philosophy. Most employees receive the same or nearly the same percentage increase. These automatic increases are often referred to as *cost-of-living raises*, even if they are not tied specifically to economic

FIGURE 11-5 Continuum of Compensation Philosophies

Entitlement	Performance
• Pay and raises based on length of service • Across-the-board raises • Pay scales increased annually • Industry comparisons of pay only • Holiday bonuses given to all employees	• Pay and raises based on performance • No raises for poor-performing employees • Market-adjusted pay scales • No raises for length of service or job tenure • Industry comparisons of total rewards

© Cengage Learning 2014

indicators. The entitlement philosophy is more prevalent in unionized settings and in public-sector employment.[22]

Performance Philosophy A **pay-for-performance philosophy** assumes that compensation decisions reflect performance differences. Organizations using this philosophy do not guarantee additional compensation for simply completing another year of service. Instead, pay and incentives are structured to reward performance differences (quantity, quality, speed of work, customer satisfaction, and so forth) among employees. Outstanding performers are compensated with substantially greater pay increases and higher variable rewards than employees who perform at only a satisfactory level. Employees who perform below standards are denied pay increases and are often placed on a performance-improvement plan. It is critical that evaluation criteria differentiate between performance levels and that employees are provided effective feedback when the performance-based compensation philosophy is used.[23]

Few organizations follow an exclusively performance-oriented compensation philosophy but the overall trend is toward greater use of pay-for-performance systems. Performance measures should reflect important outcomes to shareholders, customers, and employees. Focusing on results such as sales revenue rather than activity (number of calls placed) aligns employee effort with valued outcomes.[24] Performance-based systems do not always lead to increased employee performance because of inappropriate pay differentials, equity concerns, and poor teamwork. As a result, managers should periodically evaluate the link between pay and performance and make adjustments accordingly.[25]

11-3b Communicating Pay Philosophy

Sharing the organizational pay philosophy helps employees to recognize the value of the total reward package provided and shows how their job performance might affect their compensation. Honest, transparent communication about compensation can lead to higher employee engagement and productivity because employees better understand what is expected of them and how they will be rewarded. A variety of communication channels can be used, from one-on-one discussions with a supervisor to employee meetings and information on the company website. Before launching a communication program, it is advisable to clearly outline the company's philosophy, ensure that decisions match the philosophy, and train supervisors in how to manage the conversation.[26]

11-3c Compensation Responsibilities

HR specialists and line managers work together to administer compensation expenditures. HR specialists develop and administer the organizational compensation system and ensure that pay practices comply with all legal requirements. Because of the complexity involved, HR specialists typically conduct job evaluations and wage surveys and develop base pay programs and salary structures and policies. Line managers evaluate employee performance and participate in pay decisions. They are often the first point of contact for employees with questions about pay fairness. It is advisable to train managers about how the organization develops and administers its compensation program.

Payroll Administration Calculating pay and ensuring timely, accurate payroll processing is particularly important to assure compliance with compensation laws and maintain positive employee relations. Payroll staff may report to the company's HR function or the accounting function. Recordkeeping is critical, especially in light of the Fair Pay Act. This labor-intensive responsibility is typically among the first to be outsourced. While an organization may outsource payroll processing, liability for legal compliance remains with the company. Careful selection of a payroll service provider is therefore important.[27]

11-3d Human Resource Metrics and Compensation

MEASURE

Employers spend a substantial amount of money on employee compensation. Just like any other area of cost, compensation expenditures should be evaluated to determine their effectiveness. Metrics can be tracked to assess the compensation program's internal performance and its external competitiveness.[28] A number of widely used measures are shown in Figure 11-6.

The raw data needed to calculate various measures may be found in many organizational functions. Wage rates, total payroll costs, and overtime information can be obtained from the payroll staff or vendor. Productivity numbers may be logged by the Operations Department. Tenure and pay range information may be recorded in the HRIS. Compiling all the necessary information to make proper assessments is

FIGURE 11-6 HR Metrics for Compensation

Metric	Calculation
Average hourly rate	◆ Add the individual hourly rates of pay for all employees. ◆ Divide by the number of employees.
Number of Full Time Equivalents (FTEs)	◆ Add the annual hours paid for all employees. ◆ Divide by the number of hours a full-time employee is scheduled to work. (This is frequently 2,080 hours.)
Average tenure	◆ Add the total years of service for all employees. ◆ Divide by the number of FTEs.
Average compa-ratio (comparative ratio)	◆ Calculate the compa-ratio for each employee. ◆ Add the compa-ratios. ◆ Divide by the number of employees.
Productivity	◆ Total revenue divided by number of FTEs.
Average annual salary increase	◆ Calculate the salary increase for each employee. ◆ Add the increases. ◆ Divide by the number of FTEs.

HR PERSPECTIVE

Using Predictive Analytics to Determine Pay

For many years, companies have collected information about compensation practices within their industry and geographic locations. This information helps to ensure that the firm is paying competitively to attract and retain high-quality workers. In recent years, companies have started to use more sophisticated analytics to study employee turnover trends and determine how compensation might affect retention.

A large regional bank was experiencing high turnover among staff in front-facing positions. Before the use of predictive analytics, the bank might have simply raised the pay for these workers to reduce turnover. However, statistical modeling using a variety of metrics showed that workers were dissatisfied with career progress. Therefore, offering job changes and career development opportunities, even without additional pay,

reduced employees' intentions to quit. The bank was able to use internal employee-related data to better direct investments in human resources. Using data more effectively led to better employee retention without increasing pay rates.

The Las Vegas casino chain, Caesars Entertainment Corporation, also discovered the power of analytics by carefully studying patterns in employee turnover. The company found that employees earning less than the midpoint of their salary range were 16% more likely to quit than those earning above the midpoint. Focusing on bringing employee's pay to the midpoint but not going beyond that amount had the greatest effect on reducing turnover. Zeroing in on compensation data along with other employment measures allows companies to more precisely determine how to best use total rewards to motivate and retain employees.[29]

complex and may require HR professionals to coordinate with other organizational functions. Ideally, compensation metrics should be computed each year and compared with historic results to show how the rate of compensation changes compares with the rate of other financial changes in the organization. The accompanying HR Perspectives: Using Predictive Analytics to Determine Pay shows how progressive companies use metrics and analytics to improve their pay effectiveness.

11-4 ■ COMPENSATION SYSTEM DESIGN ISSUES

Depending on the compensation philosophies, strategies, and approaches used by an organization, many decisions are made that affect the design of the compensation system. Employee satisfaction with the compensation system can be influenced by how the organization manages these issues.

11-4a Motivation Theories and/or Compensation Philosophies

Research in the field of worker motivation was especially active during the 1960s with many well-known theories emerging. Two theories of motivation in particular influence the design of compensation systems. Expectancy theory and equity theory are especially relevant to the perceptions employees have of the total rewards provided by the organization.[30] The ideas behind these two theories were introduced in Chapter 5.

Expectancy theory
An employee's motivation is based on the probability that his or her efforts will lead to an expected level of performance that is linked to a valued reward.

Expectancy Theory The expectancy theory of motivation was first introduced by Victor Vroom at Yale in 1964 and later expanded by Porter and Lawler. **Expectancy theory** says that an employee's motivation is based on several linked concepts. Figure 11-7 shows the important relationships in expectancy theory within the context of pay. This theory emphasizes the importance of finding valued rewards for the employee. Rewards that are not appreciated by the employee have little power to motivate performance. Additionally, a break between the promise and delivery of the reward will decrease motivation. For example, an employee who is promised a bonus to increase sales and achieves the desired result, but is then told that budget cuts prevent the company from giving the bonus, will be much less likely to put extra effort into future performance. Managers who understand the key linkages in these expectations can better monitor employee motivation and adjust reward systems accordingly.[31]

Equity theory
Individuals judge fairness (equity) in compensation by comparing their inputs and outcomes against the inputs and outcomes of referent others.

Equity Theory The **equity theory** of motivation was first introduced by John Stacey Adams in 1963. This theory states that individuals judge fairness (equity) in compensation by comparing their inputs and outcomes against the inputs and outcomes of referent others. These *referent others* are workers that the individual uses as a reference point to make these comparisons. Inputs include time, effort, loyalty, commitment, skill, and enthusiasm. Outcomes include pay, job security, benefits, praise, recognition, and thanks. Figure 11-8 shows the important ratios in equity theory.

The comparisons are personal and are based on individual perceptions, not necessarily facts. Individuals who believe that they are not being rewarded fairly (such as getting lower outcomes than peers for the same inputs) can restore equity in two ways. They can reduce inputs or seek greater outcomes. Reducing inputs is a simple matter of investing less effort in work, refusing to work extra hours, or decreasing loyalty and commitment to the organization. For example, if Miranda feels that her pay is lower than her coworker, Allan, she may refuse to work overtime or stop offering ideas and suggestions to improve company operations. Seeking additional outcomes is more difficult. The individual must request a pay increase or praise and recognition from a supervisor who may or may not cooperate. Monitoring changes in employee behavior may help to uncover perceptions of inequity.

FIGURE 11-7 Expectancy Theory

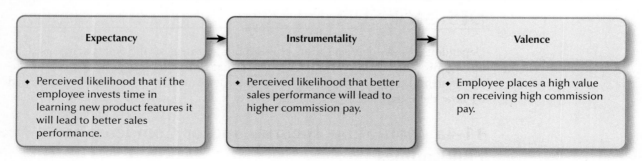

Source: Vroom, 1964.*

*Adapted from Victor Vroom, *Work and Motivation*. 1964, New York: McGraw Hill.

FIGURE 11-8 Equity Theory

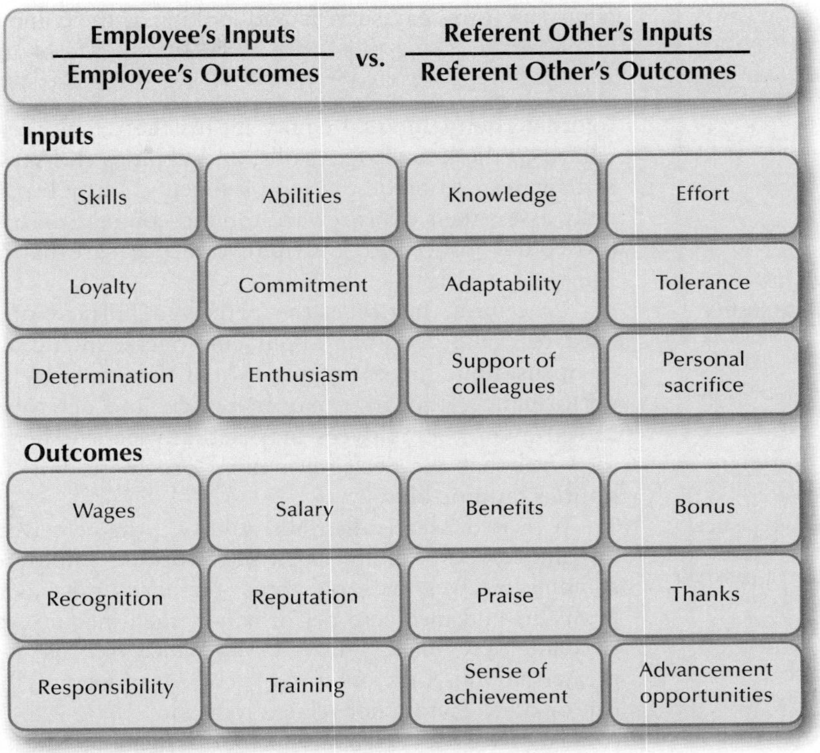

$\dfrac{\text{Employee's Inputs}}{\text{Employee's Outcomes}}$ vs. $\dfrac{\text{Referent Other's Inputs}}{\text{Referent Other's Outcomes}}$			
Inputs			
Skills	Abilities	Knowledge	Effort
Loyalty	Commitment	Adaptability	Tolerance
Determination	Enthusiasm	Support of colleagues	Personal sacrifice
Outcomes			
Wages	Salary	Benefits	Bonus
Recognition	Reputation	Praise	Thanks
Responsibility	Training	Sense of achievement	Advancement opportunities

Source: Adams, 1965.*

*Adapted from John Stacey Adams, J. S. (1965). "Inequity in social exchange." *Advances in Experimental Social Psychology*. Volume 62, 1965, 335–343.

A study by HR Solutions International found that employees often think peers at other firms earn more than they do, but in reality they are usually paid about the same.[32] A further complication is that employees may compare themselves to the wrong peer group and may not have accurate information about other employees' inputs and outcomes. These findings illustrate how perceptions influence the individual determination of fairness. Employees may make many incorrect assumptions that lead to dissatisfaction with compensation. Fostering open communication by sharing the pay philosophy and decision-making process can reduce employee unhappiness.[33]

11-4b Compensation Fairness and Equity

Most people work for monetary rewards. Whether they receive base pay or variable pay, the extent to which employees perceive their compensation to be fair often affects their performance and how they view their jobs and their employers. Employees are more likely to have lower job satisfaction and leave jobs when they feel inadequately compensated.[34]

External Equity If an employer's rewards are not viewed as equitable compared to other organizations, the employer is likely to experience higher turnover. This also creates greater difficulty in recruiting qualified and high-demand individuals. A few indicators of external inequity are low employee morale, difficulty hiring new employees, and abnormal internal pay ratios.[35] Organizations can track external equity by using pay surveys and looking at the compensation policies of competing employers.

Internal Equity Internal equity means that employees are compensated fairly with regard to the knowledge, skills, and abilities (KSAs) they use in their jobs, as well as their responsibilities, accomplishments, and job performance. Employees continually assess their effort/reward ratio in comparison to coworkers. Two key issues—procedural justice and distributive justice—are particularly important to internal equity.[36]

Procedural justice
Perceived fairness of the process and procedures used to make decisions about employees.

Procedural justice is the perceived fairness of the process and procedures used to make decisions about employees, including their pay. As it applies to compensation, the entire process of determining base pay for jobs, measuring performance, allocating pay increases, and determining incentives must be perceived as fair. Employees may actually be satisfied with lower compensation if they feel that the decision-making process is fair and not based on favoritism, politics, and/or bias.[37]

Distributive justice
Perceived fairness in the distribution of outcomes.

A related issue is **distributive justice**, the perceived fairness in how rewards are distributed. For example, if a hardworking employee whose performance is outstanding receives the same across-the-board raise as an employee with attendance problems and mediocre performance, then inequity may be perceived. Likewise, if two employees have similar performance records but one receives a significantly greater pay raise, the other may perceive an inequity because of supervisory favoritism or other factors not related to the job.

To address concerns about both types of justice, some organizations establish compensation appeals procedures. Typically, employees are encouraged to contact the HR department after discussing their concerns with their immediate supervisors and managers. Since perceptions of fairness are central to employee behavior and commitment, organizations work to monitor employee attitudes and communicate openly about compensation decision processes.[38]

Pay Secrecy Another equity issue concerns the degree of secrecy organizations have regarding their pay systems. Pay information that may be kept secret in "closed" systems relates to information about individual pay amounts, pay raises, and incentive payouts. Some firms have policies that prohibit employees from discussing their pay with other employees, and violations of these policies can lead to disciplinary action. A recent survey shows that over half of all employees feel that their employer discourages or forbids employees from sharing pay information with each other. However, such policies may violate the National Labor Relations Act, and the courts have supported employees' right to discuss pay and benefit issues.[39]

Beyond the legal issues, however, companies should examine the reasons for severely restricting employee discussion of pay. If an organization has implemented competitive pay practices and has a fair and reasonable pay structure, employee concerns about inequity can be reduced by sharing this information. Explaining pay grades and pay decision rules can enhance employee perceptions of fair treatment and help them understand why different jobs are paid at different rates. Maintaining a cloak of secrecy invites curiosity and suspicion from employees, which may result in less trust about how they are being paid.

HR SKILLS AND APPLICATIONS

Quantitative Techniques Facilitate Compensation Management

In order to effectively manage employee compensation, it is often necessary to conduct quantitative assessments of pay data. This can be challenging because many HR professionals have not been given the training required to assess compensation data. Despite this reality, an understanding of some basic statistical concepts can help organizations offer more competitive, cost-effective pay structures that attract talent, increase job satisfaction, and reduce turnover.

Central tendency measures can be used to identify important numbers. Examples include the mean (mathematical average), median (the middle number in a list), and mode (the number appearing most frequently in a group). *Distribution statistics* indicate how numbers are distributed across a particular grouping. Examples include quartiles (placing numbers into quarters), percentiles (placing numbers into hundredths), and frequency distribution (using histograms to show how frequently numbers occur). Finally, many *relationship measures* can be used to evaluate data, which include correlations that show the relationships between two or more variables and regression analyses that indicate how well a set of variables can predict another factor.

In the following sample, we show how to determine measures of central tendency.

$28,000 $30,000 $30,000 $31,000 $32,000 $35,000
$38,000 $38,000 $38,000 $42,000 $45,000

The mean is ($387,000/11) = $35,182
The median is $35,000
The mode is $38,000

When using quantitative results, one must determine which measures are most meaningful and useful for analysis. Companies should encourage HR staff to seek out additional statistical materials and training, as well as provide the proper resources when necessary.[40]

11-4c Market Competitive Compensation

Some basic statistical analysis is needed to determine the competitiveness of a company's reward practices. The HR Skills and Applications: Quantiative Techniques Facilitate Compensation Management, explains useful quantitative techniques. Whether an organization's total reward practices are competitive has a significant impact on employees' views of compensation fairness. Providing competitive compensation to employees is a concern for all employers. Organizations face the challenge of whether to adopt practices common in an industry or to differentiate the firm by using novel or distinct compensation practices. Pay practices that work for one organization may not work in other firms, so designing competitive practices should consider organizational specifics.[41]

Larger organizations may have higher compensation levels than smaller organizations because of higher productivity levels and economies of scale. The compensation mix is also affected by firm size with larger organizations spending more on indirect compensation than do small firms.[42] Managers consider compensation mix and competitive position when developing their reward strategies. Many organizations establish policies about where they wish to be positioned in the labor market using a *quartile strategy*, as illustrated in Figure 11-9. The quartile strategy reflects the overall market position where the organization sets its compensation levels.

FIGURE 11-9 Compensation Quartile Strategies

Lag-the-Market Strategy An employer using a *first-quartile* strategy chooses to "lag the market" by paying below market levels for several reasons. If the employer is experiencing financial difficulties it may be unable to pay more. Also, when an abundance of workers is available, particularly those with lower skills, a below-market approach can be used to attract sufficient workers at a lower cost. The downside of this strategy is that it increases the likelihood of higher worker turnover and lower employee morale. If the labor market supply tightens, then attracting and retaining workers becomes more difficult. Companies may be tempted to adopt this strategy during recessionary times, only to discover that when the economy improves, worker turnover increases dramatically. Using a lag-the-market strategy is risky, and a company should consider the possible consequences before adopting this approach.[43]

Lead-the-Market Strategy A *third-quartile* strategy uses an aggressive approach to "lead the market." This strategy generally enables a company to attract and retain sufficient workers with the required capabilities and be more selective when hiring. Since it is a higher-cost approach, organizations often look for ways to increase the productivity of employees receiving above-market wages.

Match-the-Market Strategy Most employers position themselves in the *second quartile* (median), the middle of the market, as determined by pay data from surveys of other employers' compensation plans. Choosing this level attempts to balance employer cost pressures and the need to attract and retain employees by providing compensation levels that "meet the market" for the company's jobs.

Selecting a Quartile Pay structures and levels can affect organizational performance and staffing quality. Deciding which quartile position to target is a function of many considerations—financial resources available, competitiveness pressures, and the market availability of employees with different capabilities. For instance, some employers with extensive benefits programs or broad-based incentive programs may choose a first-quartile strategy so that their overall compensation costs and levels are not excessive. The decisions about compensation mix and competitive position are related and should be addressed as part of a comprehensive total rewards strategy.

11-4d Competency-Based Pay

Most compensation programs are designed to reward employees for carrying out their tasks, duties, and responsibilities. The job requirements determine which employees have higher base rates. Employees receive more for doing jobs that require a greater variety of tasks, more knowledge and skills, greater physical effort, or more demanding working conditions. However, the design of some compensation programs emphasizes competencies rather than the tasks performed.

Competency-based pay
Rewards individuals for the capabilities they demonstrate and acquire.

Competency-based pay rewards individuals for the capabilities they demonstrate and acquire. In knowledge-based pay (KBP) or skill-based pay (SBP) systems, employees start at a base level of pay and receive increases as they learn to do other jobs or gain additional skills and knowledge and thus become more valuable to the employer. These plans can lead to greater workforce flexibility and productivity.[44] For example, a manufacturing firm operates plastic molding presses of various sizes. Operating larger presses requires more skills than smaller presses. Under a KBP or SBP system, press operators increase their pay as they learn how to operate the more complex presses, even though sometimes they may be running only smaller machines. However, because of higher fixed labor costs and recordkeeping demands, few companies implement these pay systems.[45]

11-4e Individual versus Team Rewards

As some organizations have shifted to using work teams, the concern is how to develop compensation programs that support the team concept. Determining how to compensate individuals whose performance may be a result of team efforts and achievements is complicated. For base pay, employers may compensate individuals on the basis of competencies, experience, and other job factors. Then they use team incentive rewards on top of base pay. Equity concerns are particularly challenging and designing team rewards requires careful thought and planning.[46] Team-based incentives are discussed in Chapter 12.

LO4 Understand the challenges of managing global compensation systems.

GLOBAL

11-5 ■ GLOBAL COMPENSATION ISSUES

All of the issues discussed here can become confusing when dealing with global compensation. The growing world economy has led to an increase in the number of employees working internationally. Therefore, organizations with employees working throughout the world face some special compensation issues.

Variations in laws, living costs, tax policies, and other factors must be considered in designing the compensation for local employees and managers, as well as managers and professionals on international assignment. Fluctuations in the values of various currencies must be tracked and adjustments made as exchange rates rise or fall. With these and numerous other concerns, developing and managing a global compensation system becomes extremely complex.

One significant global issue in compensation design is how to compensate employees from different countries. Local wage scales vary significantly among countries. Figure 11-10 shows the typical real minimum hourly wage in various countries. It is clear that there are noticeable differences between developed nations where employees earn a high level of pay and developing nations where compensation rates are a fraction of those in developed nations. Costs of living standards vary a great deal between nations and compensation differences may reflect differences in purchasing power among nations. These variations in compensation levels have led to significant **offshoring** of jobs to lower-wage countries. The movement of call center and information technology (IT) jobs to India and manufacturing jobs to China, the Philippines, and Mexico are examples.[47] However, U.S. manufacturers have begun to *reshore* (return operations to the United States) production as wages in China and Mexico have risen.[48] This shows that compensation levels certainly play a role in helping companies decide where to locate their operations.

Many organizations have started to globalize their pay policies to attract and retain employees from an international talent pool. This requires management to balance the desire for consistent practices throughout the company with the need

Offshoring
Moving jobs to lower-wage countries.

FIGURE 11-10 International Comparison of Real Minimum Hourly Wage Rate

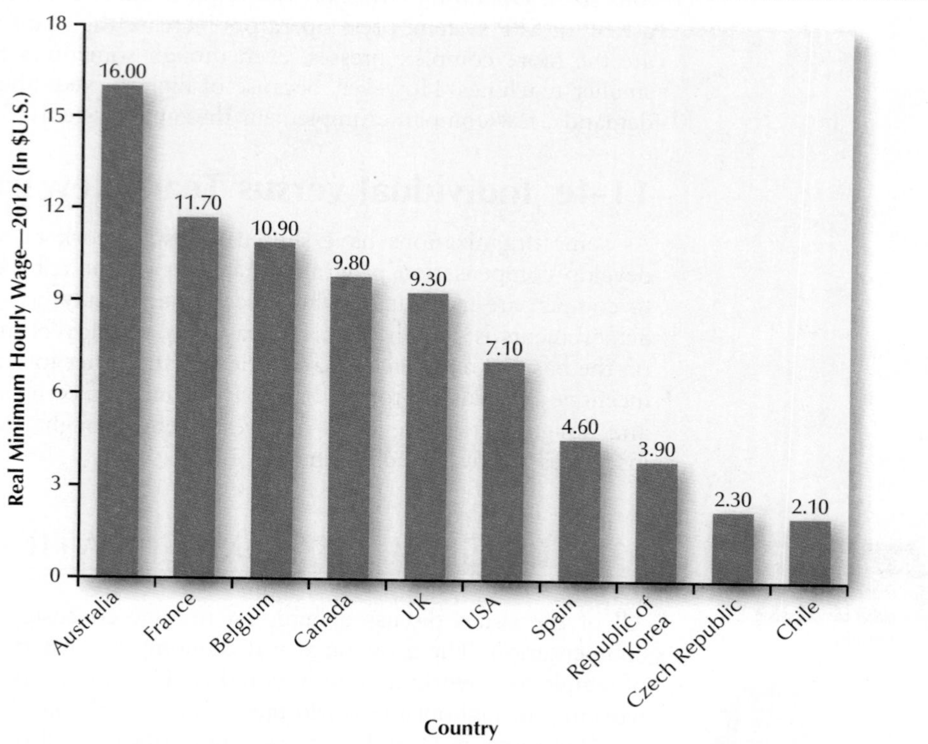

Source: OECD.statextracts.

for differentiating practices based on local input and customs. For instance, Boeing compensates locally hired employees with a competitive reward package designed to meet the requirements in each operating location while offering a uniform mix of compensation elements across the company.[49] When designing total rewards for employees around the world, culture is taken into consideration. In some cultures, pay for performance or individual incentives may be out of step with the local culture. This would reduce the effectiveness of a compensation plan that relies on such programs to attract and motivate employees.[50]

11-5a International Assignees

GLOBAL

Multinational companies may staff their operations with a mixture of employees from around the world which were defined in Chapter 1. Figure 11-11 shows the three primary types of international assignees. Compensation practices may be designed for each type of employee to maximize employee commitment and productivity. It has been estimated that the total employer costs for an expatriate, including all allowances, is three to four times the expatriate's salary with the duration of a typical expatriate assignment at two or three years. The expense of sending expatriates abroad clearly warrants special attention in the global compensation approach. Because of the intricacies of devising an effective compensation plan for international assignees, companies often use consultants knowledgeable in this field.

Expatriate employees may have unique needs and preferences in terms of how the compensation package is structured. A married employee with children might

FIGURE 11-11 Staffing Categories for International Assignees at Multinational Enterprise (MNE)

Types of International Assignment	Definition	Example
Home-country national—*Expatriate*	• Employee is a citizen of the country where the MNE is headquartered. • Employee works at an operation overseas.	• Employee is a U.S. citizen working for a U.S. company who is sent to China on assignment.
Host-country national—*Local hire*	• Employee is a citizen of the country where MNE has overseas operation. • Employee works in his or her country of citizenship.	• Employee is a citizen of China working for a U.S. company at its operation in China.
Third-country national	• Employee is a citizen of a country in which the MNE may or may not have operations. • Employee works in a country where he or she is not a citizen.	• Employee is a citizen of India working for a U.S. company at its operation in China.

Source: Adapted from McPhail, Fisher, Harvey, & Moeller, 2012 and Isidor, Schwens, & Kabst, 2011.

have drastically different requirements than an unmarried employee. Therefore, involving the expatriate in structuring the reward package may improve retention and job performance.[51]

A wide range of allowances and perquisites may be considered for inclusion in expatriate compensation. Hardship or hazard pay may be provided for expatriates assigned to dangerous or undesirable locations. Education assistance may be provided for the expatriate's dependents to make up for quality of education differences between the home and host country. Housing assistance in the form of free company-owned housing to make up for the difference in housing costs between locations may be granted. Multinational enterprises seek to find creative solutions that improve expatriate success while keeping costs under control.[52]

The two primary approaches to international compensation for expatriates are the home-country-based approach and the host-country-based approach.[53] The **home-country-based approach** is the most commonly used method. The overall objective is to maintain the expatriate's standard of living in the home country. Housing, taxes, and discretionary spending expenses are calculated based on those items in the home country. The company then pays the expatriate the difference so that he or she "remains whole." The home country approach can result in higher employer costs and more administrative complexity than other plans.

The **host-country-based approach** compensates the expatriate at the same level as workers from the host country. The company might continue to cover the employee in its retirement plan and also provide a housing allowance. If the cost of living is substantially lower in the host country than in the home country this approach might make sense because the expatriate can live comfortably while on assignment and can more effectively acclimate to the culture of the host country.

Home-country-based approach
Maintain an expatriate's standard of living in the home country.

Host-country-based approach
Compensate the expatriate at the same level as workers from the host country.

11-6 ■ DEVELOPING A BASE PAY SYSTEM

L05 Illustrate the steps in developing a base pay system.

Figure 11-12 shows how a base compensation system is developed using the compensation philosophy and job analysis. The process incorporates information gathered while valuing jobs and analyzing pay surveys—activities designed to ensure that the pay system is both internally and externally equitable and in line with the organizational philosophy. The data compiled in these two activities are used to design pay structures, including pay grades and pay ranges. After pay structures are established, individual jobs are placed in the appropriate pay grades and employee pay is determined. Finally, the pay system is monitored and updated.

Companies want their employees to perceive that they are paid fairly in relation to pay for jobs performed by others within the organization.[54] The two general approaches for valuing jobs are *job evaluation* and *market pricing*. Job evaluation looks at pay levels within the company, and market pricing looks outside the company. Both methods use relative comparisons to determine the worth of jobs in an organization. To comply with equal pay and nondiscrimination laws, companies should review the relative standing of each job to ensure that jobs held by women and minorities are not consistently ranked the lowest in the organization. Using valid methods and maintaining records regarding how ranking decisions are made can help a company defend its practices.[55]

FIGURE 11-12 Compensation Administration Process

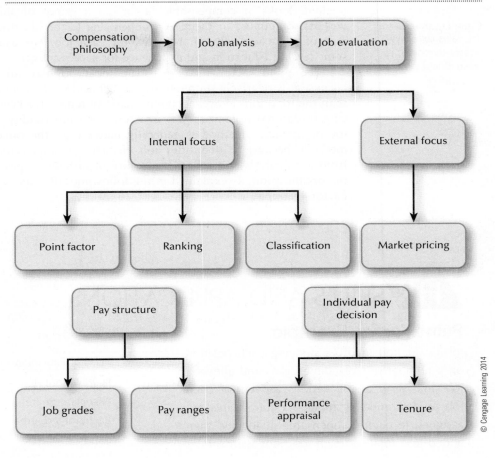

11-6a Job Evaluation Methods

Job evaluation
Formal, systematic means to identify the relative worth of jobs within an organization.

Job evaluation is a formal, systematic process to determine the relative worth of jobs within an organization. Employers can adopt one of several alternate methods.

The *ranking method* is a simple system that places jobs in order, from highest to lowest, by their value to the organization. This is a qualitative method in which the entire job is considered rather than individual components. The ranking method generally is more appropriate in a small organization that has relatively few jobs. For example, the ranking method might be used at a small family owned dry cleaning shop with only two or three distinct job titles.

The *classification method* is often used in public-sector organizations. Descriptions of job classes are written and then each job is put into a grade according to the class it best matches. A major difficulty with this method is that subjective judgments are needed to develop the class descriptions and to place jobs accurately in them.

The *factor-comparison method* is a complex quantitative method that combines the ranking and point factor methods (explained below). Organizations that use this method must develop their own key jobs and factors. The factor-comparison method is time-consuming and difficult to use, which accounts for its limited popularity in organizations.

Compensable factor
Job value commonly present throughout a group of jobs within an organization.

Point Factor Method The most widely used job evaluation method, the point factor method, looks at compensable factors in a group of similar jobs and assigns weights, or *points*, to them. A **compensable factor** identifies a dimension that is part of every job and can be rated for each job. For example, all jobs require some level of education and experience for successful performance.

The point factor method is the most popular job evaluation approach because it is relatively simple to use and considers the components of a job rather than the total job. However, point factor systems have been criticized for reinforcing traditional organizational structures and job rigidity. Although not perfect, the point factor method is generally better than the ranking and classification methods because it quantifies job elements. Compensable factors are derived from job analysis and reflect the nature of different types of work performed in the organization, as explained in the following HR Skills and Applications: Point Factor Example.

HR SKILLS AND APPLICATIONS

Point Factor Example

Job evaluation involves studying each position on a number of work dimensions and allows a job analyst to assess various aspects of each job to determine its relative value. Points are assigned to each compensable factor and then added to a total for each job. Jobs with similar point totals are considered to be relatively equal in importance.

A point factor system often uses compensable factors that reflect skill, responsibilities, social interaction, and working conditions. The skill dimension might be assessed on the basis of two compensable factors, the level of education and work experience needed for successful job performance, as illustrated in the following example. Each compensable factor is broken into degrees and each factor may have a different number of degrees. In the example, there are five degrees for education but only four degrees for experience. Further, the point values are not universal for all compensable factors. The point values indicate the weight of each factor in the evaluation of each job.

Degree	Level of Education	Point Value
1	High school diploma	20
2	Associate degree	25
3	Bachelor's degree	30
4	Master's degree	35
5	Doctoral degree	40

Degree	Years of Experience	Point Value
1	0–1	10
2	2–5	20
3	6–10	30
4	Over 10	40

The job analyst selects the appropriate levels of education and experience for each job and assigns the point value as the example shows. A similar chart is developed for each compensable factor such as responsibilities, social interaction, and working conditions. The job analyst rates each job on each compensable factor and calculates the total points. This process then leads to the placing of jobs in grades.

11-6b Market Pricing

Market pricing
Use of market pay data to identify the relative value of jobs based on what other employers pay for similar jobs.

While the point factor method has served employers well for many years, the trend is moving to a more externally focused approach. More companies are moving to **market pricing**, which uses market pay data to identify the relative value of jobs based on what other employers pay for similar jobs.

Key to market pricing is identifying relevant market pay data for jobs that are good "matches" with the employer's jobs, geographic considerations, and company strategies and philosophies about desired market competitiveness levels. The switch to market pricing as part of strategic compensation decisions can ensure market competitiveness of compensation levels and practices. However, there will not always be a perfect match for each job in the external market. For example, compensation specialists at Crosstex Energy Services, a natural gas company with 500 employees, are able to match about 85% of its jobs. The remaining 15% can be quite challenging because these jobs are unique to Crosstex. Judgment and interpretation are needed to determine the appropriate pay levels for these jobs.[56]

Advantages of Market Pricing The primary advantage cited for the use of market pricing is that it closely ties organizational pay levels to what is actually occurring in the market, without being distorted by "internal" job evaluation. An additional advantage of market pricing is that it allows an employer to communicate to employees that the compensation system is truly "market linked." Employees often see a compensation system that was developed using market pricing as having "face validity" and as being more objective than a compensation system that was developed using traditional job evaluation methods.

Disadvantages of Market Pricing The biggest disadvantage of market pricing is that pay survey data may be limited or may not be gathered in methodologically sound ways. It is also critical to understand the compensation mix that is common in the market. For example, one organization might allocate a much higher percentage of its compensation to variable pay than its competitors. If so, then a comparison on base pay would result in the organization being out of step with the market when in fact its employees might be more richly rewarded if they perform well.

Finally, tying pay levels to market data can lead to wide fluctuations on the basis of market conditions. Skills that are in great demand today can quickly become obsolete. Consider the IT job market during the past decade when pay levels varied significantly. The "hot skills" of mobile app developers are likely to be replaced as technology evolves to its next version and mobile technology falls by the wayside. The debate over the use of job evaluation versus market pricing is likely to continue because there are advantages and disadvantages to both approaches.[57]

11-6c Pay Surveys

Pay survey
Collection of data on compensation rates for workers performing similar jobs in other organizations.

Benchmark jobs
Jobs found in many organizations that can be used for the purposes of comparison.

A **pay survey** is a report based on research of compensation rates for workers performing similar jobs in other organizations. Pay surveys are an important element for establishing external pay equity. Both job evaluation and market pricing are tied to surveys of the pay that other organizations provide for similar jobs.

It is particularly important to identify common **benchmark jobs**—jobs that are found in many other organizations. Often these jobs have stable content, are common across different employers, and are performed by a large number of

employees. For example, benchmark jobs commonly used in the hospitality industry are housekeeper, front-desk clerk, concierge, and restaurant manager. Benchmark
jobs are used because they provide "anchors" against which other jobs can be
compared.

An employer may obtain surveys conducted by other organizations, access
Internet data, or conduct its own survey. The make-or-buy decision regarding pay
surveys is based on several factors such as the number of relevant competitors, the
comparability of jobs, and time and budget issues. There are many vendors that
provide general as well as custom surveys. National surveys on many jobs and
industries are provided by the U.S. DoL's Bureau of Labor Statistics, professional
and national trade associations, and various management consulting companies.
The most common source of pay data is compensation surveys conducted by third
parties that obtain data from employers. Information provided by employees (via
websites) is infrequently used by employers.[58]

Internet-Based Pay Information HR professionals can access a wide range of pay
data online. Employment-related website such as salary.com and glassdoor.com
provide data gathered from companies and employees. Use of these sources requires
caution because their accuracy and completeness may not be verifiable or may not
be applicable to individual firms and employees.

Employees have also discovered online salary information and may bring Internet data to HR professionals or their managers and to determine their current pay
is different from the pay reported on these websites. Responding to employee questions requires addressing many areas. Salary.com includes sample explanations on
its website including the following:

- *Job titles and responsibilities*: Compare the full job description, not just job titles
  and brief job summaries on the websites.
- *Experience, KSAs, and performance*: Most pay survey data on the Internet are
  averages of multiple companies and of multiple employees in those companies
  with varying experience, KSA levels, and performance.
- *Geographic differences*: Many pay survey sites on the Internet use geographic
  index numbers, not actual data from employers in a particular area.
- *Company size and industry*: Pay levels may vary significantly by company size,
  with smaller firms often having lower pay. Also, pay levels may be lower in
  certain industries, such as retail and nonprofits.
- *Base pay versus total compensation*: Employers have different benefits and
  incentive compensation programs. However, Internet data usually reflect only
  base pay amounts.

Using Pay Surveys The proper use of pay surveys involves evaluating many factors
to determine if the data are relevant and valid. The following questions should be
answered for each survey:

- *Participants*: Does the survey cover a realistic sample of the employers with
  whom the organization competes for employees?
- *Broad-based*: Does the survey include data from employers of different sizes,
  industries, and locales?
- *Timeliness*: How current are the data (when was the survey conducted)?
- *Methodology*: How established is the survey, and how qualified are those who
  conducted it?

- *Job matches*: Does the survey contain job summaries so that appropriate matches to job descriptions can be made?
- *Details provided*: Does the survey report on base pay, incentive pay, and other elements of compensation separately for comparison of the reward mix?

Pay Surveys and Legal Issues One reason for employers to use outside sources for pay surveys is to avoid charges that they are attempting to "price fix" wages as described in the opening case. The concern is that employers might collude to set wages and restrict employees from earning a true market wage. One such case involved registered nurses in Detroit who claimed that local hospitals violated the Sherman Antitrust Act by sharing compensation data that artificially held wages down. Cases in other industries have alleged that by sharing wage data, the employers attempted to hold wages down artificially in violation of the law.[59]

Organizations are permitted to participate in surveys but only if they meet the following conditions:

1. The survey must be administered by a third party such as a consultant or trade/professional association.
2. The data must be more than three months old.
3. A minimum of five employers must participate in the survey. No single employer's data may be worth more than 25% of the total.
4. All data must be aggregated and stripped of any identifying information.

In addition to antitrust considerations, companies participating in pay surveys must safeguard employee privacy and provide only de-identified data so that specific employee pay rates and names are not shared. Care must also be taken to avoid violating the National Labor Relations Act provisions that apply to disclosing wage and benefit information.

11-7 ■ PAY STRUCTURES

After job evaluations and pay survey data are gathered, pay structures can be developed. Pay structures may be created for various categories of jobs such as hourly, salaried, technical, sales, and management. Organizations may have separate pay structures for exempt and nonexempt jobs. The nature, culture, and structure of the organization are considerations for determining how many and which pay structures to have.[60]

11-7a Pay Grades

Pay grades
Groupings of individual jobs having approximately the same job worth.

Market line
Graph line that shows the relationship between job value as determined by job evaluation points and job value as determined by pay survey rates.

When establishing a pay structure, organizations use **pay grades** to group individual jobs having approximately the same job worth. Although no set rules govern the establishment of pay grades, 11 to 17 grades are generally used in small- and medium-sized companies. Two methods are commonly used to establish pay grades are job evaluation data and use of job market banding.

Setting Pay Grades Using Job Evaluation Points One approach for determining pay grades uses job evaluation points or other data generated from the traditional job evaluation methods discussed earlier in the chapter. This process ties pay survey information to job evaluation data by plotting a **market line** that shows the

FIGURE 11-13 Market Pay Line and Job Evaluation Points

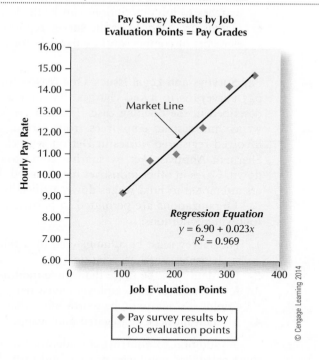

relationship between job value as determined by job evaluation points and job value as determined by pay survey rates. Market lines are developed by calculating the regression equation using statistical analysis techniques. Figure 11-13 shows an example of a market line and regression equation used in setting a particular set of pay grades. A market line uses data to place jobs having similar point values into pay grades. Pay ranges can then be computed for each pay grade.

Setting Pay Grades Using Market Banding Closely linked to the use of market pricing to value jobs, **market banding** groups jobs into pay grades based on similar market survey amounts. Figure 11-14 shows three bands for jobs in a manufacturing company. The midpoint of the survey average is used to develop pay range minimums and maximums, the methods for which are discussed later in this chapter.

Market banding
Grouping jobs into pay grades based on similar market survey amounts.

11-7b Pay Ranges

Once pay grades are determined, the pay range for each pay grade must be established. Using the market line as a starting point, the employer can determine minimum and maximum pay levels for each pay grade by making the market line the midpoint line of the new pay structure (see Figure 11-15). For example, in a particular pay grade, the maximum value may be 20% above the midpoint located on the market line, and the minimum value may be 20% below it. Once pay grades and ranges have been computed, then the current pay of employees is compared with the proposed ranges. It is common to have broader pay ranges for higher level job grades because more discretion is needed to reflect capability and performance differences.[61] For example, for entry level and production jobs the pay range may be 10% to 15% above and below the midpoint. For executive level positions the range may be 40% to 60% above and below the midpoint.

FIGURE 11-14 Market Bands for a Manufacturing Company

Grade	Job Title	Pay Survey Results	Minimum Pay	Midpoint Pay	Maximum Pay
1	Shipping Clerk	21,387	17,400	20,350	24,625
	Machine Operator	19,403			
	Utility Operator	20,723			
2	Quality Inspector	22,697	19,800	24,750	29,700
	Mechanic I	24,934			
	Scheduler	26,568			
3	Mechanic II	31,586	27,000	33,725	40,500
	Electrician I	35,914			
	Engineering Tech	33,685			

© Cengage Learning 2014

Pay rates overlap between job grades. Notice in Figure 11-15 that the minimum for Grade 2 is not at the same pay rate as the maximum for Grade 1. This overlap allows for a smoother transition when an employee is promoted from one grade to the next. Some employers have reduced the number of pay grades and expanded pay ranges by using a practice called *broadbanding*.

Broadbanding The practice of using fewer pay grades with much broader ranges than in traditional compensation systems is called **broadbanding**. Combining many grades into these broad bands is designed to encourage horizontal movement and therefore more skill acquisition. The main advantage of broadbanding is that it is more consistent with the flattening of organizational levels and the growing use of jobs that are multidimensional. A problem with broadbanding is that many

Broadbanding
Practice of using fewer pay grades with much broader ranges than in traditional compensation systems.

FIGURE 11-15 Example of Pay Grades and Pay Ranges

Grade	Point Range	Minimum Pay	Midpoint Pay	Maximum Pay
1	100–150	7.50	9.17	10.87
2	151–200	7.96	9.75	11.54
3	201–250	8.98	11.00	13.02
4	251–300	10.00	12.25	14.50
5	301–350	11.01	13.49	15.97
6	350–400	11.79	14.74	17.69

© Cengage Learning 2014

employees expect a promotion to be accompanied by a pay raise and movement to a new pay grade. By removing this grade progression, employees may feel that there are fewer promotional opportunities. Most companies continue to rely on traditional pay grade structures with only about 10% adopting a broadband structure.[62]

11-7c Individual Pay

Once pay grades and pay ranges have been established, pay can be set for each individual employee. Setting a range for each pay grade gives flexibility by allowing individuals to progress within a grade instead of having to move to a new grade each time they receive a raise. A pay range also allows managers to reward employees based on performance while maintaining the integrity of the pay system. Regardless of how well a pay structure is constructed, there can be occasions when an employee is paid outside of the range because of past pay practices, different levels of experience, or performance. There are risks in allowing these situations to persist as they are evidence of poor pay administration and might lead to claims of pay inequities.

Red-circled employee
Incumbent who is paid above the range set for a job.

Red-Circled Employees A red-circled employee is an employee who is paid above the range for the job. For example, assume that an employee in Grade 3 has a current pay rate of $13.50 an hour, but the pay range for Grade 3 is $8.98 to $13.02 an hour. The person would be red-circled and proper administration of the pay system would make the employee ineligible for a pay increase.

Several approaches can be used to bring a red-circled employee's pay into line. Although the fastest way would be to cut the employee's pay, that approach is not recommended and is seldom used. Instead, the employee's pay may be frozen until the pay range is adjusted upward. Another approach is to give the employee a small lump-sum payment but not adjust the pay rate when others are given raises. Of course, an employee being paid above the maximum range is an indicator that either the pay ranges are not keeping pace or the employee should be directed to development opportunities that will lead to a promotion to a job in a higher pay grade.

Green-circled employee
Incumbent who is paid below the range set for a job.

Green-Circled Employees An individual whose pay is below the range for a job is a **green-circled employee**. Promotion is a major contributor to this situation. Green-circled problems might also result from opportunistic hiring when employees are earning below-market pay at their former employer. Generally, it is recommended that the satisfactory green-circled individual receive fairly rapid pay increases to reach the pay grade minimum. More frequent increases can be used if the minimum is a great deal above the incumbent's current pay.

Pay compression
Occurs when the pay differences among individuals with different levels of experience and performance become small

Pay Compression One major problem many employers face is **pay compression**, which occurs when pay differences among individuals with different levels of experience and performance become small. Pay compression is frequently a result of labor market pay levels increasing faster than current employees' pay adjustments. Further contributing to the problem are pay freezes put in place during economic downturns. In the past, employees may not have been aware of these pay compression situations. However, young employees in the millennial generation are very open about pay matters and they widely discuss their pay with coworkers. So managers have to be prepared to address pay compression.[63]

In response to shortages of particular job skills in a highly competitive labor market, companies may have to pay higher amounts to hire people with those scarce skills. Microsoft increased pay and shifted more of the pay to cash than stock in an effort to retain employees who might be tempted to quit and join competitors. Software developers are in great demand and the external market is boosting compensation rapidly. If Microsoft is forced to hire from outside the company, it will have to pay new employees more than current workers. So, the boost in pay is an effort to get ahead of a possible problem and reduce pay compression.[64]

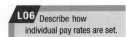

L06 Describe how individual pay rates are set.

11-8 ■ DETERMINING PAY INCREASES

Decisions about pay increases are important in the relationships between employees, their managers, and the organization. Individuals express expectations about their pay and about how much of an increase is "fair," especially compared with the increases received by other employees. Managers and HR professionals often work together to communicate pay increases and to help manage perceptions of any changes made to employees' compensation.

As part of the planning process, most organizations establish a target pay increase budget. Many factors are considered when establishing the pay budget, but economic conditions certainly play a role. In 1993 budgeted salary increases averaged 4.3%. In 2008 that average had fallen to 1.8%. Estimates at this writing are for pay increases to average 3%.[65] Employees pay close attention to the organization's pay increase budget and evaluate it in terms of inflation and their purchasing power.

Pay increases can be determined in several ways, including performance, seniority, cost-of-living adjustments, across-the-board increases, and lump-sum increases. These methods can be used separately or in combination.

11-8a Performance-Based Increases

As mentioned earlier, some employers have shifted to more pay-for-performance philosophies and strategies. Consequently, they have adopted the following means to provide employees with performance-based increases.

Targeting High Performers This approach focuses on providing the top-performing employees with significantly higher pay raises. Some organizations target the top 10% of employees for significantly greater increases while providing standard increases to the remaining satisfactory performers. According to a survey by Towers Watson, average raises for the best performers were 4.5%, satisfactory performers got 2.5%, and low performers got 0% to 1.4%.[66]

The primary reason for having such differentials is to reward and retain critical high-performing individuals. Key to rewarding exceptional performers is identifying how much their performance exceeds normal work expectations. Standard increases for average performers are usually aligned with labor market pay adjustments, keeping those individuals at a competitive level. Lower performers are given less because of their performance issues, which "encourages" them to either improve their deficiencies or leave the organization.

Pay Adjustment Matrix Integrating performance appraisal ratings with pay changes is done through the development of a pay adjustment matrix, or merit-based performance matrix. A pay adjustment matrix reflects an employee's upward movement in an organization.

The matrix considers two factors—the employee's level of performance as rated in an appraisal and the employee's position in the pay range (their current pay level quartile), which is often related to experience and tenure. An employee's placement on the chart determines his or her recommended pay increase. According to the matrix in Figure 11-16, if employee David is rated as exceeding expectations and is currently in the second quartile of the pay range, David is eligible for a raise of 3% to 5%.

Two elements of the sample matrix illustrate the emphasis on paying for performance. First, individuals whose performance is below expectations receive small to no raises. This approach sends a strong signal that poor performers will not continue to receive increases just by completing another year of service. In Figure 11-16 employees with "below expectations" ratings are eligible for 0% raises regardless of what quartile they are currently paid. Second, as employees move up the pay range, they must exhibit higher performance to earn the same percentage raise as those lower in the range performing at the same level. This approach is taken because the firm is paying above the market midpoint but receiving only satisfactory performance rather than above-market performance. Matrices can be constructed to reflect the specific pay-for-performance policies and philosophy in an organization and are typically revised based on the budgeted increase level.

FIGURE 11-16 Pay Adjustment Matrix

Recommended pay increase when budget average is 3%.

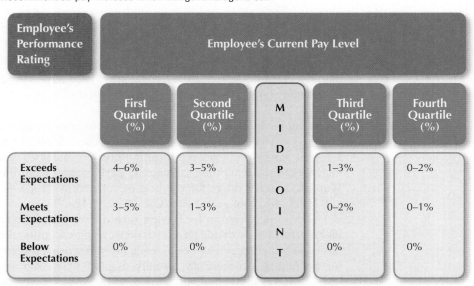

Employee's Performance Rating	Employee's Current Pay Level					
	First Quartile (%)	Second Quartile (%)	M I D P O I N T	Third Quartile (%)	Fourth Quartile (%)
Exceeds Expectations	4–6%	3–5%		1–3%	0–2%
Meets Expectations	3–5%	1–3%		0–2%	0–1%
Below Expectations	0%	0%		0%	0%

Source: Adapted from Payscale's 2012 Compensation Best Practices report.

Compa-ratio
Pay level divided by the midpoint of the pay range.

The general objective is for all employees to be paid at approximately the pay range midpoint. To determine each individual employee's standing in relationship to the midpoint, many organizations use a value called the **compa-ratio**. The compa-ratio is calculated by dividing the individual's pay rate by the midpoint of the pay range. To illustrate, the following is an example of the compa-ratio for employee Jennifer:

Jennifer is an employee in Pay Grade 3. The pay range for Grade 3 is:

Minimum = 8.98; Midpoint = 11.00; Maximum = 13.02

Jennifer earns $9.90 per hour.

Jennifer's compa-ratio is (9.90/11) = 0.90

All employees whose compa-ratio is below 1.0 are paid below the pay range midpoint; all employees whose compa-ratio is over 1.0 are paid above the pay range midpoint. Pay administrators calculate the overall compa-ratio for the entire organization to determine the general pattern of pay rates relative to midpoint levels to ensure that the pay philosophy is enforced.

11-8b Standardized Pay Adjustments

Companies that have an entitlement philosophy rely more on standardized pay increases. Several methods can be used to provide standardized pay increases to employees.

Seniority
Time spent in an organization or on a particular job.

Seniority Time spent in an organization or on a particular job, called **seniority** or tenure, can be used as the basis for pay increases. Many employers have policies that require an employee to work for a certain length of time before being eligible for pay increases. Pay adjustments based on seniority are often set as automatic steps depending on satisfactory performance during the required length of time. This is often used early in a person's employment. For example, the company may have automatic step increases at 30, 60, and 90 days to improve retention of new hires and to reward mastery of job skills.

Cost-of-Living Adjustments Another pay-raise practice is the use of a *cost-of-living adjustment (COLA)* whereby every employee's pay is increased to compensate for inflation and rising prices. Often, these adjustments are tied to changes in the Consumer Price Index (CPI) or some other general economic measure. However, the CPI may overstate the actual cost of living, and COLA increases do nothing to recognize employees for their relative contributions to the organization.

Across-the-Board Increases Unfortunately, some employers give across-the-board raises and call them *merit raises*, which they are not. They are usually given as a percentage raise based on standard market or financial budgeting determinations. If all employees get the same percentage pay increase, it is clearly not tied to merit or good performance. For this reason, employers should reserve the term *merit* for any amount above the standard raise, and they should state clearly which amount is for performance and which amount is the "automatic" portion.

Lump-Sum Increases Most employees who receive pay increases, either for merit or for seniority, receive an increase in the amount of their regular monthly or weekly paycheck. For example, an employee who makes $12.00 an hour and receives a 3% increase will move to $12.36 an hour.

Lump-sum increase (LSI)
One-time payment of all or part of a yearly pay increase.

In contrast, a **lump-sum increase (LSI)** is a one-time payment of all or part of a yearly pay increase. The pure LSI approach does not increase the base pay. Therefore, in the example of a person making $12.00 an hour, if a 3% LSI is granted, the person receives a lump sum of $748.80 ($0.36 an hour × 2,080 working hours in the year). However, the base rate remains at $12.00 an hour, which slows down the progression of the base wages.

The major advantage of an LSI plan is that it heightens employees' awareness of what their performance levels "merited." Another advantage is that the firm can use LSIs to slow down the increase of base pay and thus reduce or avoid the compounding effect on succeeding raises. One disadvantage of LSI plans is that workers who receive a lump-sum payment may become discouraged because their base pay does not change. Unions generally resist LSI programs because of their impact on pensions and benefits. And when calculating the employee's overtime pay, the LSI should be considered as part of the base wage calculation.

11-8c Compensation Challenges

A number of concerns for managers affect compensation planning and administration. Circumstances within and outside the organization can create employee dissatisfaction or turnover.

Economic Recessions During trying economic times, many organizations address shortfalls in revenue by reducing employment-related expenses. Layoffs and reductions in force may be strategies to lower costs, but some organizations take less drastic steps in the hopes of retaining employees through the downturn. Wage and salary freezes or cuts and reductions in employee benefits may be used to save money while not losing talented workers.[67] When economic circumstances improve, organizations are wise to reverse these reductions and restore employees to previous pay levels to improve employee commitment and retention.[68]

Two-Tier Wage Systems As global competition has increased and low-skilled jobs have been sent offshore, some companies have been saddled with high wage costs from decades of generous pay increases. The situation is particularly prevalent in unionized environments with entitlement approaches to compensation. One way some companies have addressed this is to institute a two-tier wage system in which new employees are paid a lower starting wage than existing workers. For example, Kohler Company's latest union contract sets the pay for new employees at 65% of the standard rate for the job. Rather than earning an hourly rate of $22.54, new hires are paid $14.65 per hour. While this approach might save the company money, there are labor relations and equity issues that develop with new hires perhaps feeling less motivated and committed.[69]

Gender Pay Gap Despite laws prohibiting pay discrimination on the basis of sex (as discussed in Chapter 3), there is a persistent pay gap between men and women in the workplace. The wage gap is wider in some industries than others. For example, female computer programmers earn 93% of the rate of male programmers, while female physicians earn 60% of male physicians' earnings. In general, women are more likely to work part-time rather than full-time jobs and to interrupt their careers to start a family.[70] Women have been gaining ground in recent years. They outpace men in terms of college attendance and women between 25 and 34 years old are more likely to have a college degree than are men of the same age. But they are less likely to study technical subjects or go into jobs that receive higher pay.[71] Continued monitoring of an organization's pay levels and career progress for female employees are ways to address these concerns. However, it will take many years to bring parity to overall pay practices.[72]

SUMMARY

- The concept of *total rewards* has become a crucial part of HR management, and includes compensation, benefits, work–life practices, and performance and talent management.
- Compensation provided by an organization can come directly through base pay and variable pay and indirectly through benefits.
- The Fair Labor Standards Act (FLSA), as amended, is the major federal law that affects pay systems. It requires most organizations to pay a minimum wage and to comply with overtime provisions, including appropriately classifying employees as exempt or nonexempt and as independent contractors or employees.
- A continuum of compensation philosophies exists, ranging from an entitlement philosophy to a performance philosophy.
- When designing and administering compensation programs, internal and external equity, organizational justice, and pay openness all must be considered.

- Compensation practices for international employees can be designed using a variety of methods to ensure equity.
- A base pay system is developed using information from valuations of jobs and pay surveys, both of which are designed to ensure that the pay system is internally equitable and externally competitive.
- The valuation of jobs can be determined using either job evaluation or market pricing.
- Once a firm has collected pay survey data, it can develop a pay structure, which is composed of pay grades and pay ranges.
- Problems involving employees paid outside of the pay range can be addressed in many ways.
- Individual pay increases can be based on performance, seniority, cost-of-living adjustments, across-the-board increases, lump-sum increases, or a combination of different approaches.

CRITICAL THINKING CHALLENGES

1. Think of an organization where you have worked. What were its compensation policies and how were they communicated to employees?

2. Congratulations you have recently been promoted and are the company's new Human Resources Manager! You have offices in several countries, how would you evaluate different compensation packages for employees who are located throughout the world?

3. Recently larger companies have been in the news because of violations of overtime regulations. How should your Human Resources department protect itself from these devastating claims? Brainstorm some ideas on how to prevent these issues from occurring.

4. You are the HR Director for an insurance company with regional offices in several states. For each office, you want to be sure that the

administrative assistants reporting to the regional manager are paid appropriately.

A. Go to www.salary.com to find geographic pay survey data for this job in Hartford, Connecticut; Atlanta, Georgia; Omaha, Nebraska; and Phoenix, Arizona.

B. Then recommend pay ranges, identifying the low, median, and high rates for each pay range.

C. To present the data, list each of the offices in order from lowest median pay to highest median pay.

CASE

Is the FLSA a Dinosaur?

Is workplace flexibility out of reach for employees? Based on the Fair Labor Standards Act, nonexempt employees and their employers are restricted by the definitions of a workweek that were established in 1938 when the law was enacted. A Congressional subcommittee on workforce protections recently held a hearing to explore calls for reform of the FLSA. High-profile companies like IBM testified that current regulations are neither employer nor employee friendly. Companies have instituted policies to restrict flexible work hours, telecommuting, and the use of mobile technology to comply with the wage and hour law.

Overtime "exemptions" were granted by the government to only a small subset of workers with an intent to require companies to pay nearly all workers an overtime premium for work hours over 40 in a week. Life was different in 1938 when the vast majority of workers were men working in manual labor jobs. These jobs took a physical toll and long work weeks could lead to injuries and fatigue. All work was done onsite under a bureaucratic organization hierarchy. Workers had little discretion and input into how the work was to be done.

Fast forward 75 years and look at today's workplace. Technology and communication tools allow workers to carry their work with them wherever they go. No longer do we have to travel to a job site to complete our work. Women make up approximately half of the U.S. workforce. Many jobs are "knowledge" jobs rather than strenuous manual labor. Employees are empowered and engaged, and their input into work design is welcomed by their employers.

While public-sector employees are allowed to take comp time rather than pay for overtime hours, it's strictly forbidden in the private sector. This limits employees from working hard early in the year in order to "bank" some time to use for summer vacation or winter holidays. It's a lose-lose because the employee can't get what she wants and neither can the employer. So, no flexibility for you!

If it's such a good deal, who could be against revising the FLSA? There are those who believe that employers would take advantage of workers and things would return to post-Depression era worker abuse. Without being forced to acknowledge and pay overtime premiums, employers might make unreasonable demands on workers' time. There continue to be major lawsuits and settlements by workers who have been underpaid for their work hours. So, perhaps companies can't be trusted to treat workers properly.[73]

It's worthy of discussion and debate. Is the FLSA an artifact of working conditions that no longer exist? You be the judge.

1. Does the 40-hour workweek still make sense? Would you recommend changing to a "pay period" calculation for overtime? For example, if a company pays workers every two weeks, should hours over 80 in a pay period be used to determine overtime rather than 40 in a week?
2. How should nonexempt workers track their time spent away from work doing tasks such as responding to e-mail or text messages?
3. Would you recommend that private-sector employers be permitted to offer nonexempt employees compensatory time off rather than pay for overtime hours worked?

SUPPLEMENTAL CASES

Compensation Changes at JC Penney

This case identifies how performance management systems might be redesigned. (For the case, go to www.cengage.com/management/mathis.)

Scientific Turmoil

This case discusses the concerns associated with having a formal base pay system and communication issues that occur. (For the case, go to www.cengage.com/management/mathis.)

Pay for Performance Enhances Employee Management at Scripps Health

This case discusses how a hospital uses pay for performance to improve employee productivity. (For the case, go to www.cengage.com/management/mathis.)

NOTES

1. Based on Ted Olsen, "Agreements Among Employers Not to Poach Others' Employees May Result in Antitrust Liability," *Sherman & Howard*, May 1, 2012; Jessica Guynn, "Apple, Google, Others to Face Antitrust Suit over Staff Poaching," *Los Angeles Times*, April 19, 2012, Marcus Wohlsen, "Suit Claims Tech Giants' Pacts on Poaching Held Down Pay," *Associated Press*, January 29, 2012; David M. Brown, "The 'No Poaching' Antitrust Litigation Case Against Several High-Tech Companies Continues," *Abbey Spanier Blog* , June 19, 2012; Jonathan Stempel, "Apple, Google, Intel Fail to Dismiss Staff-Poaching Lawsuit," *Reuters*, April 19, 2012.

2. Mike Colias, "Employee Bonuses Driven by Customer Loyalty at General Motors," *Workforce.com*, June 8, 2012.

3. Lin Grensing-Pophal, "Money vs. Happiness," *Human Resource Executive*, December, 2011, 14; Sanford E. Devoe, Byron Y. Lee & Jeffrey Pfeffer, "Hourly Versus Salaried Payment and Decisions About Trading Time and Money Over Time", *Industrial and Labor Relations Review*, Volume 63, 2010, 627–640.

4. Vas Taras, "Direct Versus Indirect Compensation: Balancing Value and Cost in Total Compensation," *Compensation & Benefits Review*, Volume 44, 2012, 24–28.

5. SangheePark & Michael C. Sturman, "How and What You Pay Matters: The Relative Effectiveness of Merit Pay, Bonuses and Long-Term Incentives on Future Job Performance," *Compensation & Benefits Review*, Volume 44, 2012, 80–85; Tom Burke, "The New Normal in Compensation Programs," *WorldatWork. org*, June 2011.

6. Lisa Beyer, "Employers Turn to Creative Strategies to Reward Employees," *Workforce.com*, January 28, 2011; Sue Shellenbarger, "Perking Up: Some Companies Offer Surprising New Benefits," *The Wall Street Journal*, March 18, 2009.

7. Andrew R. Mcllvaine, "Targeting Rewards," *Human Resource Executive Online*, June 2, 2009; Paul F. Bulter & Glen M McEvoy, "Strategy, Human Resource Management and Performance: Sharpening Line of Sight," *Human Resource Management Review*, Volume 22, 2012, 43–56.

8. "WorldatWork," September 7, 2012, http://www.worldatwork.org/waw/aboutus/html/aboutus-waw.html.

9. Joanne Sammer, "Measure Compensation's Impact." *HR Magazine*, September 2012, 85–90; Eric Marquardt & Nick Dunlap "Compensation Risk Assessments: A Process for Active Plan Management and Continuous Improvement," *Compensation & Benefits Review*, Volume 44, 2012, 6–11.

10. Kenneth W. Thomas, "The Four Intrinsic Rewards that Drive Employee Engagement," *Ivey Business Journal*, Volume 73, 2009, 9; Katie Kuehner – Hebert, "Can You Really Have it All?" *Human Resources Executive Online*, September 18, 2012.

11. "Hay Group Study Shows Slight Uptick in Use of Variable Pay," *IOMA.com*, February 2011.

12. Shelley Banjo, "Wal-Mart to Pay $4.8 Million in Back Wages, Damages," *The Wall Street Journal*, May 2, 2012; Allen Smith "Wage and Hour Enforcement Ramps Up," *HR Magazine*, June 2012, 17.

13. Melanie Trottman, "Employees Urged to Seek Wage Rights," *The Wall Street Journal*, April 6, 2010.

14. Sarah E. Needleman, "As Wages Rise, Tough Choices," *The Wall Street Journal*, December 1, 2011.

15. Matthew J. Heller, "Quicken Verdict Gives Employers Hope on Overtime," *Workforce Management*, May 2011, 6–7.

16. Allen Smith, "Ledbetter Act Adds Lengthy To-Do List for HR," www.shrm.org, February 10, 2009; Brett A. Gorovsky, "Lilly Ledbetter Fair Pay Act of 2009: What's Next for Employers?" www.CCH.com, 2009.

17. Jerry Kalish, "Worker Classification Question: Is You Is Or Is You Ain't My Employee?" *Employee Benefit News*, September 15, 2010, 44, 46.

18. "Employee misclassification can lead to big penalties for employers," www.Americanbar.org, July 2011.

19. Mark McGraw, "Reconsidering Worker Classifications," *Human Resource Executive*, November 2011; "Time to Settle Worker Classification Issues," www.shrm.org, November 2011.

20. "Employer's Supplemental Tax Guide," IRS.gov, Publication 15-A, 2012; "The IRS's 20-Factor Analysis," *US Chamber of Commerce Small Business Nation*, 2012.

21. Theodore E. Weinberger, "Assessing the Situational Awareness of Employees for Pay Practice Adherence to Compensation Philosophy," *Compensation & Benefits Review*, Volume 42, 2010, 215–221.

22. John Ferak & Matt Wynn, "Longevity Pays Off in Douglas County," *Omaha World-Herald*, August 22, 2010, 1A; Sharon Terlep "GM Rethinks Pay for Unionized Workers," *The Wall Street Journal*, January 12, 2011, B6.

23. Andrew Jacobus & Darren Shearer, "Measuring Performance, the Right Way," *Workspan Magazine*, January 2011, 57–62.

24. Eric Krell, "All for Incentives, Incentives for All," www.shrm.org, January 1, 2011.

25. Brian Levine & Haig R. Nalbantian, "Back to Base-ics: A Next-Generation Approach to Pay for Performance," *Worldatwork.org*, 2011.

26. Diane Leary, "Communications Pay Philosophy: A Key to Attracting, Keeping and Motivating Employees," *Worldatwork.org*, June 18, 2010; "Inform Employees of Your Pay Policies," *Escan Newsletter*, February 2011.

27. Princy Thomas & P K Thomas, "Payroll Outsourcing: A New Paradigm," *The IUP Journal of Business Strategy*, Volume 8, 2011.

28. Chris Ratajczyk, "A Primer on Base Pay Compensation Metrics," *Workspan Magazine*, July 2011, 31–3; John Donney, "Benchmarking Human Capital Metrics," www.shrm.org, January 4, 2012.

29. Adapted from Rachel Emma Silver, "Big Data Upends the Way Workers are Paid," *The Wall Street Journal*, September 19, 2012, B1.

30. Sefa Hayibor, "Equity and Expectancy Considerations in Stakeholder Action," *Business & Society*, Volume 51, 2012, 220–262.

31. "Expectancy Theory of Motivation," www.managementstudyguide.com, 2012; Barry A. Friedman, Pamela L. Cox & Larry E. Maher, "An Expectancy Theory Motivation Approach to Peer Assessment," *Journal of Management Education*, Volume 32, 2008, 580–612.

32. Todd Henneman, "Pay 'Philosophy' Could Prompt Workers to Stay," *Workforce Management*, March 2011, 18–19.

33. Reginald L. Bell, "Addressing Employees' Feelings of Inequity: Capitalizing on Equity Theory in Modern Management," *Supervision*, Volume 72, 2011, 3–6.

34. Alina Ileana Petrescu & Rob Simmons, "Human Resource Management Practices and Workers' Job Satisfaction," *International Journal of Manpower*, Volume 29, 2008, 651–667.

35. Steve Werner & Naomi Werner, "Indications Your Company Has External Inequity Issues," *Workspan Magazine*, September 2009, 67–70.

36. Michal Wiktor Krawczyk "A Model of Procedural and Distributive Fairness," *Theory and Decision*, Volume 70, 2011, 111–128; Hai Ming Chen & Peng Chuan Fu, "Perceptions of Justice in Extrinsic Reward Patterns," *Compensation & Benefits Review*, Volume 43, 2011, 361–370.

37. Lin Grensing-Pophal, "Addressing Perceptions of Inequities," *Human Resource Executive*, September 2, 2011.

38. Michel Tremblay, et al., "The Role of HRM Practices, Procedural Justice, Organizational Support and Trust in Organization Commitment and In-Role and Extra-Role Performance," *The International Journal of Human Resource Management*, Volume 21, 2010, 405–433; Joy H. Karriker & Margaret L. Williams, "Organizational Justice and Organizational Citizenship Behavior: a Mediated Multifoci Model," *Journal of Management*, Volume 35, 2009, 112–135.

39. Fay Hansen, "Having Their Say on Pay," *Workforce Management*, January 2011, 22–23; Kevin F. Hallock, "Pay Secrecy and Relative Pay," *Workspan Magazine*, April 2011, 10–11.

40. Based on Robert J. Greene, "Applying Analytics to Rewards Management" (Part 1), *Workspan*, January 2009, 47–51; Robert J. Greene, "Applying Analytics to Rewards Management" (Part 2), *Workspan*, February 2009, 83–86.

41. Robert J. Greene, "Rewards Strategies and Programs: Innovation Versus Emulation," *Worldatwork Journal*, 1 Qtr., 2009, 55–64.

42. Kevin F. Hallock, "Go Big: the Firm-size Pay (and Pay-Mix) Effect," *Workspan Magazine*, February 2012, 12–13.

43. Chuck Csizmar, "To Lag or Lead, or Lead-Lag: Examining the Question in the Real World," *Compensationcafe.com*, October 7, 2010.

44. Atual Mitra, Nina Gupta & Jason D. Shaw, "A Comparative Examination of Traditional and Skill-Based Pay Plans," *Journal of Managerial Psychology*, Volume 26, 2011, 278–296. Frank L. Giancola, "A Framework for Understanding New Concepts in Compensation Management," *Benefits & Compensation Digest*, Volume 46, 2009, 1–16; Frank L. Giancola, "Skill-Based Pay: Fad or Classic?" *Compensation & Benefits Review*, Volume 43, 2011, 220–226.

45. Peter A. Bamberger & Racheli Levi, "Team-Based Reward Allocation Structures and the Helping Behaviors of Outcome-Interdependent Team Members," *Journal of Managerial Psychology*, Volume 24, 2009, 330–327.

46. Peter D. Jensen & Torben Pedersen, "The Economic Geography of Offshoring: The Fit Between Activities and Local Context," *Journal of Management Studies*, Volume 48, 2011, 352–372; Arne Bigsten, Dick Durevall & Farzana Munshi, "Offshoring and Occupational Wages: Some Empirical Evidence," *Journal of International Trade & Economic Development*, Volume 21, 2012, 253–269.

47. David Wessel & James R. Hagerty, "Flat U.S. Wages Help Fuel Rebound in Manufacturing," *The Wall Street Journal*, May 29, 2012; Timothy Aeppel, "Detroit's Wages Take on China's," *The Wall Street Journal*, May 23, 2012.

48. "International Pay and Benefits," Boeing.com, 2012, http://www.boeing.com/companyoffices/empinfo/benefits/global/index.html.

49. Kimberly K. Merriman, "Lost in Translation: Cultural Interpretations of Performance Pay," *Compensation & Benefits Review*, Volume 42, 2010, 403–410.

50. Doris Warneke & Martin Schneider, "Expatriate Compensation Packages: What Do Employees Prefer?" *International Journal of Manpower*, Volume 18, 2011, 236–256.

51. G. M. McEvoy, "Reducing the Cost of Expatriation in Austere Times: A Case Study of Two Organizations," *Journal of International Management Studies*, Volume 6, 2011, 1–9.

52. "Cartus Survey Shows Employee Expectations Compete With Company Costs as Biggest Challenges for International Relocation Managers," *Yahoo! Finance*, January 23, 2012.

53. Melissa Foss, "'I Owe the Company How Much?!' How to Manage the Tax Equalization Process to Avoid Surprises," *KPMG.com*, 2009/2010.

54. Muhammad Ali El-Haji, "Job Evaluation by Committees: An Analytical Study," *International Journal of Management*, Volume 28, 2011, 730–739.

55. Angela Wright, "'Modernizing' Away Gender Pay Inequality? Some Evidence From the Local Government Sector on Using Job Evaluation," *Employee Relations*, Volume 33, 2011, 159–178; Kay Gilbert, "Promises and Practices: Job Evaluation and Equal Pay Forty Years On!" *Industrial Relations Journal*, Volume 43, 2012, 137–151.

56. Nancy Hatch Woodward, "Matching Jobs with Pay," *HR Magazine*, May 2012, 55–58.

57. Rajiv Burman, "Building a Market-Based Pay Structure From Scratch,"
shrm.org, April 10, 2012; Joseph B. Kilmartin & Andrew K. Miller, "Understanding Market Pricing," Salary.com, August 2008, 1–5.

58. "2011 Culpepper Compensation Market Pricing Practices Survey," *Culpepper.com*, October 2011.

59. Ted Olsen, "Antitrust Challenge to Employers' Exchange of Pay Information Continues," Sherman & Howard, May 1, 2012.

60. Jeff Carlsen & Barbara Manny, "Why a Job Family Approach?" *Workspan Magazine*, August 2009, 65–73.

61. "How to Establish Salary Ranges," www.shrm.org, May 17, 2010; Kerry Chou, "Making Your Salary Structure Work for You," *Worldatwork.org*, February 13, 2012.

62. "Salary Structures: An Effective Tool to Create Competitive and Equitable Pay Levels," *Culpepper.com*, November 2010.

63. Rebecca Manoli, "Addressing Salary Compression in Any Economy," *Workspan Magazine*, December 2009, 52–56.

64. Nick Wingfield, "Microsoft to Boost Cash Pay for Employees," *The Wall Street Journal*, April 22, 2011, B5.

65. Stephen Miller, "Unanimity on 2013 Salary Forecasts Holding Up," shrm.org August 15, 2012; Fay Hansen, "3 Percent Floor No More?, *Workforce Management*, March, 2011, 32–33.

66. Lisa V. Gillespie, "Moderate Pay Raises on Tap for Workers," *Employee Benefit News*, September 15, 2011, 13–14.

67. Louis Uchitelle, "Still on the Job, But at Half the Pay," *New York Times*, October 14, 2009.

68. Dana Mattioli, "Raises Creep Back Onto Salary Scene," *Wall Street Journal*, May 3, 2010; Paul Glader, "Firms Move Gingerly to Rescind Salary Cuts," *Wall Street Journal*, April 1, 2010; Fay Hansen, "Payback Time," *Workforce Management*, March, 2010.

69. Rick Romell, "Two-Tier Wage Systems No Stranger in Recessions," *Journal Sentinel*, October 10, 2010; Matthew Dolan, "Ford To Begin Hiring at Much-Lower Wages," *Wall Street Journal*, January 26, 2010; Mario Centeno & Alvaro Novo, "Excess Worker Turnover and Fixed-Term Contracts: Causal Evidence in Two-Tier System," *Labour Economics*, Volume 19, Issue 3, 2011, 320–328.

70. Carl Bailik, "Not All Differences in Earnings Are Created Equal," *Wall Street Journal*, April 10–11, 2010, A2; Fay Hansen, "Women's Pay Gap Persists," *Workforce Management*, June, 2011, 30–31.

71. Conor Dougherty, "Strides by Women, Still a Wage Gap," *Wall Street Journal*, March 1, 2011, A3.

72. Kevin F. Hallock, "Pay System Gender Neutrality," *Workspan*, November, 2011, 10–12; Meir Yaish & Haya Stier, "Gender Inequality in Job Authority: A Cross? National Comparison of 26 Countries," *Work and Occupations*, Volume 36, Number 4, 2009, 343–366.

73. Based on Allen Smith, "FLSA: The Dinosaur in the Room," *shrm.org*, July 19, 2012; "Workplace Flexibility," HR Policy Association, *www.hrpolicy.org*, 2012; "Fair Labor Standards Act Questioned," www.alfa.org/news/1872, July 19, 2011.

12

Variable Pay and Executive Compensation

Learning Objectives

After you have read this chapter, you should be able to:

1 Define variable pay and identify three elements of successful pay-for-performance plans.

2 Discuss three types of individual incentives.

3 Identify key concerns that must be addressed when designing group/team variable pay plans.

4 Specify why profit sharing and employee stock ownership are common organizational incentive plans.

5 Explain three ways in which sales employees are typically compensated.

6 Indicate the components of executive compensation and discuss criticisms of executive compensation levels.

HR HEADLINE

Variable Pay "Clawbacks"

Executives and sometimes lower level managers may receive variable pay based on how well they or the company perform in a given year. However, those payments may have resulted from wrongdoing or financial misstatement. Rules aimed at recovering variable pay go back at least a decade, as well as more recently in the Sarbanes-Oxley Act and the Dodd-Frank financial overhaul, specifying the types of situations in which that money can be "clawed back".

Clawbacks have been available, but have not been used much until recently. At Credit Suisse Group AG, the firm has used clawbacks for traders' compensation after losses during the financial crisis. The Goldman Sachs Group has used clawbacks, but will not disclose specifics. At Morgan Stanley, "the claw" has been used a handful of times, but voluntary give-backs (under pressure) are more common.

Former partners at a defunct law firm (Dewey and LeBoeuf LLP) have agreed to give back at least $50 million in past earnings in exchange for immunity from lawsuits. Banks, bondholders, and trade creditors have claims against the firm that total $560 million. The settlement had targeted 672 former partners and sought $90.4 million in past compensation and benefits.

J. P. Morgan Chase and Company is expected to try to clawback some of the variable pay awarded to executives and traders in a unit that has cost the company more than $2 billion in losses. Indeed, since clawbacks are attempts to recover previous incentive compensation from employees whose behavior has hurt the company, the idea is to bring about justice to offset the harm done to stakeholder by unethical manipulations of the variable pay system.[1]

Variable pay
Compensation that is tied to performance.

Incentives
Tangible rewards that encourage or motivate action.

Variable pay is compensation that is tied to performance. Better performance leads to greater rewards for employees. The performance considered may be an individual's, the performance of a group (a team or even a whole plant), or the performance of an entire organization. *Pay for performance* is often used interchangeably with the term *variable pay*. **Incentives** are tangible rewards that encourage or motivate action, and therefore might be related to pay or be even broader. This chapter will deal with all three concepts, and two special cases of variable pay: sales compensation and executive compensation.

Do people work harder if their pay is tied to their performance? The answer is "yes," *but* there are several caveats that make the relationship a bit less clear cut. Employers apparently believe that pay based on performance can be used to tie business objectives to compensation because performance-based compensation is increasing for a large part of the workforce.[2] Variable pay plans in some form are used by over 80% of companies.[3]

Tying pay to performance can be attractive for both employers and employees. For employers, it can mean more output per employee (productivity) lower fixed costs, and shifting some risk to the employees. For employees, it can mean more pay. But not everyone likes variable pay. For example, unions uniformly prefer being paid for the amount of time spent on the job rather than for the amount produced.

12-1 ■ VARIABLE PAY: INCENTIVE FOR PERFORMANCE

Variable pay plans attempt to provide tangible rewards, or incentives, to employees for performance beyond normal expectations. The philosophical foundation of variable pay rests on three basic assumptions:

- Some people or groups contribute more to organizational success than do others.
- Some people perform better and are more productive than are others.
- Employees or groups who perform better or contribute more should receive more compensation.

Pay for performance has a different set of assumptions than does the more traditional entitlement compensation system, in which differences in length of service are often the primary differentiating factor.

The assumptions for a pay system based on seniority are as follows:

- Time spent each day is the best measure of contribution.
- Length of service is the primary difference among people.
- Giving more rewards to some than to others is divisive and hampers cooperation.

There is evidence that variable pay broadly available to most employees does improve company performance.[4] However, not everyone wants to have their pay contingent on their performance. There is "self selection" with incentive plans attracting different people with different characteristics such as willingness to take risks and gender.[5] In fact, some economic studies suggest that some of the variance in male wage rates versus female wage rates can be attributed to this self selection regarding pay for performance. Men are more likely to choose jobs that have pay for performance than women.[6] Pay for performance has a poor record of success in the public sector where a lack of metrics, self selection of employees who choose to work in government, and other variables have contributed to the difficulty.[7]

Incentives motivate some people but not others, and they can take many forms. For example, incentives might include profit sharing, simple praise, "recognition and reward" programs that award trips and merchandise, bonuses for performance accomplishments, and money for successful team results. A variety of different possibilities are discussed throughout this chapter. A successful plan might include a combination of several types of incentives.

Figure 12-1 shows a wide variety of possible incentives for employees.

FIGURE 12-1 A Variety of Possible Incentives

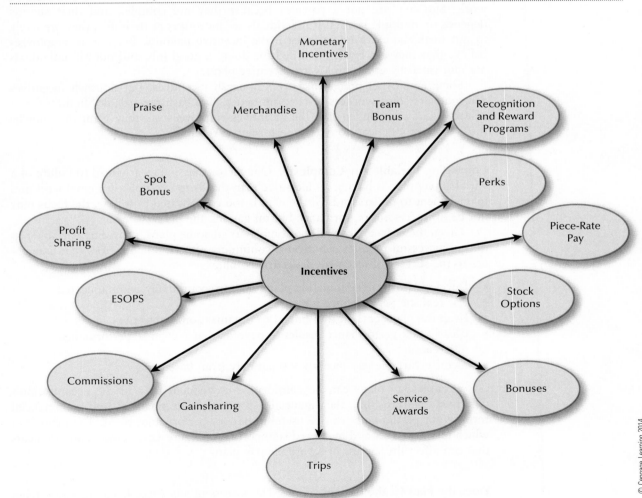

12-1a Successful Variable Pay

Employers adopt variable pay for many reasons. Some of these reasons include the following:

- Link strategic business goals and employee performance
- Enhance organizational results and reward employees financially for their contributions
- Recognize different levels of employee performance through different rewards
- Achieve HR objectives, such as increasing retention, reducing turnover, recognizing succession training, and rewarding safety
- Reduce fixed costs

As economic conditions have changed in industries and among employers, the use of variable pay incentives has changed as well. Under variable pay programs, employees are provided a greater share of the gains or declines in organizational performance results. But even though variable pay has grown in use, some attempts at developing incentives have succeeded while others have not. Incentives work, but they are not a panacea because they are complex and their success depends on multiple factors. If individuals see incentives as desirable, they are likely to put forth the extra effort to earn the incentive payouts. But not all employees believe that they are being rewarded for doing a good job, and not all individuals are motivated by their employers' incentive plans.

Some employees prefer cash over noncash incentives, but noncash incentives can motivate some workers to perform better than cash rewards do. In addition, a research study concluded that the incentives employees say they want may not be those that actually lead to higher performance results.[8]

Combating Variable Pay Complexity One factor that can clearly lead to failure of a variable pay plan is having an incentive plan that is too complex for employees and management to understand.[9] If the plan is too complicated to follow, the focus may not be on successful performance but on gaming the plan.

Given these dynamics and the complexity of some plans, providing variable pay that is successful requires significant, continuing efforts. Some factors that contribute to the success of incentive plans are as follows:

- Develop clear, understandable plans that are continually communicated
- Use realistic performance measures
- Keep the plans current and linked to organizational objectives
- Clearly link performance results to payouts that recognize performance differences
- Identify variable pay incentives separately from base pay

Variable pay plans can be considered successful if they fit the organization's objectives, culture, and the financial resources. Both financial and nonfinancial rewards for performance can be useful in pay-for-performance plans. The manner in which targets are set and measured is important.[10] Figure 12-2 shows many elements that can affect the success of a variable pay plan.

Does the Plan Fit the Organization? The success of any variable pay program relies on its consistency with the culture of the organization. For example, if an organization is autocratic and adheres to traditional rules and procedures, an incentive system

FIGURE 12-2 Factors for Successful Variable Pay Plans

that attempts to reward flexibility and teamwork will likely fail. In such a case, the incentive plan has been "planted" in the wrong environment for it to grow.

When it comes to variable pay-for-performance plans, one size does not fit all. A plan that has worked well for one company will not necessarily work well for another. For instance, in professional service firms, performance measures such as client progress and productivity, new business development revenues, client satisfaction, and profit contributions are typically linked to pay-for-performance programs. These measures might not work as well in a different industry. However, many employers find that variable pay plans make performance results a higher priority for employees. This may contribute to positive organizational results, but may result in a need to adjust the pay plan periodically to make certain it is still appropriate.[11]

Does the Plan Reward Appropriate Actions? Variable pay systems should be tied as much as possible to desired performance. Employees must see a direct relationship between their efforts and financial and nonfinancial rewards. Since people tend to produce what is measured and rewarded, organizations must make sure that what is being rewarded is clearly linked to what is needed.[12] Performance measures need to have appropriate emphasis and weights for calculating incentives for the programs to be effective. If incentive measures are perceived as manipulated or inappropriate, the variable pay systems will not be effective.

Use of multiple measures helps to ensure that important performance dimensions are not omitted. For example, assume a hotel reservation center wants to set incentives for employees to increase productivity by lowering the time they spend on each call. If the amount of time spent is the only measure, the quality of customer service and the number of reservations made might drop as employees rush callers to reduce call time. Therefore, the center should consider basing rewards on multiple measures, such as call time, number of reservations booked, and the results of customer satisfaction surveys.

Linking pay to performance may not always be appropriate. For instance, if the output cannot be measured objectively, management may not be able to correctly reward the higher performers with more pay. Managers may not even be able to accurately identify the higher performers. For example, in a hospital emergency room it may be impossible to identify the unique contributions of each team member and to reward each differently.

Further employee misconduct such as accounting irregularities, churning customer accounts, giving inappropriate gifts to a client and using company property for personal purposes, can occur when employees are trying to meet expected pay for performance goals. The opportunities to be gained from misconduct may exceed the fear of being caught. Performance contingent compensation systems may unwittingly reinforce misconduct, especially if there is little base pay and much of the compensation is variable.[13]

Is the Plan Administered Properly? A variable pay plan may be simple or complex, but it will be successful only if employees understand what they have to do to be rewarded. The more complicated a plan is the more difficult it will be to communicate it meaningfully to employees. Experts generally recommend that a variable pay plan include several performance criteria. However, having multiple areas of focus can complicate the calculations necessary for employees to determine their incentive amounts on their own.[14] Managers also need to be able to explain clearly what future performance targets need to be met and what the rewards will be.

12-1b Global Variable Pay

GLOBAL

Variable pay is expanding in global firms, as well as among employers in other countries. In Europe, Asia, and Latin America, many management professionals and general staff are eligible for broad-based variable pay plans. Programs are similar to those at U.S.-based companies, but global programs must accommodate cultural, legal, and economic differences. For firms with operations in multiple countries, having incentives requires that local managers be trained to control the reward programs.[15]

Although administering any incentive plan can be difficult, global incentive programs can be especially complex. A company may have an overarching strategy, such as growing market share or increasing the bottom line, but that strategy frequently results in different goals in different geographic regions. Also, laws and regulations differ from one country to the next. For example, in Latin America, there are mandatory profit-sharing regulations, that must be reflected in variable plans. Individual incentives are more widely used in China and India than in the United States and Europe. However, these countries have very different perspectives on incentives as the HR Perspective: Ideas on China, Incentives, and Discipline shows.

12-1c Three Categories of Variable Pay

Variable pay plans can be classified into three categories: individual, group/team, and organizational. There are advantages and disadvantages associated with using each type.

Individual incentives are given to reward the effort and performance of individuals. Some common means of providing individual variable pay are piece-rate

Ideas on China, Incentives, and Discipline

The following is adapted from the thoughts and experiences expressed in *Human Resource Executive* by Peter Cappelli, a Human Resources professor at the Wharton School.

Managers from China are not especially good at HR issues because they have not had to be. They have only been involved in a real labor market for a decade or so. But they are *determined* to learn. A question asked by some Chinese managers raised an interesting issue: "What is appropriate punishment for workers?" In some Chinese factories, the day starts with an assembly and workers who made mistakes yesterday are berated in front of everyone—this is clearly punishment. But they almost never fire employees, so what the managers were really asking was, "How can we shake up lifetime tenured employees when needed?"

We believe in incentives in the United States, but we have learned that people are much more motivated by the threat of a loss than the possible gain of an equal amount. A study in the Chicago School System found that an incentive program for teachers designed to improve student performance had virtually no impact on student performance. But when a bonus was provided that could be "clawed back" if students failed to meet achievement goals, student achievement soared.

Are clawback arrangements "punishment"? Probably. Yet several studies show that this approach significantly affects motivation and does not cost more than traditional incentive plans. However, giving people bonuses before they have earned them seems odd from an American perspective. Given the cultural differences, perhaps the Chinese can adopt these ideas and make them work better than the Americans can![16]

---

systems, sales commissions, and individual bonuses. Others include special recognition rewards such as trips or merchandise. However, with individual incentives, employees may focus on what is best for them personally, which may harm the performance of other individuals with whom they are competing. The net result might be good for an individual but less than optimal for the organization. For this reason, group/team incentives may be more appropriate in some situations.

When an organization rewards an entire group/team for its performance, cooperation among the members may increase. The most common *group/team incentives* are gainsharing (or goalsharing) plans, whereby the employees on a team that meets certain performance goals share in the gains. Such programs often focus on quality improvement, cost reduction, and other measurable results.

Organizational incentives reward people according to the performance results of the entire organization. This approach assumes that all employees working together can generate improved organizational results that lead to better financial performance. These programs often share some of the financial gains made by the firm with employees through payments calculated as a percentage of the employees' base pay. The most prevalent forms of organization-wide incentives are profit-sharing plans and employee stock plans.

FIGURE 12-3 Categories of Variable Pay

Individual Incentives	Group/Team Incentives	Organizational Incentives
◆ Piece-rate systems ◆ Bonuses ◆ Nonmonetary incentives (trips, merchandise, awards) ◆ Commissions	◆ Group team results ◆ Gainsharing/goal sharing ◆ Quality improvement ◆ Cost reduction	◆ Profit sharing ◆ Employee stock plans ◆ Executive stock options ◆ Deferred compensation

Figure 12-3 shows some of the different incentive plans that fall under each category of variable pay. These different approaches are discussed individually in the sections that follow.

L02 Discuss three types of individual incentives.

12-2 ■ INDIVIDUAL INCENTIVES

Individual incentive systems tie personal effort to additional rewards for the individual employee. Conditions necessary to use individual incentive plans are as follows:

- *Individual performance must be identifiable.* The performance of each individual must be such that it can be measured and identified. Each employee must have job responsibilities and tasks that can be separated from those of other employees.
- *Individual competitiveness must be desirable.* Since individuals generally pursue the incentives for themselves, competition among employees may occur. Therefore, independent competition in which some individuals "win" and others do not must be something the employer can tolerate.
- *Individualism must be stressed in the organizational culture.* The culture of the organization must be one that emphasizes individual growth, achievements, and rewards. If an organization emphasizes teamwork and cooperation, then individual incentives may be counterproductive.

12-2a Piece-Rate Systems

Piece-rate system
Pay system in which wages are determined by multiplying the number of units produced by the piece rate for one unit.

The most basic individual incentive systems are piece-rate systems. Under a straight **piece-rate system,** wages are determined by multiplying the number of units produced (such as garments sewn or service calls handled) by the piece rate for one unit. The wage for each employee is easy to figure, and labor costs can be accurately predicted.

A *differential piece-rate system* pays employees one piece-rate wage for units produced up to a standard output and a higher piece-rate wage for units produced over the standard. Managers can determine the quotas or standards by using time and motion studies. For example, assume that the standard production quota for a worker is set at 300 units per day and the standard rate is 25 cents per unit. However, for all units over the standard, the employee receives 30 cents per unit. Under this system, the worker who produces 400 units in one day would get $105 = (300 × 25¢) + (100 × 30¢). Many possible combinations of straight and differential piece-rate systems can be used. Not everyone responds the same to piece-rate systems. Some work hard to make more money, others do the minimum. When workers are paid with a piece-rate system inequality in pay naturally arises. This inequality can also affect how people respond to the idea of piece rates.[17]

Despite their incentive value, piece-rate systems can be difficult to apply because determining appropriate standards can be a complex and costly process for some types of jobs. In some instances, the cost of determining and maintaining the standards may be greater than the benefits derived. Also, jobs in which individuals have limited control over output or high standards of quality are necessary may be unsuited to piecework unless quality can be measured.

12-2b Bonuses

Bonus
One-time payment that does not become part of the employee's base pay.

Individual employees may receive additional compensation in the form of a **bonus**, which is a one-time payment that does not become part of the employee's base pay. Individual bonuses are used at all levels in firms and are a popular short-term incentive.

A bonus can recognize performance by an employee, a team, or the organization as a whole. When performance results are good, bonuses go up. When performance results are not met, bonuses go down or disappear. Many employers base part of an employee's bonus on individual performance and part on company results, as appropriate. CEOs can receive bonuses on the basis of specific revenue or profit results.

Bonuses can also be used to reward employees for contributing new ideas, developing skills, or obtaining professional certifications. When helpful skills or certifications are acquired by an employee, a pay increase or a one-time learning bonus may follow. For example, a financial services firm provides the equivalent of two weeks' pay to employees who master job-relevant computer skills. Another firm gives one week of additional pay to members of the HR staff who obtain professional certifications such as Professional in Human Resources (PHR), Senior Professional in Human Resources (SPHR), or Certified Compensation Professional (CCP).

Massive Kinked Bonuses A very large all or nothing bonus is called a *massive kinked bonus*. For example, golfer Darren Clarke ranked 111th in the world earned a $3 million bonus from his sponsor, Dunlop. For some time, Clarke wore the company's logo on his golf shirt and did not earn a bonus. He would be paid *only* if he won a major tournament (there are only four). When he won the British Open (odds of winning 200 to 1), he received the $1.45 million prize and the $3 million bonus from Dunlop. Did this all-or-nothing bonus motivate him more than just paying him $2,000 per tournament to be a clothes horse with logos? If so, what did it motivate him to do? Was he a better billboard for the sponsor prior to winning?[18] This kind of bonus raises questions of motivating potential.

"Spot" Bonuses A unique type of bonus is a spot bonus, so called because it can be awarded at any time. Spot bonuses are given for many reasons, perhaps for extra time worked, extra efforts, or an especially demanding project. For instance, a spot bonus may be given to an information technology employee who installed a computer software upgrade that required extensive time and effort.

Signing Bonuses on Wall Street

Signing bonuses are common in professional athletics as well as on Wall Street for successful brokers who are willing to change firms. Securities firms hired many brokers away from competitors during the last economic downturn, but some of these star financial advisors who were promised six- and seven-figure bonuses to jump ship failed to generate adequate profits to cover their bonuses. The deals look especially bad in hindsight because brokerage firms were willing to pay excessive sums. However, some firms decided they wanted their signing bonus money back because of performance issues and turnover.

The Financial Industry Regulatory Authority (FINRA), which arbitrates such cases, has issued about 165 arbitration awards, with the firms winning a high percentage of the cases. Some signing bonuses exceeded $10 million each in addition to $3 to $5 million that top brokers earned in fees and commissions. Most signing bonuses are lump-sum loans that are forgiven if the broker stays with the firm the agreed upon time, perhaps 5 to 10 years. If the broker leaves early, the firm typically wants some money back.

A UBS AG spokesman says, "It surprises me that in an industry that is all about trust, people would accept money from one firm and then walk on the obligation to pay it back." Some brokers contend that they failed to do well because the new firm did not provide them the necessary support to succeed. But that argument rarely carries much weight with the arbitrator because they signed an agreement to repay the loan if they leave the firm.[19]

Often, spot bonuses are given in cash, although some firms provide managers with gift cards, travel vouchers, or other noncash rewards. Noncash rewards vary in types and levels, but they need to be visible and immediately useful to be seen as desirable. The keys to successful use of spot bonuses are to keep the amounts reasonable and to provide them only for exceptional performance accomplishments. The downside to their use is that they can create jealousy and resentment in other employees who believe that they deserved a spot bonus but did not get one.

Other Bonuses Bonuses can be given for almost anything noteworthy, but some common examples are referral bonuses (given for referring someone who is later hired), and hiring bonuses (given when someone agrees to hire on with a firm). Retention bonuses are used to keep a valuable employee with the company, and project completion bonuses are given upon completion of difficult projects. See the HR Perspective: Signing Bonuses on Wall Street about how Wall Street's use of hiring bonuses backfired.

12-2c Nonmonetary Incentives

Numerous nonmonetary incentive programs can be used to reward individuals ranging from one-time contests for meeting performance targets to awards for performance over time. For instance, safe-driving awards are given to truck drivers with no accidents or violations on their records during a year. Although such

FIGURE 12-4 Purposes of Nonmonetary Incentives

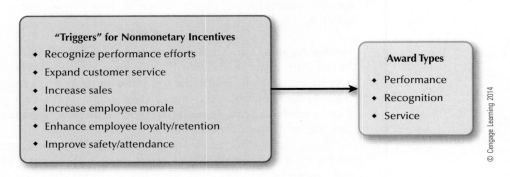

"Triggers" for Nonmonetary Incentives
- Recognize performance efforts
- Expand customer service
- Increase sales
- Increase employee morale
- Enhance employee loyalty/retention
- Improve safety/attendance

Award Types
- Performance
- Recognition
- Service

© Cengage Learning 2014

special programs can be developed for groups and for entire organizations, they often focus on rewarding individuals. Figure 12-4 shows several of the purposes for which nonmonetary incentives are used.

Advocates of nonmonetary incentives hold that there is a growing acceptance of noncash compensation for recognition purposes. In fact, they argue that recognition from an employee's manager may be highly valued including a simple "good morning" or "thank you, I really appreciate the job you are doing."[20] However, research suggests that while nonmonetary incentives may have intrinsic motivating properties, the way in which they are perceived by employees depends on several factors, especially perceptions of pay equity, organizational justice, and managerial discretion.[21]

Performance Awards Merchandise, gift certificates, and travel are the most frequently used incentives for performance awards. Cash is still highly valued by many employees because they can decide how to spend it. However, noncash incentives may be stronger motivators in some cases according to a study that considered awards such as vacation cruises, home kitchen equipment, groceries, and other noncash items.[22] For instance, travel awards appeal to many U.S. employees, particularly trips to popular destinations such as Disney World, Las Vegas, Hawaii, and international locations. These examples indicate that many employees appreciate the trophy value of such awards and the variety they provide as much as the actual monetary value.

Recognition Awards Another type of program recognizes individual employees for their work. For instance, many organizations in industries such as hotels, restaurants, and retailers have established "employee of the month" and "employee of the year" awards. Hotels often use favorable guest comment cards as the basis for providing recognition awards to front-desk representatives, housekeepers, and other hourly employees.

Recognition awards often work best when given to acknowledge specific efforts and activities that the organization has specified as important. Global employers may use recognition awards that reflect cultural differences in various countries. The criteria for selecting award winners may be determined subjectively in some situations. However, formally identified criteria provide greater objectivity and are more likely to be seen as rewarding performance rather than being based on favoritism. When giving recognition awards, organizations should use specific examples to clearly describe how those receiving the awards were selected.

Service Awards Another type of reward given to individual employees is the service award. Although service awards may often be portrayed as rewarding performance over many years, in reality the programs in most firms recognize length of service (e.g., 1, 3, 5, or 10 years) rather than employees' actual performance. Many of these awards increase in value as the length of service increases, and sometimes they are made as dollar amounts rather than as gifts.

Some firms give recipients gift cards to retail or restaurant locations, while others let qualifying employees select items from a range of merchandise choices (e.g., cameras, watches, and other items). Firms can even offer employees special trips to resorts or social events. The overall goal of these awards is to show appreciation to employees for years of service.[23]

HR PERSPECTIVE

How Dropping Commissions Affected a Car Dealership

Performance based individual compensation that includes commissions increases employees' incentives to work. What would happen if an employer shifted *away* from a strongly performance-based pay system to one with a larger salary component and less incentive?

This happened in a large car dealership that changed from totally commission based pay to a mix of fixed salary and much lower commission rates. The change to less performance sensitive compensation had several effects. First, individual sales productivity fell markedly as did salesperson's compensation. Turnover increased among the previously high producing salespeople, and low performance salespeople were attracted by the new system to replace them. This self selection shows how an incentive plan can affect both an employee's choice of employment *and* effort level. Certainly in this case, the choice of a compensation plan affected both recruitment and retention of differently performing salespeople.

Surprisingly, the turnover of high producers did not translate immediately into lower company performance. In light of the decreased individual sales performance, the company hired more salespeople in total and changed the sales mix by providing more incentive to sell higher margin cars. The total number of cars sold decreased significantly after the change to the new plan. But the increase in revenue because of the changed sales mix of higher margin cars offset the decrease in total number of cars sold leaving overall revenue for the company about the same. However, revenue is not profit and the outlook for profit long term is questionable.

The change to a less performance-related pay system had the greatest impact on highly productive employees. It resulted in those employees leaving and being replaced with poorer performers who were attracted to the new compensation system with the more certain guaranteed salary it offered. The company was able to change its sales mix and in the short run did not suffer great revenue loss although overall sales units dropped.[24] What the long run holds is unknown.

12-2d Commissions

A commission is a percentage of the revenue that is generated by sales, that is given to an agent or salesperson. As such, a commission represents a potential incentive for employees who qualify. Tips can be similar, even though they are paid by the customer rather than the employer. A straight salary has *no* additional commission incentive, while a straight commission has all compensation tied to the incentive. Finding the best mix of salary and commission to fit a situation is one of the decisions compensation managers must make.[25]

Sales and executive compensation will be discussed later in the chapter. The HR Perspective: How Dropping Commissions Affected a Car Dealership shows what happened when one employer moved from a 100% commission system to a combination commission and salary system.

12-3 ■ GROUP/TEAM INCENTIVES

The use of groups/teams in organizations has implications for incentive compensation. Although the use of groups/teams has increased substantially in the past few years, the question of how to compensate members equitably remains a challenge. Firms provide rewards for work groups or teams for several reasons, as Figure 12-5 notes.

Team incentives can take the form of cash bonuses for the team or items other than money, such as merchandise or trips. But group incentive payments can place

FIGURE 12-5 Possible Reasons for Using Group/Team Variable Pay

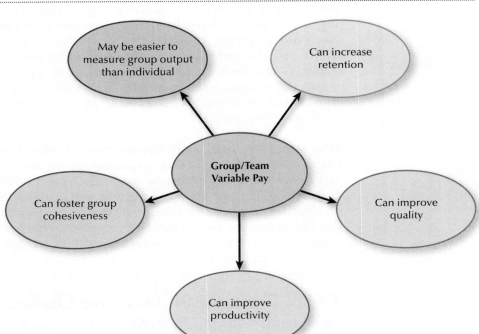

social pressure on members of the group. Everyone in the group succeeds or fails together. Therefore, some argue that team incentives should be given to team members equally, although not everyone agrees.

12-3a Design of Group/Team Variable Pay

LO3 Identify key concerns that must be addressed when designing group/team variable pay plans.

In designing group/team variable pay, organizations must consider several issues. The main concerns are how and when to distribute the incentives, and who will make decisions about the incentive amounts.

Distribution of Group/Team Incentives The two primary ways for distributing those rewards are as follows:

1. *Same-size reward for each member*: All members receive the same payout, regardless of job level, current pay, seniority, or individual performance differences. This is the most common approach.
2. *Different-size reward for each member*: Employers vary rewards given to team members depending on factors such as individual contribution to group/team results, current pay, years of experience, or skill levels of jobs performed.

The size of the group/team incentive can be determined either by using a percentage of base pay for the individuals or the group/team as a whole, or by offering a specific dollar amount. For example, one firm pays members group bonuses on the basis of a percentage of individual base rates that reflect years of experience and any additional training that they have. Alternatively, the group/team reward could be distributed to all as an equal dollar amount.

Timing of Group/Team Incentives The frequency group/team incentives pay out is another important consideration. Firms may choose monthly, quarterly, semiannually, and annually, although the most common period used is annually. Shorter time periods increase the likelihood that employees will see a link between their efforts and the performance results that trigger award payouts. For instance, employers may limit the group/team rewards to $1,000 or less, allowing them to pay out rewards more frequently. The nature of the teamwork, measurement criteria, and organizational results must all be considered when determining the appropriate time period.

Who Makes Decisions about Group/Team Incentive Amounts? To reinforce the effectiveness of working together, some group/team incentive programs allow members themselves to make decisions about how to allocate the rewards to individuals in the group. In some situations members vote and in others a group/team leader decides. Of course, the incentive "pot" can be divided equally, thus avoiding conflict and recognizing that all members contributed equally to the team results. Many companies have found that group/team members are unwilling to make incentive decisions about coworkers.

12-3b Group/Team Incentive Challenges

This difference between rewarding team members *equally* and rewarding them *equitably* triggers many of the problems associated with group/team incentives. Rewards distributed in equal amounts to all members may be perceived as unfair by employees who work harder, have more capabilities, or perform more difficult jobs. This problem is compounded when an individual who is performing poorly prevents the group/team from meeting the goals needed to trigger the incentive payment.

Free rider
A free rider is a member of the group who contributes little.

A related challenge is that of "free riders." A **free rider** is a member of the group who contributes little. Such behavior can cause hard feelings and conflict in the group. Employee perceptions of the fairness of how the group incentives handle free riders influence the trust in management and in the program.[26] Lack of trust can certainly reduce the value of any group variable pay plan. Social pressure from group members to hold down effort or results can also occur. Further, group agreement and pressure can result in cheating to dishonestly pad results.

Group size is another consideration in team incentives. If a group becomes too large, employees may feel that their individual efforts have little or no effect on the total performance of the group and the resulting rewards. But group/team incentive plans may also encourage cooperation in small groups where interdependence is high. Such plans have been used in many industries. Conditions for successful group/team incentives are shown in Figure 12-6. If these conditions cannot be met, then either individual or organizational incentives may be more appropriate.

12-3c Types of Group/Team Incentives

Group/team reward systems can use different ways of compensating the group. The two most common types of group/team incentives are team results and gainsharing.

Group/Team Results Results to be measured may include group production, cost savings, or quality improvement. Those results may be rewarded with cash bonuses,

FIGURE 12-6 Conditions for Successful Group/Team Incentives

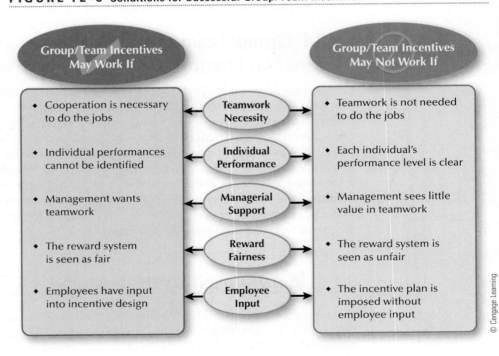

© Cengage Learning

group awards, or some other incentive. The results chosen may be part of a balanced scorecard that includes several important results in a combination approach.

Gainsharing   The system of sharing greater-than-expected gains in profits and/or productivity with employees is **gainsharing**. Also called *teamsharing* or *goalsharing*, the focus is to increase "discretionary effort," which is the difference between the maximum amount of effort a person can exert and the minimum amount of effort that he or she needs to exert to keep from being fired. Workers in many organizations believe they are not paid for additional discretionary effort, but are paid to meet the minimum acceptable level of effort required. When workers demonstrate discretionary effort, the organization can afford to pay them more than the going rate because the extra effort produces financial gains over and above the returns of minimal effort.[27] For example, in a global pharmaceutical plant, group effort was seen as contributing to improved productivity and lower direct labor costs making more money available for group variable pay.

To develop and implement a gainsharing or goalsharing plan, management identifies the ways in which increased productivity, quality, and/or financial performance can occur and decides how some of the resulting gains should be shared with employees. These group incentives may be based on a self-funding model, which means that the money to be used as rewards come from the improvement in organizational results (e.g., reduced costs). Measures such as labor costs, overtime hours, and quality benchmarks are often used.[28] Both organizational measures and departmental measures may be targeted, with the weights for gainsharing split between the two categories. Plans can also require that an individual in the group must exhibit satisfactory performance to receive the gainsharing payments.

Two older approaches similar to gainsharing are still used. One, called *Improshare*, sets group piece-rate standards and pays weekly bonuses when those standards are exceeded. The other, the *Scanlon plan*, uses employee committees to calculate and pass on savings to the employees.[29]

12-3d Group/Team Incentives and Information Sharing

Gainsharing programs provide money to be used as a cash bonus for employees on the basis of cost savings from implementing employee ideas or efforts. The increased use of employee-based knowledge in a gainsharing program may enhance organizational results, reduce production costs, and make other useful improvements. For example, at one time, bonuses at IBM were based primarily on individual performance. The result was a number of "fiefdoms" that paralyzed information exchange. People would not share valuable information with each other because "knowledge is power," so executive management changed compensation to a team-based model. The result was better information flow, which aided the growth of IBM in the decade that followed.

12-4 ■ ORGANIZATIONAL INCENTIVES

An organizational incentive system compensates all employees according to how well the organization as a whole performs during the year. The basic concept behind organizational incentive plans is that overall results depend on organization-wide efforts and cooperation. The purpose of these plans is to produce better organizational results by rewarding cooperation. For example, the inherent conflict between marketing and production might be overcome if management uses an incentive system that emphasizes organization-wide profit and productivity. To be effective, an organizational incentive program should include everyone from nonexempt employees to managers and executives. Two common organizational variable pay systems are profit sharing and employee stock plans.

12-4a Profit Sharing

LO4 Specify why profit sharing and employee stock ownership are common organizational incentive plans.

As the name implies, **profit sharing** distributes some portion of organizational profits to employees. One research study found that profit sharing plans in small firms can help to enhance employee commitment and increase job-related performances of individuals.[30] The primary objectives of profit sharing plans can include the following:

Profit sharing
System to distribute a portion of the profits of an organization to employees.

- Increase organizational performance
- Attract or retain employees
- Improve product/service quality
- Enhance employee morale
- Focus employees on organizational goals and objectives

Typically, the percentage of the profits distributed to employees is set by the end of the year before distribution, although both timing and payment levels are considerations that might be determined later. In some profit-sharing plans, employees receive their portions of the profits at the end of the year. In others, the pay outs are deferred, placed in a fund, and made available to employees at retirement or on their departure from the organization. Figure 12-7 shows how profit sharing plans can be funded and the money allocated. Often the level of profits is influenced by factors not under the employees' control, such as accounting decisions, marketing efforts, competition, and elements of executive compensation. In recent years, some labor unions have supported profit sharing plans that tie employees' pay increases to improvements in broader organizational performance measures.

Drawbacks of Profit Sharing Plans When used throughout an organization, including with lower-level workers, profit sharing plans can have some drawbacks.[31] First, employees must trust that management will accurately disclose financial and profit information. As businesspeople know, the definition and level of profit can depend on the accounting system used and on good and bad

FIGURE 12-7 Framework Choices for a Profit-Sharing Plan

Funding Choices	Allocation Choices
• Fixed percentage of profits • Sliding percentage based on sales or return assets • Unit profits • Some other formula	• Equally to all employees • Based on percent of employee earnings • Based on years of service • Based on contribution and performance

© Cengage Learning 2014

Profit Sharing and Information

The employees at the Canadian packaging manufacturer Great Little Box Company all know how well the business is doing. Management discusses business results in monthly meetings with all 213 employees. This "open book management" is tied to the company's profit sharing strategy. Fifteen percent of pre-tax earnings are split equally among everyone at Great Little Box.

The company started profit sharing in 1991 because they thought it would encourage employees to work harder and share ideas. They were correct. It is, however, rare for most management teams to share financial data with the employees. Perhaps 1% of American companies do so. The open information model is relatively rare. But one can argue that profit sharing can work better if employees know what is going on in the business.

The openness at Great Little Box causes everyone to work harder because they want to increase profits and therefore their own take home pay. They don't let others slack off because that affects them. Even the lowest level workers look for ways to save money and improve productivity. For example, a maintenance worker suggested that a quarter inch less cardboard could be used in some boxes. That one small change saved Great Little Box thousands of dollars monthly. "Less waste—more profit" is the mantra.

The company expects revenue to hit $35 million up $5 million from last year. Managers have been receptive to ideas from rank and file workers who often know exactly how to cut unnecessary costs since they see them every day. Managers find that the suggestions often improve productivity and cut costs.[32]

decisions made. To be credible, management must be willing to disclose sufficient financial and profit information to alleviate the skepticism of employees, particularly if profit sharing levels fall from those of previous years. If profit sharing communication is done well, employee pay satisfaction and commitment can be improved. See the HR Perspective: Profit Sharing and Information on opening the books with profit sharing. Profits may vary a great deal from year to year, resulting in windfalls or losses beyond the employees' control. Payoffs are generally far removed by time from employees' individual efforts; therefore, higher rewards may not be obviously linked to better performance.

12-4b Employee Stock Plans

Organizational incentive plans can use stock ownership in the organization to reward employees. The goal of these plans is to get employees to think and act like "owners."

A **stock option plan** gives employees the right to purchase a fixed number of shares of company stock at a specified exercise price for a limited period of time. If the market price of the stock exceeds the exercise price, employees can then exercise the option and buy the stock. The number of firms giving stock options to nonexecutives has declined in recent years, primarily because of changing laws and accounting regulations, but is rebounding as companies are offering the plans globally.[33]

Stock option plan
Plan that gives employees the right to purchase a fixed number of shares of company stock at a specified price for a limited period of time.

Employee stock ownership plan (ESOP)

Plan designed to give employees significant stock ownership in their employers.

Employee Stock Ownership Plans Firms in many industries have an **employee stock ownership plan (ESOP)**, which is designed to give employees significant stock ownership in their employers. According to the National Center for Employee Ownership, an estimated 11,000 firms in the United States offer broad employee-ownership programs covering about 13 million workers.[34] Firms in many industries have ESOPs. For example, a clothing designer in New York, Eileen Fisher, has an ESOP for about 600 employees. The account was established when Fisher transferred about 30% of her total shares to the ESOP. Doing this gave her employees more incentive to enhance the performance of the firm, which hopefully would raise its stock value. Even private companies that do not have stock are using LTI (long-term incentives) to do the same thing.[35]

Establishing an ESOP creates several advantages. The major one is that the firm can receive favorable tax treatment on the earnings earmarked for use in the ESOP. Another is that an ESOP gives employees a "piece of the action" so that they can share in the growth and profitability of their firm. Employee ownership may motivate employees to be more productive and focused on organizational performance.[36]

Many people approve of the concept of employee ownership as a kind of "people's capitalism."[37] However, ownership can also be a disadvantage for employees because it makes their wages/salaries and retirement benefits dependent on the performance of their employers. This concentration poses even greater risk for retirees because the value of pension fund assets may also be dependent on how well the company does or does not perform.[38] The financial downturns, bankruptcies, and other travails of some firms during tough economic times have illustrated that an ESOP does not necessarily guarantee success for the employees who become investors.

12-4c Metrics for Variable Pay Plans

Firms in the United States are spending significant amounts on variable pay plans as incentives. With incentive expenditures increasing each year, it is crucial that the results of variable pay plans be measured to determine the success of these programs.

Various metrics can be used, depending on the nature of the plan and the goals set for it. Figure 12-8 shows examples of metrics that can be used to evaluate variable pay plans.

FIGURE 12-8 Metric Options for Variable Pay Plans

Organizational Performance	Sales Programs	HR Related
• Actual change vs. planned change • Revenue growth • Return on investment • Average employee productivity change	• Increase in market share • Customer acquisition rate • Growth of existing customer sales • Customer satisfaction	• Employee satisfaction • Turnover costs • Absenteeism cost • Workers' comp claims • Accident rates

© Cengage Learning

A common metric for incentive plans is return on investment (ROI). To illustrate a general ROI example, suppose a company decides that using a program to provide rewards in the form of lottery drawing chances each month for employees who were not absent during the month will reduce absenteeism. An ROI metric would look at the dollar value of the improvement minus the cost of the program divided by the total cost. So if the value of the reduction in absenteeism was $100,000 per year, and the program cost $85,000, calculations would be $(100,000 - 85,000) \div 85,000$, for just over a 17% return on the investment.

Other metrics can also be used to evaluate programs for management decision making. Regardless of the variable pay plan, employers should collect and analyse data to determine if the expenditures are justified by increased organizational operating performance. If the measures and analyses show positive results, the plan is truly a pay-for-performance one. If not, the plan should be changed to one that is more likely to be successful.

Salespeople and executives are two employee groups unique in many ways from other employees because of the nature of their jobs, and their pay is often different as well. Both of these types of employees are typically tied to variable pay incentives more than other employees. A consideration of sales and executive pay follows.

12-5 ■ SALES COMPENSATION

The compensation paid to employees in sales functions is frequently partially or entirely tied to individual sales performance. Salespeople who sell more products and services receive more total compensation than those who sell less. Sales incentives are perhaps the most widely used individual incentives.[39] The intent is to stimulate more effort from salespeople so they sell more.

Jobs in sales in many organizations have changed in the last 20 years. Certainly the sales department is still responsible for bringing in revenue for a company, but today's customers have more choices and more information, and so the distribution of power has changed.[40] The pressure to make sales often takes place in an international environment with many complexities.[41]

Sales commission programs can effectively drive the behavior of sales representatives, especially if the sales performance measures are based wholly or mostly on sales volume and revenues. However, some sales incentives programs may encourage unethical behavior, particularly when compensation of sales representatives is based solely on commissions. For instance, there have been consistent reports that individuals in other countries buying major industrial equipment have received bribes or kickbacks from sales representatives. The bribes are paid from the incentives received by the sales representatives. This criticism may apply especially with major transactions that generate high revenues, such as aircraft contracts or major insurance coverage products.

12-5a Types of Sales Compensation Plans

Sales compensation plans can be of three general types introduced earlier in the chapter. Those general types of sales compensation and some challenges associated with each are specified in the following sections.

Salary Only Some companies pay salespeople only a salary. The *salary-only approach* is useful when an organization emphasizes serving and retaining existing accounts over generating new sales and accounts. This approach is also frequently used to protect the income of new sales representatives for a period of time while they are building up their clientele. Generally, the employer extends the salary-only approach for new sales representatives to no more than six months, at which point it implements one of the other systems discussed later in this section. Salespeople who want additional rewards often function less effectively in salary-only plans because they are less motivated to sell without additional performance-related compensation.[42]

Commission
Compensation computed as a percentage of sales in units or dollars.

Straight Commission A widely used individual incentive system in sales jobs is the **commission**, which is compensation computed as a percentage of sales in units or dollars. Commissions are integrated into the pay earned by sales workers in three common ways: straight commission, salary-plus-commission, and bonuses.

In the *straight commission system*, a sales representative earns a percentage of the value of the sales generates. Consider a sales representative working for a consumer products company who receives no compensation if that person makes no sales, but who receives a percentage of the total amount of all sales revenues she has generated. The advantage of this system is that it requires the sales representative to sell in order to earn. The disadvantage is that it offers no security for the sales staff.

Draw
Amount advanced against, and repaid from, future commissions earned by the employee.

To offset this insecurity, some employers use a **draw** system, in which sales representatives can draw advance payments against future commissions. The amounts drawn are then deducted from future commission checks. Arrangements must be made for repayment of drawn amounts if individuals leave the organization before earning their draws in commissions. The use of draws is influenced by the salary/incentive ratio. When salary is low and incentives high, draws are more common.[43]

Salary-Plus-Commission
Combines the stability of a salary with a commission.

Salary-Plus-Commission or Bonuses The form of sales compensation used most frequently is the **salary-plus-commission**, which combines the stability of a salary with the performance aspect of a commission. A common split is 80%–20% or 70%–30% salary to commission, although the split varies by industry and numerous other factors.[44] Some organizations also pay salespeople salaries and then offer bonuses that are a percentage of the base pay, tied to how well each employee meets various sales targets or other criteria. A related method is using *lump-sum bonuses*, which may lead to salespeople working more intensively to get higher sales results.

12-5b Sales Compensation Management Perspectives

Sales incentives work well, especially when they are tied to the broad strategic initiatives of the organization and its specific marketing and sales strategies.[45] However, as the economic and competitive environment has become more complex and shifted in nature, employers in many industries have faced challenges in generating sales. Therefore, firms need to more thoroughly analyze their sales compensation costs, assess how sales pay is influencing performance efforts by employees, and then evaluate the extent to which the sales and profit goals are being met.[46]

Administering Sales Compensation Programs The last few years have seen sales compensation plans with different design features. Many of them are multitiered and can be very complex. Selling over the Internet brings additional challenges to incentive compensation. Some sales organizations combine individual and group sales bonus programs. In these programs, a portion of sales incentive is linked to the attainment of group sales goals. The variable pay results can be difficult to calculate and administer.

Internet-based software has helped employers administer programs and post results daily, weekly, or monthly. Salespeople can use this information to track their results. Administering incentives globally is difficult, but HR technology has helped as incentive management software has become widespread.[47] These systems are advantageous because they can track the performance of numerous employees worldwide who may be covered by different incentive plans. Consider a company that has different product lines, geographic locations, and company subsidiaries, and imagine tracking the performance of hundreds or thousands of sales representatives for a sales incentive program. Or imagine manually tracking attendance, safety, and training incentives for firms with employees worldwide. The development of software systems to measure and record such factors has been important in helping to support and manage global sales forces more effectively.

MEASURE

12-5c Sales Performance Metrics

Successfully using variable sales compensation requires establishing clear performance criteria and measures. Figure 12-9 shows some of the possible sales metrics. Generally, no more than three sales performance measures should be used in a sales compensation plan. Otherwise, sales commission plans can become too complex to motivate sales representatives.[48] Some plans may be too simple, focusing only on the salesperson's pay, and not on wider organizational objectives. Companies may measure performance primarily by comparing an individual's sales revenue against established quotas. These plans would be better if the organizations used a variety of criteria, including total revenue, obtaining new revenue, and selling specific and/or new products or services.

FIGURE 12-9 Sales Metric Possibilities

Sales Effectiveness Metrics

- Revenue growth
- Margin growth
- New customer revenue
- Average sales revenue per salesperson
- Sales from new products
- Customer satisfaction
- Account retention
- Return on sales compensation
- Return on sales investment
- Increase in average sale
- Control of sales expenses

Considering Effectiveness of Sales Plans Considering so many organizations have sales incentive plans, it is logical to think such plans are effective. However, many sales compensation plans are not seen as effective by either salespeople or managers/executives. One problem that can occur involves making too many changes to sales incentives, resulting in confusion. Excessive complexity also reduces the effectiveness of plans and creates problems with the sales representatives and managers. For example, a financial services company was not increasing revenues and was losing market share. In discussions with the salespersons it found that none of them could explain how sales behaviors or making sales actually impacted their compensation. There were so many factors that entered into the equation that the salespeople just did the same thing each day because they could not figure out how their results actually drove their compensation.[49] HR professionals may be involved in designing, revising, and communicating sales incentive plans, as well as responding to the complaints and concerns of sales representatives.

Effective sales incentives should ideally provide extra compensation for making sales, but sales managers warn that incentive systems will fail when an "entitlement culture" takes hold in the sales force. An entitlement culture is the idea that bonuses are *deferred salary* rather than extra pay for extra sales performance. When sales incentives designed to be extra pay for top performers become reliable paychecks on which everyone can count, entitlement has taken root and motivation drops.

Failure to deal with incentive programs that no longer motivate salespeople causes variable costs (pay for performance) to actually become fixed costs (salary) from the perspective of the employer. Pay without performance, poor quota setting, and little difference in pay between top and bottom performers cause these problems. Significant efforts are needed to establish and maintain effective sales incentive plans.

12-6 ■ EXECUTIVE COMPENSATION

Executive compensation is handled differently than employee pay in most public companies, privately held companies, and even tax-exempt organizations.[50] The amounts CEOs receive are usually more than business unit heads with similar responsibilities in larger diversified companies.[51] The average CEO in the United States in a recent year made $9.6 million.[52] Others, of course, made *much* more. More of that is being tied to stock awards and less to cash bonuses than in the past. Stockholder activists argue the pay is too high and is not tied closely enough to how well the company has done—"pay for pulse" they call it.[53]

From the 1940s through the 1970s there was little relationship between executive compensation and firm growth. However, the correlation is somewhat stronger in the last 30 years.[54] Dissatisfaction over executive pay still remains. It is part of a mix of economic and social problems including the growing gap between rich and poor. Defining what is wrong with C-suite (CEO, CFO, CHRO, etc.) pay is difficult, but the highly respected management scholar Peter Ducker once said CEO's should not earn more than 20 times the average employee's salary—today it is as much as 300 times.[55] What do CEOs do to earn all that money? Ideally, they should do three things well, as Figure 12-10 shows.

Establishing strategic direction requires good judgment, knowledge of business and the industry, and a bit of a crystal ball to accurately see what is coming. *Building an organization* includes leadership skills, planning succession, developing

FIGURE 12-10 Difficult CEO Responsibilities

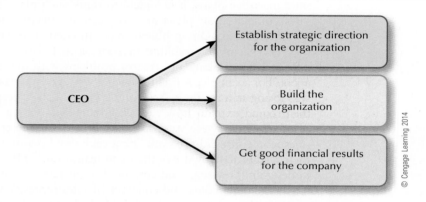

© Cengage Learning 2014

subordinates, promoting the right people, dealing with the Board of Directors, and evaluating the organizations' strengths and weaknesses accurately. *Getting good financial results* includes favorable earnings per share, total return to shareholders, ROI, and many more financial measures. Clearly a successful CEO is a special person because the job description is not one which everyone can do well.

12-6a Executive Compensation Controversy

At the heart of most executive compensation plans is the idea that executives should be rewarded if the organization grows in profitability and value over a period of years. Variable pay distributed through different types of incentives is a significant part of executive compensation in both the United States and global organizations. Executive compensation, however, like business itself should include an element of risk for the executive. Risk should be an integral part of an incentive plan—the executive suite should not be a "consequence-free" environment. When the organization under performs, senior management should see its payouts and stock holdings fall.[56]

Executive pay is in one sense a measure of the power that a CEO brings to the organizational relationship.[57] But in another it is based more on peer group practices than on a rational executive compensation strategy to make the money spent a strategic advantage.[58] Traditionally, companies have looked to other organizations in a similar industry and of similar size as comparators to determine what executive compensation should be.[59] But such approaches have led to the current situation with executive compensation portrayed as excessive, reforms being advocated, clawbacks growing, the federal government getting involved and shareholders become activist.[60]

12-6b Changes in the Context of Executive Compensation

The U.S. government has historically involved itself in executive compensation only by requiring more disclosure of compensation from companies, and changing the tax code to favor some payments over others.[61] However, incentive plans have usually been designed in ways to minimize the impact of such attempts at influencing executive pay.[62]

"Say on Pay" A provision of the Dodds-Frank Act took a proactive approach. Publicly listed companies now must allow shareholders to vote on executive compensation. The "Say on Pay" vote is nonbinding, yet ignoring the vote could certainly create stockholder relations problems for the board.[63] The main benefit to this law is the increased transparency as to how executive pay packages are designed. Votes that are over 15% negative on executive compensation packages should be viewed as a signal that shareholder concerns should be examined.[64]

Shareholders of Citigroup Inc., sent a scathing message when they rejected a board-approved pay package for its senior executives, voting 55% to 45% to oppose. Reasons given were that the bank had not anchored rewards to performance.[65] Some observers estimate that since the passage of "Say on Pay" about 25% of share owners have been opposed to executive pay practices.[66]

Clawbacks As was noted in the chapter opening case, the "clawbacks" provision in Dodds-Frank allows a company to recover any incentive-based pay that was paid out during the prior three years if it would not have been paid under restated financial statements.[67] This applies to all of a company's executive officers (typically the top two levels of a company—CEO, President, Senior Vice Presidents, CDO, CFO, CHRO, etc.). In a recent year, 17% of global banks clawed back compensation payments made to employees. The most common reasons for the clawbacks were breach of authority or ethical violations.[68]

LO6 Indicate the components of executive compensation and discuss criticisms of executive compensation levels.

12-6c Elements of Executive Compensation

Since many executives are in high tax brackets, and their compensation is often provided in ways that offer significant tax savings, their total compensation packages consist of much more than just their base pay. Executives are often interested in current compensation and the mix of items in the total package because it affects the amount of actual value after taxes. Figure 12-11 illustrates the components of executive compensation packages.

FIGURE 12-11 Components of Executive Compensation Packages

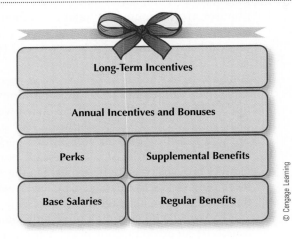

Long-Term Incentives

Annual Incentives and Bonuses

Perks   Supplemental Benefits

Base Salaries   Regular Benefits

© Cengage Learning

Executive Salaries Salaries of executives vary by the type of job, size of organization, the industry, and other factors. In some organizations, particularly nonprofits, salaries often make up 90% or more of total compensation. In contrast, in large corporations salaries may constitute less than half of the total package. Executive salaries are reviewed by boards of directors to ensure that their organizations are competitive.

Executive Benefits Many executives are covered by *regular benefits plans* that are also available to nonexecutive employees, including retirement, health insurance, and vacation plans. In addition, executives may receive *supplemental benefits* that other employees do not receive. For example, corporate-owned insurance on the life of the executive is popular; this insurance pays both the executive's estate and the company in the event of death. One supplemental benefit that has grown in popularity is company-paid financial planning for executives. Also, trusts of various kinds may be designed by the company to help executives deal with estate-planning and tax issues. *Deferred compensation* is another way of helping executives with tax liabilities caused by incentive compensation plans.

Executive Perquisites (Perks) In addition to the regular benefits received by all employees, perquisites are often received by executives. **Perquisites (Perks)** are special benefits—usually noncash items—for executives. Many executives value the status enhancement of these visible symbols, which allow the executives to be seen as "very important people" both inside and outside their organizations. Perks can offer substantial tax savings because some of them are not taxed as income.[69] Some commonly used executive perks are company cars, health club and country club memberships, first-class air travel, use of private jets, stress counseling, and chauffeur services.

Annual Executive Bonuses Annual bonuses for senior managers and executives can be determined in several ways. One way is to use a discretionary system whereby the CEO and the board of directors decide bonuses. The absence of formal, measurable targets may detract significantly from the pay for performance element of this approach. Another way is to tie bonuses to specific measures, such as return on investment, earnings per share, and net profit before taxes. More complex systems create bonus pools and thresholds above which bonuses are computed. Whatever method is used, it is important to describe it so that executives attempting to earn additional compensation understand the plan, otherwise, the incentive effect will be diminished.

Long-Term Incentives (LTI) Executive performance-based incentives should tie executive compensation to the long-term growth and success of the organization.[70] However, whether these incentives really emphasize the long term or merely represent a series of short-term successes is controversial.[71] Short-term rewards based on quarterly or annual performance may not result in the kind of long-run-oriented decisions necessary for the company to perform well over many years. As would be expected, the total amount of pay for performance incentives varies by management level, with CEOs receiving significantly more than other senior managers.

As noted, a **stock option** gives individuals the right to buy stock in a company, usually at an advantageous price. Various types of stock option plans are the most

Perquisites (Perks) Special benefits—usually noncash items—for executives.

Stock option Option that gives individuals the right to buy stock in a company, usually at an advantageous price.

Restricted stock option
Option that indicates that company stock shares will be paid as a grant of shares to individuals, usually linked to achieving specific performance criteria.

widely used executive incentive. Several types of stock option plans are used for executives, with *restricted stock options* becoming more prevalent. A **restricted stock option** indicates that company stock shares will be paid as a grant of shares to individuals, usually linked to achieving specific performance criteria. Other types of stock options include *phantom stock*, *performance shares*, and other specialized technical forms that are beyond the scope of this discussion.

Despite the prevalence of such plans, research has found little relationship between providing CEOs with stock options and subsequent firm performance. The two items may not be closely linked in some firms. Because of the corporate scandals involving executives who received outrageously high compensation due to stock options and the backdating of those options, the use of stock options has been changing.[72] Also, the recent economic difficulties in the automobile, banking, financial, investment, manufacturing, and other industries have led to more governmental and regulatory oversight of these plans.

Exit Packages and Golden Parachutes While severance payments and pension payments may not ordinarily cause headlines, special executive compensation for separation agreements and payouts as the executive is leaving are controversial. The payouts occur right at the time people are often unhappy with the executive and may appear unfair.[73] For example, a veteran executive at GE received a $28.3 million package when he left and guaranteed that he would not compete with GE. His exit allowance represented "a generous severance package in exchange for his non-compete agreement," a consultant noted.[74] Corporate boards are becoming wary of **golden parachute** severance agreements because as a study on the topic concludes they don't work the way they are supposed to work.[75]

Golden parachute
Compensation given to an executive if he or she is forced to leave the organization.

GLOBAL

12-6d Global Executive Compensation

The expansion of global business by firms based in both the United States and other countries has raised executive compensation issues. Numerous executives have responsibilities for operations throughout the world, and they are compensated for those expanded responsibilities. However, senior executives in the United States continue to earn higher salaries than similar executives in other countries.

In the United States, critics of executive pay levels point out that many U.S. corporate CEOs have a ratio value of more than 300 times that of the average workers in their firms, while in Britain the ratio is 22, in Canada it is 20, and in Japan it is 11.[76] Even though executives in other countries often have lower base pay, they also may have valuable incentives at percentage rates similar to those of U.S. executives.

12-6e "Reasonableness" of Executive Compensation

The notion of providing monetary incentives that are tied to improved performance of the company makes sense to most people. However, in the United States, there is an ongoing debate about whether executive compensation, especially that of CEOs, is truly linked to performance. Given the generous nature of some executive compensation packages, this concern is justified.[77]

The reasonableness of executive compensation is often justified by comparison to compensation market surveys, but these surveys usually provide a range of compensation data that requires interpretation. Despite the justification of this analysis, there is continued concern about the overall levels of executive compensation. Some useful questions that have been suggested for determining whether executive pay is "reasonable" include the following:

- Would another company hire this person as an executive?
- How does the executive's compensation compare with that for executives in similar companies in the industry?
- Is the executive's pay consistent with pay for other employees within the company?
- What would an investor pay for the level of performance of the executive?

Measuring Executive Compensation Of all the executive compensation issues that have been raised, the one that is discussed most frequently is whether executive compensation levels, especially for CEOs, are sufficiently linked to organizational performance. Board members of some organizations have viewed CEO compensation as not being as closely linked to performance as needed, resulting in CEO total compensation being viewed as too high.[78]

Compensation in the form of incentives is intended to motivate employees and increase corporate performance and stock values. Another common reason for using variable compensation is the ability to attract and keep employees. These reasons apply to executives as well as to other employees. But for compensation based on these reasons to be effective, it must be clearly linked to performance.

One key part of assessment is the performance measures used. In many settings, financial measures such as return on equity, return to shareholders, earnings per share, and net income before taxes are used to measure performance. However, many firms also incorporate nonfinancial organizational measures of performance when determining executive bonuses and incentives. Customer satisfaction, employee satisfaction, market share, productivity, and quality are other areas that can be measured for executive performance rewards.

Measurement of executive performance varies from one employer to another. Some executive compensation packages use a short-term focus of one year, which may lead to large rewards for executive performance in a given year even though corporate performance over a multiyear period is mediocre, especially if the yearly measures are not carefully chosen. Executives may manipulate earnings per share by selling assets, liquidating inventories, or reducing research and development expenditures.[79] All of these actions may make organizational performance look better in the short run but impair the long-term growth of the organization.

Other executive compensation issues and concerns exist. Figure 12-12 highlights some of the criticisms and counterarguments in regard to executive compensation. One of the more controversial issues is that some executives seem to get large awards for negative actions. It seems contradictory to some to reward executives who improve corporate results by cutting staff, laying off employees, changing pension plans, or increasing the deductible on the health insurance, although sometimes cost-cutting measures are necessary to keep a company afloat. However, a

FIGURE 12-12 Common Executive Compensation Criticisms

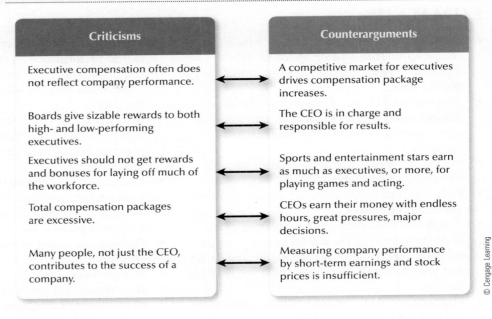

Criticisms	Counterarguments
Executive compensation often does not reflect company performance.	A competitive market for executives drives compensation package increases.
Boards give sizable rewards to both high- and low-performing executives.	The CEO is in charge and responsible for results.
Executives should not get rewards and bonuses for laying off much of the workforce.	Sports and entertainment stars earn as much as executives, or more, for playing games and acting.
Total compensation packages are excessive.	CEOs earn their money with endless hours, great pressures, major decisions.
Many people, not just the CEO, contributes to the success of a company.	Measuring company performance by short-term earnings and stock prices is insufficient.

© Cengage Learning

sense of reasonableness must be maintained. If rank-and-file employees suffer, giving bonuses and large payouts to executives appears counterproductive and even hypocritical.

Executive Compensation and Boards of Directors In most organizations, the board of directors is the major policy-setting entity and must approve executive compensation packages. The **compensation committee** usually is a subgroup of the board of directors that is composed of directors who are not officers of the firm.[80] A compensation committee generally makes recommendations to the board of directors on overall pay policies, salaries for top officers, supplemental compensation such as stock options and bonuses, and additional perquisites for executives.

> **Compensation committee**
> Subgroup of the board of directors that is composed of directors who are not officers of the firm.

One major concern voiced by many critics is that the base pay and bonuses of CEOs are often set by the members of board compensation committees, many of whom are CEOs or executives of other companies with similar compensation packages. Also, the compensation advisors and consultants to the CEOs often collect large fees, and critics charge that those fees distort the objectivity of the advice given.

To counter criticism, some corporations have changed the composition of the compensation committees by taking actions such as prohibiting insider company officers from serving on them. Also, some firms have empowered the compensation committees to hire and pay compensation consultants without involving executive management.[81] Finally, better disclosure can provide the board with a more complete picture of a chief's entire compensation package.

SUMMARY

- Variable pay, also called incentive pay, is compensation that can be linked to individual, group/team, and/or organizational performance.
- Effective variable pay plans fit both business strategies and organizational cultures, appropriately award actions, and are administered properly.
- Metrics for measuring the success of variable pay plans are available.
- Piece-rate and bonus plans are commonly used individual incentives.
- The design of group/team variable pay plans must consider how the incentives are to be distributed, the timing of the incentive payments, and who will make decisions about the variable payout.
- Organization-wide rewards include profit sharing and stock ownership plans.

- Sales employees may have their compensation tied to performance on several criteria. Sales compensation can be provided as salary only, commission only, or salary-plus-commission or bonuses.
- Measuring the effectiveness of sales incentive plans is a challenge that may require the plans to be adjusted on the basis of success metrics.
- Executive compensation must be viewed as a total package composed of salaries, bonuses, benefits, perquisites (perks), and both short- and long-term performance-based incentives.
- Performance-based incentives often represent a significant portion of an executive's compensation package.
- A compensation committee, which is a subgroup of the board of directors, generally has authority over executive compensation plans.

CRITICAL THINKING CHALLENGES

Discuss why variable pay-for-performance plans have become popular and what elements are needed to make them successful.

1. Give examples of individual incentives used by an organization in which you were employed, and then describe why those plans were or were not successful.

2. Describe the nature and components of, and the issues currently facing, executive compensation in various U.S. industries.

3. Suppose you have been asked to lead a taskforce to develop a sales incentive plan at your firm. The taskforce is to generate a list of strategies and issues to be evaluated by upper management. Using details from www.salescompensation.org and other related websites, identify and develop preliminary materials for the taskforce.

4. Your insurance company needs to update the sales incentive program for its sales/marketing representatives. Because of the growth in the volume and diversity of the products being sold, the existing system of having one incentive program for all sales marketers no longer meets the needs of the company. To maximize sales in each of the product lines, the system needs to provide an incentive and reward system to encourage employees to focus on their specific product lines while also cross-marketing the company's portfolio of other products. To identify the key facets of a sales commission program, visit websites including www. 8020salesperformance.com/sales_ compensation.html.

   A. Would a compensation program that offered only commission work for your company? Why or why not?

   B. What other incentives would assist the company in motivating the sales staff?

CASE

Best Buy Pays Big Bucks for CEO

Best Buy, the Richfield, Minnesota retailer awarded its new CEO, Hubert Joly, a pay package valued at as much as $32 million for three years. The slumping consumer-electronics chain with 1,400 stores had been without a permanent CEO for about five months.

Mr. Joly, who is a native of France, will be paid $6.25 million *if he is unable* to get a visa to work in the United States. The deal further calls for Mr. Joly to get a base salary of $1.175 million for the coming years, but guarantees him an annual long-term cash award of no less than $8.75 million for the same period. Mr. Joly insisted on payments to make up for the compensation he leaves behind as he leaves his job as CEO of the hospitality chain Carlson Companies.

Best Buy defended the arrangement saying that it had to compensate Mr. Joly for the money he left behind at Carlson, but that most of future pay is tied to incentives based on his performance for the company. According to one spokesman, the cash compensation is in the middle range of executive compensation for a company the size of Best Buy.

The founder and leading shareholder of Best Buy, Richard Schulze, has announced his intent to try to take the company private after the latest quarterly earnings fell 91%. That may require a proxy fight, although Mr. Schulze remains open to discussion. Best Buy has struggled to make changes in its business to deal with the growth of online retailers such as Amazon.com Inc.

Mr. Joly has a record of stabilizing troubled companies, but he has not previously worked before in retailing. His pay package of $32 million is primarily made up of $20 million in signing bonuses. A person familiar with the situation said, "He is a sitting CEO doing well." Another observer declared, "All he has to do is show up for three years to get most of it." "As a shareholder you would like to see more strings attached."[82]

QUESTIONS

1. Was Joly overpaid?
2. What factors probably led to this pay package?
3. If you were able to vote on this pay package ("say on pay"), how would you vote and why?

SUPPLEMENTAL CASES

Cash Is Good, Card Is Bad

Both the positive and negative issues associated with the use of an incentive plan are discussed in this case. (For the case, go to www.cengage.com/management/mathis.)

Incentive Plans for Fun and Travel

This case discusses incentive plans that stimulate employee interest and motivate them to perform well.

(For the case, go to www.cengage.com/management/mathis.)

Sodexo Incentives

This case shows how a large firm uses recognition and awards. (For the case, go to www.cengage.com/management/mathis.)

NOTES

1. Adapted from Suzanne Kapner and Aaron Lucchetti, "Pay Clawbacks Raise Knotty Issues," *The Wall Street Journal*, May 17, 2012, B1; Jennifer Smith, "Ex-Dewey Partners Agree to "Clawback"," *The Wall Street Journal*, August 12, 2012, B1.
2. Amy Lynn Flood, "High Hopes for Performance Based Equity," *Workspan*, April 2012, 27–32.
3. Allison Avalos, "Salary Budget Increases," *Workspan*, September 2009, 27–30.
4. Maya K. Kroumova and Mila B. Lazarova, "Broad Based Incentive Plans, HR Practices, and Company Performance," *Human Resource Management Journal*, 2009, 19, 355–373; Anne C. Gielen, et al., "How Performance Related Pay Affects Productivity and Employment," *Journal of Population Economics*, 2010, 23, 291–301.
5. Thomas Dohmen and Armin Falk, "Performance Pay and Multidimensional Sorting: Productivity, Preferences, and Gender," *The American Economic Review*, 2011, 101, 556–590.
6. Thomas Lemieux, et al., "Performance Pay and Wage Inequality," *The Quarterly Journal of Economics*, 2009, 124, 1–49.
7. James S. Bowman, "The Success of Failure: The Paradox of Performance Pay," *Review of Public Personnel Administration*, 2010, 30, 70–88.
8. Scott A. Jeffrey, "Justifiability and the Motivational Power of Tangible Noncash Incentive," *Human Performance*, 22 (2009), 143–155.
9. Peter A. Lupo, "Keep It Simple," *Workspan*, October 2009, 65–68.
10. Christopher Bergeron and Mark A. Szypko, "Aligning Goal Setting and Incentive Pay," *Workspan*, January 2012, 44–47.
11. Pankaj M. Madhani, "Rebalancing Fixed and Variable Pay in a Sales Organization: A Business Cycle Perspective," *Compensation and Benefits Review*, 2010, 42, 179–189.
12. Terry Satterfield, "The Role of Merit Pay in Bonuses and Incentives," *Workspan*, February 2011, 40–45.
13. James Werbel and David B. Balkin, "Are Human Resource Practices Linked to Employee Misconduct?: A Rational Choice Perspective," *Human Resource Management Review*, December 2010, 20, 317–326.
14. Peter A. Lupo, "Keep It Simple," *Workspan*, October 2009, 65–68.
15. Kevin O'Connell, "Global Sales Compensation Plans," *Workspan*, January 2009, 59–65.
16. Based on Peter Cappelli, "Rethinking Incentives and Discipline," *Human Resource Executive Online*, September 10, 2012, 1.
17. William S. Neilson and Jill Stowe, "Piece Rate Contracts for Other-Regarding Workers," *Economic Inquiry*, July 2010, 48, 575–586.
18. Kevin F. Hallock, "Massive Kinked Bonuses," *Workspan*, March 2012, 12–13.
19. Based on Aaron Lucchetti, "Signing Bonuses Haunt Wall Street," *The Wall Street Journal*, October 11, 2010, C1–C2.
20. Tom Starner, "The Value of Incentives," *Human Resource Executive Online*, April 18, 2012, 1–3.
21. Daniel L. Morrell, "Employee Perceptions and the Motivation of Nonmonetary Incentives," *Compensation and Benefits Review*, 2011, 43, 318–323.
22. Leo Jakobson, "Don't Show Me the Money," *Incentive*, September 2009, 14–19.
23. Rebecca R. Hastings, "Length-of-Service Awards Becoming More Personal," *HR Magazine Supplement on SHRM's 2009 HR Trend Book*, www.shrm.org, 43–48.
24. Based on Joanna L. Y. Ho, et al., "How Changes in Compensation Plans Affects Employee Performance, Recruitment, and Retention: An Empirical Study of a Car Dealership," *Contemporary Accounting Research*, Spring 2009, 26, 167–199.
25. Based on Scott Ladd, "May the Sales Force Be with You," *HR Magazine*, September 2010, 105–107.
26. Frances A. Kennedy, et al., "The Roles of Organizational Justice and Trust in a Gain-Sharing Control System," *Advances in Accounting Behavioral Research*, 2009, 12, 1–23.
27. Barbara Melby and Vito Petretti, "Money Matters," *Human Resource Executive Online*, March 16, 2009, 1–3.
28. Susan Helper, et al., "Analyzing Compensation Methods in Manufacturing: Piece Rates, Time Rates, or Gain-Sharing?" *NBER Working Paper #16540*, November 2010, 1–2.
29. Alexander C. Gardner, "Goal Setting and Gainsharing: The Evidence on Effectiveness," *Compensation and Benefits Review*, 2011, 43, 236–244.
30. A. Bayo-Moriones and M. Larraza Kintana, "Profit-Sharing Plans and Affective Commitment," *Human Resource Management*, March–April 2009, 207–226.
31. Harold David Stein and Romualdas Ginevicius, "Overview and Comparison of Profit Sharing in Different Business Collaboration Forms," *Journal of Business Economics and Management*, 2010, 11, 428–443.
32. Adapted from Jody Heymann, "Bootstrapping Profits by Opening the Books," *Bloomberg Business Week*, October 3, 2010, 62.
33. Valarie H. Diamond, "Global Plan Design and Compliance Strategies for ESPP," *Workspan*, September 2012, 37–40.
34. *A Statistical Profile of Employee Ownership*, February 2009, www.nceo.org.
35. Bonnie Schindler, "Incentive Pay Practices at Private Companies," *Workspan*, July 2012, 51–55.
36. "How an Employee Ownership Plan (ESOP) Works," *National Center for Employee Ownership*, 2009, www.nceo.org.
37. "Yael V. Hochberg, "Incentives, Targeting and Firm Performance: An Analysis of Non-executive Stock Options," *Review of Financial Studies*, 2010, 4148–4186.
38. Jim Hein and Michael Enos, "Navigating Underwater Stock Options," *Workspan*, May 2009, 28–33.
39. Chad Albrecht, "Sales Compensation and the Fairness Question," *Workspan*, August 2009, 16–20.

40. Lynette Ryals and Iain Davies, "Do You Really Know Who your Best Salespeople Are?", *Harvard Business Review*, December 2010, 34–35.
41. Michael Vaccaro, "Sales Compensation," *Workspan*, January 2012, 33–37.
42. Scott Barton, "Are Incentives Dead," *Workspan*, December 2009, 78–79.
43. Jerry Colletti, and Mary S. Fiss, "How to Use Compensation Draws Effectively," *Colletti-Fiss LLC*, 2012, 1.
44. Desmond Lo et al., "The Incentive and Selection Roles of Sales Force Compensation Contracts," *Journal of Marketing Research*, 2011, 48, 781–798.
45. Chinmoy Ghosh and James I. Hilliard, "The Value of Contingent Commissions in the Property-Casualty Insurance Industry," *The Journal of Risk and Insurance*, 2012, 79, 165–191.
46. Ines Küster and Pedro Canales, "Compensation and Control Sales Policies, and Sales performance: The Field Sales Manager's Points of View," *Journal of Business and Industrial Marketing*, 2011, 26, 273–285.
47. Justin Lane, "Challenges in Sales Compensation Administration," *Workspan*, August 2012, 25–27.
48. Michael J. Gibbs, et al., "Performance Measure Properties and Incentive System Design," *Industrial Relations: A Journal of Economy and Society*, 2009, 48, 237–264.
49. Steven Slutsky, "Tips for Designing the Next Generation of Sales Compensation Programs," *Workspan*, October 2012, 31–34.
50. Mark Stockwell, et al., "Pay for Performance for Executives in Tax-Exempt Organizations," *Workspan*, October 2012, 36–44.
51. Juan Santalo and Carl J. Kock, "Division Directors vs. CEO Compensation: New Insights into the Determinants of Executive Pay," *Journal of Management*, 2009, 35, 1047–1076.
52. B. Condon and C. Rexrode, "Typical U.S. CEO Makes $9.6M," *Casper Star Tribune*, May 27, 2012, C4.
53. Ibid.
54. Carola Frydman and Raven E. Saks, "Executive Compensation: A New View from a Long-term Perspective, 1936–2005," *Review of Financial Studies*, 2010, 23, 2099–2138.
55. Karen Dillon, "The Coming Battle over Executive Pay," *Harvard Business Review*, September 2009, 96–103.
56. Richard N. Ericson, "Risk and How It Affects Executive Incentive Pay, *Workspan*, May 2011, 20–27.
57. Wei Shen, et al., "The Impact of Pay on CEO Turnover," *Journal of Business Research*, 2010, 63–729–734.
58. Todd McGovern, et al., "The Evolution of Executive Compensation Strategy," *Workspan*, September 2012, 31–34.
59. Steven Van Patten, et al., "Taking Peer Group Selection to the Next Level," *Workspan*, May 2011, 48–52.
60. Michael Faulkender, et al., "Executive Compensation: An Overview of Research on Corporate Practices and Proposed Reforms," *Journal of Applied Corporate Finance*, Winter 2010, 22, 107–118.
61. Mamdough Farid, et al., "Toward a General Model for Executive Compensation," *Journal of Management Development*, 2011, 30, 61–74.
62. Mike Spector and Tom McGinty, "The CEO Bankruptcy Bonus," *The Wall Street Journal*, January 27, 2012, A1 and A12.
63. "Sounding Off on Executive Compensation," *HR Magazine*, March 2011, 68.
64. The Wharton School, "Remuneration Rumination," *Human Resource Executive Online*, January 12, 2011, 1–6.
65. Suzanne Kapner, et al., "Citigroup Investors Reject Pay Plan," *The Wall Street Journal*, April 8, 2012, A1.
66. John Borneman and Mark Emanuel, "Lessons from Say on Pay and Shareholder Engagement," *Workspan*, September 2012, 43–46.
67. Joanne Sammer, "Clawing Back Compensation," *HR Magazine*, September 2011, 105–107.
68. "17% of Banks Clawed Back Pay in 2011," *World at Work*, 2012, 1.
69. Deborah Nielsen and Christopher Knize, "Executive Perquisites in the Spotlight," *Workspan*, July 2011, 38–43.
70. James C. Sesil and Yu Peng Lin, "The Impact of Employee Stock Option Adaptation and Incidence of Productivity," *Industrial Relations: A Journal of Economy and Society*, 2011, 50, 514–534.
71. Ira T. Kay and John Sinkular, "Is Relative TSR the Right Measure?", *Workspan*, October 2012, 20–28.
72. Don Nemerov and Grant Thornton, "Are Performance Based LTI Plans Effective?", *Workspan*, June 2012, 32–38.
73. Knowledge@Wharton, "No End to Exorbitant CEO Exit Packages," *Human Resource Executive Online*, July 26, 2012, 1–3.
74. Kate Linebaugh and Joann Lublin, "For Retired GE Executive, $89,000 a Month Not to Work," *The Wall Street Journal*, August 2, 2012, A1.
75. Rebecca Vesely, "Boards Looking to Bring Golden Parachutes Back to Earth," *Workforce Management*, March 2012, 11.
76. Kevin Hallock, "Pay Ratios and Pay Inequality," *Workspan*, May 2011, 14–16; For details go to www.StandardandPoors.com.
77. Jared D. Harris, "What's Wrong with Executive Compensation?", *Journal of Business Ethics*, 2009, 85, 147–156.
78. Joann S. Lublin and Dana Mattioli, "A Few Disconnects in CEO Pay," *The Wall Street Journal*, May 21, 2012, B1.
79. Adair Morse, et al., "Are Incentive Contracts Rigged by Powerful CEO's?", *The Journal of Finance*, October 2011, 66, 1779–1800.
80. Richard Smith, "Underlying Problems in Executive Compensation," *World at Work*, October 2011, 1–4.
81. Martin J. Conyon et al., "New Perspectives on the Governance of Executive Compensation: Role of Compensation Consultants," *Journal of Management and Governance*, 2011, 15, 29–58; Martin J. Conyon et al., "Compensation Consultants and Executive Pay: Evidence from the U.S. and U.K.," *Academy of Management Perspectives*, February 2009, 23–43–55.
82. Based on Ann Zimmerman and Joann S. Lublin, "Best Buy to Pay Richly for CEO," *The Wall Street Journal*, August 23, 2012, A2.

13

CHAPTER

Managing Employee Benefits

Learning Objectives

After you have read this chapter, you should be able to:

1 Define a benefit and identify four strategic benefit considerations.

2 Analyze the differences between employee benefits in the United States and those in other countries.

3 Distinguish between mandated and voluntary benefits and list three examples of each.

4 Discuss the trend in retirement plans and compare defined benefit and defined contribution plans.

5 Explain the importance of managing the costs of health benefits and identify some methods of doing so.

6 Describe the growth of financial, family oriented, and time-off benefits and their importance to employees.

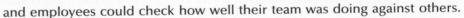

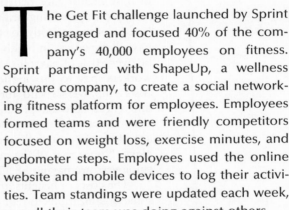

HR HEADLINE

Sprinting to Health

The Get Fit challenge launched by Sprint engaged and focused 40% of the company's 40,000 employees on fitness. Sprint partnered with ShapeUp, a wellness software company, to create a social networking fitness platform for employees. Employees formed teams and were friendly competitors focused on weight loss, exercise minutes, and pedometer steps. Employees used the online website and mobile devices to log their activities. Team standings were updated each week, and employees could check how well their team was doing against others.

Almost half of the employees who started the program finished the entire 12-week challenge. Many employees have continued to engage in the healthy behaviors adopted during the challenge. Sprint felt that employee engagement increased as a result of the program because individuals believed that the company cared about them. Innovative use of technology provided employees a way to connect with others and build a community within the company.

Using social networking allowed Sprint to involve employees at remote and smaller locations, employees previously ignored in the company's wellness efforts. Accessing team standings and posting individual results helped employees to remain accountable and feel part of a bigger movement instead of just their own health program. Sprint employees lost over 40,000 pounds of weight and walked nearly 5 billion steps during the 12-week Get Fit wellness challenge. In the end it was a win for everyone; employees got healthier and more involved with each other, and the company earned higher employee commitment and realized substantial cost savings in health benefits.[1]

Benefit
An indirect reward given to an employee or group of employees for organizational membership.

Most companies provide benefits to workers as part of a total reward package. A **benefit** is a tangible indirect reward provided to an employee or group of employees for organizational membership. Benefits often include retirement plans, paid time off, health insurance, life and disability insurance, and many more. Benefits are not typically based on employee performance, rather they are provided to all employees who meet eligibility requirements.

In the United States, employers often play a key role in providing benefits for workers. In many other nations, citizens and employers are taxed to pay for government-provided benefits, such as health care and retirement programs. Although federal and state regulations require U.S. employers to provide certain benefits, U.S. employers voluntarily provide many others. A recent major change in how health care benefits are provided means that U.S. employers may be less involved in providing health insurance.

Benefits are costly for the typical U.S. employer, averaging from 30% to 40% of payroll expenses. In highly unionized manufacturing and utility industries, they may be over 70% of payroll. At a minimum, a company will contribute more than 8% of workers' pay to provide legally required benefits.[2] Figure 13-1 shows the per-hour costs employers spend for typical benefits. The figure shows that there are large differences between private- and public-sector employee compensation costs, especially concerning retirement benefits. Health insurance represents the largest percentage of benefit costs followed by paid time off, legally required benefits, and retirement plans. Notice that of the average total compensation of $28.80 in the private sector, employers are paying $8.52 for benefits, a 30% add-on to the base pay.

The costs of benefits are increasing, sometimes faster than inflation rates, causing some organizations to require employees to pay a bigger share of these costs. Further,

FIGURE 13-1 Employer Compensation and Benefits Costs per Hour

Compensation Element	Private-Sector Employers		State and Local Government Employers	
	Dollar ($)	Percentage (%)	Dollar ($)	Percentage (%)
Total compensation	28.80		41.10	
Wages and salaries	20.28	70.4	26.72	65.0
Legally required	2.36	8.2	2.55	6.2
Paid leave	1.96	6.8	3.04	7.4
Supplemental pay	0.84	2.9	0.33	0.8
Health insurance	2.22	7.7	4.81	11.7
Defined benefit retirement	0.43	1.5	3.21	7.8
Defined contribution retirement	0.60	2.1	0.29	0.7

Source: U.S. Bureau of Labor Statistics, 2012.

the latest economic slowdown negatively affected many companies and led to changes in employer benefit offerings. These issues show why benefits are a strategic HR concern in organizations.[3]

13-1 ■ BENEFITS AND HR STRATEGY

A challenge for employers is how to balance the increasing costs of benefits against the value of those benefits to the organization. For instance, companies can choose to compete for or retain employees by providing different levels of base compensation, variable pay, and benefits. Using a total rewards philosophy may mean putting greater emphasis on indirect rewards that can differentiate the company from its competitors. Exploring new benefits options and adopting a comprehensive approach to compensation management help organizations to remain attractive places to work. This is why benefits should be an element of the total rewards package when determining organizational strategies regarding compensation.[4]

The benefits approach adopted as part of total rewards depends on many factors, such as the size of the organization, workforce competition, organizational life cycle, employee demographics, and corporate strategic approach. For example, companies employing over 500 workers are far more likely to offer insurance and retirement plans than are smaller firms. Organizations also tailor benefit programs based on employees' life stages by offering benefits that will attract younger employees (like career development opportunities) and employees with families (child-care assistance and flexible work schedules).[5]

13-1a Benefits as a Competitive Advantage

Benefits can be used to create and maintain a competitive advantage for the organization. While they represent a significant cost, benefits are an important factor in employee commitment and retention. Attracting and retaining employees and increasing productivity are business objectives that can be enhanced through effective design of benefit programs. Surveys by Aflac and Towers Watson show that over 70% of employees regard employee benefits as an important factor in their decision to join or remain with an organization. There is also a strong connection between employee satisfaction with the benefits package and overall job satisfaction.[6] Despite this, evidence also suggests that benefits do not always meet the needs of both employers and workers and therefore do not lead to improved engagement or operational effectiveness.[7]

Employers may offer benefits to aid recruiting and retention, improve organizational performance, and meet legal requirements. Some employers use benefits to reinforce the company philosophy of social and corporate citizenship. Firms that provide above average benefits are often viewed more positively within a community and the industry by customers, civic leaders, current employees, and individuals working for other firms. Conversely, employers who are seen as skimping on benefits, cutting benefits, or taking advantage of workers may be viewed more negatively.

An example of how a company can utilize benefits to improve operating results is Wegmans Food Markets, based in Rochester, New York. The company operates 79 grocery stores and has topped the Fortune 100 Best Places to Work list because of its exceptional human resource practices. In the highly competitive, low-margin retail grocery sector, Wegmans defies the odds by offering generous benefits and extensive training opportunities to its employees. Providing over $4.5 million annually in scholarships to employees, paying 85% of health care premium costs, and offering adoption assistance are just a few ways in which the company cements the bond between workers and the company. Employee engagement and retention lead the industry, and customer service in stores is legendary. This is a prime example of how an organization can leverage the total reward package for the benefit of all.[8]

Benefits can influence employees' decisions about which employer to work for, whether to stay with or leave an organization, and when to retire. What benefits are offered, the competitive level of benefits, and how those benefits are viewed by individuals all affect employee attraction and retention efforts. An additional concern is that the composition of the U.S. workforce is changing, and expectations about benefits by different generations of employees are affecting benefit decisions for employers. For instance, many baby boomers who are approaching retirement age are concerned about retirement benefits and health care, while younger workers are more interested in flexible and portable benefits and career development opportunities. Offering benefit plans that appeal to employees at different stages of life and with different needs and priorities is a way to attract and retain a diverse workforce.

13-1b Tax-Favored Status of Benefits

Providing employees benefits rather than wages can be advantageous for employees. Most benefits (except for paid time off) are not taxed as income to employees. During WWII, wage and price controls were instituted to insure appropriate use of resources and to keep inflation rates low. Wishing to attract and reward hardworking employees, companies began to offer paid fringe benefits as added incentives. Since benefits were not paid in wages, they were never taxed as income to the employee yet the company could deduct the cost as a business expense. This explains why the United States differs from many other countries in how benefits (especially health insurance) are provided to workers.

The tax-favored status means that a dollar in employee benefits is actually worth much more to an employee. For example, if Sally is an employee who is in a 25% tax bracket and earns an extra $400 as a special bonus, she will pay $100 in taxes on this amount (disregarding deductions). So, her special bonus increases Sally's total rewards by only $300. But if Sally's employer provides her with group legal insurance benefits worth $400, she receives the full value of $400 since it is not reduced by taxes. This feature makes benefits a desirable form of compensation to employees if they understand the value provided by the benefits. See the accompanying HR Skills and Applications: Gross Up Pay Calculation to learn how to "gross-up" wages.

Gross-up
To increase the net amount of what the employee receives to include the taxes owed on the amount.

13-1c Global Benefits

L02 Analyze the differences between employee benefits in the United States and those in other countries.

There are significant differences in benefits across the globe. In many countries, retirement, health, and other benefits are provided through programs administered by the government. Employers and employees are taxed heavily to pay into government funds that cover these benefits. Figure 13-2 shows the hourly pay rate, employment taxes, and other benefits paid directly by employers in selected countries. An employee in Belgium receives total hourly compensation of $50.69, made up of $24.01 in wages and $26.68 in employee benefits. Compare that to an employee in the Philippines who receives total hourly compensation of $1.90, made up of $1.41 in wages and $0.49 in employee benefits. Employee benefits make up nearly 50% of

GLOBAL

HR SKILLS AND APPLICATIONS

Gross up Pay Calculation

To determine the "true" value of employee benefits, HR professionals can calculate the "gross-up" amount that represents the equivalent pay to the employee. **Gross-up** means to increase the net amount of what the employee receives to include the taxes owed on the amount. Let's say that Harold is our employee and he is in a 38% tax bracket. His employer provides pet care insurance worth $200. Harold is given the choice of accepting the pet insurance benefit or taking the cash equivalent. To be fair, Harold should receive the grossed-up value of that benefit, not simply $200 in his paycheck. Remember that if he receives $200 in his pay, he will pay income taxes on that amount and will net $124 ($200 less taxes of $76).

To calculate how much the $200 is really worth to Harold, calculate the gross-up by following these steps:

1. 100% − tax% = Net%
   (100% − 38%) = 62%
2. Payment/Net% = Gross amount of earnings
   ($200/62%) = $322.58
3. Check by calculating Harold's gross-to-net pay
   (Payment × Net%) = Net pay
   ($322.58 × 62%) = $200

Now, Harold can make an informed decision about which option to select, knowing that he is receiving the same value no matter which way he chooses. The $200 insurance benefit is really worth $322.58 to an employee in the 38% tax bracket (if he or she has a dog).

FIGURE 13-2 Global Comparison of Hourly Compensation in U.S. Dollars

Country	Hourly Pay	Value of Mandatory Benefits Paid by Employer	Value of Voluntary Benefits Paid by Employer	Total
Belgium	24.01	16.39	10.29	50.69
Germany	25.80	9.52	8.43	43.75
France	21.06	12.95	6.55	40.56
Canada	24.23	8.03	3.42	35.68
United States	23.32	8.47	2.95	34.74
Japan	18.32	5.71	7.97	32.00
United Kingdom	21.16	4.39	3.89	29.44
Brazil	5.41	3.24	1.43	10.08
Philippines	1.41	0.18	0.31	1.90

Source: U.S. Bureau of Labor Statistics.

the compensation for workers in Belgium, France, and Brazil and only 25% of compensation to workers in the Philippines. Employers in the United States pay an average of approximately 32% on top of wages for benefits provided to workers.

Driving the high costs of benefits in many nations are generous retirement and health insurance plans coupled with an aging workforce and increasing retiree populations. Currently, the standard retirement age for workers in France is 60. In response to recent economic hardships in the Euro Zone, the French government attempted to increase the retirement age to 62, but citizens demonstrated and threatened to strike in protest.[9] In Portugal, the government was forced to drop a controversial plan to increase employee social security contributions from 11% to 18% of pay in an effort to address public deficits. An outcry by unions and workers put an end to the idea, and now the government will seek alternate ways to restore economic stability.[10] National pension programs in Germany, France, and Japan, among other countries are facing significant financial pressures because of their aging workforces and populations. The Social Security and Medicare systems in the United States face similar challenges.

Health care benefits also differ significantly worldwide. Developed nations (with the exception of the United States until very recently) are far more likely to provide compulsory, government-sponsored health plans for all citizens, regardless of employment status. Countries including Great Britain, Chile, South Korea, Thailand, Brazil, and Canada have universal health care programs. These programs are financed either by employer contributions or from income taxes paid by employees, or a combination of both. In most countries, wealthier citizens can purchase private health insurance and seek treatment from private medical providers rather than using public medical providers. Recent changes in the law mean that U.S. citizens will have universal access to health care in the coming years. This topic will be covered in greater detail later in this chapter. Figure 13-3 shows the percent of Gross Domestic Product (GDP) for health care in selected countries. Costs in the United States are the highest in the world at nearly 18% of 2010 GDP, while developing nations like Bangladesh spend less than 4% of GDP.

The amount of paid leave and vacation time also vary significantly around the globe. Employees in Brazil, Lithuania, Finland, and Russia are provided paid holiday and vacation of 40 days per year, while in Canada and China employees are provided only 20 days. India mandates that employees receive pay for 12 days of annual vacation plus 16 public holidays off work each year. The United States differs from most other nations in that federal law does not mandate pay for time not worked. Although there is no required minimum holiday allowance, the typical American receives an average of around 15 paid days off annually (paid holidays plus vacation).[11]

Paid time off for childbirth and medical disability are generous in Scandinavian and European countries and they provide lengthy paid leave for new mothers. Many also provide paid time off for new fathers as well. For example, mothers in Sweden receive 14 weeks of job-protected maternity leave with at least 80% salary paid while fathers receive 2 weeks of paternity leave at 80% of salary. In addition, parents are eligible for up to 480 additional paid days off for parental leave until the child's first year of school. Few industrialized nations do not mandate such benefits for employees.[12]

Paid sick leave policies are also more extensive around the world. The United States is the only major developed nation that does not guarantee workers paid sick leave. Nations in Europe offer substantial paid time off for illness. Luxembourg and Norway require employers to allow 50 days of paid time off for employee illness.

FIGURE 13-3 Percentage of GDP Spent on Health Care in Select Countries

Country Name	1995	2010
United States	13.56	17.89
France	10.37	11.88
Germany	10.09	11.64
Canada	9.04	11.29
Portugal	7.76	11.00
Austria	9.53	10.97
Belgium	8.52	10.71
Brazil	6.65	9.01
Korea, Rep.	3.93	6.93
Mexico	5.15	6.32
China	3.54	5.07
India	4.25	4.05
Thailand	3.53	3.88
Philippines	3.45	3.61
Bangladesh	3.52	3.48

Source: World Bank, 2012.

Many of the maternity and sick-leave benefits are funded by employer contributions although benefits are paid from a government-administered program.[13]

These examples illustrate the challenges faced by firms that have employees located in different countries. Firms provide generous benefits to be competitive in local labor markets. But finding equitable and practical solutions to the differences among national requirements are complex. Multinational companies operating in various countries must determine how to compensate both host-country nationals and expatriates so that all employees will feel that they are being treated fairly. How they handle these decisions impacts global attraction and retention of employees among international employers.

13-1d Public-Sector Benefits

Workers in the public sector have for many years enjoyed more generous benefits than those in the private sector. Many states and cities face serious budget shortfalls because of the funding requirements for employee retirement and health care plans. For example, retiree costs in the city of Providence, RI now amount to 50% of the city's tax collections.[14] Several state governments have deferred payments to pension funds because they are already in debt and do not have enough tax revenue to cover the costs. This has led to proposed and enacted legislation in several states to roll back the power of public sector unions who have successfully bargained for these benefits.

Public sector workers (police, firefighters, teachers, and other government workers) belong to labor unions at a much higher rate than do nongovernment workers. Their union contracts often include free health care and traditional defined benefit pension plans. These are costly benefits that many states and cities can no longer afford. However, because the benefits are part of negotiated labor agreements, both the union and the employer must agree on changes. Some states and their union workers are finding ways to modify benefits plans. Many others will be dealing with this issue in the coming years.

13-2 ■ MANAGING BENEFITS

Benefit programs must be designed, administered, measured, and communicated. To maximize the impact that employee benefits have on employee satisfaction and retention, careful consideration must be given to designing benefit programs with the overall organizational philosophy and strategy in mind. The HR Skills and Applications: Getting the Best Bang for the Benefits Buck offers some best practices regarding designing and communicating employee benefits.

13-2a Benefits Design

Organizations design benefit plans with a goal of providing value for employees while remaining cost-effective for the company. Many key decisions must be made as part of benefits design as highlighted in Figure 13-4.

Flexible benefits plan
Program that allows employees to select the benefits they prefer from groups of benefits established by the employer.

Flexible Benefits As part of both benefits design and administration, employers may offer employees choices in benefits. A **flexible benefits plan** allows employees to select the benefits they prefer from options established by the employer. As a result of the changing composition of the workforce, flexible benefits plans have grown in popularity. Flexible benefits systems recognize that individual employee situations differ because of age, family status, and lifestyle. For instance, dual-career couples may not want to duplicate benefits from two different employers. Under a flex plan, one of them can forgo some benefits that are available in the partner's plan and take other benefits instead.

A problem with flexibility in benefit choice is that employees may choose an inappropriate benefits package. Younger employees may decide not to participate

FIGURE 13-4 Benefit Design Decisions

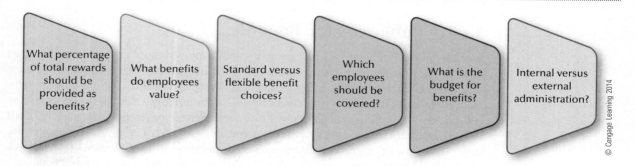

What percentage of total rewards should be provided as benefits? | What benefits do employees value? | Standard versus flexible benefit choices? | Which employees should be covered? | What is the budget for benefits? | Internal versus external administration?

© Cengage Learning 2014

HR SKILLS AND APPLICATIONS

Getting the Best Bang for the Benefits Buck

There are several recommended steps a company can take to maximize the value of employee benefits and insure that employees are attracted to the offerings.

Involve employees

Give employees an opportunity to provide input into the process. Find out what is important to them regarding their benefits. Ask for their preferences and priorities. Use employee surveys and focus groups to discover what employees want. It is good to involve diverse groups of employees because preferences may differ among individuals.

Compare but don't imitate

While imitation is the most sincere form of flattery, a company can use its benefit programs to differentiate itself in the labor market. Find unique benefits that reflect the organization's culture and values to cement the employment brand and make people want to work there. An organization should ensure that its benefits are competitive in the labor market by studying what other companies offer. But make benefits "your own" by creatively offering programs that are different than the competition.

Link benefits to business objectives

Tie benefit programs to company core values and business objectives. Use benefits like time off to reward employees who perform well or meet goals. Employees may value time off or development opportunities more than financial rewards. Think of the "total rewards" formula when focusing employees on organizational goals.

Don't let the dust build up

Employee preferences and labor markets change. Prevent benefit programs from "getting stale" by reviewing them every year. An annual checkup helps to keep benefits aligned with organizational goals and ensures that they are meeting employee needs. If turnover begins to increase or hiring becomes difficult, it's good to review benefits to make sure they are competitive and valued by employees.

Communicate the details and value of benefit plans

Companies that communicate the details of benefit plans get a much higher "bang for the buck." If benefit programs are a well-kept secret it is doubtful that they are seen as valuable by employees. Use the company website and chat rooms, especially during open enrollment periods to provide all the information employees need to get the most use of their benefits. Use employee testimonials to share stories about how employees use their benefits and why they are important.[15]

---

in the retirement plan because they believe retirement is decades away and that there is sufficient time to save in the future. However, this may result in inadequate retirement savings for the employee. Part of this problem can be overcome by requiring employees to select a core set of benefits (life, health, retirement, and disability insurance) and then offering options on other benefits.

Adverse selection
Situation in which *only* higher-risk employees select and use certain benefits.

Another problem can be **adverse selection** by employees, whereby only higher-risk employees select and use certain benefits. For example, employees with young children are far more likely to enroll in orthodontia benefit plans that provide braces than are older employees. Since insurance plans are based on a group rate, the premium rates might be higher because too few employees who do not need braces enroll in the plan.

Offering more choices leads to higher administrative costs for the organization. Since many flexible plans have become complex, they require more administrative time and information systems to track the choices made by employees. Despite the disadvantages, flex plans will likely continue to grow in popularity.

Part-Time Employee Benefits Another key design issue is whether or not to provide benefits to part-time employees. Many employers do not provide part-time employee benefits, except some paid time off. Figure 13-5 shows the percentage of full-time and part-time employees in the private sector that have access to employee benefits. Part-time employees are most likely to receive paid time off and retirement benefits and least likely to receive medical and life insurance benefits. Part-time employees who receive benefits usually do so in proportion to the percentage of full-time work they provide. Companies such as Lands' End, Lowe's, REI, and UPS have been recognized as exceptional employers because they offer generous benefits to part-time workers.[16]

Domestic Partner Benefits Under some state laws, same-sex domestic partners may be entitled to coverage on company medical insurance plans and to be recognized under retirement plans as a surviving spouse. In states where gay marriage is legal, companies must treat same-sex partners in the same manner as traditional married couples. The majority of the Fortune 500 companies offer domestic partner benefits to same-sex couples, and a significant number of local and state governments also do so. Universities tend to lead the way in providing these benefits. Offering same-sex domestic partner benefits shows that an organization is compassionate, progressive, and respectful of all employees, and these programs can be a competitive advantage in the search for talent.[17]

Older Workers Benefit Needs Hiring and retaining older workers can be an important strategy for an organization seeking high-quality talent with a wealth

FIGURE 13-5 Access to Employee Benefits for Private-Sector Workers

Benefit Category	Part-time Employee		Full-time Employee	
	Access (%)	Participation (%)	Access (%)	Participation (%)
Paid holidays	40	40	90	90
Paid vacation	35	35	91	91
Paid sick leave	23	23	75	75
Retirement plan	38	19	74	59
Medical insurance	24	13	86	64
Life insurance	13	12	73	71

Source: U.S. Bureau of Labor Statistics, 2012.

Note: "Access" means that the employee has the opportunity to enroll in the benefit plan. "Participation" means that the employee actually enrolls in the benefit plan or receives the benefit.

of knowledge and experience. Modified work schedules, part-time benefits, and simplified seasonal travel can be attractive to older workers. For example, CVS Caremark instituted a snowbird program to allow pharmacists to migrate south for the winter months and transfer to pharmacies in those locations. The pharmacists return to their northern homes during the warmer months and work in pharmacies there for the summer.[18]

Phased retirement programs allow employees to work part time and withdraw some retirement funds at the same time. Wellness programs and annual financial planning counseling are also highly valued by older workers. Since many older workers plan to remain actively employed into their later years, organizations can offer benefits targeted to this employee population and retain skilled workers for the organization.

13-3 ■ BENEFITS ADMINISTRATION, TECHNOLOGY, AND COMMUNICATION

Legal compliance, recordkeeping, enrollment, and participation issues result in a significant benefits administrative responsibility for organizations. Organizations may elect to have internal benefits professionals handle these duties, or they may use employees and vendors to streamline many of the routine clerical tasks involved. Many organizations offer an open enrollment period once a year. **Open enrollment** is a time when employees can change their participation level in various benefit plans and switch between benefit options.

Open enrollment
A time when employees can change their participation level in various benefit plans and switch between benefit options.

Third-party administrator (TPA)
A vendor that provides administrative services to an organization.

Outsourcing Benefits Administration With the myriad of benefits, it is easy to see why many organizations must make coordinated efforts to administer benefits programs. One significant trend is the outsourcing of benefits administration. **Third-party administrators** (TPA) are vendors that provide enrollment, recordkeeping, and other administrative services to companies. Over 60% of companies outsource their retirement benefits and 50% outsource their medical insurance plans.[19] Outsourcing is on the rise, and many organizations use TPAs to help manage costs and to provide expertise and efficiency in plan administration.

Technology and Employee Self-Service The spread of HR technology, particularly web-based and mobile systems, has significantly changed the benefits administration burden on HR staff. Internet and computer-based systems are being used to communicate benefits information, conduct employee benefits surveys, and facilitate benefits administration. These systems can decrease expenses, increase positive communication, and effectively connect people across many HR functions, including benefits management.

Information technology makes it possible for companies to offer self-service to employees. **Self-service** allows employees to change their benefits choices, track their benefits balances, and submit questions to HR staff members and external benefits providers. However, not all employees can easily navigate the online system for benefits enrollment and maintenance. While the ideal self-service portal includes links to medical care providers, investment funds for retirement plans, and other important information, it can easily overwhelm employees. It is therefore important that assistance is available and that employees are provided with help screens, contact information for administrators, and access to HR experts.[20]

Self-service
Technology that allows employees to change their benefits choices, track their benefits balances, and submit questions to HR staff members and external benefits providers.

FIGURE 13-6 Frequently Used Benefits Metrics

Benefits as a percent of payroll

Benefit costs per FTE

Benefit costs by employee group

Benefits administration costs

Health care costs per FTE

Retirement plan participation rate

Paid time off utilization

Tuition reimbursement costs

© Cengage Learning 2014

MEASURE

13-3a Benefits Measurement

The significant costs associated with benefits require that analyses be conducted to determine the payoffs for the expenditures. Numerous HR metrics can be used to evaluate whether benefits are providing the expected results in terms of employee retention and satisfaction. Some examples are shown in Figure 13-6.

Other metrics are used to measure the return on the expenditures for various benefits programs provided by employers. Some common benefits that employers track using HR metrics are workers' compensation, wellness programs, prescription drug costs, leave time, tuition aid, and disability insurance. The point is that both benefits expenditures generally and costs for individual benefits specifically need to be measured and evaluated as part of strategic benefits management.

13-3b Benefits Cost Control

Since benefits costs have risen significantly in the past several years, particularly for health care, employers are focusing more attention on measuring and controlling them, even reducing or dropping benefits offered to employees. Increases in employer expenditures for benefits are growing faster than increases in wages for employees.[21] For example, during economic downturns, many organizations stop contributing to the employee 401(k) plan, reduce education reimbursement, and cut training expenses. Companies are likely to wait until they are confident that they can afford the programs before benefits are reinstated. To soften the blow to employees, some companies add voluntary benefits such as group auto and home insurance programs at reduced group rates.

Another common means of benefits cost control is cost sharing, which refers to having employees pay for more of their benefits costs. The majority of firms use this strategy along with wellness programs, offering employee health education efforts, and changing prescription drug programs. Companies might also consider consolidating benefits packages into more streamlined offerings so that costs can be minimized.

13-3c Benefits Communication

Employees generally do not know much about the values and costs associated with the benefits provided by employers. This is in large measure due to ineffective communication by the company. Over 40% of benefits professionals are not sure if their benefits communication efforts are helping them to meet their goals.[22] That means the investment many companies make in employee benefits may not be helping them attract and retain workers.

Benefits communication and employees' satisfaction with benefits are linked. For instance, employees often do not fully understand their health benefits, a situation that can cause dissatisfaction. Consequently, many employers develop special benefits communication systems to inform employees about the monetary value of the benefits they provide. Employees are actually more satisfied with an employer that provides fewer benefits but does a better job of explaining them so that employees understand what they are receiving.[23]

Employers can adopt some "best practices" when designing benefit communications. Creating a clear communication strategy, using a benefits website, and being connected to social media are ways to ensure that workers can easily access information about their benefit plans.[24] Some of the important information to be communicated includes the value of the plans offered, why changes have to be made, and the fundamental financial costs of the plans. Some benefits laws include specific communication provisions.

Younger employees (Generation Y) generally give low marks to their company's benefits communications.[25] They find that the information they receive is not informative or helpful in their decision making regarding benefits participation. Companies that address this by providing personal counseling and making online content more interactive can engage this group of employees and improve the perception of value delivered by benefits.

When planning benefits communication efforts, it is important to consider factors such as the timing and frequency, the communication methods, and the specialized content. Any significant changes to benefits, such as reduction in 401(k) matches and increases in employee health plan contributions, should be communicated by the top managers in the organization. Providing the rationale for these actions helps employees understand why their benefits are being changed. These communications should be supported by HR professionals and other key managers who are well-informed to answer any questions.

Benefits Statements Some companies give individual employees a personal statement that translates benefits into dollar amounts. These statements give employees a snapshot of the total compensation they receive. They help employees to see the "hidden paycheck"—the value of their benefits. These statements can be shared with family members to emphasize the true package of rewards provided by the employer.

13-3d Types of Benefits

L03 Distinguish between mandated and voluntary benefits and list three examples of each.

A wide range of benefits are offered by employers. Some are mandated by laws and government regulations, while others are offered voluntarily by employers as part of their HR strategies. Figure 13-7 lists the major categories of benefits and highlights those that are legally required and those that are voluntarily provided by employers.

While there are many mandated benefits that employers in the United States must provide to employees, in general, the U.S. requires fewer employee benefits

FIGURE 13-7 Types of Benefits

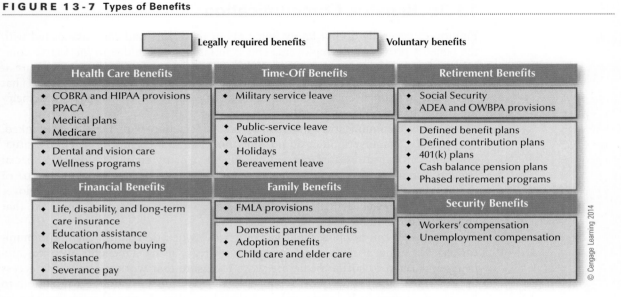

| Legally required benefits | Voluntary benefits |

Health Care Benefits	Time-Off Benefits	Retirement Benefits
• COBRA and HIPAA provisions • PPACA • Medical plans • Medicare	• Military service leave	• Social Security • ADEA and OWBPA provisions
• Dental and vision care • Wellness programs	• Public-service leave • Vacation • Holidays • Bereavement leave	• Defined benefit plans • Defined contribution plans • 401(k) plans • Cash balance pension plans • Phased retirement programs

Financial Benefits	Family Benefits	Security Benefits
• Life, disability, and long-term care insurance • Education assistance • Relocation/home buying assistance • Severance pay	• FMLA provisions • Domestic partner benefits • Adoption benefits • Child care and elder care	• Workers' compensation • Unemployment compensation

© Cengage Learning 2014

Cafeteria benefit plan
Employees are given a budget and can purchase the bundle of benefits most important to them from the "menu" of options offered by the employer.

than many other nations. However, employers voluntarily offer a broad variety of other benefits to help them compete for and retain employees. By offering additional benefits, organizations provide greater security and support to workers with diverse personal circumstances. In addition, as jobs become more flexible and varied, both workers and employers recognize that choices among benefits are necessary, as evidenced by the growth in flexible benefits and cafeteria benefit plans. A **cafeteria benefit plan** is one in which employees are given a budget and can purchase the bundle of benefits most important to them from the "menu" of options offered by the employer.

Figure 13-8 shows how the typical employer benefit dollar is spent. Legally required benefits make up about one-third of the total cost of benefits. Health care costs and time-off benefits are the most costly for companies to provide.

13-4 ■ LEGALLY REQUIRED BENEFITS

The earliest benefits law was the Social Security Act passed at the end of the Great Depression. Little was done on the federal level after that until the 1970s and later. Federal statutes have been enacted to address financial and employment security for workers, particularly those with medical problems.

13-4a Social Security and Medicare   *Hospital Suplementary insurance*

The Social Security Act of 1935 and its later amendments established a system to provide *old-age*, *survivor's*, *disability*, and *retirement* benefits. Administered by the federal government through the Social Security Administration, this program provides benefits to previously employed individuals. Medicare was implemented in 1965 to provide medical care for people over the age of 65. The Federal Insurance Contributions Act (FICA) was passed to facilitate payroll contributions in support of both programs.

FIGURE 13-8 How the Typical Benefits Dollar Is Spent

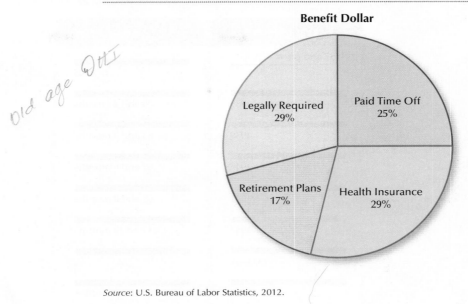

Old age OtI

Benefit Dollar

Legally Required 29%
Paid Time Off 25%
Retirement Plans 17%
Health Insurance 29%

Source: U.S. Bureau of Labor Statistics, 2012.

Social Security Employees and employers share in the cost of Social Security through a tax on employees' wages or salaries. When the law was first enacted, employers and employees each contributed 1% of worker wages to the fund. By 1990 the rate had increased to 6.2% paid by each party (for a total of 12.4%), which is the current rate of payroll tax contributions. The amount of wages subject to tax is reviewed and increased periodically. In 2013 the taxable wage base was $113,700. Earnings over that amount are not subject to Social Security tax.

Social Security is a politically sensitive program. The U.S. Congress has responded to public pressure by raising payments and introducing cost-of-living adjustments. However, concerns persist about the long-term financial viability of the program. In response, the normal retirement age to receive maximum Social Security benefits has been steadily increased from 65 to 67. Figure 13-9 shows the retirement age for employees born in various years. Increasing the retirement age is one strategy to keep the Social Security program solvent. A range of options have been considered, and it is likely that legislative action will be required to address widespread criticisms that the system is not sustainable in its current form.[26]

Medicare Medicare is the health insurance program for older Americans (age 65 and above) and for some disabled citizens. Medicare is funded by a tax on employers and employees. Each party pays 1.45% of employee earnings. Unlike the taxes paid for Social Security, there is no earnings limit on Medicare contributions. Therefore, all wages earned by workers are taxed at 2.9%.

Medicare is a comprehensive, government-operated insurance program that provides a broad spectrum of benefits. Participants share in some of the costs for hospital stays, physician visits, diagnostic tests, and prescription drugs.[27] Because of the large volume of medical expenses paid under the Medicare program, the government plays a major role in establishing pricing and limits for medical services. The future financial solvency of the program has been questioned and legislative action in the coming years is likely to be needed to address the program's continuation.

FIGURE 13-9 Normal Retirement Age for Social Security Benefits

Year of Birth	Age
1937 and prior	65
1938	65 and 2 months
1939	65 and 4 months
1940	65 and 6 months
1941	65 and 8 months
1942	65 and 10 months
1943–54	66
1955	66 and 2 months
1956	66 and 4 months
1957	66 and 6 months
1958	66 and 8 months
1959	66 and 10 months
1960 and later	67

Source: U.S. Social Security Administration, 2012.

Workers' compensation
Security benefits provided to workers who are injured on the job.

No-fault insurance
Injured workers receive benefits even if the accident was their fault.

Exclusive remedy
Workers' compensation benefits are the only benefits injured workers may receive to compensate for a work-related injury.

13-4b Workers' Compensation

Workers' compensation provides security benefits to workers who are injured on the job. State laws require most employers to provide workers' compensation coverage by purchasing insurance from a private carrier, state insurance fund, or self-insurance.

Workers' compensation regulations require employers to give cash benefits, medical care, and rehabilitation services to employees for injuries or illnesses occurring within the scope of their employment. In exchange, employees give up the right to pursue legal actions and awards. The concepts of no-fault insurance and exclusive remedy balance the rights of employers and employees under workers' compensation. **No-fault insurance** means that the injured worker receives benefits even if the accident was the employee's fault. For example, if an employee violates the safety rules and fails to wear safety shoes and drops a heavy object on his foot causing a broken toe, his medical and disability expenses will still be paid by the employer's insurance coverage. **Exclusive remedy** means that the only compensation an injured worker can receive from the employer is from the workers' compensation coverage. In most instances, an injured worker cannot file a lawsuit for additional money.

Workers' compensation programs are funded at the employer's expense; workers cannot be required to make financial contributions for this coverage. Since each state operates independently, employers must be aware of various regulations if they operate in multiple states. The Bureau of Labor Statistics reports that, on average, private-sector employers spend about $0.42 per hour or 1.5% of total payroll in workers' compensation costs.[28] Some states are much higher. Costs can vary a great deal based upon the requirements in each state and the safety record for each company. The most effective cost-control mechanism to keep premiums low is accident prevention.

13-4c Unemployment Compensation

Unemployment compensation was established as part of the Social Security Act of 1935 to provide a minimum level of benefits for workers who are out of work. Each U.S. state operates its own unemployment compensation system and benefit levels and job-search provisions differ significantly from state to state. Each company pays an unemployment tax that is based on an "experience rate," which reflects the number of claims filed by workers who leave.

Under normal circumstances, an employee who is out of work and actively looking for employment can receive up to 26 weeks of pay at the rate of 50% to 80% of normal pay. Most employees are eligible. However, workers fired for misconduct or those not actively seeking employment are generally ineligible.

During times of widespread economic hardship, the government might increase the number of weeks during which eligible workers receive benefits. In recent years, unemployed workers collected benefits for up to 99 weeks. The decision to extend benefits is often controversial and legislators struggle to find a balance between providing income security to workers against the reduced motivation for workers to seek employment.

13-4d Additional Legally Required Benefits

Besides workers' compensation and unemployment insurance, most companies must also provide additional benefits. Continued group medical benefits under COBRA regulations are discussed in the section on health care. Health care portability and medical information privacy under HIPAA are also discussed in the health care section later in this chapter. Job-protected medical leave under FMLA is discussed in the section on time-off benefits.

LO4 Discuss the trend in retirement plans and compare defined benefit and defined contribution plans.

13-5 ■ RETIREMENT BENEFITS

The aging of the workforce in many countries is affecting retirement planning for individuals and retirement plan costs for employers and governments. In the United States, the number of citizens at least 55 years or older has increased significantly in recent years, and older citizens constitute a large portion of the population. More workers are delaying retirement because of financial difficulties and decreased value of retirement savings coupled with longer life spans. Approximately 30% of workers surveyed had no plans to stop working or did not know when they would retire.[29]

Unfortunately, most U.S. citizens have inadequate savings and retirement benefits to fund their retirements. According to a study by the Employee Benefit

FIGURE 13-10 The Three-Legged Stool of Retirement Income

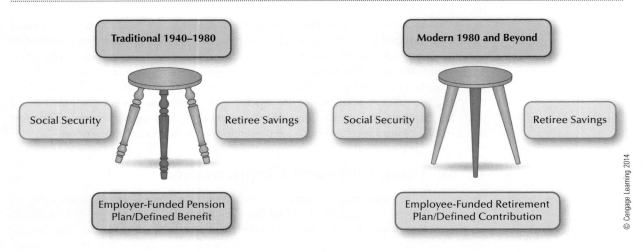

Research Institute, 60% of workers report that they have less than $25,000 in savings excluding the value of their home.[30] While traditional pension plans that provided a defined amount for retirement at a defined age were the norm for decades, since the early 1980s fewer companies have provided these benefits. Instead, employee-funded retirement accounts have become the standard. Therefore, individuals must rely on Social Security payments which were not designed to provide full retirement income. Financial planners refer to the **three-legged stool** of retirement income. Figure 13-10 shows how the model has changed over time with workers now carrying a greater burden to save for retirement.

Retirement benefits can be a valuable tool for attracting and retaining workers. Sixty percent of employees with less than two years of service at companies with traditional pension plans state that the pension plan is an important reason for their job choice. Further, 80% of workers at companies with traditional pensions plan to continue working for their employer until they retire. Over half of employees surveyed report that they would switch jobs to get better retirement benefits.[31] Therefore, the decisions a company makes about its retirement benefits can have an important and lasting impact on talent management.

13-5a Retirement Plan Concepts

Certain rights are associated with retirement plans. One such right called **vesting** means that the employee has a benefit that cannot be taken away. If employees resign or are terminated before they have been employed long enough to become vested, no pension rights accrue to them except the funds they have contributed. If employees work for the required number of years to be fully vested, they retain their pension rights and receive the amounts contributed by both the employer and themselves.

Another feature of some retirement plans is **portability**. In a portable plan, employees can move their retirement benefits from one employer to another. Instead of requiring workers to wait until they retire to move their retirement plan benefits, once workers have vested in a plan they can transfer their fund balances to other retirement plans if they change jobs.

Three-legged stool
A model showing the three sources of income to fund an employee's retirement.

Vesting
Right of employees to receive certain benefits from their pension plans.

Portability
A pension plan feature that allows employees to move their pension benefits from one employer to another.

13-5b Retirement Plans

Retirement plan
Retirement program established and funded by the employer and employees.

A **retirement plan** is a program established and funded by the employer and/or employees to fund the employee's retirement years. Organizations are not required to offer retirement plans to employees beyond contributions to Social Security. There are two broad categories of retirement plans: defined benefit plans and defined contribution plans, as shown in Figure 13-11.

Defined Benefit Pension Plans A traditional pension plan is one in which the employer makes required contributions and the employee receives a defined amount each month upon retirement. Through a **defined benefit (DB) plan**, employees are promised a pension amount based on age and years of service. Less than 10% of workers in the private sector are now covered by these plans. Small firms are less likely to offer DB plans than are larger firms. Workers in the public sector are far more likely to have a defined benefit plan with over 90% of public employers providing this benefit.[32]

Defined benefit (DB) plan
Retirement program in which employees are promised a pension amount based on age and service.

Contributions are based on actuarial calculations of the benefits to be paid to employees after retirement and the formula used to determine such benefits. A defined benefit plan gives employees greater assurance of benefits and greater predictability in the amount of benefits that will be available for retirement. These plans reward long service with a company.

Companies that provide defined benefit plans must comply with cumbersome and strict government rules regarding the funding of the plan. If the funding is inadequate to pay the benefits promised, the company must make up the shortfall. For example, Caterpillar's pension plan had $10 billion in assets, but that was $700 million less than its obligations. Because of poor investment performance in recent years, many such plans are in financial danger.[33] Therefore, many employers have dropped defined benefit plans in favor of defined contribution plans (discussed next) so that their contribution liabilities are known.

Defined benefit pension plans offer greater security to employees. The benefits are guaranteed by the Pension Benefit Guaranty Corporation (PBGC). The PBGC

FIGURE 13-11 Comparison of Defined Benefit and Defined Contribution Retirement Plans

Defined Benefit	Defined Contribution
• Typically funded at least in part by employer	• Typically funded by employee and employer
• Amount of benefit paid at retirement is pre-determined	• Amount of benefit at retirement is determined on the basis of investment performance
• Investment risk borne by employer	• Investment risk borne by employee
• Benefit guaranteed by Pension Benefit Guaranty Corporation (PBGC)	• Benefit not guaranteed
• Amount of contribution changes on the basis of actuarial assumption	• Amount of contribution is defined by employee participation level and company match
• Common in public sector and unionized workforces	• Common in private sector and non union workforces

© Cengage Learning 2014

maintains a solvency fund to pay benefits if a company goes bankrupt and cannot pay its retiree benefits. The fund is supported by employer contributions of approximately $50 per participant per year.

Defined benefit plans may see a resurgence, but in a modified form. Since so few companies offer them to new employees, reintroducing these plans could be a source of differentiation in the labor market. However, funding risk and regulatory burdens make companies wary. Companies may create new hybrid plans that will be attractive to employees without creating too great a liability for the employer.[34]

Defined contribution (DC) plan
Retirement program in which the employer makes an annual payment to an employee's pension account.

401(k) plan
Agreement in which a percentage of an employee's pay is withheld and invested in a tax-deferred account.

Auto-enrollment
Employee contributions to a 401(k) plan are started automatically when an employee is eligible to join the plan.

Defined Contribution Pension Plans In a **defined contribution (DC) plan**, contributions are made to the plan by the employer and/or employee to fund an account for the employee's retirement. The key to this plan is the contribution rate; employee retirement benefits depend on fixed contributions and investment earnings. Profit-sharing plans, employee stock ownership plans (ESOPs), and 401(k) plans are common defined contribution plans. Because these plans hinge on the investment returns on previous contributions, employees' retirement benefits are somewhat less secure and predictable. But because of their portability and other plan features, these plans are sometimes preferred by younger, shorter-term employees.

The **401(k) plan** gets its name from section 401(k) of the federal tax code. This plan is an agreement in which a percentage of an employee's pay is withheld and invested in a tax-deferred account. 401(k) plans now dominate the field of employment-based retirement programs.[35] These plans are attractive to employees because contributions are made on a tax-deferred basis, so the employee pays lower income taxes during working years. Of course, taxes must be paid when funds are withdrawn during retirement. The most common reason given by companies for offering 401(k) plans is a concern for employee financial security.[36] However, 401(k) plans mean that the employee is now the manager of investment risk and the decision-maker regarding investment options.

There are many features that companies may include in the 401(k) plan. A highly valued feature is company matching contributions. Many employers contribute to the employee's account up to a percentage of pay. Employees in plans with matching contributions are more likely to contribute themselves. Unfortunately, since employer contributions are voluntary, during economic recessions many companies reduce or stop making their matching contributions. As the economy improves, they restore the matches but set lower limits on the company's participation in the plan.[37]

A powerful feature to increase employee participation in the 401(k) plan is the use of automatic enrollment. Over half of the companies with 401(k) plans use auto-enrollment and nearly as many use automatic annual contribution increases to ensure that employees save enough for retirement.[38] **Auto-enrollment** means that employee contributions are started automatically when the employee is eligible to join the plan. Most companies set the initial contribution rate at 3% of pay. The employee has the ability to increase that rate or to stop the contributions voluntarily. Companies that use auto-increases boost the employee's contribution level by a small amount each year unless the employee voluntarily stops it.[39]

Financial education and counseling can be used to help employees understand how to manage their 401(k) and get the greatest value from the plan. People who use investment assistance earn better returns on their retirement funds than those who manage their own accounts. Employers can offer a variety of education programs designed for specific groups of employees. More than 75% of companies offer online education tools such as webinars, risk assessments, and retirement calculators.[40] Since companies have turned to 401(k) plans as the main retirement programs, educating employees is an important part of helping them to achieve financial security in retirement.

Cash Balance Pension Plans   Some employers have changed traditional pension plans to hybrids based on ideas from both defined benefit and defined contribution plans. One such plan is a **cash balance plan**, in which retirement benefits are based on an accumulation of annual company contributions, expressed as a percentage of pay, plus interest credited each year. With these plans, retirement benefits accumulate at the same annual rate until an employee retires. Since cash balance plans spread funding across a worker's entire career, these plans work better for mobile younger workers. The plans are gaining in popularity, especially among small businesses that account for 84% of these plans.[41]

> **Cash balance plan**
> Retirement program in which benefits are determined on the basis of accumulation of annual company contributions plus interest credited each year.

13-6 ■ LEGAL REGULATION OF RETIREMENT BENEFITS

Numerous laws and regulations affect retirement plans. Key regulations govern plan communications, funding, and other important aspects of retirement programs. The laws have been enacted to ensure that workers understand their plans and are assured of receiving the full value of promised benefits.

13-6a Employee Retirement Income Security Act

Widespread criticism of many pension plans led to enactment of the Employee Retirement Income Security Act (ERISA) in 1974. The purpose of this law is to insure that private pension plans meet minimum standards. ERISA requires plans to periodically provide participants with information about the plan features (such as vesting) and funding, benefit accrual amounts, and gives participants the right to file lawsuits for violations of the law. Violations of ERISA can lead to costly lawsuits and possible disqualification of a pension plan. Employers spend considerable time to comply with the provisions of pension law.

13-6b Retirement Benefits and Age Discrimination

According to a 1986 amendment to the Age Discrimination in Employment Act (ADEA), most employees cannot be forced to retire at a specific age. In many employer pension plans, "normal retirement" is the age at which employees can retire and receive full pension benefits. Employers must decide whether individuals who continue to work past normal retirement age (typically 65) are eligible for the standard benefits package provided to active employees under age 65. Changes in Social Security regulations have increased the age for full benefits past age 65, so modifications in policies may occur.

Early Retirement   Many pension plans include provisions for early retirement to allow workers to retire before the normal retirement age. Phased retirements are alternatives being used by individuals and firms. Historically, employees either worked full time or were retired full time. Phased retirement allows employees to bridge between these two states while offering the company a chance to retain important knowledge and skills. For example, BASF instituted a phased retirement plan that redeploys employees to a special skills transfer program during their phased retirement period to insure an orderly transition.[42]

Some employers use early retirement buyout programs to cut back their workforces and reduce costs. Buyout programs often include incentives such as out-placement services, health care benefits, and a severance payment. There is of course a risk that too many employees will participate, thereby leaving the company shorthanded. Employers must take care to make these early retirement programs truly voluntary and to communicate them effectively.

Older Workers Benefit Protection Act The Older Workers Benefit Protection Act (OWBPA) was enacted in 1990 as an amendment to the ADEA. It requires equal treatment for older workers in early retirement or severance situations. It also sets specific criteria that must be met if older workers are asked to sign waivers promising not to sue for age discrimination in exchange for severance benefits during layoffs.

13-7 ■ HEALTH CARE BENEFITS

L05 Explain the importance of managing the costs of health benefits and identify some methods of doing so.

Employers provide a variety of health care and medical benefits, usually through insurance coverage. Major changes brought about by the Patient Protection and Affordable Care Act (PPACA), which is still evolving, may significantly alter the involvement of employers in providing these essential benefits. This legislation is discussed in the following section.

Health plans are considered by employees to be the most important benefit that companies offer. The most common plans cover medical, dental, prescription drug, and vision care expenses for employees and their dependents.

13-7a Increases in Health Benefits Costs

For several decades, the costs of health care have escalated at rates well above those of inflation and increases in workers' earnings. The costs of health care have increased by two percentage points over increases in the GDP across many developed nations for close to 50 years.[43] As a result of these large increases many employers find that dealing with health care benefits is time consuming and expensive.

The average annual premiums for employer-sponsored health coverage for a single employee are $5,600. Premiums for family coverage are triple the cost, averaging $16,000 per family per year.[44] These staggering costs have led companies to require that employees shoulder some of the premium and benefit costs. On average, single employees pay 18% of premiums, while employees with family coverage pay 28% of premiums.[45]

13-7b Health Care Reform Legislation

Landmark legislation enacted in 2010 changed health care in the United States, making insurance available to an additional 32 million people. The Patient Protection

FIGURE 13-12 Key Provisions of the Affordable Care Act

Requires most individuals to maintain minimum essential coverage or pay a penalty

Requires companies with 50 or more employees (who work 30 hours a week or more) to provide health care coverage or pay a penalty

Extends dependent coverage up to age 26

Eliminates lifetime and unreasonable annual benefit limits

Requires coverage for preventive services

Restricts insurance companies from setting rates based on individuals' health status or medical conditions or other health-related factors

Creates state-run health care exchanges where insurance companies will offer competitive health plans

© Cengage Learning 2014

and Affordable Care Act provisions were phased in over several years, culminating in universal coverage in 2014. While the act was vehemently opposed by many, the Supreme Court ruled in 2012 that the provisions of the law were constitutional. Therefore, the landscape of employer-sponsored health benefits will undergo radical changes.

Key Provisions The PPACA includes many important provisions intended to provide affordable health care for all citizens. To achieve this goal, enrollment in health coverage is now mandated for every citizen. Key elements of the law are highlighted in Figure 13-12.

13-7c Employer-Sponsored Plans

Employers will face a decision about continuing to offer their own health insurance plans or to drop their plans in favor of government-sponsored coverage. Beginning in 2014, employers with at least 50 employees (who work at least 30 hours per week) will be required to provide minimum essential health care coverage to all full time employees. Employers that fail to provide adequate health coverage will pay an annual penalty of $2,000 per employee.

Dropping health insurance plans would result in a significant reduction in over-all employee compensation, which could have a negative effect on attracting and retaining employees. A recent survey showed that only 3% of employers are likely to discontinue health care plans for active employees as a result of the change in law.[46] Providing compensation to employees would allow them to purchase individual coverage in the health exchange market that could be far more costly than continuing employer-sponsored coverage.

Employers that provide high-cost ("Cadillac") health benefits to employees may face a 40% excise tax. If the premium cost for the benefit plan exceeds federal limits, the employer would pay additional taxes. Some employers offer high-cost plans because a generous plan is part of their attraction and retention strategy, they are located in a high-cost area, or they have collective bargaining agreements with labor unions that include these plans. Benefit reductions and cost control measures would be implemented to lower premium costs.[47]

Employers must begin reporting the value of employer-paid health coverage on employees' W-2 forms beginning with the 2012 reporting year. Discussions during the debate on health care reform included consideration of eliminating the tax-favored status of employer-sponsored health care and taxing employees on the value of their benefits. Reporting on employee W-2 forms makes this information available and may lead to further consideration of this proposal.

13-7d Controlling Health Care Benefit Costs

Employers offering health care benefits are taking a number of approaches to control and reduce their costs. The most frequently used strategies include the following:[48]

- Increasing deductibles and copayments
- Instituting high-deductible plans
- Increasing employee contributions
- Using managed care
- Limiting family coverage; excluding spouses
- Switching to consumer-driven health plans
- Increasing health preventive and wellness efforts

Deductible
Money paid by an insured individual before a health plan pays for any medical expenses.

Copayment
The portion of medical expenses paid by the insured individual.

Increasing Employee Cost Sharing A **deductible** is paid by an insured individual before the medical plan pays any expenses. Employers who raise the per-person deductible from $50 to $250 realize significant savings in health care expenses because employees use fewer health care services and prescription drugs.

Copayments are costs that an insured pays for medical treatment. For example, the health plan may require a fixed $20 co-pay for each physician visit. Alternatively the co-pay may be based on a percentage, such as 20%, of medical treatment costs up to a set dollar amount. Companies can increase the fixed co-pay amount, increase the percentage, or increase the dollar amount on which employees share costs.

13-7e Increasing Employee Contributions

Employees are usually required to pay a portion of the monthly premium to maintain health care insurance. On average, single employees pay 18% of premiums, while employees with family coverage pay 28% of premiums. Over 50% of employers plan to increase the percentage that employees contribute to health plan premiums.[49]

Managed care
Approaches that monitor
and reduce medical costs
through restrictions
and market system
alternatives.

Using Managed Care Several other types of programs attempt to reduce health care costs paid by employers. **Managed care** consists of approaches that monitor and reduce medical costs through restrictions and market system alternatives. Managed care plans emphasize primary and preventive care, the use of specific providers that charge lower prices, restrictions on certain kinds of treatment, and prices negotiated with hospitals and physicians. Preferred provider organizations (PPO) and health maintenance organizations (HMO) are the most common forms of managed care.

Spousal Exclusions Spousal exclusion provisions limit access to a company's health plan when an employee's spouse works for another company that offers health insurance. Companies may charge a premium surcharge to enroll the spouse or require that the spouse enroll in his or her own employer's plan. Approximately 20% of employers have adopted these restrictions and more companies are planning to do so.[50]

13-7f Consumer-Driven Health Plans

**Consumer-driven
health (CDH) plan**
Health plan that provides
employer financial con-
tributions to employees
to help cover their
health-related expenses.

Some employers are turning to health insurance plans where the employee chooses the insurance. The most widely used is a **consumer-driven health (CDH) plan** in which the employer provides financial contributions to employees to help cover their health-related expenses. For example, Sears Holdings Corporation and Darden Restaurants recently implemented these plans. The companies provide a fixed sum of money to employees and allow them to choose their medical coverage and insurer from an online marketplace. The employee can buy up the benefit level by paying the additional costs beyond what the employer contributes.[51]

CDH plans may represent the wave of the future by giving employees ownership of their health care dollars. Over 20% of large employers offer the plans and the trend is on the increase.[52] Successful implementation of CDH plans involves timely, accurate data for informed employee decisions. Communicating throughout the year and helping employees to make good spending decisions can achieve satisfied employees and cost savings.[53]

13-7g Dental and Vision Coverage

Additional health benefits frequently include coverage for dental and vision care expenses. Employees typically pay a portion of the premium for dental and vision plans. These plans often emphasize preventive care. Semi-annual dental visits and annual optometry visits may be covered in full or at minimal cost to the employee.

13-7h Improving Health through Wellness Initiatives

Preventive and wellness efforts can take many forms. Many employers offer programs to educate employees about health care costs and how to reduce them. Newsletters, formal classes, and many other approaches are designed to help employees understand why health care costs are increasing and what they can do to control them. A major strategy of cost reduction is wellness programs that focus on improving worker health.

The courts have ruled that financial penalties as part of an employer wellness program are permitted and do not violate the ADA if the purpose is to establish underwriting risk for the health plan. Risk assessments for employees and family members enrolled in employer health care plans are becoming more widely used with many companies requiring participation. For example, AmeriGas requires that employees obtain a medical checkup or lose their health insurance coverage. A similar approach is used by 80% of large organizations with almost two-thirds penalizing smokers with higher insurance premiums.[54] Although these programs are intended to save money, they pose some ethical issues as employees may feel that their employer is invading personal privacy or putting cost savings before individual freedom.

ETHICS

Incentives are a more positive approach. Nearly 75% of companies use incentives to engage employees in health improvement programs with an average incentive of $430 per employee.[55] Creating a "culture of health" and involving workers' family members in wellness efforts can go a long way toward lowering health care costs and improving their lives. As highlighted in the HR Headline at the start of the chapter, companies and employees can work together in ways that benefit them both.

13-7i Health Care Legislation

The importance of health care benefits to employers and employees has led to a variety of federal and state laws being created. Several laws have been enacted to provide protection for employees who leave their employers, either voluntarily or involuntarily. To date, the two most important laws passed that govern issues related to the protection of former workers are COBRA and HIPAA.

COBRA Provisions The Consolidated Omnibus Budget Reconciliation Act (COBRA) requires that most employers with 20 or more full-time and/or part-time employees offer extended health care coverage to certain groups of plan participants. The different groups are as follows:[56]

* Employees who voluntarily quit or are terminated
* Widowed or divorced spouses and dependent children of former or current employees
* Retirees and their spouses and dependent children whose health care coverage ends
* Any child who is born or adopted by a covered employee
* Other individuals involved in the plan such as independent contractors and agents/directors

Qualifying event
An event that causes a plan participant to lose group health benefits.

A **qualifying event** is an event that causes a plan participant to lose group health benefits. Typically, reduction in work hours or loss of employment constitutes a qualifying event for employees. Divorce or death of an employee constitutes a qualifying event for covered family members. When a qualifying event occurs, a complex notification process begins. There are several deadlines that the company and the employee must meet to comply with COBRA requirements. Figure 13-13 shows the timeline regarding notification and important qualifying circumstances.

The individual no longer employed by the organization must pay the premiums, but the employer may charge the individual up to 102% of the premium costs. The 2% premium addition generally falls well short of the true cost of providing this coverage. COBRA participants generally cost twice the amount in benefit payments than active employees.[57]

Compliance with COBRA regulations can be very complicated and noncompliance with the law can lead to lawsuits and substantial penalties. Consequently, COBRA requirements often mean additional paperwork and related costs for many employers. COBRA administration is frequently outsourced to a third-party administrator that has expertise and data processing capabilities.

FIGURE 13-13 Timeline of COBRA Notification Requirements

Event	Notification Deadline
1. COBRA Initial Notice must be provided	Within *30 days* after the employee first becomes enrolled in the group health plan
2. Employer to notify plan administrator	Within *30 days* after the qualifying event date
3. COBRA Qualifying Event Notice	*14 days* from the date the plan administrator receives notification from employee
4. Qualified beneficiary has right to elect COBRA Coverage	*60 days* from the date of COBRA notice
5. Qualified beneficiary initial premium due	*45 days* from the date of electing COBRA
6. Monthly COBRA premium grace period	*30 days* after the first day of each month
7. Employee/qualified beneficiary to notify plan administrator of a qualifying event	*60 days*
8. Continuation period ends	*18 months* after qualifying event for terminated employees *29 months* after qualifying event for disabled terminated employees *36 months* after qualifying event for spouse and dependent children plan participants

Source: Adapted from https://www.goigoe.com/Employers/COBRATimelines.aspx

HIPAA Provisions The Health Insurance Portability and Accountability Act (HIPAA) of 1996 allows employees to switch their health insurance plans when they change employers and to enroll in health coverage with the new company regardless of preexisting health conditions. The legislation also prohibits group insurance plans from dropping coverage for a sick employee and requires them to make individual coverage available to people who leave group plans.

One of the greatest impacts of HIPAA comes from its provisions regarding the privacy of employee medical records. These provisions require employers to provide privacy notices to employees. They also regulate the disclosure of protected health information without authorization.

LO6 Describe the growth of financial, family oriented, and time-off benefits and their importance to employees.

13-8 ■ FINANCIAL BENEFITS

Companies may offer employees a wide range of special benefits that provide financial support. Figure 13-14 illustrates some common financial benefits. Employers find that such benefits can be useful in attracting and retaining employees. Workers like receiving these benefits, which are often not taxed as income.

13-8a Insurance Benefits

In addition to health care insurance, some companies provide other types of insurance. These benefits offer major advantages for employees because employers may pay some or all of the costs. Even when employers do not pay any of the costs,

FIGURE 13-14 Common Types of Financial Benefits

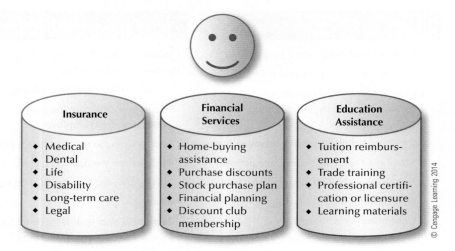

employees still benefit because of the lower rates available through group programs. The most common types of insurance benefits are the following:

- *Life insurance*: A typical level of coverage is one and one-half or two times an employee's annual salary.
- *Disability insurance*: Both *short-term* and *long-term disability insurance* provide continuing income protection for employees who become disabled and are unable to work.
- *Long-term care insurance*: Usually voluntary, these plans allow employees to purchase insurance to cover costs for long-term health care in a nursing home, an assisted-living facility, or at home. Though employees usually pay for the premiums, they may get cheaper rates through employer-sponsored group plans.
- *Legal insurance*: In these plans employees (or employers) pay a flat fee for a fixed number of hours of legal assistance each month. In return, they have the right to use the service of a network of lawyers to handle their legal problems.

13-8b Financial Services

Financial benefits include a wide variety of items. A *credit union* sponsored by the employer provides saving and lending services for employees. *Purchase discounts* allow employees to buy goods or services from their employers at reduced rates, often in a company store. *Discount programs* and *club memberships* may also be offered to allow employees to purchase goods from local vendors or "club" stores at lower rates. The programs are inexpensive for companies to implement and they are viewed positively by employees.[58]

Employee thrift plans, *savings plans*, or *stock purchase plans* may be available. To illustrate, in a *stock purchase plan*, employees may buy shares in the company at a discount, or the company pays the brokerage fees. This type of plan allows employees to benefit from the future growth of the corporation with the intention of increasing employee loyalty to the organization and interest in its success.

Financial planning and *counseling* are especially valuable services for executives, many of whom may need information on investments and tax shelters, as well as comprehensive financial counseling, because of their higher levels of compensation. The importance of these financial planning benefits will likely grow as a greater percentage of workers approach retirement age and need to plan financially for retirement.

Relocation Assistance Relocation benefits are offered by many firms. Companies may pay for temporary living expenses and moving expenses, and help a "trailing spouse" find a job. Numerous other financial-related benefits may be offered as well including the use of a company car, company expense accounts, and assistance in buying or selling a house. The HR Perspective: Helping Employees Realize the American Dream describes an innovative way that some companies help employees with home purchases.

13-8c Education Assistance

Another benefit that is popular with employees is education assistance and tuition aid, which pays some or all of the costs associated with formal education courses and degree programs. Many employers offer some form of education assistance to their employees. Some employers reimburse the employee for a percentage of tuition based on grades earned while others may require only a passing grade of C or above. Often the course of study must be related to the employee's current job or a logical career path within the company. Unless the education paid for by the employer meets certain conditions, the cost of educational aid must be counted as taxable income by employees.

Although U.S. employers spend more than $16 billion for tuition aid each year, few firms conduct analyses to determine the return on their investment of these programs. To make education benefits programs more effective, employers should measure the effect of these programs on employee retention, internal promotions, increased employee satisfaction, and other factors.[59]

13-8d Severance Pay

Companies may provide severance pay to individuals whose jobs are eliminated or who leave the company by mutual agreement. While the Worker Adjustment and Retraining Notification Act (WARN) of 1988 requires employers to give 60 days' notice of mass layoff or plant closings, it does not mandate severance pay. The amount of severance pay is often determined by an employee's level within the organization and years of service with the company. Some employers provide continued health insurance or outplacement assistance as part of the severance pay package.

13-9 ■ FAMILY ORIENTED BENEFITS

The composition of families in the United States has changed significantly in the past few decades. Two-earner families and single-parent households are now the norm. Workers therefore seek out companies that balance work and nonwork obligations and offer family-friendly benefits. To enhance recruiting and retention of high-quality talent, employers have established a variety of family-oriented benefits. The major legal requirement regarding family-oriented benefits is the Family and Medical Leave Act (FMLA), which provides for unpaid leaves of absence.

HR PERSPECTIVE

Helping Employees Realize the American Dream

Among the list of creative benefits that some companies offer, a few have implemented programs that help their employees realize the dream of home ownership. These programs are a low-cost, high-reward way to increase employee commitment and retention.

CVS Caremark, Northrop Grumman Shipbuilding, and Loyola University have all found ways to assist their employees in buying a home. Elements of their programs include the following:

- Educating workers about home ownership
- Counseling workers on how to improve their credit score
- Steering them to affordable neighborhoods with dependable public transit
- Assisting with down payment or closing costs
- Forgiving loans if the employee stays with the company for a required number of years

The city of Chicago is a hotbed of this activity because of a program started by the Metropolitan Planning Council several years ago to offer free real estate and credit counseling to employees of local firms. The program was so successful that the state of Illinois now offers tax credits and matches incentives paid by companies to help with employee home purchases. Over 50 Illinois employers now take advantage of the state's program.

Of course, companies located outside of Illinois also offer these opportunities to their employees. Aurora Health Care, a Milwaukee-based hospital system with 29,000 employees, provides a $3,000 forgivable loan to employees who buy homes in the city. Over 400 employees, including dieticians and nursing assistants, have purchased homes through the assistance program. The hospital has benefited by improved employee productivity and loyalty and a significant reduction in turnover.

CVS employees typically earn between $30,000 and $50,000 and are therefore very grateful for the counseling and financial help extended by the company. CVS uses a learning center staffed by a local faith-based organization because many of their employees don't trust banks and don't want the company to know too much about their personal finances. At Loyola University, employees must live near specific mass transit lines because the institution has a green initiative to reduce reliance on cars for commuting.

With or without government incentives, employers find that programs aimed at helping employees become homeowners is a win-win. This is an example of employers providing creative and useful benefits to employees who can really use them.[60]

13-9a Family and Medical Leave Act

The FMLA was enacted in 1993 and amended several times. It covers all federal, state, and private employers with 50 or more employees who live within 75 miles of the workplace. Only employees who have worked at least 12 months and 1,250 hours in the previous year are eligible for leave under the FMLA. The law provides for unpaid leave; however, some companies pay short-term disability benefits during FMLA leaves under certain conditions.

FMLA Leave Provisions The law requires that employers allow eligible employees to take a maximum of 12 weeks of unpaid, job-protected leave during any 12-month period for the following situations:[61]

- Birth of a child and care for the newborn within one year of birth
- Adoption or foster care placement of a child
- Caring for a spouse, child, or parent with a serious health condition
- Serious health condition of the employee
- Military family members who must handle the affairs for military members called to active duty
- 26 weeks leave to care for a military servicemember injured while on active duty

Serious health condition

Health condition requiring in-patient, hospital, hospice, or residential medical care or continuing physician care.

A **serious health condition** is an illness or injury that requires inpatient care or continuing treatment by a health care provider for medical problems that exist beyond three days. An employer may require a medical certificate from a health care provider to support the reason for the employee's leave. The Department of Labor has issued many guidelines regarding FMLA employee leaves as shown in Figure 13-15.

Noteworthy revisions were made to the FMLA in 2009 regarding military servicemembers and their families. Expanded coverage allows families of injured active military servicemembers to take caregiving leave for up to 26 weeks to assist servicemembers injured on active duty. The law was further expanded to help families of military servicemembers (National Guard or Reserves) manage their affairs while the member is on active duty in support of a contingency operation.

Impact of the FMLA Since the enactment of FMLA, a significant percentage of employees have taken family and medical leave. Many employers have not paid enough attention to the FMLA or do not fully understand its provisions, resulting in numerous costly lawsuits.[62] Although FMLA leave is unpaid, employers have to cover the workload for employees on family leave. Balancing work demands for

FIGURE 13-15 Guidelines regarding FMLA Administration

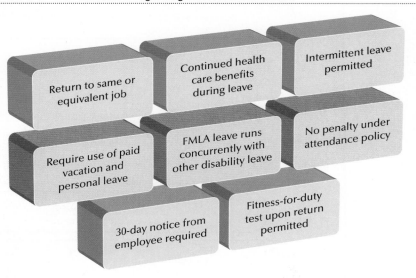

Source: http://www.dol.gov/whd/fmla

many employees and their family and medical situations has placed significant demands on HR professionals to ensure compliance with FMLA provisions.

13-9b Family-Care Benefits

Family issues are important for many organizations and workers. Companies may offer work/life balance options to all employees regardless of family status. A variety of family benefits can be provided.

Adoption Benefits Many employers provide maternity and paternity benefits to employees who give birth to children. A comparatively small number of employees adopt children, and in the interest of fairness and life enrichment, some organizations provide specific benefits to support adoption. Estimates are that approximately 55% of firms provide some type of adoption benefits. Every year more employers have added adoption assistance to their benefits package. They often include financial assistance and paid time off.[63]

Child-Care and Elder-Care Assistance Balancing work and family responsibilities is a major challenge for many workers. Whether they are single parents or dual-career couples, employees often experience difficulty obtaining high quality, affordable child care. Further, employees may be "sandwiched" between raising their own children while caring for aging parents. Figure 13-16 highlights programs to help employees deal with child-care and elder-care issues.

Employers that provide these programs have found them to be beneficial for several reasons. Employees are more likely to stay with companies that help them balance work/life issues. Child-care and elder-care benefits can produce significant savings, primarily because of decreased employee absenteeism and turnover.[64]

FIGURE 13-16 Child-Care and Elder-Care Programs

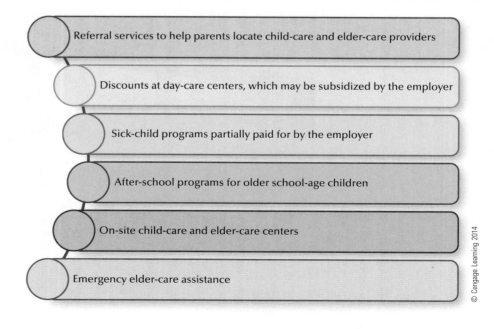

Referral services to help parents locate child-care and elder-care providers

Discounts at day-care centers, which may be subsidized by the employer

Sick-child programs partially paid for by the employer

After-school programs for older school-age children

On-site child-care and elder-care centers

Emergency elder-care assistance

13-10 ■ PAID TIME-OFF BENEFITS

Time-off benefits represent a significant portion of total benefits costs. Employers give employees paid time off for a variety of circumstances. Paid lunch breaks and rest periods, holidays, and vacations are common. But time off is given for many other purposes as well, including various leaves of absence. Employees place high value on paid time off, and some prefer time off rather than extra pay.

13-10a Vacation Pay

Paid vacations are a common benefit and over 90% of companies provide some form of paid vacation.[65] Employers often use graduated vacation-time scales based on the employees' lengths of service. Some companies have a "use it or lose it" policy whereby employees forfeit any vacation not used during the year. Other companies have policies to "buy back" unused vacation time, or they allow employees to donate unused vacation days to a pool that can be used by other workers.

13-10b Holiday Pay

Most employers provide pay for a variety of holidays. Employers in the United States commonly offer fewer paid holidays than those in many other countries. The number of paid holidays can vary depending on state/provincial laws and union contracts.

As an abuse-control measure, employers can require employees to work the last scheduled day before a holiday and the first scheduled workday after a holiday to be eligible for holiday pay. Some employers pay time-and-a-half to hourly employees who must work on holidays.

13-10c Leaves of Absence

Employers grant *leaves of absence*, taken as time off with or without pay, for a variety of reasons. All the leaves discussed here add to employer costs even if unpaid because the missing employee's work must be covered, either by other employees working additionally or by temporary employees working under contract.

Leaves are given for a variety of purposes. Some, such as *military leave*, *election leave*, and *jury leave*, are required by various state and federal laws. Employers can pay the difference between the employee's regular pay and the military, election, or jury pay. Federal law prohibits taking discriminatory action against military reservists by requiring them to take vacation time when deployed or in training.

Funeral leave or *bereavement leave* is another common type of leave offered. An absence of up to three days for the death of immediate family members is often granted. Some policies also allow unpaid time off for the death of more distant relatives.

Family Leave As mentioned earlier in the chapter, FMLA guarantees unpaid leave for certain family and medical reasons. Even though *paternity leave* for male workers is available under the FMLA, a relatively low percentage of men take it. The primary reason for the low usage is a perception that it is not as socially acceptable for men to stay home for child-related reasons. This view has begun changing as Gen X fathers are participating more actively in childrearing duties.

Sick Leave Many employers allow employees to miss a limited number of days because of illness without losing pay. The majority of U.S. workers receive paid sick leave.

Some employers allow employees to accumulate unused sick leave, which may be used in case of catastrophic illnesses. Others pay their employees for unused sick leave. Research has shown that absenteeism due to illness is lower when employees are *not* paid for sick time.[66] However, organizations that are too strict might encourage employees to come to work when they are ill, causing lower productivity or possibly spreading illness and disease. Legislation has been proposed in a number of cities to require small businesses to provide paid sick time. This is a controversial issue as small firms might find the added costs unaffordable.

Some companies have shifted the emphasis to reward employees who do not use sick leave by giving them *well pay*—extra pay for not taking sick leave. Another approach is to use a paid-time-off plan.

13-10d Paid-Time-Off Plans

Paid-time-off (PTO) plan
Plan that combines all sick leave, vacation time, and holidays into a total number of hours or days that employees can take off with pay.

A growing number of employers have made use of a **paid-time-off (PTO) plan**, which combines all sick leave, vacation time, and holidays into a total number of hours or days that employees can take off with pay. Studies have found that about 20% of all employers have PTO plans. Many employers have found PTO plans to be more effective than other means of reducing absenteeism, scheduling time off, increasing employee understanding of leave policies, and assisting with recruiting and retention. However, most employees still prefer traditional time-off programs.[67]

13-10e Employee-Paid Group Benefits

To combat the high cost of benefit programs, some companies offer employees the opportunity to purchase benefits through payroll deductions. The cost for these benefits is typically less than the employee could purchase on his or her own because the buying power of the group reduces the cost. Survey results show that Gen X and Y employees would rather pay for benefits than lose them.[68]

Adding employee-paid voluntary benefits is becoming a popular cost-effective strategy for many companies. It is part of a trend that gives employees choices but also makes them responsible for selecting and funding the benefits they find valuable. In particular, employees are willing to pay for the cost of income protection insurance in the case of disability. Other employee-paid benefits include pet health care insurance, critical-illness coverage (cancer care), and supplemental life insurance. Payroll deductions make employee participation in these plans convenient and simple.

SUMMARY

- Benefits provide additional compensation to employees as a reward for organizational membership.
- Because benefits generally are not taxed, they are highly desired by employees.
- Benefits design and cost-control actions are crucial to strategic benefits efforts.
- Companies in most nations outside the United States are required to provide more generous

benefits for their employees than are companies in the United States.
- Public-sector employees in the United States frequently receive richer benefits than employees working in the private sector.
- Benefits administration is often outsourced to third-party administrators.
- Benefits can be viewed as mandatory or voluntary. The general types of benefits

include security, health care, retirement, financial, family oriented, and time off.

- Major legally required benefits are Social Security, Medicare, workers' compensation, and unemployment compensation.
- Organizations provide retirement benefits through defined benefit or defined contribution plans. Use of defined contribution and cash balance retirement plans is growing.
- Retirement programs are governed by several federal laws including ERISA and ADEA.
- Recent federal legislation now requires employers to provide health care benefits to their employees.
- Because health care benefits costs have increased significantly, employers are managing their health benefits costs more aggressively by increasing employee copayments and employee

contributions, limiting spousal coverage, using managed care, and switching to consumer-driven health (CDH) plans.

- Federal laws allow former employees to continue their group medical insurance after leaving employment and limit the use of pre-existing condition limits for new plan participants.
- Various types of financial services, insurance benefits, relocation assistance, education assistance, and other benefits enhance the appeal of an organization to employees.
- Family oriented benefits include complying with the Family and Medical Leave Act (FMLA) of 1993 and offering adoption benefits, child-care assistance, and elder-care assistance.
- Holiday pay, vacation pay, various leaves of absence, and paid-time-off plans are another means of providing benefits to employees.

CRITICAL THINKING CHALLENGES

1. Why are benefits strategically important to employers, and what are some key strategic considerations?

2. Discuss the following statement: "Health care costs are out of control in the United States, and increasing conflicts between employers and employees are likely as employers try to reduce their health benefits costs."

3. Assume that as an HR staff member, you have been asked to research consumer-driven health plans because your employer is considering implementing one. Go to a leading benefits information resource, *Employee Benefit News*, at www.benefitnews.com, and identify the elements of a successful CDH plan and some examples of firms that use such a plan.

4. Based on the information discussed in the chapter, how would you oversee the design

(or redesign) of a benefits program in a large organization? What issues would you consider?

5. Your company now has more than 60 employees. The controller has been handling all of the HR functions including administration of the company's benefits. You are considering outsourcing the benefits administration function to enable the controller to focus more on the company's accounting needs. Information to assist you in determining the type of services to best meet the company's needs can be found at www.corbanone.com.

   A. What are the differences between the services offered by an HRO, ASO, and PEO?

   B. Based upon the company's size and the types of benefits offered, which service will best meet the needs of the company?

CASE

Creative Benefits Tie Employees to the Company

Offering employee benefits can be a cost-effective way to attract and motivate high-quality talent.

Some companies have discovered that benefits can be a creative way to connect their employees to the company, and in the process they improve employee retention, engagement, and productivity.

Gaia Online allows employees to unleash their creative potential by decorating their office space in any way they choose. The company employs many artists and creative types, so this is a natural extension of their personalities and skills. This low-cost benefit leads to more engaged and happier employees because they can express themselves and customize their work space to their tastes.

Food and energy products company, Clif Bar, helps employees commute to work in environmentally friendly ways. The company will pay a worker $500 toward the cost of a commuter bicycle for travel to work. Employees who buy hybrid, biodiesel, or natural gas engine automobiles can get up to $6,500 from the company. The company philosophy includes making employees healthier and more relaxed, an extension of its product line of healthy foods and snacks.

Imagine hanging fabulous art in your home for a fraction of its cost. If you work at the University of Minnesota Twin Cities' Weisman Art Museum, you can rent artwork for $40 per year and hang it in your home to enjoy. The museum makes pieces available to students and employees so that it can be appreciated and valued. It's a small price to pay for building the connections between employees and the museum.

Netflix empowers employees to manage their work schedules without micro-managing their time. Unlimited vacation is provided to employees with the requirement that they get their work done. Performance isn't measured by hours in the seat, but by end results. Employees must work effectively and produce expected outcomes. But no one makes them track hours or come to the office for "face time". Netflix management demands outstanding performance in exchange for this flexibility and routinely terminates employees who are "adequate" performers.

These are examples of unique benefits that companies have implemented to more closely tie employees to the company's mission and strategy. Creative benefits can be designed in ways that reflect the company's culture and philosophy. By offering employees benefits that reinforce the company's values and strategies, employees are more likely to remain engaged and productive.[69]

QUESTIONS

1. What are the advantages and disadvantages of offering unique and creative benefits to employees?

2. How would an organization determine the types of benefits that employees might want? What methods of collecting this information would you recommend a company use if the goal is to enhance the employer's ability to attract and retain high-quality talent?

3. What are the pros and cons of allowing individual managers to design and offer creative benefits to their employee group? How would it impact overall company morale if the benefit offerings are not universal?

SUPPLEMENTAL CASES

Delivering Benefits

This case explores how FedEx provides benefits to its employees. (For the case, go to www.cengage.com/management/mathis.)

Benefiting Connie

This case describes the problems that can occur when trying to coordinate time-off leaves for employees. (For the case, go to www.cengage.com/management/mathis.)

Strategic Benefits at KPMG Canada

This case explores how KPMG Canada updated its benefit program by involving employees in the design process. (For the case, go to www.cengage.com/management/mathis.)

NOTES

1. Based on Andrea Davis, "Sprint Expands Wellness Through Social Media," *Employee Benefit News*, March 2012, 44.
2. "2011 Employee Benefits - Examining Employee Benefits Amidst Uncertainty," SHRM and Colonial Life, 2011.
3. "Benefits Trends in U.S. Organizations: An Overview of the Latest Findings From the SHRM 2011 Employee Benefits Research Report," *www.shrm.org*, 2011.
4. Les Richmond and Kimberly Fox, "Aligning Benefits Strategy with Total Rewards Philosophy," *WorldatWork.org*, 2012; James H. Dulebohn, Janice C. Molloy, Shaun M. Pichler and Brian Murray, "Employee Benefits: Literature Review and Emerging Issues," *Human Resource Management Review*, 19, 2009, 86–103; "Total Reward Strategy, Alignment Study," Grahall, 2009.
5. Joe Mullich, "2011 Benefits Trends: Greater Choice, Increased Focus on Health, More Innovative Perks," *The Wall Street Journal*, April 5, 2011.
6. Lauren Weber, "Benefits Matter," *The Wall Street Journal*, April 4, 2012; "Why a Healthy Workforce May be the Next Great Employment Differentiator," *Aflac WorkForce Report*, 2012.
7. "2012 Total Rewards Survey: Transforming Potential Into Value," *AON Hewitt*, 2012; Andrea Davis, "Choosing better Benefits," *Employee Benefit News*, January 2012, 29.
8. David Rohde, "The Anti-Walmart: The Secret Sauce of Wegmans Is People," *The Atlantic*, 2012; Candace Walters, "Taking a Closer Look at Benefits: the Wegmans Way," *HR Works Inc.*, June 20, 2011.
9. Inti Landauro, "France Gives Workers More Benefits," *The Wall Street Journal*, June 7, 2010; David Gauthier-Villars and Max Colchester, "French Strikers Protest Higher Retirement Age," *The Wall Street Journal*, October 13, 2010.
10. Patricia Kowsmann, "Portugal Gives Ground on Worker Contributions," *The Wall Street Journal*, September 24, 2012.
11. Susannah Nevison, "What Countries Offer the Most Paid Time Off?" *ThomasNet News*, November 10, 2009.
12. "Family Leave – U.S., Canada, and Global," *Catalyst.org*, May 2012; Bernd Debusmann Jr., "U.S. Behind the World on Parental Leave: Report," *Thomas Reuters*, February 23, 2011; Erin Killian, "Parental Leave: The Swedes are the Most Generous," *NPR.org*, August 8, 2011; Jens Hansegard, "For Paternity Leave, Sweden Asks if Two Months is Enough," *The Wall Street Journal*, August 1, 2012.
13. Jody Heymann, Hye Jin Rho, John Schmitt and Alison Earle, "Contagion Nation: A Comparison of Paid Sick Day Policies in 22 Countries," *Center for Economic and Policy Research*, May 2009.
14. Steve Malanga, "The Local Government Pension Squeeze," *The Wall Street Journal*, June 27, 2011; Gina Chon, "States Skip Pension Payment," *The Wall Street Journal*, April 4, 2010.
15. Stephen Miller, "Study: Rewards Programs Not Tied to Business Operations," *www.shrm.org*, June 19, 2009.
16. Emily Guy Birken, "The 16 Best Part-Time Jobs with Benefits – Updated for 2012," *www.MONEY.com*, February 1, 2012.
17. "Employer's Guide to Benefits for Same-Sex Spouses and Domestic Partners," *Lockton Benefit Group*, November 2009.
18. Tamara Lytle, "Benefits for Older Workers", *HR Magazine*, March, 2012, 53–58.
19. Sixth Annual Study of Employee Benefits: Today & Beyond," *Prudential Group Insurance*, 2011.
20. Virginia Eanes, "Goodbye, Yellow-Brick Road," *Employee Benefit News*, April 1, 2009.
21. Denniss Cauchon, "Job Benefits Growing Faster Than Wages," *USA Today*, October 19–21, 2012; Joe Light, "As Labor Costs Increase, Signs Point to Benefits," *The Wall Street Journal*, May 2, 2011.
22. "Employers Missing Key Opportunities to Use Benefits Communication to Improve Program Success, Meet Strategic Goals," *Worldatwork.org*, August 16, 2012.
23. Dana Burnette, "Making the Case for Benefits Communication and Education," *Workspan Magazine*, August 2009, 21–26; "Employers' Benefits Communications Compromising Employee Engagement," *Worldatwork.org*, September 12, 2012.
24. Jennifer Benz, "Viewpoint: Get More from Your Benefits Investment," *www.shrm.org*, August 3, 2012; Andrea Ozias, "Engaging Employees with Benefits Communications," *Worldatwork.org*, October 2012.
25. SHRM Online Staff, "Gen Y: Employers Get Low Marks for Benefits Communications," *www.shrm.org*, September 12, 2011.
26. Mark Huggett and Juan Carlos Parra, "How Well Does the U.S. Social Insurance System Provide Social Insurance?" *Journal of Political Economy*, Volume 118, 2010, 76–112.
27. "What is Medicare?" *Medicare.gov*, 2012.
28. "BLS - Table 5. Private Industry, By Major Occupational Group and Bargaining Status," 2012, *http://bls.gov/news.release/ecec.t05.htm*.
29. "Changes to Retirement Benefits: What HR Professionals Need to Know in 2012," *Workplace Visions – SHRM*, Issue 1, 2012.
30. Stephen Blakely and Jack VanDerhei, "EBRI's 2012 Retirement Confidence Survey: Job Insecurity, Debt Weigh on Retirement Confidence, Savings," *Employee Benefit Research Institute*, March 13, 2012.
31. Stephen Miller, "Better Retirement Plans May Prompt Job Switching," *HR Magazine*, July 2012, 11; "Reeling Them In With Retirement Bait: Retirement Benefits Shown Effective to Attract and Retain," *Employee Benefit News*, February 2011, 58.
32. Nancy L. Bolton, "Comparing Apples to Oranges," *Employee Benefits News*, July 2011, 12; John Kador, "Factoids From the Workplace and Beyond," *Human Resources Executive*, September 16, 2011, 50.

33. Herb Greenberg, "Underfunded Pensions are Red Flag for Investors", *www.cnbc.com*, July 8, 2010.

34. Joanne Sammer, "Are Defined Benefit Plans Dead?" *HR Magazine*, July 2012, 29–32.

35. Christopher Farrell, "Fine-Tuning the 401(k)," *Bloomberg Business-week*, April 5, 2012, 80.

36. "2012 Workplace Benefits Report," *Bank of America Merrill Lynch*, 2012.

37. Jilian Mincer, "Many U.S. Employers Cut 401(k) Matches," *The Wall Street Journal*, March 26, 2009; Aleksandra Todorova, "No Match," *The Wall Street Journal*, April 7, 2009; Kelly Greene, "Retirement Plans Make Comeback with Limits," *The Wall Street Journal*, June 14, 2011.

38. Patty Kujawa, "Playing Catch-Up," *Workforce Management*, January 2010, 23–26.

39. Deborah Silver, "401(k) Savings Zoom When Employers Set Autopilot," *Workforce Management*, September 2011, 14–15.

40. Kathleen Koster, "Online or Face Time?" *Employee Benefit News*, October 2012, 20–22.

41. "Annual Adoption of Cash Balance Plans Nearly Doubled," *www.shrm.org*, July 26, 2012.

42. Roselyn Feinsod and Allen Steinberg, "Back to the Future of Phased Retirement: Developing Flexible Retirement Programs that Work," *Worldatwork.org*, October 2012.

43. "Latest Survey Finds Health Benefits Cost Growth for 2012 Likely To Be the Lowest in 15 Years," *Mercer.com*, September 21, 2011.

44. Stephen Miller, "Family Health Plan Premiums Near $16,000 in 2012," *www.shrm.org*, September 21, 2012.

45. ibid

46. "Employers Remain Committed to Benefits," *Employee Benefit News*, May 2012, 50.

47. Stephen Miller, "For Employers, Health Care Excise Tax Is the 'X Factor'," *www.shrm.org*, November 22, 2010.

48. "Health-Care Costs Projected to Increase 5.3% in 2013," *Worldatwork.org*, August 29, 2012; "U.S. Employers Revamping Health Care Benefits," *HR Magazine*, HR Trendbook, 2012.

49. Joanne Sammer, "Health Care Costs Likely to Jump in 2013," *Business Finance Magazine*, September 17, 2012; "Large Employers Plan Benefits Overhaul," *Employee Benefit News*, October 2011, 66.

50. David Tobenkin, "Spousal Exclusions on the Rise," *HR Magazine*, November 2011, 55–60.

51. Anna Wilde Mathews, "Big Firms Overhaul Health Coverage," *The Wall Street Journal*, September 27, 2012.

52. Sander Domaszewicz, "A Considered Approach," *Human Resource Executive Online*, May 2, 2009.

53. Phillip T. Powell and Ron Laufer, "The Promises and Constraints of Consumer-Directed Healthcare," *Business Horizons*, Volume 53, 2010, 171–182; Anthony T. Lo Sasso, Lorens A. Helmchen and Robert Kaestner, "The Effects of Consumer-Directed Health Plans on Health Care Spending," *The Journal of Risk and Insurance*, Volume 77, 85–103.

54. Harvey Meyer, "Getting Tough," *Human Resource Executive Online*, May 1, 2010.

55. "Dollar Value of Wellness Incentives on the Rise," *Employee Benefit News*, April 15, 2012.

56. "FAQs for Employees about COBRA Continuation Health Coverage," Employee Benefits Security Administration, *www.dol.gov*.

57. Kathleen Koster, "Will It Ever End?" *Employee Benefit News*, June 15, 2010, 1, 19–21.

58. Marli D. Riggs, "Everybody Loves a Deal," *Employee Benefit News*, October 2012, 24–25.

59. Pamela Babcock, "Always More to Learn," *HR Magazine*, September 2009, 51–56; "Turning Your Tuition Assistance Program Into a Strategic Asset," *Apollo Research Institute*, 2011.

60. James Warren, "It Pays to Help Workers Buy a Home," *Bloomberg Businessweek*, June 14–20, 2010, 28.

61. "Family and Medical Leave Act," 2012, *http://www.dol.gov/whd.fmla.index.htm*.

62. Sean T. Hayes, Jared P. Smith, Lee J. Tyner and Jennifer Barger Johnson, "$21 Billion and Counting: The Burdens of FMLA to Employers," *Compensation & Benefits Review*, Volume 44, January 2012, 18–23.

63. Carrie Boerio, "Adoption Benefits: A Smart Addition to the Work-Life Balance," *Compensation & Benefit Review*, Volume 41, 2009, 66–72.

64. Peng Wang, John J. Lawler and Kan Shi, "Implementing Family-Friendly Employment Practices in Banking Industry: Evidence From Some African and Asian Countries," *Journal of Occupational & Organizational Psychology*, Volume 84, 2011, 493–517.

65. "2012 Employee Benefits: The Employee Benefits Landscape in a Recovering Economy," *www.shrm.org*, 2012.

66. Nicolas R. Ziebarth and Martin Karlsson, "A Natural Experiment on Sick Pay Cuts, Sickness Absence, and Labor Costs," *Journal of Public Economics*, Volume 94, 2010, 1108–1122.

67. Lisa V. Gillespie, "Taking It To the Bank," *Employee Benefit News*, July 2012, 10–12.

68. Patty Kujawa, "Gen X and Y Employees: Add More Benefits to the Workforce Menu," *Workforce.com*, September 20, 2012.

69. Based on Ben Steverman, "Creative Employee Benefits," *Bloomberg.com*, September 14, 2011; Richard Rothschild, "Some Employers are Thinking Outside the Benefits Box," *Workforce Management*, December 2010, 14.

© Hemera/Thinkstock

Employee Relations

14

Risk Management and Worker Protection

Learning Objectives

After you have read this chapter, you should be able to:

1 Understand risk management and identify its components.

2 Discuss three legal areas affecting safety and health.

3 Outline the basic provisions of the Occupational Safety and Health Act of 1970 and recordkeeping and inspection requirements.

4 Recognize the activities that constitute effective safety management.

5 List three workplace health issues and how employers are responding to them.

6 Explain workplace violence as a security issue and name some components of an effective security program.

7 Describe the nature and importance of disaster preparation and recovery planning for HR.

© badahos/Shutterstock.com

HR HEADLINE

Watch Out for Disgruntled Saboteurs

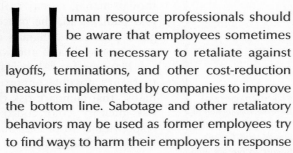

H uman resource professionals should be aware that employees sometimes feel it necessary to retaliate against layoffs, terminations, and other cost-reduction measures implemented by companies to improve the bottom line. Sabotage and other retaliatory behaviors may be used as former employees try to find ways to harm their employers in response to unpopular HR decisions. Due to an increase in the number of these negative incidents, business leaders need to be aware of the potential risks and pitfalls. Tim Dimoff, a risk expert who heads the Akron-based SACS Consulting & Investigative Services Inc., claims that such problems are common during times of job loss, and that HR must evaluate whether employees have been a problem in the past to determine if they are a risk factor. Based on his experiences, Dimoff also thinks that it is important to treat exiting employees favorably to reduce retaliation.

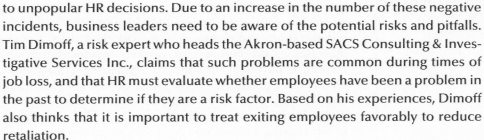

There are many real-life examples of workplace retaliation. For instance, a woman in one organization made bogus accusations about her manager sexually harassing her, in response to a likely layoff by the firm. In another company, an employee who was let go introduced a virus into the computer network that became active several weeks after he was gone. In a similar case of IT sabotage, a terminated employee gained access to and downloaded sensitive corporate information at his residence, destroying some content and dismantling critical programs. Further, a recently terminated worker was able to halt work in a company for several days by flipping a hidden switch, causing managers to believe that a computer virus had infected the system. Cases such as these, in addition to other situations involving leaked corporate secrets, equipment tampering, and workplace bullying and harassment, can be quite troubling for managers trying to protect the workplace.

HR managers can be proactive in developing policies that adequately prepare companies for possible negative consequences of terminations and layoffs. Implementing a professional and considerate approach for handling these sensitive issues, and then training managers to follow proper procedures, may deter employee revenge. Managers should also be aware of how they treat employees because abusing and disrespecting others at work can encourage sabotage and other counterproductive behaviors.[1]

L01 Understand risk management and identify its components.

Organizations can take steps to effectively anticipate a multitude of problems occurring in the normal functioning of business. These preparations, which ideally position employers to answer challenges, are the focus of *risk management*. Even though managers may realistically have a limited capacity to predict future events and plan ahead, the process is based on the idea that managers can develop a game plan that enhances a company's ability to respond to issues ranging from poor worker health and wellness to natural disasters.[2]

Planning for risk helps to mitigate the negative impacts and enhances capacity to realize possible opportunities. Managers can use various tools such as "heat maps" that compare risk factors and "traffic light" diagrams that convey levels of risk intensity (color coded as red, yellow, and green).[3] **Risk management** involves responsibility to protect both organizational and individual interests.

Risk management
Involves responsibilities to consider physical, human, and financial factors to protect organizational and individual interests.

Even though risk management is often a distinct business function, there are specific and separate risks associated with employees. In the United States and other developed nations, HR departments are included in the prevention, minimization, and elimination of workplace risks. For example, there have been increases in the numbers of workers' compensation and employment liability insurance payments because of rightsizing efforts and accusations of unfair employment practices.[4] These issues call for collaboration between risk managers and HR executives to develop plans that protect companies. For instance, the HR and risk management groups in one large U.S. company jointly assessed the risks of off-shoring various mid-level jobs to cut expenses as part of a labor savings measure. Their analysis found that doing so would limit developmental opportunities for promising individuals who could work in those jobs domestically, so the positions were not sent abroad.[5] A well-done risk management approach involving HR can reduce unnecessary expenses and perhaps enhance available opportunities.

There are a variety of risk management issues linked to HR, including the prevention of accidents and health problems at work, the protection of employees from workplace violence, and HR data security. Other issues can involve preparing for natural disasters, terrorist attacks, and global disease outbreaks. One of the most noteworthy risk issues that Human Resource professionals face today is the shortage of competent and skillful employees to fill critical openings precipitated by turnover and other staffing changes.[6]

HR managers must also consider risk management when moving employees across global borders. Personal assault, theft, natural disasters, disease, poor health care, and different laws can make international assignments challenging. Organizations in the United States and other nations such as Germany, Australia, and the

GLOBAL

United Kingdom have instituted duty-of-care requirements specifying that companies take active steps to protect the well-being of employees and their families when they are required to work and live overseas. For U.S. firms, managers must create risk management plans that educate workers and address how emergencies should be handled to avoid legal claims of negligence.[7] In addition to concerns over security and logistics, HR departments must also be aware of the tax and immigration risks that individuals potentially face when they travel abroad for shorter periods of time to conduct business.[8]

A major part of HR-based risk management in most organizations involves health, safety, and security, as shown in Figure 14-1. The terms *health*, *safety*, and *security* are closely related and can often be considered together when policies are created because they affect each other in practice. The broader and somewhat more nebulous term is **health**, which refers to a general state of physical, mental, and emotional well-being. A healthy person is free from illness, injury, or mental and emotional problems that impair normal human activity. Health management practices in organizations strive to maintain that overall well-being. For instance, a company might provide its workers free access to a local fitness center as part of a generalized health and wellness plan so that individuals are encouraged to be healthier.

Typically, **safety** refers to a condition in which the physical well-being of people is protected. The main purpose of effective safety programs in organizations is to prevent work-related injuries and accidents. For example, a manufacturing firm that utilizes combustible materials might routinely practice fire drills as part of a safety plan to ensure worker protection. Finally, the purpose of **security** is protecting employees and organizational facilities from those who may harm them. With the growth of workplace violence and issues such as terrorism and sabotage,

Health
General state of physical, mental, and emotional well-being.

Safety
Condition in which the physical well-being of people is protected.

Security
Protection of employees and organizational facilities.

FIGURE 14-1 Key Components of HR-Based Risk Management

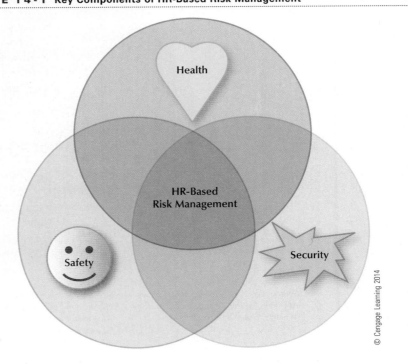

© Cengage Learning 2014

security has become a concern for employers and employees. Education can help; for instance, an insurance company could offer workplace violence seminars to educate its employees on the warning signs that often lead to danger to others on the job.

14-1 ■ CURRENT STATE OF HEALTH, SAFETY, AND SECURITY

Accidents can be costly for organizations as there are direct, indirect, and immeasurable costs associated with different incidents. Figure 14-2 shows that the direct costs of accidents are only a small part of the total costs, and organizations should

FIGURE 14-2 Examples of Direct, Hidden, and Immeasurable Costs of Accidents

Direct Costs
Medical
Compensation
Safety fines
Insurance premium
increase
Damage to work
equipment

Indirect (Hidden) Costs
Time lost away from worksite
Economic cost incurred by employee
Time lost by peers in the workplace
Reduced work group efficiency
Time lost by supervisor
Cost of training/staffing substitutes
Time lost because of faulty/offline equipment
Water, chemical, and other damage to operations
Time CEO/leaders invest in managing accident

Immeasurable Costs
Adverse harm to the reputation of an organization
Negative influence on employees' esprit de corps

Source: Based partly on Arieh Gavious, Shlomo Mizrahi, Yael Shani, and Yizhaq Minchuk, "The Costs of Industrial Accidents for the Organization: Developing Methods and Tools for Evaluation and Cost-Benefit Analysis of Investment in Safety," *Journal of Loss Prevention in the Process Industries*, 22 (2009), 434–438.

be careful to estimate all the expenses associated with accidents, particularly any indirect costs that might be overlooked. Illnesses can also generate financial and operational setbacks for companies. In a recent year, almost 3 million nonfatal job-related injuries and illnesses were recorded by private-sector organizations, with an average of 3.5 incidents being reported for every 100 full-time employees. These numbers were similar to those reported in the previous year, which represents a departure from the gradual decline in workplace accidents that have been reported over the last decade.

14-1a Snapshot of Health, Safety, and Security

Specific accident and illness rates vary depending on the industry, type of job, and other factors. For example, recently illnesses and injuries in private industry were down, but both the agriculture, forestry, and fishing and hunting industry and the accommodation and food services industry experienced an increase in cases. The health care and social assistance and retail trade sectors reported a decrease in workplace injuries and illnesses. The number of workplace injuries and illnesses also varied by employer size, with medium-sized companies having the highest reported rates and small businesses having the lowest rates.[9]

More than 50% of the injuries and illnesses that were reported in the United States were severe and called for employee time off, job changes, and and/or restrictions. Workplace injuries represented a much larger proportion of the incidents reported than did job-related illnesses (94.8% vs. 5.2% of the 3 million documented nonfatal injuries and illnesses). Just over 75% of injuries happened in service-based sectors, while 36% of work-related illnesses occurred in goods-producing sectors and just over 30% occurred in manufacturing.[10]

There is reason to believe that some organizations misrepresent how often injuries and illnesses occur in the workplace. Nearly half of employers investigated by OSHA for documentation problems failed to report accurate information about worker illnesses and injuries (figures were typically lower than they should have been). In addition, health care providers claim that companies have encouraged them to deemphasize illnesses and injuries, as well as to give inadequate treatment to employees.[11] Further, a study of employee accident reporting determined that, for each case that is properly disclosed in a company, there are roughly two and one-half incidents that go unreported, and the lack of a positive safety-oriented work climate and the uneven enforcement of safety requirements seemed to encourage underreporting.[12]

Other factors that can lead to underreporting of illnesses and injuries are:

- Lack of procedural knowledge on the part of employees and managers
- Safety policies that provide a reason not to report cases
- Belief that the company won't get inspected
- Concerns about workers' compensation claims
- Loss of business because of illness and injury

Managers must realize that companies can incur hefty fines in the millions of dollars for not properly disclosing incidents. In an effort to mitigate these concerns, OSHA could improve the situation by offering additional training about documenting illnesses and injuries, shortening the times between reports and audits, and updating the list of dangerous sectors that is used to make audit selections.[13]

14-1b Domestic Trends in Health, Safety, and Security

There are many trends in occupational health, safety, and security related to specific demographic and occupational issues that are occurring in the United States. For instance, deaths from accidents among Hispanic workers are on the rise. Many work in low-wage jobs with higher risk factors. In addition, poor English communication skills, lack of training, and other factors contribute to this situation, which runs counter to the trends for other groups.[14] Another interesting finding is that it appears more accidents occur in the spring on the day after the change to daylight savings time. Employees had almost 6% more workplace injuries on the Monday following the change to daylight savings time, presumably because of the "lost" hour of sleep. However, no significant change has been shown in the fall when everyone "gains" an hour.[15]

Self-employed workers have higher accident rates than do those who work for others. Although self-employed individuals make up less than 8% of the U.S. civilian workforce, 20% of workplace fatalities involve self-employed workers. When compared to those working for someone else, self-employed individuals were almost three times as likely to be killed. One explanation is that self-employed individuals are more likely to work in industries and occupations with higher fatality rates, especially farming. For instance, more than one out of every four self-employed people who died on the job was a farmer. A possible conclusion is that self-employed people are more willing to work in dangerous circumstances, and therefore they are more vulnerable to illnesses, injuries, and death.

GLOBAL

14-1c Global Trends in Health, Safety, and Security

Safety and health laws and regulations vary from country to country, ranging from virtually nonexistent to more stringent than those in the United States. The importance placed on health, safety, and security relates somewhat to the level of regulation and other factors in each country. However, factors may also exist in countries that lead to greater safety concerns for some individuals and groups. For example, one study determined that immigrants to Canada (compared to individuals who were born in the country) may face higher employment risks that make them more likely to be injured on the job, some of which included not being affiliated with a union, working in physically taxing jobs, and being employed on a shift-work schedule.[16]

International Emergency Health Services With more and more expatriates working internationally, especially in some less-developed countries, significant health and safety issues may exist. One consideration is provision of emergency evacuation services. For instance, evacuating and caring for an expatriate employee who sustains internal injuries in a car accident in the Ukraine or Sierra Leone may be a major issue. Many global firms purchase coverage for their international employees from an organization that provides emergency services, such as International SOS, Global Assistance & Healthcare, or U.S. Assist. If an emergency arises, the emergency services company dispatches physicians or even transports injured employees by chartered aircraft. If adequate medical assistance can be obtained locally, the emergency services company maintains a referral list and arranges for the expatriate to receive treatment. Emergency services firms may also provide legal counsel in foreign countries, emergency cash for medical expenses, and assistance in reissuing lost documents.

International Security and Terrorism As more U.S. firms operate internationally, the threat of terrorist actions against those firms and their employees increases. The extent to which employees are likely to experience security problems and violence depends on the country. The employer can regularly check the security conditions in countries where expatriates are traveling and working.

Global firms can take a variety of actions to address security concerns. For example, something as simple as removing signage identifying the location of foreign firms can reduce security concerns. Many international firms screen employees as they enter the worksite and use metal detectors to scan all packages, briefcases, and other items. Firms can also utilize physical barriers such as iron security fences, concrete barricades, bulletproof glass, and electronic surveillance devices in offices as part of their security efforts.

Kidnapping Not all violence occurs at work. Kidnapping, murder, home invasion, robberies, and carjackings happen relatively frequently in some places, such as Mexico City. In many countries throughout the world, U.S. citizens are especially vulnerable to extortion, kidnapping, bombing, physical harassment, and other terrorist activities.

To counter such threats, many global firms have *kidnap and ransom insurance*. This insurance covers the costs of paying ransoms to obtain releases of kidnapped employees and family members, paying for the bodily injuries suffered by kidnap victims, and dealing with negotiations and other expenses. Individual employees and their family members working and living abroad must also be made aware of security concerns. Both predeparture and ongoing security training should be given to all expatriates, their dependents, and employees of global firms working internationally, especially if located in high-risk areas.

LO2 Discuss three legal areas affecting safety and health.

14-2 ■ LEGAL REQUIREMENTS FOR SAFETY AND HEALTH

Employers must comply with a variety of federal and state laws when developing and maintaining healthy, safe, and secure working environments. Three major legal concerns are workers' compensation legislation, the Americans with Disabilities Act, and child labor laws.

14-2a Workers' Compensation

First passed in the early 1900s, workers' compensation laws in some form are on the books in all states today. As noted in Chapter 13, under these laws employers contribute to an insurance fund that compensates employees for injuries received while on the job. Premiums paid are experience-rated to reflect the accident rates of the employers, with employers that have higher incident rates being assessed higher premiums. Depending on the amount of lost time and the wage level in question, these laws often require payments be made to an employee for the time away from work because of an injury, payments to cover medical bills, and for retraining if a new job is required as a result of the incident. Most state laws also set a maximum weekly amount for

FIGURE 14-3 Sample of Workers' Compensation Covered Injuries

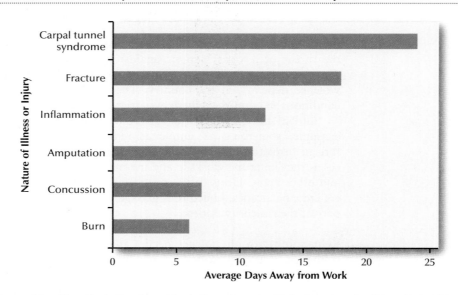

Source: Adapted from Nicole Nestoriak and Brooks Pierce, Comparing Workers' Compensation Claims with Establishments' Responses to the SOII, *Monthly Labor Review*, May 2009, 63.

determining workers' compensation benefits. Figure 14-3 shows some of the injuries covered and time lost for each.

Workers' compensation coverage has been expanded in many states to include emotional impairment that may have resulted from physical injury, as well as job-related strain, stress, anxiety, and pressure. Some cases of suicide have also been ruled to be job related in some states, with payments due under workers' compensation.

Another aspect of workers' compensation coverage relates to the use of telecommuting by employees. In most situations, while working at home for employers, individuals are covered under workers' compensation laws. Therefore, if an employee is injured while doing employer-related work at home, the employer is likely liable for the injury.

Controlling Workers' Compensation Costs Workers' compensation costs have become a major issue, and can represent from 2% to 10% of payroll for employers. Given these cost concerns, companies should focus on injury and accident prevention. A key to reducing these expenses has been *return-to-work plans*. These plans monitor employees who are off work because of injuries and illness. Also, the plans focus on returning the individuals to do *light-duty work* that is less physically demanding until they are able to perform their full range of job duties.

Workers' compensation fraud is an expensive problem. It has been estimated that about one-fourth of the workers' compensation claims filed are fraudulent. False and exaggerated claims make up the bulk of the fraud—costing employers billions of dollars annually. Employers must continually monitor their workers' compensation expenditures. Efforts to reduce workplace injuries, illnesses, and fraud can reduce workers' compensation premiums and claims costs. Many of the safety and health management suggestions discussed later in this chapter can contribute to reducing workers' compensation costs.

The Family and Medical Leave Act (FMLA) affects workers' compensation as well. Because the FMLA allows eligible employees to take up to 12 weeks of leave for their serious health conditions, injured employees may ask to use that leave time in addition to the leave time allowed under workers' compensation, even if it is unpaid. Some employers have policies that state that FMLA leave runs concurrently with any workers' compensation leave.

14-2b Americans with Disabilities Act and Safety Issues

Employers sometimes try to return injured workers to light-duty work to reduce workers' compensation costs. However, under the Americans with Disabilities Act (ADA), when making accommodations for injured employees through light-duty work, employers may undercut what are really essential job functions. Making such accommodations for injured employees for a period of time may require employers to make similar accommodations for job applicants with disabilities.

Health and safety recordkeeping practices have been affected by an ADA provision that requires all medical-related information to be maintained separately from all other confidential files. Specific access restrictions and security procedures must be adopted for medical records of all types, including employee medical benefits claims and treatment records.

HR professionals understand the ADA guidelines as they affect physical disabilities. However, it becomes more difficult where mental illness is at issue. Employees may not be aware of the extent to which their disability may impact their performance. To the extent workplace misconduct is the issue, management should follow normal procedure. Depending on the seriousness of the complaint, it should be determined if the employee presents a risk of violence, but concerns must be based on objective facts. Although no one should ignore a threat to safety, an overreaction to odd behavior could be a liability under the ADA.[17]

FIGURE 14-4 Selected Child Labor Hazardous Occupations (Minimum Age: 18)

Hazardous Work

- Manufacturing or storing explosives
- Driving a motor vehicle and being an outside helper
- Coal mining
- Logging and saw milling
- Using power-driven woodworking machines*
- Exposure to radioactive substances and to ionizing radiations
- Operating power-driven hoisting apparatus
- Operating power-driven, metal forming, punching, and shearing machines*
- Mining, other than coal mining
- Slaughtering or meatpacking, or rendering
- Using power-driven bakery machines
- Operating power-driven paper products machines*
- Manufacturing brick, tile, and related products
- Using power-driven circular saws, and guillotine shears*
- Wrecking, demolition, and shipbreaking operations
- Roofing operations*
- Excavation operations*

© Cengage Learning

*In certain cases, the law provides exemptions for apprentices and student learners in these occupations.

14-2c Child Labor Laws

Risk management includes dealing with safety concerns that have resulted in restrictions affecting younger workers, especially those under the age of 18. Child labor laws, found in the Fair Labor Standards Act (FLSA), set the minimum age for most employment at 16 years. Individuals who are 14 or 15 years old may work no more than three hours per day and a total of 18 hours in a week when school is in session, and they can only work from 7 a.m. through 7 p.m. When not in school or during the summer months, individuals can work 8 hours per day and a total of 40 hours per week, and June 1 until Labor Day they can work as late as 9 p.m. Individuals of any age can work for a family-based business that is owned and operated by their parents, but individuals who are younger than 16 cannot be employed in manufacturing or mining jobs. In addition, children of any age can deliver newspapers or work as entertainers. For hazardous occupations, 18 is the minimum age of employment.[18] Figure 14-4 lists some occupations that the federal government considers hazardous for children who work while attending school.

Two examples illustrate violations of the child labor law provisions. At a fast-food restaurant specializing in roast beef sandwiches, a teenage worker operated a meat slicer, which is a hazard covered by the FLSA. At a national discount retailer, teenage workers were found to have operated the mechanical box crushers. Both situations resulted in enforcement actions and fines for violating the FLSA.

Work-related injuries of younger workers are a significant issue for employers with many young employees. The retail and restaurant sectors consistently face safety and health issues with these workers. One characteristic of many young workers is to take more risks at work, much like they do when they drive cars. The degree to which workers engage in work-related risks is a significant factor affecting injuries and safety practices for younger workers. Companies need to (1) understand the laws associated with employing minors, (2) take the proper steps needed to reduce workplace safety concerns, (3) properly manage and train younger employees so that workplace hazards are recognized and prevented, and (4) encourage feedback from minors about their safety concerns.[19]

In addition to complying with workers' compensation, ADA, and child labor laws, most employers must comply with the Occupational Safety and Health Act of 1970. This act has had a tremendous impact on the workplace. The act is administered by the Occupational Safety and Health Administration. In an example of OSHA involvement, Tempel Grain LLC was found to be in violation of requirements when a 17-year-old was asked to clear a grain elevator without wearing a safety harness. He fell into the elevator and suffocated after being covered with grain. The company paid out settlements to the boy's family and, and as part of a five-year probationary period, could not employ anyone under the age of 18, had to develop an ongoing safety training program for new and current workers, and had to ensure that proper safety equipment would be utilized on the job.[20]

LO3 Outline the basic provisions of the Occupational Safety and Health Act of 1970 and recordkeeping and inspection requirements.

14-3 ■ OCCUPATIONAL SAFETY AND HEALTH ACT

The Occupational Safety and Health Act of 1970 was passed to ensure that the health and safety of individuals employed in organizations would be protected. Every employer that is engaged in commerce and has one or more employees is covered by the act.

Farmers having fewer than 10 employees are exempt. Employers in specific industries, such as railroads and mining, are covered under other health and safety acts. Federal, state, and local governments are covered by separate statutes and provisions.

The Occupational Safety and Health Act of 1970 established the Occupational Safety and Health Administration, known as OSHA, to administer its provisions. The act also established the National Institute for Occupational Safety and Health (NIOSH) as a supporting body to do research and develop standards. In addition, the Occupational Safety and Health Review Commission (OSHRC) has been established to review OSHA enforcement actions and to address disputes between OSHA and employers that have been cited by OSHA inspectors.

By making employers and employees more aware of safety and health considerations, OSHA has significantly affected organizations. OSHA regulations and on-site presence appear to have contributed to reductions in the number of accidents and injuries in some cases. But in other industries, OSHA has had little or no effect.

14-3a OSHA Enforcement Standards

To implement OSHA regulations, specific standards were established to regulate equipment and working environments. National standards developed by engineering and quality control groups are often used. OSHA rules and standards are frequently complicated and technical. Small business owners and managers who do not have specialists on their staffs may find the standards difficult to read and understand. In addition, the adoption of many less important minor standards has hurt OSHA's credibility.

Two provisions have been recognized as key to employers' responsibility to comply with OSHA:

- *General duty*: The act requires that the employer has a general duty to provide safe and healthy working conditions, even in areas where OSHA standards have not been set. Employers that know or reasonably should know of unsafe or unhealthy conditions can be cited for violating the general duty clause.
- *Notification and posters*: Employers are required to inform their employees of safety and health standards established by OSHA. Also, OSHA posters must be displayed in prominent locations in workplaces.

Hazard Communication OSHA has established *process safety management* (PSM) standards that focus on hazardous chemicals. As part of PSM, hazard communication standards require manufacturers, importers, distributors, and users of hazardous chemicals to evaluate, classify, and label those substances. Employers must also make information about hazardous substances available to employees, their representatives, and health professionals. This information is contained in material safety data sheets (MSDSs), which must be kept readily accessible to those who work with chemicals and certain other dangerous substances. The MSDSs indicate antidotes or actions to be taken should someone come in contact with the substances. If the organization employs many workers for whom English is not the primary language, then the MSDSs should be available in the necessary languages. Also, workers should be trained in how to access and use the MSDS information.

The Internet has made it much quicker and easier for companies to meet OSHA's hazard communication requirements because (1) employers can access safety information produced by vendors and suppliers on hazardous materials and chemicals and (2) information technology allows employers to use the Internet to maintain

MSDSs on chemicals and workplace substances. Using MSDS software, firms can update electronic MSDSs regularly rather than having to reissue printed manuals. An employer can place all MSDSs on an intranet through a hyperlink or access manufacturers' information sheets. Many MSDSs can also be found on websites.

As part of hazard communications, OSHA has established *lockout/tag-out regulations*. To comply with these regulations, firms must provide mechanics and tradespeople with locks and tags to use to make equipment inoperable during repair or adjustment to prevent accidental start-up of defective machinery. Only the person whose name is printed on the tag or engraved on the lock may remove the device.

Bloodborne Pathogens OSHA has issued a standard regarding exposure to the hepatitis B virus (HBV), the human immunodeficiency virus (HIV), and other bloodborne pathogens. This regulation was developed to protect employees who regularly are exposed to blood and other such substances from contracting AIDS and other serious diseases. Obviously, health care laboratory workers, nurses, and medical technicians are at greatest risk. However, all employers covered by OSHA regulations must comply in workplaces where cuts and abrasions are common. Regulations require employers with the most pronounced risks to have written control and response plans and to train workers in following the proper procedures.

Personal Protective Equipment One goal of OSHA has been to develop standards for personal protective equipment (PPE). These standards require that employers analyze job hazards, provide adequate PPE to employees in hazardous jobs, and train employees in the use of PPE items. Common PPE items include safety glasses, hard hats, and safety shoes. Employers are required to provide PPE to all employees (at no cost) who are working in an environment that presents hazards or who might have contact with hazardous chemicals and substances on the job.[21] In addition, a recent court ruling specified that employees should be paid at the proper hourly rate for the time it takes to put on and take off protective equipment, including any potential overtime that is incurred beyond a 40-hour workweek.[22]

Pandemic Guidelines In addition to regulations, OSHA issues guidelines that can help to protect people at work in matters of health or safety. One such set of guidelines can help employers to prepare for a pandemic disease. These guidelines provide information about how the organization can manage a serious disease outbreak with proper procedures and safety equipment. In addition, guidelines are provided that help a company continue operations with a depleted workforce.

14-3b Ergonomics and OSHA

Ergonomics
Study and design of the work environment to address physical demands placed on individuals.

Cumulative trauma disorders (CTDs)
Muscle and skeletal injuries that occur when workers repetitively use the same muscles to perform tasks.

Ergonomics is the study and design of the work environment to address physical demands placed on individuals. In a work setting, ergonomic studies look at factors such as fatigue, lighting, tools, equipment layout, and placement of controls. Ergonomics can provide economic value to employers as it can reduce injuries.

For many years, OSHA focused on the large number of work-related injuries that occur because of repetitive stress and repetitive motion, such as cumulative trauma disorders, carpal tunnel syndrome, and other injuries. **Cumulative trauma disorders (CTDs)** are muscle and skeletal injuries that occur when workers repetitively use the same muscles to perform tasks. *Carpal tunnel syndrome*, a cumulative trauma disorder, is an injury common to people who put their hands through repetitive motions such as typing, playing certain musical instruments, cutting, and sewing.

Problems caused by repetitive and cumulative injuries occur in a variety of work settings. The meatpacking industry has a very high level of CTDs. Grocery cashiers experience CTDs from repetitively twisting their wrists when they scan bar codes on canned goods. Office workers experience CTDs too, primarily from doing extensive typing and data entry on computers and computer-related equipment. Most recently, attention has focused on the application of ergonomic principles to the design of workstations where workers extensively use personal computers, portable message devices, cell phones, and video display terminals for extended periods of time.

OSHA has approached ergonomics concerns by adopting voluntary guidelines for specific problem industries and jobs, identifying industries with serious ergonomic problems, and giving employers tools for identifying and controlling ergonomics hazards. Among the industries receiving guidelines are nursing homes, poultry processors, and retail grocery stores.

Successful Ergonomics Programs A successful ergonomics program has several components. First, management must commit to reducing injuries caused by repetition and cumulative trauma, including providing financial and other resources to support the efforts. Involvement of employees is key to getting employee support. Other actions should include reviewing jobs where CTD problems could exist and ensuring that proper equipment, seating, lighting, and other engineering solutions are utilized. Also, supervisors and managers should be trained to observe signs of CTD and on how to respond to employee complaints about musculoskeletal and repetitive motion problems.

14-3c Work Assignments and OSHA

The rights of employees regarding work assignments have been addressed as part of OSHA regulations. Two primary areas where work assignments and concerns about safety and health meet are reproductive health and unsafe work.

Work Assignments and Reproductive Health Assigning employees to work in areas where their ability to have children may be affected by exposure to chemical hazards or radiation is an issue. Women who are able to bear children or who are pregnant have presented the primary concerns, but in some situations the possibility that men might become sterile has also been involved. On the basis of standards specified in the Civil Rights Act and Pregnancy Discrimination Act, employers should not prevent women (or men) from working in hazardous jobs because of reproductive concerns. Although employers have no absolute protection from liability, the following actions can help:

- Maintain a safe workplace for all by seeking the safest working methods.
- Comply with all state and federal safety laws.
- Inform employees of any known risks.
- Document employee acceptance of any risks.

Refusing Unsafe Work Both union and nonunion workers have refused to work when they considered the work unsafe. In many court cases, that refusal has been found to be justified. The conditions for refusing work because of safety concerns include the following:

- The employee's fear is objectively reasonable.
- The employee has tried to have the dangerous condition corrected.
- Using normal procedures to solve the problem has not worked.

14-3d OSHA Recordkeeping Requirements

Employers are generally required to maintain a detailed annual record of the various types of injuries, accidents, and fatalities for inspection by OSHA representatives and for submission to the agency. OSHA guidelines state that facilities where accident records are below the national average rarely need inspecting. But those with high "days away from work scores" may get letters from OSHA and perhaps an inspection.[23] Most organizations must complete OSHA Form 300 to report workplace accidents and injuries. As stated previously, however, many incidents go unreported for a variety of reasons.

Reporting Injuries and Illnesses Four types of injuries or illnesses are defined by the Occupational Safety and Health Act. They are as follows:

* *Injury- or illness-related deaths*: fatalities at workplaces or caused by work-related actions must be reported within 8 hours
* *Lost-time or disability injuries*: job-related injuries or disabling occurrences that cause an employee to miss regularly scheduled work on the day following the accident
* *Medical care injuries*: injuries that require treatment by a physician but do not cause an employee to miss a regularly scheduled work turn
* *Minor injuries*: injuries that require first aid treatment and do not cause an employee to miss the next regularly scheduled work turn

The recordkeeping requirements for these injuries and illnesses are summarized in Figure 14-5. Notice that only very minor injuries do not have to be recorded for OSHA. For example, an employee was repairing a conveyor belt when his hand slipped and hit the sharp edge of a steel bar. His hand was cut, and he was taken to the hospital. He received five stitches and was told by the doctor not to use his hand for three days. This injury was recorded and reported to OSHA because the stitches and restricted duty required that it be recorded.

14-3e OSHA Inspections

The Occupational Safety and Health Act provides for on-the-spot inspections by OSHA representatives, called compliance officers or inspectors. In *Marshall v. Barlow's, Inc.*, the U.S. Supreme Court held that safety inspectors must produce a search warrant if an employer refuses to allow an inspector into the plant voluntarily. The Court also ruled that an inspector does not have to show probable cause to obtain a search warrant. A warrant can be obtained easily if a search is part of a general enforcement plan.[24]

Dealing with an Inspection When an OSHA compliance officer arrives, managers should ask to see the inspector's credentials. Next, the company HR representative or safety professional should insist on an opening conference with the compliance officer. The compliance officer may request that a union representative, an employee, and a company representative be present while the inspection is conducted. During the inspection, the officer checks organizational records to see if they are being maintained and to determine the number of accidents that have occurred. Following this review of the safety records, the officer conducts an on-the-spot inspection and may use a wide variety of equipment to test compliance with standards. After the inspection, the compliance officer can issue citations for any violations of standards and provisions of the act.

FIGURE 14-5 Guide to Recordability of Cases under the Occupational Safety and Health Act

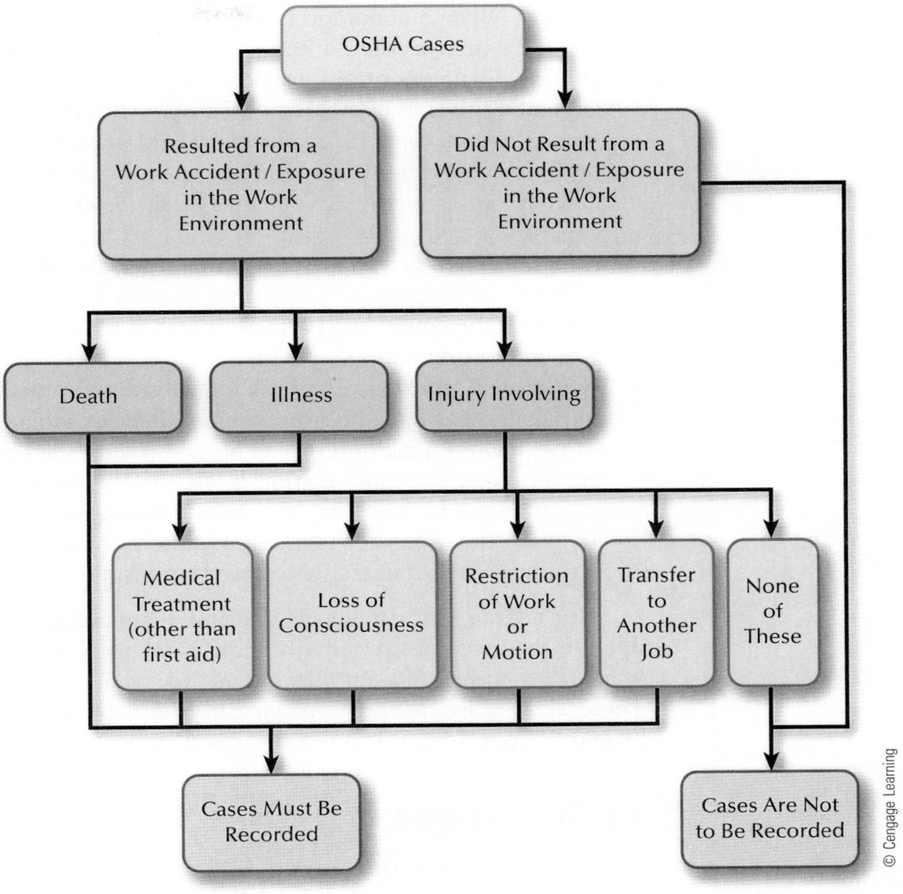

Citations and Violations Although OSHA inspectors can issue citations for violations of the act, whether or not a citation is issued depends on the severity and extent of the problems, and on the employer's knowledge of them. In addition, depending on the nature and number of violations, monetary penalties can be assessed against employers. The nature and extent of the penalties depend on the type and severity of the violations as determined by OSHA officials.

Many types of violations are cited by OSHA. Ranging from the most severe to minimal, including a special category for repeated violations, the most common are as follows:

- *Imminent danger*: When there is reasonable certainty that the condition will cause death or serious physical harm if it is not corrected immediately, an imminent-danger citation is issued and a notice posted by an inspector. Imminent-danger situations are handled on the highest-priority basis. They are reviewed by a regional OSHA director, and the condition must be corrected immediately. If the condition is serious enough and the employer does not cooperate, a representative of OSHA may obtain a federal injunction to close the company until the condition is corrected. The absence of guardrails to prevent employees from falling into heavy machinery is one example of an imminent danger.

- *Serious*: When a condition could probably cause death or serious physical harm, and the employer should know of the condition, OSHA issues a serious-violation citation. Examples of serious violations are the absence of a protective screen on a lathe and the lack of a blade guard on an electric saw.
- *Other than serious*: Violations that could impact employees' health or safety but probably would not cause death or serious harm are called "other than serious." Having loose ropes in a work area might be classified as an other-than-serious violation.
- *De minimis*: A *de minimis* condition is one not directly and immediately related to employees' safety or health. No citation is issued, but the condition is mentioned to the employer. Lack of doors on toilet stalls is a common example of a *de minimis* violation.
- *Willful and repeated*: Citations for willful and repeated violations are issued to employers that have been previously cited for violations. If an employer knows about a safety violation or has been warned of a violation and does not correct the problem, a second citation is issued. The penalty for a willful and repeated violation can be high. For example, if death results from an accident that involves such a safety violation, a jail term of six months can be imposed on the executives or managers who were responsible.

Consider a case in which a metal manufacturer instructed its employees to operate the machines differently than usual when OSHA conducted an inspection. It also hid pieces of equipment, and management lied about its usual practices. These actions led to a willful violation and large fines for numerous violations, primarily because the firm tried to cover up its noncompliance.

14-3f Critique of OSHA

OSHA has been criticized on several fronts. Because the agency has so many worksites to inspect, employers have only a relatively small chance of being inspected. Some suggest that employers pay little attention to OSHA enforcement efforts for this reason. Labor unions and others have criticized OSHA and Congress for not providing enough inspectors. For instance, it is common to find that many of the worksites at which workers suffered severe injuries or deaths had not been inspected in the previous five years.

Employers, especially smaller ones, continue to complain about the complexity of complying with OSHA standards and the costs associated with penalties and with making changes required to remedy problem areas. Larger firms can afford to hire safety and health specialists and establish more proactive programs. However, smaller firms that cannot afford to do so still have to comply with the regulations, meaning that managers need to be more involved in safety management.

LO4 Recognize the activities that constitute effective safety management.

14-4 ■ SAFETY MANAGEMENT

Well-designed and effectively managed safety programs can result in reduced accidents and associated costs. Further, a variety of safety problems often decline as a result of management efforts that emphasize a safe work environment. A recent

FIGURE 14-6 Typical Division of HR Responsibilities for Health, Safety, and Security Issues

HR Unit	Operating Managers
• Coordinate health and safety programs	• Monitor the health and safety of employees daily
• Develop safety reporting system	• Coach employees to be safety conscious
• Provide accident investigation expertise	• Investigate accidents
• Provide technical expertise on accident prevention	• Monitor workplace for security problems
• Develop restricted-access procedures and employee identification systems	• Communicate with employees to identify potentially difficult employees
• Assist with disaster and recovery planning efforts	• Implement disaster and recovery plan

© Cengage Learning 2014

study determined that safety management is associated with an increase in organization-based safety performance, a stronger competitive orientation, and an enhanced financial position.[25] Often, the difference between high-performing firms with good occupational safety records and other firms is that the former have effective safety management programs. As Figure 14-6 indicates, both the HR unit and operating managers must be involved in coordinating health, safety, and security efforts.

Successful safety management has been researched extensively. A summary of what is known about managing safety effectively and reducing accidents includes the following important components of a safety management program:

- Organizational commitment to safety
- Safety policies, discipline, and recordkeeping
- Safety training and communication
- Effective safety committees
- Inspection, investigation, and evaluation

14-4a Organizational Commitment to Safety

At the heart of safety management is an organizational commitment to a comprehensive safety effort that should be coordinated at the top level of management and include all members of the organization. It should also be reflected in managerial actions. A president of a small electrical manufacturing firm who does not wear a hard hat in the manufacturing shop can hardly expect to successfully enforce a requirement that all employees wear hard hats in the shop.

14-4b Safety Policies, Discipline, and Recordkeeping

Designing safety policies and rules and disciplining violators are important components of safety efforts. Frequently reinforcing the need for safe behavior and frequently supplying feedback on positive safety practices are also effective ways of improving worker safety. Such safety-conscious efforts must involve employees, supervisors, managers, safety specialists, and HR staff members.

For policies about safety to be effective, good recordkeeping about accidents, causes, and other details is necessary. Without records, an employer cannot track its safety performance, compare benchmarks against other employers, and may not realize the extent of its safety problems.

14-4c Safety Training and Communication

Safety training can be conducted in various ways to effectively reduce accidents. Regular sessions with supervisors, managers, and employees are often coordinated by HR staff members. Communication of safety procedures, reasons why accidents occurred, and what to do in an emergency is critical. Without effective communication about safety, training is insufficient. To reinforce safety training, continuous communication to develop safety consciousness is necessary. Merely sending safety memos is not enough. Producing newsletters, changing safety posters, continually updating bulletin boards, and posting safety information in visible areas are also recommended.

Employers may need to communicate in a variety of media and languages. Such efforts are important to address the special needs of workers who have vision, speech, or hearing impairments; who are not proficient in English; or who are challenged in other ways. Many approaches might be needed in training to enhance individual learning, including the use of role-playing and other active practice exercises, behavioral examples, and extensive discussion.

14-4d Effective Safety Committees

Employees frequently participate in safety planning through safety committees, often composed of workers from a variety of levels and departments. A safety committee generally meets at regularly scheduled times, has specific responsibilities for conducting safety reviews, identifies risks, and makes recommendations for changes necessary to avoid future accidents. Usually, at least one member of the committee comes from the HR department.

Companies must take care to ensure that managers do not constitute a majority on their safety committees. Otherwise, they may be in violation of provisions of the National Labor Relations Act, commonly known as the Wagner Act. That act, as explained in detail in Chapter 16, prohibits employers from "dominating a labor organization." Some safety committees have been ruled to be labor organizations because they deal with working conditions.

In approximately 32 states, all but the smallest employers may be required to establish safety committees. From time to time, legislation has been introduced at the federal level to require joint management/employee safety committees. But as yet, no federal provisions have been enacted.

14-4e Inspection, Investigation, and Evaluation

It is not necessary to wait for an OSHA inspector to check the work area for safety hazards. Regular inspections may be done by a safety committee or by a company safety coordinator. Problem areas should be addressed immediately to prevent accidents and keep work productivity at the highest possible levels. Also, OSHA inspects organizations with above-average rates of lost workdays more frequently. Therefore, reducing accidents can lower the frequency of on-site OSHA visits.

The phases of accident investigation are shown in Figure 14-7. Identifying why an accident occurred is extremely useful. However, taking the proper steps to prevent

FIGURE 14-7 Phases of Accident Investigation

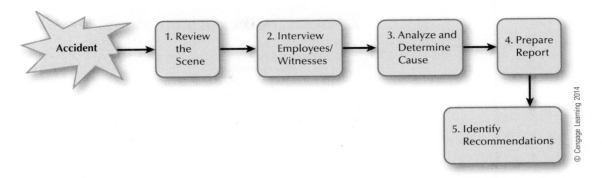

similar accidents from occurring is even more important when it comes to effectively managing safety in the workplace.

Closely related to accident investigation is research to determine ways of preventing accidents. Employing safety engineers or having outside experts evaluate the safety of working conditions may be useful. If many similar accidents seem to occur in an organizational unit, a safety training program may be necessary to emphasize safe working practices. As an example, a medical center reported a greater-than-average number of back injuries among employees who lifted heavy patients. Installation of patient-lifting devices and safety training on the proper way of using them was initiated. As a result, the number of worker injuries was reduced.

14-4f Approaches for Effective Safety Management

Three approaches are typically used by employers to manage safety. Figure 14-8 shows some of the organizational, engineering, and individual approaches and their components. Successful programs may use all three when dealing with safety issues.

Organizational Approach Companies can effectively manage safety by designing safer jobs and by creating policies that encourage safety. Safety committees can be used to increase awareness of important safety issues, and guidelines for accident investigations can help managers identify the causes of safety violations. All of these approaches build a strong commitment to safety in the organization, encouraging a safety culture that leads to many positive work outcomes. Firms such as Johnson & Johnson, DuPont Chemical and Energy Operations, and Frito-Lay are well known for emphasizing safety as part of their organizational cultures. A recent meta-analysis found that a good safety climate precipitated greater safety knowledge, motivation, and performance in organizations and decreased workplace injuries and accidents.[26] Another study determined that a safety-oriented work climate was associated with an improved physical and psychological work context, as well as decreased accidents in the workplace.[27]

Engineering Approach Employers can prevent some accidents by designing machines, equipment, and work areas so that workers who perform potentially dangerous jobs cannot injure themselves and others. Providing safety equipment and guards on machinery, installing emergency switches, installing safety rails, keeping aisles clear, and installing adequate ventilation, lighting, heating, and air conditioning can all help to make work environments safer.

FIGURE 14-8 Approaches for Effective Safety Management

> **Organizational Approach**
> - Designing safe jobs
> - Developing/implementing safety policies
> - Using safety committees
> - Coordinating accident investigations
> - Creating safety culture
>
> **Engineering Approach**
> - Designing work settings and equipment
> - Evaluating and using equipment
> - Applying ergonomic principles
> - Implementing safety procedures in workplace
>
> **Individual Approach**
> - Reinforcing safety motivation and attitudes
> - Providing employee safety training
> - Rewarding safety through incentive programs
> - Discussing safety in meetings and at worksites

© Cengage Learning 2014

Designing a job properly requires consideration of the physical setting of the job. The way the work space surrounding a job is utilized can influence the worker's performance of the job itself. Several factors that affect safety have been identified, including size of work area, kinds of materials used, sensory conditions, distance between work areas, and interference from noise and traffic flow.

Individual Approach Engineers approach safety from the perspective of redesigning the machinery or the work area. Industrial psychologists and human factors experts see safety differently. They address the proper match of individuals to jobs and emphasize employee training in safety methods, fatigue reduction, and health awareness.

Numerous field studies with thousands of employees have looked at the human factors in accidents. The results have shown a definite relationship between cognitive factors and occupational safety. Behavior-based safety (BBS) approaches are efforts to reduce *risky behavior* and increase safe behavior by defining unsafe behavior and attempting to change it. While BBS is beneficial, it does not constitute a complete approach to dealing with safety.

Work schedules can be another cause for accidents. The relationship between work schedules and accidents can be explained as follows: Fatigue based on physical exertion sometimes exists in the industrial workplace of today. Boredom, which occurs when a person is required to do the same tasks for a long period of time, is rather common. As fatigue or boredom increases, motivation decreases, and when motivation decreases, workers' attention wanders, possibly leading to more accidents on the job. A particular area of concern is overtime in work scheduling. Overtime work has been consistently related to accident incidence because the more overtime worked, the higher the incidence of severe accidents.

MEASURE

14-4g Measuring Safety Efforts

Organizations should monitor and evaluate their safety efforts. Just as organizational accounting records are audited, a firm's safety efforts should be audited periodically as well. Accident and injury statistics should be compared with previous accident patterns to identify any significant changes. This analysis should be designed to measure progress in safety management.

Various safety efforts can be measured. Common metrics are workers' compensation costs per injury/illness; percentage of injuries/illnesses by department, work shifts, and job categories; and incident rate comparisons with industry and benchmark targets. Regardless of the specific measures used, it is critical to track and evaluate safety management efforts using relevant HR metrics.

Employers in a variety of industries have found that emphasizing health and safety pays off in many ways. Lower employee benefits costs for health care, fewer work-related accidents, lower workers' compensation costs, and more productive employees can all be results of employer efforts to stress health and safety.

14-5 ■ EMPLOYEE HEALTH

L05 List three workplace health issues and how employers are responding to them.

Employee health problems are varied—and somewhat inevitable. They can range from minor illnesses such as colds to serious illnesses related to the jobs performed. Some employees have emotional health problems; others have alcohol or drug problems. Some problems are chronic; others are transitory. All may affect organizational operations and individual employee productivity.

Employers face a variety of workplace health issues. Previously in this chapter, cumulative trauma injuries and exposure to hazardous chemicals were discussed because OSHA has addressed these concerns through regulations or standards. Other concerns associated with employee health include substance abuse, emotional/mental health, older workers, smoking, and obesity.

14-5a Substance Abuse

Substance abuse
Use of illicit substances or misuse of controlled substances, alcohol, or other drugs.

Use of illicit substances or misuse of controlled substances, alcohol, or other drugs is called **substance abuse**. The millions of substance abusers in the workforce cost global employers billions of dollars annually, although recently there has been a decline in illegal drug use by employees. Employers' concerns about substance abuse stem from the ways it alters work behaviors, causing increased tardiness and absenteeism, a slower work pace, a higher rate of mistakes and accidents, and less time spent at work. It can also cause an increase in withdrawal (physical and psychological) and antagonistic behaviors, which may lead to workplace violence. Consequently, many companies have a drug screening policy that focuses on pre-employment testing.[28]

A company should also consider relying on employee assistance programs (EAPs) for support and counseling related to substance abuse, as well as craft zero-tolerance policies that address employees' use of alcohol and drugs. EAPs are programs that assist troubled employees. Unfortunately, many employers turn a blind eye to these issues because of the threat of bad publicity, increased costs, and fears concerning discrimination lawsuits. This is why HR professionals must get involved in substance abuse cases by (1) preparing supervisory personnel to implement a progressive penalty process that

FIGURE 14-9 Common Signs of Substance Abuse

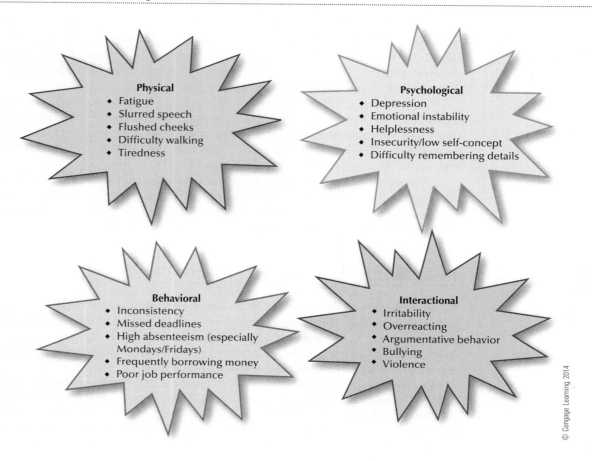

Physical
- Fatigue
- Slurred speech
- Flushed cheeks
- Difficulty walking
- Tiredness

Psychological
- Depression
- Emotional instability
- Helplessness
- Insecurity/low self-concept
- Difficulty remembering details

Behavioral
- Inconsistency
- Missed deadlines
- High absenteeism (especially Mondays/Fridays)
- Frequently borrowing money
- Poor job performance

Interactional
- Irritability
- Overreacting
- Argumentative behavior
- Bullying
- Violence

© Cengage Learning 2014

gives substance abusers a chance to seek assistance, (2) encouraging managers to confront problems head on, (3) preventing supervisors from diagnosing problems and providing counseling, and (4) choosing the right EAPs and monitoring the quality of support provided.[29] In addition, Figure 14-9 shows common signs of substance abuse that HR professionals and managers can monitor. However, not all signs may manifest in any one case. A pattern that includes some of these behaviors should be a reason to pay closer attention.[30]

Alcohol testing and drug testing are used by many employers, especially following an accident or some other reasonable cause. A recent poll determined that a majority of companies (over 70%) make some or all applicants take a drug test before securing employment, with 71% of larger firms using pre-employment drug testing, 40% of smaller firms, and almost 75% of global companies using such assessments. The study also showed that using such tests increased employee productivity and reduced workers' compensation claims.[31] Some employers also use random testing programs.

The U.S. Department of Transportation *requires* drug testing for aviation workers, truck drivers, railroad workers, mass transit employees, pipeline employees, and commercial vessel operators. The U.S. Department of Health and Human Services suggests that companies follow these guidelines when managing drug testing in the workplace:[32]

Always
- be aware of current laws and talk to union leaders and appropriate government contacts
- create a program that ensures confidentiality, and identify one individual to receive lab results
- let employees know about drug testing program 30–60 days before implementation and follow all specified requirements once the program in under way
- use certified labs to conduct and evaluate tests
- follow-up an initial positive result with a confirmatory test

Avoid
- inconsistencies in the implementation of drug testing policies
- sharing lab results with individuals other than those who are required to know about drug testing figures
- making personnel decisions on the basis of initial test results
- focusing all efforts on drug abuse, while ignoring alcohol-related problems
- addressing drug- and alcohol-related problems without a witness
- letting impaired individuals drive themselves to their place of residence

Types of Drug Tests There are several types of tests to detect drug use: urinalysis, radioimmunoassay of hair, surface swiping, and fitness-for-duty testing. The innovative fitness-for-duty tests can be used alone or in conjunction with drug testing. These tests can identify individuals under the influence of alcohol or prescription drugs to the extent that their abilities to perform their jobs are impaired. Some firms use fitness-for-duty tests to detect work performance safety problems before permitting an employee to operate dangerous equipment. As an example, in one firm when a crew of delivery truck drivers comes to work, they are asked to "play" a video game—one that can have serious consequences. Unless the video game machine presents receipts saying they passed the test, they are not allowed to drive their trucks that day. It works like this—the computer has an established baseline for each employee. Subsequent testing measures the employees against their baselines. Interestingly, most test failures are not drug or alcohol related. Rather, fatigue, illness, and personal problems more frequently render a person unfit to perform a hazardous job.

Handling Substance Abuse Cases The Americans with Disabilities Act (ADA) affects how management can handle substance abuse cases. Currently, users of *illegal* drugs are specifically excluded from the definition of *disabled* under the act. However, those addicted to *legal* substances (e.g., alcohol and prescription drugs) are considered disabled under the ADA. Also, recovering substance abusers are considered disabled under the ADA.

To encourage employees to seek help for their substance abuse problems, a *firm-choice option* is usually recommended and has been endorsed legally. In this procedure, a supervisor or a manager confronts the employee privately about unsatisfactory work-related behaviors. Then, in keeping with the disciplinary system, the employee is offered a choice between help and discipline. Treatment options and consequences of further unsatisfactory performance are clearly discussed, including what the employer will do. Confidentiality and follow-up are important when employers use the firm-choice option.

Using Drug Testing to Determine Medication Use

Urine analysis is viewed as an effective means for determining if employees are taking prescription drugs given to them after an injury. In addition, these tests can also show whether or not an employee is using other drugs as supplemental medication. It can also indicate if the individual is failing to take medication perhaps so that the drugs can be sold illegally. Drug testing might be used to learn how well workers are following worker's compensation regimes, ultimately reducing the expenses associated with filling prescriptions.

For Marriott International Inc., evidence collected from a recent rollout of a urine testing program indicated that many employees are not taking prescription medication in a way that helps their health and wellness. For instance, only a little over one-third of individuals were taking their medication the way they should be, and over half of employees didn't have enough medication in their systems, or had traces of other drugs that were not given to them by doctors. These results suggest the following:

- Many employees don't really need the prescription drugs to help manage pain and recover.
- Employees could be either over-medicating or under-medicating, thus generating peculiar lab results.
- The employees could be taking illegal drugs to supplement the effects of the medication provided by doctors or simply for recreation.

The use of drug testing to monitor prescription drug use in worker's compensation situations has become more economically viable in recent years. Some of the comprehensive tests cost between $300 and $500, which is far less than single doses of some prescription drugs. One potential outcome might involve providing incentives to doctors who can cut back on prescriptions when tests show that patients are not taking the proper drugs.[33]

Medical Marijuana The use of marijuana for medical reasons, mainly as a mechanism for relieving severe physical pain, has been authorized in some states including Alaska, California, Colorado, Hawaii, Maine, Michigan, Montana, Nevada, New Jersey, New Mexico, Oregon, Rhode Island, Vermont, and Washington. However, use of this drug has raised several important implications about how to manage situations where employees are found to be using an illegal substance, when a company policy clearly stands against the use and/or abuse of drugs and alcohol. The question is whether a company should discipline or terminate an individual who tests positive for marijuana consumption in a medical marijuana state. The HR Perspective: Using Drug Testing to Determine Medication Use discusses how urinalysis can be used to determine whether employees are taking the proper prescription medications while adhering to a treatment program.

An organization might consider developing a zero-tolerance policy if employers are not currently required by states to make accommodations to medical marijuana users. Consumption of the drug is still illegal under federal law. Another option involves placing medical marijuana users on disability leave (or time off associated with the Family and Medical Leave Act) so that individuals can assess their current situation in the company. Finally, companies could choose to make some exceptions for situations where medical marijuana is being used because of an individual disability, but fitness-for-duty assessments should still be conducted to make sure the employees can perform their duties effectively, and accommodations should not cause undue hardship for employers.[34] There may be liability if an employee who is known by the employer to be using marijuana is involved in an accident.

14-5b Emotional/Mental Health

A variety of emotional/mental health issues arise at work that must be addressed by employers. Many individuals are facing work, family, and personal life pressures. Although most people manage these pressures successfully, some individuals have difficulty handling the demands. Specific events, such as death of a spouse, divorce, or medical problems, can affect individuals who otherwise have been coping successfully with life pressures. Depression is another common emotional/mental health concern. The effects of depression are seen at all organizational levels, from warehouses and accounting offices to executive suites.

Beyond trying to communicate with the employees and relieving some workload pressures, it is generally recommended that supervisors and managers contact the HR staff, who can intervene and then refer affected employees to outside resources through employee assistance programs. Employees who appear to be depressed can be guided to employee assistance programs, if one exists, and helped with obtaining medical treatment. It is also important to note that emotional/mental illnesses such as schizophrenia and depression are considered disabilities under the ADA.

14-5c Health and Older Employees

The graying of the workforce has been mentioned previously, but there are implications for health and safety. All signs point to an abundance of older workers, and many work beyond age 65. There is a diminishing pool of successful younger workers to replace them. Data show that older workers have fewer injuries, but are out of work longer when they do, and these injuries cost more to fix. Musculoskeletal disorders, when they occur, are more severe. Key practices for dealing with older workers include:[35]

- Preventing slips and falls
- Eliminating repetitive stress and heavy lifting
- Using ergonomically sound workspaces
- Emphasizing driver safety/retraining
- Providing means for healthy gradual transitions back to work after injury

14-5d Smoking at Work

In response to health studies, complaints by nonsmokers, and resulting state laws, many employers have instituted no-smoking policies throughout their workplaces. Other organizations such as Alaska Airlines, Turner Broadcasting, and Union Pacific have had such policies in place for many years. The rationale for doing so is that organizations want to improve job performance, reduce health-related expenses, and promote healthier lifestyles. Despite such interest, some states have created laws that protect individuals from discrimination if they do smoke, with some exemptions granted to health-based firms and nonprofit organizations. Companies may opt to develop initiatives that encourage workers to quit or cut back on smoking.[36] Some employers offer smoking cessation workshops as part of health promotion efforts.[37]

14-5e Health Promotion

Employers concerned about maintaining a healthy workforce try to move beyond simply providing healthy working conditions and begin promoting employee health and wellness in other ways. **Health promotion** is a supportive approach of facilitating and encouraging healthy actions and lifestyles among employees. Health promotion efforts can range from providing information and increasing employee awareness of health issues to creating an organizational culture supportive of employee health enhancements, as Figure 14-10 indicates. Going beyond simple compliance with workplace safety and health regulations, organizations engage in health promotion by encouraging employees to make physiological, mental, and social choices that improve their health.

The first level of health promotion (information and awareness) leaves much to individual initiatives for following through and making changes in actions and behaviors. Employers provide information on topics such as weight control, stress management, nutrition, exercise, and smoking cessation. Even though such efforts may be beneficial for some employees, employers that wish to impact employees' health must offer second-level efforts, such as more comprehensive programs and actions that focus on the lifestyle/wellness of employees. The third level requires a commitment to wellness that is seldom seen in employers.

Obesity Nearly one-third of U.S. adults are obese and another one-third are overweight. Obesity is a fact of modern life and a concern to employers, and a movement to involve employers in employee weight management is apparently gaining momentum. The reason employers are concerned is cost. The economic costs of obesity include doctor visits, diabetes, high blood pressure, higher health care premiums, and lost workdays. Companies can take steps to address the increasing problem of obese employees. Some firms are offering incentives to workers who are involved in physical fitness programs and lose weight. In one firm with an active program focusing on obese employees, more than 2,000 employees lost over 61,000 pounds as part of the program.

Wellness Programs Employers' desires to improve productivity, decrease absenteeism, and control health care costs have come together in the wellness movement.[38] **Wellness programs** are designed to maintain or improve employee health before problems arise. They encourage self-directed lifestyle changes, including reduced cholesterol and heart

Health promotion
Supportive approach of facilitating and encouraging healthy actions and lifestyles among employees.

Wellness programs
Programs designed to maintain or improve employee health before problems arise.

FIGURE 14-10 Health Promotion Levels

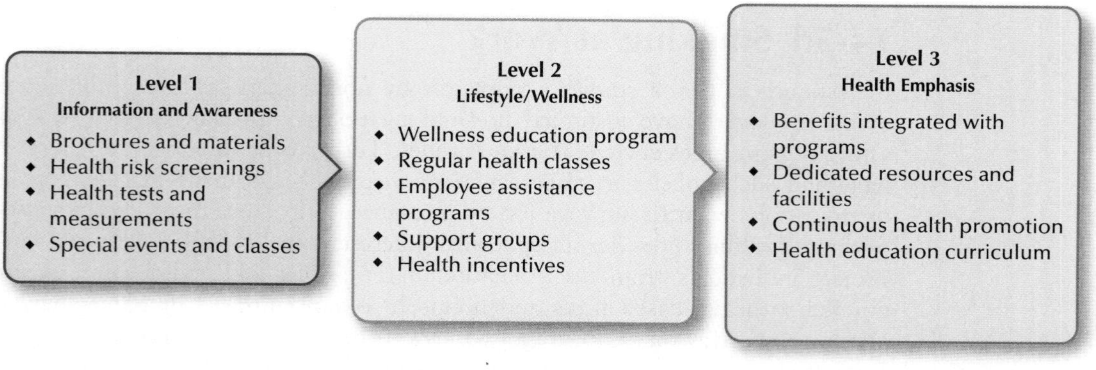

Level 1
Information and Awareness
- Brochures and materials
- Health risk screenings
- Health tests and measurements
- Special events and classes

Level 2
Lifestyle/Wellness
- Wellness education program
- Regular health classes
- Employee assistance programs
- Support groups
- Health incentives

Level 3
Health Emphasis
- Benefits integrated with programs
- Dedicated resources and facilities
- Continuous health promotion
- Health education curriculum

© Cengage Learning 2014

disease risks and individualized exercise programs and follow-up. Employer-sponsored support groups have been established for individuals dealing with health issues such as weight loss, nutrition, and breaking unhealthy habits. The top-rated topics for wellness programs are stress management, exercise/fitness, screenings/checkups, health insurance education, disease management (heart disease, diabetes, etc.), nutrition and diet, and smoking cessation.[39]

The management of employee health may involve offering incentives to individuals who participate in wellness programs and meet or exceed various health targets and metrics. A recent study of over 500 large firms showed that over half offered such incentives to encourage greater interest in wellness and to combat the often low rates of participation. Offering individuals ongoing incentives seems to be the key to sustaining these programs in the long term.[40] Another key is offering different kinds of incentives that keep diverse groups of people motivated to work toward wellness goals, as well as having champion employees, or evangelists, in the company who promote wellness programs.[41] However, participation in rewards-based wellness programs needs to be voluntary to comply with the American with Disabilities Act and the Genetic Information Nondiscrimination Act.[42]

Online and Web-based wellness programs have grown in popularity. Ford, Microsoft, Chevron, and Watson Wyatt are just a few of the companies that offer online wellness programs. These programs use information and subtle psychology to motivate people to live healthier lifestyles. They typically focus on exercise, nutrition, sleep, stress, and life balance.

Employee assistance program (EAP)
Program that provides counseling and other help to employees having emotional, physical, or other personal problems.

Employee Assistance Programs As mentioned, organizations can respond to specific and difficult health issues with an **employee assistance program (EAP)**, which provides counseling and other help to employees having emotional, physical, or other personal problems. In such a program, an employer typically contracts with a counseling agency for the service. Employees who have problems may then contact the agency, either voluntarily or by employer referral, for assistance with a broad range of problems. Counseling costs are paid for by the employer, either in total or up to a preestablished limit.[43]

EAPs ideally help improve employee performance (lower absenteeism/turnover and higher involvement), reduce expenses associated with benefits (decreased claims and workers' comp costs), and enhance organizational well-being (better wellness, lower risk/security problems, drug testing follow-up).[44] These programs often provide help for troubled employees, problem identification, short-term intervention, and referral for more complex services. The most common employee issues dealt with by EAPs are (1) depression and anxiety, (2) marital and relationship problems, (3) legal difficulties, and (4) family and children concerns. Other areas commonly addressed as part of an EAP include substance abuse, financial counseling, and career advice. EAP participation rates by employees are only 5% to 7%. This figure indicates that many individuals are not using this health benefit as often as would be expected.[45] Companies can encourage employees to use these resources when needed and protect individual confidentiality so that they feel safe in using the EAP.

LO6 Explain workplace violence as a security issue and name some components of an effective security program.

14-6 ■ SECURITY CONCERNS AT WORK

Traditionally, when employers have addressed worker risk management, they have been concerned about reducing workplace accidents, improving safety practices, and reducing health hazards at work. However, providing security for employees has become important. Notice that virtually all of the areas considered in the following discussion have significant HR implications. Heading the list of security concerns is workplace violence.

14-6a Workplace Violence

Workplace violence is violent acts directed at someone at work or on duty. For example, physical assault, threats, harassment, intimidation, and bullying all qualify as violent behaviors at work. Workplace violence can be instigated by several individuals:

- *Criminal*: a crime is committed in conjunction with the violence by a person with no legitimate relationship with the business (e.g., robbery, arson, trespassing).
- *Customer*: a person with a legitimate relationship with the business becomes violent (e.g., patients, students, inmates, customers).

HR SKILLS AND APPLICATIONS

Defining Workplace Violence

Even though workplace violence usually involves inappropriate conduct of a physical kind, guidelines issues by the U.S. Occupational Safety Commission indicate that such violence can also include verbal assaults of others in the workplace. Such guidance complicates the management of this issue because actions such as excessive use of profanity and abusive language could be considered by some to be violent acts, as well as clear violations of the general duty clause specified by OSHA. For instance, if two employees had a serious argument on the job, and one individual called the other a name in an aggressive manner, then the victim could claim that they were subjected to violent conduct. Consequently, workplace violence can be a troubling for HR professionals since many acts, both verbal and nonverbal, might be broadly interpreted to fall under the definition of violence in the workplace.

However, the standards offered by the Occupational Safety and Health Act specify that, while verbal abuse can be considered workplace violence in some instances, claiming that the general duty clause has been violated when such actions occur is incorrect because circumstances resulting in considerable physical harm or death are not present. In other words, the general duty clause does not cover situations involving mental or emotional harm. Yet, HR managers may still elect to do something about these situations even though physical violence is not the issue.

The following best practices can help HR professionals handle such a complaint, particularly if OSHA has been notified and sends an inspector to investigate:

- Discuss the issue with an attorney well-versed in OSHA compliance and regulation and get advice.
- Rely on a well-written policy of workplace violence and understand the proper interpretation of the general duty clause.
- Convey that the issue is considered serious, but that the situation is not considered workplace violence.
- Show how misconduct is being handled internally and offer to get back to OSHA with the resulting consequences of the situation.[46]

- *Coworker*: a current or past employee attacks or threatens another employee (e.g., contractor, temp).
- *Domestic*: a person who has no legitimate relationship with a business but has a personal relationship with the victim commits some form of violence against an employee (e.g., family member, boyfriend).

The inherent complexities of workplace violence are covered in the HR Skills and Applications: Defining Workplace Violence.

Workplace Violence Warning Signs There is reason to believe that some people might downplay the risks associated with violent colleagues.[47] However, there are warning signs and characteristics of potentially violent persons at work that should be recognized by employees. Individuals who have committed the most violent acts have had the profile depicted in Figure 14-11. Someone with some of these signs and characteristics may cope for years until a trauma pushes that person over the edge. A profound humiliation or rejection, the end of a marriage, the loss of a lawsuit, termination from a job, or other sources of stress may make a difficult employee turn violent.[48]

Workplace Incivility
Rude behavior that offends other employees.

Workplace Incivility and Bullying Workplace incivility occurs when rude behavior by ill-mannered coworkers or bosses makes the targets of incivility feel annoyed, frustrated, or offended. Most employees do not find incivility serious enough for formal action.[49] But incivility can escalate into bullying, which is more likely to require action.[50]

Bullying is behavior that the victim perceives as oppressive, humiliating, threatening, or infringing on the target's human rights that occurs over an extended period of time. Bullying, especially by supervisors, can result in damage to the employee and to the organization, leading to increased turnover.[51] Research exploring a random sample of 45 bullying cases that were heard in U.S. courts found that almost 20% of situations contained violence were often precipitated by a manager, and that public organizations experienced a majority of the problems. Just over one-third of organizations had crafted an anti-bullying policy.[52] This finding suggests a need for management attention to the problem through training, policies, and codes of conduct.[53]

FIGURE 14-11 Profile of Potentially Violent Employees

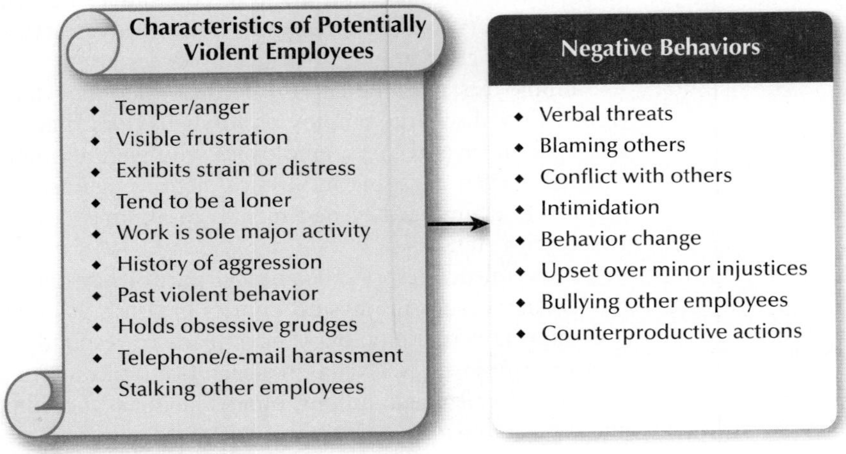

Domestic Causes of Workplace Violence Too often violence that begins at home with family or friends can spill over into the workplace. Many abused women report being harassed frequently at work, by telephone or in person, by abusing partners. Such behavior can disrupt the workplace and create a negative work environment for all parties involved.

Domestic violence can harm work attitudes, and even worse, put the well-being of employees in jeopardy. One survey determined that 21% of workers claimed that they had suffered from domestic abuse, and well over half indicated that this violence adversely impacted them on the job. Another study found that approximately 10% of surveyed employees claimed that they were currently dealing with domestic violence, with 19% of those claiming that the abuse was taking place on the job.[54] The fact that 70% of employers have not developed workplace violence policies, and of those that do, only 30% focus on domestic abuse at work, tends to make matters worse. Organizations need to be proactive about teaching supervisors about the dangers of such misconduct and get victims proper counseling and assistance.[55]

Domestic violence is particularly troubling if HR professionals find it difficult to take action because of concerns over personal privacy.[56] A reaction by employers is to sometimes ignore obvious signs of domestic violence. In fact, some employers have been sued and found liable for ignoring pleas for help from employees who later were victims of domestic violence in company parking lots or on employer premises.

Dealing with Workplace Violence The increase in workplace violence has led many employers to develop policies and practices for trying to prevent and respond to it. Policies can identify how workplace violence is to be dealt with in conjunction with disciplinary actions and referrals to EAPs. Training of managers and others is an important part of successful practice. Employees in some occupations such as nursing routinely receive training on dealing with violent behaviors.[57] There is reason to believe that workplace violence involves learned behaviors, which requires training that refocuses individuals' definitions of the misconduct instead of merely familiarizing them with the organization's anti-violence policies.[58] An appropriate organizational climate can also mitigate concerns about workplace bullying and other counterproductive behaviors.[59]

One application of these policies is a *violence response team*. Composed of security personnel, key managers, HR staff members, and selected employees, this team functions much like a safety committee, but with a different focus. Such a team conducts analyses, responds to and investigates employee threats, and may even help to calm angry, volatile employees.

Employers must be careful because they may face legal action for discrimination if they discharge employees for behaviors that often precede violent acts. For example, in several cases, employees who were terminated or suspended for making threats or even engaging in physical actions against their coworkers then sued their employers claiming they had mental disabilities covered under the Americans with Disabilities Act.

Post-violence response is another part of managing workplace violence. Whether the violence results in physical injuries or death or just intense interpersonal conflicts, it is important that employers have plans to respond afterward. Their response must reassure employees who may be fearful of returning to work or who experience anxiety and sleeplessness, among other reactions. Providing referrals to EAP resources, allowing employees time to meet with HR staff, and arranging for trained counselors on-site are all possible elements of post-violence response efforts.

14-6b Security Management

A comprehensive approach to security management is needed to address a wide range of issues, including workplace violence. HR managers may have responsibility for security programs or may work closely with security managers or consultants.

Security audit
Comprehensive review of organizational security.

Security Audit A **security audit** is a comprehensive review of organizational security. Sometimes called a *vulnerability analysis*, such an audit uses managers inside the organization (e.g., the HR manager and the facilities manager) and outsiders (e.g., security consultants, police officers, fire officials, and computer security experts) to assess security issues and risks.

Typically, a security audit begins with a survey of the area around the facility. Factors such as lighting in parking lots, traffic flow, location of emergency response services, crime in the surrounding neighborhood, and the layout of the buildings and grounds are evaluated. The audit may also include a review of the security available within the firm, including the capabilities of guards. Another part of the security audit reviews disaster plans, which address how to deal with events such as earthquakes, floods, tornadoes, hurricanes, and fires.

Controlled Access A key part of security involves controlling access to the physical facilities of the organization. Many workplace homicides occur during robberies. Therefore, employees who are most vulnerable, such as taxi drivers and convenience store clerks, can be provided bulletproof partitions and restricted access areas.

Many organizations limit access to facilities and work areas by using electronic access or keycard systems. Although not foolproof, these systems can make it more difficult for an unauthorized person, such as an estranged spouse or a disgruntled former employee, to enter the premises. Access controls can also be used in elevators and stairwells to prevent unauthorized people from entering designated areas within a facility.

Controlling computer access may be an important part of securing IT resources. Coordination with information technology resources to change passwords, access codes, and otherwise protect company information may also be important. The inappropriate use of information resources is a common problem in companies today. A recent study determined that making employees aware of security measures, providing instruction that heightens understanding of security, and monitoring the use of computers could reduce improper use of information systems through tougher and more certain perceived punishments.[60]

Violence Training Managers, HR staff members, supervisors, and employees should be trained on how to recognize the signs of a potentially violent employee and what to do when violence occurs.[61] During training at many firms, participants learn the typical profile of potentially violent employees and are trained to notify the HR department and to refer employees to outside counseling professionals. Such training requires observers to notice verbal and nonverbal reactions by individuals that may indicate anger or hostility, and to listen to individuals exhibiting such reactions.

Specific suggestions addressed in training for dealing with potentially violent employees typically include the following:

- Ask questions requiring explanations and longer answers that allow individuals to vent.
- Respond calmly and nonthreateningly to individuals' emotions, acknowledge concerns, and demonstrate understanding about how the individuals feel.

- Get assistance from others, perhaps a manager not directly affected by the situation being discussed.
- Indicate the need for time to respond to the concerns voiced, and then set up another time for follow-up.
- Notify security personnel and HR staff members whenever employees' behaviors change dramatically or when job disciplinary action may provoke significant reactions by employees.

14-6c Employee Screening and Selection

A key facet of providing security is screening job applicants. HR management is somewhat limited by legal constraints on what can be done, particularly regarding the use of psychological tests and checking of references. However, firms that do not screen employees adequately may be subject to liability if an employee commits crimes later. For instance, an individual with a criminal record for assault was hired by a firm to maintain sound equipment in clients' homes. The employee used a pass-key to enter a home and assaulted the owner; consequently, the employer was held responsible for not doing an adequate background check. Of course, when selecting employees, employers must be careful to use only valid, job-related screening means and to avoid violating federal EEO laws and the Americans with Disabilities Act.

14-6d Security Personnel

Providing adequately trained security personnel in sufficient numbers is a part of security management. Many employers contract with firms specializing in security. If security is handled in-house, security personnel must be selected and trained to handle a variety of workplace security problems, ranging from dealing with violent behavior by an employee to taking charge in natural disasters.

LO7 Describe the nature and importance of disaster preparation and recovery planning for HR.

14-7 ■ DISASTER PREPARATION AND RECOVERY PLANNING

During the past several years, many significant disasters have occurred. Some have been natural disasters, such as hurricanes, major snowstorms, flooding in various states, tornadoes, and wild fires. There has also been concern about terrorism, and some firms have been damaged by fires and explosions. According to a SHRM study, the 9/11 attacks encouraged many organizations to revisit and update the plans used to prepare employees for various disasters, and while not every kind of problem can be foreseen, just having such a plan can be very beneficial for building confidence.[62] All of these issues have led to an expanded role for HR staff in disaster planning.

To prepare for any instance in which organizations and their employees are impacted by such events, crisis management has become important. Learning how to effectively manage a crisis that a company faces can be described in three basic steps:[63]

- *Pre-crisis phase*: Managers should identify how crises can be avoided through proper preparation, risk assessment, and disaster prevention.
- *Crisis phase*: Craft a plan that enables the firm to adequately identify and respond to a crisis.

- *Post-crisis phase*: Identify how an organization can better respond to the crisis if it ever happens again.

GLOBAL

For a discussion about how disaster response plans can be developed and updated, see the HR Perspective: Response Plans Should Be Current and Viable. Such planning and preparation is particularly important when sending employees abroad for overseas assignments. Proper planning should be conducted before individuals leave their worksites. If possible, HR professionals should visit foreign locations and discuss security with employees, and the degree to which a security presence and personal weapons are needed for protection should be determined. Finally, a crisis management team should be developed, along with a clear set of responsibilities to enhance safety and employee well-being.[64]

HR PERSPECTIVE

Response Plans Should Be Current and Viable

The natural disasters that organizations face have led to increased interest in the development of disaster response plans. HR professionals should be intricately involved in the creation and implementation of such plans because they are often the key champions of employee safety. By ensuring that proper planning has been conducted, a company should be better prepared to handle issues of employee well-being and operational control when disasters occur. For instance, when the deadly tsunami and earthquake struck Japan, many U.S. organizations that had employees and families living in the country turned to the highly regarded EAP firm ACI Specialty Benefits to get help. The firm helped with the disaster response effort by offering referrals for emergency supplies and lodging.

The first step a company should take is conducting an audit of vulnerability to determine the risks associated with potential disasters. This requires businesses not only to identify the potential for large-scale disasters including earthquakes, tornadoes, tsunamis, but to also determine the likelihood of less serious setbacks such as utilities problems, fires, losses of power and electricity, IT crashes, and theft of property

and other resources. An organization should also try to determine how well it would handle a natural disaster using its current recovery plan (if it indeed has one).

If a company does not have a disaster plan, or its current plan needs to be revised, then managers need to craft an effective guide for handling organizational crises. Such a plan should be flexible enough to provide guidance in all types of disasters, and safety, evacuation, damage control, communication, equipment use, and contingency concerns should be covered in depth. HR professionals should also make sure that employees receive critical training on the standards articulated in the response plan.

One company that has successfully relied on sound response and recovery plan when dealing with natural disasters is Ruth's Chris Steak House. After Hurricane Katrina, Ruth's Chris Steak House was able to locate almost all of its employees by relying on individual texting. The firm also takes active steps to prepare its restaurants for organizational disasters such as trimming trees around food outlets to minimize wildfire danger, using disaster kits, and outlining security concerns.[65]

14-7a Disaster Planning

For effective disaster planning to occur, the three components shown in Figure 14-12 must be addressed. Imagine that a hurricane destroys the work facility where employees work, as well as many of the employees' homes. Or picture an explosion or terrorist attack that prohibits workers from getting to their workplaces. Such situations illustrate why each of the components in Figure 14-12 has human dimensions to be addressed.

Organizational Assessment Organizational assessment includes establishing a disaster planning team, often composed of representatives from HR, security, information technology, operations, and other areas. The purpose of this team is to conduct an organizational assessment of how various disasters might affect the organization and its employees. Then a disaster-recovery plan is developed to identify how the organization will respond to different situations.

Human Impact Planning Certain areas are part of human impact planning (the impact of events on people). Issues, such as having backup databases along with employee contact information, are key considerations of such planning. Who will take responsibility for various duties and how these efforts will be coordinated must also be identified.

Some organizations have done an effective job with such planning. For instance, following Hurricane Katrina, many employers could not reach employees, nor could employees contact their employers. However, firms such as Home Depot and Wal-Mart had databases outside of the Gulf Coast area. Employees could contact any other company location or a national hot line and learn about receiving paychecks, ask benefits questions, and even find out about continuing employment elsewhere. Home Depot allowed evacuees to become employees at any other U.S. location, and these stores had access to employment history and payroll data, making the worker transition easier. After losing power and Internet service because of Hurricane Sandy, ICS Software, Ltd., the New York-based provider of health administration programs, used cloud phone services offered by 8x8, Inc., so that employees could continue talking to customers from their residences.[66]

FIGURE 14-12 Disaster Planning Components

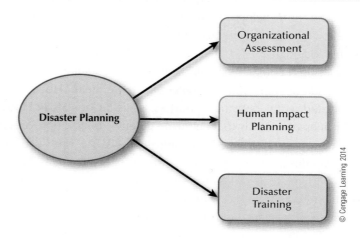

Disaster Training All of the planning efforts may be wasted if managers and employees are not trained on what to do when disasters occur. This training covers a wide range of topics, including the following:

- First aid/CPR
- Hazardous materials containment
- Disaster escape means
- Employer contact methods
- Organizational restoration efforts

But this training is not sufficient without conducting exercises or simulations for managers and employees to use the training.[67] Much like public schools have tornado evacuation exercises, employers may have site evacuation drills. Regular tests to ensure that information technology and databases are security accessible outside of the main location should occur. Testing responses for when an attack occurs may identify additional activities needed in an organization. Training must be a continuing consideration, and must reflect updated disaster planning efforts.[68]

14-7b Disaster Planning for Disease

A significant worldwide concern is the occurrence of different environmental risks. One issue during the past few years has been the spread of various kinds of viruses and flu throughout the world. The global nature of business travel has increased the likelihood of the spread of a deadly virus. Two key issues are whether to evacuate expatriate employees from locations where flu occurs and how to protect local employees if the flu symptoms occur within an area.[69]

The concerns about flu and other pandemic diseases have led OSHA to establish guidelines for employers to use. The guidelines have special sections for firms in the poultry production industry because of their higher vulnerability. Relatively few U.S. employers and other worldwide organizations are prepared for the spread of pandemic flu or any other critical environmental disease. Many of the recommendations for preparations are similar to other types of disaster planning, but specialized policies, programs, and training may be needed. Experts project that there could be a major epidemic disease spread, whether a natural one or one instigated by terrorism. Thus, risk management preparation for this specialized area is part of broader disaster preparation and recovery planning efforts.

SUMMARY

- The four components of risk management are workplace safety and health, employee health/wellness promotion, workplace and worker security, and disaster preparation and recover planning.
- Health is a general state of physical, mental, and emotional well-being. Safety is a condition in which the physical well-being of people is protected. Security is the protection of employees and organizational facilities.
- Global security is of growing importance, and emerging health services, terrorism, and kidnapping are key concerns.
- Workers' compensation coverage is provided by employers to protect employees who suffer job-related injuries and illnesses.
- Both the Family and Medical Leave Act (FMLA) and the Americans with Disabilities Act (ADA) affect employer health and safety policies and practices.

- The Fair Labor Standards Act (FLSA) limits the types of work that younger employees, especially those under the age of 18, can perform.
- The Occupational Safety and Health Act states that employers have a general duty to provide safe and healthy working conditions.
- The Occupational Safety and Health Administration (OSHA) has established enforcement standards to aid in many areas, including hazard communication.
- Ergonomics looks at the physical demands of work.
- OSHA addresses employee work assignments, requires employers to keep records on occupational illnesses and injuries, inspects workplaces, and can issue citations for several levels of violations.
- Effective safety management requires integrating three approaches: organizational, engineering, and individual.
- Developing safety policies, disciplining violators, keeping safety records, conducting safety training, communicating on safety issues, establishing safety committees, inspecting work areas for safety concerns, investigating accidents, and

- evaluating safety efforts are all part of comprehensive safety management.
- Substance abuse, emotional/mental health, workplace air quality, and smoking at work, as common health issues, are growing concerns for organizations and employees.
- Employee health is promoted by employers at several levels to improve organizational operations and individual employee productivity.
- Employers have responded to health problems by establishing and supporting wellness programs and employee assistance programs.
- Establishing and maintaining an organizational culture of health continues to pay off for many employers.
- Security of workplaces is important, particularly as the frequency of workplace violence increases.
- Employers can enhance security by conducting a security audit, controlling access to workplaces and computer systems, screening employees adequately during the selection process, and providing security personnel.
- Disaster preparation and recovery planning have grown as important HR concerns.

CRITICAL THINKING CHALLENGES

1. How does one go about controlling workers' compensation costs, and why is that important?

2. What should an employer do when facing an OSHA inspection?

3. As the HR manager of a distribution and warehouse firm with 600 employees, you plan to discuss a company wellness program at an executive staff meeting next week. The topics to cover include what a wellness program is, how it can benefit the company and employees, and the process for establishing it. To aid in developing your presentation to the executives, consult the website www.welcoa.org and other applicable websites you can locate.

4. What should be included in disaster planning for a big employer in New York City that is concerned about terrorism attacks that

might shut down the company and part of the city?

5. Employee layoffs, poor economic conditions, increased workplace violence, and increases in domestic restraining orders have caused management to develop a workplace violence action plan. There are many factors to consider, as your company has three locations and more than 500 employees. For information to assist you in identifying workplace violence categories and prevention strategies, visit the website at www.fbi.gov/publications/violence.pdf.

   A. Which workplace violence categories are of most concern to your company?

   B. What steps and provisions do you need to include in your workplace violence action plan?

CASE

Wellness Programs Help the Bottom Line

Employee wellness programs can be designed in a manner that brings about many positive individual and organizational benefits. In fact, a focus on well-being should be seen as a strategic advantage since employees who feel and think better can lead to an improved bottom line. The problem is that some firms see wellness as an additional employee benefit, rather than a tool for improving the workplace in the long run. Companies such as H-E-B and SAS Institute are changing how these programs are being viewed strategically by managers.

The United States government provides funding and tax breaks to organizations that develop wellness programs, and evidence suggests that healthier employees save firms money through reduced health-related costs. Indeed, research shows that a focus on a healthy work environment can significantly decrease workers' compensation premiums, lost work time, and other health care expenses. Other similar studies have determined that healthy employees tend to exhibit higher levels of retention in companies that show an interest in supporting positive lifestyles.

Based on responses from approximately 300 employees and top-level leaders representing 10 different companies in varied business sectors (Biltmore, Chevron, Comporium, Healthwise, H-E-B, Johnson & Johnson, Lowe's, MD Anderson Cancer Center, Nelnet, and SAS Institute), a recent investigation identified many factors that make wellness programs effective:

- Wellness programs must be supported by leaders from all different levels of the organization, including the CEO and other top officials. In addition, a good wellness program needs enthusiastic leaders who develop and coordinate wellness activities, as well as employees who build excitement for the program at the worksite level.

- Initiatives should be closely aligned to the company's sense of purpose and future business plans.
- Wellness programs need to build excitement among employees through comprehensive, quality activities.
- Initiatives should be provided to employees at little or no cost, and programs should be offered at the worksite so that individuals can easily access wellness benefits.
- Partnerships can be developed internally and externally with other key parties to make wellness programs more viable and desirable.
- Wellness programs need to be communicated with messages that fit the needs of the target participants. In addition, using a variety of communication methods can reach different audiences.

Companies tend to experience many positive benefits from their wellness initiatives. For example, both H-E-B and SAS Institute have determined that enhanced employee well-being leads to decreased overall costs. Companies also see higher job performance and esprit de corps among workers when wellness is championed in the workplace.[70]

QUESTIONS

1. What are some factors that you consider to be important predictors of successful wellness programs?

2. What types of activities should companies include in a wellness initiative to increase employee participation?

3. Which of the success factors for wellness programs identified in the case do you think is the most important? Which factor is the least important?

SUPPLEMENTAL CASES

Data Security

This case explores the different challenges associated with the management of data security. (For the case, go to www.cengage.com/management/mathis.)

What's Happened to Bob?

This case concerns warning signs of possible alcohol use and the consequences at work. (For the case, go to www.cengage.com/management/mathis.)

Communicating Safety and Health Success

This case provides information on the success of safety and health efforts in the workplace. (For the case, go to www.cengage.com/management/mathis.)

NOTES

1. Based on Lin Grensing-Pophal, "Getting Even," *Human Resource Executive Online*, July 1, 2009, www.hreonline.com.
2. Nassim N. Taleb, Daniel G. Goldstein, and Mark W. Spitznagel., "The Six Mistakes Executives Make in Risk Management," *Harvard Business Review*, October (2009), 78–81.
3. Ravin Jesuthasan, Angel Hoover, and Towers Watson, "Exploiting Workforce Risks to Transform You HR Function," *Workspan*, March 2012, 39–42.
4. Andrew Van Brimmer, "Risky Business," *HR Magazine*, March 2012, 50–51.
5. Andrew R. McIlvaine, "The HR/Risk Connection," *Human Resource Executive Online*, April 4, 2011, www.hreonline.com.
6. David Shadovitz, "Rethinking Risk," *Human Resource Executive*, January/February 2012, 22.
7. Lisbeth Claus, "International Assignees at Risk," *HR Magazine*, February 2010, 73–75.
8. Eric Krell, "Be a Global Risk Manager," *HR Magazine,* March 2012, 81–84; *Jay* Sternberg and Brett Guiley, "Business Travelers," *Workspan*, April 2012, 75–78.
9. "Workplace Injuries and Illnesses— 2011," New Release, Bureau of Labor Statistics, October 25, 2012, 1–3.
10. Ibid.
11. Roy Maurer, "GAO: Workplace Injuries, Illnesses Underreported," *HR*

Magazine, January 2010, 11; Dave Zielinski, "What's Safe? Employers Underreport Injuries and Illnesses," *HR Magazine*, February 2012, 12.
12. Tahira M. Probst and Armando X. Estrada, "Accident Under-Reporting among Employees: Testing the Moderating Influence of Psychological Safety Climate and Supervisor Enforcement of Safety Practices," *Accident Analysis & Prevention*, 42 (2010), Issue 5, 1438–1444.
13. Roy Maurer, "GAO: Workplace Injuries, Illnesses Underreported," *HR Magazine*, January 2010, 11; Dave Zielinski, "What's Safe? Employers Underreport Injuries and Illnesses," *HR Magazine*, February 2012, 12.
14. Rick Jervis, "Hispanic Worker Deaths Up 76%," *USA Today*, July 20, 2009, 1A.
15. Catherine Rampell, "Why 'Falling Back' Is Better than 'Springing Forward,'" *New York Times.com*, November 2, 2009, http://economix. blogs.NYTimes.com, 2.
16. Peter M. Smith and Cameron A. Mustard, "The Unequal Distribution of Occupational Health and Safety Risks among Immigrants to Canada Compared to Canadian-Born Labour Market Participants: 1993–2005," *Safety Science*, 48 (2010), Issue 10, 1296–1303.
17. Robert Fisher, "Legal Implications of Mental-Health Issues," *Human Resource Executive Online*, May 2, 2009, www.hreonline.com, 1–3.

18. Alice Andors, "Keeping Teen Workers Safe," *HR Magazine*, June 2010, 76–80.
19. Ibid.
20. Caitlin Gibbons, "Grain Firm Fined in Death," *Denver Post*, August 6, 2011, 1B, 4B.
21. Bill Leonard, "OSHA Issues Final Rule on Personal Protective Equipment," *HR News*, November 19, 2007, www.shrm.org, 1.
22. Amy Onder, "Donning and Doffing Protective Gear Was 'Work' Under FLSA," *HR Magazine*, September 2011, 113.
23. "OSHA Flags High Injury and Illness Rates," *HR Magazine*, June 2009, 24.
24. *Marshall v. Barlow's, Inc.*, 98 S. Ct. 1816 (1978).
25. Beatriz Fernandez-Muniz, Jose Manuel Montes-Peon, and Camilo Jose Vasquez-Ordas, "Relation Between Occupational Safety Management and Firm Performance," *Safety Science*, 47 (2009), 980–991.
26. Michael S. Christian, Jill C. Bradley, J Craig Wallace, and Michael J. Burke, "Workplace Safety: A Meta-Analysis of the Roles of Person and Situation Factors," *Journal of Applied Psychology*, 94 (2009), No. 5, 1103–1127.
27. Anne Mette Bjerkan, "Health, Environment, Safety Culture and Climate—Analyzing the Relationships to Occupational Accidents," *Journal of Risk Management*, 13 (2010), No. 4, 445–477.

28. Corrie Lykins, "Why Should Employers Just Say Yes to Drug Screening?" *Trendwatcher*, July 31, 2009, 1–3.

29. Robert J. Grossman, "What to Do About Substance Abuse," *HR Magazine*, November 2010, 33–38.

30. Richard Marcus, "Warning Signs," *Human Resource Executive Online*, May 2, 2009, 1–2, www.hreonline.com.

31. Bill Leonard, "Poll: Majority Favors Drug Testing Applicants," *HR Magazine*, November 2011, 87.

32. Rita Zeidner, "'Putting Drug Screening to the Test," *HR Magazine*, November 2010, 25–30.

33. Based on Dan Reynolds, "Screening with Meaning," *Human Resource Executive Online*, March 10, 2011, www.hreonline.com.

34. Diane Cadrain, "The Marijuana Exception," *HR Magazine*, November 2010, 40–42.

35. Roy Maurer, "The Future of Work: Safety and Health Issues of an Aging Workforce," July 9, 2009, www.shrm.org, 1–2.

36. Joanne Deschenaux, "Is a 'Smoker-Free' Workplace Right for You," *HR Magazine*, July 2011, 43–45; Wendy Koch, "Workplaces Expand Smoking Bans," *USA Today*, January 6, 2012, 3A; A.G. Sulzberger, "Cigarette Habit Could Burn Chances at a Job," *The Denver Post*, February 13, 2011, Business, 4K.

37. Michael O'Brien, "Different Smokes for Different Folks," *Human Resource Executive Online*, October 26, 2009, www.hreonline.com, 1–2.

38. Robert Langreth, "Use Bribes to Stay Healthy," *Forbes Magazine*, August 24, 2009, 37–39.

39. Dorette Nysewander, "The Business of Wellness," *American Fitness*, 27 (2009) 22–28.

40. Tom Abshire, "An Incentives-Based Approach to Employee Health," *Workspan*, April 2011, 64–68.

41. Jennifer Turgiss, "Corporate Wellness Programs Reinvented," *Workspan*, August 2009, 45–49.

42. Michael Booth, "Workers' Wellness Can Turn a Profit," *The Denver Post*, December 25, 2011, 1A, 18A; Frank Ferreri, "Voluntariness Required for Wellness Programs,"

Human Resource Executive Online, September 13, 2011, www.hreonline.com.

43. Greg Hudson, "Oil and Alcohol: Too Potent a Mix," *Canadian Business*, October 13, 2009, 24.

44. Mark Attridge et al., "The Business Value of EAP: A Conceptual Model," *EASNA Research Notes*, 1 (2010), Number 10, 1–5.

45. Dave Sharar and Richard Lennox, "A New Measure of EAP Success," September 24, 2009, www.shrm.org.

46. Based on Arthur G. Sapper, "Sticks and Stones," *HR Magazine*, September 2011, 115–118.

47. Frank S. Perri and Richard G. Brody, "The Sallie Rohrbach Story: Lessons or Auditors and Fraud Examiners," *Journal of Financial Crime*, 18 (2011), Issue 1, 93–104.

48. Pamela Babcock, "Workplace Stress? Deal with It!" *HR Magazine*, May 2009, 67–70.

49. Lilia Cortina and Vicki Magley, "Patterns and Profiles of Responses to Incivility in the Workplace," *Journal of Occupational Health Psychology*, 14 (2009), 272–288.

50. Brad Estes and Jia Eang, "Integrative Literature Review: Workplace Incivility," *Human Resource Development Review*, 7 (2008) 218–240.

51. Vincent Roscigno, et al., "Supervisory Bullying, Status Inequities, and Organizational Context," *Social Forces*, 87, (2009) 1561–1589.

52. William Martin and Helen LaVan, "Workplace Bullying: A Review of Litigated Cases," *Employee Responsibilities and Rights Journal*, 22 (2010) 175–194.

53. Jack Howard, "Employee Awareness of Workplace Violence Policies," *Employee Responsibility and Rights Journal*, 21, 2009, 7–19.

54. Dori Meinert, "Out of the Shadows," *HR Magazine*, October 2011, 50–55.

55. Ibid.

56. Ibid.

57. Kari Aquino and Stefan Thau, "Workplace Victimization: Aggression from the Target's Perspective," *Annual Review of Psychology*, 60 (2009) 717–741.

58. Brian Altman, "Workplace Bullying: Application of Novak's (1998)

Learning Theory and Implications for Training," *Employee Responsibilities and Rights Journal*, 22 (2010) 21–32.

59. Gabriele Giorgi, "Workplace Bullying Risk Assessment in 12 Italian Organizations," *International Journal of Workplace Health Management*, 2 (2009), Issue 1, 34–47.

60. John D'Arcy, Anat Hovav, and Dennis Galletta, "User Awareness of Security Countermeasures and Its Impact on Information Systems Misuse: A Deterrence Approach," *Information Systems Research*, 20 (2009), Issue 1, 79–98.

61. Carol Hymowitz, "Bosses Have to Learn How to Confront Troubled Employees," *The Wall Street Journal*, April 23, 2007, B1.

62. Tamara Lytle, "Rising from the Rubble," *HR Magazine*, September 2011, 64–69.

63. Daniel Laufer, "Charting a Course Through Crisis," *BizEd*, September/October 2010, 46–50.

64. Aliah D. Wright, "Extreme HR," *HR Magazine*, May 2011, 28–31.

65. Based on Ann D. Clark, "Being Prepared When Disaster Strikes," *Human Resource Executive Online*, May 23, 2011, www.hreonline.com.

66. "Businesses Affected by Hurricane Sandy Turn to 8x8 Cloud Communications Services to Enable Business Continuity," Yahoo! Finance, November 12, 2012, http://finance.yahoo.com.

67. Jason Moats, et al., "Using Scenarios to Develop Crisis Managers," *Advances in Developing Human Resources*, 38, (2008) 1–25.

68. Dian-Yan Liou and Chin-Huang Lin, "Human Resources Planning on Terrorism and Crises in the Asia Pacific Region," *Human Resource Management*, Spring 2008, 49–72.

69. Donald Benson and Katherine Dix, "Pandemic Preparations for the Workplace," *The Colorado Lawyer*, May 2009, 49–56.

70. Based on Leonard L. Berry, Ann M. Mirabito, and William B. Baun, "What's the Hard Return on Employee Wellness Programs," *Harvard Business Review*, December (2010), 104–112.

15

Employee Rights and Responsibilities

Learning Objectives

After you have read this chapter, you should be able to:

1 Define employment-at-will and discuss how wrongful discharge, just cause, and due process are interrelated.

2 Identify employee rights associated with access to employee records and free speech.

3 Discuss issues associated with workplace monitoring, employer investigations, and drug testing.

4 List elements to consider when developing an employee handbook.

5 Understand the use of employee discipline in companies and differentiate between the positive and progressive approaches to discipline.

6 Outline the issues and procedures related to employee termination.

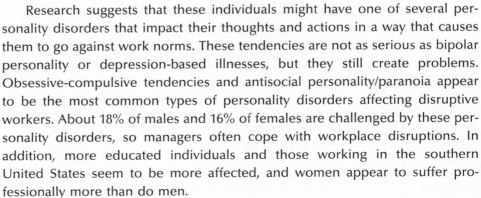

HR HEADLINE

Supervising Problem Workers with Personality Disorders

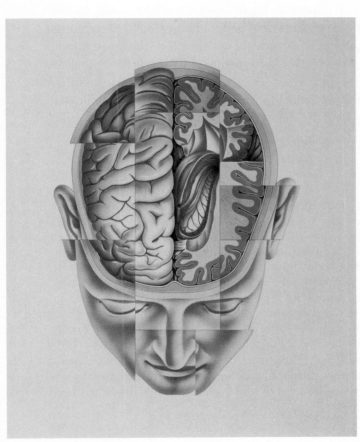

John Bavosi/Science Source/Photo Researchers Inc

A ll managers deal with problem employees during their careers. Leaders think they spend 80% of their time with 20% of their workers who cause significant work conflict. These individuals operate in counterproductive ways, such as relating poorly with managers, disagreeing with colleagues, being selfish, believing others are out to get them, being inflexible in the face of change, misinterpreting workplace communication, and using intimidation/threats. These inappropriate behaviors can make work unpleasant for others, so organizations might provide counseling assistance or redesign jobs to deal with disruptive employees. At the University of Pennsylvania Health System, a group was established to review such cases.

Research suggests that these individuals might have one of several personality disorders that impact their thoughts and actions in a way that causes them to go against work norms. These tendencies are not as serious as bipolar personality or depression-based illnesses, but they still create problems. Obsessive-compulsive tendencies and antisocial personality/paranoia appear to be the most common types of personality disorders affecting disruptive workers. About 18% of males and 16% of females are challenged by these personality disorders, so managers often cope with workplace disruptions. In addition, more educated individuals and those working in the southern United States seem to be more affected, and women appear to suffer professionally more than do men.

521

Managers should recognize that employees with personality disorders are protected by the Americans with Disabilities Act, and that with the proper treatment programs, the disorders can be effectively managed. Managers can sometimes make reasonable accommodations for individuals by changing the nature and requirements of their jobs, or use employee assistance programs if available to get them help. Expectations for appropriate workplace conduct should be upheld, and a company's legal counsel might need to be approached to determine the best courses of action. Penn Health System created a "professionalism committee" to provide assistance in these situations. According to Jody Foster, developer and leader of the Professionalism Program at Penn Medicine and chair of the psychiatry department at Philadelphia-based Pennsylvania Hospital, disruptive employees are evaluated on the basis of personality, and treatment is provided to help them better function in the workplace.[1]

This chapter explores many interrelated issues that affect the management of Human Resources: *employee rights*, *HR policies*, and *discipline*. Employees come to work with some rights, but their rights at work are further influenced by the HR policies and rules established by an employer. For instance, disciplinary policies establish standards about how managers should correctly deal with those who fail to follow organizational requirements. The variations in how these policies are managed illustrate how the concepts of rights, policies, and discipline evolve as laws, societal, and organizational values change. At one time, the right of an employer to operate an organization as it saw fit was very strong. However, leaders must now consider a multitude of laws and employee rights issues to manage human resources. HR professionals must help create a work environment that honors fairness, protects individual privacy, and provides a just situation that protects the well-being of employees, while at the same time allowing the business to succeed.

15-1 ■ EMPLOYER AND EMPLOYEE RIGHTS AND RESPONSIBILITIES

Rights
Powers, privileges, or interests derived from law, nature, or tradition.

Statutory rights
Rights based on laws or statutes passed by federal, state, or local governments.

Rights generally do not exist in the abstract. Instead, **rights** are powers, privileges, or interests derived from law, nature, or tradition. Of course, defining a right presents considerable potential for disagreement. For example, does an employee have a right to privacy of communication in personal matters when using the employer's computer on company time? Moreover, *legal rights* may or may not correspond to certain *moral rights*, which opens "rights" up to controversy and lawsuits.

Statutory rights are the result of specific laws or statutes passed by federal, state, or local governments. Various laws have granted employees certain rights at work, such as equal employment opportunity, collective bargaining, and workplace safety. These laws and their interpretations have also been the subjects of a considerable number of court cases because employers also have rights.

Responsibilities
Obligations to perform certain tasks and duties.

Rights are offset by **responsibilities**, which are obligations to perform certain tasks and duties. Employment is a reciprocal relationship in that both the employer and the employee have rights and obligations. For example, if an employee has the right to a safe working environment, then the employer must have an obligation to provide a safe workplace. If the employer has a right to expect uninterrupted, high-quality work from the employee, then the worker has the responsibility to be on the job and to meet job performance standards. The reciprocal nature of rights and responsibilities suggests that both parties in an employment relationship should ideally regard the other as having rights and should treat the others' rights with respect.

15-1a Contractual Rights

When individuals become employees, they encounter both employment rights and responsibilities. Those items can be spelled out formally in written employment contracts or more likely in employer handbooks and policies disseminated to employees. Contracts formalize the employment relationship. For instance, when hiring an independent contractor or a consultant, an employer should use a contract to spell out the work to be performed, expected timelines, parameters, and costs and fees to be incurred.

Contractual rights
Rights based on a specific contract between an employer and an employee.

An employee's **contractual rights** are based on a specific contract with an employer. For instance, a union and an employer may agree on a labor contract that specifies certain terms, conditions, and rights that employees who are represented by the union have with the employer. The contract also identifies employers' agreed-upon actions and restrictions.

Employment contract
Formal agreement that outlines the details of employment.

Employment Contracts Traditionally, employment contracts have been used for executives and senior managers, but the use of employment contracts is filtering down in the organization to include highly specialized professional and technical employees who have scarce skills. An **employment contract** is a formal agreement that outlines the details of employment. Depending on the organization and individuals involved, employment agreements often contain many provisions that detail the nature of the exchanges that are expected to occur between companies and employees. A study determined that less than 50% of CEOs working for S&P 500 companies actually had explicit employment contracts with their employers, and that the agreements were more long-term in nature. Findings also showed that explicit employment contracts were more likely to be used when the following conditions were present:

- The CEO was hired from outside the organization instead of being promoted from within the ranks.
- The company environment and employment situation was risky for the CEO because of uncertainty.
- The CEO received higher-than-normal compensation, and much of that was performance-based.[2]

An employment contract typically has the following sections. An *identification section* lists the parties to the contract and the general nature of the employee's job duties. The level of compensation and types of benefits are often addressed, including any special compensation, benefits, incentives, or perquisites to be provided by the employer. The employment contract may also note whether the employment

FIGURE 15-1 Provisions in Employment Contracts

Employment Contract

- Parties to the contract
- General job duties and expectations
- Compensation and benefits
- Terms and conditions of employment
- Termination/resignation factors
- Noncompete and nonpiracy agreements
- Nonsolicitation of current employees
- Intellectual property and trade secrets

Date:

Employee's signature:

Company representative's signature:

Seal

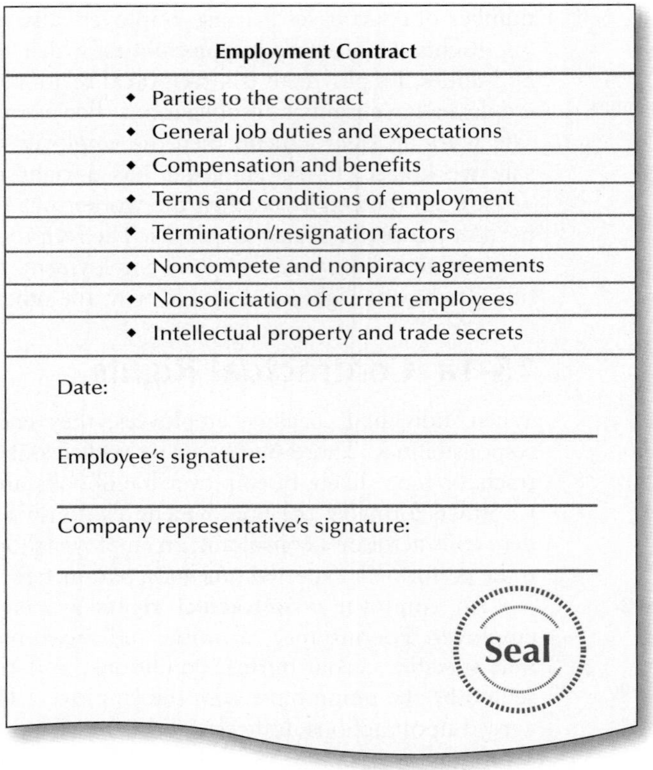

© Cengage Learning

relationship is to be in place for an indeterminate time, or whether it can be renewed automatically after a specified period. Finally, the contract may spell out a severance agreement, continuation of benefits, and other factors related to the employee's leaving the employer. Figure 15-1 shows some common provisions that are found in employment contracts.

Noncompete agreements

Agreements that prohibit individuals who leave an organization from working with an employer in the same line of business for a specified period of time.

Noncompete Agreements Employment contracts may include **noncompete agreements,** which prohibit individuals who leave an organization from working with an employer in the same line of business for a specified period of time. A noncompete agreement may be presented as a separate contract or as a clause in an employment contract. Though primarily used with newly hired employees, some firms have required existing employees to sign noncompete agreements. The use of such contracts can help companies. For instance, a study found that the use of noncompete agreements can enhance the stability of managers, reduce employee costs, and encourage greater expenditures on human capital.[3]

Court decisions have ruled both for and against employers that have fired employees for refusing to sign noncompete agreements or violating them. Consider a manager working for a national clothing retail store who was hired to do stock work at a local competitor's store, or a restaurant manager working for a Hyatt hotel who accepted a job at an Olive Garden location as a part-time assistant manager. Either can lead to legal actions if these individuals signed noncompete agreements. Google hired one of Microsoft's computer scientists Dr. Kai-Fu Lee to run its research and development site in China. Microsoft took Google to court, and a court order was passed to prevent Lee from overseeing certain activities based on a noncompete contract he had signed years previously.[4]

To create employment contracts with enforceable noncompete agreements, the criteria specified must take into consideration the well-being of both employees and employers.[5] Reasonable geographical and time limitations should be imposed, and the agreement should be confined to jobs of a similar type. Noncompete agreements are usually evaluated on the following specific criteria to determine whether or not they are acceptable:

- Shows reasonableness about the expectations of an employee not looking for work elsewhere.
- Typically covers a period of time from one to two years.
- Operates under an acceptable geographic scope and is not too far-reaching.
- Provides employees something extra beyond just having a job (i.e., more compensation or opportunities for promotion as a quid pro quo).
- Does not generally prevent employees from working in new areas of employment that are different from the current job.[6]

Such contracts may contain *nonpiracy agreements*, which bar former employees from soliciting business from former customers and clients for a specified period of time. Clauses requiring *nonsolicitation of current employees* can be incorporated into the employment agreement. These are written to prevent a former employee from contacting or encouraging coworkers at the former employer to join a different company, often a competitor.[7]

Intellectual Property An additional area often covered in employment contracts is protection of *intellectual property* and *trade secrets*. A 1996 federal law made the theft of trade secrets a federal crime punishable by fines up to $5 million and 15 years in jail. Employer rights in this area include the following:

- The right to keep trade secrets confidential
- The right to have employees bring business opportunities to the employer first before pursuing them elsewhere
- A common-law copyright for works and other documents prepared by employees for their employers

The primary objectives of outlining trade secrets in the employment contract are to have workers understand that they will be privy to sensitive information on the job, to limit employees' discussion of trade secrets and competitive actions, and to indicate that advances made by employees on the job fall under the management and control of the organization.[8]

15-1b Implied Contracts

The idea that a contract (even an implied or unwritten one) exists between individuals and their employers affects the employment relationship. The rights and responsibilities of the employee may be spelled out in a job description, an employment contract, HR policies, or a handbook, but often they are not. The rights and responsibilities of the employee may exist *only* as unwritten employer expectations about what is acceptable behavior or performance on the part of the employee. Some court decisions have held that if an employer hires someone for an indefinite period or promises job security, the employer has created an implied contract. Such promises establish employee expectations, especially if there has been a long-term business relationship.

When the employer fails to follow up on the implied promises, the employee may pursue remedies in court. Numerous federal and state court decisions have held that such implied promises, especially when contained in an employee handbook, constitute a contract between an employer and its employees, even without a signed contract document. Many employers acquire special insurance to cover the costs of responding to such legal actions.

15-2 ■ RIGHTS AFFECTING THE EMPLOYMENT RELATIONSHIP

As employees have increasingly regarded themselves as free agents in the workplace and as the power of unions has changed in the United States, the struggle between individual employee and employer "rights" has become heightened. Employers often do not fare well in court in employee rights cases. Not only is the employer liable in many cases, but also individual managers and supervisors have been found liable when hiring or promotion decisions have been based on discriminatory factors, or when they have had knowledge of such conduct and have not taken steps to stop it. Several concepts from law and psychology influence rights in the employment relationship: employment-at-will, wrongful or constructive discharge, just cause, due process, and distributive and procedural justice.

15-2a Employment-at-Will (EAW)

Employment-at-will (EAW)

A common-law doctrine stating that employers have the right to hire, fire, demote, or promote whomever they choose, unless there is a law or a contract to the contrary.

Employment-at-will (EAW) is a common-law doctrine stating that employers have the right to hire, fire, demote, or promote whomever they choose, unless there is a law or a contract to the contrary. Conversely, employees can quit whenever they want and go to another job. An employment-at-will statement in an employee handbook usually contains wording such as the following:

This handbook is not a contract, express or implied, guaranteeing employment for any specific duration. Although we hope that your employment relationship with us will be long term, either you or the Employer may terminate this relationship at any time, for any reason, with or without cause or notice.

National restrictions on EAW include prohibitions against the use of race, age, sex, national origin, religion, and disabilities as bases for termination. Restrictions on other areas vary from state to state. Nearly all states have enacted one or more statutes to limit an employer's right to discharge employees. Also, numerous states allow employees to file breach-of-contract lawsuits because of certain provisions in employee handbooks.[9]

EAW and the Courts The courts have recognized certain rationales for hearing EAW cases. The three key ones are as follows:

- *Public policy exception*: This exception to EAW holds that employees can sue if fired for a reason that violates public policy. For example, if an employee refused to commit perjury and was fired, the employee can sue the employer.

- *Implied contract exception*: This exception to EAW holds that employees should not be fired as long as they perform their jobs. Long service, promises of continued employment, and lack of criticism of job performance imply continuing employment.
- *Good-faith and fair-dealing exception*: This exception to EAW suggests that a covenant of good faith and fair dealing exists between employers and at-will employees. If an employer breaks this covenant by unreasonable behavior, the employee may seek legal recourse.

Over the past several decades many state courts have revisited and revised the employment-at-will contractual components. Some courts have placed limits on the doctrine, including situations when employers act harmfully toward workers.

Wrongful discharge
Termination of an individual's employment for reasons that are illegal or improper.

Wrongful Discharge Employers that run afoul of EAW restrictions may be guilty of **wrongful discharge**, which is the termination of an individual's employment for reasons that are illegal or improper. Employers can take several precautions to reduce wrongful-discharge liabilities. Having a well-written employee handbook, training managers, and maintaining adequate documentation are key. The HR Skills and Applications: Stopping Wrongful Discharge Claims provides further advice about how to reduce the likelihood of wrongful discharge claims.

A landmark court case in wrongful discharge was *Fortune v. National Cash Register Company*. The case involved the firing of a salesperson (Mr. Fortune) who had been with National Cash Register (NCR) for 25 years.[10] The employee's termination came shortly after he got a large customer order that would have earned him a big commission. Based on the evidence, the court concluded that he was wrongfully discharged because NCR dismissed him to avoid paying the commission, thus violating the covenant of good faith and fair dealing. Given the increase in wrongful-discharge lawsuits based on different interpretations of the law, companies are much more concerned today about the potential for litigation. Organizations need an appropriate defense against wrongful-discharge lawsuits, some of which are highlighted in Figure 15-2.

Constructive discharge
Process of deliberately making conditions intolerable to get an employee to quit.

Constructive Discharge Closely related to wrongful discharge is **constructive discharge**, which is deliberately making conditions intolerable to get an employee to quit. Under normal circumstances, an employee who resigns rather than being dismissed cannot later collect damages for violation of legal rights. An exception to this rule occurs when the courts find that the working conditions were made so intolerable as to *force* a reasonable employee to resign. Then, the resignation is considered a discharge.[11] Dangerous duties, insulting comments, and failure to provide reasonable work are examples of actions that can lead to a claim of constructive discharge.

15-2b Just Cause

Just cause
Reasonable justification for taking employment-related action.

Just cause is reasonable justification for taking employment-related action. The need for a "good reason" for disciplinary actions such as dismissal usually can be found in union contracts, but not in at-will situations. Even though definitions of *just*

HR SKILLS AND APPLICATIONS

Stopping Wrongful Discharge Claims

The EAW doctrine has long been recognized as a key component of the employment relationships that exist between employers and employees. This working relationship operates under the assumption that individuals and their firms can simply "go their separate ways" at any time they wish, with or without reason. There are cases when exceptions to EAW can be invoked, such as when employment contracts are broken, employees act in good faith while performing work, companies abuse their power, or societal expectations are violated. In addition, EEO legislation still covers employees based on protected characteristics such as gender, religion, and disability. Despite these protections, EAW provides many advantages to companies, and comparatively fewer benefits to workers, which is why EAW is often challenged in court. As a result, organizations must also support firing employees with "just cause" arguments.

The following steps can be implemented to help organizations better manage employee terminations to avoid claims of wrongful discharge:

STEP 1: GET READY

- Discuss EAW with employees through regular channels in the organization.

- Develop fair discipline policies and communicate these approaches to employees.
- Use performance evaluations to regularly discuss performance problems and opportunities.

STEP 2: GET SET

- Be sure to document all performance-related issues so that a paper trail is established.
- Treat employees fairly and be respectful in all interactions.
- Don't put termination decisions off just because they make people feel uncomfortable.

STEP 3: GO

- Make sure documentation has been adequately compiled and is organized in a way to give proper feedback.
- Follow established disciplinary policies when dealing with terminations.
- Value employee privacy by not discussing cases with other individuals.
- Explain reasons for decision without showing any regret, and allow time for an employee to make brief comments.
- Get help from security if needed, and require terminated employees to leave the worksite.[12]

---

cause vary, the overall concern is fairness. To be viewed by others as *just*, any disciplinary action must be based on facts in the individual case. Violations of these requirements can result in legal action. For instance, a court could easily rule that a high-performing worker was not fired for just cause if he had been terminated for poor performance after taking unpaid time off associated with the Family and Medical Leave Act to help a sick relative.

15-2c Due Process

Due process
Requirement that the employer use a fair process to determine employee wrongdoing and that the employee have an opportunity to explain and defend his or her actions.

Due process, like just cause, is about fairness. Due process is the requirement that the employer use a fair process to determine if there has been employee wrongdoing and that the employee has an opportunity to explain and defend his or her actions. Often times, this requires a company to properly investigate the reasons for personnel

FIGURE 15-2 Keys for Preparing a Defense against Wrongful Discharge

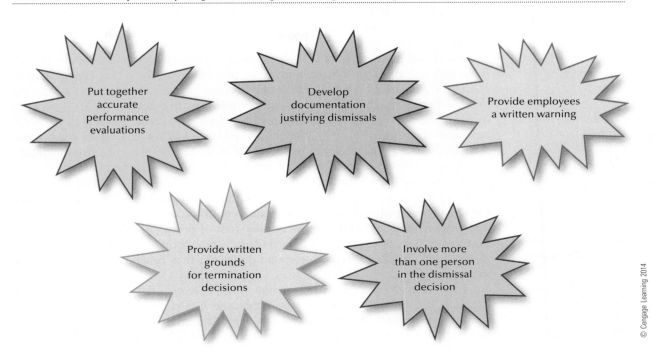

decisions, and to give individuals an opportunity to express their concerns to unbiased reviewers of the situations in question. Organizational justice is a key part of due process.

Figure 15-3 shows some factors to be considered when combining an evaluation of just cause and due process. How HR managers address these factors determines whether the courts perceive employers' actions as fair.

FIGURE 15-3 Criteria for Evaluating Just Cause and Due Process

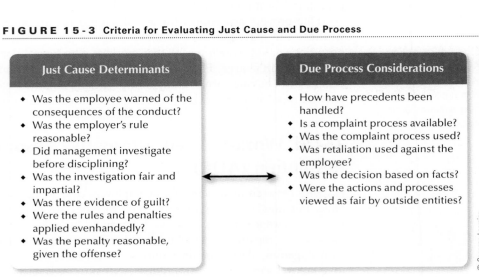

Just Cause Determinants

- Was the employee warned of the consequences of the conduct?
- Was the employer's rule reasonable?
- Did management investigate before disciplining?
- Was the investigation fair and impartial?
- Was there evidence of guilt?
- Were the rules and penalties applied evenhandedly?
- Was the penalty reasonable, given the offense?

Due Process Considerations

- How have precedents been handled?
- Is a complaint process available?
- Was the complaint process used?
- Was retaliation used against the employee?
- Was the decision based on facts?
- Were the actions and processes viewed as fair by outside entities?

Organizational Justice Most people want to feel that the organization treats employees justly. A wide range of HR activities can affect these perceptions of justice, including selection processes, job performance reviews and appraisals, and disciplinary actions.

Individual perceptions of fairness or justice in the workplace depend on at least three different types of assessments. First, people obviously prefer favorable outcomes for themselves. They decide the favorability of their outcomes by comparing them with the outcomes of others, given their relative situations. This decision involves the concept of **distributive justice**, which deals with the question "Were outcomes distributed fairly?" Disciplinary action based on favoritism when some are punished and others are not would likely be viewed as unfair. Fairness is dependent on employee perceptions, and is ultimately a subjective determination.

The second factor, procedural justice, focuses on whether the procedures that led to an action were appropriate, clearly understood, and provided an opportunity for employee input. **Procedural justice** deals with the question "Was the decision-making *process* fair?" Due process is a key part of procedural justice when making promotion, pay, discipline, and other HR decisions. If organizations provide procedural justice, employees tend to respond positively, thus benefiting the organization in return.

Interactional justice is based on the way a person interacts with others. For example, if a manager is perceived as rude and insults another person, their relationship may be affected negatively. But if a manager treats the other person with respect and shares information truthfully, then individuals are more likely to see justice in interactions with managers.

Due Process and Complaint Procedures Procedures to deal with complaints are provided by employers to resolve employee complaints or grievances. In most cases, the complaint procedures used to provide due process for unionized employees differ from those for nonunion employees. For unionized employees, due process usually refers to the right to use the formal grievance procedure specified in the union contract. Due process may involve following specific steps in the grievance process, imposing time limits, following arbitration procedures, and providing knowledge of disciplinary penalties. More discussion of the grievance process and procedures in unions can be found in Chapter 16.

Due process procedures for at-will employees are more varied than for union workers and may address a broader range of issues. Numerous employers use an **open-door policy**, which means that workers who have a complaint can talk directly to someone in charge. However, this policy can be mishandled, so nonunion firms benefit from having formal complaint procedures that are well-defined because they provide more systematic due process for employees than do open-door policies.

15-2d Work-Related Alternative Dispute Resolution (ADR)

Disputes between management and employees over work issues are normal and inevitable, but how the parties resolve their disputes are important. Open-door policies, formal grievance procedures, and lawsuits provide several resolution methods. However, companies are looking to alternative means of settlement. Dissatisfaction with expenses, delays in the court system when lawsuits are filed, and damages to employer–employee relationships have prompted growth in alternative dispute

Distributive justice
Perceived fairness in the distribution of outcomes.

Procedural justice
Perceived fairness of the processes used to make decisions about employees.

Interactional justice
Perceived fairness about how a person interacts with others.

Open-door policy
A policy in which anyone with a complaint can talk with a manager, an HR representative, or an executive.

resolution (ADR) methods such as arbitration, peer review panels, ombuds, and mediation.[13] However, these methods must be considered fair by employees if disputes are to be effectively handled. Research determined that appropriate communication of decisions, giving employees a chance to provide input, and the membership composition of the panel strongly influenced individual perceptions of overall fairness.[14]

Arbitration Disagreements between employers and employees can result in lawsuits and large legal bills for settlements. Most employees who believe they have experienced unfair treatment do not get legal counsel, but their discontent and complaints are likely to continue. Consequently, to settle disputes, employers can use arbitration in nonunion situations. The HR Perspective: Arbitration Used in Sexual Harassment Cases discusses how arbitration is used in organizations to handle situations involving sexual harassment.

Arbitration

Process that uses a neutral third party to make a decision.

Arbitration is a process that uses a neutral third party to make a binding decision, thereby eliminating the necessity of using the court system. Arbitration has been a common feature in union contracts. However, it must be set up carefully if employers want to use it in nonunion situations. Since employers often select the arbitrators, and because arbitrators may not be required to issue written decisions and opinions, some see the use of arbitration in employment-related situations as unfair.

HR PERSPECTIVE

Arbitration Used in Sexual Harassment Cases

Sexual harassment has been a recurring problem in organizations for many years, despite the many attempts to educate employees and develop policies that dissuade individuals from acting unprofessionally on the job. Firms have invested many millions of dollars in training and seminars to better inform workers about the different types of sexual harassment, and many companies and lawyers specialize in how to handle cases once they have occurred. Unfortunately, these efforts have only partially reduced the frequency of sexual harassment cases. Even though the number of incidents has gone from almost 16,000 in 1997 to slightly below 12,000 in 2010, some experts believe these figures don't paint an accurate picture of the current state of sexual harassment in companies.

There is reason to believe that the declining numbers are influenced by an increase in the use of arbitration to handle claims of sexual harassment. Many firms are now requiring job candidates to sign mandatory arbitration agreements to handle problems such as sexual harassment to secure employment. Unfortunately, cases handled through arbitration/mediation are not made public, making it difficult to develop an accurate case count because few are even aware of the allegations. Arbitration usually speeds up the hearing process and results in a much quicker resolution for all individuals involved.

A recent SHRM survey indicated that almost 60% of companies offered sexual harassment training to staff, and over 80% of those required all workers to attend these sessions. The EEOC also offers training seminars for companies in an effort to mitigate concerns about inappropriate behavior. Such training will continue because serious cases of sexual harassment still occur, and evidence suggests that hostile work environment harassment (i.e., jokes, sexual comments, unprofessional communication) is quite common in the workplace.[15]

Some firms use *compulsory arbitration*, which requires employees to sign a pre-employment agreement stating that all disputes will be submitted to arbitration; employees waive their rights to pursue legal action until the completion of the arbitration process. Requiring arbitration as a condition of employment is legal, but employers must follow it rather than try to waive it in some cases. However, a legal check of compulsory arbitration as part of ADR should be done before adopting the practice. In addition, companies should ensure that arbitrators function in an equitable manner, arbitration decisions and awards are reflective of the law, and proper attempts should be made by organizations to communicate arbitration agreements to employees.[16]

Peer Review Panels   Some employers allow their employees to appeal disciplinary actions to an internal committee of employees. This panel reviews the actions and makes recommendations or decisions. Peer review panels use fellow employees and perhaps a few managers to resolve employment disputes. Panel members are specially trained volunteers who sign confidentiality agreements, after which the company assigns them to hear appeals.

These panels have several advantages including reduced lawsuits, provision of due process, decreased costs, and management and employee development. Also, peer review panels can compliment a formal complaint process for nonunion employees because solutions can be identified and made binding without court action. If an employee does file a lawsuit, the employer presents a stronger case when a group of the employee's peers previously reviewed the employer's decision and found it to be appropriate.

Ombuds

Individuals outside the normal chain of command who act as problem solvers for both management and employees.

Ombuds   Some organizations ensure process fairness through **ombuds**—employees outside the normal chain of command who act as independent problem solvers for both management and employees. At many large and medium-sized firms, ombuds have effectively addressed complaints about unfair treatment, employee/supervisor conflicts, and other workplace behavior issues. Ombuds address employees' complaints and operate with a high degree of confidentiality. Any follow-up to resolve problems is often handled informally, except when situations include unusual or significant illegal actions.

Mediation   Ombuds, as well as other individuals and groups who oversee dispute cases, will sometimes use *mediation* as a tool for developing appropriate and fair outcomes for all parties involved. Facilitative and directive forms of mediation rely on an approach that ultimately helps identify resolutions to the problems collectively explored. Transformative mediation is more exploratory in nature, with participants identifying their own problems, fixing damaged relationships, and developing realistic solutions. The focus of transformative mediation is to settle disputes and figure out how employees can more effectively interact with each other on the job.[17]

15-3 ■ MANAGING INDIVIDUAL EMPLOYEE AND EMPLOYER RIGHTS ISSUES

Employees who join organizations in the United States bring with them certain rights, including *freedom of speech*, *due process*, and *protection against unreasonable search and seizure*. Although the U.S. Constitution grants these and other rights to citizens, over the years, laws and court decisions have identified limits on them in the workplace. Globally, laws and policies vary, which means more issues for employers with expatriates and local workers in different countries. Balancing both employers' and employees' rights is a growing HR concern because of increased legal cases and expanding global workforces. Employers have legitimate rights and needs to ensure that employees are doing their jobs and working in a secure environment, while employees expect their rights, both at work and away from work, to be protected.

Right to privacy
An individual's freedom from unauthorized and unreasonable intrusion into personal affairs.

The **right to privacy** is defined in legal terms as an individual's freedom from unauthorized and unreasonable intrusion into personal affairs. Although the right to privacy is not specifically identified in the U.S. Constitution, past U.S. Supreme Court cases have established that such a right must be considered. Also, several states have enacted right-to-privacy statutes. A scope of privacy concerns exists in other countries as well.

The dramatic increase in Internet communications, blogging, twitters, social media, specialized computers, and telecommunications systems is changing the nature of privacy issues in many workplaces. The use of technology by employers to monitor employee actions also increases concerns that the privacy rights of employees are being threatened.

LO2 Identify employee rights associated with access to employee records and free speech.

15-3a Privacy Rights and Employee Records

As a result of concerns about protecting individual privacy rights in the United States, the Privacy Act of 1974 was passed. It includes provisions affecting HR recordkeeping systems. This law applies *only* to federal agencies and to organizations supplying services to the federal government. However, similar laws in some states, somewhat broader in scope, have also been passed. For the most part, state rather than federal law regulates private employers on this issue. In most states, public-sector employees are permitted greater access to their files than are private-sector employees.

Employee Medical Records Recordkeeping and retention practices have been affected by the following provision in the Americans with Disabilities Act (ADA):

> *Information from all medical examinations and inquiries must be kept apart from general personnel files as a separate confidential medical record available only under limited conditions specified in the ADA.*

As interpreted by attorneys and HR practitioners, this provision requires that all medical-related information be maintained separately from all other confidential files. The Health Insurance Portability and Accountability Act also contains regulations designed to protect the privacy of employee medical records. Both regular and confidential electronic files must be considered. As a result of all the legal restrictions, many employers have established several separate files on each employee, as illustrated in Figure 15-4.

Security of Employee Records It is important to establish access restrictions and security procedures for employee records. These restrictions and procedures are designed to protect the privacy of employees and protect employers from potential liability for improper disclosure of personal information. Individuals' social security numbers, personal addresses, and other contact information should be protected.

FIGURE 15-4 Employee Record Files

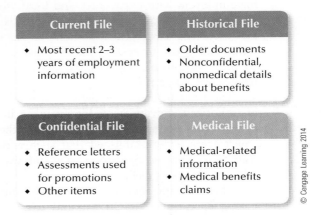

A legal regulation called the Data Protection Act requires employers to keep personnel records up-to-date and keep only the details that are needed.[18] The following guidelines are offered regarding employer access and storage of employee records:

- Restrict access to records to a limited number of individuals.
- Use confidential passwords for accessing employee records in various HR databases.
- Set up separate files and restricted databases for especially sensitive employee information.
- Inform employees about which types of data are retained.
- Purge employee records of outdated data.
- Release employee information only with employee consent.

Personnel files and records are usually maintained for three years. However, different types of records should be maintained for shorter or longer periods of time based on various legal and regulatory standards.

Electronic Records Another concern is how electronic records are maintained and secured, given the changes in software, e-mail, and other technology. Estimates are that more than 200 billion company e-mails are sent daily. Many of these e-mails may relate to records and worker actions. As a result, employers should establish an electronic records policy to ensure legal compliance and avoid violating individuals' personal rights.[19]

15-3b Employees' Free Speech Rights

The right of individuals to freedom of speech is protected by the U.S. Constitution. However, that freedom is *not* an unrestricted one in the workplace, so employees and companies need to be aware of appropriate boundaries. Three situations in which employees' freedom of speech might be restricted include expressing controversial views, whistle-blowing, and using the Internet and other communication-based technology.

Employee Advocacy of Controversial Views Questions of free speech arise over the right of employees to advocate controversial viewpoints at work. Numerous examples can be cited. For instance, can an employee of a tobacco company join in anti-smoking demonstrations outside of work? Can a disgruntled employee at a nonunion employer wear a union badge on a cap at work? Is it acceptable for workers to discuss their feelings about controversial social issues such as abortion or government-backed contraception programs in the workplace? In situations such as these, employers must follow due process procedures and demonstrate that disciplinary actions taken against employees can be justified by job-related reasons. In one U.S. case, a court decision ruled against a white worker who displayed Confederate flags on his toolbox, which offended some African-American employees. The court said that the worker's free speech right was not violated when the employer fired him for refusing to remove the flags.[20]

However, simply because an employer *might be able* to punish employees who make inappropriate statements that embarrass the company, should the employer do so? Perhaps not, because this sort of managerial action might be viewed as an overreaction by employees. It may cause other employees to quit their jobs, or to lose respect for the employer. The best way to handle these concerns is to (1) attempt informal resolution first, (2) clearly outline the boundaries and standards for appropriate behavior in a formalized policy that addresses work expectations, and (3) have a signed nondisclosure privacy agreement.

ETHICS

Whistle-blowers
Individuals who report real or perceived wrongs committed by their employers.

Whistle-Blowing and Employee Protection Individuals who report real or perceived wrongs committed by their employers are called **whistle-blowers**. Many well-known whistle-blowing incidents have occurred in past years. For instance, it was found that Bank of America Corp. violated the Sarbanes-Oxley Act when the company terminated an employee who blew the whistle on extensive fraud that had occurred at Countrywide Financial Corp., a firm that had merged with Bank of America.[21]

However, whistle-blowers are less likely to lose their jobs in public employment than in private employment because most civil service systems follow rules protecting whistle-blowers. A U.S. federal amendment said that for private employers to receive federal stimulus funding, they must have the same whistle-blowing regulations as the federal government.[22] However, no comprehensive whistle-blowing law fully protects the right to free speech of both public and private employees.

There are laws that protect whistle-blowers in the corporate setting such as the Sarbanes-Oxley Act and Dodd-Frank Wall Street Reform and Consumer Protection Act.[23] For instance, the Sarbanes-Oxley Act is intended to remedy company ethical breaches by requiring organizations to properly report financial figures, encouraging ethical business practices, and providing protection for whistle-blowers. But an antiretaliation provision covers *only* complaints made to certain entities, such as a manager/executive and federal regulatory or law enforcement agencies. The Dodd-Frank Act also protects whistle-blowers and provides financial incentives to individuals who report wrongdoing. In addition to paying fines, a company that is found guilty of retaliation is required to (1) give the individual back his or her job, (2) provide back pay or double back pay to make up for lost compensation, and (3) cover any costs associated with legal counsel.[24]

Employers need to address two key questions in regard to whistle-blowing: (1) When do employees have the right to speak out with protection from retribution? (2) When do employees violate the confidentiality of their jobs by speaking out? Even though the answers may be difficult to determine, retaliation against whistle-blowers is clearly not appropriate. Whistle-blowing is viewed as a lack of loyalty on the part of an employee, although that may or may not be a correct interpretation.[25] Whistle-blowers are often treated poorly by their employers because they are seen as a significant threat to the stability of the organization. This is why an ethical culture that includes reporting mechanisms that encourage employees to tell managers about problems and retaliation policies that prevent mistreatment of whistle-blowers are beneficial.[26] The culture of the organization often affects the degree to which employees report inappropriate or illegal actions internally or resort to using outside contacts.

15-3c Technology and Employer–Employee Issues

The extensive use of technology by employers and employees is constantly creating new issues to be addressed. For instance, ethical issues surrounding blogs and how they can lead to termination are highlighted in the HR Online: Ethical HR Issues on Blogs. However, terminating workers for openly complaining about an employer on social media has come under scrutiny based on recent court rulings. As a result of a lawsuit brought by the National Labor Relations Board, American Medical Response of Connecticut Inc., agreed to pay a settlement and modify its online communications policies for terminating an employee after she posted negative comments about her manager on Facebook. However, interpretation of the ruling

Ethical HR Issues on Blogs

Blogs provide an easy way for people to post opinions or views on any subject—including work, the boss, the company, company products, and people at work. Blogs may also be created by outsiders, and both positive and negative publicity can be submitted. Another major use of blogs for employers is providing information to employees about activities, policies, and practices within the organization. Thus, communication from HR and other departments, as well as from individual employees, can be delivered efficiently and effectively.

Misuse of blogs by employees may lead to disciplinary action and even termination. Because HR policies on blogs may not be established or current, ethical problems can occur in blogs that are personal and not job-related, as well as those that are work-related. For

example, an employee may communicate harmful information about friends, family members, and other employees. Blogs can even directly insult managers and coworkers. As such, blogs can violate employer policies and lead to the termination of employees.

Firing employees for innocuous, harmless blog actions can be seen as inappropriate and creates ethical concerns. However, terminating individuals for negative work-related comments might be viewed more favorably. Consequently, HR executives and professionals are advised to establish and communicate ethical requirements about blogging. Training of all managers and employees on HR requirements must be continuous, not just a one-time occurrence. If HR policies regarding blogs are clearly communicated, problems can be minimized.[27]

suggests that it does not condone excessive disloyalty or communication of highly sensitive content.[28]

Monitoring Electronic Communications The use of e-mail has become a major issue regarding employee and workplace privacy. Employers have good reason to monitor what is said and transmitted through their Internet and voicemail systems, despite employees' concerns about free speech. Organizations want to reduce employee misconduct, protect corporate resources, make sure that employees are working, and follow federal guidelines.[29] Many employers have specialized software that can retrieve deleted electronic communications and e-mail, and some even record each keystroke made on their computers.

There are many challenges that can be encountered when companies monitor e-mails and other electronic communications. For instance, one problem is that most people express themselves more casually in e-mail than they would in formal memos, a tendency that can lead to inappropriate communication. Another problem is that jokes are sometimes forwarded through e-mails that contain unprofessional content, and these electronic messages can be sent rapidly to multiple (and sometimes unintended) recipients. The use of monitoring, while perhaps needed, can harm esprit de corps and trust among employees.[30]

Employees have varying opinions about electronic monitoring based on different situational factors, which can present many challenges. For example, a recent study found that individuals were more accepting of electronic monitoring in companies than in universities.[31] Another study determined that increased e-mail monitoring resulted in privacy concerns among employees, which could harm relationships in the workplace.[32] Further, the standards and acceptance of monitoring vary greatly in different nations (i.e., France vs. the United Kingdom), so companies need to consider these factors and inform managers about what actions are considered appropriate.[33] Organizations need to consider such issues when developing policies regarding the monitoring of electronic communications.

HR Policies on Electronic Communications Given all the time and effort individuals spend on technology through both work and personal activities, it is important for HR professionals to provide guidance to executives, managers, and employees. Many employers have developed and disseminated electronic communications policies. Figure 15-5 depicts recommended employer actions for such policies including monitoring. These policies should describe to employees why monitoring is needed, the methods used, and the amount of monitoring planned. Employees should also sign off indicating that they understand their purpose and scope. Inappropriate communication and material should be clearly discussed, and individuals should receive guidance about the company's standards for using communication systems to send and receive private messages. With regard to the implementation of procedures, employers should monitor just enough to be prudent, and audits can be conducted to determine if policies are being enforced.[34]

Employers' efforts can also guard against employees' accessing pornographic or other websites that could create problems for the employer. If law enforcement investigations find evidence of such access, the employer could be accused of aiding and abetting illegal behavior. Many employers have purchased software that tracks the websites accessed by employees, and some employers use software programs to block certain websites that are inappropriate for business use.

FIGURE 15-5 Recommended Employer Actions regarding Electronic Communications

1. Develop an Electronic Communications Policy

↓

2. Communicate the Policy to Employees

↓

3. Obtain Signed Permission from Employees

↓

4. Monitor for Business Purposes Only

↓

5. Enforce the Policy through Disciplinary Procedures

© Cengage Learning

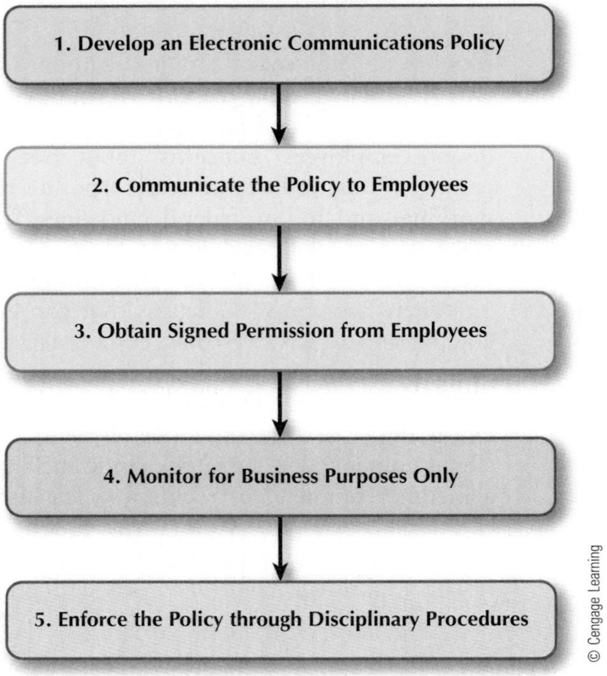

15-3d Employee Rights and Personal Behavior Issues

Another area employers should watch is employee personal behavior. Personal behavior on or off the job can be at issue. For example, if an employer investigates off-the-job charges of illegal behavior an invasion-of-privacy claim might result. Failure to do due diligence can jeopardize disciplinary actions that should be taken by employers, or can result in liability for negligent retention. Some of the more prevalent concerns in this area are discussed next.

Reviewing Unusual Behavior Employers may decide to review unusual behavior by employees both on and off the job. For instance, if an employee is suddenly wearing many new clothes and spending lavishly, inquiries as to the reasons why and the resources used might be warranted. Another issue is the presence of various counterproductive behaviors such as bullying, substance abuse, stealing, and sabotage that can potentially hurt companies and its employees. Some of these behaviors run counter to the law, some are used to reach a desired consequence (i.e., a promotion or high organizational performance), and still others prevent the completion of work.[35]

Organizations and HR must also deal with employees and/or managers being inappropriately angry, insulting, or extremely rude to customers, suppliers, and employees at different levels. Jokes or comments that are inconsiderate can create problems. To respond to such actions, managers and HR professionals should document inappropriate behaviors and meet privately with individuals to discuss concerns and give feedback. Identifying what are acceptable and unacceptable behaviors and communicating standards to all employees is also helpful. A recent court ruling even suggests that, in an effort to reduce volatile behavior, companies can require employees to pass a fitness-for-duty test before reporting for work, particularly in occupations that are considered dangerous.[36]

Dress and Body Appearance Limitations Employers have put limits on employees' dress and appearance in some situations, including items such as visible tattoos, certain clothing and accessories, and body piercings. Many managers have unwritten dress policies, but for legal reasons it is recommended that firms have written dress and appearance policies and codes.[37] The key is to give adequate notice to employees and managers, and to answer their concerns before a dress and appearance code is implemented.

One industry in which dress and appearance codes and policies are important is the food and beverage industry. For instance, a pizza firm prohibits visible tattoos and many kinds of body piercing. However, employers must be careful that the codes do not discriminate against women, racial and ethnic minorities, those with disabilities, or religious individuals. Appearance issues can be the subject of HR policies if they are job related.[38]

Off-Duty Behavior An additional employee rights issue concerns personal behavior off the job. Employers encounter special difficulty in establishing "just cause" for disciplining employees for their off-the-job behavior. Most people believe an organization should not control the lives of its employees off the job except in the case of clear job-related consequences. For example, can employees be disciplined for drinking or using tobacco or drugs on their own time away from work? Or, what should an employer do if an employee is an acknowledged transvestite, a member of an activist environmental group, a leader in a racist group, or an exotic dancer on weekends? In some of these cases, the answer should be "nothing"; in others, action might be taken. The HR Skills and Applications: Managing Employees off the Clock explores the issue of managing employees off the clock.

15-4 ■ BALANCING EMPLOYER SECURITY AND EMPLOYEE RIGHTS

Balancing employer and employee rights is difficult. On one side, employers have a legitimate need to ensure that employees are performing their jobs properly in a secure environment. On the other side, employees expect the rights that they have both at work and away from work to be protected. The monitoring of e-mail and voicemail is only one way employers watch the workplace. Technology gives employees who leave an employer the opportunity to take a great deal of valuable company secrets or data with them. For this reason (and others as well), workplace monitoring has increased.

15-4a Workplace Monitoring

LO3 Discuss issues associated with workplace monitoring, employer investigations, and drug testing.

In the United States, the right of protection from unreasonable search and seizure only protects an individual against activities of the government. Thus, employees of private-sector employers can be monitored, observed, and searched at work by

HR SKILLS AND APPLICATIONS

Managing Employees off the Clock

Companies expect employees to act in a professional manner while on the job, but managing their behaviors outside of work can be more problematic because of concerns over privacy. Certainly, individuals should be able to live their lives without fear of supervisors micromanaging their actions off the clock, but their personal conduct can sometimes run counter to what is considered acceptable by the organization. In some cases, companies have to take action to protect their reputations as employers. In one instance, a university professor was terminated for working part-time as an exotic dancer.

Employee misconduct off the job has the potential to seriously damage the reputation of a business, especially if individuals are wearing clothing and other identifying badges and logos that show the general public where they work. Organizations need to be particularly careful because embarrassing information can be easily disseminated to millions of interested parties over the Internet, radio, and television, as well as through print media. In some cases, managers must make sure that employees behave professionally when they are on their own free time.

There are several steps an employer can take to ensure that workers act appropriately:

- Companies should make hiring decisions based on an individual's ability to demonstrate good personal ethics and behavior. Integrity should be a key factor that is assessed during the recruitment and selection processes.
- Employee orientation should focus on the proper ethical values that encourage individuals to make ethical decisions. Such training should introduce workers to the behavioral expectations that are valued by the firm.
- Policies should be developed that set specific standards for on-the-job and off-the-job behaviors. A code of conduct can be created that summarizes important behavioral guidelines.
- Behavioral standards and norms should be reinforced with guidelines communicated in job-related training. Companies should communicate ethical standards on a consistent basis.
- Codes of conduct must be supported by positive managerial action and role modeling. Managers should take the proper steps to reinforce the standards that are outlined in ethics codes.[39]

representatives of the employer. Several court decisions have reaffirmed the principle that both private-sector and government employers may search desks, files, lockers, and computer files without search warrants if they believe that work rules have been violated. Also, the terrorist attacks of September 11, 2001, led to passage of the USA PATRIOT Act, which expanded legislation to allow government investigators to engage in broader monitoring of individuals, including workplaces, to protect national security.

Conducting Video Surveillance at Work Numerous employers have installed video surveillance systems in workplaces. Some employers use these systems to ensure employee security, such as in parking lots, garages, and dimly lit exterior areas. Other employers have installed them on retail sales floors and in production areas, parts and inventory rooms, and lobbies. When video surveillance is extended into employee restrooms, changing rooms, and other more private areas, employer rights and employee privacy collide. It is important that employers develop a video surveillance policy, inform employees about the policy, perform the surveillance only for legitimate business purposes, and strictly limit those who view the surveillance results. Use of monitoring systems should also not run counter to legitimate union activities. Finally, morale should also be considered when developing policies because monitoring systems can be viewed negatively by employees.[40]

Monitoring Employee Performance Employee activity may be monitored to measure performance, ensure performance quality and customer service, check for theft, or enforce company rules or laws. The common concerns in a monitored workplace usually center not on whether monitoring should be used, but on how it should be conducted, how the information should be used, and how feedback should be communicated to employees. Research points to other considerations. A recent study determined that electronic monitoring processes that were utilized for employee development, that were adequately explained, and that provided good feedback resulted in more positive perceptions of organizational justice, which lead to many positive work outcomes such as supervisor trust, work satisfaction, and work performance.[41]

At a minimum, employers should obtain a signed consent form that indicates that the employee knows performance will be monitored and phone calls will be taped regularly. Also, it is recommended that employers provide employees with feedback on monitoring results to help employees improve their performance and to commend them for good performance. For example, one major hotel reservation center allows employees to listen to their customer service calls and rate their own performance. Then, the employees meet with their supervisors to discuss both positive and negative performance issues.

15-4b Employer Investigations

Another area of concern regarding employee rights involves workplace investigations. The U.S. Constitution protects public-sector employees in the areas of due process, search and seizure, and privacy at work, but private-sector employees are not protected. Whether it occurs on or off the job, unethical or illegal behavior can be a serious problem for organizations. Examples of employee misconduct include illegal drug use, falsification of documents, misuse of company funds, disclosure of organizational secrets, workplace violence, employee harassment, and theft of corporate resources. The HR Ethics: Proper Investigations looks at the use of investigations and whistle-blowing to reduce concerns about misconduct in companies.

Conducting Work-Related Investigations Workplace investigations can be conducted by internal or external personnel. Often, HR staff and company security personnel lead internal investigations. Until recently, the use of outside investigators such as the police, private investigators, or attorneys was restricted by the Fair Credit Reporting Act. However, passage of the Fair and Accurate Credit Transactions (FACT) Act changed the situation. Under FACT, employers can hire outside investigators without first notifying the individuals under investigation or getting their permission.

Proper Investigations

The French car manufacturing company Renault recently terminated three managers who were suspected of corporate espionage. These individuals were allegedly passing on trade secrets about the company's electric car production to China, and many public statements were made about the misconduct and the company's handling of the incident. However, an internal investigation of the situation indicated that no espionage had occurred, leading to a public apology that hurt France's relationship with China and embarrassed executives at Renault (the Chief Operating Officer and one of the HR staffing managers were let go). The three managers who were terminated were offered their jobs back (only one returned) and the head of HR was promoted onto the executive committee to help with future issues. This situation shows the importance of conducting proper investigations to avoid corporate missteps.

Having a sound business process in place that helps internal investigations is one critical step organizations should take to minimize risk and security concerns. Another important step involves helping employees blow the whistle on wrongdoing so that problems can be indentified before they become serious. Tyco International and Ingersoll Rand are examples of companies that are using websites and hotlines to encourage employees to report workplace misconduct. In the United States, the Dodd-Frank Wall-Street Reform and Consumer Protection Act provides additional protection and incentives to employees who choose to blow the whistle, so more individuals should feel motivated to do so in the future.[42]

Workplace investigations are frequently conducted using technology. This allows employers to review e-mails, access computer logs, conduct video surveillance, and use other investigative tactics. When using audiotaping, wiretapping, and other electronic methods, care should be taken to avoid violating privacy and legal regulations. In addition to these considerations, the following best practices should be used when conducting workplace investigations:

- Develop a good working plan that guides how the company should respond to crises before they occur. Confidentiality should be a high priority throughout investigations, and all important incidents should be properly documented.
- Specify whether HR or another party (i.e., an attorney or accountant) will conduct the actual investigation of workplace incidents. If possible, select an objective and impartial investigator who does not have any professional connections with the individuals being investigated.
- Investigate problems quickly before evidence can be tampered with or destroyed and begin interviewing key witnesses. Investigate wrongdoing within several days after being made aware of the incident, and try to finish the investigation within a timeframe of two weeks.
- The credibility of individuals providing information in an investigation must be assessed by looking at the following factors: personal demeanor, reliability,

chronology, and credibility of answers provided, whether information can be corroborated, and past and present motives.

- Use the stories and information collected to conclude the investigation and recommend any remedial steps that should be taken. Present the results of investigations to key decision-makers and make appropriate recommendations.[43]

E T H I C S

Employee Theft and Fraud Employee theft of property and company secrets do occur, and white-collar theft through embezzlement, accepting bribes, and stealing company property are also concerns. Evidence suggests that fraud is a significant challenge for businesses in the United States, with around 7% of revenues and a total of a trillion dollars being lost every year because of fraudulent activities.[44] If the organizational culture encourages or allows such questionable behavior, then employees are more likely to see theft as acceptable. In addition, the more there are pressures to achieve, opportunities to act unethically, and ways to rationalize misconduct, the more likely fraud will be experienced in organizations.[45]

Employee theft and other workplace misconduct can be addressed using many methods.[46] Typical methods may include doing an investigation before hiring, using applicant screening, and conducting background investigations. Honesty tests may also be used both before and after a person is hired. After hire, workplace monitoring can review unusual behaviors. Companies can also consider developing an ethics code that outlines appropriate behaviors, and managers and business owners should be good role models. Finally, sound internal control mechanisms that split up critical job functions across different positions and random audits of inventory can help reduce employee fraud.[47]

Honesty and Polygraph Tests Pencil-and-paper honesty tests are alternatives to polygraph testing, as mentioned in Chapter 7. These tests are widely used, particularly in the retail industry and others. More than two dozen variations are available. For current employees, polygraph testing (performed with "lie detectors") is used by some organizations. The Employee Polygraph Protection Act prohibits the use of polygraphs for most preemployment screening and also requires that employees must

- be advised of their rights to refuse to take a polygraph exam;
- be allowed to stop the exam at any time; and
- not be terminated because they refuse to take a polygraph test or solely because of the exam results.

15-4c Substance Abuse and Drug Testing

Employee substance abuse and drug testing have received a great deal of attention. Concern about substance abuse at work is appropriate, given that absenteeism, accident/damage rates, and theft/fraud are higher for workers using illegal substances or misusing legal substances such as prescription drugs and alcohol. Estimates by the U.S. Office of National Drug Control Policy are that about 8% of employees are drug abusers, and those persons create significantly more employer medical and workers' compensation claims.[48] Figure 15-6 identifies some of the financial effects of substance abuse. Ways to address substance abuse problems were discussed in Chapter 14. Employee rights issues associated with these actions are discussed in the following sections.

FIGURE 15-6 How Substance Abuse Affects Employers Financially

Increased Absenteeism

- Pay for absent employee
- Pay for fill-in staff

More Accidents/Damage

- Downtime
- Medical expenses
- Wages of temporary employees
- Replacement of damaged equipment
- Legal/investigation fees

Higher Health Care Needs

- Increased insurance costs
- Employee time lost
- Administrative costs

Increased Theft/Fraud

- Unproductive hours
- Replacement of stolen items
- Fees for hiring security services
- Legal fees and investigative costs

© Cengage Learning 2014

Americans with Disabilities Act and Other Laws The Americans with Disabilities Act (ADA) specifies that alcoholism is a disability, but that dependency on illegal drugs is not. However, someone who currently recovering from any kind of substance abuse is protected based on the provisions specified in the ADA. Managers may still reprimand individuals who break a company's substance abuse policies, are not capable of working because they are under the influence, or are poor performers regardless of their drinking and/or drug problems. A substance abuser might be covered under the Family and Medical Leave Act because the consumption of drugs and alcohol is considered a significant health concern. HR professionals should also be aware of state statutes that might protect individuals.[49]

Drug-Free Workplace Act of 1988 The U.S. Supreme Court has ruled that certain drug-testing plans do not violate the Constitution. Private-employer programs are governed mainly by state laws, which can be a confusing hodgepodge. The Drug-Free Workplace Act of 1988 requires government contractors to take steps to eliminate employee drug use. Failure to do so can lead to government contract termination. Tobacco and alcohol do not qualify as controlled substances under the act, and off-the-job drug use is not included. Additionally, the U.S. Department of Transportation requires regular testing of truck and bus drivers, train crews, mass-transit employees, airline pilots and mechanics, pipeline workers, and licensed sailors.

Drug Testing and Employee Rights Unless federal, state, or local law prohibits testing, employers have a right to require applicants or employees to submit to a drug test. Preemployment drug testing is widely used. A recent study conducted in the U.S. construction industry determined that many companies use both preemployment and random drug testing, and the most commonly consumed drugs were marijuana and cocaine. Urine analysis was the primary type of test used to determine substance abuse among workers, and cheating on administered drug tests was a significant challenge in construction companies.[50] In the transportation industry, firms that operate under DOT guidelines must use preemployment, post-accident, and random drug exams to verify that individuals involved in transportation activities are fit for duty. When employees fail an exam or refuse to participate, they are barred from working and must sign up for treatment. They must also pass a separate "return-to-duty" urine exam, as well as be randomly tested six additional times over a 12-month period. DOT regulations specify that observers must be present during urine tests to verify that no cheating has occurred.[51]

When employers conduct drug testing of current employees, they generally use one of three policies: (1) random testing of everyone at periodic intervals, (2) testing only in cases of probable cause, or (3) testing after accidents. Means of testing include urinalysis and hair testing, among others. If testing is done for probable cause, it needs to be based on performance-related behaviors, such as excessive absenteeism or poor performance, and not just the substance usage itself. From a policy standpoint, it is most appropriate to test for drugs when the following conditions exist:

- Job-related consequences of the abuse are severe enough that they outweigh privacy concerns.
- Accurate test procedures are available.
- Written consent of the employee is obtained.
- Results are treated confidentially, as are any medical records.
- Employer offers a complete drug rehabilitation program, including an employee assistance program.

Employers win many drug-testing cases in courts, including cases in which a person has been terminated for violating drug policy provisions. However, not all employers are enamored with drug testing, and some claim the rate of testing is dropping because it shows no demonstrable return on investment. Also, drug testing for certain employers may restrict the hiring of sufficient numbers of new employees, so some employers have reexamined their drug policies.

15-5 ■ HUMAN RESOURCE POLICIES, PROCEDURES, AND RULES

Policies
General guidelines that focus organizational actions.

Procedures
Customary methods of handling activities.

HR policies, procedures, and rules greatly affect employee rights (just discussed) and discipline (discussed next). Where there is a choice among actions, **policies** act as general guidelines that help focus those organizational actions. Policies are general in nature, whereas procedures and rules are specific to the situation. The important role of all three requires that they be reviewed regularly.

Procedures provide customary methods of handling activities and are more specific than policies. For example, a policy may state that employees will be given vacations according to years of service, and a procedure establishes a specific method for authorizing vacation time without disrupting work.

Rules
Specific guidelines that regulate and restrict the behavior of individuals.

Rules are specific guidelines that regulate and restrict the behavior of individuals. They are similar to procedures in that they guide action and typically allow no discretion in their application. Rules reflect a management decision that action be taken—or not taken—in a given situation, and they provide more specific behavioral guidelines than do policies. Certain rules may be violated more than others, and violations may occur more frequently if individual and organizational performance is not what is expected.[52] An example of a rule might be that a vacation day may not be scheduled the day before or after a holiday.

Perhaps more than any other part of the organization, the HR function needs policies, procedures, and rules. People react strongly to differential treatment regarding time off, pay, vacation time, discipline, and other factors. New and smaller employers often start without many of these HR issues well defined. But as these companies grow, issues become more complex, with policy decisions being made on an "as needed" basis. Before long the inconsistency and resulting employee complaints bring on the need for clear policies, procedures, and rules that apply to everyone. Therefore, it is necessary that specific HR policies, procedures, and rules be established and enforced.

Coordination is necessary between the HR unit and operating managers for HR policies, procedures, and rules to be effective. As Figure 15-7 shows, managers are the main users and enforcers of rules, procedures, and policies, and they should receive training and explanation in how to carry them out. The HR unit supports managers, reviews policies and disciplinary rules, and trains managers to use them. Often policies, procedures, and rules are provided in employee handbooks.

LO4 List elements to consider when developing an employee handbook.

15-5a Employee Handbooks

An employee handbook can be an essential tool for communicating information about workplace culture, benefits, attendance, pay practices, safety issues, and discipline. The handbooks are sometimes written in a formal legalistic fashion, but need not be. More common language can make the handbook less negative. Even small organizations can prepare handbooks relatively easily using available computer software with sample policies. When preparing handbooks, management should consider legal issues, readability, and use. Handbooks may

FIGURE 15-7 Typical Division of HR Responsibilities: Policies, Procedures, and Rules

HR Unit	Managers
• Designs formal mechanisms for coordinating HR policies • Assists in development of organization-wide HR policies, procedures, and rules • Provides information on application of HR policies, procedures, and rules • Trains managers to administer policies, procedures, and rules	• Help in developing HR policies and rules • Review policies and rules with all employees • Apply HR policies, procedures, and rules • Explain rules and policies to all employees • Give feedback on effectiveness of policies and rules

© Cengage Learning

contain many areas, but some policies commonly covered in them include the following:

- At-will prerogatives
- Harassment
- Electronic communication
- Pay and benefits
- Discipline
- Hours worked

Legal Considerations and Best Practices As mentioned earlier, the courts have used employee handbooks against employers in lawsuits by charging a broken "implied" contract. This should not eliminate the use of employee handbooks as a way of communicating policies to employees. In fact, not having an employee handbook with HR policies spelled out understandably can leave an organization open to costly litigation as well. A sensible approach is to first develop sound HR policies and employee handbooks to communicate them, and then have legal counsel review the language contained in the handbooks. Legal experts also note that overuse of legal wording can make handbooks less useful for employees.[53]

There are many best practices that companies should consider when developing employee handbooks. Managers should view handbooks as a mechanism that enables the firm to better communicate standards to workers. Given this viewpoint, handbooks should be customized to fit a company's current situation instead of being too generalized. Also, the more personalized, easy-to-understand, and well-organized (with many headings/subheadings) a handbook is, the more likely it will be accepted and appreciated by employees. While a variety of issues should be covered, benefits should be discussed earlier in the manual, followed by discussions of security, safety, and workplace standards and expectations.[54] Several other recommendations include the following:

- *Eliminate controversial phrases.* For example, the phrase "permanent employee" may be used to describe a person who has passed a probationary period. This wording can lead to disagreement over what the parties meant by *permanent*. A more appropriate phrase is "regular employee."
- *Use disclaimers.* Courts generally uphold disclaimers, but only if they are prominently shown in the handbook.[55] To ensure that disclaimers are appropriate and create a positive image in the handbook, they should be done carefully. For instance, a disclaimer in the handbook can read as follows:

  This employee handbook is not intended to be a contract or any part of a contractual agreement between the employer and the employee. The employer reserves the right to modify, delete, or supplement any policies set forth herein without notice and reserves the right to terminate an employee at any time with or without a specific cause.

- *Keep the handbook current.* The content in employee handbooks must be revisited and revised when new issues are encountered or the conditions of the workplace change. Doing so prevents employee grievances and complaints. Consequently, assessments of employee handbooks and HR policies should be conducted on an ongoing basis.

To communicate and discuss HR information, a growing number of firms are distributing employee handbooks electronically using an intranet, which enables employees to access policies in employee handbooks at any time. It also allows changes in policies to be made electronically rather than distributed as paper copies. Companies should require employees to verify that they have received handbooks and other employment information by signing an appropriate form or by responding through e-mail.[56]

15-5b Communicating Human Resource Information

HR communication focuses on the receipt and dissemination of HR data and information throughout the organization. *Downward communication* flows from top management to the rest of the organization, informing employees about what is and will be happening in the organization, and what the expectations and goals of top management are. For instance, organizations communicate with employees through internal publications and media, including newspapers, company magazines, organizational newsletters, videotapes, Internet postings, and e-mail announcements. Whatever the formal means used, managers should make an honest attempt to communicate information employees need to know.

Upward communication enables managers to learn about the ideas, concerns, and information needs of employees. Companies use surveys and employee-suggestion programs to encourage the upward communication of good ideas.[57] For instance, the creation of Subway's $5 foot-long sandwich and promotion of the company's healthier menu items were ideas started by franchise owners that were later adopted companywide. Managers must make an attempt to respond to employee suggestions if they want to encourage suggestions in the future.[58]

15-6 ■ EMPLOYEE DISCIPLINE

L05 Understand the use of employee discipline in companies and differentiate between the positive and progressive approaches to discipline.

Discipline
Form of training that enforces organizational rules.

The earlier discussion about employee rights and organizational rules provides an appropriate introduction to the topic of employee discipline, because employee rights often are a key issue in disciplinary cases. **Discipline** is a form of training that enforces organizational rules. Those most often affected by the discipline systems may be problem employees. Common disciplinary issues caused by problem employees include absenteeism, tardiness, productivity deficiencies, alcoholism, and insubordination. Fortunately, problem employees represent a small number of the workplace. However, if managers fail to deal with problem employees because they choose not to confront disciplinary issues in a timely manner, work groups are often negatively affected.

15-6a Reasons Why Discipline Might Not Be Used

Managers may be reluctant to use discipline for many reasons. Some of the main reasons include the following:

- *Organizational culture of avoiding discipline*: If the organizational "norm" is to avoid penalizing problem employees, then managers are less likely to use discipline or to dismiss problem employees.
- *Lack of support*: Some managers do not want to use discipline because they fear that their decisions will not be supported by higher management. Upper management must understand what happens when they do not support discipline decisions.

- *Guilt*: Managers realize that before they became managers, they may have committed the same violations as their employees, and therefore they do not discipline others for similar actions because of their previous conduct.
- *Fear of loss of friendship*: Managers may fear losing friendships or damaging personal relationships if they discipline employees.
- *Avoidance of time loss*: Discipline often requires considerable time and effort. Sometimes it is easier for managers to avoid taking the time required for proper discipline, especially if their actions may be overturned on review by higher management.
- *Fear of lawsuits*: Managers are sometimes concerned about being sued for disciplining an employee, particularly if the discipline leads to termination.

15-6b Effective Discipline

Because of legal concerns, managers must understand discipline and know how to administer it properly. Effective discipline should be aimed at the problem behaviors, not at the employees personally, because the goal is to improve performance. Distributive and procedural justice notions suggest that if a manager tolerates unacceptable behavior, other employees may resent the unfairness of that tolerance.

Role of Human Resources The changing nature of HR to a more strategic orientation in some organizations likely impacts the discipline process. For instance, HR managers will likely be called on to oversee disciplinary procedures to ensure that remedial actions follow corporate policy, are done appropriately, and are fair. A recent study conducted in the United Kingdom found that line managers were expected to handle discipline cases instead of HR personnel. Alternatively, HR was expected to function in a more objective, advisory role, performing activities such as assisting inexperienced line managers during hearings and guiding the actions of managers. However, evidence suggested that many managers were not capable of handling some disciplinary situations, which meant that HR had to step in and manage cases in a more formal manner.[59] These findings show that HR professionals must be adequately prepared to function as trainers and mediators in cases where discipline must be administered to employees.

Training of Supervisors Training supervisors and managers on when and how discipline should be used is crucial. Employees see disciplinary action as more fair when given by trained supervisors who base their responses on procedural justice than when discipline is done by untrained supervisors. Training in counseling and communications skills provides supervisors and managers with the tools necessary to deal with employee performance problems, regardless of the disciplinary approaches used.

15-6c Approaches to Discipline

The disciplinary system can be viewed as an application of behavior modification to a problem or unproductive employee. The best discipline is clearly self-discipline, and most people can be counted on to do their jobs effectively when they understand what is required at work. But for some people, the prospect of external discipline helps their self-discipline. One approach to discipline is called positive discipline.

Positive Discipline Approach The positive discipline approach builds on the philosophy that violations are actions that usually can be corrected constructively without penalty. In this approach, managers focus on using fact finding and guidance to encourage desirable behaviors, rather than using penalties to discourage undesirable behaviors. The four steps to positive discipline are as follows:

1. *Counseling*: The goal of this phase is to heighten employee awareness of organizational policies and rules. Often, people simply need to be made aware of rules, and knowledge of possible disciplinary actions may prevent violations.
2. *Written documentation*: If an employee fails to correct behavior, then a second conference becomes necessary. Whereas the first stage took place as a conversation between supervisor and the employee, this stage is documented in written form, and written solutions are identified to prevent further problems from occurring.
3. *Final warning*: If the employee does not follow the written solutions noted in the second step, a final warning conference is held. In that conference, the supervisor again emphasizes to the employee the importance of correcting the inappropriate actions. Some firms require the employee to take a day off with pay to develop a specific written action plan to remedy the problem behaviors. The decision day off emphasizes the seriousness of the problem and the manager's determination to see that the behavior is changed.
4. *Discharge*: If the employee fails to follow the action plan that was developed, and further problems exist, then the supervisor can discharge the employee.

The advantage of this positive approach to discipline is that it focuses on problem solving. The greatest difficulty with the positive approach to discipline is the extensive amount of training required for supervisors and managers to become effective counselors, and the need for more supervisory time with this approach than with the progressive discipline approach, which is discussed next.

Progressive Discipline Approach Progressive discipline incorporates steps that become progressively more stringent and are designed to change the employee's inappropriate behavior. Figure 15-8 shows a typical progressive discipline process; most progressive discipline procedures use verbal and written reprimands and suspension before resorting to dismissal. For example, at a manufacturing firm, an employee's failure to call in when being absent from work might lead to a suspension without pay after the third offense in a year. Suspension sends employees a strong message that undesirable job behaviors must change or termination is likely to follow.

Although it appears to be similar to positive discipline, progressive discipline is more administrative and process oriented. Following the progressive sequence ensures that both the nature and the seriousness of the problem are clearly communicated to the employee. Not all steps in progressive discipline are followed in every case. Certain serious offenses are exempted from the progressive procedure and may result in immediate termination. Typical offenses leading to immediate termination include intoxication at work, alcohol or drug use at work, fighting, and theft. However, if a firm has a written progressive disciplinary policy, it should be followed when immediate termination is not appropriate because failing to do so can cause an employee's dismissal to be considered outside the normal disciplinary procedures.

FIGURE 15-8 Progressive Discipline Process

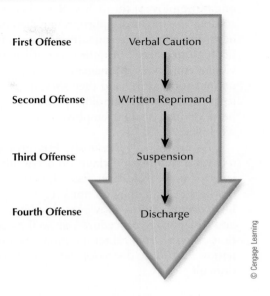

First Offense — Verbal Caution

Second Offense — Written Reprimand

Third Offense — Suspension

Fourth Offense — Discharge

© Cengage Learning

Discharge
When an employee is removed from a job at an employer.

15-6d Discharge: The Final Disciplinary Step

The final stage in the disciplinary process may be called *discharge, firing, dismissal,* or *termination,* among other terms. Regardless of the word used, **discharge** is when an employee is removed from a job at an employer. Both the positive and the progressive approaches to discipline clearly provide employees with warnings about the seriousness of their performance problems before dismissal occurs.

One difficult phase of employee termination is the removal of dismissed employees and their personal possessions from company facilities. The standard advice from legal experts is to physically remove the employee as quickly as possible. Ex-employees are often escorted out of the building by security guards. Some firms allow terminated employees to return to their desks, offices, or lockers to retrieve personal items under the observation of security personnel and the department supervisor/manager, but this means the ex-employee may be seen by and talk to coworkers while still upset or angry.

Termination Issues Termination happens for a wide range of reasons. For instance, excessive violations of attendance policies commonly lead to employee terminations. Other causes involve breaking company rules, behavioral issues such as sexual harassment and other unethical acts, and poor execution of work-related duties. Addiction to alcohol and drugs and substance-related convictions (such as a DUI) can also lead to terminations, particularly in jobs that require driving. While the ADA indicates that alcohol abuse is considered a disability, companies can reprimand and terminate employees who cannot drive a vehicle because of this impairment. EEOC guidelines also indicate that criminal convictions can also be sufficient enough to terminate an employee, just so the seriousness of the offense, the amount of time transpired after the offense, and the nature of the position in question are considered.[60]

There are other issues that can be examined. Some managers might elect to terminate employees through videoconferencing, telephone, or e-mail, but face-to-face sessions are the most appropriate when dealing with terminations. Managers should never use e-mail to terminate employees because it is too impersonal and can be difficult to manage.[61] Another concern is when managers must terminate potentially violent employees. Managers must be careful not to move forward with these terminations too hastily, and they should get assistance from others in security, HR, and legal counsel when handling such cases. Finally, a workplace violence policy should be developed so that employees are trained to identify potential problems in the workplace.[62]

As mentioned previously, HR professionals and managers may be faced with *wrongful termination* claims and lawsuits following terminations. These legal challenges can be based on federal, state, and local laws. At face value, terminating workers because they do not keep their promises would seem equitable and defensible in many courts. However, employers need to follow appropriate HR processes and disciplinary procedures, as well as consistently document reasons for termination, to win wrongful termination lawsuits. The HR Skills and Applications: Termination Procedure discusses some practices that can make employee termination less difficult.

Separation agreement

Agreement in which a terminated employee agrees not to sue the employer in exchange for specified benefits.

Separation Agreements In some termination situations, formal contracts may be used. One type is a **separation agreement**, in which an employee who is being terminated agrees not to sue the employer in exchange for specified benefits, such as additional severance pay or other "considerations."

For such agreements to be legally enforceable, the considerations are usually additional items not part of normal termination benefits. For international

HR SKILLS AND APPLICATIONS

Termination Procedure

Dismissal of an employee can be problematic. The following practices can make it less difficult:

1. *Review evidence.* The disciplining manager, that manager's superior, and an HR representative should review the documentation and make the final determination.
2. *Select a neutral location.* Termination should occur in a neutral location, not in the supervisor/manager's office.
3. *Conduct the termination meeting.* The HR representative and/or the manager informs the employee of the reason for the termination. The manager and the HR representative should remain professional and calm, not apologetic or demeaning.
4. *Have HR discuss termination benefits.* The HR representative explains the employee's final payroll and benefits. A specific letter can serve as evidence that the employee was notified of the termination decision and details of those rights.
5. *Escort the employee from the building.* This phase is controversial. The goal is to ensure that the employee, who is likely to be upset, is removed from the premises quickly without obvious conflicts or concerns about security.
6. *Notify the department staff.* The manager notifies the department staff that the individual is no longer employed. No details or explanations should be provided.[63]

employees, different legal requirements may exist in various countries, including certain requirements for severance pay and benefits. When using separation agreements, care must be taken to avoid the appearance of constructive discharge of employees. Use of such agreements should be reviewed by legal counsel.

SUMMARY

- The employment relationship is a reciprocal one in which both employers and employees have statutory and contractual rights, as well as responsibilities.
- Contractual rights can be spelled out in an employment contract or be implied as a result of employer promises.
- Employment-at-will gives employers the right to hire and terminate employees with or without notice or cause.
- Courts are changing aspects of employment-at-will relationships through exceptions for violations of public policy, an implied contract, and good faith and fair dealing.
- Wrongful discharge occurs when an employer improperly or illegally terminates an individual's employment.
- Constructive discharge is the process of making conditions intolerable to get an employee to "voluntarily" quit a job.
- Just cause for employment-related activities should exist for taking appropriate employment-related actions.
- Although both due process and organizational justice are not guaranteed for the at-will employees, the courts expect to see evidence of due process in employment-related cases.
- Complaint procedures and due process is important for both unionized and nonunion employees. In nonunion situations, alternative dispute resolution (ADR) means may be used.

- Arbitrations, peer review panels, and ombuds also can be used to address disciplinary actions.
- Balancing employer and employee rights becomes an issue when dealing with privacy rights, access to employee records, free speech, and whistle-blowing situations.
- Employers increasingly are facing privacy, free speech, and other issues in electronic communications, including e-mails, twitters, blogs, wikis, voicemail, and other technology means.
- The rights of employees for personal behavior must be balanced by employers' rights, particularly in regard to individuals' display of behaviors, unique dress or appearance, and questionable off-duty actions.
- Employer investigations protect both employer and employee rights.
- Drug testing provides a useful and legal method for employers to deal with increasing drug problems at work.
- HR policies, procedures, and rules should be in employee handbooks and other communications means. Courts sometimes view employee handbooks as implied contracts.
- Although employee self-discipline is the goal, positive or progressive discipline is sometimes necessary to encourage self-discipline.
- The final disciplinary phase is discharge of an employee through termination, which might include a separation agreement.

CRITICAL THINKING CHALLENGES

1. Identify how the issues of due process and just cause are linked to employer disciplinary actions.

2. Discuss the following statement: Even though efforts to restrict employees' free speech at work may be permissible, such

efforts raise troubling questions affecting individual rights.

3. Give some examples of how technology is creating employer/employee rights and policy issues. Then suggest some possible actions that may be needed.

4. Assume that as the HR manager, you have decided to prepare some guidelines for supervisors to use when they have to discipline employees. Gather the information needed, using Internet resources such as www.blr.com and www.workforce.com for sample policies and other details. Then prepare a guide for supervisors on implementing both positive and progressive discipline.

5. In developing a company workplace violence prevention program, management has become aware of concerns regarding a drug-free workplace. Several employees have recently come to

HR requesting a leave of absence to enter a drug rehabilitation program. The managers were not aware of the substance abuse issues relating to these employees. Consequently, management recognizes that a drug-free workplace program will help improve workplace safety and health. These programs also play an important role in fostering safer and drug-free families and communities. To assist HR in developing a drug-free workplace program, visit this website at www .dol.gov/workingpartners.

A. What are the key components that should be included in your company's drug-free workplace program to best meet the needs of both employees and the company?

B. Identify the steps a manager should take if an employee's actions create a suspicion that the employee has reported to work under the influence of substances.

CASE

"Evaluate" before "Terminate"

The move to terminate potentially violent or dangerous employees can be a difficult one. If the decision is made haphazardly or hastily, firing problem employees can open up an organization to claims of wrongful termination or even illegal discrimination. If individuals are retained, a company can be found negligent, ultimately being held responsible for any wrongdoing and harm that occurs as a result of keeping them around. Consequently, companies must try to strike a reasonable balance between being too proactive, and not being judicious enough.

Such decision-making difficulties and dilemmas are illustrated in the recent court case *Mary Wolski v. City of Erie*. The City of Erie had fired Ms. Wolski, a fire truck driver who had been employed in the fire fighting group for many years, because the organization believed that she was a safety problem in the workplace. Years previously, her mother had passed away, causing Ms. Wolski to become very depressed. As a result, she took extensive leave from work to seek treatment and

recover from her psychological troubles. While on leave, she attempted to poison herself with carbon monoxide by starting a fire at her father's house and consuming an overdose of medication.

Such conduct was considered highly dangerous by her employer, and an investigation was initiated by the City of Erie. The findings of the inquiry resulted in her termination, so Ms. Wolski subsequently filed a lawsuit claiming that the organization's decision to terminate her violated requirements of the ADA. The court ruled in her favor because the organization did not conduct an "individualized assessment" of Ms. Wolski before the termination decision. The move to fire her appeared to be based largely on an evaluation of her conduct, which was likely caused by her documented depression.

This case presents many important implications for HR professionals. For instance, employers should get the proper input from medical professionals who understand the mental and physical challenges that impair employees' ability to perform their work. HR also needs to talk with employees to determine whether individual impairments negatively impact their performance of essential job activities. In addition, reasonable accommodations should be identified, and employee requests for assistance should be secured in writing. Finally, retention and termination decisions should be business-related and objective in nature.[64]

QUESTIONS

1. Based on your work experiences, identify examples of behaviors that might be considered dangerous by managers, supervisors, and/or coworkers. How did your employers respond, and was anyone terminated?

2. If you were an HR professional, how would you handle the termination of a potentially dangerous employee? What policies might you create to make your organization less susceptible to wrongful termination or discrimination lawsuits?

SUPPLEMENTAL CASES

Dealing with Workplace Bullying

This case explores the problems that occur when "bullying" bosses or employees are present in the workplace. (For the case, go to www.cengage.com /management/mathis.)

George Faces Challenges

This case describes the problem facing a new department supervisor when HR policies and discipline have been handled poorly in the past. (For the case, go to www.cengage.com/management /mathis.)

Employer Liable for "Appearance Actions"

This case discusses a California court ruling on terminating a female for her personal appearance. (For the case, go to www.cengage.com/management /mathis.)

NOTES

1. Based on Peter Cappelli, "Managing the 'Difficult' Employee," *Human Resource Executive Online*, June 20, 2011, www.hreonline.com; "How Disruptive Behavior by Employees Can Devastate a Workplace," Knowledge@Wharton website, The Wharton School, University of Pennsylvania, March 27, 2013, www.knowledge.wharton.upenn. edu.

2. Stuart L. Gillan, Jay C. Hartzell, and Robert Parrino, "Explicit versus Implicit Contracts: Evidence from CEO Employment Agreements," *The Journal of Finance*, 64 (2009), Issue 4, 1629–1655.

3. Mark J. Garmaise, "Ties that Truly Bind: Noncompetition Agreements, Executive Compensation, and Firm Investment," *Journal of Law, Economics, and Organization*, 27 (2011), Issue 2, 376–425.

4. Matthias Krakel and Dirk Sliwka, "Should You Allow Your Employee to Become Your Competitor? On Noncompete Agreements in Employment Contracts," *International Economic Review*, 50 (2009), 117–141.

5. Chris Arbery, "Noncompete Valid if Reasonable and Balanced," *HR Magazine*, August 2010, 81.

6. Robert J. Orelup and Christopher S. Drewry, "Judicial Review and Reformation of Noncompete Agreements," *The Construction Lawyer*, Summer 2009, 29–32, 44, 52–55.

7. Emily B. York, "Does a Noncompete Agreement Really Offer Any Protection?" *Workforce Management*, October 13, 2009, www.workforce. com.

8. Roger M. Milgram and Eric E. Benson, "Use of Agreements to

Protect Trade Secrets in the Employment Relationship," *Milgram on Trade Secrets*, 2011.

9. For details, go to "Contract Disclaimers and Employment-at-Will Policies," *Ceridian Abstracts*, www.hrcompliance.ceridian.com.

10. *Fortune v. National Cash Register Co.*, 373 Mass. 96, 36 N.E.2d 1251 (1977).

11. Tomlinson and Bockanic, 2009.

12. Based on Edward C. Tomlinson and William N. Bockanic, "Avoiding Liability for Wrongful Termination: 'Ready, Aim, … Fire'," *Employee Responsibilities and Rights Journal*, 21 (2009), 77–87.

13. Donna Maria Blancero, Robert G. DelCampo, and George F. Marron, "Just Tell Me! Making Alternative Dispute Resolution Systems Fair," *Industrial Relations*, 49 (2010), 524–542.

14. Ibid.

15. Based on Jeff Green, "The Silencing of Sexual Harassment," *Bloomberg Businessweek*, November 21–November 27, 2011, 21–22.

16. Michael Delikat, "Arbitrating Workplace Disputes," *Human Resource Executive Online*, June 16, 2010, www.hreonline.com.

17. Jim Hanley, "Transformative Mediation," *HR Magazine*, April 2010, 64–65.

18. For details on the retention of employee records and documents, go to www.hrcompliance.ceridian.com.

19. Michelle V. Rafter, "Electronic Records Management," *Workforce Management Online*, May 2009, www.workforce.com; "Can You Identify the Elements of an Effective Electronic Communications Policy?" *HR Compliance*, July 2009, www.hrcompliance.ceridian.com.

20. *Dixon v. Coburg Dairy Inc.*, No. 02-1266 (4th Cir., May 30, 2003).

21. "Bank of America Firing Violated Rights of Whistle-Blower," *HR Magazine*, November 2011, 18.

22. Jessica Marquez, "Firms Getting Stimulus Face Tougher Whistle-Blower Law," *Workforce Management*, April 6, 2009, 4.

23. Drew Harker and Matthew D. Keiser, "Whistleblower Incentives and Protections in the Financial Reform Act," Advisory, Arnold &

Porter LLP, July 2010, 1–3; Dori Meinert, "Whistle-Blowers: Threat or Asset?" *HR Magazine*, April 2011, 27–32.

24. Harker and Keiser, 2010.

25. Jukka Varel, "Is Whistle-Blowing Compatible with Employee Loyalty?" *Journal of Business Ethics*, 85 (2009), 263–275.

26. Meinert, 2011.

27. Based on information from Sean Valentine, et al., "Exploring the Ethicality of Terminating Employees Who Blog," *Human Resource Management*, 20 (2010), 82–108.

28. Sam Hananel, "Facebook: Protected Speech," *The Denver Post*, February 8, 2011, 7B.

29. William P. Smith and Filiz Tabak, "Monitoring Employee E-Mails: Is There Any Room for Privacy?" *Academy of Management Perspectives*, 23 (2009), 33–48.

30. Ibid.

31. Frances S. Grodzinsky, Andra Gumbus, and Stephen Lilley, "Ethical Implications of Internet Monitoring: A Comparative Study," *Information Systems Frontiers*, 12 (2010), 433–441.

32. Jason L. Snyder, "E-Mail Privacy in the Workplace," *Journal of Business Communication*, 47 (2010), 266–294.

33. Joanne Deschenaux, "Europeans Demand Greater Privacy," *HR Magazine*, June 2010, 99–104.

34. Ibid.

35. Nathan A. Bowling and Melissa L. Gruys, "Overlooked Issues in the Conceptualization and Measurement of Counterproductive Work Behavior," *Human Resource Management Review*, 20 (2010), 54–61.

36. Maria Greco Danaher, "Fitness-for-Duty Exam Can Be Based on Concern About Volatile Behavior," *HR Magazine*, November 2010, 72.

37. Kathleen Koster, "What Not to Wear: Legal, Communication, and Enforcement Tips for Introducing a Dress Code," *Employee Benefit News*, September 1, 2009, 56–57.

38. Steve Taylor, "'Look' Policies Pose Risks," *HR Disciplines*, July 15, 2009, www.shrm.org.

39. Based on Lin Grensing-Pophal, "How 'Free Time' Can Cost Millions," *Human Resource*

Executive Online, April 7, 2011, www.hreonline.com.

40. Clifford H. Nelson and Leigh Tyson, "HR Undercover," *HR Magazine*, October 2010, 107–110.

41. Laurel A. McNall and Sylvia G. Roch, "A Social Exchange Model for Employee Reactions to Electronic Performance Monitoring," *Human Performance*, 22 (2009), 204–224.

42. Based on Jared Shelly, "To Find the Truth," *Human Resource Executive Online*, September 2, 2011, www.hreonline.com.

43. Jared Shelly, "To Find the Truth," *Human Resource Executive Online*, September 2, 2011, www.hreonline.com; David I. Weissman, "Proper Workplace Investigations," *HR Magazine*, May 2011, 71–76.

44. Kristoffer R. Jackson, Daniel V. Holland, Chad Albrecht, and Dave R. Woolstenhulme, "Fraud Isn't Just for Big Business: Understanding the Drivers, Consequences, and Prevention of Fraud in Small Business," *The Journal of International Management Studies*, 5 (2010), 160–164.

45. Kristoffer R. Jackson et al., 2010.

46. Keisha-Ann G. Gray, "Searching for Employee Misconduct," *Human Resource Executive Online*, May 18, 2009, www.hreonline.com.

47. Kristoffer R. Jackson et al., 2010.

48. Kathleen Koster, "Drug Tests: Accurate Measures of Impairment or Ineffective Invasions of Privacy?" *Employee Benefit News*, November 2009, 16.

49. Jonathan Segal, "Elephant in the Living Room," *HR Magazine*, March 2012, 95–98.

50. Svetlana Olbina, Jimmie Hinze, and Christopher Arduengo, "Drug Testing in the US Construction Industry in 2008," *Construction Management and Economics*, 29 (2011), 1043–1057.

51. Chris Arbery and Robert Dumbacher, "Direct Observation Rule for Urine Tests Upheld," *HR Magazine*, August 2009, 66.

52. David W. Lehman and Rangaraj Ramanujam, "Selectivity in Organizational Rule Violations," *Academy of Management Review*, 34 (2009), 643–657.

53. John T. Hansen and Radhika Sood, "A Lighter Touch for Handbooks," *HR Magazine*, May 2009, 91–97.

54. D. Albert Brannen, "Tips on Writing an Employee Handbook," Employee Benefits News Legal Alert, March 4, 2011, ebnbenefitnews@e.benefit news.com.

55. *Compton v. Rent-a-Center*, No. 08-6264 (10th Cir., Oct. 20, 2009).

56. Carolyn m. Plump, "Dealing with Problem Employees: A Legal Guide for Employers," *Business Horizons*, 53 (2010), 607–618.

57. Tamara Lytle, "Give Employees a Say," *HR Magazine*, October 2011, 68–72; Michael O'Brien, "Beyond Engagement," *Human Resource Executive*, March 2012, 40–42.

58. Tamara Lytle, 2011.

59. Carol Jones and Richard Saundry, "The Practice of Discipline: Evaluating the Roles and Relationship Between Managers and HR Professionals," *Human Resource Management Journal*, 22 (2012), Issue 3, 252–266.

60. Margaret Fiester, "Drunk Driving," *HR Magazine*, November 2009, 20.

61. Yvette Lee, "Tele-Terminating," *HR Magazine*, June 2010, 31.

62. Kathryn Tyler, "Safer Separations," *HR Magazine*, December 2011, 43.

63. Provided by Nicholas Dayan, SPHR, and Saralee Ryan.

64. Based on Mark McGraw, "Predicting the Potential for Violence," *Human Resource Executive Online*, December 6, 2012, www.hreonline.com.

16

Union/ Management Relations

Learning Objectives

After you have read this chapter, you should be able to:

1 Discuss what a union is and explain why employees join and employers resist unions.

2 Outline the current state of union activity in the United States.

3 Identify several reasons for the decline in union membership.

4 Explain the nature of each of the major U.S. labor laws.

5 Describe the stages of unionization and the typical collective bargaining process.

6 Define a grievance and identify the stages in a grievance procedure.

7 Understand how unions have been involved in the global arena.

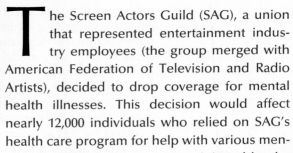

HR HEADLINE

Union Decides to Drop Mental Health Coverage

The Screen Actors Guild (SAG), a union that represented entertainment industry employees (the group merged with American Federation of Television and Radio Artists), decided to drop coverage for mental health illnesses. This decision would affect nearly 12,000 individuals who relied on SAG's health care program for help with various mental health and substance abuse problems. The action was precipitated by the passing of the Mental Health Parity and Addiction Equity Act, a law that requires many changes to health plans.

A majority of health insurance programs specify that 24 months of long-term disability payments is the maximum amount given for outpatient treatments of mental health or substance abuse problems when a claimant is not working. In addition, use of the benefit accumulates over time and stays in effect for as long as the insurance policy exists. If an individual cannot work and continues to accept policy payouts, benefits will cease at the 24-month cap.

The Mental Health Parity and Addiction Equity Act requires health policies to equalize coverage benefits for mental health problems so that they are on par with those provided for other medical issues. The actuaries for the union health plan determined that complying with this law would double the expenses of providing health care insurance to members. Consequently, the organization decided to drop the coverage. Some states have even seen decreases in health care expenses after equalizing benefits, while others have not.[1]

559

Union
Formal association of
workers that promotes
the interests of its
members through collec-
tive action.

L01 Discuss what a union is and explain why employees join and employers resist unions.

Union
Formal association of
workers that promotes
the interests of its
members through collec-
tive action.

A **union** is a formal association of workers that promotes the interests of its members through collective action. In the United States, unions typically try to increase compensation, improve working conditions, and influence workplace rules. When a union is present, these issues are decided through collective bargaining agreements and specified in formal contracts that have been ratified by management and labor.

Unions did not seem to have a bright future in the 1930s when the National Labor Relations Act (NLRA) was passed, giving unions a legal right to exist. Then they grew to represent about 36% of the workforce in the 1950s, only to see their strength in the private sector drop to less than 8% recently. However, in the public sector, union strength continues to grow. These trends illustrate the inherent political nature of unionization, particularly because government and public opinion play such prominent roles in union strength.

The very existence of unions depends upon laws and legal action.[2] As such, the ability of unions to function as bargaining entities is based on how they gain and keep favor with politicians who represent their interests in government. For instance, in the state of Wisconsin intense political jockeying over the role of public-sector unions occurred, with some politicians favoring a reduction in their collective bargaining abilities and workers expressing their desire for union representation though recall campaigns and the political process.[3] Unions also donate funds directly to political candidates, as well as indirectly through union voter mobilization drives and large political action committees (PACs). PACs are organized by both major political parties and represent either a platform of pro-labor with stronger union representation or a position of pro-management with a smaller union presence. While unions must indicate how much money is gathered from members for PACs, politicians, and other political entities, they don't have to report how much money is used for other union-based political pursuits.[4]

Unions' ability to survive also depends on public opinion of their role in influencing business organizations. Such opinion can be expressed through the political process, and people vote for the political parties and candidates that represent their views on the proper balance between labor and management. Evidence suggests that the general public's views on unionization may be changing, and this is often reflected in the way people vote. Recently, the approval of union representation has declined.[5]

Exactly how political, economic, and workforce changes affect employers and unions will be factors in the future of the labor/management relationship. Even though fewer workers have chosen to be union members in recent years than in the past, employers and HR professionals still need to understand the system of laws, regulations, court decisions, and administrative rulings related to the nature of unions. This is important because unions remain a strong alternative for employees in the event of poor HR management.

16-1 ■ PERSPECTIVES ON UNIONIZATION

Union representation has many advantages and disadvantages. For instance, unions give employees an opportunity to provide feedback to employers about their concerns and suggestions that would be difficult to express otherwise. Unions can provide a balance to the unchallenged decision-making power of management when needed. Increases in job performance and employee earnings are also often associated with unionization. Alternatively, unions can negatively impact the allocation of organizational resources, cause decreases in profitability, and hurt productivity as a result of increased compensation. These points should be considered when exploring why employees join unions and why employers resist unionization.

16-1a Why Employees Unionize

Whether a union targets a group of employees for organization, or the employees request union assistance, the union must win support from the employees to become their legal representative. Over the years employees have joined unions for two general reasons: (1) they are dissatisfied with how they are treated by their employers, and (2) they believe that unions can improve their work situations. If employees believe they are being treated unfairly by their companies, they may turn to unions to get assistance with their concerns. As Figure 16-1 shows, the major factors that can trigger unionization are issues of compensation, working conditions, management style, and employee treatment.

One of the primary reasons why employees want to unionize is based on how well their companies are managed. Unions function as a watchdog for workplace equity and make sure that employees are treated fairly. When unions are not present, inequalities in the way compensation is distributed to workers can occur.[6] Employees expect to receive reasonably competitive compensation, a good working environment, effective management and supervision, and fair and responsive treatment of workers. When these basic expectations are not met, employee interest in organized labor increases. Unionization often occurs when employees feel disrespected, unsafe, underpaid, and unappreciated, and see a union as a viable option for change.

Even though actions of management influence whether or not employees vote for unionization, individuals' overall perceptions of unions is a driver of intentions

FIGURE 16-1 Factors Leading to Employee Unionization

Desirability of Unionization

1. Working Conditions
- Inadequate staffing
- Mandatory overtime
- Unsatisfactory work requirements
- Unrealistic expectations

2. Compensation
- Noncompetitive pay
- Inadequate benefits
- Inequitable pay raises
- Unfair allocation of resources

3. Management Style
- Arbitrary decision making
- Use of fear/intimidation
- Lack of recognition
- Autocratic leadership

4. Employee Treatment
- Job insecurity
- Unfair discipline/policies
- Lack of response to complaints
- Harassment/abusive behaviors

© Cengage Learning 2014

to organize.[7] This implies that general opinions of organized labor creates a certain mindset among workers either for or against unions, regardless of the practices they immediately experience on the job. Once unionization occurs, the ability of the union to foster commitment from members and to remain as their bargaining agent depends on how well the union succeeds in providing the services that its members want, which can further strengthen or weaken workers' perceptions of unions.

16-1b Why Employers Resist Unions

Some employers would rather not have to negotiate with unions because they affect how employees and workplaces are managed. Unions are criticized for creating inefficiencies at work that cause waste and poor performance. For instance, the rebuilding of Ground Zero in New York Center after the 9/11 attacks has been plagued with high labor costs and overstaffing, excessive overtime expenses, and the employment of unneeded trade professionals making six-figure salaries, problems caused directly by unionization. As a result, many union contractors and developers in New York are moving toward nonunion or other arrangements.[8]

Union workers frequently get compensated better than do nonunion workers, but on the flipside, higher pay and benefits might be related to higher job performance. Despite this higher productivity, managers still try to identify labor-saving ways of doing work to offset increased expenses. For instance, performance-based compensation and profit sharing was explored at General Motors as a way of increasing productivity and reducing the risks associated with non-incentive based raises.[9]

Once established, some employers pursue a strategy of good relations with unions, while others choose an aggressive, adversarial approach.[10] However, there are numerous strategies that can be employed to prevent unionization from occurring in the first place. As stated previously, employees become interested in organized labor when they feel mistreated by their employers and/or operate in unfair, undesirable, or even dangerous work environment. Companies can develop good employment practices, encourage greater employee feedback, offer better compensation, and build good rapport with workers to make unions unnecessary in employees' eyes.[11] In addition, companies can be careful about how they handle unions when they approach workers to organize the company. The TIPS acronym provides some sound guidelines about how not to deal with organizing attempts:[12]

- *Threaten*: Do not bully employees because they talk to union officials.
- *Interrogate*: Never pry into and aggressively ask about union–employee discussions.
- *Promise*: Never provide incentives to employees in an effort to dissuade them from organizing.
- *Spy*: Do not secretly listen to employees' interactions with union representatives.

Human Resource Professionals and Unionization To prevent unionization, as well as to work effectively with unions already representing employees, both HR professionals and operating managers must be attentive and responsive to employees. The pattern of dealing with unionization varies among organizations. In some firms, management handles labor relations and HR has limited involvement. In other organizations, the HR unit takes primary responsibility for resisting unionization or dealing with unionized employees.[13]

L02 Outline the current
state of union activity in the
United States.

16-2 ■ UNION MEMBERSHIP IN THE UNITED STATES

The statistics on union membership over the past several decades tell a dishearten-ing story for organized labor in the United States. As shown in Figure 16-2, union membership covered more than 30% of the workforce from 1945 to 1960. But most recently, union membership in the United States represented only 11.8% of wage and salary workers in 2011 and 11.3% in 2012. In the public section, mem-bership in unions was 35.9% of the workforce in 2012, and membership was only 6.6% of the workforce in the private sector.[14] The actual number of members has declined in most years.

However, it's not all bad news for unions, with some unions prospering. In the past several years, unions have organized thousands of janitors, health care work-ers, cleaners, and other low-paid workers using publicity, pickets, boycotts, and strikes. In some states, membership in unions functioning under the AFL-CIO has steadily increased over the last several years, which is attributed to the economy turndown and concerns about poor work opportunities.[15] The Bureau of Labor Statistics disclosed that union membership among employees working in the private sector had recently increased by approximately 50,000, for a total of almost 15 mil-lion individuals.[16]

FIGURE 16-2 Union Membership as a Percentage of the U.S. Civilian Workforce/Wage and Salary Workers

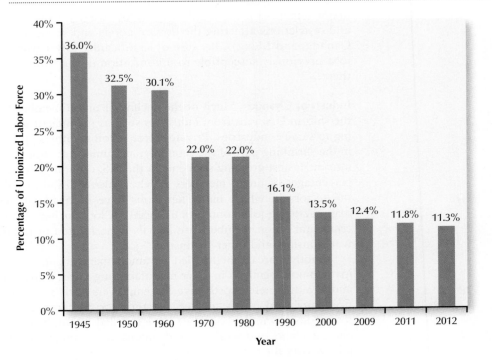

Source: Bureau of Labor Statistics.

L03 Identify several reasons for the decline in union membership.

16-2a Reasons for U.S. Union Membership Long-Term Decline

Several general trends have contributed to the decline of U.S. union membership, including deregulation, foreign competition, a larger number of people looking for jobs, and a general perception by firms that dealing with unions is expensive compared with nonunion alternatives. Management at many employers has taken a much more activist stance against unions than during the years of union growth, and economic downturns have also had negative impacts.[17]

To some extent, unions may be victims of their own successes. Unions in the United States historically have emphasized helping workers obtain higher wages and benefits, shorter working hours, job security, and safe working conditions from their employers. Some believe that one cause for the decline of unions has been their success in getting those important issues passed into law for everyone. Therefore, unions may no longer be seen as necessary by many workers, even though they enjoy the results of past union efforts to influence legislation that has been beneficial to them.

Geographic Changes During the past decade, job growth in the United States has been the greatest in states located in the South, the Southwest, and the Rocky Mountains. Most of these states have little tradition of unions, more "employer-friendly" laws, and relatively small percentages of unionized workers.

Another geographic issue involves the movement of many low-skill jobs outside the United States. Primarily to take advantage of cheaper labor, many manufacturers with heavily unionized U.S. workforces have moved a significant number of low-skill jobs to the Philippines, China, Thailand, and Mexico. For instance, the passage of the North American Free Trade Agreement provided a major impetus for moving low-skill, low-wage jobs to Mexico. It removed tariffs and restrictions affecting the flow of goods and services among the United States, Canada, and Mexico. Because of significantly lower wage rates in Mexico, many jobs previously susceptible to unionization in the United States have been moved there.

Industrial Changes Much of the decline of union membership can be attributed to the shift in U.S. jobs from industries such as manufacturing, construction, and mining to service industries. Private-sector union membership is primarily concentrated in the shrinking part of the economy, and unions are not making significant inroads into the fastest-growing segments in the U.S. economy. For example, there are small percentages of union members in wholesale/retail industries and financial services, the sectors in which many new jobs have been added, whereas the number of manufacturing jobs continues to shrink. A look at Figure 16-3 shows that nongovernmental union members are heavily concentrated in utilities, transportation and warehousing, and other "industrial" jobs.

Another area that has led to union membership decline is the retirement of many union members in older manufacturing firms. Extremely high retiree pensions and health benefits costs have led employers such as Goodyear Tire, Ford Motor Company, and others to face demands for cuts in benefits for both current and retired union employees. They have also led to employers reducing the number of current plants and workers, and unions attempting to maintain benefits costs and job security for remaining workers.

FIGURE 16-3 Union Membership by Industry in 2011

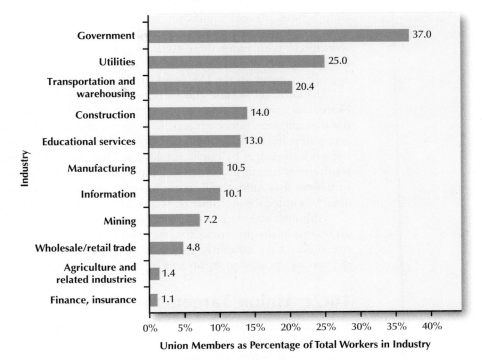

Source: Information compiled from "Union Members Summary" report, *Bureau of Labor Statistics*, January 27, 2012.

Workforce Changes Many of the workforce changes discussed in earlier chapters have contributed to the decrease in union representation of the labor force. The decline in many blue-collar jobs in manufacturing has been especially significant. For instance, the United Auto Workers' membership has dropped from 1.5 million in 1980 to about 600,000 currently.

There are growing numbers of white-collar employees such as clerical workers, insurance claims representatives, data input processors, mental health aides, computer technicians, loan officers, auditors, and retail sales workers. Unions have increased efforts to organize white-collar workers because advances in technology have boosted their numbers in the workforce. However, unions have faced challenges in organizing these workers. Many white-collar workers see unions as resistant to change and not in touch with the concerns of the more educated workers in technical and professional jobs. In addition, many white-collar workers exhibit attitudes and preferences quite different from those held by blue-collar union members, and they tend to view unions as primarily blue-collar oriented.

The growing percentage of women in the U.S. workforce presents another challenge to unions. In the past, unions have not been as successful in organizing female workers as they have been in organizing male workers. Some unions are trying to focus more on recruiting female members, and unions have been in the forefront in the push for legislation on such family-related goals as child care, maternity and paternity leave, pay equity, and flexible work arrangements. Women in "pink-collar," low-skill service jobs have been somewhat more likely to join unions than women working in white-collar jobs.

16-2b Public-Sector Unionism

Unions have enjoyed significant success with public-sector employees. The government sector (federal, state, and local) is the most highly unionized part of the U.S. workforce, with more than 40% of government workers represented by unions. Local (city and county) government workers have the highest unionization percentage of any group in the U.S. workforce.

Unionization of state and local government employees presents some unique problems and challenges. First, some employees work in critical service areas, and it is felt that allowing police officers, firefighters, and sanitation workers to strike endangers public health and safety. Consequently, more than 30 states have laws prohibiting work stoppages by public employees. These laws also identify a variety of ways to resolve negotiation impasses, including arbitration. But government employees seem to believe that unions still give employees in these areas greater security and better ability to influence decisions on wages and benefits compared to nonunion workers.

Although unions in the federal government hold the same basic philosophy as do unions in the private sector, they still differ somewhat. Previous laws and executive orders have established methods of labor/management relations that consider the special circumstances present in the federal government.

16-2c Union Targets for Membership Growth

The continuing losses have led to disagreements among unions about how to fight the decline. Rather than remaining a part of the traditional AFL-CIO labor organization, seven unions split into a new group in 2005. The AFL-CIO is a federation of individual unions that has been the main force in organized labor. Calling itself Change to Win, this association has a goal of taking a more aggressive approach to adding union members and affecting U.S. political legislation.

To attempt to counteract the overall decline in membership, unions are focusing on many industries and types of workers. One reason why Change to Win split off from the AFL-CIO was to more effectively organize individuals working for low wages in the retail, hospitality, home health care, and other service industries.[18]

Professionals Traditionally, professionals in many occupations have been skeptical of unionization. However, the health care industry has experienced a growth in the unionization of professionals such as physicians, physical therapists, and nurses. The primary reason these employees consider union membership is the growth of managed care. A frequent complaint of health care professionals is that they have lost control of patient-care decisions as a result of managed care and the drive to reduce health care costs.

Low-Skilled Workers On the other end of the labor pay scale, unions have targeted low-skilled workers, many of whom have lower-paying, less desirable jobs. Janitors, building cleaners, nursing home aides, and meatpacking workers are examples of groups successfully targeted by unions. For instance, in the health care industry workers in nursing homes dealing with the elderly are a fast-growing segment of the workforce. Many employees in this industry are relatively dissatisfied. The industry is often noted for its low pay and difficult, heavy work, and many employees are women who work as nurses' aides, cooks, and launderers and in other low-wage jobs.

Another group of individuals targeted by unions is immigrant workers in low-skill jobs. Some unions also have been politically active regarding legislation to allow illegal immigrant workers to get work permits and citizenship over time. Although these efforts are not always successful, unions are likely to continue pursuing industries and employers with numerous low-skill jobs and low-skilled workers. The advantages of unionization are especially strong for these employees.

Contingent and Part-Time Workers Since many employers have added contingent workers instead of full-time employees, unions have tried to target part-time, temporary, and other employees. A decision by the National Labor Relations Board (NLRB) allows temporary workers to be included in attempts to unionize firms. Time will tell if the efforts to unionize part-time workers and other groups will halt the decline of union membership in the United States. When unions are present, collective bargaining agreements frequently limit the amount of contingent labor that may be used.

16-3 ■ UNION HISTORY AND STRUCTURE IN THE UNITED STATES

The union movement in the United States has existed in some form or another for more than two centuries. During that time, the nature of unions has evolved because of legal and political changes.

16-3a Evolution of U.S. Unions

The union movement in the United States began with early collective efforts by workers to address job concerns and counteract management power. As early as 1794, shoemakers organized a union, picketed, and conducted strikes. In those days, unions in the United States received very little support from the courts. In 1806, when the shoemakers' union struck for higher wages, a Philadelphia court found union members guilty of engaging in a "criminal conspiracy" to raise wages.

The *American Federation of Labor (AFL)* united several independent national unions in 1886. Its aims were to organize skilled craft workers and to emphasize economic issues and working conditions. As industrialization increased in the United States, many factories used semiskilled and unskilled workers. However, it was not until the *Congress of Industrial Organizations (CIO)* was founded in 1938 that a labor union organization focused on semiskilled and unskilled workers. Years later, the AFL and the CIO merged to become the AFL-CIO. That federation is still the major organization coordinating union efforts in the United States today despite the split described previously.

16-3b Union Structure

Craft union
Union whose members do one type of work, often using specialized skills and training.

Industrial union
Union that includes many persons working in the same industry or company, regardless of jobs held.

Labor in the United States is represented by many unions. Regardless of size and geographic scope, two basic types of unions have developed over time. In a **craft union,** members all do one type of work, often using specialized skills and training. Examples are the International Association of Bridge, Structural, Ornamental and Reinforcing Iron Workers, Electricians, Plumbers, and the American Federation of Television and Radio Artists. An **industrial union** includes many persons working in the same industry or company, regardless of jobs held. The United Food and Commercial Workers, the United Auto Workers, and the American Federation of State, County, and Municipal Employees are examples of industrial unions.

Federation
Group of autonomous unions.

AFL-CIO Federation Labor organizations have developed complex organizational structures with multiple levels. The broadest level is the **federation,** which is a group of autonomous unions. A federation allows individual unions to work together and present a more unified front to the public, legislators, and members. The most prominent federation in the United States is the AFL-CIO, which is a confederation of unions currently representing over 9 million workers.

Change to Win The establishment of Change to Win meant that seven unions with over 5 million members left the AFL-CIO. The primary reason for the split was a division among different unions about how to stop the decline in union membership, as well as some internal organizational leadership and political issues. Prominent unions in the Change to Win are the Teamsters, the Service Employees International Union, and the United Food and Commercial Workers.[19]

National and International Unions National and international unions are not governed by a federation even if they are affiliated with it. They collect dues and have their own boards, specialized publications, and separate constitutions and bylaws. Such unions as the United Steelworkers of America and the American Federation of State, County, and Municipal Employees determine broad union policy and offer services to local union units. They also help maintain financial records and provide a base from which additional organizing drives may take place. Political infighting and corruption sometimes pose problems for national unions, as when the federal government stepped in and overturned the results of an officer election held by the Teamsters Union several years ago.

Like companies, unions find strength in size. In the past several years, about 40 mergers of unions have occurred, and some other unions have considered merging. For smaller unions, these mergers provide financial and organizing resources. Larger unions can add new members to cover managerial and administrative costs rather than having to recruit more members.

Local Unions Local unions may be centered around a particular employer organization or a particular geographic location. The members of local unions elect officers who are subject to removal if they do not perform satisfactorily. For this reason, local union officers tend to be concerned with how they are perceived by the union members. They often react to situations as politicians do because their positions depend on obtaining votes. The local unions are the focus and the heart of labor/management relations in most U.S. labor organizations.

Local unions typically have business agents and union stewards. A **business agent** is a full-time union official who operates the union office and assists union members. The agent runs the local headquarters, helps negotiate contracts with management, and becomes involved in attempts to unionize employees in other organizations. A **union steward** is an employee who is elected to serve as the first-line representative of unionized workers. Stewards address grievances with supervisors and generally represent employees at the worksite.

Business agent
A full-time union official who operates the union office and assists union members.

Union steward
Employee elected to serve as the first-line representative of unionized workers.

L04 Explain the nature of each of the major U.S. labor laws.

16-4 ■ U.S. LABOR LAWS

The right to organize workers and engage in collective bargaining offers little value if workers cannot freely exercise it. Management has consistently developed practices to prevent unions from organizing employees. Over a period of many years, the federal government has taken action both to hamper unions and to protect them.

16-4a Early Labor Legislation

Beginning in the late 1800s, federal and state legislation related to unionization was passed. The two most prominent acts are discussed next.

Railway Labor Act The Railway Labor Act (RLA) of 1926 represented a shift in government regulation of unions. The result of a joint effort between railroad management and unions to reduce transportation strikes, this act gave railroad employees "the right to organize and bargain collectively through representatives of their own choosing." In 1936, airlines and their employees were added to those covered by the RLA. Some experts believe that some of the labor relations problems in the airline industry stem from the provisions of the RLA, and that those problems would be more easily resolved if the airlines fell within the labor laws covering most other industries.

The RLA mandates a complex and cumbersome dispute-resolution process. This process allows either the unions or the management to use the National Labor Relations Board, a multistage dispute-resolution process, and even the power of the President of the United States to appoint an emergency board. The end result of having a prolonged process that is subject to political interference has been that unions often work for two or more years after the expiration of their old contracts because the process takes a long time.

Norris-LaGuardia Act The crash of the stock market and the onset of the Great Depression in 1929 led to massive cutbacks by employers. In some industries, the resistance by employees led to strikes and violence. Under laws at that time, employers could go to court and have a federal judge issue injunctions ordering workers to return to work. In 1932, Congress passed the Norris-LaGuardia Act, which guaranteed workers some rights to organize and restricted the issuance of court injunctions in labor disputes.

The Next Stage The economic crises of the early 1930s and the continuing restrictions on workers' ability to organize into unions led to the passage of landmark labor legislation, the Wagner Act, in 1935. Later acts reflected other pressures and issues that required legislative attention. Three acts passed over a period of almost 25 years constitute the U.S. labor law foundation: (1) the Wagner Act, (2) the Taft-Hartley Act, and (3) the Landrum-Griffin Act. Each act was passed to focus on some facet of the relations between unions and management. Figure 16-4 indicates the primary focus of each act. Two other pieces of legislation, the Civil Service Reform Act and the Postal Reorganization Act, also have affected only the governmental aspects of union/management relations.

16-4b Wagner Act (National Labor Relations Act)

The National Labor Relations Act, more commonly referred to as the Wagner Act, has been called the Magna Carta of labor and was, by anyone's standards, pro-union. Passed in 1935, the Wagner Act was an outgrowth of the Great Depression. With employers having to close or cut back their operations, workers were left with little job security. Unions stepped in to provide a feeling of solidarity and strength for many workers. The Wagner Act declared, in effect, that the official policy of the U.S. government was to encourage collective bargaining. Specifically, it established the right of workers to organize, unhampered by management interference, through unfair labor practices.

FIGURE 16-4 Major National Labor Laws

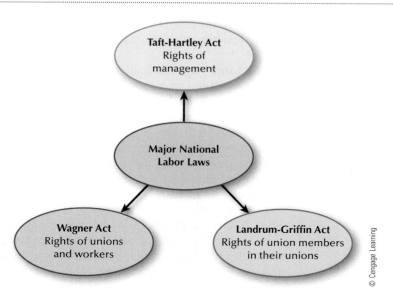

Unfair Labor Practices To protect union rights, the Wagner Act prohibited employers from using unfair labor practices. Five of those practices were identified as follows:

- Interfering with, restraining, or coercing employees in the exercise of their right to organize or to bargain collectively
- Dominating or interfering with the formation or administration of any labor organization
- Encouraging or discouraging membership in any labor organization by discriminating with regard to hiring, tenure, or conditions of employment
- Discharging or otherwise discriminating against an employee because the employee filed charges or gave testimony under the act
- Refusing to bargain collectively with representatives of the employees

National Labor Relations Board The Wagner Act established the National Labor Relations Board as an independent entity to enforce the provisions of the act. The NLRB administers all provisions of the Wagner Act and of subsequent labor relations acts. The primary functions of the NLRB include conducting unionization elections, investigating complaints by employers or unions through its fact-finding process, issuing opinions on its findings, and prosecuting violations in court. The five members of the NLRB are appointed by the President of the United States and confirmed by the U.S. Senate.

16-4c Taft-Hartley Act (Labor Management Relations Act)

The passage in 1947 of the Labor Management Relations Act, better known as the Taft-Hartley Act, was accomplished as a means to offset the pro-union Wagner Act by limiting union actions. It was considered to be pro-management and became the second of the major labor laws.

The new law amended or qualified in some respect all the major provisions of the Wagner Act and established an entirely new code of conduct for unions. The Taft-Hartley Act forbade unions from engaging in a series of unfair labor practices, much like those prohibitions on management behavior. Coercion, discrimination against nonmembers, refusing to bargain, excessive membership fees, and other practices were not allowed by unions. A 1974 amendment extended coverage of the Taft-Hartley Act to private, nonprofit hospitals and nursing homes.

The Taft-Hartley Act also established the Federal Mediation and Conciliation Service (FMCS) as an agency to help management and labor settle labor-contract disputes. The act required that the FMCS be notified of disputes over contract renewals or modifications if they were not settled within 30 days after the designated date.

National Emergency Strikes The Taft-Hartley Act allows the President of the United States to declare that a strike presents a national emergency. A national emergency strike is one that would impact an industry or a major part of it in such a way that the national economy would be significantly affected. The act allows the U.S. President to declare an 80-day cooling-off period during which union and management continue negotiations. Only after that period can a strike occur if settlements have not been reached.

Over the decades, national emergencies have been identified in the railroad, airline, and other industries. For example, the national emergency provisions were involved in a strike of transportation and dock workers throughout the U.S. West Coast states. During the 80-day period, a contract agreement was reached, so a strike was averted.

Right-to-Work Provision One provision of the Taft-Hartley Act, section 14(b), deserves special explanation. This section allows states to pass laws that restrict compulsory union membership. Accordingly, several states have passed **right-to-work laws**, which prohibit requiring employees to join unions as a condition of obtaining or continuing employment. The laws were so named because they allow a person the right to work without having to join a union.

The states that have enacted these laws are shown in Figure 16-5. After much political jockeying, Indiana became the 23rd state, and the first in the Rust Belt, to enact a right-to-work provision, and similar battles are being staged in Montana and New Hampshire.[20] Union representatives encouraged members to keep paying their union dues in new right-to-work status so that organized labor still has a strong voice in the state. However, many members may be motivated to drop their memberships because of their political beliefs or personal finances.[21] Michigan voted to become the 24th right-to-work state, and the HR Perspective: Michigan Passes 24th Right-to-Work Provision discusses this development.

In states with right-to-work laws, employers may have an **open shop**, which indicates workers cannot be required to join or pay dues to a union. Thus, even though a union may represent a group of employees at a company, individual workers cannot be required or coerced to join the union or pay dues. Consequently, in many of the right-to-work states, individual membership in union groups is significantly lower.

The National Right to Work Legal Defense Foundation is an organization that has lobbied for more states to become right-to-work states. Also, that organization

Right-to-work laws
State laws that prohibit requiring employees to join unions as a condition of obtaining or continuing employment.

Open shop
Firm in which workers are not required to join or pay dues to a union.

FIGURE 16-5 Right-to-Work States

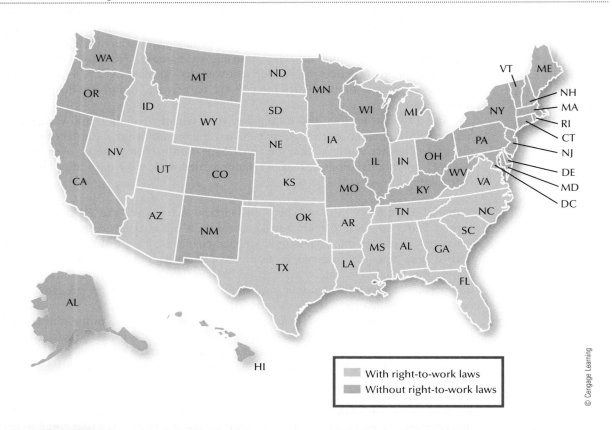

With right-to-work laws

Without right-to-work laws

© Cengage Learning

HR PERSPECTIVE

Michigan Passes 24th Right-to-Work Provision

Michigan became the 24th right-to-work state, which will greatly reduce the role of unions representing workers in both public and private organizations in this traditionally prolabor area of the country. The State House of Representatives voted 58-51 in favor of a provision that prevents unions from requiring government employees to become members to get hired. In other words, membership dues can be paid by workers on a voluntary basis to support union activities. A similar bill was voted in 58-52 for employees operating in the private sector and establishes similar standards. Governor Rick Snyder was supportive of the legislation because it empowers workers to make their own choices.

The passage of this legislation is not without its detractors. Thousands of protestors gathered outside the Capitol building to express their concerns about the state's new right-to-work agenda. Access to the Capitol was closed because the building was beyond capacity, so individuals had to gather in the surrounding areas. The debate in the House prompted negative outcries from some protestors, and some individuals expressed their discontent outside Snyder's office. Many demonstrators even became aggressive and unruly, requiring police to make several arrests to reduce tensions. These incidents show just how heated debates over right-to-work provisions can become.[22]

has become involved in lawsuits where workers have claimed to have been coerced to join unions. According to one official from the National Right to Work Committee, politicians who are against right-to-work provisions or are union-friendly make passing such legislation difficult.[23]

Closed shop
Firm that requires individuals to join a union before they can be hired.

The nature of union/management relations is affected by the right-to-work provisions of the Taft-Hartley Act. Right-to-work generally prohibits the **closed shop**, which requires individuals to join a union before they can be hired. Because of concerns that a closed shop allows a union to control who may be considered for employment and who must be hired by an employer, section 14(b) prohibits the closed shop except in construction-related occupations.

In states that do not have right-to-work laws, different types of arrangements exist. Three of the different types of "shops" are as follows:

- *Union shop*: Arrangement requires that individuals join the union, usually 30 to 60 days after being hired.
- *Agency shop*: Arrangement makes workers who don't join the union to make payments equal to union dues and fees to get union representation services.
- *Maintenance-of-membership shop*: Requires workers to remain members of the union for the period of the labor contract

The nature of the shop is negotiated between the union and the employer. Employees who fail to meet the requirements are often terminated from their jobs.

16-4d Landrum-Griffin Act (Labor Management Reporting and Disclosure Act)

The third of the major labor laws in the United States, the Landrum-Griffin Act, was passed in 1959. Since a union is supposed to be a democratic institution in which union members freely vote, elect officers, and approve labor contracts, the Landrum-Griffin Act was passed in part to ensure that the federal government protects the democratic rights of the members. Under the Landrum-Griffin Act, unions are required to establish bylaws, make financial reports, and provide union members with a bill of rights. The law appointed the U.S. Secretary of Labor to act as a watchdog of union conduct.

There is a need for such legislative oversight to protect individual union members. For instance, in some situations union officers have been known to physically harass individuals who didn't like them. In other cases, officials have seized union resources and used them for their own personal gain.

16-4e Civil Service Reform and Postal Reorganization Acts

Passed as part of the Civil Service Reform Act of 1978, the Federal Service Labor Management Relations statute made major changes in how the federal government deals with unions. The act also identified areas subject to bargaining and established the Federal Labor Relations Authority (FLRA) as an independent agency similar to the NLRB. The FLRA, a three-member body, was given the authority to oversee and administer union/management relations in the federal government and investigate unfair practices in union organizing efforts.

In a somewhat related area, the Postal Reorganization Act of 1970 established the U.S. Postal Service as an independent entity. Part of the 1970 act prohibited postal workers from striking and established a dispute-resolution process for them to follow.

16-4f Proposed Employee Free Choice Act

The Employee Free Choice Act would allow unions to sign up workers on cards (referred to as "card check") and become recognized without an election by secret ballot.[24] As a result, the "campaigns" to organize that unions dislike would be eliminated because simply getting 50% of the workers in a unit to sign a card would be sufficient to bring in the union.[25] Further, the proposed law would require a contract to be negotiated within a certain time period or one could be imposed by an arbitrator.[26] Employers take issue with this approach because it goes against the U.S. tradition in which negotiated contracts must be agreed to by both parties.

L05 Describe the stages of the unionization process and the typical collective bargaining process.

16-5 ■ THE UNIONIZATON PROCESS

The typical union organizing process is outlined in Figure 16-6. The process of unionizing an employer may begin in one of two primary ways: (1) a union targeting an industry or a company, or (2) employees requesting union representation. In the first case, the local or national union identifies a firm or an industry in which it believes unionization can succeed. The logic for targeting is that if the union succeeds in one firm or a portion of the industry, then many other workers in the industry will be more willing to consider unionizing. In the second case, the impetus for union organizing occurs when individual workers at an employer contact a union and express a desire to unionize. The employees themselves—and/or the union—may then begin to campaign to win support among the other employees.

16-5a Organizing Campaign

Like other entities seeking members, a union usually mounts an organized campaign to persuade individuals to join. As would be expected, employers respond to unionization efforts by taking various types of opposing actions.

Employers' Union Prevention Efforts Management representatives may use various tactics to defeat a unionization effort. Such tactics often begin when union publicity appears or during the distribution of authorization cards. Some employers such as Con Agra, Coca-Cola, and Wal-Mart hire consultants who specialize in combating unionization efforts. Using these "union busters," as they are called by unions, appears to enhance employers' chances of winning the representation election. Union prevention efforts that may be conducted by

FIGURE 16-6 Typical Unionization Process

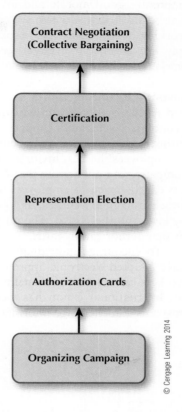

consultants or done by management and outside labor attorneys include the following:[27]

- Holding mandatory employee meetings
- Distributing antiunion leaflets at work and mailing antiunion letters to employees' homes
- Providing and using antiunion videos, e-mails, and other electronic communications

Many employers have created a "no-solicitation" policy to restrict employees and outsiders from distributing literature or soliciting union membership on company premises. Employers without such a policy may be unable to prevent those acts. A policy against solicitation must be a long-term, established approach, not a single action taken to counter a specific and immediate unionization attempt. For example, a Steelworkers union sought certification by the NLRB to be the bargaining agent at an Ohio facility. After the union lost the election by one vote, it protested that the company had interfered with the right to organize when just before the election it adopted a rule prohibiting the posting of pro-union material on an employee bulletin board. The NLRB set aside the first election, and the company lost the second election.

Employers may make strategic decisions and take aggressive steps to remain nonunion. Such a choice is perfectly rational, but may require some specific

HR policies and philosophies. For example, "preventive" employee relations may emphasize good morale and loyalty based on concern for employees, competitive wages and benefits, a fair system for dealing with employee complaints, and safe working conditions. Other issues may also play a part in employees' decisions to stay nonunion, but if employers adequately address the points just listed, fewer workers are likely to feel the need for a union to represent them.

Unions' Organizing Efforts The organizing and negotiating successes of unions are tied to the economy and economic trends. For example, see the HR Perspective: Economic Cycles and Unions. The persuasion efforts by unions can take many forms, including personally contacting employees outside work, mailing materials to employees' homes, inviting employees to attend special meetings away from the company, and publicizing the advantages of union membership. Brochures and leaflets can be given to employees as they leave work, mailed to their homes, or even attached to their vehicles, as long as the union complies with the rules established by laws and the NLRB. The purpose of all this publicity is to encourage employees to sign authorization cards.

To encourage individuals to become involved in unionization efforts, unions have adopted electronic approaches, such as establishing websites where interested workers can read about benefits of unionization. For instance, the Service Employees International Union has websites and chat rooms where nurses at nonunion hospitals can exchange information with unionized nurses. Change to Win and the

HR PERSPECTIVE

Economic Cycles and Unions

Employees get involved with unions because they believe these organizations can help improve their situations in the workplace. Under some circumstances, unions can function as a positive sounding board for the concerns of employees, and union representation can encourage employers to better support their workers. Even though there has been an overall reduction in union membership, unions might be able to once again improve employees' work experiences.

Such conditions could be present now. For instance, the recession weakened employees' bargaining power, a trend that is likely to continue. More jobs in the United States will be freelance and temporary with less emphasis on permanent positions, similar to the situation in

Europe. Employers create just-in-time workforces that can be turned on and off, allowing them to reduce fixed costs. That means companies have an edge in bargaining power, and the risks are pushed to employees.

Certainly not all workers are pleased with such jobs, but in bad times they have little choice, and unions have little opportunity. However, looking into the future, it is possible to see that better times may be coming for labor. In a decade, retirement of the baby boomers could cause labor shortages. A shortage of workers was widely noted before the last recession, and the underlying dynamic has not gone away. The idea of loyalty to an employer has effectively disappeared in many places, and the mechanisms for labor's return remain intact—waiting for better times.[28]

AFL-CIO both have weblinks and blogs available through their websites to provide union information online. These sites explain workers' rights and give examples of the advantages of being union members. Successes in unionizing groups of employees are described. Also, the differences between wages, benefits, and job security are contrasted before and after unionization occurred.

Salting
Practice in which unions hire and pay people to apply for jobs at certain companies to begin organizing efforts.

Unions sometimes pay organizers to infiltrate a targeted employer and try to organize workers. In this practice, known as **salting,** the unions hire and pay people to apply for jobs at certain companies; when the people are hired, they begin organizing efforts. The U.S. Supreme Court has ruled that refusing to hire otherwise-qualified applicants, solely because they are also paid by a union, violates the Wagner Act. However, employers may refuse to hire "salts" for job-related and nondiscriminatory reasons.[29]

16-5b Authorization Cards

Union authorization card
Card signed by employees to designate a union as their collective bargaining agent.

A **union authorization card** is signed by employees to designate a union as their collective bargaining agent. At least 30% of the employees in the targeted group must sign authorization cards before an election can be called.

Union advocates have lobbied for changing laws so that elections are not needed if more than 50% of the eligible employees sign authorization cards. As mentioned earlier, the proposed Employee Free Choice Act would eliminate the secret ballot for electing union representation and make it so that the union would automatically represent all workers if more than 50% of the employees signed authorization cards. Some states have enacted such laws for public-sector unionization. Also, some employers have taken a neutral approach and agreed to recognize unions if a majority of workers sign authorization cards. Some employers' agreements allow for authorization card checks to be done by a neutral outside party to verify union membership.

However, the fact that an employee signs an authorization card does not necessarily mean that the employee is in favor of a union. It means only that the employee would like the opportunity to vote on having a union. Employees who do not want a union might sign authorization cards because they want management to know they are disgruntled or because they want to avoid upsetting coworkers who are advocating unionization.

Employers and some politicians argue that eliminating elections violates the personal secrecy and democracy rights of employees. The extent of legislative changes will depend on the political composition of the U.S. Congress and presidential reactions to such efforts.

16-5c Representation Election

An election to determine if a union will represent the employees is supervised by the NLRB for private-sector organizations and by other legal bodies for public-sector organizations. If two unions are attempting to represent employees, the employees will have three choices: union A, union B, and no union.

Bargaining unit
Employees eligible to select a single union to represent and bargain collectively for them.

Bargaining Unit Before any election, the appropriate bargaining unit must be determined. A **bargaining unit** is composed of all employees eligible to select a single union to represent and bargain collectively for them. If management and the union do not agree on who is and who is not included in the unit, the regional office of the NLRB must make the determination. A major criterion in deciding the composition of a bargaining unit is what the NLRB calls a "community of interest." For example, at a warehouse distribution firm, delivery drivers, accounting clerks, computer programmers, and mechanics would probably not be included in the same bargaining unit; these employees have widely varying jobs, areas of work, physical locations, and other differences that would likely negate a community of interest. Employees who constitute a bargaining unit have mutual interests in the following areas:

- Wages, hours, and working conditions
- Traditional industry groupings for bargaining purposes
- Physical location and amount of interaction and working relationships between employee groups
- Supervision by similar levels of management

Supervisors and Union Ineligibility Provisions of the National Labor Relations Act exclude supervisors from voting for or joining unions. As a result, supervisors cannot be included in bargaining units for unionization purposes, except in industries covered by the Railway Labor Act. But who qualifies as a supervisor is not always clear. The NLRB expanded its definition to identify a supervisor as any individual with authority to hire, transfer, discharge, discipline, and use independent judgment with employees. Numerous NLRB and court decisions have been rendered on the specifics of different situations. A major case decided by the U.S. Supreme Court found that charge nurses with RN degrees were supervisors because they exercised independent judgment. This case and others have provided employers and unions with some guidance about who should be considered supervisors and thus excluded from bargaining units.[30]

Election Unfair Labor Practices Employers and unions engage in many activities before an election. Both the Wagner Act and the Taft-Hartley Act place restrictions on these activities. Once unionizing efforts begin, all activities must conform to the requirements established by applicable labor laws. Both management and the union must adhere to those requirements, or the results of the effort can be appealed to the NLRB and overturned. The HR Skills and Applications: Unionization Do's and Don'ts highlights some of the legal and illegal actions managers must be aware of during unionization efforts.

Election Process If an election is held, the union needs to receive only a majority of the votes. For example, if a group of 200 employees is the identified bargaining unit, and only 50 people vote, only 26 (50% of those voting plus 1) need to vote yes for the union to be named as the representative of all 200 employees. Typically, the smaller the number of employees in the bargaining unit, the higher the likelihood that the union will win.

If either side believes that the other side used unfair labor practices, the election results can be appealed to the NLRB. If the NLRB finds evidence of unfair practices, it can order a new election. If no unfair practices were used and the union obtains a majority in the election, the union then petitions the NLRB for certification.

16-5d Certification and Decertification

Official certification of a union as the legal representative for designated private-sector employees is given by the NLRB, or for public-sector employees by an equivalent body. Once certified, the union attempts to negotiate a contract with the employer. The employer *must* bargain; refusing to bargain with a certified union constitutes an unfair labor practice.

HR SKILLS AND APPLICATIONS

Unionization Do's and Don'ts

Employers can take numerous actions to prevent unionization. All managers and supervisors must adhere to NLRB and other requirements to avoid unfair labor practices. Listed below are some common do's and don'ts.

✓ DO (LEGAL)

- Tell employees how current wages and benefits compare with those in other firms.
- Tell employees why the employer opposes unionization.
- Tell employees the disadvantages of having a union (dues, assessments, etc.)
- Show employees articles about unions and relate negative experiences elsewhere.
- Explain the unionization process to employees accurately.
- Forbid distribution of union literature during work hours in work areas.

- Enforce disciplinary policies and rules consistently and appropriately.

✗ DON'T (ILLEGAL)

- Tell employees that they will be given pay increases or promotions if they vote against the union.
- Suggest that the company will close down or move if a union is voted in.
- Monitor union meetings.
- Make a speech to employees or groups at work within 24 hours of the election. (Before that, it is allowed.)
- Ask employees how they plan to vote or if they have signed authorization cards.
- Encourage employees to persuade others to vote against the union.
- Tell employees that they will be terminated or disciplined if they advocate the union.

Decertification
Process whereby a union is removed as the representative of a group of employees.

When members no longer wish to be represented by the union, they can use the election process to sever the relationship between themselves and the union. Similar to the unionization process, **decertification** is a process whereby a union is removed as the representative of a group of employees. Employees attempting to oust a union must obtain decertification authorization cards signed by at least 30% of the employees in the bargaining unit before an election may be called. If a majority of those voting in the election want to remove the union, the decertification effort succeeds. Some reasons that employees might decide to vote out a union are that the treatment provided by employers has improved, the union has been unable to address the changing needs of the organizational workforce, or the image of the union has declined. Current regulations prohibit employers from initiating or supporting decertification because it is a matter between employees and unions, and employers must stay out of the process.

Collective bargaining
Process whereby representatives of management and workers negotiate over wages, hours, and other terms and conditions of employment.

16-5e Contract Negotiation (Collective Bargaining)

Collective bargaining, the last step in unionization, is the process whereby representatives of management and workers negotiate over wages, hours, and other terms and conditions of employment. This give-and-take process between representatives

FIGURE 16-7 Continuum of Collective Bargaining Relations

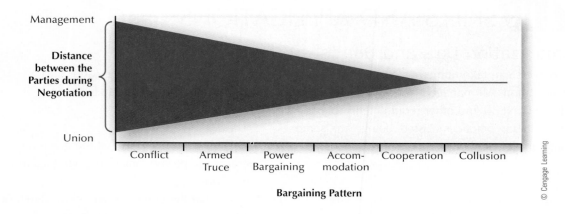

of the two organizations attempts to establish conditions beneficial to both. It is also a relationship based on relative power.

Management/union relations in collective bargaining can follow one of several patterns. Figure 16-7 depicts them as a continuum, ranging from conflict to collusion. On the left side of the continuum, management and the union see each other as enemies. On the right side, the two entities join in collusion, which is relatively rare in U.S. labor history and is illegal. Most positions fall between these two extremes.

The power relationship in collective bargaining involves conflict, and the threat of conflict seems necessary to maintain the relationship. But perhaps the most significant aspect of collective bargaining is that it is a continuing relationship that does not end immediately after agreement is reached. Instead, it continues for the life of the labor agreement and beyond.[31] Therefore, the more cooperative management is, the less hostility and conflict with unionized employees will be present to carry over into the workplace. However, this cooperation does not mean that the employer agrees to all union demands.

16-6 ■ COLLECTIVE BARGAINING ISSUES

A number of issues can be addressed during collective bargaining. Although not often listed as such in the contract, management rights and union security are two important issues subject to collective bargaining. These and other issues, common to collective bargaining, are discussed next.

16-6a Management Rights

Management rights
Rights reserved so that the employer can manage, direct, and control its business.

Virtually all labor contracts include **management rights**, which are rights reserved so that the employer can manage, direct, and control its business. By including such a provision, management attempts to preserve its unilateral right to make changes in areas not identified in a labor contract. A typical provision might read as follows:

> *The employer retains all rights to manage, direct, and control its business in all particulars, except as such rights are expressly and specifically modified by the terms of this or any subsequent agreement.*

16-6b Union Security

A major concern of union representatives when bargaining is the negotiation of **union security provisions,** which are contract clauses to help the union obtain and retain members. One type of union security clause in labor contracts is the *no-layoff policy,* or *job security guarantee.* Such a provision is especially important to many union workers because of all the mergers, downsizings, and job reductions taking place in many industrial, textile, and manufacturing firms. However, for these very reasons, management is often unwilling to consider this type of provision.

Union Dues Issues A common union security provision is the *dues checkoff* clause, which provides for the automatic deduction of union dues from the payroll checks of union members. The dues checkoff provision makes it much easier for the union to collect its funds, and without it, the union must collect dues by billing each member separately.

However, unions' ability to use such checkoff clauses for contributions to political and congressional candidates has been challenged in federal court. A U.S. Supreme Court case supported the constitutionality of state laws that require labor unions to get written consent before using nonmember fees for political purposes. The court noted that agency shop agreements were acceptable, and that public-sector unions could levy fees on nonmember employees. However, it was also noted that unions need to obtain authorization from nonmembers when agency fees are being used to support political campaigns.

Types of Required Union Membership Another form of union security provision is *requiring union membership* of all employees, subject to state right-to-work laws. As mentioned earlier, a closed shop is illegal except in limited situations within the construction industry. But other types of arrangements can be developed, including union shops, agency shops, and maintenance-of-membership shops, which were discussed earlier.

16-6c Classification of Bargaining Issues

The NLRB has defined collective bargaining issues in three ways. The categories it has used are mandatory, permissive, and illegal.

Mandatory Issues Issues identified specifically by labor laws or court decisions as subject to bargaining are **mandatory issues.** If either party demands that issues in this category be subject to bargaining, then that must occur. Generally, mandatory issues relate to wages, benefits, nature of jobs, and other work-related subjects. Mandatory subjects for bargaining include the following:

- Discharge of employees
- Grievances
- Work schedules
- Union security and dues checkoff
- Retirement and pension coverage
- Vacations and time off
- Rest and lunch break rules
- Safety rules
- Profit-sharing plans
- Required physical exam

Permissive issues
Collective bargaining issues that are not mandatory and that relate to certain jobs.

Illegal issues
Collective bargaining issues that would require either party to take illegal action.

Permissive Issues Issues that are not mandatory and that relate to certain jobs are **permissive issues**. For example, the following issues can be bargained over if both parties agree: benefits for retired employees, product prices for employees, and performance bonds.

Illegal Issues A final category, **illegal issues**, includes those issues that would require either party to take illegal action. Examples would be giving preference to union members when hiring employees or demanding a closed-shop provision in the contract. If one side wants to bargain over an illegal issue, the other side can refuse.

16-7 ■ COLLECTIVE BARGAINING PROCESS

The collective bargaining process involved in negotiating a contract consists of four possible stages: preparation and initial demands, negotiations, settlement or impasse, and strikes and lockouts. Throughout the process, management and labor deal with the terms of their relationship.

16-7a Preparation and Initial Demands

Both labor and management representatives spend considerable time preparing for negotiations.[32] Employer and industry data concerning wages, benefits, working conditions, management and union rights, productivity, and absenteeism are gathered. If the organization argues that it cannot afford to pay what the union is asking, the employer's financial situation and accompanying data become relevant to the process. However, the union must request such information before the employer is obligated to provide it. Typical bargaining includes initial proposals of expectations by both sides. The amount of rancor or calmness exhibited may set the tone for future negotiations between the parties.

Core Bargaining Issues The primary focus of bargaining for both union and management is on the core areas of wages, benefits, and working hours and conditions. The importance of this emphasis is seen in several ways.

Union wages and benefits generally are higher in unionized firms than in nonunionized firms. As shown in Figure 16-8, in a recent year median earnings for union members were $938/week compared with the nonunion amount of $729/week. The additional $209/week represents over $10,000/year more for union members' wages than nonunion wages. It is common for wages and benefits to be higher in unionized firms.

16-7b Continuing Negotiations

After taking initial positions, each side attempts to determine what the other side values highly so that the best bargain can be struck. For example, the union may be asking the employer to pay for dental benefits as part of a package that also includes wage increases and retirement benefits. However, the union may be most interested in the retirement benefits and may be willing to trade the dental payments for better retirement benefits. Management must determine what the union has as a priority and decide exactly what to give up.

FIGURE 16-8 Weekly Earnings of Union and Nonunion Workers

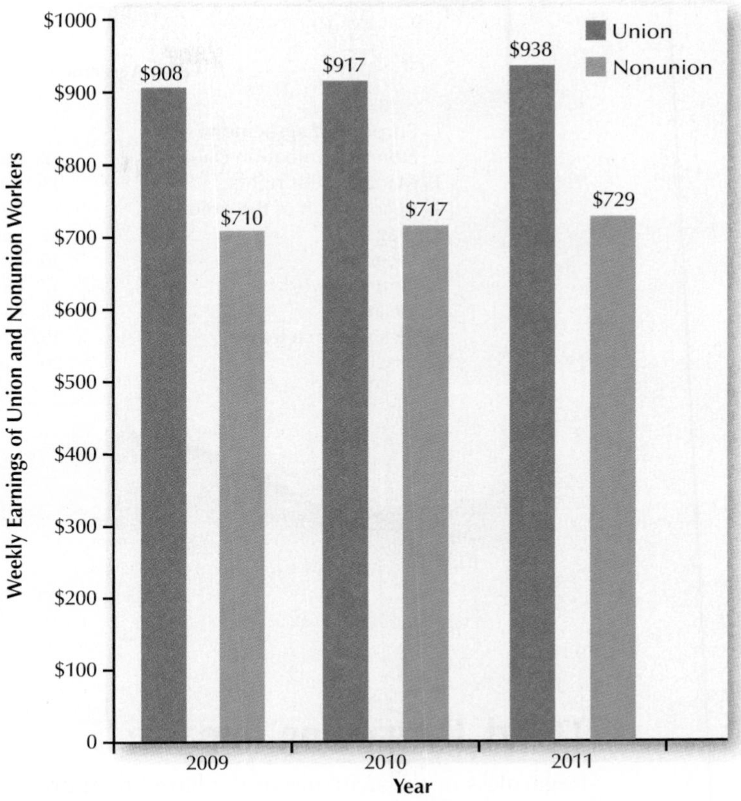

Source: Information compiled from "Union Members Summary" report, *Bureau of Labor Statistics*, January 27, 2012.

Good Faith Provisions in federal law require that both employers and union bargaining representatives negotiate in good faith. In good-faith negotiations, the parties agree to send negotiators who can bargain and make decisions, rather than people who do not have the authority to commit either group to a decision. To be more effective, meetings between the parties should be conducted professionally and address issues, rather than being confrontational. Refusing to bargain, scheduling meetings at absurdly inconvenient hours, and using other conflicting tactics may lead to employers or unions filing complaints with the NLRB.

16-7c Settlement and Contract Agreement

Ratification
Process by which union
members vote to accept
the terms of a negotiated
labor agreement.

After reaching an initial agreement, the bargaining parties usually return to their respective constituencies to determine if the informal agreement is acceptable. A particularly crucial stage is **ratification** of the labor agreement, which occurs when union members vote to accept the terms of a negotiated labor agreement. Before ratification, the union negotiating team explains the agreement to the union members and presents it for a vote. If the members approve the agreement, it is then formalized into a contract. Figure 16-9 lists the typical items in a labor agreement.

FIGURE 16-9 Typical Items in a Labor Agreement

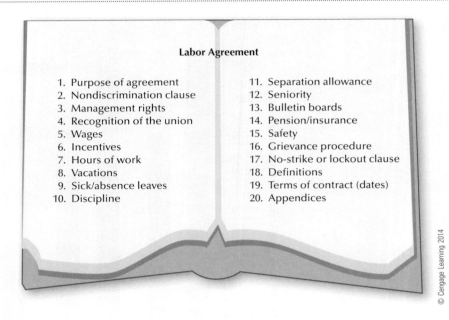

Labor Agreement

1. Purpose of agreement
2. Nondiscrimination clause
3. Management rights
4. Recognition of the union
5. Wages
6. Incentives
7. Hours of work
8. Vacations
9. Sick/absence leaves
10. Discipline

11. Separation allowance
12. Seniority
13. Bulletin boards
14. Pension/insurance
15. Safety
16. Grievance procedure
17. No-strike or lockout clause
18. Definitions
19. Terms of contract (dates)
20. Appendices

© Cengage Learning 2014

16-7d Bargaining Impasse

Regardless of the structure of the bargaining process, labor and management do not always reach agreement on the issues. If they reach an impasse, then the disputes can be taken to conciliation, mediation, or arbitration.

Conciliation

Process by which a third party assists union and management negotiators to reach a voluntary settlement.

Conciliation and Mediation When an impasse occurs, an outside party such as the Federal Mediation and Conciliation Service may help the two deadlocked parties to continue negotiations and arrive at a solution. In **conciliation**, the third party assists union and management negotiators to reach a voluntary settlement, but makes no proposals for solutions. In **mediation**, the third party may suggest ideas for solutions to help the negotiators reach a settlement.

In conciliation and mediation, the third party does not attempt to impose a solution. Sometimes fact finding helps to clarify the issues of disagreement as an intermediate step between mediation and arbitration.

Mediation

Process by which a third party helps the negotiators reach a settlement.

Arbitration

Process that uses a neutral third party to make a decision.

Arbitration In **arbitration**, a neutral third party makes a decision. Arbitration can be conducted by an individual or a panel of individuals. "Interest" arbitration attempts to solve bargaining impasses, primarily in the public sector. This type of arbitration is not frequently used in the private sector because companies generally do not want an outside party making decisions about their rights, wages, benefits, and other issues. However, grievance or "rights" arbitration is used extensively in the private sector. Fortunately, in many situations, agreements are reached through negotiations without the need for arbitration. When disagreements continue, strikes or lockouts may occur.

16-7e Strikes, Lockouts, and Other Tactics

Strike
Work stoppage in which union members refuse to work in order to put pressure on an employer.

If a deadlock cannot be resolved, an employer may revert to a lockout—or a union may revert to a strike. During a **strike**, union members refuse to work to put pressure on an employer. Often, the striking union members picket or demonstrate against the employer outside the place of business by carrying placards and signs. Despite current trends, evidence suggests some employees are using the strike because they believe their interests are not being adequately considered by politicians, organizations, and managers. According to information compiled by the Bureau of Labor Statistics, there were 11 significant work stoppages in one recent year and 19 incidents occurred in the next year. Recent strikes have occurred at many Wal-Mart stores because employees believe that company does not care enough about its workers. In addition, employers are concerned about compensation and scheduling.[33] See the HR Perspective: No More Twinkies, At Least for Now for another example of an employee strike at Hostess Brands.

HR PERSPECTIVE

No More Twinkies, At Least for Now

The 83-year-old company Hostess Brands, makers of Twinkies, Ho Hos, Ding Dongs, Sno Balls, Hostess Cupcakes, and many other well-known baked products, recently decided to close its doors because of failed negotiations with one of its major unions, the Bakery, Confectionery, Tobacco Workers and Grain Millers International Union. Members participated in a strike that was prompted by grievances over wage and benefit cuts, which adversely impacted the company's ability to manufacture and ship goods. Employees would need to take an 8% decrease in pay and a 20% increase in what they pay for benefits to help the company turnaround.

Hostess shut down several manufacturing plants in response to the strike, and several days after the closings, stated that the firm would cease operating completely and liquidate if enough employees did not come back to their jobs. An agreement unfortunately was not reached, and the company halted all of its operations and sought permission from the U.S. Bankruptcy Court to liquidate its brands and other assets, as well as to lay off its workforce of 18,500 employees.

The company blamed the closure on union involvement in wage and benefit disagreements and rising debt. The union blamed the company's woes on low interest in technological advancements and an overemphasis on generating profits for the hedge funds that own Hostess Brands. CEO Gregory F. Rayburn indicated that he was optimistic about the firm being able to sell it product lines to other organizations, and there is speculation that other food producers such as McKee Foods (makers of Little Debbie products), Bimbo Bakeries (makers of Entenmann's baked goods), and ConAgra could be involved in brand buy outs.

The closure of Hostess Brands prompted a buying spree among customers. Retail stores saw their remaining stock of Twinkies and other Hostess products fly off the shelves because people didn't know when or if they would be able to enjoy these snacks again. Customers' feelings about the shut down were also downbeat, which illustrates the negative impact of failed union-management negotiations for all concerned.[34]

Lockout
Shutdown of company operations undertaken by management to prevent union members from working.

In a **lockout**, management shuts down company operations to prevent union members from working. This action may avert possible damage or sabotage to company facilities or injury to employees who continue to work. It also gives management leverage in negotiations.

Types of Strikes Five types of strikes can occur:

- *Economic strikes* happen when the parties fail to reach agreement during collective bargaining.
- *Unfair labor practices strikes* occur when union members leave their jobs over what they feel are illegal employer actions, such as refusal to bargain.
- *Wildcat strikes* occur during the life of the collective-bargaining agreement without approval of union leadership and violate a no-strike clause in a labor contract. Strikers can be discharged or disciplined.
- *Jurisdictional strikes* exist when members of one union walk out to force the employer to assign work to them instead of to members of another union.
- *Sympathy strikes* take place when one union chooses to express support for another union involved in a dispute, even though the first union has no disagreement with the employer.

As a result of the decline in union power, work stoppages due to strikes and lockouts are relatively rare. In a recent year, all national strikes were settled quickly. Many unions are reluctant to go on strike because of the financial losses their members would incur or the fear that a strike would cause the employer to go bankrupt. In addition, management has shown its willingness to hire replacements, and some strikes have ended with union workers losing their jobs.

Replacement of Workers on Strike Management retains and sometimes uses its ability to simply replace workers who strike. These replacements are called "scabs." Workers' rights vary depending on the type of strike that occurs. For example, in an economic strike, an employer is free to replace the striking workers. But with an unfair labor practices strike, the workers who want their jobs back at the end of the strike must be reinstated.

Other Tactics Besides picketing and strikes, unions and their members might resort to unorthodox or even aggressive practices to express their discontent about employer practices and advance their pro-labor agenda. For instance, many organizations located in Wisconsin have been threatened with boycotts (or have actually been boycotted) because they supported anti-union politicians or did not show strong support for organized labor.[35] In another case, a grain terminal operator based at a port in Washington state was targeted by hundreds of longshoreman after the organization decided to hire nonunion workers to save money. The employees broke into the facility, held several security guards hostage, and vandalized company equipment and resources. These actions prompted the NLRB to reprimand the union members for their inappropriate conduct and secure a restraining order from a federal judge.[36]

16-7f Trends in Union/Management Negotiations

As we have seen, unions are having a tougher time representing employees' interests. A decline in membership, increased competition for business, and the availability of more attractive options for handling employee issues have severely weakened interest in unions. These realities have encouraged unions in both the public and private sectors to make more concessions when negotiating with management. For example, the United Auto Workers agreed to a $1-billion reduction in employee benefits and agreed to other significant concessions to help American automotive companies after they were bailed out by the federal government.[37] There even has been interest in cooperative arrangements between labor organizers and companies so that both parties achieve success, which is discussed in the next section.

In addition, courts have also played a prominent role in clarifying the parameters of collective bargaining arrangements. For instance, in the landmark case *14 Penn Plaza vs. Pyett (2009)* the Supreme Court determined that arbitration agreements negotiated by unions should be honored when claims of employment discrimination are made by employees. Employees are still protected by discrimination legislation, but they are expected to use arbitration to handle such disputes when such arrangements exist. Given the informal nature of arbitration (compared to the formality of court cases), it is expected that more companies will seek to develop arbitration agreements.[38] Courts have also enforced the requirements of collective bargaining agreements. For example, the 2nd U.S. Court of Appeals determined that Pratt & Whitney Division's (of United Technology Corporation) plans to close two of its Connecticut-based airplane repair shops breached a collective bargaining arrangement made with the District Lodge 26 union. The ruling was based on the idea that the company had not fully considered labor issues when deciding to close the facilities.[39]

16-8 ■ UNION/MANAGEMENT COOPERATION

The adversarial relationship that naturally exists between unions and management may lead to strikes and lockouts. However, as noted, such conflicts today are relatively rare. Even more encouraging is the recognition on the part of some union leaders and employer representatives that cooperation between management and labor unions offers a useful route if organizations are to compete effectively in a global economy.

During the past decade, firms have engaged in organizational and workplace restructuring in response to competitive pressures in their industries. Restructurings have had significant effects, such as lost jobs, changed work rules, and altered job responsibilities. When restructurings occur, unions can take different approaches, ranging from resistance to cooperation. When unions have been able to obtain information and share that information with their members to work constructively with the company management at various levels, then organizational restructurings have been handled more successfully.

16-8a Employee Involvement Programs

It seems somewhat illogical to suggest that union/management cooperation or involving employees in making suggestions and decisions could be bad, and yet some decisions by the NLRB appear to have done just that. Some historical perspective is required to understand the issues that surrounded the decisions.

In the 1930s, when the Wagner Act was written, certain employers would form sham company unions, coercing workers into joining them to keep legitimate unions from organizing the employees. As a result, the Wagner Act contained prohibitions against employer-dominated labor organizations. These prohibitions were enforced, and company unions disappeared. But the use of employee involvement programs in organizations today has raised new concerns along these lines.

Because of the Wagner Act, employee-involvement programs set up in past years may be illegal, according to an NLRB decision dealing with Electromation, an Elkhart, IN, firm. Electromation used teams of employees to solicit other employees' views about such issues as wages and working conditions. The NLRB labeled these teams *labor organizations*, in line with requirements of the Wagner Act. It further found that the teams were dominated by management, which had formed them, set their goals, and decided how they would operate. The results of this and other decisions have forced many employers to rethink and restructure their employee-involvement efforts.

Federal court decisions have upheld the NLRB position in some cases and reversed it in others. One key to decisions allowing employee involvement committees and programs seems to be that these entities should not deal directly with traditional collective bargaining issues such as wages, hours, and working conditions. Other keys are that the committees should be composed primarily of workers and that they have broad authority to make operational suggestions and decisions.

16-8b Unions and Employee Ownership

Unions in some situations have encouraged workers to become partial or complete owners of the companies that employ them. These efforts were spurred by concerns that firms were preparing to shut down, merge, or be bought out. Such results were likely to cut the number of union jobs and workers.

Employee stock ownership plans for union members have even become popular. Such programs have been successful in some situations because members have purchased all or part of an organization. However, such programs might undermine union support by creating a closer identification with the concerns and goals of employers, instead of union solidarity.

L06 Define a grievance and identify the stages in a grievance procedure.

Complaint
Indication of employee dissatisfaction.

Grievance
Complaint formally stated in writing.

16-9 ■ GRIEVANCE MANAGEMENT

Employee dissatisfaction is a potential source of trouble for employers, whether it is expressed or not. Hidden dissatisfaction grows and creates reactions that may be completely out of proportion to the original concerns. Therefore, it is important that dissatisfaction be given an outlet. A **complaint**, which is merely an indication of employee dissatisfaction, is one outlet. If an employee is represented by a union, and the employee says, "I should have received the job transfer because I have more seniority, which is what the union contract states," and she submits it in writing, then that complaint becomes a grievance. A **grievance** is a complaint formally stated in writing whether or not a union is involved.

Management should be concerned with both complaints and grievances because both indicate potential problems within the workforce.[40] Without a grievance procedure, management may be unable to respond to employee concerns because managers are unaware of them. Therefore, a formal grievance procedure provides a valuable communication tool for organizations, whether a union is present or not. In North America, a wide variety of grievance procedures and dispute resolution approaches are used to address employee dissatisfaction, particularly in

FIGURE 16-10 Typical Division of HR Responsibilities: Grievance Management

HR Unit	Managers
◆ Assists in designing the grievance procedure ◆ Monitors trends in grievance rates for the organization ◆ May assist in preparing grievance cases for arbitration ◆ May have responsibility for settling grievances	◆ Operate within provisions of the grievance procedure ◆ Attempt to resolve grievances where possible ◆ Document grievance cases for the grievance procedure ◆ Engage in grievance prevention efforts

workplaces that do not deal with a union presence. For instance, alternative dispute-resolution techniques such as mediation, panel assessments, open-door policies, and peer reviews can be effective. But when employees are organized, companies often use some form of arbitration to tackle grievances.[41]

16-9a Grievance Responsibilities

The typical division of responsibilities between the HR unit and operating managers for handling grievances is shown in Figure 16-10. These responsibilities vary considerably from one organization to another, even among unionized firms. But the HR unit usually has more general responsibilities. Managers must accept the grievance procedure as a possible constraint on some of their decisions.

16-9b Grievance Procedures

Grievance procedures

Formal channels of communication used to resolve grievances.

Grievance procedures are specific communication channels that are used to resolve grievances between employees and employers. Many times, first-line supervisors are usually closest to a problem and should be one of the primary problem solvers in employee-grievance cases. However, supervisors can be distracted by other work matters and may even be the subject of an employee's grievance. Consequently, grievances need to be handled with a specified resolution approach so that problems are appropriately resolved.

Union Representation in Grievance Procedures A unionized employee generally has a right to union representation if the employee is being questioned by management and if discipline may result. If these so-called *Weingarten rights* (named after the court case that established them) are violated and the employee is dismissed, the employee usually will be reinstated with back pay. Employers are not required to allow nonunion workers to have coworkers present in grievance-procedure meetings. However, employers may voluntarily allow such presence.[42]

16-9c Steps in a Grievance Procedure

Grievance procedures can vary in the steps included. Figure 16-11 shows a typical grievance procedure, which consists of the following steps:

1. The employee discusses the grievance with the union steward (the representative of the union on the job) and the supervisor.

FIGURE 16-11 Steps in a Typical Grievance Procedure

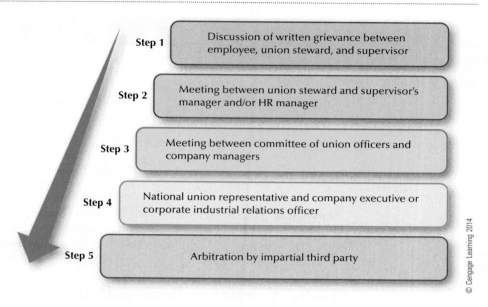

Step 1 — Discussion of written grievance between employee, union steward, and supervisor

Step 2 — Meeting between union steward and supervisor's manager and/or HR manager

Step 3 — Meeting between committee of union officers and company managers

Step 4 — National union representative and company executive or corporate industrial relations officer

Step 5 — Arbitration by impartial third party

© Cengage Learning 2014

2. The union steward discusses the grievance with the supervisor's manager and/or the HR manager.
3. A committee of union officers discusses the grievance with appropriate company managers.
4. The representative of the national union discusses the grievance with designated company executives or the corporate industrial relations officer.
5. If the grievance is not solved at this stage, it goes to arbitration. An impartial third party may ultimately dispose of the grievance.

Grievance arbitration
Means by which a third party settles disputes arising from different interpretations of a labor contract.

   Grievance arbitration is a means by which a third party settles disputes arising from different interpretations of a labor contract.[43] This process should not be confused with contract or issues arbitration, discussed earlier, in which arbitration is used to determine how a contract will be written. The U.S. Supreme Court has ruled that grievance-arbitration decisions issued under labor contract provisions are enforceable and generally may not go to court to be changed. Grievance arbitration includes many topic areas, with discipline and discharge, safety and health, and security being common concerns.

L07 Understand how unions have been utilized in the global arena.

G L O B A L

16-10 ■ UNIONS IN THE GLOBAL ARENA

Globalization increases the degree to which there is economic competition among workers, companies, and nations. As such, the ability of a country to remain competitive (i.e., increasing the availability of jobs and attracting foreign direct investment) is often influenced by its union-bargaining arrangements and labor laws. In some nations, union-bargaining power is notably weaker compared to the bargaining power of employers. However, in other countries this is not the case. Diverse legal requirements and social mores have created very different situations around the world, so HR professionals should be aware of these variations when operating globally.

Laws that make it easier and cheaper to hire and fire employees may reduce unemployment. But in many countries, such laws cause discomfort because of the great inequality they create in the balance of power in the employer–employee relationship.[44] As the world economy becomes more integrated, unions worldwide are facing changes. The status of global unions is being affected in several ways.

16-10a International Union Membership

The percentage of union membership varies significantly from country to country. The highest is in the Scandinavian countries. Collective bargaining is set in law as the way wages are to be determined in Europe. However, in many European countries, artificially high wages and generous benefits have kept the unemployment rate high. The pressures for change are increasing. The range of labor concerns is quite wide and varies from country to country, with child labor an issue in some countries, and changes in participatory employment practices issues in others.

In some countries, unions do not exist at all, are relatively weak, or are closely tied to political parties. For instance, in Italy and France national strikes occur regularly to protest proposed changes in government policy on retirement, pension programs, and regulations regarding dismissal of employees. In the Irish telecommunications industry, there is growing use of contingent workers, which required the Communications Workers Union to employ different approaches to sustain membership. The organizing officer convinced contract workers that the union could play a key role in shaping their employment experiences, and discussed how challenges at work could be addressed with union representation.[45]

Some countries require that firms have union or worker representatives on their boards of directors. This practice, called **codetermination**, is common in European countries. Differences from country to country in how collective bargaining occurs are also quite noticeable. In the United States, local unions bargain with individual employers to set wages and working conditions. In Australia, unions argue their cases before arbitration tribunals. In Scandinavia, national agreements with associations of employers are the norm. In France and Germany, industry-wide or regional agreements are common. In Japan, local unions bargain but combine at some point to determine national wage patterns. Workers are banding together and using technology to reform the way work gets done in factories located in China, as discussed in the HR Perspective: Technology Helps Work Reform in China.

Codetermination
Practice whereby union or worker representatives are given positions on a company's board of directors.

16-10b Global Labor Organizations

Global labor relations standards are being addressed by several organizations. The International Labour Organization, based in Switzerland, coordinates the efforts of labor unions worldwide and has issued some principles about rights at work. Such coordination is occurring as unions deal with multinational firms having operations in multiple countries.

Unions separately and sometimes together push import quotas and other measures to their benefit.[46] Throughout the world unions are also linking up as part of global labor federations. The Union International Network (UIN) is an entity composed of unions from numerous countries. This organization and other international groups are working to establish international policies on child labor, worker safety and health, and training. The UIN is also providing aid and guidance to

HR PERSPECTIVE

Technology Helps Work Reform in China

In the past, Chinese authorities were fairly effective at squashing labor protests by making arrests, offering concessions to disgruntled workers, and preventing more organized demonstrations. However, there is a movement among migrant workers in China to speak out against unfair labor practices in a much more coordinated way. Large rallies of Chinese employees with musical groups and individuals reciting poetry are sometimes organized to provide collective feedback about poor working conditions at different companies such as Foxconn. These rallies are provided additional support by various law firms, universities, aid groups, and nongovernmental entities that are pushing for businesses to operate in a more socially responsible manner.

The different technologies available today help Chinese workers organize more effectively. There are almost 800 million individuals who use cell phones, and over 300 million use the Internet, which gives people access to information about different labor developments around globe. Technology use has also made more workers understand the tougher labor requirements passed in 2008 that require businesses to consider worker rights.

In addition, more Chinese workers are getting a college education, which has given them more knowledge about workers' rights. There is also strong support on university campuses for worker activism and greater awareness of positive HR practices. This collective awareness has led to strikes at different plants and worksites, from cotton manufacturing firms to larger organizations such as Honda Motor. These demonstrations will likely continue as more individuals communicate with each other online and through cell phones.[47]

---

unions in developing countries, such as those in Africa and Asia. Unions in the United States are very active in these global entities. In some situations, establishing agreements with employers based in the European Union has led to more U.S. union membership in multinational firms.

16-10c United States and Global Differences

Union management relations in the United States approached some issues differently from other countries. In the United States, the key union focuses have been the following:

- *Economic issues vs. other concerns*: In the United States, unions have typically focused on improving the bread-and-butter issues for their members—wages, benefits, job security, and working conditions. In some other countries, integration with ruling governmental and political power and activism are equal concerns along with economic issues. In the United Kingdom, union organizations have developed training and other learning opportunities for workers that directly benefit the organizations that employ these individuals. Apprenticeships, Internet training, and self-assessments are used to enhance employees' preparedness for work, which helps employers reach their own learning objectives.[48]
- *Organization by kind of job and employer*: In the United States, carpenters often belong to the carpenters' union, truck drivers to the Teamsters, teachers to the American Federation of Teachers or the National Education Association, and so

on. Also, unionization can be done on a company-by-company basis. In other countries, national unions bargain with the government or with employer groups.

- *Collective agreements as "contracts"*: In the United States, collective bargaining contracts usually spell out compensation, work rules, and the conditions of employment for several years. In other countries, the agreements are made with the government and employers, sometimes for only one year because of political and social issues.
- *Competitive relations*: In the United States, management and labor traditionally take the roles of competing adversaries who often clash to reach agreement. In many other countries, tripartite bargaining occurs between the national government, employers' associations, and national labor federations with little clashing.

SUMMARY

- A union is a formal association of workers that promotes the interests of its members through collective action.
- Workers join unions primarily because of management's failure to address organizational and job-related concerns.
- The history of unions in the United States indicates that they primarily focus on wages, hours, and working conditions.
- In the United States, current union membership as a percentage of the workforce is down dramatically, being less than 12% of the civilian workforce.
- While public-sector unions have grown, unions in general have experienced a decline in membership because of geographic, industrial, and workforce changes.
- In attempts to grow, unions are targeting professionals, low-skilled workers, and contingent and part-time workers.
- The history of unions in the United States has evolved, and the structural levels of U.S. unions include federations, national and international unions, and local unions.
- The National Labor Code is composed of three laws that provide the legal basis for labor relations today: the Wagner Act, the Taft-Hartley Act, and the Landrum-Griffin Act.
- The Wagner Act was designed to protect unions and workers; the Taft-Hartley Act restored some powers to management; and the Landrum-Griffin Act was passed to protect individual union members.

- Issues addressed by the different acts include unfair labor practices, national emergency strikes, and right-to-work provisions.
- The unionization process includes an organizing campaign, authorization cards, a representation election, certification and decertification, and contract negotiation through collective bargaining.
- Collective bargaining occurs when management negotiates with representatives of workers over wages, hours, and working conditions.
- The issues subject to collective bargaining fall into three categories: mandatory, permissive, and illegal.
- The collective bargaining process includes preparation and initial demands, negotiations, and settlement and contract agreement.
- Once an agreement (contract) is signed between labor and management, it becomes the document governing what each party can and cannot do.
- When an impasse occurs, work stoppages through strikes or lockouts can be used to pressure the other party.
- Union/management cooperation has been beneficial in many situations, although care must be taken to avoid violations of NLRB provisions.
- Grievances express workers' written dissatisfactions or differences in contract interpretations.
- A grievance procedure begins with the first-level supervisor and may end—if the grievance is not resolved along the way—with arbitration by a third party.
- Unions are becoming more global as the world economy expands, and global labor federations are expanding, despite differences in approaches.

CRITICAL THINKING CHALLENGES

1. Discuss the following statement: If management gets a union, it deserves one.

2. Suppose a coworker just brought you a union leaflet urging employees to sign an authorization card. What may happen from this point on?

3. As the HR Manager, you have heard rumors about potential efforts to unionize your warehouse employees. Use the www.genelevine.com website to develop a set of guidelines for supervisors if they are asked questions by employees about unionization as part of a "union prevention" approach.

4. Public-sector unions now account for more than half of union members, while the private sector accounts for less than half. Why has this change occurred?

5. There has been some discussion among the employees in your company's manufacturing plant about forming a union. Company management recognizes the discussions may be because of the absence of a formal grievance procedure to assist employees with reporting their concerns and grievances to management. HR has been asked to develop a formal grievance procedure in an effort to develop better labor relations between the employer and the employees and as an avoidance measure to the formation of a union. To assist HR in developing a formal grievance procedure, visit several websites including the ADR/Conflict Resolution link at http://community.linchr.com /employmentguide.

A. Employees in the shipping department have requested the implementation of a "suggestion box" system to help them bring their concerns to the attention of management and to help improve labor relations. Identify the advantages and disadvantages of such a system.

B. If company management determines that the "suggestion box" request will be more cumbersome than helpful, what are some alternative solutions that management can suggest to the employees?

CASE

Just Let Them Strike

Detonation Media is a successful gaming software firm located in California that is responsible for many successful software titles. Despite these achievements, the company is currently experiencing a backlash from many of its unionized employees about various compensation issues. Almost 50% of Detonation's employees are members of the Software Engineers Guild, which has enabled workers to develop a unified voice about their concerns. Another major problem is that many professionals have been working for the organization for some time without a contract, an unacceptable situation in an industry known for high burnout and corporate layoffs. This current state of affairs has encouraged union representatives and employees to picket the organization in an effort to rally support for better working conditions.

Making matters worse is the current volatility of the industry. Software companies have experienced labor disputes, and the industry as a whole is suffering from a gradual downturn in the economy. To many, these trends foreshadow changes at Detonation, none of which are viewed positively by employees. Lower wages, reduced control over the workplace, and increased dissatisfaction are some of the likely outcomes. One superstar software developer, Tetsui Wakatanabe, has even threatened to leave the company to start his own software firm (taking key Detonation employees with him) if negotiations between management and the Software Engineers Guild break down further.

The situation has gotten even worse because the original compensation-based concessions offered to employees cannot be met because of weak sales projections. It is therefore up to Detonation's general counsel and lead negotiator Carol Lee to work with the union's lead negotiator Dan Hontz to try to find some middle ground. This could be quite difficult given that the company is offering considerably smaller pay increases over the next three years compared to amounts originally proposed, all of which will not be implemented on a retroactive basis. In addition, management wants to move compensation away from a revenue-sharing approach to profit-sharing, shifting more risk to employees.

Ultimately, Carol and Dan couldn't reach an immediate deal that would satisfy all parties involved. After discussing the situation with CEO Emilio Teti several times, Carol was surprised by his reaction to recent negotiations. He wanted to offer no additional concessions and dared union members to strike. Carol left his office trying to figure out how a win-win solution could be identified for both the employees and the company.[49]

QUESTIONS

1. Should CEO Emilio Teti stick with his proposed plan to reduce the original concessions offered to unionized employees? Should no concessions be offered?

2. Does changing compensation from a revenue-sharing approach to profit-sharing represent a viable business strategy?

3. How else might the Software Engineers Guild and Detonation Media reach a fair deal for employees?

SUPPLEMENTAL CASES

Teamsters and the Fraternal Order of Police (FOP)

The case discusses how unions sometimes compete to represent workers and explores experiences at the Denver Sheriff's Department. (For the case, go to www.cengage.com/management/mathis.)

Wal-Mart and Union Prevention

This case covers Wal-Mart efforts to stay non-union. (For the case, go to www.cengage.com/management/mathis.)

The Wilson County Hospital

This case deals with labor disputes in a unionized hospital. (For the case, go to www.cengage.com/management/mathis.)

NOTES

1. Carol Harnett, "The Screen Actors Guild Abandons Mental-Health Benefits," *Human Resource Executive Online*, January 17, 2011, www.hreonline.com.

2. Melanie Trottman, "Unions Look to Labor Board Picks to Reverse Bush Rulings," *The Wall Street Journal*, June 3, 2009, A2.

3. Tim Jones, "Worked-Up Unions," *Bloomberg Government Insider*, October 31–November 6 (Winter) 2011, B18.

4. Melanie Trottman and Brody Mullins, "Unions Rejigger Political Spending," *The Wall Street Journal*, February 27, 2012, A4.

5. Peter Cappelli, "Puzzling Out Union Impact," *Human Resource Executive Online*, March 28, 2011, www.hreonline.com.

6. Kristen B. Frasch, "As Unions Decline, So Do Wages," *Human Resource Executive Online*, August 17, 2011, www.hreonline.com.

7. Arthur D. Martinez and Jack Fiorito, "General Feelings Toward Unions and Employers as Predictors of Union Voting Intent," *Journal of Labor Research*, 30 (2009), 120–134.

8. Julia Vitullo-Martin, "How Unions are Stifling America," *USA Today*, July 13, 2011, 9A.

9. Sharon Terlep, "GM Rethinks Pay for Unionized Workers," *The Wall Street Journal*, January 12, 2011, B6.

10. Carol Gill, "Union Impact on the Effective Adoption of High Performance Work Practices," *Human Resource Management Review*, 19 (2009), 39–50.

11. Erin Patton, "Union Organizing (How Can We Prevent a Union from Organizing in Our Company?)," *HR Magazine*, September 2009, 28.

12. Ibid., 28.

13. Mark Schoeff, "A Step Back," *Workforce Management*, January 19, 2009, 18–22.

14. "Union Members Summary," Economic News Release, January 23, 2012, Bureau of Labor Statistics website, United States Department of Labor, www.bls.gov.

15. Steve Raabe, "Unions Facing Tough Times," *The Denver Post*, September 15, 2010, 1K, 6K.

16. Sam Hananel, "Private Sector Unions Add to Ranks, Reversing Long Slide in Membership Numbers," *The Denver Post*, January 28, 2012, www.denverpost.com.

17. Kris Maher, "Concessions Foreshadow a Tough Year for Unions," *The Wall Street Journal*, January 5, 2009, A3.

18. Victor G. Devinatz, "Does the Change to Win Federation Represent U.S. Labor's Third Movement? Evidence from National Labor Relations Board Certification Elections, 2003–2005," *Employee Responsibilities and Rights Journal*, 22 (2010), 161–173.

19. Ibid.

20. Tom LoBianco, "Indiana House Deals Blow to Labor Unions," *Casper Star-Tribune*, January 26, 2012, A8; Tom LoBianco, "Indiana Joins Right-to-Work Ranks," *Casper Star-Tribune*, February 2, 2012, A9.

21. Tim LoBianco, "Unions Hoping Workers Pay Dues," *Casper Star-Tribune*, February 12, 2012, 6A.

22. Based on Alex Johnson, "Snyder Signs Michigan Anti-Union 'Right to Work' Measures over Protests of Thousands," U.S. News on NBC News, December 11, 2012, http://usnews.nbcnews.com.

23. Tom LoBianco, "Indiana Joins Right-to-Work Ranks," *Casper Star-Tribune*, February 2, 2012, A9.

24. John Hollon, "A Poor 'Choice,'" *Workforce Management*, January 19, 2009, p. 42; Steve Raabe, "Unions Facing Tough Times," *The Denver Post*, September 15, 2010, 1K, 6K.

25. John Matchulat, "The Unions Rejoice Act: An Examination of the Intent and Potential Impact of EFCA," *Employee Relations Law Journal*, Spring 2009, 16–55.

26. Douglas Seaton and Emily Ruhsam, "The Employee Free Choice Act: No Choice for Employer or Employee," *Employer Relations Law Journal*, Spring 2009, 3–15.

27. For example, Jackson Lewis, a law firm with 29 offices nationwide, represents management exclusively; see www.jacksonlewis.com.

28. Based on Peter Coy, et al., "The Disposable Worker," *BusinessWeek*, January 18, 2010, 32–39.

29. *Toering Electric Co.*, 351 NLRB No. 18 (Sept. 29, 2009).

30. Leigh Tyson and W. Jonathan Martin, "NLRB Clarifies When an Employee Is a 'Supervisor,'" *Ceridian Abstracts*, www.hrcompliance.ceridian.com.

31. *14 Penn Plaza LLCV v. Pyett*, No. 07-581 (S. Ct. 2009).

32. Eric Krell, "The Rebirth of Labor Relations," *HR Magazine*, February 2009, 57–60.

33. Mark Koba, "Beyond Twinkies: Why More Workers are Striking," US Business News, CNBC, November 16, 2012, www.cnbc.com.

34. Based on Adam Bernstein, "A Eulogy for the Humble Hostess Twinkie," *The Washington Post* (Style Section), November 16, 2012, www.washingtonpost.com. Patrick Rizzo, "Hostess, Makers of Twinkies and Ding Dongs, Says Closing Business," Business on NBCNews.com, November 16, 2012, www.nbcnews.com; Martha C. White, "Relax, Twinkies Likely to Live On," Business on NBCNews.com, November 16, 2012, www.nbcnews.com.

35. Kris Maker and Douglas Belkin, "Boycott Threats Fly in Union Rights Fight," *The Wall Street Journal*, April 6, 2011, A4.

36. "A Union Goes too Far," *The Wall Street Journal*, September 9, 2011, A18.

37. Dale Kasler, "Unions Fight to Retain Role in Workplace," *The Denver Post*, May 6, 2012, 4K.

38. Paul Salvatore, "New Avenues for Arbitration," *Human Resource Executive Online*, May 16, 2009, www.hreonline.com.

39. Angela H. France, "Plant Closure Plan Halted for Violation of Collective Bargaining Agreement," *HR Magazine*, October 2010, 102.

40. Nancy Woodward, "New Guidelines Adopted for Workplace Grievances," *HR Magazine*, June 2009, 32.

41. Bernard Walker and Robert T. Hamilton, "Employee-Employer Grievances: A Review," *International Journal of Management Reviews*, 13 (2011), 40–58.

42. "Resolving Workplace Disputes Internally," *SHRM*, 2009, www.shrm.org.

43. Matthew Franckiewicz, "How to Win Your Arbitration Case Before It Even Starts," *Labor Law Journal*, 2009, 115–120.

44. S. Dankov and R. Ramalho, "Employment Laws in Developing Countries," *Journal of Comparative Economics*, 37, (2009), 3–13.

45. Robert MacKenzie, "Why Do Contingent Workers Join a Trade Union? Evidence from the Irish Telecommunications Sector," *European Journal of Industrial Relations*, 16 (2010), 153–168.

46. Kris Maher, "Steelworkers Press the U.S. for Trade Relief," *The Wall Street Journal*, June 3, 2009, B3.

47. Based on Dexter Roberts, "A New Labor Movement is Born in China," *Bloomberg Businessweek*, June 14–June 20, 2010, 7–8.

48. Ann Pace, "Union-Led Learning: A Success Story for the UK," *T + D*, July 2010, 18.

49. Based on Jon Healey (Commentary by Richard l. Trumka, Richard B. Freeman, and Jeffrey Anderson), "The Knowledge Workers' Strike," HBR Case Study, *Harvard Business Review*, July–August 2009, 27–34.

APPENDIX A

PHR® AND SPHR® BODY OF KNOWLEDGE

The Professional in Human Resources (PHR®) and Senior Professional in Human Resources (SPHR®) exams are created using the PHR and SPHR Body of Knowledge, which outlines the responsibilities of and knowledge needed by today's HR professional. The PHR and SPHR Body of Knowledge is created by HR subject matter experts through a rigorous practice analysis study and validated by HR professionals working in the field through an extensive survey instrument. It is updated periodically to ensure it is consistent with current practices in the HR field.

FUNCTIONAL AREAS:

01: Business Management & Strategy (11%/30%)

Developing, contributing to, and supporting the organization's mission, vision, values, strategic goals and objectives; formulating policies; guiding and leading the change process; and evaluating organizational effectiveness as an organizational leader.

Responsibilities:

01 Interpret and apply information related to the organization's operations from internal sources, including finance, accounting, business development, marketing, sales, operations, and information technology, to contribute to the development of the organization's strategic plan.

02 Interpret information from external sources related to the general business environment, industry practices and developments, technological advances, economic environment, labor force, and the legal and regulatory environment, to contribute to the development of the organization's strategic plan.

03 Participate as a contributing partner in the organization's strategic planning process (e.g., provide and lead workforce planning discussion with management, develop and present long-term forecast of human capital needs at the organizational level). *SPHR only*

04 Establish strategic relationships with key individuals in the organization to influence organizational decision making.

05 Establish relationships/alliances with key individuals and outside organizations to assist in achieving the organization's strategic goals and objectives (e.g., corporate social responsibility and community partnership).

06 Develop and utilize business metrics to measure the achievement of the organization's strategic goals and objectives (e.g., key performance indicators, balanced scorecard). *SPHR only*

07 Develop, influence, and execute strategies for managing organizational change that balance the expectations and needs of the organization, its employees, and other stakeholders.

08 Develop and align the human resource strategic plan with the organization's strategic plan. *SPHR only*

09 Facilitate the development and communication of the organization's core values, vision, mission, and ethical behaviors.

10 Reinforce the organization's core values and behavioral expectations through modeling, communication, and coaching.

11 Provide data such as human capital projections and costs that support the organization's overall budget.

12 Develop and execute business plans (i.e., annual goals and objectives) that correlate with the organization's strategic plan's performance expectations to include growth targets, new programs/services, and net income expectations. *SPHR only*

13 Perform cost–benefit analyses on proposed projects. *SPHR only*

14 Develop and manage an HR budget that supports the organization's strategic goals, objectives, and values. *SPHR only*

15 Monitor the legislative and regulatory environment for proposed changes and their potential impact to the organization, taking appropriate proactive steps to support, modify, or oppose the proposed change.

16 Develop policies and procedures to support corporate governance initiatives (e.g., whistle-blower protection, code of ethics). *SPHR only*

17 Participate in enterprise risk management by ensuring that policies contribute to protecting the organization from potential risks.

18 Identify and evaluate alternatives and recommend strategies for vendor selection and/or out-sourcing. *SPHR only*

19 Oversee or lead the transition and/or implementation of new systems, service centers, and outsourcing. *SPHR only*

20 Participate in strategic decision-making and due-diligence activities related to organizational structure and design (e.g., corporate restructuring, mergers and acquisitions [M&As], divestitures). *SPHR only*

21 Determine strategic application of integrated technical tools and systems (e.g., new enterprise software, performance management tools, self-service technologies). *SPHR only*

Knowledge of:

01 The organization's mission, vision, values, business goals, objectives, plans, and processes.

02 Legislative and regulatory processes

03 Strategic planning process, design, implementation, and evaluation

04 Management functions, including planning, organizing, directing, and controlling

05 Corporate governance procedures and compliance (e.g., Sarbanes–Oxley Act)

06 Due diligence processes (e.g., M&A, divestitures). *SPHR only*

07 Transition techniques for corporate restructuring, M&A, offshoring, and divestitures. *SPHR only*

08 Elements of a cost–benefit analysis during the life cycle of the business (such as scenarios for growth, including expected, economic stressed, and worst-case conditions) and the impact to net worth/earnings for short-, mid-, and long-term horizons

09 Business concepts (e.g., competitive advantage, organizational branding, business case development, corporate responsibility)

02: Workforce Planning and Employment (24%/17%)

Developing, implementing, and evaluating sourcing, recruitment, hiring, orientation, succession planning, retention, and organizational exit programs necessary to ensure the workforce's ability to achieve the organization's goals and objectives.

Responsibilities:

01 Ensure that workforce planning and employment activities are compliant with applicable federal laws and regulations.

02 Identify workforce requirements to achieve the organization's short- and long-term goals and objectives (e.g., corporate restructuring, workforce expansion or reduction).

03 Conduct job analyses to create and/or update job descriptions and identify job competencies.

04 Identify, review, document, and update essential job functions for positions.

05 Influence and establish criteria for hiring, retaining, and promoting on the basis of job descriptions and required competencies.

06 Analyze labor market for trends that impact the ability to meet workforce requirements (e.g., federal/state data reports).

07 Assess skill sets of internal workforce and external labor market to determine the availability of qualified candidates, utilizing third-party vendors or agencies as appropriate.

08 Identify internal and external recruitment sources (e.g., employee referrals, diversity groups, social media) and implement selected recruitment methods.

09 Establish metrics for workforce planning (e.g., recruitment and turnover statistics, costs).

10 Brand and market the organization to potential qualified applicants.

11 Develop and implement selection procedures (e.g., applicant tracking, interviewing, reference and background checking).

12 Develop and extend employment offers and conduct negotiations as necessary.

13 Administer post-offer employment activities (e.g., execute employment agreements, complete I-9/E-Verify process, coordinate relocations, and immigration).

14 Develop, implement, and evaluate orientation and on-boarding processes for new hires, rehires, and transfers.

15 Develop, implement, and evaluate employee-retention strategies and practices.

16 Develop, implement, and evaluate the succession planning process. *SPHR only*

17 Develop and implement the organizational exit/off-boarding process for both voluntary and involuntary terminations, including planning for reductions in force (RIF).

18 Develop, implement, and evaluate an affirmative action plan (AAP) as required.

19 Develop and implement a record-retention process for handling documents and employee files (e.g., preemployment files, medical files, and benefits files).

Knowledge of:

11 Applicable federal laws and regulations related to workforce planning and employment activities (e.g., Title VII, ADA, EEOC Uniform Guidelines on Employee Selection Procedures, Immigration Reform and Control Act)

12 Methods to assess past and future staffing effectiveness (e.g., costs per hire, selection ratios, adverse impact)

13 Recruitment sources (e.g., employee referral, social networking/social media) for targeting passive, semi-active and active candidates

14 Recruitment strategies

15 Staffing alternatives (e.g., outsourcing, job sharing, phased retirement)

16 Planning techniques (e.g., succession planning, forecasting)

17 Reliability and validity of selection tests/tools/methods

18 Use and interpretation of selection tests (e.g., psychological/personality, cognitive, motor/physical assessments, performance, assessment center)

19 Interviewing techniques (e.g., behavioral, situational, panel)

20 Impact of compensation and benefits on recruitment and retention

21 International HR and implications of global workforce for workforce planning and employment. *SPHR only*

22 Voluntary and involuntary terminations, downsizing, restructuring, and outplacement strategies and practices

23 Internal workforce assessment techniques (e.g., skills testing, skills inventory, workforce demographic analysis)

24 Employment policies, practices, and procedures (e.g., orientation, on-boarding, and retention)

25 Employer marketing and branding techniques

26 Negotiation skills and techniques

03: Human Resource Development (18%/19%)

Developing, implementing, and evaluating activities and programs that address employee training and development, performance appraisal, and talent and performance management to ensure that the knowledge, skills, abilities, and performance of the workforce meet current and future organizational and individual needs.

Responsibilities:

01 Ensure that human resources development activities are compliant with all applicable federal laws and regulations.

02 Conduct a needs assessment to identify and establish priorities regarding human resource development activities.

03 Develop/select and implement employee training programs (e.g., leadership skills, harassment prevention, computer skills) to increase individual and organizational effectiveness.

04 Evaluate effectiveness of employee training programs through the use of metrics (e.g., participant surveys, pre- and post-testing). *SPHR only*

05 Develop, implement, and evaluate talent-management programs that include assessing talent, developing career paths, and managing the placement of high-potential employees.

06 Develop, select, and evaluate performance appraisal processes (e.g., instruments, ranking

and rating scales) to increase individual and organizational effectiveness.

07 Develop, implement, and evaluate performance management programs and procedures (includes training for evaluators).

08 Develop/select, implement, and evaluate programs (e.g., telecommuting, diversity initiatives, repatriation) to meet the changing needs of employees and the organization. *SPHR only*

09 Provide coaching to managers and executives regarding effectively managing organizational talent.

Knowledge of:

27 Applicable federal laws and regulations related to Human Resources development activities (e.g., Title VII, ADA, Title 17 [Copyright law])

28 Career development and leadership development theories and applications (e.g., succession planning, dual career ladders)

29 Organizational development (OD) theories and applications

30 Training program development techniques to create general and specialized training programs

31 Facilitation techniques, instructional methods, and program delivery mechanisms

32 Task/process analysis

33 Performance appraisal methods (e.g., instruments, ranking and rating scales)

34 Performance management methods (e.g., goal setting, relationship to compensation, job placements/ promotions)

35 Applicable global issues (e.g., international law, culture, local management approaches/practices, societal norms). *SPHR only*

36 Techniques to assess training program effectiveness, including use of applicable metrics (e.g., participant surveys, pre- and post-testing)

37 Mentoring and executive coaching

04: Compensation and Benefits (19%/13%)

Developing/selecting, implementing/administering, and evaluating compensation and benefits programs for all employee groups in order to support the organization's goals, objectives, and values.

Responsibilities:

01 Ensure that compensation and benefits programs are compliant with applicable federal laws and regulations.

02 Develop, implement, and evaluate compensation policies/programs (e.g., pay structures, performance-based pay, internal and external equity).

03 Manage payroll-related information (e.g., new hires, adjustments, terminations).

04 Manage outsourced compensation and benefits components (e.g., payroll vendors, COBRA administration, employee recognition vendors). *PHR only*

05 Conduct compensation and benefits programs needs assessments (e.g., benchmarking, employee surveys, trend analysis).

06 Develop/select, implement/administer, update and evaluate benefit programs (e.g., health and welfare, wellness, retirement, stock purchase).

07 Communicate and train the workforce in the compensation and benefits programs, policies and processes (e.g., self-service technologies).

08 Develop/select, implement/administer, update, and evaluate an ethically sound executive compensation program (e.g., stock options, bonuses, supplemental retirement plans). *SPHR only*

09 Develop, implement/administer and evaluate expatriate and foreign national compensation and benefits programs. *SPHR only*

Knowledge of:

38 Applicable federal laws and regulations related to compensation, benefits, and tax (e.g., FLSA, ERISA, FMLA, USERRA)

39 Compensation and benefits strategies

40 Budgeting and accounting practices related to compensation and benefits

41 Job evaluation methods

42 Job pricing and pay structures

43 External labor markets and/or economic factors

44 Pay programs (e.g., variable, merit)

45 Executive compensation methods. *SPHR only*

46 Noncash compensation methods (e.g., equity programs, noncash rewards)

47 Benefits programs (e.g., health and welfare, retirement, Employee Assistance Programs [EAPs])

48 International compensation laws and practices (e.g., expatriate compensation, entitlements, choice of law codes). *SPHR only*

49 Fiduciary responsibilities related to compensation and benefits

05: Employee and Labor Relations (20%/14%)

Developing, implementing/administering, and evaluating the workplace in order to maintain relationships and working conditions that balance employer/employee needs and rights in support of the organization's goals and objectives.

Responsibilities:

01 Ensure that employee and labor relations activities are compliant with applicable federal laws and regulations.

02 Assess organizational climate by obtaining employee input (e.g., focus groups, employee surveys, staff meetings).

03 Develop and implement employee-relations programs (e.g., recognition, special events, diversity programs) that promote a positive organizational culture.

04 Evaluate effectiveness of employee relations programs through the use of metrics (e.g., exit interviews, employee surveys, turnover rates).

05 Establish, update, and communicate workplace policies and procedures (e.g., employee handbook, reference guides, or standard operating procedures), and monitor their application and enforcement to ensure consistency.

06 Develop and implement a discipline policy on the basis of organizational code of conduct/ethics, ensuring that no disparate impact or other legal issues arise.

07 Create and administer a termination process (e.g., reductions in force [RIF], policy violations, poor performance) ensuring that no disparate impact or other legal issues arise.

08 Develop, administer, and evaluate grievance/dispute-resolution and performance-improvement policies and procedures.

09 Investigate and resolve employee complaints filed with federal agencies involving employment practices or working conditions, utilizing professional resources as necessary (e.g., legal counsel, mediation/arbitration specialists, investigators).

10 Develop and direct proactive employee relations strategies for remaining union-free in nonorganized locations. *SPHR only*

11 Direct and/or participate in collective bargaining activities, including contract negotiation, costing, and administration.

Knowledge of:

50 Applicable federal laws affecting employment in union and nonunion environments, such as laws regarding antidiscrimination policies, sexual harassment, labor relations, and privacy (e.g., WARN Act, Title VII, NLRA)

51 Techniques and tools for facilitating positive employee relations (e.g., employee surveys, dispute/conflict resolution, labor/management cooperative strategies)

52 Employee involvement strategies (e.g., employee management committees, self-directed work teams, staff meetings)

53 Individual employment rights issues and practices (e.g., employment at will, negligent hiring, defamation)

54 Workplace behavior issues/practices (e.g., absenteeism and performance improvement)

55 Unfair labor practices

56 The collective bargaining process, strategies, and concepts (e.g., contract negotiation, costing, and administration)

57 Legal disciplinary procedures

58 Positive employee relations strategies and non-monetary rewards

59 Techniques for conducting unbiased investigations

60 Legal termination procedures

06: Risk Management (8%/7%)

Developing, implementing/administering, and evaluating programs, procedures, and policies in order to provide a safe, secure working environment and to protect the organization from potential liability.

Responsibilities:

01 Ensure that workplace health, safety, security, and privacy activities are compliant with applicable federal laws and regulations.

02 Conduct a needs analysis to identify the organization's safety requirements.

03 Develop/select and implement/administer occupational injury and illness prevention programs (i.e., OSHA, workers' compensation). *PHR only*

04 Establish and administer a return-to-work process after illness or injury to ensure a safe workplace (e.g., modified duty assignment, reasonable accommodations, independent medical exam).

05 Develop/select, implement, and evaluate plans and policies to protect employees and other individuals, and to minimize the organization's loss and liability (e.g., emergency response, workplace violence, substance abuse).

06 Communicate and train the workforce on security plans and policies.

07 Develop, monitor, and test business continuity and disaster recovery plans.

08 Communicate and train the workforce on the business continuity and disaster recovery plans.

09 Develop policies and procedures to direct the appropriate use of electronic media and hardware (e.g., e-mail, social media, and appropriate Web site access).

10 Develop and administer internal and external privacy policies (e.g., identity theft, data protection, workplace monitoring).

Knowledge of:

61 Applicable federal laws and regulations related to workplace health, safety, security, and privacy (e.g., OSHA, Drug-Free Workplace Act, ADA, HIPAA, Sarbanes–Oxley Act)

62 Occupational injury and illness prevention (safety) and compensation programs

63 Investigation procedures of workplace safety, health and security enforcement agencies

64 Return-to-work procedures (e.g., interactive dialog, job modification, accommodations)

65 Workplace safety risks (e.g., trip hazards, bloodborne pathogens)

66 Workplace security risks (e.g., theft, corporate espionage, sabotage)

67 Potential violent behavior and workplace violence conditions

68 General health and safety practices (e.g., evacuation, hazard communication, ergonomic evaluations)

69 Organizational incident and emergency response plans

70 Internal investigation, monitoring, and surveillance techniques

71 Employer/employee rights related to substance abuse

72 Business continuity and disaster recovery plans (e.g., data storage and backup, alternative work locations, procedures)

73 Data integrity techniques and technology (e.g., data sharing, password usage, social engineering)

74 Technology and applications (e.g., social media, monitoring software, biometrics)

75 Financial management practices (e.g., procurement policies, credit card policies and guidelines, expense policies)

Core Knowledge

76 Needs assessment and analysis

77 Third-party or vendor selection, contract negotiation, and management, including development of requests for proposals (RFPs)

78 Communication skills and strategies (e.g., presentation, collaboration, sensitivity)

79 Organizational documentation requirements to meet federal and state guidelines

80 Adult learning processes

81 Motivation concepts and applications

82 Training techniques (e.g., virtual, classroom, on-the-job)

83 Leadership concepts and applications

84 Project management concepts and applications

85 Diversity concepts and applications (e.g., generational, cultural competency, learning styles)

86 Human relations concepts and applications (e.g., emotional intelligence, organizational behavior)

87 Ethical and professional standards

88 Technology to support HR activities (e.g., HR Information Systems, employee self-service, e-learning, applicant tracking systems)

89 Qualitative and quantitative methods and tools for analysis, interpretation, and decision-making purposes (e.g., metrics and measurements, cost/benefit analysis, financial statement analysis)

90 Change management theory, methods, and application
91 Job analysis and job description methods
92 Employee records management (e.g., electronic/paper, retention, disposal)
93 Techniques for forecasting, planning, and predicting the impact of HR activities and programs across functional areas
94 Types of organizational structures (e.g., matrix, hierarchy)
95 Environmental scanning concepts and applications (e.g., Strengths, Weaknesses, Opportunities, and Threats [SWOT], and Political, Economic, Social, and Technological [PEST])
96 Methods for assessing employee attitudes, opinions, and satisfaction (e.g., surveys, focus groups/panels)
97 Budgeting, accounting, and financial concepts
98 Risk-management techniques

The HR Certification Institute, established in 1976, is an internationally recognized certifying organization for the human resource profession. Today, more than 115,000 HR professionals worldwide proudly maintain the HR Certification Institute's credentials as a mark of high professional distinction.

The HR Certification Institute is a global leader in developing rigorous exams to demonstrate mastery and real-world application of forward-thinking HR practices, policies and principles.

To learn more, visit www.hrci.org

APPENDIX B

HUMAN RESOURCE MANAGEMENT RESOURCES

Students are expected to be familiar with the professional resources and literature in their fields of study. Five groups of resources are listed in this appendix.

A. Research-Oriented Journals

In HR management, the academic journals can be a communication link between researchers and the practicing managers. These journals contain articles that report on original research. Normally, these journals contain quantitative verifications of the author's findings, or conceptual models and literature reviews of previous research.

Academy of Management Journal
Academy of Management Review
Administrative Science Quarterly
American Behavioral Scientist
American Journal of Health Promotion
American Journal of Psychology
American Journal of Sociology
American Psychological Measurement
American Psychologist
American Sociological Review
Annual Review of Psychology
Applied Psychology: An International Review
British Journal of Industrial Relations
British Journal of Management
Business Ethics
Decision Sciences
Dispute Resolution Quarterly
Employee Responsibilities and Rights Journal
Entrepreneurship Theory and Practice
Ethics and Critical Thinking Journal
Human Organization
Human Relations
Human Resources Development Quarterly
Human Resource Development Review
Human Resource Management Journal
Human Resource Management Review
Human Resources Abstracts
Industrial and Labor Relations Review

Industrial Relations
Industrial Relations Journal
Industrial Relations Law Journal
International Journal of Entrepreneurial Behavior and Research
International Journal of Human Resource Management Education
International Journal of Management Reviews
International Journal of Selection and Assessment
International Journal of Training and Development
Journal of Abnormal Psychology
Journal of Applied Behavioral Science
Journal of Applied Business Research
Journal of Applied Psychology
Journal of Business
Journal of Business and Industrial Marketing
Journal of Business and Psychology
Journal of Business Communication
Journal of Business Ethics
Journal of Business Research
Journal of Business Strategy
Journal of Collective Negotiations
Journal of Communication
Journal of Comparative International Management
Journal of Compensation and Benefits
Journal of Counseling Psychology
Journal of Experimental Social Psychology
Journal of Human Resources

Journal of Industrial Relations
Journal of International Business Studies
Journal of International Management
Journal of Knowledge Management
Journal of Labor Economics
Journal of Labor Research
Journal of Leadership and Organizational Studies
Journal of Management
Journal of Management Development
Journal of Management Education
Journal of Management Studies
Journal of Managerial Psychology
Journal of Organizational Behavior
Journal of Organizational Change Management
Journal of Organizational Excellence
Journal of Personality and Social Psychology
Journal of Quality and Participation
Journal of Social Issues
Journal of Workplace Learning
Journal of Workplace Rights
New Technology, Work, and Employment
Organization Behavior and Human Decision
　　Processes
Personnel Psychology
Personnel Review
Psychological Bulletin
Psychological Review
Public Personnel Management
Quarterly Review of Distance Education
Social Forces
Social Science Research
Work and Occupations

B. Selected Professional/ Managerial Journals

These journals generally cover a wide range of subjects. Articles in these publications are normally aimed at HR professionals and managers. Most articles in these publications are written to interpret, summarize, or discuss the implications of research. They also provide operational and administrative ideas.

Academy of Management Executive
Australian Journal of Management
Benefits and Compensation Solutions
Berkeley Journal of Employment and Labor Law
Business Horizons

Business Journal
Business Week
California Management Review
Columbia Journal of World Business
Compensation and Benefits Review
Corporate Governance
Directors and Boards
Economist
Employee Benefit Plan Review
Employee Benefits News
Employee Relations
Employment Relations Today
Forbes
Fortune
Global HR
Harvard Business Review
Health Resources and Services Administration
HR Magazine
Human Capital Management
Human Resource Development International
Human Resource Executive
Human Resource Management
Human Resource Management International Digest
IHRIM Link
INC.
Industry Week
International Management
Journal of Network and Systems Management
Labor Law Journal
Long Range Planning
Management Research News
Management Review
Management Today
Managers Magazine
Monthly Labor Review
Nation's Business
Occupational Health and Safety
Occupational Outlook Quarterly
Organizational Dynamics
Pension World
Personnel Management
Psychology Today
Public Administration Review
Public Manager
Public Opinion Quarterly
SAM Advanced Management Journal
Security Management
Sloan Management Review
Training
Training and Development

Workforce Management
Working Woman
Workplace Visions
Workspan
WorldatWork Journal

C. Selected Human Resource Associations/Organizations

Academy of Management
www.aom.pace.edu
American Arbitration Association
www.adr.org
American Federation of Labor/Congress of
Industrial Organizations (AFL-CIO)
www.aflcio.org
American Institute for Managing Diversity
www.aimd.org
American Payroll Association
www.americanpayroll.org
American Psychological Association
www.apa.org
American Society for Industrial Security
www.asisonline.org
American Society for Training and Development
www.astd.org
Australian Human Resource Institute
www.ahri.com.au
Chartered Institute of Personnel and Development
(UK)
www.cipd.co.uk
CPR International Institute for Conflict Prevention
and Resolution
www.cpradr.org
Employee Benefit Research Institute
www.ebri.org
Foundation for Enterprise Development
www.fed.org
Hong Kong Institute of Human Resource
Management
www.hkihrm.org
Human Resource Certification Institute
www.hrci.org
International Association for Human Resource
Information Management
www.ihrim.org
International Association of Industrial Accident
Boards and Commissions
www.iaiabc.org

International Foundation of Employee Benefit Plans
(IFEBP)
www.ifebp.org
International Institute of Human Resource
Management
www.iihrm.org
International Personnel Assessment Council
www.ipacweb.org
International Personnel Management Association
www.ipma-hr.org
Labor and Employment Relations Association
www.lera.uiuc.edu
National Center for Employee Ownership
www.nceo.org
National Health Information Resource Center
www.nhirc.org
Social Media Policies
www.socialmediagovernance.com
Society for Human Resource Management
www.shrm.org
Union Resource Network
www.unions.org
World at Work
www.worldatwork.org

D. Selected Government Agencies Related to HR

Bureau of Labor Statistics
www.stats.bls.gov
Census Bureau
www.census.gov
Department of Labor
www.dol.gov
Employment and Training Administration
www.doleta.gov
Equal Employment Opportunity Commission
www.eeoc.gov
FedStats
www.fedstats.gov
National Institute of Environmental Health Sciences
www.niehs.nih.gov
National Institute for Occupational Safety and
Health (NIOSH)
www.cdc.gov/niosh
National Labor Relations Board
www.nlrb.gov
Occupational Safety and Health Administration
www.osha.gov

Office of Personnel Management
www.opm.gov
Pension and Welfare Benefits Administration
www.dol.gov/ebsa
Pension Benefit Guaranty Corporation
www.pbgc.gov
Small Business Administration
www.sba.gov
Social Security Administration
www.ssa.gov
U.S. House of Representatives
www.house.gov
U.S. Senate
www.senate.gov

E. Abstracts, Indices, and Databases Related to HR

ABI Inform Global
ACM Digital
ArticleFirst
Arts and Humanities Search
Book Review Digest
Books in Print
Business and Company ASAP
ComAbstracts

ContentsFirst
Criminal Justice Abstracts
Dissertation Abstracts
Ebsco Masterfile Premier
Ebsco Online Citations
ECO: Electronic Collections Online
EconLit
Education
ERIC
Essay and General Literature Index
Expanded Academic Index ASAP
Government Periodicals
GPO Monthly Catalog
Health Reference Center
HRAF: Human Relations Area Files
Human Resource Abstracts
Index to Legal Periodicals and Books
Internet and Personal Computing Abstracts
NCJRS Justice Information Center
NetFirst
Newspaper Source from Ebsco
PAIS: Public Affairs Information Service
PapersFirst
PsycInfo
Readers Guide Abstracts
Sociological Abstracts

APPENDIX C

MAJOR FEDERAL EQUAL EMPLOYMENT OPPORTUNITY LAWS AND REGULATIONS

Act	Year	Key Provisions	Covered Employers
Broad-Based Discrimination			
Title VII, Civil Rights Act of 1964	1964	Prohibits discrimination in employment on basis of race, color, religion, sex, or national origin	Employers with 15+ employees
Executive Orders 11246 and 11375	1965 1967	Require federal contractors and sub-contractors to eliminate employment discrimination and prior discrimination through affirmative action	Federal contractors with 50+ employees and a Government contract of $50,000 or more
Civil Rights Act of 1991	1991	Overturns several past Supreme Court decisions and changes damage claims provisions	Employers with 15+ employees
Congressional Accountability Act	1995	Extends EEO and Civil Rights Act provisions to U.S. congressional staff	U.S. Congress
Military Status			
Vietnam Era Veterans' Readjustment Assistance Act	1974	Prohibits discriminations against Vietnam-era veterans by federal contractors and the U.S. government and requires affirmative action	
Uniformed Services Employment and Reemployment Rights Act	1994	Protects members of the uniformed services from discrimination in employment and provides for reinstatement to their job upon return from active duty.	All employers
National Origin Discrimination			
Immigration Reform and Control Act	1986 1990 1996	Establishes penalties for employers who knowingly hire illegal aliens; prohibits employment discrimination on the basis of national origin or citizenship	Employers with 15+ employees

(Continued)

Act	Year	Key Provisions	Covered Employers
Gender/Sex Discrimination			
Equal Pay Act	1963	Requires equal pay for men and women performing substantially the same work	All employers
Pregnancy Discrimination Act	1978	Prohibits discrimination against women affected by pregnancy, childbirth, or related medical conditions; requires that they be treated as all other employees for employment-related purposes, including benefits	Employers with 15+ employees
Age Discrimination			
Age Discrimination in Employment Act (as amended in 1978 and 1986)	1967	Prohibits discrimination against persons over age 40 and restricts mandatory retirement requirements, except where age is a bona fide occupational qualification	Employers with 20+ employees
Older Workers Benefit Protection Act of 1990	1990	Prohibits age-based discrimination in early retirement and other benefits plans	Employers with 20+ employees
Disability Discrimination			
Vocational Rehabilitation Act and Rehabilitation Act of 1974	1973 1974	Prohibits federal contractors from discriminating against individuals with disabilities	Federal contractors with a contract of $25,000 or more
Americans with Disabilities Act	1990	Requires employer accommodations for individuals with disabilities	Employers with 15+ employees
Genetic Information Nondiscrimination Act	2009	Prohibits employers and health insurers from using genetic information in employment and insurance coverage decisions	Employers with 20+ employees

APPENDIX D

UNIFORM GUIDELINES ON EMPLOYEE SELECTION

The 1978 Uniform Guidelines on Employee Selection Procedures are used by the U.S. EEOC, the U.S. Department of Labor's OFCCP, the U.S. Department of Justice, and the U.S. Office of Personnel Management. These guidelines attempt to explain how an employer should deal with hiring, retention, promotion, transfer, demotion, dismissal, and referral. Under the uniform guidelines, if sued, employers can choose one of two routes to prove they are not illegally discriminating against employees: no disparate impact and job-related validity.

"No Disparate Impact" Approach

Generally, the most important issue regarding discrimination in organizations is the *effect* of employment policies and procedures, regardless of the *intent* of the employer. *Disparate impact* occurs when protected-class members are substantially underrepresented in employment decisions. Under the guidelines, disparate impact is determined with the *4/5ths rule*. If the selection rate for a protected group is less than 80% (4/5ths) of the selection rate for the majority group or less than 80% of the majority group's representation in the relevant labor market, discrimination exists. Thus, the guidelines have attempted to define discrimination in statistical terms. The use of the statistical means has been researched and some methodological issues have been identified. However, the guidelines have continued to be used because disparate impact is checked by employers both internally and externally.

Internal Metrics for Disparate Impact   Internal disparate impact metrics compare the results of employer actions received by protected-class members with those received by nonprotected-class members inside the organization. HR activities that can be checked most frequently for internal disparate impact include the following:

- Selection of candidates for interviews from those recruited
- Pass rates for various selection tests
- Performance appraisal ratings as they affect pay increases
- Promotions, demotions, and terminations
- Identification of individuals for layoffs

   The calculation that follows computes the internal disparate impact for men and women who were interviewed for jobs at a firm. In this case, the figure indicates that the selection process does have a disparate impact internally. The practical meaning of these calculations is that statistically, women have less chance of being selected for jobs than men do. Thus, illegal discrimination may exist unless the firm can demonstrate that its selection activities are specifically job related.

External Metrics for Disparate Impact   Employers can check for disparate impact externally by comparing the percentage of protected-class members in their

Internal Disparate Impact Example

Female applicants: 25% were selected for jobs
Male applicants: 45% were selected for jobs

Disparate Impact Determination (4/5 = 80%)

• Male selection rate of 45% × (80%) = 36%
• Female selection rate = 25%

Disparate impact exists because the female selection rate is less than 4/5 of the male selection rate.

workforces with the percentage of protected-class members in the relevant labor markets. The relevant labor markets consist of the areas where the firm recruits workers, not just where those employed live. External comparisons can also consider the percentage of protected-class members who are recruited and who apply for jobs to ensure that the employer has drawn a "representative sample" from the relevant labor markets. Although employers are not required to maintain exact proportionate equality, they must be "close." Courts have applied statistical analyses to determine if any disparities that exist are too high.

The following illustrates external disparate impact metrics using impact analyses for a sample metropolitan area, Valleyville. Assume that a firm in that area, Acme Company, has 500 employees, including 50 African Americans and 75 Latinos/Hispanics. To determine if the company has external disparate impact, it is possible to make the following comparisons:

Protected Class	% of Total Employees at Acme Company	4/5ths of Group in the Population	Disparate Impact?
African American	10% (50/500)	13.6%	Yes (10% < 13.6%)
Latino/Hispanic	15% (75/500)	14.4%	No (15% > 14.4%)

At Acme, external disparate impact exists for African Americans because the company employs fewer of them than the 4/5 threshold of 13.6%. However, because Acme has more Latino/Hispanic employees than the 4/5 threshold of 14.4%, there is no disparate impact for this group.

Statistical comparisons for determining disparate impact may use more complex methods. HR professionals need to know how to do such calculations because external disparate impact must be computed and reported in affirmative action plans that government contractors submit to regulatory agencies.

Racial Distribution in Valleyville (Example)

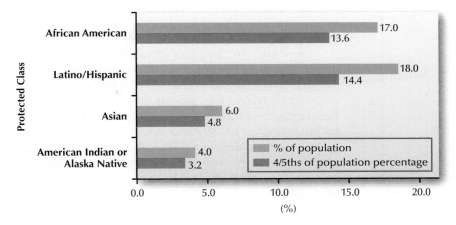

Job-Related Validation Approach

Under the job-related validation approach, virtually every factor used to make employment-related decisions is considered an employment "test." Such activities as recruiting, selection, promotion, termination, discipline, and performance appraisal all must be shown to be job related. Hence, two basic concepts, validity and reliability, affect many of the common means used to make HR decisions.

Validity and Reliability   The first concept, *validity,* is simply the extent to which a test actually measures what it says it measures. The concept relates to inferences made from tests. For instance, it may be valid to assume that performance on a mechanical knowledge test may predict performance of a machinist in a manufacturing plant. However, it is probably not valid to assume that the same test scores indicate general intelligence or promotability for a manufacturing sales representative. Another instance would be a general intelligence test; for it to be valid, it must actually measure intelligence, and not just a person's vocabulary. Therefore, an employment test that is valid must measure the person's ability to perform the job for which she or he is being hired.

Ideally, employment-related tests will be both valid and reliable. *Reliability* refers to the consistency with which a test measures an item. For a test to be reliable, an individual's score should be about the same every time the individual takes the test (allowing for the effects of practice). Unless a test measures a factor consistently (reliably), it is of little value in predicting job performance.

Validity and Equal Employment

If a charge of discrimination is brought against an employer on the basis of disparate impact, a *prima facie* case must be established. The employer then must be able to demonstrate that its employment procedures are valid and job related. A key element in establishing job relatedness is conducting a *job analysis* to identify the *knowledge, skills, and abilities (KSAs)* and other characteristics needed to perform a job satisfactorily. In one sense, then, current requirements have done management a favor by forcing employers to use job-related employment procedures.

There are two categories of validity in which employment tests attempt to predict how well an individual will perform on the job. In measuring *criterion-related validity,* a test is the *predictor,* and the measures for job performance are the *criterion variables.* Job analysis determines as exactly as possible what KSAs and behaviors are needed for each task in the job. Two types of criterion-related validity are *predictive validity* and *concurrent validity.*

Content validity is validity measured by a logical, nonstatistical method to identify the KSAs and other characteristics necessary to perform a job. Then managers, supervisors, and HR specialists must identify the most important KSAs needed for the job. Finally, a "test" is devised to determine if individuals have the necessary KSAs. The test may be an interview question about previous supervisory experience, or an ability test in which someone types a letter using a word-processing software program, or a knowledge test about consumer credit regulations.

A test has content validity if it reflects an actual sample of the work done on the job in question. For example, an arithmetic test for a retail cashier might contain problems about determining amounts for refunds, purchases, and merchandise exchanges. Content validity is especially useful if the workforce is not large enough to allow other, more statistical approaches.

Many practitioners and specialists see content validity as a commonsense standard for validating staffing and other employment dimensions, and as more realistic than other means. Research and court decisions have shown that content validity is consistent with the Uniform Guidelines also. Consequently, content validity approaches are growing in use.

APPENDIX E

PREEMPLOYMENT INQUIRIES

Given all the protected-category groups, many EEO complaints arise because of inappropriate preemployment inquiries. Questions asked of applicants may be viewed as discriminatory or biased against protected-class applicants. This appendix identifies preemployment inquiries that may or may not be discriminatory. The preemployment inquiries labeled "may be discriminatory" have been so designated because of findings in a variety of court cases. Those labeled "may not be discriminatory" are legal, but only if they reflect a business necessity or are job related. Once an employer tells an applicant he or she is hired (the "point of hire"), inquiries that were prohibited earlier may be made. After hiring, medical examination forms, group insurance cards, and other enrollment cards containing inquiries related directly or indirectly to sex, age, or other bases may be requested.

Guidelines to Lawful and Unlawful Preemployment Inquiries

Subject of Inquiry	It May Not Be Discriminatory to Inquire about …	It May Be Discriminatory to Inquire about …
1. Name	a. Whether applicant has ever worked under a different name	a. The original name of applicant whose name has been legally changed b. The ethnic association of applicant's name
2. Age	a. If applicant is over the age of 18 b. If applicant is under the age of 18 or 21 if that information is job related (e.g., for selling liquor in a retail store)	a. Date of birth b. Date of high school graduation
3. Residence	a. Applicant's place of residence b. Alternative contact information	a. Previous addresses b. Birthplace of applicant or applicant's parents c. Length lived at current and previous addresses
4. Race or Color		a. Applicant's race or color of applicant's skin

(Continued)

Subject of Inquiry	It May Not Be Discriminatory to Inquire about ...	It May Be Discriminatory to Inquire about ...
5. National Origin and Ancestry		a. Applicant's lineage, ancestry, national origin, parentage, or nationality b. Nationality of applicant's parents or spouse
6. Sex and Family Composition		a. Sex of applicant b. Marital status of applicant c. Dependents of applicants or child-care arrangements d. Whom to contact in case of emergency
7. Creed or Religion		a. Applicant's religious affiliation b. Applicant's church, parish, mosque, or synagogue c. Holidays observed by applicant
8. Citizenship	a. Whether the applicant is a U.S. citizen or has a current permit/visa to work in the United States	a. Whether applicant is a citizen of a country other than the United States b. Date of citizenship
9. Language	a. Language applicant speaks and/or writes fluently, if job related	a. Applicant's native tongue b. Language used at home
10. References	a. Names of persons willing to provide professional and/or character references for applicant b. Previous work contacts	a. Name of applicant's religious leader b. Political affiliation and contacts
11. Relatives	a. Names of relatives already employed by the employer	a. Name and/or address of any relative of applicant b. Whom to contact in case of emergency
12. Organizations	a. Applicant's membership in any professional, service, or trade organization	a. All clubs or social organizations to which applicant belongs
13. Arrest Record and Convictions	a. Convictions, if related to job performance (disclaimer should accompany)	a. Number and kinds of arrests b. Convictions, unless related to job requirements and performance

(Continued)

14. Photographs		a. Photographs with application, with résumé, or before hiring
15. Height and Weight		a. Any inquiry into height and weight of applicant, except where a BFOQ exists
16. Physical Limitations	a. Whether applicant has the ability to perform job-related functions with or without accommodation	a. The nature or severity of an illness or physical condition b. Whether applicant has ever filed a workers' compensation claim c. Any recent or past operations, treatments, or surgeries and dates
17. Education	a. Training applicant has received, if related to the job b. Highest level of education applicant has attained, if validated that having certain educational background (e.g., high school diploma or college degree) is needed to perform the specific job	a. Date of high school graduation
18. Military	a. Branch of the military applicant served in and ranks attained b. Type of education or training received in military	a. Military discharge details b. Military service records
19. Financial Status		a. Applicant's debts or assets b. Garnishments

APPENDIX F

EEO ENFORCEMENT

Enforcement of EEO laws and regulations in the United States is viewed as a work in progress that is inconsistent and confusing at times. The court system is left to resolve the disputes and interpret the laws. Often the lower courts have issued conflicting rulings and interpretations. The ultimate interpretation has often rested on decisions by the U.S. Supreme Court, although those rulings have also been interpreted differently.

EEO Enforcement Agencies

Government agencies at several levels can investigate illegal discriminatory practices. At the federal level, the two most prominent agencies are the Equal Employment Opportunity Commission (EEOC) and the Office of Federal Contract Compliance Programs (OFCCP).

Equal Employment Opportunity Commission The EEOC has enforcement authority for charges brought under a number of federal laws. Further, the EEOC issues policy guidelines on many topics influencing the EEO. Although the policy statements are not "law," they are "persuasive authority" in most cases.

Office of Federal Contract Compliance Programs While the EEOC is an independent agency, the OFCCP is part of the U.S. Department of Labor and ensures that federal contractors and subcontractors use nondiscriminatory practices. A major thrust of OFCCP efforts is to require that covered employers take affirmative action to counter prior discriminatory practices.

State and Local Agencies In addition to federal laws and orders, many states and municipalities have passed their own laws prohibiting discrimination on a variety of bases, and state and local enforcement bodies have been established. Compared with federal laws, state and local laws sometimes provide greater remedies, require different actions, or prohibit discrimination in more areas.

EEO Compliance

Employers must comply with a variety of EEO regulations and guidelines. To do so, it is crucial that all employers have a written EEO policy statement. They should widely communicate this policy by posting it on bulletin boards, printing it in employee handbooks, reproducing it in organizational newsletters, and reinforcing it in training programs. The contents of the policy should clearly state the organization's commitment to equal employment and incorporate a listing of the appropriate protected classes.

Additionally, employers with 15 or more employees may be required to keep certain records that can be requested by the EEOC, the OFCCP, or numerous other state and local enforcement agencies. Under various laws, employers are also required to post an "officially approved notice" in a prominent place for employees. This notice states that the employer is an equal opportunity employer and does not discriminate.

EEO Records Retention   All employment records must be maintained as required by the EEOC. Such records include application forms and documents concerning hiring, promotion, demotion, transfer, layoff, termination, rates of pay or other terms of compensation, and selection for training and apprenticeship. Even application forms or test papers completed by unsuccessful applicants may be requested. The length of time documents must be kept varies, but generally three years is recommended as a minimum. Complete records are necessary to enable an employer to respond should a charge of discrimination be made.

EEOC Reporting Forms

Many private-sector employers must file a basic report annually with the EEOC. Slightly different reports must be filed biennially by state/local governments, local unions, and school districts. The following private-sector employers must file the EEO-1 report annually:

• All employers with 100 or more employees, except state and local governments
• Subsidiaries of other companies if the total number of all combined employees equals 100 or more
• Federal contractors with at least 50 employees and contracts of $50,000 or more
• Financial institutions with at least 50 employees, in which government funds are held or saving bonds are issued

Recent changes require that details on employees must be reported by gender, race/ethnic group, and job levels. The most significant change was adding the phrase "two or more races," to reflect the multidiverse nature of a growing number of employees.

Applicant-Flow Data

Under EEO laws and regulations, employers may be required to show that they do not discriminate in the recruiting and selection of members of protected classes. Because employers are not allowed to collect such data on application blanks and other preemployment records, the EEOC allows them to do so with a separate applicant-flow form that is not used in the selection process. The *applicant-flow form* is filled out voluntarily by the applicant, and the data must be maintained separately from other selection-related materials. With many applications being made via the Internet, employers must collect this data electronically to comply with regulations on who is an applicant. Analyses of the data collected in applicant-flow forms may help to show whether an employer has underutilized a protected class because of an inadequate flow of applicants from that class, in spite of special efforts to recruit them. Also, these data are reported as part of affirmative action plans that are filed with the OFCCP.

Stages in the Employer's Response to an EEO Complaint

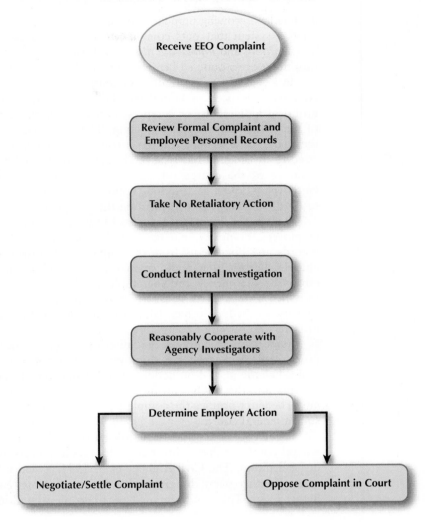

EEOC Compliance Investigation Process

When a discrimination complaint is received by an employer, it must be processed whether it is made internally by a disgruntled employee or by an outside agency. The chart shows the steps required in an employer's response to an EEO complaint.

Notice that the employer should have a formal complaint process in place and should be sure that no retaliatory action occurs. Internal investigations can be conducted by HR staff, but HR staff often utilize outside legal counsel to provide expert guidance in dealing with agency investigations. Internal investigations should also occur when employees make complaints without filing them with outside agencies. Once the employer's investigation is completed, then the decision must be made within to negotiate and settle the complaint or oppose the complaint.

EEOC Complaint Process

To handle a growing number of complaints, the EEOC and other agencies have instituted a system that puts complaints into three categories: *priority*, *needing further investigation*, and *immediate dismissal*. If the EEOC decides to pursue a complaint, it uses the process outlined here, and an employer must determine how to handle it.

In a typical situation, an EEO complaint goes through several stages before the compliance process is completed. First the charges are filed by an individual, a group of individuals, or a representative. A charge must be filed within 180 days of the alleged discriminatory action. Then the EEOC staff reviews the specifics of the charge to determine if it has *jurisdiction*, which means that the agency is authorized to investigate that type of charge. If the EEOC has jurisdiction, it must serve a notice of the charge on the employer within 10 days of the filing; then the employer is asked to respond. Following the charge notification, the major effort of the EEOC turns to investigating the complaint.

During the investigation, the EEOC may interview the complainants, other employees, company managers, and supervisors. Also, it can request additional records and documents from the employer. If sufficient cause is found to support charges that the alleged discrimination occurred, the next stage involves mediation efforts by the agency and the employer. *Mediation* is a dispute-resolution process in which a third party helps negotiators reach a settlement. The EEOC has found that use of mediation has reduced its backlog of EEO complaints and has resulted in faster resolution of complaints.

If the employer agrees that discrimination has occurred and accepts the proposed settlement, then the employer posts a notice of relief within the company and takes the agreed-on actions. If the employer objects to the charge and rejects conciliation, the EEOC can file a suit or issue *a right-to-sue letter* to the complainant. The letter notifies the complainant that he or she has 90 days to file a personal suit in federal court.

In the court litigation stage, a legal trial takes place in the appropriate state or federal court. At that point, both sides retain lawyers and rely on the court to render a decision. The Civil Rights Act of 1991 provides for jury trials in most EEO cases. If either party disagrees with the court ruling, either can file appeals with a higher court. The U.S. Supreme Court becomes the ultimate adjudication body.

SAMPLE HR-RELATED JOB DESCRIPTIONS

Sample Job Description for Human Resource Manager

Identification Section:
Position Title: Human Resource Manager
Department: Human Resources   EEOC Class: O/M
Reports to: President   FLSA Status: Exempt

General Summary: Directs HR activities of the firm to ensure compliance with laws and policies, and assists President with overall HR planning

Essential Job Functions:
1. Manages compensation and benefits programs for all employees, resolves compensation and benefits questions from employees, and negotiates with benefits carriers (20%)
2. Ensures compliance with both internal policies and applicable state and federal regulations and laws, including EEO, OSHA, and FLSA (20%)
3. Identifies HR planning issues and suggested approaches to President and other senior managers (15%)
4. Assists managers and supervisors to create, plan, and conduct training and various development programs for new and existing employees (15%)
5. Recruits candidates for employment over telephone and in person. Interviews and selects internal and external candidates for open positions (10%)
6. Reviews and updates job descriptions, assisted by department supervisors, and coordinates performance appraisal process to ensure timely reviews are completed for all employees (10%)
7. Administers various HR policies and procedures and helps managers resolve employee performance and policy issues (10%)
8. Performs other duties as needed and directed by President

Knowledge, Skills, and Abilities:
- Knowledge of HR policies, HR practices, and HR-related laws and regulations
- Knowledge of company products and services and policies and procedures
- Knowledge of management principles and practices
- Skill in operating equipment, such as personal computer, software, and IT systems
- Skill in oral and written communication
- Ability to communicate with employees and various business contacts in a professional and courteous manner
- Ability to organize multiple work assignments and establish priorities
- Ability to negotiate with others and resolve conflicts, particularly in sensitive situations
- Ability to pay close attention to detail and to ensure accuracy of reports and data
- Ability to make sound decisions using available information while maintaining confidentiality
- Ability to create a team environment and sustain employee commitment

Education and Experience: Bachelor's degree in HR management or equivalent, plus 3–5 years' experience

Physical Requirements:	Percentage of Work Time Spent on Activity			
	0%–24%	25%–49%	50%–74%	75%–100%
Seeing: Must be able to read computer screen and various reports				X
Hearing: Must be able to hear well enough to communicate with employees and others				X
Standing/walking	X			
Climbing/stooping/kneeling	X			
Lifting/pulling/pushing	X			
Fingering/grasping/feeling: Must be able to write, type, and use phone system				X

Working Conditions: Good working conditions with the absence of disagreeable conditions

Note: The statements herein are intended to describe the general nature and level of work performed by employees, but are not a complete list of responsibilities, duties, and skills required of personnel so classified. Furthermore, they do not establish a contract for employment and are subject to change at the discretion of the employer.

Sample Job Description for Compensation Manager

Job Title: Compensation Manager	**JOB CODE:** _____
Supervisor's Title: Vice President of Human Resources	**GRADE:** _____
Department: Human Resources	**FLSA STATUS:** <u>Exempt</u>
	EEOC CLASS: <u>O/M</u>

General Summary: Responsible for the design and administration of all cash compensation programs, ensures proper consideration of the relationship of compensation to performance of each employee, and provides consultation on compensation administration to managers and supervisors

Essential Duties and Responsibilities:
1. Prepares and maintains job descriptions for all jobs and periodically reviews and updates them. Responds to questions from employees and supervisors regarding job descriptions (25%)
2. Ensures that Company compensation rates are in line with pay structures. Obtains or conducts pay surveys as necessary and presents recommendations on pay structures on an annual basis (20%)
3. Develops and administers the performance appraisal program and monitors the use of the performance appraisal instruments to ensure the integrity of the system and its proper use (20%)
4. Directs the job evaluation process by coordinating committee activities and resolves disputes over job values. Conducts initial evaluation of new jobs prior to hiring and assigns jobs to pay ranges (15%)
5. Researches and provides recommendations on executive compensation issues. Assists in the development and oversees the administration of all annual bonus payments for senior managers and executives (15%)
6. Coordinates the development of an integrated HR information system and interfaces with the Management Information Systems Department to achieve departmental goals for information needs (5%)
7. Performs related duties as assigned or as the situation dictates

Required Knowledge, Skills, and Abilities:
1. Knowledge of compensation and HR management practices and approaches
2. Knowledge of effective job analysis methods and survey development and interpretation practices and principles
3. Knowledge of performance management program design and administration
4. Knowledge of federal and state wage and hour regulations
5. Skill in writing job descriptions, memorandums, letters, and proposals
6. Skill in use of word processing, spreadsheet, and database software
7. Ability to make presentations to groups on compensation policies and practices
8. Ability to plan and prioritize work

Education and Experience: Equivalent of a college degree in Business Administration, Psychology, or related field plus 3–5 years' experience in HR management, 2–3 of which should include compensation administration experience. An advanced degree in Industrial Psychology, Business Administration, or HR Management preferred, but not required.

Physical Requirements:	**Rarely (0%–12%)**	**Occasionally (12%–33%)**	**Frequently (34%–66%)**	**Regularly (67%–100%)**
Seeing: Must be able to read reports and use computer				X
Hearing: Must be able to hear well enough to communicate with coworkers				X
Standing/walking	X			
Climbing/stooping/kneeling	X			
Lifting/pulling/pushing	X			
Fingering/grasping/feeling: Must be able to write, type, and use phone system				X

Working Conditions: Normal office working conditions with the absence of disagreeable elements

Note: The statements herein are intended to describe the general nature and level of work being performed by employees, and are not to be construed as an exhaustive list of responsibilities, duties, and skills required of personnel so classified. Furthermore, they do not establish a contract for employment and are subject to change at the discretion of the employer.

GLOSSARY

A

Absenteeism Any failure by an employee to report for work as scheduled or to stay at work when scheduled.

Acceptance rate Percent of applicants hired divided by total number of applicants offered jobs.

Active practice Performance of job-related tasks and duties by trainees during training.

Adult learning Ways in which adults learn differently than younger people.

Adverse selection Situation in which *only* higher-risk employees select and use certain benefits.

Affirmative action Proactive employment practices to make up for historical discrimination against women and minorities.

Affirmative action program (AAP) A document reporting on the composition of an employer's workforce, required for federal contractors.

Alternate work arrangements Non-traditional schedules that provide flexibility to employees.

Applicant pool All persons who are actually evaluated for selection.

Applicant population A subset of the labor force population that is available for selection using a particular recruiting approach.

Arbitration Process that uses a neutral third party to make a decision.

Assessment centers Collections of instruments and exercises designed to diagnose individuals' development needs.

Attitude survey A survey that focuses on employees' feelings and beliefs about their jobs and the organization.

Attraction-selection-attrition (ASA) theory Job candidates are attracted to and selected by firms where similar types of individuals are employed and individuals who are different quit their jobs to work elsewhere.

Auto-enrollment Employee contributions to a 401(k) plan are started automatically when an employee is eligible to join the plan.

Autonomy Extent of individual freedom and discretion in the work and its scheduling.

B

Balanced scorecard A framework used to report a diverse set of performance measures.

Bargaining unit Employees eligible to select a single union to represent and bargain collectively for them.

Base pay Basic compensation that an employee receives, usually as a wage or salary.

Behavioral interview Interview in which applicants give specific examples of how they have performed a certain task or handled a problem in the past.

Behavioral modeling Copying someone else's behavior.

Behaviorally anchored rating scale Scales describe specific examples of job behavior, which are then measured against a performance scale.

Benchmark jobs Jobs found in many organizations that can be used for the purposes of comparison.

Benchmarking Comparing the business results to industry standards.

Benefit Indirect reward given to an employee or group of employees as part of membership in the organization.

Blended learning Learning approach that combines methods such as short, fast-paced, interactive computer-based lessons and teleconferencing with traditional classroom instruction and simulation.

Bona fide occupational qualification (BFOQ) Characteristic providing a legitimate reason why an employer can exclude persons on otherwise illegal bases of consideration.

Bonus One-time payment that does not become part of the employee's base pay.

Broadbanding Practice of using fewer pay grades with much broader ranges than in traditional compensation systems.

Burden of proof What individuals who file suit against employers must prove to establish that illegal discrimination has occurred.

Business agent A full-time union official who operates the union office and assists union members.

Business necessity A practice necessary for safe and efficient organizational operations.

C

Cafeteria benefit plan Employees are given a budget and can purchase the bundle of benefits most important to them from the "menu" of options offered by the employer.

Career paths Represent employees' movements through opportunities over time.

Career Series of work-related positions a person occupies throughout life.

Cash balance plan Retirement program in which benefits are determined on the basis of accumulation of annual company contributions plus interest credited each year.

Central tendency error Occurs when a rater gives all employees a score

625

within a narrow range in the middle of the scale.

Closed shop Firm that requires individuals to join a union before they can be hired.

Coaching Observation with suggestion.

Codetermination Practice whereby union or worker representatives are given positions on a company's board of directors.

Cognitive ability tests Tests that measure an individual's thinking, memory, reasoning, verbal, and mathematical abilities.

Collective bargaining Process whereby representatives of management and workers negotiate over wages, hours, and other terms and conditions of employment.

Commission Compensation computed as a percentage of sales in units or dollars.

Compa-ratio Pay level divided by the midpoint of the pay range.

Compensable factor Job value commonly present throughout a group of jobs within an organization.

Compensation committee Subgroup of the board of directors that is composed of directors who are not officers of the firm.

Competencies Individual capabilities that can be linked to enhanced performance by individuals or teams.

Competency-based pay Rewards individuals for the capabilities they demonstrate and acquire.

Complaint Indication of employee dissatisfaction.

Compressed workweek A work-week in which a full week's work is accomplished in fewer than five 8-hour days.

Conciliation Process by which a third party assists union and management negotiators to reach a voluntary settlement.

Concurrent validity Measured when an employer tests current employees and correlates the scores with their performance ratings.

Constructive discharge Process of deliberately making conditions intolerable to get an employee to quit.

Consumer-driven health (CDH) plan Health plan that provides employer financial contributions to employees to help cover their health-related expenses.

Contingent worker Someone who is not an employee, but a temporary or part-time worker for a specific period of time and type of work.

Contractual rights Rights based on a specific contract between an employer and an employee.

Contrast error Tendency to rate people relative to others rather than against performance standards.

Copayment The portion of medical expenses paid by the insured individual.

Core competency A unique capability that creates high value in which an organization excels.

Correlation coefficient Index number that gives the relationship between a predictor variable and a criterion variable.

Cost–Benefit Analysis Comparison of costs and benefits associated with training.

Craft union Union whose members do one type of work, often using specialized skills and training.

Cross training Training people to do more than one job.

Cumulative trauma disorders (CTDs) Muscle and skeletal injuries that occur when workers repetitively use the same muscles to perform tasks.

D

Decertification Process whereby a union is removed as the representative of a group of employees.

Deductible Money paid by an insured individual before a health plan pays for any medical expenses.

Defined benefit (DB) plan Retirement program in which employees are promised a pension amount based on age and service.

Defined contribution (DC) plan Retirement program in which the employer makes an annual payment to an employee's pension account.

Development Efforts to improve employees' abilities to handle a variety of assignments and to cultivate employees' capabilities beyond those required by the current job.

Disabled person Someone who has a physical or mental impairment that substantially limits life activities, who has a record of such an impairment, or who is regarded as having such an impairment.

Discharge When an employee is removed from a job at an employer.

Discipline Form of training that enforces organizational rules.

Disparate impact Occurs when members of a protected category are substantially underrepresented as a result of employment decisions that work to their disadvantage.

Disparate treatment Occurs when members of a group are treated differently from others.

Distributive justice Perceived fairness in the distribution of outcomes.

Draw Amount advanced against, and repaid from, future commissions earned by the employee.

Dual-career ladder System that allows a person to advance up either a management or a technical/professional ladder.

Due diligence A comprehensive assessment of all aspects of the business being acquired.

Due process Requirement that the employer use a fair process to determine employee wrongdoing and that the employee have an opportunity to explain and defend his or her actions.

Duty Work segment composed of several tasks that are performed by an individual.

E

Effectiveness The ability to produce a specific desired effect or result that can be measured.

Efficiency The degree to which operations are done in an economical manner.

Employee assistance program (EAP) Program that provides counseling and other help to employees having emotional, physical, or other personal problems.

Employee engagement The extent to which an employee's thoughts and behaviors are focused on the employer's success.

Employee stock ownership plan (ESOP) Plan designed to give employees significant stock ownership in their employers.

Employment brand Image of the organization that is held by both employees and outsiders.

Employment contract Formal agreement that outlines the details of employment.

Employment-at-will (EAW) A common-law doctrine stating that employers have the right to hire, fire, demote, or promote whomever they choose, unless there is a law or a contract to the contrary.

Entitlement philosophy Assumes that individuals who have worked another year are entitled to pay increases, with little regard for performance differences.

Environmental scanning The assessment of external and internal environmental conditions that affect the organization.

Equal employment opportunity Employment that is not affected by illegal discrimination.

Equity The perceived fairness of what the person does compared with what the person receives.

Equity theory Individuals judge fairness (equity) in compensation by comparing their inputs and outcomes against the inputs and outcomes of referent others.

Ergonomics Study and design of the work environment to address physical demands placed on individuals.

Essential job functions Fundamental job duties.

Exclusive remedy Workers' compensation benefits are the only benefits injured workers may receive to compensate for a work-related injury.

Exempt employees Employees who are not paid overtime.

Exit interview An interview in which individuals who are leaving an organization are asked to give their reasons.

Expatriate A citizen of one country who is working in a second country and employed by an organization headquartered in the first country.

Expectancy theory An employee's motivation is based on the probability that his or her efforts will lead to an expected level of performance that is linked to a valued reward.

F

Federation Group of autonomous unions.

Feedback The amount of information employees receive about how well or how poorly they have performed.

Flexible benefits plan Program that allows employees to select the benefits they prefer from groups of benefits established by the employer.

Forced distribution Performance appraisal method in which ratings of employees' performance levels are distributed along a bell-shaped curve.

Forecasting Using information from the past and the present to identify expected future conditions.

Free rider A free rider is a member of the group who contributes little.

401(k) plan Agreement in which a percentage of an employee's pay is withheld and invested in a tax-deferred account.

G

Gainsharing System of sharing with employees greater-than-expected gains in profits and/or productivity.

Games Exercises that entertain and engage.

Garnishment A court order that directs an employer to set aside a portion of an employee's wages to pay a debt owed to a creditor.

Glass ceiling Discriminatory practices that have prevented women and minorities from advancing to executive-level jobs.

Glass ceiling Situation in which women fail to progress into top and senior management positions.

Global tax equalization plan Compensation plan used to protect expatriates from negative tax consequences.

Golden parachute Compensation given to an executive if he or she is forced to leave the organization.

Graphic rating scale Scale that allows the rater to mark an employee's performance on a continuum.

Green-circled employee Incumbent who is paid below the range set for a job.

Grievance arbitration Means by which a third party settles disputes arising from different interpretations of a labor contract.

Grievance Complaint formally stated in writing.

Grievance procedures Formal channels of communication used to resolve grievances.

Gross-up To increase the net amount of what the employee receives to include the taxes owed on the amount.

H

Halo effect Occurs when a rater scores an employee high on all job criteria because of performance in one area.

Headhunters Employment agencies that focus their efforts on executive, managerial, and professional positions.

Health General state of physical, mental, and emotional well-being.

Health promotion Supportive approach of facilitating and encouraging healthy actions and lifestyles among employees.

High-pos Individuals who show high promise for advancement in the organization.

Home-country-based approach Maintain an expatriate's standard of living in the home country.

Horns effect Occurs when a low rating on one characteristic leads to an overall low rating.

Host-country national A citizen of one country who is working in that country and employed by an organization headquartered in a second country.

Hostile environment Sexual harassment in which an individual's work performance or psychological well-being is unreasonably affected by intimidating or offensive working conditions.

HR analytics An evidence-based approach to making HR decisions on the basis of quantitative tools and models.

HR audit A formal research effort to assess the current state of HR practices.

HR generalist A person who has responsibility for performing a variety of HR activities.

HR metrics Specific measures of HR performance indicators.

HR specialist A person who has in-depth knowledge and expertise in a limited area of HR.

Human capital return on investment (HCROI) Directly shows the operating profit derived from investments in human capital.

Human capital The collective value of the capabilities, knowledge, skills, life experiences, and motivation of an organizational workforce.

Human capital value added (HCVA) Calculated by subtracting all operating expenses *except* for labor expenses from revenue and dividing by the total full-time head count.

Human economic value added (HEVA) Wealth created per employee.

Human Resource (HR) management The design of formal systems in an organization to manage human talent for accomplishing organizational goals.

Human Resource planning The process of analyzing and identifying the need for and availability of people so that the organization can meet its strategic objectives.

I

Illegal issues Collective bargaining issues that would require either party to take illegal action.

Immediate confirmation Based on the idea that people learn best if reinforcement and feedback are given as soon as possible after training.

Incentives Tangible rewards that encourage or motivate action.

Individual-centered career planning Career planning that focuses on an individual's responsibility for a career rather than on organizational needs.

Industrial union Union that includes many persons working in the same industry or company, regardless of jobs held.

Informal training Training that occurs through interactions and feedback among employees.

Intangible rewards Elements of compensation that cannot be as easily measured or calculated.

Interactional justice Perceived fairness about how a person interacts with others.

Islamaphobia Hatred or fear of Muslims.

J

Job analysis Systematic way of gathering and analyzing information about the content, context, and human requirements of jobs.

Job description Identification of the tasks, duties, and responsibilities of a job.

Job design Organizing tasks, duties, responsibilities, and other elements into a productive unit of work.

Job duties Identify the important elements in a given job.

Job enlargement Broadening the scope of a job by expanding the number of different tasks to be performed.

Job enrichment Increasing the depth of a job by adding responsibility for planning, organizing, controlling, or evaluating the job.

Job evaluation Formal, systematic means to identify the relative worth of jobs within an organization.

Job Grouping of tasks, duties, and responsibilities that constitutes the total work assignment for an employee.

Job posting System in which the employer provides notices of job openings and employees respond by applying for specific openings.

Job redesign Taking an existing job and changing it to improve it.

Job rotation Process of moving a person from job to job.

Job satisfaction A positive emotional state resulting from evaluating one's job experiences.

Job sharing Scheduling arrangement in which two employees perform the work of one full-time job.

Job specifications The knowledge, skills, and abilities (KSAs) an individual needs to perform a job satisfactorily.

Just cause Reasonable justification for taking employment-related action.

K

Knowledge management The way an organization identifies and leverages knowledge to be competitive.

L

Labor force participation rate The percentage of the population working or seeking work.

Labor force population All individuals who are available for selection if all possible recruitment strategies are used.

Labor markets External supply pool from which employers attract employees.

Leniency error Occurs when ratings of all employees fall at the high end of the scale.

Lockout Shutdown of company operations undertaken by management to prevent union members from working.

Loyalty Being faithful to an institution or employer.

Lump-sum increase (LSI) One-time payment of all or part of a yearly pay increase.

M

Make-or-buy Develop competitive Human Resources or hire individuals who are already developed from somewhere else.

Managed care Approaches that monitor and reduce medical costs through restrictions and market system alternatives.

Management by objectives (MBO) Performance appraisal method that specifies the performance goals that an individual and manager identify together.

Management mentoring A relationship in which experienced managers aid individuals in the earlier stages of their careers.

Management rights Rights reserved so that the employer can manage, direct, and control its business.

Mandatory issues Collective bargaining issues identified specifically by labor laws or court decisions as subject to bargaining.

Marginal job functions Duties that are part of a job but are incidental or ancillary to the purpose and nature of the job.

Market banding Grouping jobs into pay grades based on similar market survey amounts.

Market line Graph line that shows the relationship between job value as determined by job evaluation points and job value as determined pay survey rates.

Market pricing Use of market pay data to identify the relative value of jobs based on what other employers pay for similar jobs.

Massed practice Practice performed all at once.

Mediation Process by which a third party helps the negotiators reach a settlement.

Motivation The desire within a person causing that person to act.

Multinational corporation (MNC) A corporation that has facilities and other assets in at least one country other than its home country.

N

Negligent hiring Occurs when an employer fails to check an employee's background and the employee injures someone on the job.

Negligent retention Occurs when an employer becomes aware that an employee may be unfit for work but continues to employ the person, and the person injures someone.

Nepotism Practice of allowing relatives to work for the same employer.

No-fault insurance Injured workers receive benefits even if the accident was their fault.

Noncompete agreements Agreements that prohibit individuals who leave an organization from working with an employer in the same line of business for a specified period of time.

Nondirective interview Interview that uses questions developed from the answers to previous questions.

Nonexempt employees Employees who must be paid overtime.

O

Offshoring Moving jobs to lower-wage countries.

Offshoring The relocation of a business process or operation by a company from one country to another.

Ombuds Individuals outside the normal chain of command who act as problem solvers for both management and employees.

On-the-job training The most common training because it is flexible and relevant.

Open enrollment A time when employees can change their participation level in various benefit plans and switch between benefit options.

Open shop Firm in which workers are not required to join or pay dues to a union.

Open-door policy A policy in which anyone with a complaint can talk with a manager, an HR representative, or an executive.

Organizational commitment The degree to which employees believe in and accept organizational goals and desire to remain with the organization.

Organizational culture Consists of the shared values and beliefs that give members of an organization meaning and provide them with rules for behavior.

Organizational mission The core reason for the existence of the organization and what makes it unique.

Organization-centered career planning Career planning that focuses on identifying career paths that provide for the logical progression of people between jobs in an organization.

Orientation Planned introduction of new employees to their jobs, coworkers, and the organization.

Outsourcing Transferring the management and performance of a business function to an external service provider.

P

Paid-time-off (PTO) plan Plan that combines all sick leave, vacation time, and holidays into a total number of hours or days that employees can take off with pay.

Panel interview Interview in which several interviewers meet with candidate at the same time.

Pay compression Occurs when the pay differences among individuals with different levels of experience and performance become small.

Pay equity The idea that pay for jobs requiring comparable levels of knowledge, skill, and ability should be similar, even if actual duties differ significantly.

Pay grades Groupings of individual jobs having approximately the same job worth.

Pay survey Collection of data on compensation rates for workers performing similar jobs in other organizations.

Pay-for-performance philosophy Assumes that compensation changes reflect performance differences.

Performance appraisal Process of determining how well employees do their jobs relative to a standard and communicating that information to them.

Performance management Series of activities designed to ensure that the organization gets the performance it needs from its employees.

Performance standards Define the expected levels of employee performance.

Performance standards Indicators of what the job accomplishes and how performance is measured in key areas of the job description.

Permissive issues Collective bargaining issues that are not mandatory and that relate to certain jobs.

Perquisites (Perks) Special benefits—usually noncash items—for executives.

Person/job fit Matching the KSAs of individuals with the characteristics of jobs.

Person–job fit Matching characteristics of people with characteristics of jobs.

Person/organization fit The congruence between individuals and organizational factors.

Phased retirement Approach in which employees gradually reduce their workloads and pay level.

Physical ability tests Tests that measure an individual's abilities such as strength, endurance, and muscular movement.

Piece-rate system Pay system in which wages are determined by multiplying the number of units produced by the piece rate for one unit.

Placement Fitting a person to the right job.

Policies General guidelines that focus organizational actions.

Portability A pension plan feature that allows employees to move their pension benefits from one employer to another.

Predictive validity Measured when test results of applicants are compared with subsequent job performance.

Predictors of selection criteria Measurable or visible indicators of selection criteria.

Prevailing wage An hourly wage determined by a formula that considers the rate paid for a job by a majority of the employers in the appropriate geographic area.

Primacy effect Occurs when a rater gives greater weight to information received first when appraising an individual's performance.

Procedural justice Perceived fairness of the process and procedures used to make decisions about employees.

Procedures Customary methods of handling activities.

Productivity Measure of the quantity and quality of work done, considering the cost of the resources used.

Profit sharing System to distribute a portion of the profits of an organization to employees.

Protected characteristic An attribute about an individual that is protected under EEO laws and regulations.

Psychological contract The unwritten expectations employees and employers have about the nature of their work relationships.

Psychomotor tests Tests that measure dexterity, hand–eye coordination, arm–hand steadiness, and other factors.

Q

Qualifying event An event that causes a plan participant to lose group health benefits.

Quid pro quo Sexual harassment in which employment outcomes are linked to the individual granting sexual favors.

R

Ranking Performance appraisal method in which all employees are listed from highest to lowest in performance.

Rater bias Occurs when a rater's values or prejudices distort the rating.

Ratification Process by which union members vote to accept the terms of a negotiated labor agreement.

Realistic job preview Process through which a job applicant receives an accurate picture of a job.

Reasonable accommodation A modification to a job or work environment that gives a qualified individual an equal employment opportunity to perform.

Recency effect Occurs when a rater gives greater weight to recent events when appraising an individual's performance.

Recruiting Process of generating a pool of qualified applicants for organizational jobs.

Red-circled employee Incumbent who is paid above the range set for a job.

Reinforcement Based on the idea that people tend to repeat responses that give them some type of positive reward and to avoid actions associated with negative consequences.

Repatriation Planning, training, and reassignment of global employees back to their home countries.

Rerecruiting Seeking out former employees and recruiting them again to work for an organization.

Responsibilities Obligations to perform certain tasks and duties.

Restricted stock option Option that indicates that company stock shares will be paid as a grant of shares to individuals, usually linked to achieving specific performance criteria.

Retaliation Punitive actions taken by employers against individuals who exercise their legal rights.

Retirement plan Retirement program established and funded by the employer and employees.

Return on investment (ROI) Calculation showing the value of an investment.

Right to privacy An individual's freedom from unauthorized and unreasonable intrusion into personal affairs.

Rights Powers, privileges, or interests that belong by law, nature, or tradition.

Right-to-work laws State laws that prohibit requiring employees to join unions as a condition of obtaining or continuing employment.

Risk management Involves responsibilities to consider physical, human, and financial factors to protect organizational and individual interests.

Rules Specific guidelines that regulate and restrict the behavior of individuals.

S

Sabbatical Time off the job to develop and rejuvenate oneself.

Safety Condition in which the physical well-being of people is protected.

Salary Consistent payments made each period regardless of the number of hours worked.

Salary-Plus-Commission Combines the stability of a salary with a commission.

Salting Practice in which unions hire and pay people to apply for jobs at certain companies to begin organizing efforts.

Security audit Comprehensive review of organizational security.

Security Protection of employees and organizational facilities.

Selection criterion Characteristic that a person must possess to successfully perform work.

Selection rate Percentage hired from a given group of candidates.

Selection The process of choosing individuals with the correct qualifications needed to fill jobs in an organization.

Self-directed team Organizational team composed of individuals who are assigned a cluster of tasks, duties, and responsibilities to be accomplished.

Self-efficacy People's belief that they can successfully learn the training program content.

Self-service Technology that allows employees to change their benefits choices, track their benefits balances, and submit questions to HR staff members and external benefits providers.

Seniority Time spent in an organization or on a particular job.

Separation agreement Agreement in which a terminated employee agrees not to sue the employer in exchange for specified benefits.

Serious health condition Health condition requiring in-patient, hospital, hospice, or residential medical care or continuing physician care.

Severance benefits Temporary payments made to laid-off employees to ease the financial burden of unemployment.

Sexual harassment Actions that are sexually directed, are unwanted, and subject the worker to adverse employment conditions or create a hostile work environment.

Simulations Reproduce parts of the real world so they can be experienced, manipulated, and learning can occur.

Situational interview Structured interview that contains questions about how applicants might handle specific job situations.

Situational judgment tests Tests that measure a person's judgment in work settings.

Skill variety Extent to which the work requires several activities for successful completion.

Spaced practice Practice performed in several sessions spaced over a period of hours or days.

Special-purpose team Organizational team formed to address specific problems, improve work processes, and enhance the overall quality of products and services.

Status blind A concept that emphasizes that differences among people should be ignored and everyone should be treated equally.

Statutory rights Rights based on laws or statutes passed by federal, state, or local governments.

Stock option Option that gives individuals the right to buy stock in a company, usually at an advantageous price.

Stock option plan Plan that gives employees the right to purchase a fixed number of shares of company stock at a specified price for a limited period of time.

Strategic HR management Entails providing input into organizational strategic planning and appropriate use of HR management practices to gain competitive advantage.

Strategic Planning The process of defining organizational strategy and allocating resources toward its achievement.

Strategic talent management The process of identifying the most important jobs in a company that provide a long-term competitive advantage, and then creating appropriate HR policies to develop employees so that they can effectively work in these jobs.

Strategy A plan an organization follows for how to compete successfully, survive, and grow.

Stress interview Interview designed to create anxiety and put pressure on applicants to see how they respond.

Strictness error Occurs when ratings of all employees fall at the low end of the scale.

Strike Work stoppage in which union members refuse to work in order to put pressure on an employer.

Structured interview Interview that uses a set of standardized questions asked of all applicants.

Substance abuse Use of illicit substances or misuse of controlled substances, alcohol, or other drugs.

Succession planning Preparing for the inevitable movements of personnel that creates holes in the hierarchy that need to be filled by other qualified individuals.

Succession planning The process of identifying a plan for the orderly replacement of key employees.

T

Tangible rewards Elements of compensation that can be quantitatively measured and compared between organizations.

Task Distinct, identifiable work activity composed of motions.

Task identity Extent to which the job includes a "whole" identifiable

unit of work that is carried out from start to finish and that results in a visible outcome.

Task significance Impact the job has on other people.

Team interview Interview in which applicants are interviewed by the team members with whom they will work.

Third-country national A citizen of one country who is working in a second country and employed by an organization headquartered in a third country.

Third-party administrator (TPA) A vendor that provides administrative services to an organization.

Three-legged stool A model showing the three sources of income to fund an employee's retirement.

Total rewards Monetary and non-monetary rewards provided by companies to attract, motivate, and retain employees.

Training Process whereby people acquire capabilities to perform jobs.

Turnover The process in which employees leave an organization and have to be replaced.

U

Undue hardship Significant difficulty or expense imposed on an employer in making an accommodation for individuals with disabilities.

Union authorization card Card signed by employees to designate a union as their collective bargaining agent.

Union Formal association of workers that promotes the interests of its members through collective action.

Union security provisions Contract clauses to help the union obtain and retain members.

Union steward Employee elected to serve as the first-line representative of unionized workers.

Unit labor cost Computed by dividing the average cost of workers by their average levels of output.

V

Variable pay Compensation linked directly to individual, team, or organizational performance.

Vesting Right of employees to receive certain benefits from their pension plans.

Virtual team Organizational team includes individuals who are separated geographically but who are linked by communications technology.

W

Wages Payments calculated directly from the amount of time worked by employees.

Wellness programs Programs designed to maintain or improve employee health before problems arise.

Whistle-blowers Individuals who report real or perceived wrongs committed by their employers.

Work Effort directed toward accomplishing results.

Work flow analysis Study of the way work (inputs, activities, and outputs) moves through an organization.

Work sample tests Tests that require an applicant to perform a simulated task that is a specified part of the target job.

Work-life balance Employer-sponsored programs designed to help employees balance work and personal life.

Workers' compensation Security benefits provided to workers who are injured on the job.

Wrongful discharge Termination of an individual's employment for reasons that are illegal or improper.

Y

Yield ratio Comparison of the number of applicants at one stage of the recruiting process with the number at the next stage.

AUTHOR INDEX

SUBJECT INDEX

Equal employment opportunity (EEO) (*continued*)
- Civil Rights Act of 1991, 78–79
- concepts of, 75–78, 75f
- considerations for, 228
- defined, 72
- disabilities discrimination and, 88–94
- discrimination issues and, 97–100
- diversity training and, 100–101
- efforts for, 191–192
- Executive Orders for, 79
- gender discrimination laws/regulations and, 81–86
- managing affirmative action, 79–80
- managing racial and ethnic discrimination issues, 80–81
- nature of, 72–73
- recruiting diversity and, 192
- religion and, 96–97
- sex laws/regulations and, 81–86
- spirituality and, 96–97

Equal Employment Opportunity Commission (EEOC), 73, 76–78, 81, 85, 87, 89–90, 93, 95, 97, 99–100, 192, 228
Equal Opportunity Employer, 192
Equal pay, 82
Equal Pay Act of 1963, 82, 374
Equity, 381–382
- defined, 151

Equity theory, 150–151, 380, 381f
Ergonomics, 492–493
Error-based examples method, 275
Essays, 355
Essential job functions, 90, 137
Ethical HR issues on blogs, 536
Ethics/ethnicity, equal employment opportunity and
- affirmative action and, 79, 80
- Cisco systems, on, 26
- Civil Rights Act of 1964, Title VII, 78, 80
- Civil Rights Act of 1991, 79
- and culture, 25–26
- and global differences, 26
- managing, 80–81
- role of human resources in organizational, 27–28
- in workforce, 22

Ethics Idol, 26
Ethics Resource Center, 25
Evaluation, 498–499
E-video, 196–197
Exclusive remedy, 456
Executive compensation, 429–435
- benefits of, 432
- board of directors and, 435
- bonuses as, 432
- changes in the context of, 430–431
- controversy, 430
- criticisms of, 435f
- elements of, 431–433
- global, 433
- measuring and, 434–435
- perquisites as, 432
- reasonableness of, 433–435
- salaries as, 432

Executive education, 326
Executive Masters of Business Administration (EMBA), 326
Executive Orders, 79
Executive salaries. *See* Executive compensation
Exempt employees, 372
Exempt status, 372, 372f
Exit interviews, 174
Ex-offenders, hiring of, 243
Expatriate, 20
Expectancy theory, 151–152, 380, 380f
External equity, 381–382
External recruiting, 199–204
- advantages/disadvantages of, 200f
- competitive, 200–201
- creative, 202
- at educational institutions, 202–204, 203f
- job fairs for, 202
- labor unions and, 202
- through employment agencies, 201–202
- through media, 199–200

External training, 279–280
External workforce, 47–49
- changing workforce considerations, 48–49
- economic and governmental factors, 48
- geographic/competitive evaluations, 48

Exxon/Mobil, 19, 40

F

Facebook, 195, 197, 198, 199, 205, 242
FACT. *See* Fair and Accurate Credit Transactions (FACT) Act
Factor-comparison method, 389
Failure rates, 248
Fair and Accurate Credit Transactions (FACT) Act, 541–542
Fair Credit Reporting Act, 244
Fair-dealing exception, 527
Fair Labor Standards Act (FLSA), 137, 371–373
- child labor provisions in, 372
- exempt/nonexempt status and, 372–373
- minimum wage and, 372
- overtime and, 373

Fair Minimum Wage Act, 372
Fairness, compensation, 381–382
Fake references, 247
Fake warning, 233
Faking personality tests, 233
False positives, 234
Family and Medical Leave Act (FMLA), 82, 470–472
- eldercare assistance and, 472
- family leave and, 473
- family-oriented benefits and, 469
- glass ceiling and, 313
- impact of, 471–472
- pregnancy discrimination, 81–82
- provisions to, 471
- workers compensation and, 488–489

Family-care benefits, 472
Family-career issues, 313
Family concerns, 248
Family leave, 473
Family-oriented benefits, 469–472
Fears, 136
Federal Insurance Contributions Act (FICA), 454
Federal Labor Relations Authority (FLRA), 573
Federal Mediation and Conciliation Service (FMCS), 571, 584
Federation, 568
FedEx, 263
Feedback, 122, 307
Feedback strategy, 274–275
Final warnings, 550
Financial assets, 5
Financial benefits, 467–496, 468f
Financial counseling, 468–469
Financial measures, 63
Financial planning, 468–469
Financial services, 468–469
Firing, 551
Firm-choice option, 503
First-quartile strategy, 384

First-year turnover evaluations, 175
Fisher, Eileen, 425
Fitness-for-duty tests, 503
Fitz-Enz, Jac, 61
Flexible benefits plan, 448–450
Flexible staffing, regular *vs.*, 189–191
Flexible work, managing, 127
Flex plan, 448–450
Flextime, 127
FLRA. *See* Federal Labor Relations Authority (FLRA)
FMCS. *See* Federal Mediation and Conciliation Service (FMCS)
Follow-ups, 175
Forced distribution, 353–354, 354f
   advantages and disadvantages of, 354–355
   defined, 353
Ford Motor Company, 507, 564
Formal succession planning, 303
Former applicant recruits, 207
Former employees recruits, 207
Fortune v. National Cash Register Company, 527
14 Penn Plaza vs. Pyett (2009), 587
401(k) plan, 280, 452, 453, 460, 461
Fraud and theft, employee, 543
Free agents, 167
Freedom of speech, 532
Free-form essays, 355
Free speech rights, 534–536
Frito-Lay, 499
Functional job analysis, 134
Functional turnover, 163
Funeral leave, 473

G

Gainsharing, 422
Games, 282, 283
Gap analysis, 272
Garnishment, 376
Gender, in workforce, 22
Gender pay gap, 400–401
General Aptitude Test Battery (GATB), 231
General Electric (GE), 19, 204, 263, 297, 324, 354
General job fairs, 202
General Motors (GM), 19, 562
General recruiting process metrics, 210–212
General summary, 139
Generational differences, 115

baby boomers, 115
   generation Xers, 115
   generation Yers, 115
   mature, 115
Generation Xers, 115
Generation Yers, 115
Genetic bias regulations, 93–94
Genetic information, 93–94
Genetic Information Nondiscrimination Act (GINA), 93–94
Geographic changes, and U.S. union membership long-term decline, 564
Geographic labor markets, 187
Gerber Products Company, 231
Glass ceiling, 84–85, 313
Glass elevators, 85
Glass walls, 85
Global assignments, 248–249
Global assignment training, 265–265
Global Assistance & Healthcare, 486
Global benefits, 444–447
Global career issues, 314–315
Global compensation, 385–388
Global competitiveness, 42–44, 265–267
Global development, 314–315
Global differences, and United States, 592–593
Global employees, 248–249, 249f
Global executive compensation, 433
Global health services, 486–487
Global issues, 385–388
Globalization, 19–21
   common challenges for global human resource, 21
   legal and political factors, 21
   and unions, 590–593
   wage comparisons, 20–21
Global labor markets, 187
Global labor organizations, 591–592
Global legal factors, 21
Global political factors, 21
Global Professional in Human Resources (GPHR), 29
Global safety, 486–487
Global security, 486–487
Global staffing, 43–44, 248–249
Global succession planning, 299
Global teams, 123
Global unions, 591
Global variable pay, 412
Goals, 80, 339
Good-faith exception, 527
Good-faith negotiations, 583

Good *vs.* bad strategy, 39–40
Goodyear Tire & Rubber, 564
Google, 525
Government codes, 27
Government-supported job training, 279–280
Grade point average (GPA), 203
Great Depression, 569
Green-circled employees, 396
Grievance, 588–590
   arbitration, 590
   and HR responsibilities, 589f
   management, 588–590
   procedures, 589, 590f
   responsibilities, 589
   steps in procedure of, 589–590, 590f
   union representation in procedure of, 589
Griggs v. Duke Power, 75
Gross Domestic Product (GDP), 446, 447f
Gross-up, 445
Group results, 421–422
Group/team incentives, 419–422
   challenges of, 420–421
   decision making about, 420
   design of, 420
   distribution of, 420
   information sharing and, 422
   timing of, 420
   types of, 421–422
Growth activities, 64

H

Halo effects, 241, 358
Handbook, employee, 546–548
Harassment, 81
Hazard communication, 491–492
Headhunters, 201–202
Health
   defined, 483
   domestic trends in, 486
   global trends in, 486–487
Health care benefits, 462–467
   consumer-driven health plans for, 465
   controlling, 464
   cost of, 462, 464
   dental and vision coverage, 465
   key provisions, 463, 463f
   legislation for, 466–467
   preventive/wellness efforts and, 465–466
   reform legislation, 462–463